W.H.P.

OCTOBER.

1985.

CIRENCESTER.

MODERN
ENGLISH LAND LAW

AUSTRALIA
The Law Book Co. Ltd.
Sydney : Melbourne : Brisbane

CANADA AND U.S.A.
The Carswell Company Ltd.
Agincourt, Ontario

INDIA
N. M. Tripathi Private Ltd.
Bombay
and
Eastern Law House Private Ltd.
Calcutta and Delhi
M.P.P. House
Bangalore

ISRAEL
Steimatzky's Agency Ltd.
Jerusalem : Tel Aviv : Haifa

MALAYSIA : SINGAPORE : BRUNEI
Malayan Law Journal (Pte.) Ltd.
Singapore

NEW ZEALAND
Sweet & Maxwell (N.Z.) Ltd.
Auckland

PAKISTAN
Pakistan Law House
Karachi

MODERN ENGLISH LAND LAW

by

MICHAEL HARWOOD, B.A., LL.B.,

Solicitor

LONDON
SWEET & MAXWELL
1982

First Edition 1975
Second Edition 1982

Published in 1982 by
Sweet & Maxwell Ltd. of
11 New Fetter Lane, London
Computerset by Promenade Graphics Ltd., Cheltenham
and printed in Great Britain by
Richard Clay (The Chaucer Press) Ltd., Bungay, Suffolk

British Library Cataloguing in Publication Data

Harwood, Michael
   Modern English land law.—2nd ed.
   1. Real property—England
   I. Title   II. Harwood, Michael. English land law
   344.2064'3   KD829

   ISBN 0-421-27890 0
   ISBN 0-421-27900 1 Pbk

To My Seventh Sister

PREFACE

This book is intended as a basic introductory text book for those university and other students embarking on the study of land law, whether as part of a law degree or of some other course.

I have attempted to set out and explain (giving factual illustrations from decided cases where possible) the fundamental rules and machinery of the modern law; what the law is today, not what it was 15, 50 or more years ago. Whilst it is sometimes necessary, even for the practitioner, to know what the law was at some point of time in the past—for example, when seeking to establish the present ownership of a plot of unregistered land—it is, in my view, neither practicable nor desirable to include the details of such earlier law in a relatively short, basic text book.

There is a further, more important reason why, in my view, it is important to adopt a standpoint set firmly in the present-day law. There is still a tendency amongst teachers and text writers to view land law as an edifice built solely on the principles and policies contained in the 1925 property legislation; and to regard all developments since then, judicial and legislative, as little more than modifications of detail. The continued primary importance of the 1925 legislation is not denied; but such an approach tends to underrate the far-reaching developments—not only of detail but of principle and purpose—that have taken place in the law since then.

The Rent Acts are as important and integral a part of landlord and tenant law as the doctrine of leasehold estates. The social control of land use contained in the Town and Country Planning legislation cannot simply be treated as a catalogue of incursions into the fundamental principle of private ownership and enjoyment, to be treated (frequently with obvious distaste) as a mere appendix to be "tacked on" to an exposition of the law. It has its own principles, purposes and dynamic which should be recognised. I am not arguing here for or against such developments; but today, land law consists of a private law and, equally important, a public law aspect; and any general exposition should seek to accord each its proper place in the totality of the structure.

Similarly, in the field of private law itself, there have been major shifts which a fixation with the 1925 legislation tends to neglect. For example, the 1925 legislation was designed with the traditional standing mortgage in mind; this law has had to be adapted by lawyers and the courts to cope with today's overwhelmingly common instalment mortgage. The trust for sale as envisaged by the 1925 legislation has developed, in some situations, into something more like a trust for occupation. The protection of rights of occupation behind the trust for sale, the licence, proprietary estoppel and statutes such as the Rent Act 1977, the Matrimonial Homes Act 1967 and the Domestic Violence and Matrimonial Proceedings Act 1976, have gone some way to undermine the chief underlying rationale of the 1925 legislation, namely the free alienability and marketability of land as a commodity.

I have continued, in this second edition, to attempt what I see as a more modern approach; and have devoted more space to instalment mortgages, licences and proprietary estoppel, the rights of beneficiaries under a trust for sale; and to registration of title.

As before, I have tried to give some indication of the process by which the judicial mind interprets and moulds the law and to give adequate treatment to areas where the law is uncertain. It is possible, particularly for students and academic lawyers, to exaggerate the uncertainty of the law. The vast majority of land transactions are completed without dispute in reliance on relatively certain rules of law and common sense; and practitioners are, one hopes, trained to adopt practices which, where possible, keep their clients safely away from contentious points.

Nevertheless, disputes do arise, litigating clients have to be advised, there are areas and points of law which are uncertain, particularly where social conditions and behaviour are changing. There is a need to appreciate that law is not static; that judges are continuously developing it; and it is necessary to be able to plot the course of such development.

Again, as before, I have tried to give some indication of what I see as the historical, economic and social forces which are the reality behind the law.

This reality is not just the fact that an abstract concept such as "the fee simple owner of Blackacre" may relate to your neighbour's back yard; or that "a chattel found on another's land" may be Mr. Wainwright's pipe turned up on the summit of Fountain's Fell. Such a relation *is* important if the study of land law is to be interesting and comprehensible to students. But a more important aspect of the reality is that the law, as fashioned by Parliament and the judges, is a tool used to further certain economic and social interests; and to restrict others. The law reflects these interests and cannot be fully understood apart from them. In my view, to suggest that law can be taught "as a self contained system . . . concerned with abstractions, abstractions built into a great pyramid of reasoning, crowned by logically satisfying conclusions" is not very meaningful and would not help the courts in deciding most cases.

The abstractions derive their only meaning from the reality.

Necessarily, the limits of space have severely restricted the amount of attention that I have been able to give to the above matters; and even the exposition of the rules of law themselves has often been more curtailed than I would have wished. As before, some areas, such as the revenue implications of land transactions, have had to be ignored altogether.

I wish to thank all those who reviewed and commented on the first edition; and have tried to give their views careful consideration in preparing the present edition. I have not, as has frequently been suggested, dealt with the relationship between law and equity earlier in the book. I still feel it preferable to deal first with the simplest units of ownership—beneficial freehold and leasehold—before progressing to the trust which must be one of the most difficult aspects of land law to grasp. I have also not altered the position of licences and proprietary estoppel. To the extent that they protect possession they should, perhaps, be in Part II; but because they constitute one of the uncertain areas of law on the difficult boundary between personal and property rights, I feel they are best left to the later place in the book.

I also wish to thank Mr. Porter and Mrs. McCormack, the librarians at Leeds University Law Library, for all their help.

I have endeavoured to state the law as at the date of this preface.

Michael Harwood

May Day 1982.

CONTENTS

xi

TABLE OF CASES

xiii

TABLE OF STATUTES

PART 1. INTRODUCTION

CHAPTER 1

NATURE AND CLASSIFICATION OF INTERESTS IN LAND

GENERAL INTRODUCTION

If you buy a pound of sugar, there is not, as a rule, any need to stop and consider just what legal interest you have in that packet of sugar. It is yours; you take it home and eat it and that is that. But with chattels of a somewhat more permanent nature, a car or a television set, for example, it might become necessary to consider just what your interest is.

If a person buys a television set and pays cash he becomes the absolute owner of it. He can do what he likes with it, throw it away if he wishes. But he might have a more limited interest, something less than absolute ownership. If he buys the television on hire purchase, he will find that although he is given possession of the set, he does not become its owner. He merely hires it for an agreed period, probably from the finance company which has in turn bought it from the dealer. Throughout the hire period the finance company remains owner of the set. But the ownership of the finance company is limited by the rights of the hirer, who does have some sort of legal interest in the set. And this interest entitles him to retain possession of it so long as he keeps up the hire payments. Moreover, because it is a hire-purchase and not just a hire agreement, he has the right to purchase the set at the end of the hire period, generally for a nominal sum, thus becoming its absolute owner, the finance company giving up all interest.[1]

Alternatively, he may simply rent the set, in which case he will have no right to make himself owner of it by purchase.

Again, the absolute owner of a television set might send it to be repaired. Clearly he remains the owner whilst it is being repaired, although temporarily having given up possession; but the repairer does have a valuable interest in the set. He is a bailee and has what is called a lien, that is, the right to retain the set until his charges have been paid.

Similarly, the law recognises many different interests which can exist in land; and a person's rights in respect of a piece of land—how he can enjoy it, how far he can dispose of it, how long

---

[1] For the law of hire-purchase, see A. G. Guest and E. Lomnicka; *An Introduction to the Law of Credit and Security* (1978).

his interest will last, and so on, depend on the precise nature of his interest. It is not good enough to say that George owns Blackacre or that he has an interest in Whiteacre. The precise nature of his ownership or interest must be identified.

The law classifies interests in land in a number of different ways.

Each of these classifications is significant in determining the scope of and rights which go with any particular interest.

The purpose of the first part of this book is to review some of the more important classifications which provide the framework on which English land law is built.

Principle 1. Ownership and third party rights

Interests in land can be divided into those which carry the right to possession, either immediately or at some time in the future, which can be described as ownership interests; and those which merely give the right to use or restrict the use of another person's land without taking possession of it; these can be described as third party rights.

Explanation

In this book the term "ownership" will in general be used to describe those interests which give possession of the land either immediately or at some time in the future. Possession means the right to exclusive occupation[2]; that is not only to occupy but also to exclude others. The right to possession is protected by the courts and can be recovered if wrongfully taken away.

In modern land law the term "possession" generally also includes the right to receive the rents and profits from the land[3]; so that a freeholder who has let his land to a tenant is still regarded as being in possession though it is the tenant who has actual physical possession and he can exclude the landlord from the premises.

The word "ownership" is a word which can be used in many different senses. It is necessary therefore to elaborate a little on the meaning given to it here.

---

[2] For the meaning of possesion in English law, see Pollock and Wright, *Essays on Possession in the Common Law*; Lightwood, *Possession of Land*; Paton, *Jurisprudence* (3rd ed.), Chap 22; Dias, *Jurisprudence* (3rd ed.), Chap 12; Harris, "The Concept of Possession in English Law," *Oxford Essays on Jurisprudence*, at p. 69. For fuller bibliography, see Dias, *Bibliography of Jurisprudence*. See further below, p. 398.

[3] See L.P.A. 1925, s. 205 (1) (xix).

The splitting up of ownership. Ownership is commonly thought of as indicating certain rights over a piece of property such as a chattel or a piece of land. These rights, associated with ownership, include the right to possession, the right to enjoy (*e.g.* if it is a television set, the right to watch it; if it is agricultural land, the right to collect and sell the crops or receive the rent if it is let); and the right of disposition (*e.g.* to sell, to give away, to use as a security for a loan and, in the case of a chattel, to destroy it). The difficulty with land law (and indeed with the law of chattels to a lesser extent) is that it has always recognised that these ownership rights need not be vested in the same person; that they can be split up and shared between a number of different persons. To take a simple example: if X is the freehold owner of Blackacre and leases it to T, which of them is the owner? X is collecting the income from the land in the form of rent; but T is enjoying physical possession; whilst X will gain physical possession at some time in the future when the lease expires. To take another example: suppose that I make my will stipulating that I want my wife to enjoy my property Blackacre on my death for the rest of her life—assuming that she survives me—and that I then want my son to have it absolutely: is it possible to say, whilst my widow is alive, that my son is the owner? Or is she the owner though only for her lifetime? As will be seen when this sort of disposition is considered below,[4] she does not obtain, even for her lifetime, all the rights associated with ownership. She cannot sell the land and keep the proceeds of sale for herself. She may have possession but her rights of enjoyment will be limited. She may not be allowed to cut timber on the land. If the land is sold, she will get the income from the investment of the proceeds for the rest of her life, and then the son will get all the proceeds. But until the widow dies, he will get nothing at all.

It might be concluded that the freeholder and his tenant, the widow with her life interest and the son entitled on her death, have little in common. But they do have one thing in common, the right to possession in the sense defined above. The right to possession, rather than some abstract concept of ownership, has always played a central role in English law and it is convenient and natural to regard all these persons—all persons with the right to possession—as having ownership interests.[5]

It must however be emphasised right here at the start, that not every person with possession will be entitled to possession for the

---

[4] Chap 6.
[5] See further below, p. 503 *et seq.*

same period or at the same time; and not every right to possession carries with it identical rights of enjoyment and disposal of the land. Each type of possession, that is, each ownership interest, will have to be explained separately to see what rights it attracts.

The doctrine of tenure: possession and not ownership as the basis of the land law

So far it has been explained that the term "ownership" will be used of interests which carry the right to possession immediately or at some time in the future. This emphasis on possession is justified by the development of English land law. In fact, unlike Roman law,[6] English land law never bothered much with the idea of ownership. It was the protection of possession and the development of the rules governing the right to possession which exercised the minds of the early lawyers and provided the foundation of today's land law.

Although Roman law did recognise that many individuals could have interests in the same piece of land, it started from the premise that there could only be one ownership. To the Roman lawyers ownership, *dominium*, was a single indivisible right; by its nature it could not be chopped up into little bits and shared between many persons.

For various reasons English law concerned itself with the fact of possession rather than the abstract right of ownership. The most important reason was the feudal system of land tenure which confronted the royal judges in the two centuries following the Norman Conquest. It was a fact of feudal life as found by these judges that a man with land did not have unfettered control but held it of some lord; he did not own it outright but held it of his lord as tenant on condition that he performed the feudal services due to the lord. But this did not make his lord the owner. For he too in turn held it of *his* lord subject to services and incidents. This pyramid of lordships and tenants with the King at the apex—since he had tenants in chief holding of him but no lords above—was feudal society.

There was no place for ownership in this scheme of things; except possibly in the King since he held of no one.

The tenant at the bottom of the pyramid, the one in actual occupation of the land, could be thought of as having possession of the land; and this lawful possession was something which the courts could recognise and protect. The tenant's lord had the right

---

[6] See Buckland, *Manual of Roman Private Law* (2nd ed.), p. 110.

to receive services and incidents from this and other tenants. This right (or collection of rights) was regarded by the courts as a piece of property, a lordship or a seignory or an honur. The lord was recognised as having possession of the lordship, etc., and this possession too could be protected by the courts. But it could hardly be thought of as ownership of the land since the lord himself in turn was only the tenant of a superior land.

This principle, that a man does not own land but merely holds it as tenant, either directly or indirectly of the Crown, is the doctrine of tenure.[7] It is still with us but only as a ghost. The substance has disappeared. The individual can still only hold land, *i.e.* have possesion of it as a tenant. He cannot own it. But two things have happened to tenure in the course of centuries:

(a) Almost all the intermediate lordships standing between the tenant in actual possession of the land and the Crown have disappeared leaving, in most cases, the tenant holding directly of the Crown.

(b) All the feudal burdens—services and incidents—attached to the land and owed to the lord have disappeared. And all tenures, except leasehold, have been converted into a single tenure, free and common socage.

The result of these changes is that tenure no longer has any practical significance as a limit on ownership. As has been said, the first thing to teach a student of land law is the doctrine of tenure, the second is that it has no importance. Unfortunately, it cannot be ignored completely because the ghost of tenure has left its imprint on the language of modern law. The language of

---

[7] However, it should be said that mediaeval lawyers themselves, in the times of Glanvil and Bracton, saw no inconsistency in using the term *dominium* to describe both the interest of the tenant in demesne (holding the land itself) and the lordship of the lord in the same land. It was "those severe feudalists of the seventeenth and later centuries" (Pollock and Maitland, *History of English Law* (2nd ed., Milsom, 1968), Vol. 2, at p. 4), who, developing the theory to explain the fact of tenure, discovered what they considered to be an inconsistency, and blamed Bracton "for never having stated the most elementary rule of English land law, and for having ascribed *proprietas* and *dominium rei* to the tenant in demesne" (*ibid.* at p. 4). See generally, Pollock and Maitland, *History of English Law*, Chap IV, particularly pp. 2—5. In the seventeenth century, Coke wrote (Co. Litt. 1b): "for in the law of England we have not, properly, *allodium*, that is, any subject's land that is not as it is holden; unless you will take *allodium* for *ex solido*, often taken in the book of Domesday; and tenants in fee simple are there called *alodarii* or *aloarii*. And he is called a tenant because he holdeth of some superior lord by some service. And therefore the King in this sense cannot be said to be a tenant, because he hath no superior but God Almighty; *praedium domini regis est directum dominium, suius nullus autor est nisi Deus* . . . But though a subject hath not properly *directum*, yet hath he *utile dominium*."

possession is still used. Today, the student will find sometimes the language of possession, sometimes that of ownership. He will find both the expressions "freehold owner" and "freehold tenant." He will read both that a freeholder owns the land and that he holds it as tenant. Again a life tenant may be described as a limited owner. Theoretically, the language of possession is more correct[8]; in practice the language of ownership is more apt.

One or two final points on this subject:

(1) The term "owner" or "absolute owner" is sometimes used, in a more limited sense than that given above, to indicate the person who holds the fee simple absolute in possession, giving the most complete rights of enjoyment and disposition over the land of all interests.

(2) Even though tenure is no longer significant as a limit on the ownership of land, ownership can still be split up in many important ways. It can, for example, under the doctrine of estates, be limited in duration; and all the rights of enjoyment and disposition may not be vested in one person.

(3) Tenure is still of practical importance in the case of leasehold ownership. The tenure which has been spoken of so far is the feudal tenure attached to freehold land. The early feudal law treated leasehold as altogether different from freehold interests in land. Leaseholds grew up outside the framework of the traditional land law and were governed by the rules used to govern chattels.[9] To this day, leaseholds are still technically classified together with chattels as personal property whereas freehold interests are classified as real property.

Nevertheless, today, the leasehold is regarded as a tenure in that it involves the relationship between (land)lord and tenant. The land is granted by the landlord to the tenant to hold for some specified leasehold interest—*e.g.* a term for 21 years. The lease or tenancy agreement will contain a whole series of continuing obligations governing the relationship between landlord and tenant. These rights and obligations (the obligation of the tenant to pay the agreed rent, perhaps to keep the premises in repair; the obligation of the landlord to let the tenant have quiet enjoyment), are obviously very real obligations which will continue to be enforceable throughout the duration of the lease.[10]

---

[8] But see n. 7 above.
[9] See Pollock and Maitland (n. 7 above) at p. 106 *et seq.*
[10] But see below, p. 91.

Third party rights.[11] In contrast to ownership interests, a person may have an interest which entitles him to use or to restrict the use of a piece of land in a particular way—to use a footpath across it for example—but which does not entitle him to take possession of it. The right of way is indeed one of the commonest examples. Suppose that D has a right of way on foot across S's land. S is the owner. He is entitled to possession. But D does have the right to enter for this particular purpose and no other, that is, to use the footpath.

These third party rights are dealt with in Part IV of this book.

Principle 2. The doctrine of estates

An estate is an interest in land which will continue for a particular duration.

The law recognises the following estates in land:

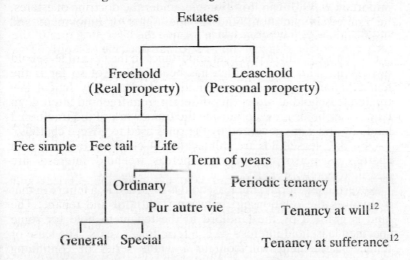

Freehold estates are classified as real property. Leasehold estates are classified as personal property.

The doctrine of estates applies to ownership and third party rights.

In the case of ownership the estate held determines not only the duration of the interest but also the rights of enjoyment.

---

[11] See further, below, p. 353.

[12] Strictly these may not be estates. See Megarry and Wade, *Law of Real Property* (4th ed.), at p. 45.

Explanation

The doctrine of estates and ownership. The precise rights which go with possession depend in the first place upon what estate a person has. Since the doctrine of estates is the product of a continous process of legal development from the earliest days, an historical explanation may help.

Estates and tenure. English land law as part of the common law was developed by the royal judges in the two or so centuries after the Norman Conquest in 1066.

To some extent the royal judges, when deciding disputes and formulating common principles relating to land, at Westminster and on circuit, drew on local custom, that is the traditional practices of the people in their local communities. These customs had developed long before the Conquest, founded on the economic and social needs of the local community and enforced in the courts of hundred and shire.

But it was feudalism which dominated the post-Conquest period and the ideas of feudalism which formed the basic structure of the early common land law in the guise of the doctrine of tenure. This was a period of social immobility. A man was tied to his village, and to the land which he worked, by every circumstance. His well-being, probably his survival, depended on the relationship between himself and the lord of whom he held his land. He held his land not because he owned it but because he gave his support to and performed services for the lord. In return he was allowed to continue to hold the land and was given the lord's protection, if only against other lords. He was a tenant not an owner.[13] The terms upon which the tenant held his land, the services and incidents attached to his holding (and the obligations owed by the lord to the tenant), constituted the tenure. Feudal lawyers recognised different possible tenures, each tenure involving specified services and incidents, tenure by knight service, socage tenure, unfree tenure, and so on. It is not intended to examine the details of the different tenures in this book.

The tenurial relationship was economic in somewhat the same way as a modern lease. It supplied the lord's needs in the form of money and services, and gave the tenant the means—in the form of land—of providing for his own needs. But it was a personal as well as an economic relationship, which the modern lease is not. A leaseholder today with, say, a 21-year lease has a property right which he can, with certain limitations, dispose of as he pleases. He

[13] But see n. 7 above.

can sell and assign the residue of the term; he can let it pass to his next-of-kin on his intestacy; or he can choose to leave it by will to whom he wishes. It will continue for its allotted 21-year period regardless of his death. In contrast, tenure represented a personal relationship between a particular man, a particular lord and a particular piece of land. Under feudalism a tenant did not have a property right which was at his own free disposal. He held it for life and on condition that he fulfilled his obligations to his feudal lord. He had no right to dispose of the land by will. Indeed, the right to leave land by will was not formally recognised until the Statute of Wills in 1540. When he died the land passed to his heir. The right to alienate *inter vivos* without the lord's consent was very restricted. A lord could not have a new tenant who might be worthless forced upon him in place of the present one. Where alienation could and did take place it was generally by subinfeudation—not by substitution, that is outright transfer as happens today. This meant that the alienating tenant created something like a sub-tenancy, another rung in the feudal ladder, the purchaser held the land of him as a tenant and he became the purchaser's lord. Payment or services would be reserved to the vendor. The vendor would himself remain tenant of his own lord in respect of that piece of land and their relationship would not, directly at least, be affected.

The position during the early post-Conquest period can perhaps be summarised as follows.[14]

The only significant question about a man's interest in land was its tenure, the terms on which he held it of his lord. The doctrine of estates is concerned with the duration and alienability of ownership. In this early period there was no place for a doctrine of estates. So far as alienabiltiy and duration were concerned every tenant was in the same position and subject to the same rule. He held for his life and on his death his heir would be entitled.

By a gradual process, spotlighted in the statute *Quia Emptores* 1290 but continuing over centuries, the machinery of tenure was dismantled and replaced by the doctrine of estates as the basis of land ownership in this country.

Land became alienable and it became alienable for different durations. It was this which led to the formulation of a doctrine of estates. The important question ultimately came to be not of whom and on what terms did he hold the land but rather for how long did he hold it. In this period of land law it is impossible to say that land became alienable—or that any other change occurred—

---

[14] Compare J.L. Barton, The Rise of the Fee Simple, (1976) 92 L.Q.R. 108.

on any specific date. But the statute *Quia Emptores* was a major milestone marking the triumph of the principle of free alienability. It gave the tenant the right to alienate outright, by susbstitution and not subfeudation, without the consent of his lord. This gave the tenant the absolute right to break the personal tenurial bond by transferring the land and the bond to someone else.

By this time too it was accepted that by alienation he could defeat the claims of his own heirs. Originally, if land was granted, "To A and his heirs," this meant what it said. It gave an interest to the heirs which A could not defeat by alienating the land. But as part of the progress towards free alienability it became accepted that A could alienate so as to defeat his heirs. The words "and his heirs" came to mean that if he did not alienate during his lifetime then, on his death, the land would go to his heirs. The words distinguished it from a mere grant to A for life in which case the land would go back to the lord and could not pass to the heirs on death. If land was granted "To A and his heirs" and A did alienate the land "To B and his heirs" then B would be in the same position. If he in turn did not alienate during his lifetime then his heirs would inherit. In modern terminology, the words "and his heirs" (this form of wording still can be but is not in practice used), are words of limitation. They indicate what estate is to be taken, in this case a fee simple and not just a life interest.[15]

The fee simple and the life interest. Thus, it can be seen that at this stage ownership of two possible durations, that is two possible estates, have emerged: the fee simple created by making a grant "To A and his heirs," and the life interest. The person with an estate in fee simple could alienate his ownership, *i.e.* his estate, *inter vivos*. If he did alienate there was nothing left to pass to his heirs. If he did not it passed on his death to his heir. If he died not having alienated and not leaving any heir, the fee simple came to and end and the land escheated to the lord. Today, the position is essentially the same. The fee simple owner can alienate *inter vivos* or, today, by will. If he dies intestate without having alienated, then the estate passes to his next of kin (no longer to the heir). Failing next of kin, the fee simple comes to an end and the land passes to the Crown—by statute, escheat for lack of heirs having been abolished.[16]

It was recognised that the grantor could prevent this from happening by simply giving the land to the grantee for his life, that

---

[15] See further below, p. 19 as to words of limitation.
[16] A.E.A. 1925, s. 45(1).

Crown = Absolute Owner.
Estate = Rights over land.

is by giving him what came to be recognised as a life estate. Again, the life estate (or interest as it should now be called)[17] is essentially the same now as then. The life tenant has the land only for his lifetime. He can alienate but not for longer than his own lifetime since that is when his interest expires. If he does alienate it, the grantee obtains an interest *pur autre vie*, an interest for life of another (in this case the life of the transferor). Of course, he has nothing to leave by will or to pass on his intestacy.

The fee tail. In 1285, by the statute *De Donis Conditionalibus*, a further possible estate was recognised. This was the fee tail.

The fee tail represents a more limited type of ownership than the fee simple. It is, like the fee simple, an estate of inheritance—this is what the word "fee" means; and so it does not automatically come to an end on the death of the tenant in tail. But the tenant in tail, unlike the fee simple owner, cannot control the destiny of his interest. He cannot dispose of it *inter vivos* or by will[18]; on his death it can only pass to his heir. And the word tail (from the french *taillé* meaning limited or cut down) indicates that the heir can only be selected—according to the common law rules for selecting a person's heir—from a limited class of surviving relatives, namely his descendants. The heir entitled to a fee simple on intestacy could, before 1926, be selected from a much wider class, namely descendant, ascendant or collateral blood relatives. Today, the next-of-kin entitled on intestacy constitutes a similarly wide group. It includes not just descendants but also spouses, parents, brothers and sisters, grandparents, uncles and aunts. The fee tail is still governed by the old rule.

If the tenant in tail leaves no surviving descendant entitled, then the fee tail comes to an end. What happens then is considered below.[19]

According to the rules, the person entitled to inherit the fee tail will be the eldest surviving son if there is one, and this indeed was the whole purpose of the fee tail when it was first developed as a type of ownership. The landowner wanted to be able to ensure that after his death, the land would remain in his family, passing unsold and undivided, from generation to generation, from eldest son as the representative of the family to eldest son. The family was to be immortalised so far as the possession of a landed estate could make it immortal. All this is considered below in the Chapters dealing with settlements.

---

[17] See L.P.A., s. 1. Strictly the word estate now only applies to legal estates.
[18] But he may be able to turn it into a fee simple by barring it. See below, p. 249.
[19] Principle 3; below, p. 15.

Types of fee tail. The law recognises four types of fee tail:

(a) The fee tail general: In this case descent is traced, that is the heir is found, among descendants from any spouse of the grantee.

(b) The fee tail male general: Here descent can only be traced through males.

(c) The fee tail female general: Rarely if ever found in practice. Here descent can only be traced through females.

(d) Special tail: In this case the heir can only be selected from descendants from a specified spouse.[20]

To illustrate these types: Blackacre is granted to P in fee tail. He marries W and they have an only child, a daughter, who in turn has a son and a daughter, GS and GD. Subsequently, W dies and P marries W2 but they do not have any children. The daughter then dies. On the death of P the question is who is entitled to the fee tail? If it is a fee tail general, descent can be traced through males or females. Daughter would have been heir but she is already dead. Her children represent her, males being preferred to females. GS will be the heir. If it is a fee tail male descent can only be traced through the male line; since P does not have a son, there is no heir and the fee tail determines. If on the other hand it were a fee tail female, GD would be the heir. Finally, if it is a special tail, "To P and the heirs of his body of W2" then again there will be no heir from the required class and the fee tail will determine.

If events occur so that, whilst the entail is still in existence, it becomes impossible for there to be any heirs of the right class, the fee tail is said to be a fee tail after possibility of issue extinct, a fee tail after possibility for short. This can happen, for example, where there is a special tail limited to the descendants by a specified spouse who dies leaving no surviving descendants. The main feature of such a tenancy in tail is that it cannot be barred.[21]

Freehold and leasehold estates: Real and personal property. Estates are either freehold or leasehold.

The fee simple, the life interest and the fee tail in land are classified as freehold estates. They could only be created in land held by one of the free tenures. Hence they came to be called, and still are called, freehold estates. The term "freehold" thus refers to both the tenure and the estate. If a person offers land for sale today, describing it as freehold, it means that it is held in free and common socage (the only freehold tenure left) for one of the three

---

[20] Two further varieties are: special tail male and special tail female. As with the fee tail general, the special tail may be further limited to the male or female line.

[21] See below, p. 249 for barring of entails.

freehold estates; and usually it is the fee simple absolute in possession estate which is indicated.

The term "leasehold" likewise refers to both the estate and the tenure. Apart from free and common socage, leasehold is the only tenure left.[22] Thus if Rupert is said to be a leasehold owner of Blackacre it will mean that he holds Blackacre as tenant of a landlord for one of the possible leasehold estates, for example a term of years.

Freehold estates in land are classified as real property; leasehold estates are classified as personal property. This distinction, no longer so important, is considered below.[23]

The doctrine of estates and third party rights. The doctrine of estates applies to both ownership and third party rights. Thus, for example, X may hold (that is have ownership, or possession of) Blackacre for an estate in fee simple. And he may hold, or own, a right of way in fee simple over neighbouring Whiteacre.

When applied to third party rights, the doctrine of estates does no more than determine the duration of the interest. When applied to ownership it determines not only the duration but also the rights of enjoyment which go with the interest.

It is common in practice to use the name of the estate by itself to refer to an ownership interest. Thus, it may be said that A holds or owns the fee simple in Blackacre, meaning that he holds Blackacre for an estate in fee simple. Where the doctrine is being applied to third party rights this should be clear from the context.

Principle 3. Estates in possession and future interests (remainders and reversions)

The fee simple is the greatest estate recognised by English law and represents what is in effect absolute ownership of the land.

The fee simple tenant can carve any number of the lesser estates, fee tails, life interests and leases, out of his fee simple; but once he has disposed of the fee simple he ceases to have any interest in the land at all.

Whilst any number of these lesser estates can be carved out of the fee simple, only one estate at a time can enjoy the right to immediate possession of the land. An estate which carries with it

---

[22] Copyhold, formerly villein or unfree tenure, was finally abolished by L.P.A. 1922, Pt. V, as amended by the L.P. (Amendment) Act 1924, coming into force on January 1, 1926. For the preservation of some of the incidents attached to copyhold land, see L.P.A. 1922, s. 128 and Sched. 12.

[23] See p. 583.

the right to immediate possession of the land is called an interest (or estate)[24] in possession. An estate which carries with it the right to possession at some time in the future on the determination of estates with a prior right to possession, is said to be a future interest (or future estate).[25]

A future interest may be a reversion or a remainder.

Where the original grantor has not disposed of his whole estate, his estate is said to be a reversion (or in reversion) since possession will revert back to him or his successors on the determination of all estates which have been created.

Where the future interest is held by anyone other than the original grantor or his successors, it is called a remainder since possession will remain away from the original grantor.

Explanation

The fee simple as the largest estate. So far it has been explained that the law recognises three possible freehold estates, the fee simple, the fee tail and the life interest. Each type represents ownership for a particular duration and carries with it certain rights of enjoyment of the land. A life interest is ownership for a single lifetime. A fee tail represents ownership which continues after death, but which can only pass on death to the descendant heir. On the other hand, the fee simple represents ownership which can be transferred freely *inter vivos* or by will, and which is not likely to fail on intestacy for want of surviving next-of-kin. In other words it is ownership which is likely to continue indefinitely and carries with it the widest powers of disposition and enjoyment. Further, the other two freehold estates, and leases of any duration, can be carved out of the fee simple. So it is reasonable to think of the fee simple as amounting to absolute ownership of the land, and the tenant in fee simple as the absolute owner.

Estates in possession, reversion and remainder. If G, the fee simple owner, sells Blackacre to P, what he is doing in law is to transfer the fee simple to P. The result is that he will cease to have any interest in the property. Similarly, if he makes a will leaving Blackacre to A. When the will takes effect on the death of G, the whole ownership of the land, the fee simple, will be vested in A.

Suppose, however, that instead he grants the land to A for life, that is, gives him a life interest. He is able to do this because the life interest, like the fee tail and the lease, is a more limited form of

---

[24] See n. 17 above.
[25] *Ibid.*

ownership than the fee simple. In this case G has not disposed of his whole ownership, but merely a part of it represented by the life interest.

It is very important to understand what has happened and also how English law describes what has happened. In effect, what G has done is to transfer possession of the land to A for life together with the rights of enjoyment which go with an interest limited to a person's lifetime.[26] In legal language G has granted A a life estate in possession. And as soon as the grant takes effect, as soon as G has executed the necessary document, A will be entitled to take possession of the land, and this means that he can exclude G as well as everyone else.

The question which then arises is what has G got left? His position is that he has given up possession for A's lifetime but he has not made any further disposition of the land. He has not provided for possession to go to any one else when A dies. Consequently, when this happens, the right to possession will revert back to G. The English law doctrine of estates explains this by saying that G still has his fee simple, but a fee simple which does not give the right to possession until another estate, A's life interest, determines. In other words, G has a fee simple in reversion.

The important point to grasp is that G has given up possession for the time being but he has not given up his fee simple estate. The right to future possession of the land is as much a property right as the right to immediate possession. G's reversion, since it is a fee simple reversion, can be sold, left by will, pass on intestacy and settled. The value of the reversion lies, of course, in the fact that ultimately, on the death of A, it will give actual possession of the land. Its precise value will obviously depend in part on the likely longevity of A. If he is 105 tommorow and in decline then the value cannot be much less than the value of the fee simple in possession.

To return to the start, with G holding the fee simple in possession. Suppose that this time he executes the necessary documents giving Blackacre to A for life and providing that it is then to go to B in fee tail (remainder to B in fee tail, as it is put), remainder to C in fee tail. As before A is first in line and will have possession for his lifetime. When A dies and his life interest determines, possession will attach to the next estate in line, that is B's fee tail. Since, when this happens, possession will remain away from the grantor and his successors. B's future interest is called a

---

[26] For a life tenant's rights of enjoyment, see below, p. 243 *et seq.*

remainder—a fee tail in remainder. When A does die it will become a fee tail in possession. Similarly, C also has a fee tail in remainder. G as before has a fee simple in reversion.

What has been said about reversions is true about remainders: they are from the start existing property rights and their value will depend in part on the probability of their falling into possession. If the original grantee is not still holding the estate when it falls into possession, it will be necessary to trace who has become entitled to it through sale, intestacy, etc.

The arrangements of the sort that have been illustrated above—the creation of two or more estates in property, each carrying the right to possession in succession—are known as settlements. These are considered in more detail in Part III.

What can be said in conclusion is this: Any number of lesser estates (but only one fee simple) can exist in the same piece of land at the same time; but only one freehold estate at a time can be in possession.[27] The others must be future interests and either in reversion or remainder.

The above ignores the fact that estates can exist in both law and equity. This is considered later at page 160 *et seq.*

Reversions on leaseholds. A fee simple landlord who grants a lease is said to have a reversion on the lease in that he will recover actual physical possession of the land when the lease expires. But he still has a fee simple in possession—because possession is deemed to include the right to receive the rents.[28] Confusion arising from this use of the word "reversion" should be avoided.

Principle 4. Absolute, determinable and conditional interests

Any of the estates may be absolute, determinable or conditional.

Explanation

An estate which is not determinable and not subject to a condition is absolute. An estate is determinable if the grant stipulates that it is to come to an end automatically if and when a stipulated event happens. An estate is conditional if the grant provides that it is liable to be determined by re-entry if and when a stipulated event happens. For example, a gift to A in fee simple,

---

[27] This is not entirely correct, since two or more estates can be created both giving the right to possession at the same time. This would then be a case of co-ownership. See below, p. 311, n.1.

[28] L.P.A. 1925, s. 205 (1) (xix).

"provided that he does not marry a person who has been a domestic servant,"[29] creates a conditional fee. On the other hand, if the gift is to A in fee simple "until he marries a person who has been a domestic servant," the result is a determinable fee.

The distinction is considered further in the context of the rule against perpetuities.[30]

General note on Principles 3 and 4

Any one of the recognised estates may be:
1. In possession, remainder or reversion.
2. Absolute, determinable or conditional.

For example, Blackacre could be granted "To A for life until he marries, remainder to B in fee simple." A has a determinable life interest in possession. B has a fee simple absolute (since nothing to the contrary is stated) in remainder.

Principle 5. Words of limitation and words of purchase

The words in a grant of land which identify the grantee (the purchaser) are words of purchase.

The words which define (delimit) the estate which is to be taken are words of limitation.

The following rules, governing words of limitation, apply to grants *inter vivos* and by will:

(1) In the absence of evidence of a contrary intention, the grantee will obtain the fee simple or the other whole interest of the grantor.

(2) Any words will be sufficient to create a life interest provided they show such an intention.

(3) To create a fee tail strict words of limitation must be used, namely, either:
  (a) The words "heirs" followed by words of procreation; *e.g.* "To A and the heirs of his body."
  (b) The words "in tail" following the name of the grantee.

Principle 6. Splitting up ownership: settlements; co-ownership; leases

The beneficial ownership of land can be split up in three ways:
  (1) By settlement; with the right to possession being enjoyed in succession.

---

[29] See *Jenner* v. *Turner* (1880) 16 Ch.D. 188.
[30] See below, p. 307. Determinable fees also play an important part in protective trusts; see below, p. 297.

    (2) Co-ownership; with the right to possession being shared by two or more persons at the same time.

    (3) By lease; with the lessee receiving possession and the reversioner receiving rent.

Explanation

If A is the benficial fee simple absolute in possession owner of Blackacre, he can if he wishes transfer that ownership outright. On the other hand, there are three possible ways in which he can carve up the ownership so that it is shared by more than one person.

First, he may settle the land. For example, he may make a will leaving it to A for life remainder to B in fee simple.

Secondly, he may create co-ownership. He may, for example, sell it to a married couple and convey it "To H and W in fee simple." Whereas beneficiaries under a settlement enjoy the right to possession in turn, co-owners share the right to possession at the same time.

It is possible to have a settlement involving co-ownership. For example, Blackacre is settled on "A and B for life remainder to C in fee simple."

Finally, he may simply lease the land for a longer or shorter period, reserving the right to receive a rent. As will be seen,[31] land subject to a settlement or co-ownership can be leased subject to certain conditions. In the example above, it may be possible for A and B,as joint tenants for life, to join together and lease the land to T for 21 years.

Principle 7. Legal and equitable interests[32]

.   Any interest in land will be legal or equitable.

Explanation

Legal and equitable ownership. Today, only two forms of legal ownership are possible[33]:

    the fee simple absolute in possession;

    the term of years absolute.

    Any other ownership interest (*e.g.* a fee simple in remainder) must be equitable.

---

[31] See below, p. 214.
[32] For the distinction between common law and equity see below, p. 156 *et seq.*
[33] L.P.A. 1925, s.1.

Third party rights. Only a limited number of third party rights can be legal; all others must be equitable. Whether a third party right is legal or equitable may determine whether it is enforceable against a transferee of the land.[34]

Principle 8. Beneficial and trust ownership

Each piece of land must have a legal freehold owner—someone who holds the legal fee simple absolute in possession.

In general, this legal ownership carries with it the rights to deal with the land, to sell, lease, mortgage it, etc. These rights may be more or less limited. Equitable ownership represents the rights of enjoyment.

The legal owner may hold the land for his own benefit, in which case he will be owner in law and equity and known as beneficial owner.[35]

Alternatively, he may hold the legal estate as trustee for the benefit of others, the benficiaries, who will be the equitable owners. In this case the trustee can only deal with the land in the limited way permitted by the law for the benefit of the beneficiaries.

Part II of this book deals with beneficial ownership.

Part III deals with the various forms of trust ownership including—since today these can only exist in equity behind a trust—settlements and co-ownership.

Principle 9. The 1925 legislation

A great many of both the principles and details of modern land law are contained in the property legislation of 1925 which was the culmination of the nineteenth century statutory reforms, and made many fundamental changes in the land law as developed by the courts of common law and equity over the centuries:

This legislation, commonly referred to as the 1925 legislation, includes the following statutes[36]:

The Settled Land Act;
The Trustee Act;
The Law of Property Act;
The Land Registration Act;
The Land Charges Act;
The Administration of Estates Act.

---

[34] See below, p. 511 *et seq.*
[35] There can be up to four joint owners of the legal fee simple; see below, p. 170.
[36] Commonly abrreviated, by use of their initials.

Although many of the rules and principles contained in the 1925 legislation are derived from earlier statutes, for the sake of simplicity this book will in general ignore the earlier legislation.

Principle 10. What is land?

The term "land" includes not only the surface of the earth but also[37]:

(1) The soil beneath the surface and the right to the airspace above the surface.

(2) Buildings and any chattels which have by sufficient attachment to the soil or to buildings, become fixtures.[38]

(3) *Fructus naturales* (natural crops); but not *fructus industriales* (industrial growing crops).

The term also includes any interest in the land as defined above, whether freehold or leasehold, ownership or third party right. It does not include rights, such as personal licences, which may relate to the land but which are mere personal rights and not property interests.[39]

Explanation

The distinction between what is and what is not land is important because—although as with other classifications the dividing line may be arbitrary at times—a number of important rules and rights depend on this classification. To mention some:

(a) Any contract for the sale of land needs to be evidenced in writing.[40]

(b) A contract for the sale of land and a conveyance of land will automatically include everything which is part of the land unless expressly excluded.[41]

(c) The person who owns the surface of the land is presumed to own also whatever in law is part of the land.[42]

(d) Where a person attaches a chattel to the land so that it becomes a fixture, it automatically becomes the property of the

---

[37] See L.P.A. 1925, s. 205 (1) (ix).

[38] See next Principle, p. 24, for fixtures.

[39] As to whether it includes an interest under a trust for sale see below, p. 327 *et seq.* As to licences, see below, p. 400.

[40] L.P.A. 1925, s. 40(1); see below, p. 555.

[41] See, *e.g. Kelsen v. Imperial Tobacco Co. Ltd.* [1957] 2 Q.B. 334.

[42] See further, below, p. 33.

landowner and passes with the land. This principle has a number of important applications and is considered separately in the next Principle.

The courts have frequently found difficulty in drawing the line between what is to be treated as land and what as chattels. One of the problems is that nothing by its nature is one or the other. The line can be crossed either way. Bricks in a builder's yard—obviously chattels—can be built into a house and so become fixtures and therefore part of the land; but the building can be demolished, and the bricks become chattels again.[43] In deciding, the courts will consider all the relevant circumstances, including the purpose for which the classification is being made; indeed, it is possible that the same thing may at the same time be regarded as land for one purpose and yet as a chattel for some other purpose.[44]

Fructus naturales. This term refers to the natural products of the soil, such as grass, timber, fruit from fruit trees, which do not require annual labour to produce a crop. Industrial growing crops (*fructus industriales*) on the other hand, such as corn and potatoes, requiring annual labour for their production are not regarded as part of the land.[45]

Severance. A landowner is always entitled to sever his own *fructus naturales* or other fixtures so as to convert them into chattels. If he agrees to sell them after severance he is clearly selling chattels and not land. However, the law has gone further. Even where the agreement is for the purchaser to sever, so that at the time of the contract they are still part of the land, the courts have classified it as a sale of chattels—at least for the purposes of section 40 of the Law of Property Act 1925, which requires that contracts for the disposal of land or any interest in land should be in writing or evidenced by some note or memorandum in writing. In *Marshall* v. *Green*[46] there was an oral contract for the sale of trees to be felled and removed by the purchaser. After he had taken six, the vendor purported to cancel the sale. Undaunted the purchaser carried on and removed the rest of the trees whereupon the vendor sued him. The vendor's attempt to avoid the consequences of the contract—by arguing that this was a contract

---

[43] See *Holland* v. *Hodgson* (1872) L.R. 7 C.P. 328 at p. 334, *per* Lord Blackburn.
[44] See *Lee* v. *Gaskell* (1876) 1 Q.B.D. 700.
[45] Compare emblements, below, p. 248.
[46] (1875) 1 C.P.D. 35.

for the sale of land which should have been evidenced in writing—was rejected by the court.[47]

Possibly, for other purposes, fixtures might be considered part of the land until actual severance.

Principle 11. Fixtures

A fixture is a chattel which has been attached to the land or to a building (which itself is a fixture) in such a way as to be regarded by the law as part of the land.

The courts apply two main tests in deciding whether a chattel has become a fixture:

The degree of annexation test. If the chattel has been physically attached to the property in any way, there is a presumption that it has become a fixture; the greater the degree of annexation and the greater the damage that would be done by removal then the greater is the presumption. Conversely, if the chattel rests on its own weight there is a presumption that it is still a chattel.

The purpose of annexation test. This test is the decisive test. If the circumstances show that the purpose of annexation was merely to enable the chattel to be enjoyed as a chattel, it will be treated as still being a chattel. If the purpose was to make a permanent improvement to the property, then the chattel will be treated as a fixture and part of the land.

If a chattel becomes a fixture, it becomes (if not so already) the property of the landowner and, in the absence of express exclusion, passes on any transfer of the land. This rule applies even if the chattel was affixed by someone other than its owner or if it was affixed by one person on another's land.

Explanation

The two tests. Many judges have commented on the difficulty of reconciling the many conflicting cases on fixtures.[48] In *Lyon & Co.* v. *London City and Midland Bank*[49] the plaintiffs supplied on hire to the owner and occupier of the Brighton Hippodrome "345

---

[47] Note also s. 61 of the Sale of Goods Act 1979, which defines goods to include "things attached to or forming part of the land which are to be severed before or under the contract of sale."

[48] In *Reynolds* v. *Ashby* [1904] A.C. 466, Lord Lindley said (at p. 473); "My Lords, I do not profess to be able to reconcile all the cases on fixtures, still less all that has been said about them."

[49] [1903] 2 K.B. 135 (Joyce J.).

buttoned back lift-up seat crimson velvet armchairs and 344 plain back ditto. . . . " The agreement included an option to purchase the chairs. The chairs were delivered and fitted in accordance with the regulations of the town council; that is each seat was fitted between two cast iron standards and each standard was fixed to the floor by four screws through the base. In 1901 the owner mortgaged the Hippodrome to the defendant bank. Things did not go well, and in 1902 the bank took possession under its mortgage and at the same time the plaintiffs demanded the return of the chairs. The issue was this: had the chairs become fixtures? If so, they had ceased to be the property of the plaintiffs and the defendants were entitled to retain them as part of the mortgaged land. Or had they retained their character a chattels and thus remained the property of the plaintiffs?

Joyce J. said: "No doubt a chattel on being attached to the soil or to a building prima facie becomes a fixture, but the presumption may be rebutted by showing that the annexation is incomplete so that the chattel can easily be removed without injury to itself or to the premises to which it is attached, and that the annexation is merely for a temporary purpose for the more complete enjoyment and use of the chattel as a chattel. . . . The mode of annexation of these chairs to the freehold is analogous rather to the mode in which a carpet is fastened to the floor. . . ."

He held that the chairs were still chattels.

The last sentence of Joyce J. is interesting in the light of the more recent Canadian case of *La Salle Recreations* v. *Canadian Camdex Investments*[50] which did in fact concern fitted carpets held down by the "Roberts' smooth edge or tackless method." This was a dispute between the owner of the carpets who hired them to an hotel and the mortgagee of the hotel. But here the British Columbia Court of Appeal held that the carpets had become fixtures. The physical attachment was negligible. The carpets rested at their edges on short nails pointing upwards and slanting towards the wall. As to the purpose of annexation, McFarlane J.A. said[51] that it was a question of "whether the goods were affixed to the building, though slightly, for the better use of the goods as goods, or for the better use of the building as an hotel building."

One other case is worth mentioning in the present context: *Vaudeville Electric Cinema Ltd.* v. *Muriset*.[52] Here, tip-up chairs

---

[50] (1969) 4 D.L.R. (3rd) 549.
[51] *Ibid.* at p. 554.
[52] [1923] 2 Ch. 74 (Sargant J.).

were fixed into a cinema in exactly the same way as the chairs in *Lyon's* case. The plaintiffs, the owners of the cinema, mortgaged it to the defendant. Subsequently, they went into liquidation and the mortgagees sold the cinema together with the chairs. In the present case the plaintiffs were claiming that the chairs were not fixtures and so not included in the mortgage and that the defendants were therefore acting wrongfully in selling them. Sargant J. held that they were fixtures and found it possible to distinguish *Lyon's* case on the ground that "the owner of the property (*i.e.* the cinema) was the owner of the chairs and that the chairs were being affixed for the permanent benefit and equipment of the property. . . . ." It will be remembered that in the *Lyon's* case the chairs had been owned by the hire company. But there is no doubt that a chattel can become a fixture even if put there by someone other than its owner.

It is impossible to reconcile all the cases relating to fixtures and the many conflicting decisions do suggest that the two tests—although commonly used in court—cannot be applied to give any predictable result. After all, the purpose of introducing most chattels is partly to make a more or less permanent improvement to what is already there and partly because that is the only way of enjoying them as chattels. A house is improved by a fitted carpet—permanent no doubt until the owner decides or can afford to get a new one; but, on the other hand, how else can a carpet be enjoyed? Similarly, a cinema would not be much of a cinema without seats; but if you have 345 tip-up seats, how else can you make use of them as chattels?[53]

Situations in which the distinction between fixture and chattels is important. The distinction is important wherever the distinction between land and chattels is important. In addition to the cases listed above,[54] the following are some of the situations in which the courts have had to distinguish between fixtures and chattels:

(a) On the expiry of a lease: Any chattel added by the tenant so as to become a fixture becomes part of the landlord's freehold. However, on the expiry of his lease, the tenant does have the right to remove trade fixtures, domestic or ornamental fixtures and agricultural fixtures which he has added.

(b) On the termination of a life interest: Again, fixtures added by the life tenant becomes part of the land and pass with the land to the next tenant entitled. However, the tenant's personal

---

[53] See also *Berkley* v. *Poulett* (1976) 241 E.G. 911 (C.A.).
[54] See above, p. 22.

representatives—or, in the case of an interest *pur autre vie*, the tenant himself—have the right to remove trade fixtures and domestic or ornamental fixtures added by the tenant.

(c) If land is mortgaged, the security will include (in the absence of agreement to the contrary) fixtures, whether put there before or after the creation of the mortgage.

Principle 12. Registered and unregistered title.

The ownership of land may be registered or unregistered.

Explanation.

If a landowner wishes to sell his land or an interest in it, he will need to be able to prove to the purchaser that he owns whatever interest he has agreed to sell, that is, he will need to prove his title. In general, a transferee of property cannot acquire a better title than the transferor. If V has a 21-year lease in Blackacre, he cannot transfer the fee simple. If he has a fee simple subject to a mortgage, he cannot effectively tansfer it free of that mortgage.

Before the legislation culminating in the Land Registration Act 1925, the title to all land was unregistered. A vendor could only prove his title by tracing the ownership back through the title deeds, showing how it had passed lawfully from one person to another until it became vested in him.

The legislation, now contained mainly in the Land Registration Act 1925, contains a scheme for the registration of title. The principle is that the owner of any piece of land will be registered as such in a central register; and this registration as proprietor will provide a guarantee of his title. A vendor whose title is registered proves his title to a purchaser simply by showing that he is the registered proprietor. As more and more titles are registered, so is the system of unregistered conveyancing disappearing.

At present the two systems still operate side by side. In general, the same basic rules of land law apply whether the title is registered or unregistered. The differences lie mainly in the field of conveyancing, that is, the rules governing the transfer of interests in land, and are dealt with in Chapters 24, 25 and 26. But where there are relevant differences, these are noted in the other chapters.

PART 2. BENEFICIAL OWNERSHIP

CHAPTER 2

BENEFICIAL FREEHOLD OWNERSHIP

SECTION I. THE NATURE OF BENEFICIAL OWNERSHIP

Principle 1. Beneficial and trust ownership

Since 1925 the only possible forms of legal ownership of land (*i.e.* the only possible legal estates) have been the fee simple absolute in possession and the term of years absolute.

Every piece of land—unless it is held directly by the Crown—must have a legal fee simple absolute in possession owner.[1] (He is commonly referred to as the freeholder.) It may also be subject to any number of legal leases.

The person who holds the legal estate is known as the estate owner.[2]

An estate owner may hold the land (*i.e.* the legal estate) for his own benefit. Technically he is said to own the estate in law and equity (or to hold the whole legal and equitable interest); such a person is called the <u>beneficial owner</u>.

Alternatively, the estate owner may be a trustee. That is he may hold the legal estate and the rights which go with it for the benefit of others, known as the beneficiaries. Technically, he holds the legal estate while the equitable interest is vested in one or more beneficiaries.[3]

The leasehold estate may similarly be held beneficially or in trust for others.

Explanation

This chapter is concerned with the beneficial freehold owner—the person who holds the fee simple absolute in law and equity. He is the sole owner of the land and the nearest thing possible in English law to an absolute owner. In theory he is not absolute owner because (as already explained)[4] he merely holds it as tenant for an estate in fee simple. But, as also explained,[4] his tenure imposes no obligation on him at all. Further, his estate is the greatest estate known to English law and so he can be thought of

---

[1] There may be up to four joint owners of the legal estate.
[2] L.P.A. 1925, s.1(4).
[3] A person who holds an equitable interest may similarly hold it beneficially or on trust.
[4] See above, pp. 6, 7.

as absolute owner of the land. Often he is simply referred to as the landowner or the freeholder.

Three aspects of the beneficial ownership need to be considered:

(a) *The physical extent of ownership.* Before considering a landowner's rights it is necessary to consider over exactly what area those rights extend. This is considered in the next Principle.

(b) *The rights of enjoyment.* It is necessary to consider the rules which govern what a landowner can and cannot do with his land. The mere fact that a person is owner does not entitle him to do exactly what he likes with the land. Suppose for example that he wants to keep pigs. In the first place he will have to consider planning law.[5] He may need planning permission from the local planning authority and this may not be forthcoming. Further, there is the law of nuisance.[6] If the smell from the pigs is more than a reasonble neighbour can be expected to tolerate, he may find the neighbour applying to the court for an injunction to stop this activity. Again, the property might be subject to a restrictive covenant against the keeping of animals.[7]

Rights of enjoyment are considered in the next two Sections.

(c) *The right to deal with the land.* The right of the beneficial freehold owner to deal with the land is largely unrestricted. As holder of the (legal) fee simple he can dispose of the land *inter vivos* or by will; he can subject the land to what third party rights he likes such as easements and restrictive covenants in favour of his neighbour; he can mortgage it as security for a loan; he can obtain an income from it by leasing it; or make provision for his family by settling it; and so on.

Since he holds for his own benefit there are no beneficiaries whose interests are liable to be affected by his dealings with the land. So his dealings are not governed by the restrictions which affect a trustee owner. For example, the beneficial freeholder can sell the land for as little or as much as he wishes; or he can give it away. A trustee owner, on the other hand, can sell but he must obtain the best price reasonably possible.[8] Again, the beneficial freeholder can mortgage the land as security for a loan and use the borrowed money for whatever purpose he likes; but a trustee estate owner can only raise money by mortgaging the trust land for

---

[5] See below, p. 60.
[6] See below, p. 42.
[7] See below, Chap. 20.
[8] See below, p. 213.

certain authorised purposes—such as authorised improvements to the land.[9]

The restrictions which affect trustees when dealing with trust land are considered in the next part of this book. Since there are no special restrictions on the beneficial freeholder there is no need to say more about his powers of dealing. He can create any of the interests and deal with the land in any of the ways described in the various parts of this book.

The rights of the beneficial leaseholder are considered in the next chapter. His rights depend mainly on the duration and the express or implied terms of the lease.

Principle 2. The physical extent of ownership

The landowner is presumed to own not only the surface of the soil but also everything which in law is deemed to be part of the land.

He is also in general entitled to any chattels (other than treasure trove) found on his land where the real owner cannot be found.

Explanation

Cujus est solum ejus est usque ad coelum et ad inferos. There is a presumption that *cujus est solum ejus est usque ad coelum et ad inferos*[10]: the person who owns the land also owns everything up to the sky and down to the centre of the earth. This is only a presumption which prevails in the absence of evidence to the contrary. Land can be divided horizontally as well as vertically.[11] Suppose that Rupert owns two fields—Blackacre and Whiteacre. He could, of course, sell off one of the fields, or part of one, thus dividing the land vertically. But equally he could sell off the minerals beneath both fields thus dividing his land horizontally.[12] He would then no longer be owner *ad inferos*. Or he could build a block of flats and sell off the freehold of each flat, except the bottom one, to a separate purchaser. His ownership would then no longer be *ad coelum*. Here each freeholder would have the freehold in a cube of space surrounded by bricks and held up, one hopes, by easements of support from the lower parts of the building.[13]

The landowner may, for example when he is selling, have to

---

[9] See below, p. 217.
[10] *Mitchell* v. *Moseley* [1914] 1 Ch. 438, at p. 450.
[11] See *Comr. for Railways* v. *Valuer General* [1973] 3 All E.R. 268.
[12] See *e.g. Forster* v. *Elvet Colliery Co. Ltd.* [1908] 1 K.B. 629.
[13] See E.F. George and A. George, *Sale of Flats,* (4th ed.), at p. 83 *et seq.*

prove his ownership of the land as a whole.[14] On particular occasions he may be required to prove his ownership of some specific part of the land—the minerals perhaps or a boundary feature dividing his property from a neighbour's. In *Davey* v. *Harrow Corporation*[15] the corporation would not have been liable for the enroaching roots of the hedgerow trees if they had not owned the hedge. In *Kelsen* v. *Imperial Tobacco Co.* (*of Great Britain and Ireland*) *Ltd.*[16] one of the defendants' arguments was tha the airspace above the shop had not been included in the demise to the plaintiff and that therefore the projection of their advertising sign into this space was not a wrong against *him*.

In general, however, the landowner is entitled to rely on the principle *Cujus est solum ejus est usque ad coelum et ad inferos*. This means that in general:

(a) If he is selling the land, although he must prove his ownership of the land as a whole before he can require the purchaser to complete, yet he does not have to prove his ownership of every separate part.

(b) Contracts and conveyances of land do not refer specifically to the air space above and the soil beneath the surface. The land is described in terms sufficient to identify it accurately on the ground. For example, "All that piece or parcel of land known as 22 Acacia Avenue, Trotsup, in the County of West Yorkshire." It is, however, usual practice to state expressly that the buildings on the land are included. In *Kelsen's* case, McNair J. said[17]: "It is common ground that, prima facie, the lease of land includes the lease of air space above it, and it seems to me also, prima facie, that the lease of a single-storey ground floor premises would include the lease of the air space above it."

(c) Prima facie the landowner can exercise his rights of ownership over whatever is above and whatever is below the surface and whatever is attached to the land as a fixture.[18]

Exceptions.   It has already been explained that in any particular case the evidence may show that some part of the land has passed into separate ownership. Apart from this, there are certain limitations which apply to all land. Some of these—such as river water which is not owned until lawfully appropriated—are dealt with below. Some others will be mentioned here.

[14] See below, p. 563.
[15] [1958] 1 Q.B. 60.
[16] [1957] 2 Q.B. 334. See below, p. 42.
[17] [1957] 2 Q.B. 334, at p. 339.
[18] See above, p. 24.

First, certain minerals are publicly owned. By the Petroleum (Production) Act 1934, s.1(1), "the property in petroleum existing in its natural condition in strata in Great Britain is hereby vested in [Her] Majesty, and [Her] Majesty shall have the exclusive right of searching and boring for and getting such petroleum." In this Act "petroleum" includes natural gas as well as oil. Under section 3 of the Coal Act 1938 and section 38 of the Coal Industry Nationalisation Act 1946, the National Coal Board "shall acquire in accordance with the provisions of this Part of this Act the fee simple in all coal and mines of coal together with such property and rights annexed thereto and such rights to withdraw support as are hereinafter mentioned. . . . "[19] Similarly, the Crown is entitled to gold and silver in mines.[20]

Secondly, the landowner does not own wild animals on his land; though he does have the exclusive right to catch and so make them his own. But the Crown has a prerogative right to white swans and royal fish (sturgeon and whales)[21]; and certain wild creatures are now protected by statute.[22]

Thirdly, while his right to the air space is protected by the ordinary laws of tort, the Civil Aviation Act 1949, s.40, protects the right of aircraft to fly over at a reasonable height. Further, the decision in *Bernstein of Leigh (Lord)* v. *Skyviews and General Ltd.*[23] suggests that, quite apart from statute, the landowner's right to the airspace extends only to such height as is necessary for ordinary use and enjoyment of the land and buildings on it; and that above this he has no greater right than any other member of the public.

Chattels found on the land. The landowner will in fact probably own most of the chattels on his land. But the point is that ownership of chattels is not normally governed by the ownership of the land on which they happen to be at any time—unless of course they have been converted into fixtures and so become part of the land.[24] In *Moffatt* v. *Kazana*[25] a Mr. Russell had hidden £1,987 in £1 notes in a biscuit tin which he had hidden in a false flue in the chimney of his bungalow. Subsequently he sold the bungalow to the defendant apparently having forgotten all about

---

[19] Coal Act 1938, s.3(1).
[20] At common law and by the Royal Mines Acts 1688, 1693.
[21] See Wild Creatures and Forest Laws Act 1971.
[22] See, *e.g.* Wildlife and Countryside Act 1981, Pt. I.
    Wild Plants Act 1975.
[23] [1977] 2 All E.R. 902 (Griffiths J.).
[24] See above, p. 24.
[25] [1969] 2 Q.B. 152.

his little "nest egg." When the defendant was having an Aga cooker installed in the kitchen the workmen dislodged some bricks in the chimney and down came the tin. The workmen who found the tin made no claim to it.[26] Wrangham J. held that the tin undoubtedly had belonged to Mr. Russell before the sale; that in the absence of agreement to the contrary the sale of land only conveys what is part of the land—not chattels; and that therefore Mr. Russell's widow was entitled to the money.

If the facts had been different and Mr. Russell had used the notes to paper the walls of the bungalow then no doubt they would have become fixtures and passed to the purchaser automatically as part of the land.[27]

Where chattels are found on land and the real owner cannot be traced, the general rule[28] seems to be that the owner of the land is entitled to them as against the finder. In *City of London Corporation* v. *Appleyard*[29] workmen on a site in the City of London found a safe built into a wall of a building they were demolishing. In the safe was £5,728 in notes. But honest toil was not to be rewarded. It was held that the lessees who were in lawful possession of the premises under their lease were also in possession of the safe which in the circumstances formed part of the premises—even though they were not aware of its existence until found. They were therefore entitled, as against the finders, to the safe and the money which it contained.[30]

Treasure trove, that is gold or silver in coin, plate or bullion form which has been hidden, where the real owner cannot be traced, is subject to special rules and belongs to the Crown.[30a]

SECTION II.   THE RIGHTS OF ENJOYMENT: THE LANDOWNER AND HIS NEIGHBOUR

Principle 3.   The principle of self-interest

Subject to the limits referred to in the following Principles, the landowner can do what he likes on his own land and enjoy it in

---

[26] Any claim by them could not have been better than the defendant's and so must have failed.

[27] This case also shows that s.62 of the L.P.A. 1925 does not apply to chattels. See below, p. 375, for s.62.

[28] But see *Hannah* v. *Peel* [1945] K.B. 509 and cases and article cited there. And *Parker* v. *British Airways Board* [1982] 1 All E.R. 834 (C.A.) which does little to make the law more certain.

[29] [1963] 1 W.L.R. 982.

[30] But under an express term in their lease they had to hand it over to their lessors, the Corporation of London.

[30a] See *Att.-Gen. of the Duchy of Lancaster* v. *G. E. Overton Farms Ltd.* [1982] 1 All E.R. 524 (C.A.).

whatever way he pleases. He will not be liable merely because his action causes loss to a neighbour or to the public generally.[31]

Explanation

After the Norman Conquest and during the period of the mediaeval common law, the pattern of land ownership was a complex, interwoven network of mutual rights and obligations. For a start there was a tenure, which has already been mentioned.[32] The tenant's holding necessarily involved him in the rights and obligations which formed the tenurial relationship between himself and his lord.

Not only that; the tenant had to regulate the enjoyment of his land in every detail—in particular his agricultural practices—to comply with the local pattern. This was a necessary consequence of the open field system of agriculture and the need for mutual co-operation between all local landholders throughout the agricultural year from ploughing to reaping. There was no room for individualism in land usage. If a tenant sowed winter wheat in his strips in the open fields, it was because all the other villagers were doing likewise.

Further, a large part of the land area used to support the village was common—either meadow or waste—in that each tenant shared the common right to use it; to receive a portion of the hay crop; to pasture his animals on it; to cut turf there for fuel; and so on.

Much of this system predated the common law and continued to be regulated in the local courts outside the common law machinery. But it has left its mark on the common law. Some of the rules of a simple agricultural community were received into and became part of the developing common law. Even today, some of the basic principles which still govern such matters as common rights, highways, the use of river and stream water, derive from this source.

However, by the nineteenth century, the essential pattern of land usage and therefore of land ownership had changed. The system of tenure had been dismantled. The methods introduced during the industrial and agricultural revolutions in the eighteenth

---

[31] See Friedmann, at p. 103, who contrasts the English attitude with the Continental doctrine of abuse of rights; but notes that even on the Continent *abus de droit* does not subject the use of property to the needs of the community. W. Friedmann, *Law in a Changing Society* (2nd ed.).

[32] See above, p.6.

and nineteenth centuries made possible, if not unavoidable,[33] the exploitation of land on an individualistic basis. Maximum profit depended on maximum control of his land by the landowner,[34] unfettered by tenure or common rights, and unfettered by any interference from the state.[35] The spirit of *laissez-faire* capitalism which gripped the country and drove the agricultural and industrial revoluations along, meant working against, not in co-operation with, the neighbour.

The pattern of land ownership by the nineteenth century had thus become a collection of separate, absolutely-owned holdings, rather than the interlocking jigsaw pattern of the earlier age. The principle governing enjoyment came to be the principle of self-interest and the right of the landowner to do what he wanted with his land. Even today, this is still generally stated as the basic premise of property law.

The classic example of judicial support for the principle of self-interest is the much quoted case of *Bradford Corporation* v. *Pickles*.[36] Here the plaintiffs had become owners of a public water undertaking by compulsory purchase. The reservoir was partly fed by water percolating through the defendant's adjoining land. The trouble arose when the defendant, by digging down into his own land, diverted the percolating water so that it never reached the reservoir. The Corporation sued. The defendant gave evidence that his motive was simply to drain his own land so that he could work the minerals; but it is clear from the report that his real reason was to deprive the Corporation of the water and thus force them to purchase his land at an attractive (for him) price. It was on this basis that the case was decided.

The House of Lords held that Pickles was not liable. A landowner, they reasoned, is entitled to abstract water percolating through his land even if he exhausts the supply and even if a neighbouring landowner suffers loss as a result. Further—and this was the real point in issue—his motive is irrelevant. He will not be liable even if his sole motive is to injure his neighbour, and even if that neighbour represents the local community. The following, from the judgment of Lord MacNaghten, probably expresses the general attitude of the court.[37]

[33] See *Land Reform and Economic Development* (Peter Dorner, 1972), for some modern systems of land usage on a co-operative basis.

[34] And also maximum freedom of contract, except between labourers; see Combination Acts 1799, 1801.

[35] And also unfettered by the claims of subsequent generations under settlements. See below, Chap. 5.

[36] [1895] A.C. 587.

[37] At p. 600.

"Well, he has something to sell, or, at any rate, he has something which he can prevent other people enjoying unless he is paid for it. Why should he, he may think, without fee or reward, keep his land as a storeroom for a commodity which the corporation dispense, probably not gratuitously, to the inhabitants of Bradford? He prefers his own interests to the public good."

This case has been followed in recent years, in *Langbrook Properties Ltd.* v. *Surrey County Council*.[38] In this case the plaintiffs, property developers, owned a three-acre site at Sunbury-on-Thames on which they had built shops, offices and residences. The defendant council were constructing a section of the M3 motorway on adjoining land. They had to keep the excavations dry by pumping out water as the work proceeded. The effect of pumping, however, was to draw off water which was percolating under the adjoining site and to cause settlement of the buildings and thus loss to the plaintiffs. Plowman J. followed *Bradford Corporation* v. *Pickles*[39] and decided that the County Council was not liable. There was, of course, no suggestion that the defendants in this case were motivated by any sort of desire to cause loss to the plaintiffs.

This principle of self-interest, that a landowner can do just what he likes on his land, has been applied in contexts other than that of percolating water. For example, the courts have held that it is not wrong for a person to build a bridge over a river even though this causes loss of trade to a nearby ferry. In another case it was held lawful for a landowner to set up a decoy for ducks with the object of attracting ducks from his neighbour's decoy. And, of course, it is quite generally the rule that commercial competition is legitimate even if it causes the bankruptcy of one of the competitors.

However, the principle is far from universal. There is another general principle which is sometimes used by the courts and which directly contradicts the principle of self-interest. This is the principle *sic utere tuo ut alienum non laedas*—use your property so as not to injure that of others. It is this principle which has inspired the development of the tort of nuisance—restricting a landowner's enjoyment so as to protect his neighbour's. Nuisance and other torts are considered below,[40] but it is convenient to mention in the present context two types of limitation imposed by the law of nuisance on the principle of self-interest.

---

[38] [1970] 1 W.L.R. 161.
[39] See above, n. 36.
[40] See below, p. 41.

⫨ First, there are some things which a landowner cannot do on his
land however good his motive. For example, *Bradford Corporation* v. *Pickles*[41] was concerned with percolating water. The rule
for rivers is quite different.[42] A landowner never had more than a
limited right to abstract such water. Even a local authority
endeavouring to supply a town's water needs must obtain statutory
authority before taking the water.

⫨ Secondly, in some situations, the motive of the defendant has in
fact been held to be relevant. In other words there are some things
which a landowner can do provided that his motive is not
considered by the courts to be unlawful. For example, in the case
of *Hollywood Silver Fox Farm* v. *Emmett*[43] the plaintiff had started
a silver fox farm on his land. The defendant owned an adjoining
field which he was about to develop and he was afraid that the
advertising sign that the plaintiff had put up and which could be
seen from his land would be detrimental to its value. The plaintiff
refused to remove the sign. The defendant did not remain idle.
During the spring, the mating time for silver foxes, he went on a
number of occasions and stood on his land near the boundary with
the plaintiff's land and discharged his 12-bore shot gun into the air.
As anyone will tell you, vixens are very sensitive creatures during
the mating season. They were more than upset by the noise. At
least one of them devoured her cubs. Others refused to mate at all.
The plaintiff sued for nuisance; and the court held that it was
entitled to consider the motive of the defendant; that his sole
motive was to injure the plaintiff and that therefore he was liable
for nuisance.[44] If he had been shooting at the same time and in the
same place but with the object of shooting rabbits on his land he
would not, it seems, have been liable.

Most disputes which arise between neighbouring landowners
will be more or less covered by binding authority. But where there
is no authority, the courts must decide between the two principles,
between the freedom of the landowner and the protection of his
neighbour. As it has been said, "a balance has to be maintained
between the right of the occupier to do what he likes with his own
and the right of his neighbour not to be infered with."[45]

---

[41] See above, n. 36.
[42] See below, p. 51.
[43] [1936] 2 K.B. 468.
[44] Friedmann (above, n. 31), at p. 103, treats this as an exceptional case.
[45] *Sedleigh-Denfield* v. *O'Callaghan* [1940] A.C. 880, at p. 903, *per* Lord Wright.

Principle 4.   Restrictions on enjoyment

A landowner's rights of enjoyment may be restricted:
(a)   In the interests of subsequent owners of the land.
(b)   In the interests of neighbouring landowners.
(c)   In the interests of the public at large.

Explanation

It is convenient to consider the possible restrictions on a landowner's rights of enjoyment under the above headings. The first can be dealt with briefly since there is no limit to a beneficial freeholder's rights of enjoyment on these grounds. Unlike the limited owner, such as the life tenant, the beneficial freeholder can dispose of his land as he wishes *inter vivos* or by will; and he is not considered by the law to have any responsibility to those who may succeed to ownership of that piece of land.[46] He may pull down buildings, cut trees, exhaust the mineral wealth and generally depreciate its capital value. In contrast, a life tenant is much more limited in his rights of enjoyment. He is regarded as a temporary owner, entitled to enjoy the fruits of the land for his lifetime, but nothing more. The buildings, trees, minerals, etc. are regarded as part of the capital inheritance, which must be preserved for the equal enjoyment of each succeeding generation of beneficiaries. The rights of enjoyment of limited owners are considered later.[47]

The rest of this Section II is concerned with limits on enjoyment imposed for protection of neighbours.

Limits imposed for the benefit of the public at large are considered in the next Section III.

Principle 5.   Restrictions imposed by the law of torts [48]

A landowner must not use his land in any way that constitutes a tort against a neighbouring landowner.[49]

Explanation

The law or torts is the oldest limit on a landowner's rights of enjoyment. It has always been recognised, even in the period

---

[46] He is subject to the more general responsibility to the public imposed by planning law.

[47] Below, p. 243.

[48] See generally, Winfield and Jolowicz on *Tort* (11th ed., 1979) and other standard books on tort.

[49] The law of torts also protects enjoyment of third party rights such as easements and profits. See *Weston* v. *Lawrence Weaver Ltd.* [1961] 1 Q.B. 402.

which most favoured the idea of unrestricted ownership, that one landowner must be prepared to limit the enjoyment of his land in the interests of neighbouring landowners. The absolute freedom of each landowner is limited to make life reasonably tolerable for all. Thus, although the law of torts limits a landowner's enjoyment, at the same time it does protect the limited enjoyment which is permitted. If a river runs through my land, I will be liable in nuisance to riparian owners lower down stream if I pollute the water. But at the same time I will have a remedy if the water reaching me is polluted by those owning land higher up.

The torts most likely to concern the landowner are trespass to land and nuisance; but he must also bear in mind negligence, the Rule in *Rylands* v. *Fletcher*, his liability to visitors and others on his land (generally referred to as occupiers' liability) and liability for damage done by animals.

The rest of this explanation is intended to do no more than give some indication of the application of these torts in practice.

Trespass to land and nuisance. Trespass to land has been defined as that form of trespass which is constituted by unjustifiable interference with the possession of land.[50]

In *Kelsen* v. *Imperial Tobacco Co. Ltd.*[51] the plaintiff held the lease of a tobacconist's shop. The owners of the adjoining three storey building had allowed the defendants to affix to the side of their wall a large sign which thus projected over the plaintiff's single storey building. The sign said: "Players Please." It was large, being some twenty feet by eight feet, but being affixed to the wall it projected over the plaintiff's property by eight inches at most. And it was not causing the plaintiff any actual damage of any sort. Nevertheless, he complained and it was held that he was entitled to an injunction ordering the removal of the sign.

This case also illustrates the principle that a plaintiff suing in trespass does not have to prove damage in order to succeed. Trespass is said to be actionable *per se*. If someone walks across your land without permission that is trespass and you can sue him. However, before you rush out and issue a writ against him one or two points should be considered.

First, the common law remedy of damages is designed to compensate a plaintiff for his loss. You may win your case, get judgment in your favour, but if in fact the defendant has not damaged your property in any way, you can only get nominal

---

[50] Winfield and Jolowicz (n. 48 above), at p. 335.
[51] [1957] 2 Q.B. 334.

damages[52]—a token sum which shows that technically your right has been infringed. This may be all you are seeking. Trespass is commonly employed simply as a device for settling disputes as to the ownership of land. The court will decide whether you are the owner and the defendant the trespasser, or vice versa.

Secondly, it needs to be remembered that the court always has a discretion as to costs and a successful plaintiff may not be awarded costs if the court considers that he should not have brought the action.[53]

Thirdly, the alternative to damages as a remedy for trespass is the injunction, ordering the trespass to cease. As *Kelsen's* case shows it may be perfectly proper to ask for an injunction even where you cannot prove damage. A man is entitled to protect the integrity of his boundaries. But, on the other hand, the injunction is an equitable and therefore discretionary remedy. Even if you prove the trespass, the court may still consider it proper to refuse the injunction. In *Woollerton & Wilson Ltd.* v. *Richard Costain Ltd.*[54] the plaintiffs owned premises and the defendants were building contractors developing the adjoining site. It was a confined site in a built up area and they had no alternative but to swing the jib of their tower crane over the plaintiffs' building. There was no danger but the plaintiffs were seeking to "exploit the artificial value which their air space had acquired as a result of the defendants' needs."[55] The defendants had offered to pay £250 a week but this was apparently not enough and the plaintiffs started the present proceedings claiming an injunction. The court produced a neat solution. It granted the injunction but suspended its operation until the date when the building operations were due to be completed.

Nuisance has been defined as the "unlawful interference with a person's use or enjoyment of land, or some right over it or in connection with it."[56] In general, it arises from the use, or rather misuse, of land.

---

[52] As to exemplary or punitive damages see Winfield and Jolowicz (above, n. 48). at p. 592; and see below, p. 117, n. 40.

[53] This is unlikely to happen. See the *Supreme Court Practice* (1979), (the "White Book"), Ord. 62, r.2.

[54] [1970] 1 W.L.R. 411 (doubted in *Charrington* v. *Simons & Co. Ltd.* [1971] 1 W.L.R. 598).

[55] Winfield and Jolowicz (above n. 48), at p. 341, n. 43.

[56] Winfield and Jolowicz (above n. 48), at p. 355. This section is concerned with private nuisance which should be distinguished from public nuisance. Private nuisance arises from an interference with the individual land owner's enjoyment. Public nuisance arises from interference with the rights or comforts of the public

The main distinction between nuisance and trespass to land is that in the case of trespass the wrongful interference must be direct and immediate; in the case of nuisance it is indirect and consequential. If I throw the branch of a tree onto your land that is trespass; if I plant a tree with the result that the branch grows over your boundary, that is nuisance.

Davey v. *Harrow Corporation*[57] illustrates nuisance. The plaintiff owned a property in Pinner, Middlesex; next door was a cemetery owned by the defendant corporation and the two properties were divided by a hedge also owned by the corporation. The hedge contained elm trees the roots of which had spread into the plaintiff's land causing subsidence and damage to his house and garage. It was held that the plaintiff was entitled to damages in nuisance.

Nuisance is a wide ranging tort. It covers not only physical damage to the plaintiff's property but also any substantial interference with his enjoyment of the property or his personal comfort. In the well-known case of *St. Helens Smelting Co.* v. *Tipping*[58] the plaintiff's trees and shrubs were damaged by fumes from the defendants's smelting works. This was physical damage to the property. In *Hollywood Silver Fox Farm* v. *Emmett*[59] there was interference with the plaintiff's business. In *Christie* v. *Davey*[60] the defendant caused the plaintiff personal discomfort by hammering and beating trays against the dividing wall. In all these cases the defendants were held liable for nuisance.

Nuisance includes damage caused by, amongst other things, water, smoke, smells, fumes, gas, heat vibrations, electricity, germs, vegetation, and so on.

On the other hand, not every activity which happends to offend a neighbouring landowner or even damage his property will constitute nuisance. If this were so the ordinary enjoyment of land would be seriously hampered. "The affairs of life in a dense neighbourhood cannot be carried on without mutual sacrifice of comfort."[61] Nuisance only arises where the interference results from the defendant exceeding the bounds of what the courts consider to be the reasonable use of his property. Whether one landowner's activity is unreasonable and so constitutes a nuisance

or a section of the public. For example, obstruction of the highway. Public nuisance is a crime and the individual can only sue in tort if he suffers special damage.

[57] [1958] 1 Q.B. 60.   [58] (1865) 11 H.L.C. 642.
[59] [1936] 2 K.B. 468.   [60] [1893] 1 Ch. 316.
[61] Street on *Torts* (6th ed. 1976), at p. 225, citing Erle C.J. in *Cavey* v. *Ledbitter* (1863) 13 C.B.N.S. 470, at p. 476; and see *Kennaway* v. *Thompson* [1980] 3 All E.R. 329 (C.A.).

against his neighbour depends basically on the degree of interference which it causes; but the permissible degree of interference depends in turn on many factors which will vary from case to case. It is not possible to say that X decibels of noise will constitute a nuisance at all times and in all places.

The defendant's motive may be relevant,[62] so too will the locality—noise, smoke, etc., are far more likely to be considered a nuisance in a residential than an industrial area. The noise from a confectioner's pestle and mortar is more likely to be adjudged a nuisance in an area largely devoted to medical practitioners than in an industrial area.[63] It has been stated judicially that: "What would be a nuisance in Belgrave Square would not necessarily be so in Bermondsey. . . . [64] However, where there is material damage to the plaintiff's property it is not likely to be excused by the nature of the locality.

Fault and strict liability. The general principle in both trespass and nuisance is that liability is not strict but based on fault; the defendant will only be liable if the wrong was intended or the result of his negligence.

The nature of trespass is such, being a direct or immediate interference, that the wrongful act is usually intended. But it may be the result of negligence only. In *National Coal Board* v. *J.E. Evans & Co. (Cardiff) Ltd.*[65] the defendants were contractors and in the course of excavating a trench, struck the plaintiff's electric cable. It was held that as the damage was neither intentional nor negligent they were not liable. This was a case of trespass to goods but it seems likely that the same principle applies to trespass to land.[66]

The same general principle applies in nuisance. Occasionally, as in *Hollywood Silver Fox Farm* v. *Emmett*[67] the damage will have been intended. More usually it is a question of negligence. Did the landowner take reasonable steps to avoid or minimise the effects of his activity. If he did the plaintiff will have no claim even if he has suffered substantial damage or interference. In *Bolton* v. *Stone*[68] a cricket match was being played on the defendant's land. An unusually big hit by one of the batsmen flew over the fence

[62] See above, p. 40.
[63] See *Sturges* v. *Bridgeman* (1879) 11 Ch.D. 852.
[64] *Sturges* v. *Bridgeman, ibid.,* at p. 865, *per* Thesiger L.J.
[65] [1951] 2 K.B. 861 (C.A.).
[66] See also *Fowler* v. *Lanning* [1959] 1 Q.B. 426, (Diplock J.); also Winfield and Jolowicz (n. 48 above), at p. 107, and cases and authorities cited there.
[67] Above, n. 59.
[68] [1951] A.C. 850.

which was 75 yards from and 17 feet above the level of the wicket, on a further 100 years and struck the plaintiff who was standing in the highway. The risk of the ball being hit out of the ground was remote. It had happened before but only on a very few occasions; about six times in the last 30 years. The risk of it hitting someone outside the ground was even more remote. The activity as carried on could not be regarded as dangerous and so the defendants were not liable.

Where the danger results not from the landowner's activity but from something happening naturally on his land,[69] he is only expected to do what is reasonably possible in all the circumstances to remove the cause of the nuisance once he has or should have discovered its existence. The courts will take into account the fact that the situation is not of his own making.[70]

However, there are certain dangerous activities which the landowner carries on at his own risk regardless of fault. It is not enough for him to take care to avoid the damage. His only proper course is not to carry on the activity at all. In these cases there is said to be strict liability: that is, the person "acts at his peril and is responsible for the consequences how ever careful he may have been to prevent them."[71]

Thus, in *Castle* v. *St. Augustine's Links*,[72] for example, the defendants owned and ran a golf course. The thirteenth tee was close to a busy public road and it was apparently quite common for players to slice their shots from the tee onto the road. This is exactly what the second defendant did but on this occasion the ball smashed through the windscreen of the plaintiff's taxi, causing a glass splinter to enter his eye and the eventual loss of the eye. The second defendant emigrated to Australia and so the action proceeded against the owners of the course. They were held liable in nuisance. They were not responsible for the damaging shot—indeed, there was no evidence that the player had not used all reasonable care in making it. The judge was satisfied that "many a ball had been sliced onto this public road, and he did not think that would be said to be the result of careless and bungling playing. . . . "[73] What they were responsible for was creating the

---

[69] Or from the activity of a trespasser. See *Sedleigh-Denfield* v. *O'Callaghan* [1940] A.C. 880.
[70] See *Goldman* v. *Hargrave* [1967] 1 A.C. 645; and see *Leakey* v. *National Trust for Places of Historic or Natural Beauty* [1980] 1 All E.R. 17 (C.A.).
[71] *Salmond on Torts* (17th ed.), at p. 61.
[72] (1922) 38 T.L.R. 615 (Sankey J.).
[73] At p. 616.

dangerous situation in the first place by putting the thirteenth tee near a busy public road where damage was likely to be caused.

Similarly, an occupier may be liable regardless of fault if he places artificial projections such as lamps overhanging the highway which cause injury to a passer-by through failure to repair.[74]

The right to sue in nuisance and trespass to land. One of the general principles of English land law is that the law protects possession rather than ownership.[75] This means that, in the case of nuisance and trespass to land, the ownership of the land is not relevant. The plaintiff merely has to show that he was in possession when the tort was committed. And the defendant cannot defeat his claim by proving that some third party, not the plaintiff, was the real owner. This last principle is sometimes expressed by saying that *jus tertii* (third party's right) is no defence.[76]

For the same reasons, a landlord cannot sue a person committing a tort against the land unless the tort damages his reversionary interest in some way.

Whether or not the courts will recognise a plaintiff as having sufficient possession to entitle him to sue may be a difficult question to which there is no simple answer.[77]

Who can be sued for nuisance and trespass to land. In the case of trespass to land the person liable is the person who commits the tresapass.

Nuisance arises from the wrongful use of land. Again the person who commits the nuisance will be liable. Generally, he will also be the occupier of the land where the nuisance arises; but in some cases the occupier of the land will be liable even though he himself did not create the nuisance. For example, the occupier will be liable for a nuisance created by his servants, agents and others under his control. In certain exceptional cases he may be liable for a nuisance created by his independent contractor. Again he may be liable for the act of a trespasser if he knows or should know about the nuisance and yet fails to abate it.[78]

Conversely, in certain cases, a landlord who is not in possession may be liable for nuisances created by his tenant. Broadly

---

[74] *Tarry* v. *Ashton* (1876) 1 Q.B.D. 314. But see Winfield and Jolowicz (n. 48 above), at p. 392. And see Defective Premises Act 1972, s.4.
[75] See below, p. 503.
[76] For *jus tertii* principle see Winfield and Jolowicz (above, n. 48), at p. 337.
[77] See Winfield and Jolowicz (above n. 48), at p. 336 and books mentioned there at n. 12.
[78] *Sedleigh-Denfield* v. *O'Callaghan* [1940] A.C. 880.

speaking, this will be the case if he is or was in a position to enter and abate the nuisance.[79]

Rylands v. Fletcher. The most important instance of strict liability affecting the landowner is the tort referred to as the Rule in *Rylands* v. *Fletcher*.[80] It has been defined as follows: "The occupier of land who brings and keeps upon it anything likely to do damage if it escapes is bound at his peril to prevent its escape, and is liable for all the direct consequences of its escape, even if he has been guilty of no negligence."[81] In the case which gave its name to this tort, the defendants constructed a reservoir on their land. It was constructed on the top of old mine workings. But the defendants employed independent contractors to do the work and the latter negligently failed to discover these workings. As a result, the water escaped from the reservoir and flooded the plaintiff's mine causing him damage. The defendants themselves had not been negligent in any way. Nevertheless, they were held liable for the loss suffered.

Rylands v. *Fletcher* is an offshot of nuisance. They overlap and it is sometimes difficult to draw the dividing line between them. The important point is this: in certain circumstances, the courts will regard a landowner's activity as creating a special danger—that is "a more than ordinary risk of accidents or a risk of more than ordinary damage if accidents in fact result."[82] In these cases it does not matter whether they are classified as *Rylands* v. *Fletcher* or nuisance, the courts will impose strict liability. The fault of the landowner lies not in the way he conducts the activity, but in starting it in the first place.

The landowner's liability for animals illustrates further the distinction between strict and fault liability. Under the Animals Act 1971, the landowner will be strictly liable if his livestock stray onto the land of another. Further, there is strict liability for damage done by animals which belong to a dangerous species or by any other animal if, known to its keeper, it has dangerous characteristics which make it likely to do the damage complained of. Apart from these special cases, liability for animals is based on fault and will be dealt with by the courts under the ordinary rules of trespass, nuisance or negligence.

---

[79] See *Brew Bros. Ltd.* v. *Snax (Ross) Ltd.* [1970] 1 Q.B. 612.
[80] (1868) L.R. 3 H.L. 330.
[81] Salmond on Torts (17th ed.), at p. 314.
[82] Law Com.No. 32, at para. 7.

Principle 6.   Support for the soil

A landowner has a natural right[83] to have his soil supported by the soil of his neighbour's land. Any interference with that support will constitute an actionable nuisance.

He does not have any natural right to have his buildings supported by his neighbour's buildings or by his neighbour's soil[84] but such a right may be acquired as an easement.[85]

Explanation

Suppose that A and B are the respective owners of a pair of old semi-detached cottages which support each other. A demolishes his cottage and this causes B's to collapse. B's natural right of support for his soil has not been interfered with. He will only be able to claim damages if he can show (which in fact will generally be possible in such cases) that at some time in the past he has acquired an easement of support for his building from A's.

Suppose instead that X and Y own adjoining plots of land and that X excavates the clay from his land to use to make bricks. Y uses his land as a market garden. As a result of X's excavations too close to the boundary, Y's land starts to slip. X will be liable for removing the support from Y's soil. This is precisely what happened in the case of *Redland Bricks Ltd.* v. *Morris*.[86]

If buildings are damaged as a result of removing the support for the soil, then the plaintiff will be entitled to compensation in respect of both the soil and the buildings. But if the soil only collapses because of the extra weight of the plaintiff's buildings, there will be no claim in respect of either.

Principle 7.   Water: classification and ownership

At common law water can be classified into the following categories:

(1) Non tidal:

    (a)   Rivers and streams.[87]
    (b)   Percolating water.[88]
    (c)   Lakes and ponds.
    (d)   Water in artificial channels.

[83] See below, p. 57 for distinction between natural and acquired rights.
[84] See *Ray* v. *Fairway Motors* (*Barnstaple*) *Ltd.* (1968) 20 P. & C.R. 261, (C.A.).
[85] See Chap. 15, below, for easements.
[86] [1970] A.C. 652.
[87] Whether above or below the ground.
[88] *Ibid.*

(2) Tidal rivers and the sea.

Under the Water Resources Act 1963 the main classification is as follows:

(i) Inland waters; this includes surface waters in categories (1) (a) (c) (d) and (2) above.[89]

(ii) Water in any underground strata.

The water itself while flowing in its natural state is not in general owned by anyone. The bed over which the water flows is capable of ownership and ownership is normally proved in the same way as the ownership of any other land.[90] However, in the absence of evidence to the contrary the following presumptions apply:

(a) The landowner is presumed to own the bed of any non-tidal river running through his land.

(b) Where a non-tidal river divides two properties the boundary is presumed to run down the middle of the river.

(c) The bed of the sea and tidal water is presumed to be vested in the Crown up to ordinary high water mark.

(d) The landowner is presumed to own both the bed and the water of ponds and lakes situated wholly on his land.

Explanation

Water, like wild animals, does not naturally recognise the boundaries of private ownership. A single stream or river will generally cross, and percolating water lie beneath, many differently owned properties. The natural conclusion drawn from this by the law is that the water itself is not owned by any landowner.

On the other hand, the bed does not move. It is simply land with water flowing over it. There is no reason why the bed should not be subject to the ordinary rules of land ownership. Any person claiming ownership of the bed will have to prove his ownership in the same way that he proves his ownership of any piece of land, from the title deeds (or register of title), from possession, etc. In the absence of evidence to the contrary the presumptions mentioned above will apply.

In *Fowley Marine (Emsworth) Ltd.* v. *Gafford*[91] the plaintiffs claimed to be owners of Fowley Rythe, a tidal creek used by small boats for navigation and mooring. The defendants had used a mooring in the creek since 1961 and resisted when the plaintiffs

[89] But ponds and lakes will not generally be sources of supply. See s.2(3) of the Act.

[90] See below, p. 563.

[91] [1968] 2 Q.B. 618.

started trying to make them pay a mooring fee. The result was the present action in trespass. It is ownership of the bed which entitles one to make a charge for mooring, and the presumption in the case of tidal waters is that ownership is vested in the Crown. However, the plaintiffs claimed that they had acquired ownership as a result of an original grant, the Wandesford Grant of 1628, from the Crown coupled with subsequent conveyances going back 60 years to a good root of title. Alternatively they claimed ownership on the grounds of adverse possession[92] against the Crown. There was evidence that from time to time the plaintiffs had laid moorings in the Rythe and given permission to others to do the same. For six years before 1913 it had been let by the plaintiffs' predecessors. Since they bought it in 1963 the plaintiffs had actively asserted their ownership.

The defendants did not claim ownership of the Rythe. They simply argued that the plaintiffs did not own it and therefore had no title to sue them in trespass. In the event the court neatly side-stepped the question of who owned the Rythe—the plaintiffs, the Crown, or someone else. They simply decided that the plaintiffs had shown sufficient exclusive possession to entitle them to sue. "Thus it is well established that a person in possession of land has a perfectly good title against all the world but the rightful owner. . . . It is equally well estabished that as against the party in possession a defendant cannot set up the title of a third party unless he himself claims under it."[93]

Principle 8. Water: abstraction

Under the Water Resources Act 1963, a person wishing to abstract or impound water from any source of supply—that is from any inland water other than a lake or from any underground strata—must first obtain a licence from the regional water authority. Any person with a right of access to the source of supply can apply for a licence which, if granted, will specify the quantity of water which can be abstracted, the means and purpose of the abstraction and the period for which the licence is to continue.

A licence is not required to abstract water from an inland water for use on land contiguous to the point of abstraction for domestic and agricultural purposes (other than spray irrigation).

A licence is also not required to abstract water for domestic purposes from an underground strata.

---

[92] See below, p. 503 *et seq.*

[93] *Per* Willmer L.J., at p. 634. For principle that *jus tertii* is no defence to action in trespass or nuisance, see above, p. 47.

If a person abstracts water without the necessary licence he will be guilty of an offence.

If a landowner abstracts water from a stream or river he will be liable to a lower riparian owner in nuisance without proof of damage unless his abstraction is authorised by licence or is permissible at common law.

Explanation

Abstraction at common law. From earliest times water has been an essential commodity—for use in the household and for agriculture; for the discharge of sewage and waste; for the supply of fish and as a means of transport; and, increasingly important, as a source of power and for other industrial uses.

Thus, although the water itself could not be owned, the courts had to regulate to competing claims to make use of it.

In the case of non-tidal rivers, the basic principle was that the right to use the water went with ownership of riparian land—that is land on the river bank together with some part of the river bed.[94] This really followed from the fact that no one else had access to the river without committing trespass. However, this riparian right could not be absolute in all respects. The common law courts had to strike some sort of balance between several riparian owners all interested in the same river. These rules were laid down in an age when the industrial use of water, apart from its use for driving mills, was uncommon. They were also laid down in an age before the growth of large urban populations without immediate access to a sufficient natural water supply. Consequently, from a modern viewpoint, the rules are very restrictive. The riparian landowner was entitled to abstract water from a river for use on the riparian land for domestic purposes and the watering of his cattle, even if this use exhausted the supply. Any other use was considered extraordinary. And such extraordinary use was permitted but only on riparian land and only if the water was returned to the river substantially unaltered in quantity and quality.

Subject to this permitted use by those higher up stream, each riparian owner was entitled to the flow of river water through his

---

[94] As to whether ownership of part of the bed is necessary for exercise of riparian rights see *Lord* v. *Sydney Commissioners* (1859) 12 Moo.P.C. 473; 14 E.R. 991, where the point was expressly left open: see also *Jones* v. *Llanrwst U.D.C.* [1911] 1 Ch. 393, which decided that there is right of flow of unpolluted water past plaintiff's land even without ownership of river bed; and see *per* Lord Cairns in *Lyon* v. *Fishmongers' Co.* (1876) 1 App.Cas. 662, at p. 673.

land, undiminished, unchecked and unaltered in quality.[95] Any wrongful interference with the flow was a nuisance actionable without proof of damage.

As to percolating water and water in ponds, the rule at common law was that the landowner had an absolute right of abstraction.[96]

The Water Resources Act 1963.[97] The case of *Rugby Joint Water Board* v. *Walters*[98] demonstrates the inadequacy of these common law rules in today's industrial and urban society. The defendant was abstracting water from the river for the spray irrigation of his crops. He was sued by the Water Board and held liable. For reasons not relevant here the case was governed by the pre-Water Resources Act common law rules. The point was this. If he had been using the traditional ditch irrigation method, the water would apparently have drained back into the river more or less undiminished and he would have been within his rights. But spray irrigation, though it might be more efficient, was not permissible because it did not return the water to the stream.

Again, at common law, a water company owning land on the bank of a river has no right to abstract water to provide a water supply for a neighbouring town since the water is not being used on riparian land.[99]

The law governing abstraction and pollution of water has been changed substantially by statute, in particular the Water Resources Act 1963.[1]

This Act has set up machinery to govern the use of water on a national basis. In formulating legislation Parliament has had to consider a number of factors:

(1) The prospect of a national water shortage. It has been said that: " . . . there seems to be no obvious limit to the growth in the demand for water from statutory water undertakings both to meet the increased domestic consumption consequent upon rising social standards and to serve the growing demands of industry . . . It is inevitable that in the future increasing quantities of water must be moved over long distances and radically new plans examined."[2]

---

[95] In contrast there is no natural right to the flow of air over land. See below, p. 359. See *Harris* v. *De Pinna* (1866) 33 Ch.D. 238.

[96] See above, p. 38 *et seq.*

[97] See M. Harwood, "The Effect of the Water Resources Act 1963 on the Common Law Right to Abstract Water"; (1969) 33 Conv.(N.S.) 14.

[98] [1967] Ch. 397 (Buckley J.).

[99] *Swindon Water Works Co. Ltd.* v. *Wilts. and Berks.Canal Navigation Co.* (1875) L.R. 7 H.L. 697.

[1] See also Water Resources Act 1968, Water Resources Act 1971 and Water Act 1973.

[2] Report of the Central Advisory Water Committee: *The Future Management of Water in England and Wales* (1971), paras. 102, 103.

The use of any particular source of supply can no longer be regarded as a privilege to be shared between those who happen to own adjacent land; the water resources of one river basin are of interest to the inhabitants of other river basins; and every available source of supply is a matter of public concern.

(2) This shortage of water has created the need to conserve and, equally important, to protect the purity of, existing supplies; to develop new sources of supply—for example by the desalination of sea water; and to plan for the transfer of water from areas with excess to areas with shortage.

(3) The need to extend the uses permitted by the common law.

The Water Act 1973 has set up a system of regional water authorities[3] under central government control to be responsible within the framework of a national water policy for the conservation and proper use, the augmentation and the redistribution of all water resources in the country, and also for the supply of water, the disposal of sewage, land drainage, the protection of fisheries and the use of water for recreation.[4]

This book is about the private landowner—though it is hoped seeing him with his face to the public—and it is possible to deal specifically only with the effect of this legislation on the landowner's rights to abstract water from inland water and underground strata.[5]

The licensing system enables the water authorities to control the amount of water abstracted from any available source of supply and to raise revenue by charging both a fee for the issue of a licence and a rate for the water abstracted.

The effect on the landowner is that he must generally apply for a licence if he wishes to abstract water for any purpose from any source of supply.[6] But in some ways at least, his rights of abstraction are extended rather than restricted. In the first place he does not need a licence to abstract water from an inland water if the water is going to be used on contiguous land for domestic or agricultural purposes other than spray irrigation—these more than cover the cases in which he had an unlimited right of abstraction at common law. Secondly, a licence may be granted to authorise abstractions which would not have been possible at common law. For example, a licence may authorise abstraction from a river by a non-riparian owner; abstraction for use on non-riparian land; and

[3] Replacing the local river authorities set up under the 1963 Act.
[4] Water Act 1973, s.1; as amended by Wales Act 1978, Sched. 11.
[5] See particularly Pt. IV of the 1963 Act.
[6] Water Resources Act 1963, s.23.

it may authorise an extraordinary use such as spray irrigation without the water having to be returned to the river.

This does mean that the rights of a lower riparian owner may be more limited. At common law he could complain if any water was removed permanently by a higher owner for any but ordinary use. Now in addition he must tolerate any other abstraction which is licensed.[7]

To a large extent, the Water Resources Act 1963 has removed this aspect of land law from the sphere of private to that of public law, from the relationship between the landowner and his neighbour to that between the landowner and the state.[8]

Principle 9. Water: pollution

A landowner will be liable in nuisance if he pollutes or alters the natural quality of river, percolating or lake water flowing through his neighbour's land.

It is in general an offence to discharge any "poisonous, noxious or polluting matter"[9] into any river or coastal water or, in some cases, underground water.[10]

The discharge of trade effluent and sewage effluent into rivers, underground strata and tidal water[11] is generally an offence[12] unless authorised by the water authorities who can impose conditions as to the amount, temperature, purity, etc., of the discharge.[13]

Explanation

Under common law a riparian owner is entitled to the flow of water through or past his land "in its natural state of purity undeteriorated by noxious matters discharged into it by others." Anyone who fouls this water infringes his right of property, and, therefore, he can maintain an action without proving that he has been actually damaged.[14]

In *Green* v. *Matthews & Co.*[15] the plaintiff was a farmer and

---

[7] If he has a "protected right" he may claim compensation from the water authority. See Water Resources Act 1963, ss.26, 29(2), 50.
[8] For relationship between common law and the Act, see *Cargill* v. *Gotts* [1981] 1 All E.R. 682 (C.A.).
[9] Control of Pollution Act 1974, s.31(1).
[10] See, generally, Control of Pollution Act 1974, Pt. II.
[11] Control of Pollution Act 1974, ss.56, 31(1).
[12] Control of Pollution Act 1974, s.32.
[13] *Ibid.*, s.34.
[14] *Per* Parker J. in *Jones* v. *Llanrwst U.D.C.* [1911] 1 Ch. 393, 402.
[15] (1930) 46 T.L.R. 206 (Eve J.).

lessee of a dairy farm known as Culver's Farm, Gillingham,
Dorset. The defendants owned nearby land which included a
brewery, stables and some cottages. The plaintiff's complaint was
that the defendants had polluted a stream running through the
farm by discharging into it the drainage from the brewery
including trade waste and sewage from the cottages "and had
rendered the water unfit for cattle to drink, and noxious and
offensive by reason of smells, making the farmhouse unwholesome
and unpleasant." The defendants were held liable.[16]

The same principle applies to percolating water. In this case, at
common law, the landowner has no right to stop his neighbour
abstracting water percolating under both their properties. But he
does have a right to stop him polluting it. In *Ballard* v.
Tomlinson[17] the defendant disposed of his sewage by putting it
down a disused well on his property. Unfortunately, the sewage
polluted the percolating water which was supplying the plaintiff's
well on neighbouring land. Again, the defendant was held liable.

Pollution like abstraction has become a matter of public
concern. It is no good conserving water if it is polluted. Under
various statutes pollution of any river or underground strata is
likely to constitute an offence. This means that the person
polluting the water will be liable to prosecution as well as a civil
action at the suit of the injured person.

Trade effluent and sewage effluent is dealt with by separate
statutory provision. Here in most cases the discharge is allowed
but only under the licence and control of the regional water
authority.

Principle 10.   Water: navigation and fishing

The right to fish and navigate in non-tidal waters belongs to the
owner of the bed.

There is a public right to fish and navigate in tidal waters. The
public may acquire the right to navigate—but not to fish—in
non-tidal waters.

A public navigable river is a public highway and subject to the
same general rules including the right of access of the owner of
land adjoining the river.

Principle 11.   Water: acquired rights

The landowner's natural rights in respect of water may be

[16] See further, on this case, below, p. 58.
[17] (1885) 29 Ch.D. 115.

increased or restricted by the creation of various acquired (third party) rights and licences.

Such rights may be private third party rights (such as easements or profits), customary rights, public rights or licences.

By way of example:

(1) A landowner may acquire an easement to pollute, or abstract, or interfere with the water flowing naturally through his neighbour's land.

(2) The right to fish in non-tidal waters in another person's land can be acquired as a profit.

(3) The right to navigate another person's non-tidal river or lake can be acquired as an easement.

The above rights may also exist as customary rights[18] or licences[19] and, in the case of navigation, as a public right.[20]

Explanation

Natural rights and acquired rights. Natural rights—sometimes referred to as natural servitudes—are those rights which a landowner has simply and automatically by virtue of his ownership of the land. The right to have his soil supported by his neighbour's soil is such a natural right[21]; so are the rights which he has in the water flowing naturally through his land. Indeed, any right of enjoyment which goes with the ownership of land can be called a natural right, though the term is usually confined to those rights which have the appearance of easements.

On the other hand, acquired (sometimes known as third party) rights are those which have to be created. The law recognises certain ways in which acquired rights can come into existence in respect of a piece of land. If a person is claiming such an acquired right he must show that the right was in fact created at some time in the past against that particular piece of land.

Easements[22] relating to a neighbour's water. Any interference with a neighbour's natural rights in water is an actionable nuisance or other tort. But the right to interfere can be acquired as an easement[23]—thus becoming lawful.

At common law the right to pollute water flowing through a

[18] See below, p. 393 for customary rights.

[19] As to which see below, p. 395.

[20] See below, p. 356 for public rights.

[21] See above, p. 49.

[22] See below, Chap. 15 for easements.

[23] But only where the interference is capable of existing as an easement. See Winfield and Jolowicz (above, n. 48), at p. 385, n. 10; and below, p. 358.

neighbour's land can be acquired as an easement. However, it is not possible to acquire an easement to commit a crime or a public nuisance—which is a crime; and since pollution of water is now generally a criminal offence it is not often that such easements will arise in the future. In *Green* v. *Matthews & Co.*[24] the defendant brewery claimed to have acquired an easement under the Prescription Act 1832 based on 40 years' user. The claim failed and one of the reasons given by Eve J. was that the pollution was an offence under the Rivers (Pollution) Prevention Act 1876.[24a]

There may still be cases where easements can exist where the pollution does not constitute a crime; for example, the right to pollute a lake lying across the boundary with a neighbour's property.

And it may be possible to interfere with the quality of the water in a way that does not amount to pollution. In *Young* v. *Bankier Distillery Co.*[25] the plaintiffs were using water from Doup's Burn to distil their whisky, the water being very soft and so suitable for the purpose. The defendants pumped hard but otherwise pure water into the stream from their mine. They were held liable for changing the quality of the water. Possibly pumping hard into soft water is not pollution and so could be legalised by easement.

Abstraction of water, like pollution, has also been removed to a great extent from the sphere of private to that of public law and so become less likely to form the subject-matter of easements. But, again, there are situations where criminal sanctions do not apply and easements may still arise. For example, a non-riparian owner will have to have access before he can apply for a licence to abstract; and such a right of access could be created as an easement. Or a right to abstract water from a neighbour's pond, which does not require a licence, could exist as an easement.

Customary rights in respect of water. Customary rights are dealt with later[26] but two illustrations will show the sort of customs that might exist in respect of water.

In *Harrop* v. *Hirst*[27] the inhabitants of the village of Tameworth in Yorkshire were asserting a customary right to take water for their domestic purposes from a spout in the village street. The spout was fed from a stream passing through the defendant's land;

---

[24] (1930) 46 T.L.R. 206 (Ch.D. Eve J.). See above, p. 55, for facts.
[24a] Compare *Cargill* v. *Gotts* [1981] 1 All E.R. 682 (C.A.) – easement to abstract water acquired *before* abstraction became illegal.
[25] [1893] A.C. 691.
[26] See below, p. 393.
[27] (1868) L.R. 4 Ex. 43.

and the complaint was that he had diminished the flow by abstracting water from the stream.

Mercer v. *Denne*[28] was a more involved case. The fishermen of Walmer were claiming a customary right to dry their nets on 11 acres of private land next to the foreshore. There was no doubt that they *had* had such a customary right but its present validity was challenged on two grounds: First, that about 30 years earlier they had adopted a new method of treating their nets before drying them on the beach in readiness for the fishing season. It was argued that the new method, oiling instead of cutching or tanning as previously, imposed a greater burden on the land and was an unlawful extension of the customary right. It was held that the custom was not defeated on these grounds. Stirling L.J. said[29] that " . . . those who are entitled to the benefit of a custom ought not to be deprived of ,hat benefit simply because they take advantage of modern inventions or new operations so long as they do not thereby throw an unreasonable burden on the landowner."

Secondly, it was argued that the custom could not attach to the land in question since this land had grown out of the sea by accretion[30] during the last 50 years or so.[31] This argument too was rejected. It was held that the custom attached to the land which was for the time being immediately behind the foreshore, a sort of shifting custom.[32]

Principle 12.   Water in artificial channels

There are no natural rights in respect of water flowing in artificial channels. But such water can become subject to easements.[33]

Explanation

All the rules which have been considered so far concern water flowing in its natural state. Water flowing in artificial channels is subject to the ordinary laws of nuisance. If a landowner discharges

---

[28] [1905] 2 Ch. 538.

[29] At p. 581.

[30] For ownership of land arising by accretion see A.S. Wisdom, *Water Rights* (1969), at p. 125. And see *Southern Centre of Theosophy* v. *State of South Australia* [1982] 1 All E.R. 283 (P.C.).

[31] In other words, that the only valid custom was in respect of land which was now some distance inland.

[32] Compare *Baxendale* v. *Instow Parish Council* [1981] 2 All E.R. 620 which concerned the construction of a grant of part of foreshore.

[33] See, *e.g. Ivimey* v. *Stocker* (1866) 1 Ch.App. 396 (right to receive flow of water from neighbour's artificial channel); *Harvey* v. *Walters* (1873) L.R. 8 C.P. 162 (right to allow rainwater to flow from eaves onto a neighbour's land).

water, or allows it to drip from his eaves, or escape from his reservoir, onto his neighbour's land, then he will probably be liable in nuisance or under *Rylands* v. *Fletcher*.

Equally, as with other private nuisances, the right to commit such a nuisance can be acquired as an easement and so become lawful.

SECTION III.   THE RIGHTS OF ENJOYMENT: THE LANDOWNER AND
THE PUBLIC: PLANNING LAW[34]

Introduction

The purpose of planning.   Town and country planning law is the machinery by which national, regional and local planning policy is enforced.

Planning, in this context, means controlling the use of land in the public interest. The right of the landowner to do what he wishes with his land provided only that he does not commit a nuisance against his neighbour, has had to be subordinated to the need to plan its use in accordance with local and national requirements. Every piece of land must, to some extent, serve a public as well as an individual need.

It was suggested in 1948 that "the community cannot allow land to be regarded merely as a matter of commerce. A people live by as well on the land and the land must serve the people. Where a nation is one of shopkeepers land may matter less than to others, but even to such a nation its habit of living is conditioned by the use of its land. For example, it may live out of imported tins or on home grown beef; it may be a nation of slum dwellers or live in homes fit for heroes. If the nation is to determine these things for itself and not leave it to the chance will of existing landowners, then some relationship between the State and the landowner must be built up. We have decided, right or wrongly, to give the State an opportunity to play a part. Hence we have our planning legislation, culminating in the Agricultural Act, Town and Country Planning Act and New Towns Act, which we have ventured to dub the new tenures."[35]

[34] See generally, J.P.W.B. McAuslan, *Land, Law and Planning* (2nd ed.); A.E. Telling, *Planning Law and Procedure* (5th ed.); N.A. Roberts, *The Reform of Planning Law* (1976); P. McAuslan, *The Ideologies of Planning Law* (1980).

[35] Potter, *Historical Introduction to English Law* (3rd ed.), at p. 488. And in 1973 the Secretary of State for the Environment said: "It is now widely realised that it is no longer possible for land, in particular, to be regarded as a commodity, for its owners to do with it as they please." [1973] J.P.L. 1.

Planning seeks, by controlling the use of land, to achieve a number of different—sometimes conflicting—objectives. Some of these are:

(1) Zoning: This means the allocation of separate areas for each different type of activity, housing, agriculture, industry, recreation, etc. It is not generally considered desirable to have homes in the shadow of factories, buildings scattered throughout the countryside, and so on.

(2) The satisfactory location of office building and industrial development from a national economic and social point of view. Thus, for example, to attract industry to areas of unemployment; and to prevent the congestion of city centres by too much office building.

(3) The conservation of natural resources, including minerals, water, the air and agricultural land.

(4) To ensure that development takes place where services, power, communications, and educational, shopping and waste disposal facilities can be supplied, and to ensure that they are in fact supplied.

(5) The preservation of the countryside both for agriculture and for recreation of town dwellers. And this includes providing access to open land in the country.

(6) Restoring to usefulness land left derelict by mining operations.

(7) The preservation of amenities. This means keeping the place looking beautiful—preserving trees, and buildings of architectural or historic interest; and requiring new buildings to conform to high standards of design.

It is not within the scope of this book to consider how far achievement has fallen short of these objectives. It is worth noting, however, that planning may involve not only conflict between the landowner and the public authority; there may also be a conflict between one planning objective and another. Witness the presence of a nuclear electricity generating station and a pumped storage installation in the Snowdonia National Park; two oil refineries and an oil terminal on Milford Haven.[36] These examples show one way of resolving the conflict!

Public health law. Public health and housing are usually treated as subjects distinct from planning. Each has its own code of legislation. But in practice they overlap[37] and merge into each

---

[36] See J.B. Cullingworth, *Town and Country Planning in England and Wales* (4th ed.), at p. 208.

[37] See, *e.g. Birmingham Corporation* v. *Minister of Housing and Local Government and Habib Ullah* [1964] 1 Q.B. 178, at p. 188.

other and of course they are all likely to affect the landowner. This section is primarily concerned with planning but some idea can be given here of the scope of the other two.

Whilst planning decides what use is permissible for a piece of land, the public health code is designed to ensure that the permitted use is carried on without danger to the health of others. The public health legislation contains many and detailed regulations dealing with such matters as the prevention and control of disease, assistance for the physically and mentally handicapped, hygiene and sanitation (including the removal of refuse and the emptying of cesspits), atmospheric purity, the destruction of pests, sewage disposal, building regulations and statutory nuisances (such as "keeping of an animal in such a place or manner as to be prejudicial to health"),[38] and the regulation of dangerous and offensive trades.

Public health law is not, of course, confined to landowners; but an example will illustrate the sort of way in which it might affect him in this capacity. Section 83(1) of the Public Health Act 1936[39] provides:

> "Where a local authority, upon consideration of a report from any of their officers, or other information in their possession, are satisfied that any premises:
> (a) are in such a filthy or unwholesome condition as to be prejudicial to health, or
> (b) are verminous,

the local authority shall give notice to the owner or occupier of the premises requiring him to take such steps as may be specified in the notice to remedy the condition of the premises by cleaning and disinfecting them, and the notice may require among other things the removal of wallpaper or other covering of the walls, or, in the case of verminous premises, the taking of such steps as may be necessary for destroying or removing the vermin."

By subsection (1A):
> "A notice under the foregoing subsection may require
> (a) the interior surface of premises used for human habitation or as shops or offices to be papered, painted or distempered, and
> (b) the interior surface of any other premises to be painted, distempered or whitewashed."

Section 83(5) goes on to provide that if the notice is not

[38] Public Health Act 1936, s.92(1).
[39] As amended by the Public Health Act 1961.

complied with the authority may carry out the work itself and recover the reasonable cost from the owner.

Section 287 of the same Act gives a right of entry to any "authorised officer" who can produce a duly authenticated document showing his authority in order, *inter alia,* to discover whether there has been any breach of the Act and to do any work authorised by the Act.

An area of public health law very closely related to planning is that dealing with the building regulations. A landowner who is proposing to develop his land must not only obtain planning permission; he must also comply with the building regulations which control, *e.g.* the construction and materials; the lighting, ventilation and space about buildings; the provision of sanitary conveniences, drainage and the means for the disposal of foul matter; and the supply of water and the prevention of fire.[40]

Housing law. This deals with a particular and important community need. As a separate subject, it is generally understood to include both matters which could be described as planning matters and those which could be regarded as within the scope of public health. The scope of housing law has been described as follows:[41]

(1) To provide new housing accommodation.

(2) To provide for the inspection and repair of individual houses.

(3) To provide for the removal by demolition or closing of unfit houses not capable of being made fit at a reasonable expense.

(4) To provide for the clearance of areas of unfit houses (slum clearance).

(5) To secure the abatement of overcrowded houses.

(6) To ensure that multi-occupied property is in fit condition for the number of people occupying it.

(7) In areas where it is needed, to provide for the improvement of housing accommodation.

(8) To provide financial assistance by way of grants and loans to local authorities and to private persons to help them with the building of new housing accommodation or the improvement, reconditioning and repair of existing accommodation.

(9) To provide rent rebates to tenants of local authority houses and rent allowances to tenants of other landlords.

The growing need for planning. Before the nineteenth century and the fantastic growth in industry, population and traffic, there

---

[40] See Public Health Act 1936, s.61; Public Health Act 1961, ss.4–11.
[41] See *Halsbury's Laws of England* (4th ed.), Vol.22, at p. 254.

was in general no need for town and country planning as it is
known today. Most of England consisted of a patchwork of
agricultural village communities. Each family more or less
controlled the means of production—land whether freehold,
copyhold or leasehold, together with common rights and access to
a water supply—sufficient to guarantee it a great measure of
economic self sufficiency. Most conflicts over the use of resources,
for example, the use of water, the use of common land, and the
liability to repair highways, could be regulated by the common law
courts. There was no acute shortage of open space or agricultural
land.

There were of course problems, mostly of a public health
nature: drainage, disease, etc. And there was inequality of wealth
as there is today. But those needs which today planning law does
seek to satisfy, could then be satisfied by each family for itself.

By the end of the nineteenth century the country was urbanised
and industrialised, with a vast landless population, becoming
larger each decade, more overcrowded and more short of land; a
population dependent on the fortunes and location of industrial
development for employment and a living; and living further and
further away from open countryside and the fresh air as industrial
towns grew and spread uncontrolled.

Twentieth century town and country planning has made some
attempt to rectify the errors of the nineteenth century and to plan
its own development on some sort of rational basis.

Modern planning policy: the development plan. A landowner
or a person thinking of buying land may wish to know how
planning policy is likely to affect his land. Perhaps he fears
compulsory purchase, or "planning blight" from the building of a
motorway nearby; perhaps he wants to know whether he will be
allowed to build a house or open a shop; or perhaps he lives in a
quiet country area and fears housing estates springing up all round
him.

The trouble is that planning law merely gives certain powers to
the planning authority. It is planning policy which decides whether
or not and how those powers will be exercised in relation to any
piece of land; and planning policy is neither altogether certain nor
unchangeable. A landowner can never be completely sure that his
land will not one day be compulsorily purchased; or that a
particular activity will or will not be allowed on his land.

However, planning policy is at least intended as a long term plan
to be used as a guide to the day to day decision making; and so it is
possible for the private landowner to get some notion of how any
particular piece of land is likely to be affected in the near future.

The most important expression of this planning policy available to the landowner is the *development plan*. This consists of a *structure plan* together with more detailed *local plans*.

It is the duty of each local planning authority to draw up a structure plan.[42] This is a statement (not a map) "formulating the local planning authority's policy and general proposals in respect of the development and other use of land in that area (including measures for the improvement of the physical environment and the management of traffic)."[43] The plan must take into account current regional economic planning and development policies and the available resources.[44] It must be accompanied by an explanatory memorandum justifying each policy in the plan and stating its relationship to the expected development of neighbouring areas.[45]

This structure plan is not likely to give much indication of the proposed future of any specific piece of land. The landowner is more likely to find such information in the local plans. A local plan will consist of a map and a detailed statement showing the proposals for a specific local area.[46] A local plan may be prepared for particular areas ("action areas") selected for comprehensive development, redevelopment, or improvement.[47] Such areas are likely to be town centres and inner city areas considered in need of early and wholesale redevelopment.

It is probably true to say that there has been a gradual downgrading of the strategic importance of the structure plan between its inception in 1968 and the present, culminating in the Local Government, Planning and Land Act 1980; and that "overall, the reforms to the regulatory planning system, when considered in historical context and together with recent departmental regulations and advice, indicate an intention to establish a speedier but simpler and less rigorous planning system which will confine itself to the consideration of narrow land use issues."[48]

The machinery of modern planning policy. The legal

---

[42] Town and Country Planning Act 1971, s.7, as amended by Local Government, Planning and Land Act 1980, s.89 and Sched. 14.

[43] *Ibid.* s.7(1A), as amended.

[44] *Ibid.* s.7(4)

[45] *Ibid.* s.6A, as amended.

[46] *Ibid.* s.11, as amended.

[47] *Ibid.* s.11(4A), as amended.

[48] See M. Loughlin, Local Government in the Welfare Corporate State, (1981) 44 M.L.R. 422, at p. 438; and see this article generally for a review of the provisions and policy of the Local Government, Planning and Land Act 1980. See also, "Structure Plans as Instruments of Social and Economic Policy," J. Jowell and D. Noble, [1981] J.P.L. 466.

machinery available to modern planning authorities to implement their policies can perhaps be divided into three categories:

(1) Regulatory control of the use to which the landowner puts his land. This includes:

(a) Planning permission control.

(b) Additional regulatory control available in special cases.

(2) Rights of access to private land.

(3) Acquisition of the land itself either for development or redevelopment (by public authority or private developer) or for some other public purpose.

These three categories will be dealt with in the Principles which follow.

Principle 13. Planning: regulatory control: planning permission

With certain exceptions, any landowner who wishes to carry out any development on his land must first obtain planning permission from his local planning authority.[49]

Development consists of:

(a) The carrying out of building, engineering, mining or other operations;

(b) any material change of use of the land.[50]

By way of exception the Act lists certain developments which do not need planning permission.[51]

The Town and Country Planning General Development Order 1977 gives a general permission for the developments listed in the Order which therefore do not need specific planning permission.[52]

The Town and Country Planning (Use Classes) Order 1972[53] lists a number of different classes of use; and provides that a change from one to another use within the same class will not constitute development. Again, therefore, there will be no need to obtain permission to make such a change.

Where a landowner applies for planning permission the local planning authority may either:

— refuse permission;

— grant it unconditionally;

— grant it subject to such conditions "as they think fit."[54]

---

[49] Town and Country Planning Act 1971, s.23(1).
[50] *Ibid.* s.22(1).
[51] *Ibid.* s.23(2)–(10).
[52] S.I. 1977, No. 289., as amended by S.I. 1980, No. 1946; made under the T.C.P.A. 1971, s.24.
[53] S.I. 1972, No. 1385. Made under T.C.P.A. 1971, s.22(2) (*f*).
[54] Town and Country Planning Act 1971, s.29(1).

Explanation

Meaning of development. This Principle is the linchpin of all planning control. It means in effect that the landowner can continue the existing use of his land[55] but that he cannot change the use unless he first persuades the planning authority that his proposal is consistent with the authority's planning policy for the area as a whole.

Development includes not only building, mining and works which change the appearance of the land; but any change of activity.

It is quite obvious that if a man builds a house or a factory on his land, that is development. Equally if he turns his existing house into a shop or if he converts an old mill into a house. But, as in all areas of the law, difficult borderline cases may have to be decided. In *Birmingham Corporation* v. *Ministry of Housing and Local Government and Habib Ullah*,[56] Habib Ullah owned two private dwelling-houses at Mary Road, Stetchford, Birmingham. Formerly each had been used as a residence for a single family. Habib Ullah used them for multiple occupation, letting various rooms separately to different tenants. At No.33 two families occupied the rooms on the ground floor sharing a kitchen and cooking facilities. The first floor rooms were occupied by two more families sharing a cooker on the landing. The attic was occupied by a single man. And all the occupants of the house shared a single lavatory.

Birmingham Corporation, the local planning authority, served an enforcement notice requiring discontinuance on the grounds that there had been a material change of use. The owner appealed to the Minister who upheld his appeal. The Corporation then appealed to the court. The court held that the Minister had been wrong to base his decision on the view that there could not be a material change of use so long as the use remained residential. Whether or not there was a material change of use was a question of degree and fact depending on the circumstances of each case. The appeal was allowed and the case sent back to the Minister to reconsider his decision in the light of this judgment.[57]

Exceptional cases. There are certain things which a landowner can do because they are not considered sufficiently significant from

---

[55] Assuming the existing use has not been started in breach of planning law.

[56] [1964] 1 Q.B. 178 (Div. Ct of Q.B.D.); applied in *Blackpool Borough Council* v. *Sec. of State for Environment* (1980) 40 P. & C.R. 104.

[57] Contrast, *e.g. Lewis* v. *Secretary of State for the Environment* (1971) 23 P. & C.R. 125. (Workshops used for repair of fleet of vans used in the heat business, were then used for ordinary motor repair business. Held that this was not a material change of use.)

a planning point of view to require permission. Either they are of a very minor nature, or incidental to an existing permitted use, or they are considered always to be unobjectionable from a planning point of view (*e.g.* the use of land for agriculture).

Section 22(2) of the Town and Country Planning Act 1971 lists certain operations and uses which are not to be regarded as development. For example, section 22(2)(*a*) states that the maintenance, improvement or alteration of the interior of a building so long as it does not materially affect the external appearance will not be regarded as development.

Similarly, the Town and Country Planning (Use Classes) Order lists different classes of use. The uses listed in each class are closely related. And a change from one use to another in the same class will not be regarded as development. Class I, for example, relates, with certain exceptions, to use as a shop for any purpose. The exceptions include the sale of motor vehicles and the sale of tripe and hot food. Thus, if a trader is selling fruit and vegetables he can change to selling do-it-yourself products without applying for planning permission. But if he wants to start selling fish and chips, he will need permission. Class XIII relates to use as a building for public worship. So if the Protestants take over from the Catholics, or vice versa, their God may, but the planners will not, be concerned.

Under the Town and Country Planning General Development Order 1977, certain developments are given blanket approval. Class I in this Order, for example, permits extensions of a limited size to dwelling-houses including the erection of such ancillary buildings as garages and stables provided the extension does not project beyond the front of the original buildings towards a highway. Class VI allows the erection of buildings for use in agriculture.

Under the Local Government, Planning and Land Act 1980,[58] a local authority can prepare a scheme for the development of a particular area with a view to its being designated an enterprise zone by the minister. The effect of designation is, *inter alia,* to grant planning permission for all or specified development within the scheme.

The decision of the planning authority. In deciding whether to grant planning permission, the local planning authority must take into consideration the provisions of the development plan and "any other material considerations."[59] The authority may grant or

[58] s.179 and Sched. 32.
[59] T.C.P.A. 1971, s.29(1).

refuse permission or grant it subject to such conditions "as u.., think fit." Any permitted development must begin within five years of the granting of permission.[60] If a person is refused permission or granted it subject to conditions the authority must give in writing the reasons for their refusal or conditions.[61]

Any conditions to be valid must "fairly and reasonably relate to the permitted development. The planning authority are not at liberty to use their powers for an ulterior object, however desirable that object may seem to them to be in the public interest."[62]

The Ministry of Housing and Local Government suggested[63] that: "It may well be expedient that, on building a factory, the developer should be required to provide parking facilities for the workers in it on a piece of land which he owns adjoining the site. A condition to this effect would be in order. It would be out of order, however, to grant permission for the factory, subject to a condition requiring the applicant to provide a car park to serve an existing factory which he owns on the other side of the street."[64] Similarly, permission to extend an existing building cannot properly be granted subject to a condition that a car park be provided large enough to cater for the employees in the extension and the existing building.

Conditions must be precise, not meaningless. Thus, a condition to improve an access "if the growth of the traffic makes it desirable," would be unacceptable.[65]

If an applicant is not satisfied with a planning decision he can appeal within six months to the Secretary of State[66] who can, in some cases after holding a public inquiry, uphold the decision or substitute for it any other decision which the authority could have made. The decision of the Secretary of State can be challenged in the courts on the ground that it is *ultra vires* or that all the relevant requirements have not been complied with. But the application to the court must be made within six weeks of the decision; and,

---

[60] *Ibid.* s.41.
[61] T.C.P. (General Development) Order, S.I. 1977, No. 289, Art. 7(7).
[62] *Pyx Granite Co.* v. *Ministry of Housing and Local Government* [1958] 1 All E.R. 625, at 633, *per* Lord Denning; and see *Fawcett Properties Ltd.* v. *Buckingham C.C.* [1960] 3 All E.R. 503 (H.L.); also *Newbury District Council* v. *Sec. of State for Environment* [1980] 1 All E.R. 731 (H.L.).
[63] Circular 5/68; see *Encyclopedia of Planning Law and Practice.*
[64] But a condition will not be void merely because it involves the cessation of some existing use: *Kingston on Thames L.B.C.* v. *Secretary of State,* [1974] 1 All E.R. 193; applied in *Penwith District Council* v. *Sec. of State for Environment* (1977) 34 P. & C.R. 269.
[65] Circular 5/68.
[66] T.C.P.A. 1971, s.36; T.C.P.G.D.O. 1977, Art.20 (S.I. 1977, No. 289).

apart from this right of appeal, the decision "shall not be questioned in any legal proceedings whatever."[67]

Principle 14.   Planning; other regulatory control

In addition to the general planning permission requirement, various particular types of development, or particular areas, may be subject to special control.

Explanation

The requirement as to planning permission applies to all development in all areas. But in special cases additional controls have been imposed. It is not possible here to do more than give some illustrations. Most of this additional control falls into two categories:

(1) **Conservation of particular areas and features.**[67a]   There are certain areas which are given special protection. The ordinary law requiring planning permission applies and there is no rule which says that development cannot take place. But special provisions apply to any application with regard to consultation with interested bodies, publicity, and special weight to be given to the desirability of conserving the area. A landowner in such an area will therefore probably find it extremely difficult to get planning permission. These areas include:

(a) *National Parks*: These are extensive tracts of country designated as National Parks by the Countryside Commission by reason of their natural beauty and the opportunities they afford for open air recreation.[68]

(b) *Areas of outstanding natural beauty.*[69]

(c) *Conservation Areas.*   These are areas designated by the local planning authority as being areas of special architectural or historic interest.[70]

(2) **Regulation of particular types of development**

(a) *Location of offices and industry.*   The location of industry and office development has become an issue of national significance affecting such matters as employment and the character of

---

[67] T.C.P.A. 1971, ss.242, 245; see below, p. 84.

[67a] See, generally, National Parks and Access to the Countryside Act 1949, Countryside Act 1968 and Wildlife and Countryside Act 1981.

[68] National Parks and Access to the Countryside Act 1949, s.5; Wales Act 1978, s.62.

[69] *Ibid.* ss.87, 88; Wales Act 1978, s.62.

[70] Town and Country Amenities Act 1974, s.1.

the major city centres. Therefore, at times it has been considered necessary to impose control over and above that represented by ordinary planning permission control. Thus, until 1979, in the case of office development, in addition to planning permission, an office development certificate had to be obtained from the Secretary of State who had a discretion but had to pay particular regard to "the need for promoting the better distribution of employment in Great Britain."[71]

Similarly, until 1982 an application for planning permission for industrial development had to be supported by an industrial development certificate issued by the Secretary of State stating that the proposed development can be carried out consistently with the proper distribution of industry.[72]

(b) *Other activities subject to special control.* These include caravan sites, advertising and mining.

Principle 15. Planning: rights of access to private land[73]

Private land may be subject to various rights of access. These may be created, *inter alia*:

(1) In favour of local authorities to enforce planning law.
(2) In favour of the public for enjoyment and recreation.
(3) In favour of statutory undertakers for the provision of electricity and other services.

Explanation

Enforcement of planning law. A right of access for officials is necessary to the effective operation of the public health and planning machinery. To give an example: under the Public Health Act 1936, s.287(1):

> "Subject to the provisions of this section, any authorised officer of a council shall, on producing, if so required, some duly authenticated document showing his authority, have a right to enter premises at all reasonable hours:
>
> (a) For the purpose of ascertaining whether there is, or has been, on or in connection with the premises any contravention of the provisions of this Act, or of any by-laws or building regulations made thereunder being provisions which it is the duty of the council to enforce."

---

[71] T.C.P.A. 1971, s.74; and Control of Office Development Act 1977. See now Control of Office Development (Cessation) Order 1979 (S.I. 1979, No. 908).
[72] T.C.P.A. 1971, s.67. See now T.C.P. (Industrial Development Certificates) (Prescribed Classes of Building) Regulations 1981, S.I. 1981 No. 1826.
[73] See above, p. 66.

The subsection goes on to give this right of entry also for the purpose of carrying out any authorised works under the Act.

Under section 280 of the Town and Country Planning Act 1971, any authorised person has a right of entry where this is necessary for the effective operation of the Act.

Access for public recreation. At common law private land may be subject to a right of way, an easement, in favour of a neighbouring landowner. It may also be subject to a public right of way in favour of the public at large. The common law rights of way, ancient public footpaths, etc., are important; and there is legislation in existence designed to give them some measure of protection.[74] But the satisfaction of modern public needs, particularly the need for open air recreation, requires new rights of access onto private land. And of course more is needed than the right to travel from one point to another, which is all that the common law right of way provides. For example, the use of land is required for camp sites, refreshments, parking, picnic sites, etc. In some cases the land itself will be acquired by the local authority; in others, a public right of access will be sufficient without taking over the land.

The Countryside Commission has the job of drawing up proposals for long distance routes, for use on foot, horseback or pedal cycle.[75] Where these do not pass along existing public rights of way, the local authority has powers under sections 25, 26 of the Highways Act 1980. It can make a "public footpath creation agreement" with the landowner concerned. Where this fails it can make a "public footpath creation order." Indeed, it is a common feature of planning law that the authority can proceed by agreement where possible with compulsory powers available in reserve.

Part V of the 1949 National Parks and Access to the Countryside Act contains provisions for the making of access agreements and access orders for open air recreation to open country. Open country is defined to include mountain, moor, heath, down, cliff and foreshore, and now also, under the 1968 Countryside Act, woodland, rivers and canals, and expanses of water.

Access for statutory undertakers. A statutory undertaker is "any person authorised by Parliament to construct, work or carry

---

[74] See, *e.g.* Highways Act 1980, ss.134, 136; National Parks and Access to the Countryside Act 1949, ss. 27–38; and Wildlife and Countryside Act 1981, Pt. III.

[75] See National Parks and Access to the Countryside Act 1949, s.51; Countryside Act 1968, s.21(2); and see Wales Act 1978, s.62.

on, any railway, canal, inland navigation, dock, harbour, tramway, gas, electricity, water, or other public undertaking."[76]

By way of example, electricity boards have the statutory power to place electricity lines below and (subject to exceptions) above private land. They must serve notice on the owner and if he does not consent obtain the approval of the Minister.[77]

Principle 16.   Planning: acquisition of the land by public authorities[78]

Private land may be compulsorily purchased by various public authorities for various purposes. For example:

(1) A local authority may compulsorily acquire land to facilitate the development, redevelopment, improvement or proper planning of an area as a whole.[79] The authority may itself develop the land acquired or release it to private developers.[80]

(2) The Minister and local highway authorities have powers to compulsorily purchase land for the construction of highways.[81]

(3) In the countryside there are powers to compulsorily purchase land in open country to provide access for public recreation[82]; and land anywhere to provide country parks, camping and picnic sites and to create nature reserves.[83]

In general the procedure on compulsory purchase is governed by the Acquisition of Land Act 1981.

Explanation

Positive and negative control.   The control which the planning authorities exercise over the use of land is essentially regulatory or negative. They can tell a landowner what he cannot do. But they cannot force him to do something else. They can draw up a development plan for their area; and they can prevent new development which is not in accordance with the plan; but the positive implementation of the plan will depend to a large extent on the initiative of private developers.[84] And this in turn means,

[76] Public Health Act 1925, s.7(3).
[77] Electricity Supply Act 1919, s.22.
[78] See above, p. 66.
[79] T.C.P.A. 1971, s.112, as amended by Local Government, Planning and Land Act 1980.
[80] *Ibid.* ss.123, 124; as amended by L.G.P.L.A. 1980, s.118.
[81] See, *e.g.* Highways Act 1980, s.239.
[82] See, *e.g.* National Parks and Access to the Countryside Act 1949, s.77.
[83] See Countryside Act 1968, ss.7–10 and National Parks and Access to the Countryside Act 1949, ss.17, 18.
[84] For use of planning permission control in a positive way see J.C. Almgill in *Journal of Town Planning Institute* (1967), Vol. 53, at pp. 303, 412, 461.

that the development plan in the first place, if it is ever going to be realised, must be attractive to these people. The shape of development which actually takes place in any area, is the product of some sort of process of interchange of ideas, influence and co-operation between the planners, the developers and the public.

However, in certain spheres, particularly where compulsory purchase powers exist, the planners can if they wish adopt a more positive role by acquiring the land and carrying out the development themselves. This is true, for example, of a state-owned enterprise such as the Atomic Energy Commission which can take the initiative in deciding when and where to locate new power stations.

It is true of new roads built by the Minister of Transport or local highway authorities.

It is also true to some extent of areas chosen for comprehensive development.

Acquisition of land for comprehensive development. These areas are likely to be town centres considered ripe for redevelopment as a whole or in large sections. It is in these areas, because of their value and social importance, that the relationship between planning authority and private developer is particularly significant.

The authority can acquire the land by compulsory purchase and carry out the development itself. Much of Coventry City Centre was redeveloped in this way after the Second World War. At the other extreme it can leave it entirely to private enterprise to acquire the land by ordinary purchase when it can and redevelop subject only to planning permission control by the local authority.

What is more likely to happen is that the actual development will be carried out by private enterprise but that the planning authority will assist in various ways (thus obtaining, no doubt, a greater influence over the style and content of the development), for example, by using its powers of compulsory purchase to assemble the land together into a single ownership and providing services such as roads.

In 1962 the Minister of Housing and Local Government gave the following example of a scheme. The local planning authority would define a comprehensive development area and prepare proposals for its redevelopment in agreement with the development company. The company would acquire as much land as possible by agreement. The authority would only use its compulsory purchase powers if essential to complete the redevelopment unit. The company would then transfer the freehold of its acquired land to the authority who would in return grant a long lease of all the land to be developed by the development company. The terms of the lease would provide for the periodic revision of the ground rent to enable account to be taken of the increasing value resulting from the development. Finally, of course, the company would carry out the agreed development.[85]

The relationship between the local planning authority and the private developer has been described as a "partnership."

It has also been said[86] that private development "is a valuable part of the life of the town and yet it often fails to meet all the community's needs. It is irreplaceable; but if it is not carefully supervised it will run wild like a weed and choke itself with its own congestion. Yet if the private developer is 'supervised' too vigorously and unwisely, he is apt to conclude that regulation is making his chance of profit too uncertain and he will simply cease to build with very serious consequences for the life of the town. . . . The town planner must study the conditions of growth of all the valuable forms of development and must endeavour to create those conditions as far as he can. At the same time he must try to cut back and control the unsatisfactory forms of growth without hindering growth in general."

This is just one opinion; but it probably reflects the philosophy now governing the use of English town planning machinery.[87]

In recent years, with the restrictive view taken by the courts of what planning authorities can legally achieve by attaching conditions to planning permissions, the authorities have placed some more reliance on agreements made with private developers (under the Town and Country Planning Act 1971, s.52), sometimes referred to as planning gain agreements. These agreements, based on bargaining and negotiation, rather than narrow, judicial criteria, enable the authority to obtain social benefits from the developer (for example, the provision of a community centre as part of a private, residential estate) in return for planning permission and perhaps assistance with land assembly.[88]

In September 1974, the Labour government declared that "the key to positive planning, and to a successful attack on betterment problems, is acquisition of land by the community."[89] The same

---

[85] See Ministry of Housing and Local Government Planning Bulletin, No. 1.
[86] F.B. Gillie, *An Approach to Town Planning* (1971), at p. 81.
[87] See Local Authority Private Enterprise Partnership Schemes (H.M.S.O., 1972).
[88] For a review of the use of such agreements, see J.N. Hawke, [1981] J.P.L. 5, 86; see also Planning "Bargaining – The Pros and Cons," D. Heap and A. Ward, [1980] J.P.L. 631. For examples of such agreements under judicial scrutiny, see *L.A.H. Ames Ltd.* v. *North Bedfordshire B.C.* (1980) 253 E.G. 55 (C.A.); and *Royal Borough of Windsor and Maidenhead* v. *Brandrose Investments Ltd.* [1981] 3 All E.R. 38 (Fox J.).
[89] Land, Cmnd 5730, para. 15.

government then introduced what became the Community Land Act 1975, the declared object of which was "to establish a permanent means:

(a) to enable the community to control the development of land in accordance with its needs and priorities; and

(b) to restore to the community the increase in value of land arising from its efforts."[90]

In 1980, after the Conservative Party had gained control of central government, the Community Land Act was repealed.[91]

This repeal, and the provisions of the Local Government, Planning and Land Act 1980, mark a shift away from positive planning. It has been suggested that there has been a " . . . distinct shift towards the private sector. This shift is towards acceptance of the pre-eminence of the market mechanism and the consequent modification in the role of the state to that of a market aid rather than as an alternative allocative system." And the same writer remarks that " . . . the primary effect seems to be to redirect the scope and modify the nature of the planning system so as to make it more supportive of the private sector."[92]

SECTION IV. THE ROLE OF THE JUDICIARY

Principle 17. Interpretation of legislation affecting landowners

The courts have in the past tended to give a restrictive interpretation to public welfare legislation which affects the rights of landowners either directly or by the creation of administrative agencies with statutory powers; that is, when faced with an ambiguous provision in such legislation, they have interpreted it in a way that interferes least with the landowner's existing rights. In general, they have failed to develop any principles of interpretation which recognise and give priority to the public purposes behind such legislation.

The courts have justified this restrictive approach by the development and application of various principles of statutory interpretation. In particular, they have used the following presumptions as to the intention of Parliament.

(1) That Parliament does not intend to make any important change in the law except by express provision.

(2) That Parliament does not intend to take away private property rights without providing compensation.

---

[90] *Ibid.* para. 16.
[91] Local Government, Planning and Land Act 1980, s.101.
[92] Martin Loughlin, Local Government in the Welfare Corporate State, (1981) 44 M.L.R. 422, at pp. 444, 445.

(3) That Parliament does not intend to interfere with freedom of contract.

(4) A presumption, in the case of a power delegated to a local authority or other administrative agency, that Parliament intends that power to be exercised (a) reasonably and (b) only for the purposes for which the enabling Act as a whole was passed.

The courts do not in general allow themselves to look outside the Act itself in order to find evidence of Parliament's intention.

In general, the courts have resisted attempts to exclude their control over the exercise of planning powers.

Explanation

In the nineteenth century the basic premise of the common law was what has been described above as the principle of self interest—the absolute freedom of a person to acquire land (and other forms of property) by contract or gift; and, having acquired it, to exploit it for his personal profit, pleasure or any other purpose, limited only—by the law of torts—to the extent necessary to preserve the similar right of other property owners.

As to the effect of this attitude on the public welfare it was widely believed that "By following the dictates of their own interests, the landowners and farmers became in the natural order of things the best trustees and guardians of the public."[93]

Indeed, it is possible that this attitude is just as widespread today. But the legislative history of the last century undoubtedly shows Parliament confronting the judiciary with an increasingly large corpus of legislation designed to promote the public welfare by limiting the freedom of the landowner to follow the dictates of his own self interest. The common law was designed largely to protect the individual in his capacity as a landowner. Parliament has come forward with legislation designed to protect the individual in his capacity as a worker in the landowner's factory, consumer of the landowner's produce, dweller in the landowner's house, and the seeker of recreation in the landowner's fields, and so on.

The attitude of the judiciary to this legislation has in general been hostile.

Where the meaning of a statutory provision is clear, then the court can only give effect to that meaning. The courts have not, in modern times, openly challenged the sovereignty of Parliament.

---

[93] J.L. and Barbara Hammond, *The Town Labourer* (Longman's, 1966), at p. 198.

Equally, where Parliament has given statutory power to an administrative agency (for example, to grant or refuse planning permission; to confirm compulsory purchase orders), the court must recognise the legality of that power so long as its exercise is within the authority of the statute.

But there can be few expressions in the English language which are entirely unambiguous and not capable of at least two possible meanings. The expression "well done" may be said in praise. But it may be said sarcastically with the opposite meaning. Wherever a judge is required to apply a statutory provision and comes to the conclusion that it is ambiguous, his job is to decide which of the possible meanings represents the intention of Parliament.

In this situation the courts do not generally allow themselves to look at reports of Parliamentary proceedings and other evidence, outside the Act itself, of what Parliament did in fact intend. What they frequently do is to employ one or more of the presumptions set out above.

These presumptions and the attitudes behind them are epitomised in the principle as stated in one of the leading text books on statutory interpretation[94]: "Statutes which encroach on the rights of the subject, whether as regards person or property, are subject to a strict construction in the same way as penal Acts. It is a recognised rule that they should be interpreted, if possible, so as to respect such rights and if there is any ambiguity the construction which is in favour of the freedom of the individual should be adopted."

Before illustrating the application of these presumptions it should be emphasised that they are not the only presumptions used by the courts when interpreting statutes; and that the whole of the present section is no more than a brief glimpse at some aspects of what has been called "an extremely complex subject with intricate ramifications."[95] It is merely an attempt to give some idea of the significance of the judicial involvment in the context of planning legislation.

The presumption against changing the law. The case ,of *Mixnam's Properties Ltd.* v. *Chertsey U.D.C.*,[96] dealing with the

---

[94] Maxwell, *On the Interpretation of Statutes* (12th ed.), at p. 251.

[95] S.A. de Smith, *Constitutional and Administrative Law* (4th ed.), at p. 558. For detailed studies of the judicial review of administrative action, see that book, Chapters 28, 29; also J.F. Garner, *Administrative Law* (5th ed.), particularly Chapter 6; and S.A. de Smith, *Judicial Review of Administrative Action* (4th ed.). On statutory interpretation in general, see R. Cross, *Statutory Interpretation* (1976).

[96] [1965] A.C. 735.

control of caravan sites, illustrates the courts at work interpreting and applying public welfare legislation affecting the landowner.

Caravan sites are subject to ordinary planning legislation and normally anyone who wishes to run a site must first obtain planning permission from the local planning authority. If it grants permission the planning authority may impose such conditions "as it thinks fit."[97] However, in the case of caravan sites there is additional control imposed by the Caravan Sites and Control of Development Act 1960. This additional control was necessary because this type of development caused more litigation under the Town and Country Act 1947 than any other. The main provision under this Act is that the intending site owner must, in addition to getting planning permission, obtain a licence from the local authority.

Section 5(1) of the 1960 Act provides that the licence may be issued "subject to such conditions as the authority may think it necessary or desirable to impose on the occupier of the land in the interests of persons dwelling thereon in caravans, or of any other class of persons, or of the public at large; and in particular, but without prejudice to the generality of the foregoing, a site licence may be issued subject to conditions. . . . "

The section then goes on to give specific types of condition which may be imposed. These include conditions limiting the maximum number of caravans, controlling the types of caravan on the site by reference to size or state of repair, regulating the position of caravans on the site, and for securing the amenities by requiring such things as the planting of trees, and so on.

In the *Chertsey U.D.C.* case[98] the respondents had applied for and obtained a site licence from the appellants, but subject to a number of conditions. These conditions, obviously designed to protect the caravan tenants, provided that the site rents must be agreed with the local authority, that security of tenure must be given to the tenants, that the site rules must be restricted to those normally found in a tenancy agreement and necessary for the proper administration of the site, that there was to be no restriction on the shops to be used by the tenants, that no premiums were to be charged and that there was to be no restriction on membership of political or other associations by the tenants.[99]

The respondents were challenging these conditions as being

[97] T.C.P.A. 1971, s.29(1).
[98] Above, n. 96.
[99] See now, Mobile Homes Act 1975.

ultra vires on the grounds that section 5 did not give the local authority power to impose conditions of this sort.

The court of first instance decided in favour of the local authority; but both the Court of Appeal and the House of Lords decided for Mixnam's, the site owners. It is noteworthy, in passing, that in the Court of Appeal Willmer L.J. dissented in part by holding that the first three conditions set out above were void; whilst in the House of Lords, Lord Guest also dissented in part but he considered the last four conditions to be void.

The case is not only interesting, however, for this diversity of judicial understanding. It is also a good illustration of the jealous and restrictive attitude which the courts have frequently adopted, in their position as statutory interpreters, towards powers delegated by Parliament to local authorities—powers to make bye-laws; to order landowners to cease certain activities; to attach conditions to other permitted activities; to compulsorily acquire land; and so on.

On the face of it, Parliament had in section 5(1) delegated to the local authorities very wide powers of controlling caravans by attaching conditions to licences. The only express limitation was that the conditions must be for the benefit of the caravan dwellers, any other class of person, or the public at large. Nevertheless, the House of Lords was ready to read into his language a further limitation that "permissible conditions must relate to the user of the licensed site; not to the user of the licensee's legal powers of letting or licensing caravan spaces."[1] They then decided that the conditions in question fell into the latter category and were therefore void.

Lord Reid,[2] supported by Lord Donovan, justified this interpretation by citing with approval the statement of Lord Goddard C.J.[3]; that: "It may be presumed that the legislature does not intend to make a substantial change in the law beyond what it expressly declares." Lord Upjohn preferred the presumption in favour of freedom of contract: "Freedom to contract between the subjects of this country is a fundamental right even today and if Parliament intends to empower a third party[4] to make conditions which regulate the terms of contracts to be made between others . . . then it must do so in quite clear terms."[5] It could perhaps be argued that in the present case Parliament had in fact

---

[1] [1965] A.C. 735, headnote.
[2] *Ibid.* at p. 751.
[3] In *National Assistance Board* v. *Wilkinson* [1952] 2 Q.B.D. 648, at pp. 658, 659.
[4] Even if that "third party" is an elected local authority.
[5] [1965] A.C. 735, at p. 764.

"expressly declared" the power claimed by the local authority in "quite clear terms."

Viscount Radcliffe did recognise that the presumption against any change in the law might no longer have much validity. He said[6]:

> "Of course conditions which limit an occupier's use of land as a caravan site interfere with what would otherwise be his unlimited common law rights (subject to nuisance). But then that is exactly what they are meant to do. Caravan sites as such had been a subject of legislative control, interfering with some common law rights, since the Public Health Act 1936. There were good reasons why they should be. The range of control conditions thereby authorised was confined to considerations of public health. Then in 1947 they were dealt with as fit subjects of planning control . . . and no doubt the permissible considerations under that Act were planning considerations. Now by 1960 they are important enough as a legislative subject to have an Act to themselves."

Nevertheless, Viscount Radcliffe considered that read in the context of the Act as a whole, section 5 must be limited in the way stated in the headnote quoted above.[7]

The presumption against taking away property rights without compensation. The case of *Esdell Caravan Parks Ltd.* v. *Hemel Hempstead R.D.C.*[8] also concerned section 5 of the Caravan Sites and Control of Development Act 1960. Section 5 expressly authorises the licensing authority to include a condition limiting the number of caravans on the site. In this particular case, it so happened that the plaintiffs were entitled under general planning law to keep an unlimited number of caravans on the site without planning permission.[9] But they did need to obtain a licence under the 1960 Act and the Rural District Council attached a condition to the licence which they granted limiting the number of caravans on the site to 24. This, claimed the plaintiffs, was taking away a property right—the right to have an unlimited number of

---

[6] *Ibid.* at p. 754; compare *Johnson* v. *Moreton* [1978] 3 W.L.R. 538, particularly *per* Lord Simon at p. 559; and see (1979) 95 L.Q.R. 4.

[7] Compare *Newbury District Council* v. *Sec. of State for the Environment* [1980] 2 W.L.R. 379 (H.L.).

[8] [1966] 1 Q.B. 895.

[9] Because the use as a caravan site had dated back to before the Town and Country Planning Act 1947. But Lord Denning M.R. (at p. 921), doubted the number of caravans could be increased from 24 to 78 without there being a material change of use requiring planning permission.

caravans—without compensation. Harman L.J. was sympathetic to the argument, saying, "It needs strong statements in a statute to deprive the private owner of rights of property without compensation."[10] But the court was driven to hold that section 5 did give express authority to limit numbers and there was no room for a restrictive interpretation. The remarkable fact is perhaps that the plaintiff's counsel must have thought that there was some chance of persuading the court to make such a restrictive interpretation.[11]

In another case, *Britt* v. *Buckinghamshire County Council,*[12] Harman L.J. was less well-disposed to a landowner who sought a restrictive interpretation of a statute on the grounds that it took away property rights without compensation. Under section 33 of the Town and Country Planning Act 1947, a local authority was enabled to serve a notice on the owner and occupier of "any garden, vacant site or other open land" whose "condition" was seriously injuring the amenity of the adjoining area. The plaintiff had bought the land in question at Prestwood in the Chilterns when it was being used as a market garden. He was a scrap car dealer and had gradually taken more and more land out of cultivation until most of it was being used as a dump for lorries and spare parts. When the council served a section 33 notice on him to clean up the land, he appealed to the court arguing that the section only applied where the condition of the land arose from inactivity and not where it was the result of some activity.

Harman L.J. said[13]: "It is said that the man who is told to abate an eyesore ought to be compensated for it.[14] That seems to me a most astonishing doctrine . . . I can see no reason why this man, who has for many years made the country hideous by his goings on, should not be made to put his house in order, and no reason at all why he should be paid by the public for doing it." The court held in favour of the local authority that the section did cover the condition arising from the plaintiff's activities.

Powers delegated to local authorities: reasonableness.   In the

---

[10] [1966] 1 Q.B. 895, at p. 929.

[11] The effect of planning permission requirements is that, in a sense, the land owner no longer owns the development rights in his land, but if he obtains planning permission this valuable property right is *given* (subject to capital gains and development land taxation) back to him.

[12] [1964] 1 Q.B. 77.

[13] *Ibid.* at p. 88.

[14] The plaintiff was arguing that the County Council should have ordered him to discontinue his activity under a different statutory provision which required them to pay compensation.

case of *Mixnam's Properties Ltd.* v. *Chertsey U.D.C.*[15] Lord Upjohn resorted to the principle of reasonableness as well as the presumption in favour of freedom of contract. "Conditions such as these must be reasonable . . . they are like bye-laws. . . . It seems to me that they (*i.e.* the conditions being challenged) all involve such oppressive and gratuitous interference with the rights of the occupier subject to them that they can find no justification in the minds of reasonable men."[16]

In the case of *Fawcett Properties Ltd.* v. *Buckinghamshire County Council*[17] Lord Denning resorted to the same principle of reasonableness but with somewhat more sympathy for the local authority. He said:[18] "As with bye-laws so with planning conditions. The court can declare them void for unreasonbleness but they must remember that they are made by a public representative body in the public interest. When planning conditions are made, as here, to maintain the green belt against those who would invade it, they ought to be supported if possible. And credit ought to be given to those who have to administer them that they will be reasonably administered."

Powers delegated to local authorities: The purpose of the Act.

Fawcett's case[19] shows the court prepared to limit a statutory power to those acts designed to achieve what they, the judges, saw as the purpose of the Act. In fact in this particular case the House of Lords held that the local authority had not exceeded the power in question.

The facts were that under section 14(1) of the Town and Country Planning Act 1947 the local planning authority when dealing with an application for planning permission was enabled to grant permission unconditionally, or subject to such conditions "as they think fit," or to refuse permission. The appellants owned two cottages at Chalfont St. Giles in Buckinghamshire. They had purchased them from the previous owner who had built them under a planning permission which was granted subject to a condition that the "occupation of the houses shall be limited to persons whose employment or latest employment is or was employment in agriculture . . . or in forestry, or in any industry

[15] Above, n. 96. See also *Westminster Bank Ltd.* v. *Beverly B.C.* [1971] A.C. 508 (H.L.); and *R.* v. *London Borough of Hillingdon* [1974] 2 All E.R. 643 (C.A.).
[16] [1965] A.C. 735, at p. 765.
[17] [1961] A.C. 636.
[18] At p. 679.
[19] Above, n. 17.

mainly dependent on agriculture and including also dependants of such persons as aforesaid."

The appellants claimed that this condition was *ultra vires* the local authority under section 14(1). The court held that it was within the scope of the Act. But the interesting point in the present context is that the judges were prepared to limit the apparently general powers given by this section by reference to the scope of the Act. It was a planning Act and the court was prepared to interfere if conditions did not relate to planning. Lord Keith said: "There might be personal attributes or circumtances required of the occupants which had no conceivable relevance to planning policy and, if so, such requirements would be bad. But that cannot, in my opinion, be said here."[20] Similarly, a number of the judges approved the principle, as stated by Lord Denning in a previous case, that any conditions must relate to the "permitted development."[21]

It has been said that, "However wide in the abstract, general words and phrases are more or less elastic, and admit of restriction or extension to suit the legislation in question. For it is a canon of interpretation that all words, if they be general and not precise, are to be restricted to the fitness of the matter, that is, to be construed as particular if the intention be particular."[22]

Exclusion of judicial review. As the cases and judicial statements quoted above show, the courts have sometimes been sympathetic and sometimes hostile to the activities of local authorities. But on the whole it is probably fair to say that the judiciary has exercised its function as official interpreter of statute law, in order to protect the property of the private landowner. To some minds at least, the courts have represented the repeated frustration of Parliament's policy.

In *Britt* v. *Buckinghamshire County Council*,[23] Harman L.J. said: "Local authorities, until they have recently been rescued,[24] have had practically to employ conveyancing counsel to settle these notices which they serve in the interests of planning the countryside or the towns which they control. Instead of trying to make this thing simpler, lawyers succeeded day by day in making it more difficult and less comprehensible until it has reached the stage where it is very much like the state of the land which the

---

[20] *Ibid.* at p. 675.
[21] See Lord Denning, at p. 674.
[22] Maxwell, *Interpretation of Statutes* (12th ed.), at p. 86.
[23] [1964] 1 Q.B. 77, at p. 87.
[24] See T.C.P.A. 1962, ss. 176, 177.

plaintiff landowner has brought about by his operations—an eyesore, a wilderness and a scandal."

And in some cases Parliament has replied by using its sovereign power to limit the right of the ordinary courts to review its legislation and define the limits of powers delegated to local authorities.

Thus, the Acquisition of Land (Authorisation Procedure) Act 1946 provides[24a]:

> "Subject to the provisions of the last foregoing paragraph, a compulsory purchase order . . . shall not, either before or after it has been confirmed, made or given, be questioned in any legal proceedings whatever . . . "

The Act does give a right to challenge the compulsory purchase order in the courts but for a period of only six weeks from its confirmation by the Minister.

In *Smith* v. *East Elloe R.D.C.*[25] the plaintiff's land had been purchased compulsorily six years earlier for the building of council houses. The statutory six weeks had long since passed and she was too late to apply to the courts. She claimed however that the purchase order had been made as a result of fraud and bad faith on the part of the council and its clerk and that the exclusion clause did not apply to such cases. On this preliminary question of jurisdiction the House of Lords held—but only by a bare majority—that the clause did apply even where fraud and bad faith were alleged and that the courts had no jurisdiction to consider her claim to have the purchase order declared void.

Viscount Simonds said[26]: "There is nothing ambiguous about paragraph 16; there is no alternative construction that can be given to it; there is in fact no justification for limiting words such as 'if made in good faith' . . . "

However, in the much discussed case of *Anisminic* v. *Foreign Compensation Commission*,[27] the House of Lords reasserted the right of the ordinary courts to review and delimit the exercise of statutory powers even in the face of such exclusion clauses. Section 4(4) of the Foreign Compensation Act 1950 provided[28]: "The

---

[24a] Now consolidated in Acquisition of Land Act 1981.

[25] [1956] A.C. 736. See also *Square Meals Frozen Foods Ltd.* v. *Dunstable B.C.* [1974] 1 All E.R. 441 (C.A.).

[26] *Ibid.* at p. 751.

[27] [1969] 2 A.C. 147 (H.L.). The case concerned a claim for compensation for property sequestrated by the Egyptian government after the Suez crisis in 1956.

[28] By s.3 of the Foreign Compensation Act 1969, replacing the 1950 Act, appeals from the Commission on most questions of law are now possible to the Court of Appeal.

determination by the Commission of any application made to them under the Act shall not be called in question in any court of law." On the face of it, a more comprehensive, obvious exclusion of judicial review can hardly be imagined. And yet the House of Lords decided that the word " 'determination' . . . should not be construed as including anything which purported to be a determination but was not in fact a determination because the Commission had misconstrued the provision of the Order defining their jusisdiction. Accordingly, the court was not precluded from inquiring whether or not the Order of the Commission was a nullity."[29]

It is beyond the scope of this book to follow the "protracted debate" and attempts at "conceptual reconciliation" of *Smith* v. *East Elloe R.D.C.* and *Anisminic* v. *Foreign Compensation Commission*[30] and the question whether the former decision can stand in the face of the latter. But a number of points can perhaps be suggested.

First, there are two stages to the judicial logic in *Anisminic*: that there is a distinction between making an error of law whilst acting within the jurisdiction conferred by a statute and acting outside the conferred jurisdiction; and that there is a valid presumption that by exclusion provisions Parliament intended to exclude review in the former but not the latter case. This logic has been formulated as follows by Lord Diplock in extolling the *Anisminic* decision[31]: "It proceeds on the assumption that where Parliament confers on an administrative tribunal or authority as distinct from a court of law,[32] power to decide particular questions defined by the Act conferring the power, Parliament intends to confine that power to answering the question as it has been so defined; and if there has been any doubt as to what the question is, this is a matter for the courts of law to resolve in fulfilment of their constitutional role as interpreters of the written law and expounders of the common law and rules of equity."

The judicial distinction between errors of law made whilst acting

---

[29] [1969] 2 A.C. 147, Headnote.

[30] See N.P. Gavells, Time Limit Clauses and Judicial Review – The Relevance of Context, (1980) 41 M.L.R. 383. And see *R.* v. *Sec. of State for the Environment, Ex p. Ostler* [1977] 1 Q.B. 122 (C.A.) (in which, as in *Smith*, the right to challenge was given for a limited period) which did attempt such a conceptual reconciliation with *Anisminic*. See also N.P. Gavells, Time Limit Clauses and Judicial Review – Some Second Thoughts, (1980) 43 M.L.R. 173.

[31] *Re Racal Communications Ltd.* [1980] 3 W.L.R. 181, at p. 186.

[32] In *Re Racal Communications Ltd.* [1980] 3 W.L.R. 181, the House of Lords held that the presumption against excluding judicial review did not apply to a judge in chambers.

within a statute given jurisdiction and acting in excess of that jurisdiction, is not new (though it is perhaps an example of the legal and linguistic sophistry typical in this area of the law); but it may seem that in their endeavour to nullify the effects of such exclusion provisions, the courts are adopting an expanding definition of what is a matter of jurisdiction.[33] In other words, to adopt Lord Diplock's phraseology, it may seem that they are inclining towards saying that if the administrative agency has got the answer wrong, it must be because it was asking the wrong question. It has been said that "The paradox is that the more Parliament tries to exclude judicial review, the more its scope is extended by the evasive logic to which the courts are driven in their desire to circumvent the statutory barriers."[34] And it has been said that "One is left wondering what kind of error of law would have been held *not* to go to jurisdiction."[35]

Lord Denning has recognised the artificiality and evasiveness of the logic and has suggested that the distinction be abandoned.[36] But the point, perhaps better appreciated by the Privy Council in disapproving of Lord Denning's suggestion,[37] is that the distinction can hardly be abandoned without revealing that the issue is not just one of correct statutory interpretation but of the respective constitutional roles of Parliament and the courts. One writer has defended the "strong, it might be said rebellious stand" of the courts against legislation seeking to exclude judicial review[38]; and the same writer has described judicial control over discretionary powers as "a constitutional fundamental,"[39] and has said that "the judges have almost given us a constitution, establishing a kind of entrenched provision to the effect that even Parliament cannot deprive them of their function. This may be discovering a deeper constitutional logic than the crude absolute of statutory omnipotence."[40]

It is true to say that since the constitutional settlement of the

---

[33] See *Pearlman* v. *Keepers and Governors of Harrow School* [1978] 3 W.L.R. 736 (C.A.); disapproved in *Re Racal Communications Ltd.* [1980] 3 W.L.R. 18 (H.L.).

[34] (1979) 95 L.Q.R. 163, at p. 167 (H.W.R. Wade).

[35] S.A. de Smith, *Constitutional and Administrative Law* (2nd ed.), at p. 572, referring to the *Anisminic* decision.

[36] In *Pearlman* v. *Keepers and Governors of Harrow School* [1978] 3 W.L.R. 736 (C.A.).

[37] In *S.E. Asia Fire Bricks SDN BHD* v. *Non-Metallic Mineral Products Manufacturing Employees' Union* [1980] 3 W.L.R. 318.

[38] H.W.R. Wade, *Constitutional Fundamentals* (Hamlyn Lecture), at p. 66.

[39] *Ibid*, at p. 68.

[40] *Ibid*, at p. 68; and see a review of this lecture in "Parliamentary Supremacy and the Judiciary," G. Winterton, (1981) 97 L.Q.R. 265.

seventeenth century, the ordinary courts (by which today is meant the Supreme Court of Judicature and the House of Lords) have asserted their right to interpret and therefore delimit statute and statutory powers. It is equally true that since Dicey,[41] this central position of these courts has commonly been regarded as an essential element in the rule of law,[42] which is seen as standing between the state and not only the private person but also private property; and that the judicial review of administrative powers is seen as adjudication in a "conflict between, on the one hand, the constitutional priorities of fairness and the rule of law and, on the other, the administrator's priorities of expediency and finality."[43]

It is beyond the scope of this book to challenge (or defend) this sort of view which is so well entrenched among the judiciary and academic and professional lawyers. But a few final points may be suggested.

In general the courts continue to apply the principles of the private law of contract, tort, land, landlord and tenant, etc., derived from the nineteenth century,[44] to areas such as planning law and the Rent Acts without sufficiently recognising that local and planning authorities, etc., are not just private persons created by statute; and that the aim of the administration of such laws is not "expedience and finality" but the achievement of some "socially proclaimed value."[45]

To give one or two examples. Covenants relating to the use of land made with local authorities have been subjected by the courts to the same principles as covenants between private landowners. Thus, they will only be enforceable against successors in title of the original covenantor if the authority has retained land to be

---

[41] See *Introduction to the Study of the Law of the Constitution* (10th ed.).

[42] See, *e.g.* C. Harlow, "Public" and "Private" Law: Definition Without Distinction, (1980) 43 M.L.R. 241, who, like Dicey, argues against a separate system of administrative law. Compare J.F. Garner, Public Law and Private Law, [1978] P.L. 230.

[43] N.P. Gavells, "Time Limit Clauses and Judicial Review – The Relevance of Context," (1980) 41 M.L.R. 383.

[44] Principles which have been described as an "amalgam of classical economics, of Benthamite radicalism, of liberal political ideals and of the law, itself created and moulded in the shadow of these movements"; see P.S. Atiyah, "Contracts, Promises and the Law of Obligations," (1978) 94 L.Q.R. 193.

[45] P.S. Atiyah, *The Rise and Fall of Freedom of Contract* (1979), at p. 633. And see the comment of Professor Garner on *R.* v. *London Borough of Hillingdon* [1974] 2 All E.R. 643, that "It could well be argued that social policy is relevant to planning considerations, but this was not accepted by the Court." *Administrative Law* (5th ed.), at p. 159; and see also on this case, J. Jowell, "The Limits of Law in Urban Planning," (1977) 30 C.L.P. 63, at p. 69. Contrast the Court of Appeal's decision (reversing Willis J.) in *Clyde & Co.* v. *Sec. of State for the Environment* [1977] 1 W.L.R. 926.

benefitted by the covenant.[46] Section 52 of the Town and Country Planning Act 1971 now provides that the local planning authority may enter into agreements with landowners for the purpose of restricting or regulating the development or use of land; and the section provides that such covenants will be enforceable as if made for the benefit of adjoining land owned by the authority. But it has been said that "the orthodox view assumes . . . that this subsection (s.52(2)) means that the agreement is to be construed as a conveyance,"[47] that is according to private law principles, which means that it is unlikely, for instance, that the courts would enforce positive covenants in such agreements against successors in title of the covenantor.[48]

A similar point has been made about the judicial interpretation of section 32 of the Housing Act 1961.[49]

A recent decision in landlord and tenant law is, perhaps, a classic example of the point being made. *Liverpool City Council* v. *Irwin*[50] was concerned with the respective obligations of landlord and tenant to repair and maintain a local authority residential tower block. It has been said, in the context of this decision, that "a council house tenant is treated as having a contract with the local authority, even though the contract is of a very peculiar nature and ressembles a public law relationship rather than a private one."[51] The decision may suggest that if such a relationship in such a context is at all amenable to adjudication in accordance with fixed legal rules, suitable legal rules have not yet been developed by the courts.[52]

This leads to the next point which is whether the ordinary courts

---

[46] *L.C.C.* v. *Allen* [1914] 3 K.B. 642. For the enforceability of covenants relating to land, see below, p. 410 *et seq.*

[47] M. Aves, Enforcing s.52 Agreements, [1976] J.P.L. 216, at p. 218. Similarly, a compulsory purchase order has been subject to the same principles as a private conveyance, see *Sovmots Investments* v. *Sec. of State for the Environment* [1979] A.C. 144.

[48] See R.W. Suddards, Section 52 Agreements: A Case for New Legislation, [1979] J.P.L. 661.

[49] See below, p. 119; and see J.I. Reynolds, Statutory Covenants of Fitness and Repair: Social Legislation and the Judges, (1974) 37 M.L.R. 377. In a sense the problem is circular. Parliament, with one eye to the judiciary, tends to draft such legislation in the language of private law familiar to the judiciary whose response can therefore be forecast with at least some degree of certainty; the judiciary, in turn, will take this cue and import all the assumptions of private law into the statute.

[50] [1977] A.C. 239; see below, p. 120.

[51] P.S. Atiyah, *The Rise and Fall of Freedom of Contract* (1979), at p. 720.

[52] The matter is now even more important since, under the Housing Act 1980, local authority tenants have been given security of tenure under the control of the courts.

are the most suitable bodies for delimiting the extent of statutory powers. Legislation which changes established property rights has, like all legislation, to be interpreted by someone. And, of course, local authorities (and other administrators) are interpreting it every day in the ordinary exercise of their delegated powers. And it has been said that "the administration prefers negotiation to litigation."[53] Since the Franks Committee Report,[54] the prevalent view has been in favour of judicial review by the ordinary courts; but it has been suggested that since " . . . many of the 'principles' of private law are based upon the subjective notions of past generations of individualistic judges, and modern local government is essentially collectivist, conflicts are not uncommon."[55] There are those who favour a separate system of administrative courts; and it has been suggested that there should be machinery for referring disputes as to statutory interpretation back to Parliament. Another suggestion, in the case of local authority powers, is to allow them to interpret their own powers and face the consequences from the local electorate.[56]

What should be emphasised, in conclusion, is that the judge, when interpreting particularly such as planning legislation, is not and cannot simply exercise the role of neutral umpire. To some extent he is a legislator "deciding what *should* be the limits on the discretion of an authority which is conferred in very wide terms. This is a political question."[57] "Judges are up to their necks in policy as they have been all throughout history."[58] And it has been said that "Planning law provides the framework of the planning process and its values permeate and inevitably shape the way the process operates."[59] In other words, in this (or any) area of law, it is not enough to know what the law is. It is necessary to examine also what economic and social values it reflects and, under the control of Parliament and the judges, is developing to reflect.

---

[53] C. Harlow, " 'Public' and 'Private' Law: Definition Without Distinction." (1980) 43 M.L.R. 241.
[54] Report of the Committee on Tribunals and Enquiries, 1957, Cmnd 218.
[55] W.I. Jennings, 51 L.Q.R. 180, at p. 181.
[56] See G. Ganz, 27 M.L.R. 611. And see generally, G. Ganz, *Administrative Procedures* (1974).
[57] *Ibid*, at p. 613.
[58] H.W.R. Wade, *Constitutional Fundamentals*, at p. 62.
[59] P.W.B. McAuslan, "Planning Law's Contribution to the Problems of an Urban Society," (1974) 37 M.L.R. 134.

CHAPTER 3

LEASEHOLD OWNERSHIP

SECTION 1. DEFINITION AND CLASSIFICATION

Principle 1. Definition[1]

Leasehold ownership[2] exists where one person (the tenant or lessee) is given:

   (a) exclusive possession of land by another (the landlord or lessor),

   (b) with the intention that he should hold it as a tenant and not in some other capacity.

   (c) for a determinate period of time less than that held by the landlord himself.

Explanation

Leasehold as a tenure. Leasehold like freehold is a tenure.[3] The relationship of (land)lord and tenant exists between the parties. The tenure of the freeholder, the relationship between him and the lord of whom in theory he holds the land, is no longer of any practical significance. But the tenure of the leaseholder is still significant in that there is a continuing relationship between the landlord and the tenant for the duration of the lease with continuing rights and obligations on both sides as contained in the lease or tenancy agreement. However, the modern tendency in the courts is to determine the rights and obligations in the light of commercial, contractual principles (subject to statutory controls) rather than the old, common law rules of tenure. In *Bailey (C.H.)* v. *Memorial Enterprises Ltd.*[4] the issue was the validity of a retrospectively operating rent review clause. The lessees argued that rent was an incident of tenure, that, as such, it could be distrained[5] for and so must be fixed and certain when due. The

---

[1] See Hill and Redman, *Landlord and Tenant* (16th ed.), at p. 3.
[2] For distinction between leasehold and freehold ownership see below, Chap. 28.
[3] See above, p. 6, for tenure.
[4] [1974] 1 All E.R. 1003 (C.A.).
[5] For distress, see below, p. 135.

court rejected this argument. Sir Eric Sachs said[6]: "The objective of the courts in cases relating to office leases is naturally to determine the intended commercial effect of the particular agreement between the parties. In this respect a lease is no less a contract relating to the use of premises than an agreement in relation to the supply of furniture for those premises is also a contract."[7]

Although it is still common, and correct, for lawyers to talk of freehold tenants, tenants in fee simple, etc., the layman normally understands the word tenant to mean the leasehold tenant; and the expression "landlord and tenant" is invariably used even by lawyers to mean leasehold ownership.

Exclusive possession. The essence of leasehold ownership is that the landlord lets the tenant into exclusive possession of the land for one of the recognised leasehold estates.[8]

If we find T in exclusive possession of Blackacre owned in fee simple by L, T *may*[9] be a leasehold tenant. If he does not have exclusive possession he *cannot* be a leasehold tenant; and will probably only be a licensee with some sort of occupation licence.[10]

It may therefore be necessary, in order to determine a person's legal position, to decide whether or not he has been given exclusive possession. The principle is simple. Exclusive possession[11] means the right, for the time being,[12] to exclude all others from the premises. And in most cases there is no room for argument. It will be quite clearly understood that the tenant is entitled to exclude anyone including the landlord from the premises. But in borderline cases there is hardly any sure guide to whether or not a person is in exclusive possession. Possession does not cease to be exclusive merely because the land is subject to easements[13] or other third party rights; otherwise third party rights could not exist. Equally it does not cease to be exclusive merely because the landlord himself reserves a right of entry for specified purposes. For example, a standard long term lease of a flat in a Mansion is likely to contain a covenant by the tenant, on the following lines, to:

---

[6] At p. 1009.
[7] And see *United Scientific Holdings Ltd.* v. *Burnley B.C.* [1978] A.C. 904 (H.L.).
[8] See below, p. 102.
[9] But not necessarily; he may fall into some other category; see below, p. 96.
[10] See below, p. 395, for licences.
[11] See above, p. 4, n. 2, for reading on nature of possession in English law. For a further discussion of the meaning of exclusive possession, see below, p. 398.
[12] The right to possession may be determinable by the landlord; *e.g.* in the case of a monthly tenancy, by giving one month's notice.
[13] See below, Chap. 15.

"Permit the lessors and others authorised by them with or without workmen and others at all reasonable times on notice (except in cases of emergency) to enter into and upon the premises hereby demised or any part thereof for the following purposes namely: (a) to repair any part of the Mansion or adjoining or contiguous premises and to make repair maintain rebuild cleanse and keep in order and good condition all sewers drains pipes cable watercourses gutters wires party structures or other conveniences belonging to or serving or used for the same and to lay down and maintain repair and test drainage gas and water pipes and electric wires and cables and for similar purposes and the Lessors or other persons exercising such right (as the case may be) doing no unnecessary damage and making good all damage occasioned thereby to the premises hereby demised."[14]

In *Bracey* v. *Read*[15] the plaintiff agreed to "let on lease to [the defendant] the right to train and exercise racehorses on the gallops."[16] These "gallops" were sretches of land on the plaintiff's downs varying in length from three-quarters to one and one-quarter miles and 15 to 20 yards wide. They stretched in different directions and, although not fenced off from the rest of the downland, they were quite distinct. The plaintiff reserved the right to cross the gallops with his implements whenever necessary to get to his farmland on the other side. The plaintiff was claiming possession as a tenant and, as so often in the modern cases, the question was whether the defendant was protected by the statutory protection now commonly given to tenants—in this case under the Landlord and Tenant Act 1954; or whether he was not in possession but a mere licensee and so not protected. As Cross J. put it,[17] was the true view that the defendant was in possession of the gallops subject to the right of the plaintiff to cross with his farm implements; or was it that the plaintiff was in possession subject to the right of the defendant to train his horses on them? Cross J. considered all the relevant factors and came to the conclusion that

[14] George and George, *Sale of Flats* (4th ed.), at pp. 274, 291. See George and George, at p. 274 for rest of this precedent which reserves this right of entry for additional purposes, *e.g.* to view the state of repair.

[15] [1962] 3 All E.R. 472 (Cross J.). Also reported, but not on this point, at [1963] Ch. 88.

[16] [1962] 3 All E.R. 472 headnote.

[17] [1962] 3 All E.R. 472, at p. 475.

the defendant was in possession and therefore a tenant[18] protected by the Act.[19]

Where there is a dispute all the relevant factors have to be taken into account in deciding whether there is exclusive possession. As Davies L.J. said in *Appah* v. *Parncliffe Investments Ltd.*[20] one has to construct some sort of balance sheet, putting on the one side those facts which suggest exclusive possession and a tenancy and on the other, those which suggest the opposite. Thus, in *Bracey* v. *Read,*[21] there was the fact that no part of the gallops had been used by the plaintiff for agriculture and that any such use would quite obviously have been a breach of the agreement; that the defendant had the sole right to use the gallops and license others to use them; that he was under an obligation to and did maintain them in good condition. "He has been in fact in complete control of the gallops."[22]

On the other hand, in *Appah* v. *Parncliffe Investments Ltd.*[23] the plaintiff took a room at an establishment owned by the defendants "whose outside facia board proclaimed itself to be the Emperor's Gate Hotel." It was rather less grand than this name suggested. For 75p a day or £5 a week—she took it at £5 a week—she got a room with a Yale lock, a gas ring, the use of a common bathroom and toilet, and the charge included the daily cleaning of the rooms, bedmaking, fresh linen and the supply of electricity and hot water. Her room was broken into, some of her property stolen and she was suing the defendants for negligence. Unknown to her but known to the defendants the previous occupant had also had a break-in and the police had advised the defendants to replace the defective Yale lock; this they had not done. The issue was this: if she was a tenant the landlords were under *no* obligation to look after her property; if on the other hand she was a mere lodger (*i.e.* a licensee) then they retained control of the room and owed her a duty of care to look after her property. The Court of Appeal decided that she did not have exclusive possession, that she was

---

[18] But today exclusive possession does not necessarily indicate a tenancy; see below, p. 96.

[19] It is possible to create an easement, such as a right of way, for one of the leasehold estates; see below, p. 382; but such an interest does not give possession or occupation of the land, and so cannot be protected under the Landlord and Tenant Act 1954, Part II. Compare *Land Reclamation Co. Ltd.* v. *Basildon D.C.* [1978] 2 All E.R. 1162 (Brightman J.).

[20] [1964] 1 W.L.R. 1064, at p. 1069.

[21] Above, n. 15.

[22] [1962] 3 All E.R. 472, at p. 474.

[23] [1964] 1 W.L.R. 1064 (C.A.).

only a lodger and that the defendants had been negligent. This sort of case illustrates that a distinction which is clear when stated as a legal principle may prove more difficult to apply in practice; and that at times the courts have perhaps been influenced by a desire to make a principle fit what, in their view, was a desirable and just result. This case also illustrates a situation in which it was to the occupant's advantage to prove that she was *not* a tenant. More usually, the occupant will be trying to establish that he does have exclusive possession and that he is a tenant.[24]

In *Heslop* v. *Burns*[25] the owner of a cottage had allowed the defendants, a young married couple, to occupy the cottage rent free between 1954 and 1968 when he died. He had done it out of some sort of charitable motive (apparently being infatuated with the wife). He visited the couple almost every day and told the wife on several occasions that when he died the cottage would be hers. After his death (the cottage not having been left to her in his will) the executors were claiming possession. The defendants argued that they had become tenants (at will since they were not paying rent and no other type of tenancy could be implied); and that by virtue of the Limitation Act 1939, s.9(1), they had acquired title (ownership) by adverse possession.[26] The evidence showed that the deceased had treated the cottage as a second home and that he could come and go whenever he wanted to. The court held that the defendants did not have exclusive possession and so could not be tenants. They were only bare occupation licensees[27] and as such could not acquire title by limitation. The licence had been terminated, so they were ordered to give up possession.[28]

The fact that exclusive possession is essential to a tenancy has at times been used by residential landlords successfully to avoid the Rent Acts (which in general only give full security to tenants and

---

[24] But with the modern protection given by the courts to the contractual licence having at least many of the characteristics of a property interest, the occupant's security may lie in showing that he has an occupation licence rather than, *e.g.* a tenancy at will or a weekly tenancy—both of which can (unless protected by statute) be determined by the landlord giving notice at any time; see, *e.g. Errington* v. *Errington* [1952] 1 K.B. 290; and see below, p. 402.

[25] [1974] 1 W.L.R. 1241 (C.A.).

[26] S.9(1) provided, in effect, that at the end of the first year a tenancy at will was deemed to have ended and the tenant to be in adverse possession. S.9(1) was repealed by the Limitation (Amendment) Act 1980, s.3(1). Time will not now run in favour of a tenant at will until the tenancy has in reality been determined. For adverse possession, see below, p. 503.

[27] See below, p. 399 for bare licences.

[28] Compare *Cobb* v. *Lane* [1952] 1 T.L.R. 1037, an earlier case under the same section.

not to licensees).[29] In *Somma* v. *Hazlehurst*,[30] H and S, an unmarried couple, were going to share a room. Each signed a separate, though identical, agreement with the owner. Each agreement was expressed as a licence and reserved the right to the owner himself to share the room and to introduce one (at any one time) other licensee to share the use of the room. The court *held* that neither H nor S had exclusive possession, nor did they together share exclusive possession (because of the owner's right to share); so they did not between them have a joint tenancy.[31] They were therefore not protected by the Rent Acts.

Possession as tenant and not in some other capacity. It is possible that the common law view was[32] that whenever a person was put into exclusive possession of property by another without the grant of a freehold interest, then he would be treated as a tenant—that is a tenant of the person putting him into possession. If he was not given any specific term of years or a periodic tenancy, then he would be a tenant at will,[33] at the will of his lord.

This view must now perhaps be modified in two directions:

(a) A person with exclusive possession may have an interest in the land which does not belong to any of the commonly recognised freehold or leasehold estates. Some of these less common interests are dealt with elsewhere.[34]

(b) A person may be in exclusive possession without having any interest in the land at all, that is having only a personal licence, a mere personal right against the person who allowed him into possession.[34a]

The distinction between property and personal rights (and the nature of licenses) is dealt with in more detail later[35]; but the most

---

[29] Licences may be given a limited degree of protection as restricted contracts; see Rent Act 1977, ss. 19 and 20; 76–85, 98–102, below, p. 142.

[30] [1978] 2 All E.R. 1011; see also *Shell-Mex and B.P. Ltd.* v. *Manchester Garages Ltd.* [1971] 1 W.L.R. 612; and *Aldrington Garages* v. *Fielder* (1978) 247 E.G. 557 (C.A.); compare *Demuren* v. *Seal Estates* (1978) 249 E.G. 440 (C.A.).

[31] See below, p. 312 for joint tenancies. A joint tenancy was held to be negatived also by the absence of joint liability for the total payment for the room; but on this point compare *Demuren* v. *Seal Estates* (1978) 249 E.G. 440 (C.A.).

[32] See A.D. Hargreaves (1953) 69 L.Q.R. 466, particularly at pp. 466–470.

[33] See below, p. 104.

[34] See below, p. 405 (proprietary estoppel); and p. 399 (contractual licences). The correct classification of the contractual licence (as a proprietary or mere personal interest) is the subject of much argument; see below, p. 399. See also, below, p. 344 (spouse's right of occupation); and below, p. 141 (the right of a statutory tenant under the Rent Act 1977).

[34a] See M. Partington, *Landlord and Tenant* (2nd ed.), pp. 96–151.

[35] Below, pp. 395.

important aspect is that a property right is capable of binding subsequent owners of the land affected, whilst a personal right is only enforceable against the person who created it according to the rules of contract law. Thus, in *Booker* v. *Palmer,*[36] the appellant's house had been destroyed by a wartime bomb, and a landowner had told a Mrs. Goldsmith (who was acting as intermediary) that she could let the appellant occupy an empty cottage on his estate, rent free,[37] for the duration of the war.[38] The appellant argued that a tenancy had been granted to Mrs. Goldsmith for the duration of the war. Such a tenancy would have bound the respondent, who had subsequently taken a lease of the land, and the appellant would in turn have been protected either as sub-tenant or licensee of Mrs. Goldsmith. It was *held* that Mrs. Goldsmith had only a personal licence which had been terminated. The appellant's interest necessarily disappeared with the interest out of which it had been created, and so she had to give up possession.

Where a person is in exclusive possession (and does not have any other property interest) there is a presumption that he is there as a tenant. But the courts will examine all the circumstances and these may show that he is there in some other capacity. Two types of case are worth mentioning:

First, he may be in possession as an employee to make possible the better performance of his duties as an employee.[39] If this is the case he is presumed to be a licensee. Thus the porter of a block of flats who occupies a flat in the building would probably provide an example. But the occupation must be necessary for the proper performance of the job, otherwise he will be a tenant regardless of the employment. In *Leslie Parsons & Sons* v. *Griffiths,*[40] the defendant was in danger of losing his home because his mortgagees were threatening to foreclose. His employers decided to help him by buying the house for £650 the amount need to pay off the mortgage and allowing him to remain there on paying £2 a week; but they stipulated that he was only to remain there whilst in their employ. There was also an understanding which the employers refused to put into writing that if he paid off the £650 together with an unspecified amount of interest, they would

[36] [1942] 2 All E.R. 674 (C.A.).

[37] A tenancy can exist without the reservation of a rent.

[38] In *Lace* v. *Chantler* [1944] K.B. 368, it was held that a lease "for the duration of the war" was void for uncertainty; but the point was not raised in *Booker* v. *Palmer*; see below, p. 102.

[39] See Hill and Redman, *Landlord and Tenant* (16th ed.), p. 31.

[40] (1966) 110 S.J. 908 (C.A.).

convey the house back to him. Subsequently the employers dismissed him and in the present action they were suing for possession. It was held by a majority in the Court of Appeal that he was in possession as a tenant and not just as an employee; he was therefore protected under the Rent Acts.[41]

The second case worth mentioning is that of the person let into possession as an act of charity or friendship, a special favour. In *Facchini* v. *Bryson*,[42] Denning L.J. said[43] that: "In all the cases where an occupier has been held to be a licensee there has been something in the circumstances, such as a family arrangement, an act of friendship or generosity, or such like to negative any intention to create a tenancy." In *Booker* v. *Palmer*[44] Lord Greene M.R. said[45] "That the landowner had the charitable intention of allowing these evacuees to stop in the cottage for the duration of the war is, I think, quite clear." In *Cobb* v. *Lane*,[46] there was what Lord Denning described as a "family arrangment." The sister of the defendant purchased a house in which the defendant lived rent (and for most of the time, rate) free until the sister died. It was *held* that the defendant was a bare licensee, not a tenant at will,[47] and so could be evicted by the sister's executors.

There is, of course, nothing to stop an informal family, or other, agreement from creating a tenancy if such intention is clearly enough shown.[48] Conversely, the existence of a commercial arrangement does not *necessarily* indicate the existence of a tenancy. In *Marchant* v. *Charters*[49] M owned a house divided into bed-sitting rooms. Each had its own hot water and cooking

---

[41] As to agricultural labourers in tied cottages, see the Agricultural Holdings Act 1948, which excludes from its protection (s.1(1)), any contract under which the land is let to the tenant during his continuance in any office, appointment or employment if held under the landlord. And for protection now given to agricultural labourers in tied cottages see below, p. 146.

[42] [1952] 1 T.L.R. 1386.

[43] *Ibid.* p. 1389.

[44] [1942] 2 All E.R. 674; see also, *Heslop* v. *Burns* [1974] 3 All E.R. 406; above p. 95.

[45] At p. 677.

[46] [1952] 1 All E.R. 1199 (C.A.). See also *Marcroft Wagons Ltd.* v. *Smith* [1951] 2 K.B. 496; *Shell-Mex and B.P. Ltd.* v. *Manchester Garages Ltd.* [1971] 1 All E.R. 841.

[47] Which would have given title under the Limitation Act 1939; see above, p. 95.

[48] And the circumstances surrounding an informal, family arrangement for the occupation of land may (even where a tenancy does not exist) give rise to protection under the rules of proprietary estoppel, contractual licences or constructive trusts; see, *e.g. Re Sharpe* [1980] 1 All E.R. 198; see below, pp. 408.

[49] [1977] 3 All E.R. 918 (C.A.).

facilities. There was a resident housekeeper who cleaned all the rooms daily and provided clean linen once a week. The bathroom and lavatory were shared. The defendant occupied one of the rooms. It was *held* that he was not a tenant but a contractual licensee[50] and so not protected under the Rent Acts.[51]

In such commercial, residential cases, there is some sort of spectrum from, say, the one night stay hotel guest at one extreme, through all the more or less permanent types of lodging arrangement to, say, the long term, unfurnished flat tenant at the other extreme.

As already stated, the courts will look at all the circumstances in deciding whether or not there is a tenancy. In *Marchant* v. *Charters* Lord Denning said[52]: "What is the test to see whether the occupier of one room in a house is a tenant or a licensee? It does not depend on whether he or she has exclusive possession or not. It does not depend on whether the room is furnished or not. It does not depend on whether the occupation is permanent or temporary. It does not depend on the label which the parties put on it. All these are factors which may influence the decision but none of them is conclusive. All the circumstances have to be worked out. Eventually the answer depends on the nature and quality of the occupancy. Was it intended that the occupier should have a stake in the room or did he only have permission for himself personally to occupy the room whether under contract or not in which case he is a licensee?"

The courts frequently refer to the intention of the parties; but caution has to be used here. It is not the label used by the parties that determines the status of the occupation.[53] This means that if in fact there is a tenancy, the landlord cannot deprive the tenant of the legal consequences by calling it something else.[54] In *Facchini* v.

---

[50] It was further held that, even if he was a tenant, the substantial provision of attendance excluded the tenancy from protection; see now, Rent Act 1977, s.7.

[51] See also, *Appah* v. *Parncliffe Investments Ltd.* [1964] 1 W.L.R. 1064; above, p. 94; *Luganda* v. *Service Hotels* [1969] 2 All E.R. 692 (C.A.), where the occupant was not in fact claiming to be a tenant but only to have sufficient "exclusive occupation" to give him the limited protection of (what is now) a restricted contract under the Rent Act 1977.

[52] [1977] 3 All E.R. 918, at p. 922. Note that until the Rent Act 1974, in the earlier Rent Acts, Parliament drew a distinction between unfurnished and furnished accommodation, the latter having only limited temporary security.

[53] At least not the label alone, though this may be some evidence of the capacity in which the property is held.

[54] Similarly, in the case of mortgages, the mortgagee cannot exclude the protection given by equity to mortgagors by calling the transaction something else; see below, p. 470.

Bryson[55] the agreement contained a term that nothing in it was to be construed as creating a tenancy. The court held, nevertheless, that there was a tenancy. Conversely, a sympathetic owner cannot protect a licensee by calling him a tenant. In *Booker* v. *Palmer*[56] the landowner gave evidence that he regarded the appellant as a tenant.

In other words the question is not (or should not be), did the parties intend to create a tenancy[57]; but did the relationship which they intended to create have the objective characteristics of a tenancy? The courts will not allow a sham to be used to avoid the Rent Acts.[57a] On the other hand, if the parties create something which is not a tenancy, the courts will recognise it as valid. The courts have not developed a rule of public policy against avoidance of such protective legislation. In *Somma* v. *Hazlehurst*[58] Cumming-Bruce J. said: "We can see no reason why an ordinary landlord, not in any of these special circumstances [hostel, hotel, family arrangement], should not be able to grant a licence to occupy an ordinary house. If that is what both he and the licensee intend and if they can frame any written agreement in such a way as to demonstrate that it is not really an agreement for a lease masquerading as a licence, we can see no reason in law or justice why they should be prevented from achieving that object."[59]

---

[55] [1952] 1 T.L.R. 1386 (C.A.).
[56] [1942] 2 All E.R. 674.
[57] Nor is it, did they intend to create legal relations? As pointed out by Scarman L.J. in *Heslop* v. *Burns*, a licence is a legal relationship; [1974] 2 All E.R. 406, at p. 414.
[57a] There is the further question, how far the courts will examine evidence extrinsic to a written agreement to ascertain the real intention of the parties. See generally, M. Partington, Non-exclusive Occupation Agreements, (1979) 42 M.L.R. 331; A. Nicol, Outflanking Protective Legislation – Shams and Beyond, (1981) 44 M.L.R. 21; and D. Tiplady, Recent Developments in the Law of Landlord and Tenant, (1981) 44 M.L.R. 129.
[58] [1978] 2 All E.R. 1011 (C.A.), at p. 1020.
[59] Contrast *Walsh* v. *Griffiths-Jones* [1978] 2 All E.R. 1003, decided by Lambeth C.C. on similar facts but with two occupants signing a single document. This case was referred to in *Somma* but no basis of distinction was offered. What is perhaps remarkable about *Somma* is that the court, whilst accepting at face value an agreement clearly designed to avoid the Rent Act, was at the same time prepared to assist the owner by implying terms designed to keep it within the bounds of legality—namely, that the owner would not use his express rights to force a person of the opposite sex on the occupier. See also *Aldrington Garages* v. *Fielder* (1978) 249 E.G. 440 (C.A.) and *Demuren* v. *Seal Estates* (1978) 249 E.G. 440 (C.A.). On non-exclusive occupation agreements, see M. Partington, *Landlord and Tenant* (2nd ed.), pp. 119–148. On the attitude of the courts to an agricultural tenancy agreement designed to avoid the Agricultural Holdings Act 1948, see *Johnson* v. *Moreton* [1978] 3 W.L.R. 538.

The difficulty is, as the cases so far referred to show, that a licence can exist with all the features of a tenancy, including exclusive possession. There is no objective characteristic that necessarily identifies an agreement as one or the other; so there is no certain guide for predicting the outcome of cases. It may seem that, for various reasons, the courts have developed the concept of the occupation licence without, as yet, being able to identify what they have developed.

Rent. Although the reservation of a rent is usual, it is not essential to the existence of a leasehold interest. But in some cases whether or not a rent is reserved may have legal significance.[60]

Importance of distinction between leases and licenses. It may be important to distinguish between a lease and a licence for a number of reasons; for example:

(1) In general, full protection under the Rent Act 1977, is only available to those who are residential tenants. Similarly, only business tenancies, and not licences, are protected under the Landlord and Tenant Act 1954, Part II.[61]

(2) The licensor, but not a tenant's landlord, may owe a duty of care to look after the licensee's goods on the premises.

(3) More generally, a lease is, and has all the characteristics of, a property interest. In particular, it is capable of binding subsequent owners of the land. A licence (or such is the traditional view) is a purely personal right, in general enforceable only against the licensor. But, as already indicated, this view may have to be modified in the light of modern judicial developments.

(4) A lease can only exist for one of the leasehold estates. The licence has far more flexibility in terms of possible duration and conditions of occupation that can be attached; and can be used today to give, at least limited, proprietary protection to occupation agreements that could not be fitted into the traditional doctrine of estates.[62]

---

[60] For example, in the case of lease for lives; see below p. 585. See also below, p. 215. For rent review clauses, important in periods of inflation, see *United Scientific Holdings Ltd.* v. *Burnley B.C.* [1978] A.C. 904. And see generally, D. G. Barnsley, *Land Options* (1979), pp. 250-278.

[61] See *Shell-Mex and B.P. Ltd.* v. *Manchester Garages Ltd.* [1971] 1 All E.R. 841. For the position of a tenancy at will under the Landlord and Tenant Act 1954, Part II, see *Hagee (London) Ltd.* v. *A.B. Erikson & Larson* [1975] 3 All E.R. 234 (C.A.). In contrast, agricultural occupation licences may be protected under the Agricultural Holdings Act 1948; and the Rent (Agriculture) Act 1976 extends to licences.

[62] See below, p. 403.

Principle 2. Duration: the leasehold estates

A lease must be for a determinate period. The law recognises four main leasehold estates:
(1) Terms of years. (2) Periodic tenancy. (3) Tenancy at will. (4) Tenancy at sufferance.

The rules governing the duration of these estates are now subject to the statutory security of tenure given in many cases.

Explanation

The term of years.[63] The term of years exists where a leasehold interest is created for a fixed period of time—even if it is determinable earlier on the happening of some specified event. "Therefore this estate is called a term, a terminus, because its duration or continuance is bounded, limited and determined."[64]

For there to be a valid term of years, the date of commencement and the maximum duration must be fixed with certainty before the term takes effect (*i.e.* in possession).[65] For example, if L grants T a lease "to take effect from January next for such period as may be stipulated by X," the lease will be valid if, before January 1, X stipulates, *e.g.* 10 years.

During World Wars I and II, it was common practice to grant leases expressed to be for the duration of the war. In *Lace* v. *Chantler*[66] such a lease was *held* to be void for uncertainty. By the Validation of War Time Leases Act 1944, such leases were converted into ten-year terms determinable at the end of the war.

In some cases, the courts have cured uncertainty by implying a term fixing the duration. In *Great Northern Ry.* v. *Arnold*[67] Rowlatt J. thought that the "law was ingenious enough to get round the difficulty." The intention was to create a valid lease for the duration of the war; he could give effect to this intention by construing the agreement as a lease for a long term of years determinable at the end of the war, and he ordered rectification accordingly.[68]

---

[63] For the special meaning given to "term of years absolute" in L.P.A. 1925, S.1, see below, p. 108.

[64] 2 Bl.Comm. 143.

[65] See below, p. 107, for the meaning of a lease taking effect.

[66] [1944] K.B. 368.

[67] [1916] 33 T.L.R. 114; and see *Siew Soon Wah* v. *Yong Tong Hong* [1973] 2 W.L.R. 713 (P.C.).

[68] The readiness of the courts to make a guess at and implement the unexpressed intentions of the parties to an agreement, gives them a very wide and flexible power to achieve (what they consider to be) a desirable result in a particular case. Compare *Somma* v. *Hazlehurst* [1978] 2 All E.R. 1011; above p. 100.

It is only the maximum duration that must be certain. It does not matter that the lease is liable to be determined at some earlier date. For example, many modern terms contain what is commonly called a break clause. This gives the landlord or tenant (or both) the right to determine the lease at stipulated intervals. Again, every well drawn lease will contain a forfeiture[69] clause giving the landlord the right to re-enter and determine the lease for non-payment of rent or breach of covenant.

A term of years will, in the absence of express provision and statute, continue for the full term and then expire automatically.

Periodic tenancies. A periodic tenancy is one which continues for an original period and then for subsequent like periods until determined by either party giving the necessary notice to quit. It is a single tenancy which grows in duration as the periods pass—not a series of separate tenancies. In the absence of notice, it does not end automatically at the end of any period. Like the term of years, it does not end automatically on the death of either party. In *Youngmin* v. *Heath*[70] the weekly tenant of a house died. Her administrators were held liable (to the extent of the deceased's assets) to pay rent for the period after death until proper notice had been given. The commonest periodic tenancies are tenancies from year to year, monthly and weekly tenancies. But they may be based on any other agreed period.

Such a tenancy may be created expressly or by implication. For example, if a person is allowed into possession as a tenant and pays rent on a weekly basis, there will be a strong presumption that he is a weekly tenant.

Subject to statute[71] and the terms of the lease, a periodic tenancy can only be determined by the appropriate notice. In the case of a yearly tenancy this means one half year's notice expiring at the end of some year of the tenancy. Any other lesser periodic tenancy must be determined by a full period's notice.

Whilst the duration of the basic period must be certain, it is not possible to say how long a periodic tenancy will last until one party gives notice. Nor will such a tenancy be void for uncertainty because it contains a term which precludes the landlord from giving notice either until some event happens or at all. But such a term might *itself* be void as being repugnant to the tenancy

---

[69] See below, p. 133.

[70] [1974] 1 All E.R. 461 (C.A.); and see *Hale* v. *Hale* [1975] 2 All E.R. 1090, showing that a weekly tenancy is property which can be assigned.

[71] *e.g.* Protection From Eviction Act 1977, s.5 which requires a minimum of four weeks' notice in the case of a residential tenancy.

created. In *Centaploy* v. *Matlodge*[72] there was a weekly tenancy which was "to continue until determined by the lessee." It was *held* that the provision that only the tenant could determine it by notice was void as being repugnant to the essential nature of a weekly tenancy thus leaving an ordinary weekly tenancy (which was protected by the Landlord and Tenant Act 1954, Part II).

Tenancy at will.[73]   A tenancy at will exists where a person is let into possession as tenant on the basis that either party may determine the tenancy at any time. Common cases are where a purchaser of land is let into possession before completion[74]; or an intending lessee is allowed into possession pending negotiations for the lease; and where a tenant for a term of years is allowed by the lessor to remain in possession on the expiry of his lease until a new term is created.

A tenancy at will can be determined immediately by either party simply notifying the other. A landlord giving notice, merely has to give the tenant reasonable time to vacate the premises.

A tenancy at will is hardly an estate at all. There is certainly tenure, the personal relationship of landlord and tenant, but no certain duration, freehold or leasehold, has been provided for. It is for this reason—that it is really no more than the tenurial relationship—that the tenancy ends automatically on the death of either party,[75] or on any attempted assignment by the tenant or any assignment of the reversion. In the absence of agreement the landlord is entitled to claim from his tenant a reasonable sum for the use and occupation of the premises.

If a tenant at will (or at sufferance) starts to pay rent he will normally become a periodic tenant by reference to the periods for which the rent is paid.

Generally, a tenancy at will arises because the courts recognise that a tenancy exists but no other freehold or leasehold interest has been created. But in *Hagee (London) Ltd.* v. *A.B. Erikson & Larson*[76] the court accepted that a tenancy at will could be created

---

[72] [1973] 2 W.L.R. 832. Contrast *Charles Clay and Son Ltd.* v. *British Railways Board* [1971] Ch. 725.

[73] As to origins of the tenancy at will see R.H. Tawney, *The Agrarian Problem in the Sixteenth Century,* at p. 23.

[74] See B.M. Hoggett, *Houses on the Never-Never,* (1972) 36 Conv.(N.S.) 325; 39 Conv.(N.S.) 343. Note Law Society's General Conditions of Sale (1980 ed.), Condition 18; and see *Hyde* v. *Pearce* [1982] 1 All E.R. 1029 (C.A.).

[75] Contrast *Youngmin* v. *Heath* [1974] 1 All E.R. 461.

[76] [1975] 3 All E.R. (C.A.).

by express agreement as a commercial tenancy (with a rent reserved).[77]

Tenancy at sufferance. A tenancy at sufferance exists where a tenant, having entered under a valid tenancy, wrongfully holds over without the landlord's assent or dissent after the expiry of his lease. The tenant at sufferance, unlike the tenant at will, is there without the agreement of the owner. Today, he is more or less in the same position as a squatter. He really has no estate and he can hardly be said to have a tenure. Time under the Limitation Act 1980 begins to run in his favour and against the landlord from the start of the tenancy; and the landlord can claim possession at any time without even having to give notice.

Principle 3. Some special types of lease

The following types of lease should be noted:

(1) **Sub-lease** (also known as an under-lease or sub-tenancy). This is a lease derived out of and shorter than another leasehold interest.

(2) **Concurrent lease.** This is a lease created by the landlord out of his reversion on an existing lease. It exists side by side with another lease.

(3) **Future lease.** This is an existing lease which carries the right to possession not immediately but at some specified time in the future.

(4) **Leases for lives or until marriage.** A lease at a rent or in consideration of a fine[78] for life or lives, or for a term of years determinable with life or lives or on the marriage of the lessee, is converted into a term of 90 years. When the relevant death or marriage occurs either party can determine the lease by giving at least one month's notice in writing.[79]

(5) **Perpetually renewable leases.** Any lease which is perpetually renewable by the tenant is converted into a term of 2,000 years which can be determined by the tenant, not by the landlord,

---

[77] And with the consequence that the security generally available to fixed term and periodic business tenancies under the Landlord and Tenant Act 1954, Part II, was effectively excluded.

[78] *i.e.* a premium; see below, p. 110.

[79] L.P.A. 1925, s.149(6); see further, below, p. 585.

giving at lease ten days' notice to expire on one of the renewal dates.[80]

(6) **Long leases under section 153 of the Law of Property Act 1925.** A long lease originally granted for at least 300 years of which at least 200 years are unexpired and in respect of which no rent of any money value is payable can be enlarged by the lessee into a fee simple.

(7) **Tenancy by estoppel.** If a person purports to grant a lease which he has no right to grant, the intended tenant will have a tenancy by estoppel. The landlord and his succesors in title will not be allowed to deny the validity of the lease; nor will the tenant or his successors in title; but others will not be bound by it.[81]

Explanation

Sub-leases. A sub-lease should be distinguished from the assignment of a lease. If L, the freeholder, leases Blackacre to T for 21 years, it is possible for T to dispose of his whole leasehold interest. Suppose that he sells and transfers (*i.e.* assigns) the residue of his term to P. P now steps into T's shoes. T is no longer interested in the land and no longer a tenant (though he may continue liable in contract). If, instead, T grants to ST a term less than his own—say seven years—this is a sub-lease. The relationship of landlord and tenant (privity of estate) between L and T continues. There is also now the relationship of landlord and tenant (another privity of estate) between T and ST.

ST could in turn sublet his seven-year term (or he could assign it) and there is in law no limit to the number of sub-leases that can be created in this way.

If a tenant attempts to create a sub-lease for a term equal to or longer than his own, it will operate as an assignment whatever he calls it.

Concurrent Leases. A landlord can create more than one lease of his land to exist side by side at the same time. If L grants T1 a 21-year lease in possession of Blackacre, T1 will be entitled to immediate possession of the land for the 21 years. But there is nothing to stop L granting another lease to T2 for any period, say 31 years. T2 cannot of course disturb T1's actual possession of the land, but he will be entitled to receive the rent from him for the rest of the 21-year period. And then for the rest of the 31 years he

---

[80] *Ibid.* s.145, Sched. 15.
[81] See *Industrial Properties (Barton Hill) Ltd.* v. *Associated Electrical Industries Ltd.* [1977] 2 All E.R. 293 (C.A.).

will be entitled to actual possession. L has in effect leased his reversion.

Future or reversionary leases. If a lease is in possession it gives the right to immediate possession. Possession means the right to exclusive occupation or the right to receive the rents.[82] Thus a freeholder who leases his land is still deemed to be in possession, just as is a sub-lessor who creates a sub-lease. Similarly, a concurrent lease may be in possession.

However, it is possible to create a lease (as it is a freehold interest) to take effect in possession at some time in the future. It is important to realise that it is the possession which is in the future, not the lease. The lessee has an immediate ownership interest in the land (which may be legal).[83] What he does not yet have is possession.

The immediate grant of a future lease should be distinguished from an agreement to grant a lease in the future. The distinction may be important. An illustration might help: on August 1, 1972, L, the freeholder, executes a lease in the usual form containing the following words: " . . . the Lessor Hereby Demises unto the Tenant All That dwellinghouse and premises (hereinafter called 'the Premises') situate at Little Chittering in the County of Kent and known as Blackacre To Hold unto the Tenant from the 1st day of August 1972." Here the term is to run from and the lessee to have possession from the date of the grant. It is a lease in possession. If, on the other hand, it said "To Hold unto the Tenant from the 1st day of August 1973." then the tenant has a future lease. He has an immediate legal lease but will not be entitled to possession until the term starts to run on August 1, 1973, from which date the lease is said to take effect.

Finally, suppose that L and T make an agreement by which L agrees that he will, on August 1, 1973, grant T a lease for 21 years. Now T has an agreement to create a lease.[84] When the day arrives L will be under an obligation to execute the necessary deed.

Under section 149(3) of the Law of Property Act 1925, a future lease which is to take effect in possession more than 21 years from

---

[82] L.P.A. 1925, s.205(1) (xix).
[83] See below, p. 108.
[84] An agreement for a lease should be distinguished from "a tenancy agreement" which latter term is usually used to signify an informal legal lease (see below, p. 110); an agreement for a lease is a contract but, where it imposes an obligation to execute a lease immediately, it may in addition constitute an equitable lease (see below, p. 110).

its date of creation will be void (unless it operates in equity under a settlement).[85]

SECTION II.   CREATION OF LEASES

Principle 4.   Creation of legal leases

Leases may be legal or equitable.

A leasehold estate will only be legal if it satisfies the following two conditions:

(1) It must be for a term of years absolute; but it does not have to be in possession.[86]

(2) It must in general have been created by deed.[87]

However, a legal lease (commonly referred to as a tenancy agreement) can be created under hand or orally if it takes effect in possession for a term not exceeding three years at the best rent which can reasonably be obtained without taking a fine.[88]

Explanation

The term of years absolute.   The Law of Property Act 1925 provides that the only possible legal leasehold estate is the term of years absolute.[89] But this expression is defined so widely that there are not many leasehold estates which are incapable of being legal. In most cases the distinction between legal and equitable leases depends on the formalities used for their creation.[90]

The expression "term of years absolute" is defined by the Law of Property Act 1925, s.205(1) (xxvii) to include a term for less than one year. The section further provides that a term of years does not cease to be absolute because it is liable to be determined by notice, re-entry, operation of law, or by a provision for cesser on redemption or in any other event, other than the dropping of a life or the determination of a determinable life interest.[91] Fixed terms do invariably contain provisos for re-entry on breach,[92] and of course periodic tenancies are liable to be determined on notice.

---

[85] See *Weg Motors Ltd.* v. *Hales* [1961] 3 All E.R. 181.

[86] L.P.A. 1925, s.1(1).

[87] L.P.A. 1925, s.52(1).

[88] L.P.A. 1925, s.54(2).

[89] *Ibid.* s.1(1).

[90] But note position as to a lease for lives (below, p. 585). As to tenancies at will and sufferance, see Megarry and Wade, *Law of Real Property* (4th ed.), pp. 639, 641.

[91] See n. 90 above.

[92] See George and George, *Sale of Flats* (4th ed.), p. 293.

It has been suggested that the word "absolute" is "here used in no intelligible sense,"[93] and that a term of years absolute may "consist of a tenancy which is neither a 'term of years' nor 'absolute' according to the natural meaning of the words, *e.g.* a monthly tenancy liable to be forfeited for non payment of rent."

A legal lease does not have to be in possession. As already explained, leases like freehold interests may be in possession or future. But whereas a fee simple absolute can only be legal if it is in possession, a term of years absolute can be legal whether it is in possession or future. The significance of this is considered later.[94]

No limit to number of legal leases. There can only be one legal freehold estate in a piece of land at any one time: the legal fee simple absolute in possession. There can be any number of legal leases. Again the significance of this is considered below.[95]

Creation by deed. "There are three things of the essence and substance of a deed, that is to say, writing on paper or parchment, sealing and delivery."[96]

In addition to the above, by the Law of Property Act 1925, s.73, the signature or mark of the person executing the deed is essential.

It has been suggested that " . . . at the present day if a party signs a document bearing a wax or a wafer or other indication of a seal with the intention of executing the document as a deed, that is sufficient adoption or recognition of the seal to amount to due execution as a deed."[97]

Delivery does not mean "handed over" to the other side; but an act done so as to evince an intention to be bound.

In modern times, the practice on signing, sealing and delivery has become informal, with little regard for the strict requirements of the law; this involves uncertainty as to when execution actually takes effect and possible risks in consequence for the person executing. It has been said that "some change in the law is urgently required."[98]

---

[93] Megarry and Wade (n. 90 above), p. 140.
[94] p. 584.
[95] *Ibid.*
[96] *Goddard's Case* (1584) 2 Co. Rep. 4b, at 5a.
[97] *Stromdale and Ball Ltd.* v. *Burden* [1952] Ch. 223 at p. 230, *per* Danckwerts J. And see *First National Securities Ltd.* v. *Jones* [1978] 2 W.L.R. 475 (C.A.). For criticism of this latter case, see D. Hoath, The Sealing of Documents – Fact or Fiction, (1980) 43 M.L.R. 415.
[98] See Barnsley, *Conveyancing Law and Practice*, (1973), at p. 386.

Parol leases. The general rule is that a deed is needed to create or transfer a legal estate in land.[99] One of the exceptions is the parol lease for a term not exceeding three years at the best rent which can reasonably be obtained without taking a fine and taking effect in possession.[1] Such a lease can be legal whether created under hand or even orally. The common examples are periodic weekly, monthly and yearly tenancies which have been held to be within the definition since it is not certain that they will continue beyond three years.

It is common for a lease not exceeding three years to be referred to as a tenancy agreement; whilst the word lease is reserved for a legal term of more than three years created by deed. But when used in this context, a tenancy agreement is *not* just a contractual agreement; it is as much a lease and a legal estate in the land as a term created by deed for 3,000 years. It will be seen from this that a future lease for however short a period must be made by deed.

The consideration must be rent only—not a fine—and it must be the best rent reasonably obtainable. A fine (or premium) is a lump sum "paid by the tenant on the commencement of his tenancy in order that his rent may be small or nominal."[2] But a lump sum paid at the beginning of a tenancy may represent, not a fine, but rent paid in advance. Conversely, a periodic payment may represent the payment of a premium by instalments. The distinction may be difficult to make in practice. In *Grace Rymer Investments Ltd.* v. *Waite*[3] the landlord had insisted on the tenant paying three years' rent in advance before letting her into possession. It was held that although paid as a lump sum nevertheless it represented rent.

Principle 5.   Equitable leases.   The doctrine of Walsh v. Lonsdale

A lease which fails to satisfy the requirements necessary to create a legal lease, may nevertheless be a valid equitable lease if the following requirements are satisfied:

(1) There must be a valid contract to create a lease.

(2) This contract must be specifically enforceable.

If these conditions are satisfied, equity will not only grant specific performance but will treat the contract itself as creating a valid lease.

---

[99] L.P.A. 1925, s.52(1).
[1] L.P.A. 1925, s.54(2). A deed is necessary to transfer such a lease at law.
[2] Shorter Oxford English Dictionary.
[3] [1958] Ch. 831 (C.A.).

Explanation

One of the important contributions of equity to land law has been to recognise interests created without the formalities necessary at law.[4]

At common law a deed was, and still is, generally necessary to create or transfer an interest in land.[5] Equity was prepared to give effect to less formal transactions and might recognise a lease as valid even though created without a deed. This distinction between a formal and informal (legal and equitable) lease is perhaps somewhat artificial today—since the sealing of a deed today is little but a formality; in both deeds and documents under hand it is the signature which identifies it.[6] Nevertheless, the distinction has been preserved by the 1925 legislation and whether a lease is legal or equitable may still be a vital question.[7]

The principle behind equity's intervention is as follows: there is a contract to create a lease. For some reason the deed necessary to create a lease in accordance with the contract has not been executed. At law therefore the intended lessee has no interest in the land at all—though if he is let into possession and pays rent on a periodic basis that will even at law give him a periodic tenancy. Equity, in order to do what is fair, will intervene. First, it will grant specific performance of the contract—that is it will order the necessary deed to be executed. Secondly, acting on the principle that equity treats as done that which ought to be done, it will treat the deed as having been executed and the intended lessee as already having the agreed lease, but, being a creature of equity, it is an equitable lease.

This principle is not confined to leases. It applies to the informal creation of equitable mortgages[8] and other equitable third party rights in land such as easements.[9]

As set out in the Principle above, two conditions must be satisfied for the equitable doctrine to operate.

There must be a contract.   There must be a contract to create a lease; and, if there is not a contract, equity will not intervene to aid a volunteer—*i.e.* it will not enforce a gratuitous promise to grant a

---

[4] For the distinction between common law and equity see below, p. 156.
[5] The most important exceptions are the short lease mentioned above and the assent by a personal representative, for which see below, p. 580. For other exceptions see L.P.A. 1925, s.52(2).
[6] L.P.A. 1925, s.73; see further, above, p. 109.
[7] See below, p. 114.
[8] See below, p. 479.
[9] See below, p. 370.

lease. However, (in the absence of an actual contract) if there is a purported lease which for some reason is not valid at law (if, for example, not created by deed) equity will treat this *as a* contract[10] and apply the doctrine in *Walsh* v. *Lonsdale.*

The contract must be specifically enforceable.   Under section 40 of the Law of Property Act 1925 any contract for the sale or disposition of land or any interest in land will be unenforceable unless in writing or evidenced in writing by a memorandum signed by the person sued on it or his authorised agent. However, even in the absence of sufficient written evidence, the contract may still be specifically enforceable if there has been a sufficient act of part performance by the plaintiff.[11]

The creation of equitable leases can be traced to the case of *Walsh* v. *Londsdale*[12] which has given its name to the principle. In that case there was an agreement in writing to grant a seven year lease of a mill, Providence Mill, to T at a rent. The agreement provided that if demanded the rent would be paid one year in advance. No deed was executed, but T was let into possession and paid rent in arrears. This gave him a yearly tenancy at law. The landlord demanded rent in advance under the agreement and when it was not paid he distrained. The tenant sued for damages for wrongful distress. It was held that although at law he might only be a yearly tenant liable to pay in arrears, in equity he had a seven-year term and was liable to pay rent in advance under the agreement. The distress was therefore lawful.

It will be noted that in this case there was both written evidence and part performance. The taking of possession by the plaintiff with the consent of the landlord is invariably a sufficient act of part performance.[13]

In *Kingswood Estates Co. Ltd.* v. *Anderson,*[14] there was an oral agreement to give the elderly widow and her invalid son a flat for the rest of their lives in return for them giving up their existing flat in which they had security of tenure. The agreement was oral but it was held that there was a sufficient act of part performance by the plaintiffs—moving flats—and they were therefore protected in equity.[15]

Even if the requirement as to written evidence or part performance is satisfied, there may still be some reason which

---

[10] *Parker* v. *Taswell* (1858) 2 De G. and J. 559.
[11] See below, p. 558.
[12] (1882) 21 Ch.D. 9 (C.A.).
[13] See below, p. 558.
[14] [1963] 2 Q.B. 169 (C.A.).
[15] Presumably they had an equitable 90-year lease under L.P.A. 1925, s.149(6).

would bar a claim for specific performance. If this is so, there will be no equitable lease. For example, in *Cornish* v. *Brook Green Laundry*,[16] there was a contract in writing to grant a tenancy conditional on the intended lessees carrying out certain repairs. These repairs were not carried out; the contract was therefore not specifically enforceable and there was no lease in law or equity. *Warmington* v. *Miller*[17] is another example. M. held under a 24-year lease which contained a covenant not to assign or part with possession of the premises. In breach of this covenant he agreed to execute a sub-lease in favour of the plaintiff W. He let W. into possession but failed to execute the sub-lease and the plaintiff claimed: (a) specific performance; and (b) a declaration that he had an equitable sub-lease in accordance with the agreement. The court rejected both claims. To order specific performance would be to order the defendant to break the covenant in his lease. The agreement was therefore not specifically enforceable and so did not give rise to an equitable lease.

A more doubtful case is *Tottenham Hotspur Football and Athletic Co. Ltd.* v. *Princegrove Publishers*.[18] Here there was an agreement for a business tenancy for a fixed term of one year. Such a tenancy is normally subject to the security of tenure provisions of the Landlord and Tenant Act 1954, Part II, ss.24–28; and any agreement to exclude these provisions is void. However, under s.38(4),[19] on a joint application of landlord and tenant, the court can authorise the exclusion of ss.24–28 provided the agreement is then endorsed on "the instrument creating the tenancy."[20] The authorisation of the court was obtained and the tenant took possession, paying the agreed rent, but no lease was executed and so no endorsement made. It was *held* that the doctrine in *Walsh* v. *Lonsdale* applied; that therefore equity would treat the lease (including the statutory endorsement) as having been executed. Consequently, the tenant was not entitled to security. The decision has been described as a "remarkable translation of the doctrine of *Walsh* v. *Lonsdale*."[21] Further, it has been suggested[22] that since the agreed term had expired at the

---

[16] [1959] 1 Q.B. 394.
[17] [1973] 2 W.L.R. 654 (C.A.).
[18] [1974] 1 All E.R. 17 (Lawson J.).
[19] Added by L.P.A. 1969, s.5.
[20] Apparently to warn possible assignees of the lease.
[21] (1974) 90 L.Q.R. 149.
[22] *Ibid.* See also *Industrial Properties (Barton Hill) Ltd.* v. *Associated Electrical Industries Ltd.* [1977] 2 All E.R. 293 (C.A.).

time of the hearing, the agreement was no longer specifically enforceable.

The doctrine has also been applied where the lessor held not the legal state but only the benefit of a specifically enforceable contract to purchase the legal estate.[23]

A final point: The doctrine of *Walsh* v. *Lonsdale* only operates where the contract is overdue for performance. It does not convert a contract to create a lease in the future into a present equitable lease. But if there is a specifically enforceable contract to create a lease on the first of January next, there will be an equitable lease from that date even if the deed is not executed.[24]

Principle 6. Comparison of legal and equitable leases

In general an equitable lease is as good as a legal lease. It is said that "a contract for a lease is as good as a lease." The equitable lease will be subject to the same terms as would have governed the legal lease;[25] and it will be enforceable in the same way. However, there are a number of differences, including the following:

(1) Whilst an equitable lease does not require a deed, it does require a specifically enforceable contract. A legal lease requires a deed but does not depend on consideration or the existence of a contract.

(2) A legal lease in unregistered land[26] is good against all the world. An equitable lease, if not registered under the Land Charges Act 1972 as an estate contract, will be void against a purchaser for money or money's worth of a legal estate in the land.

In the case of registered land,[27] what matters is not whether the lease is legal or equitable but whether it is a registrable, a minor or an overriding interest. A legal lease exceeding 21 years may be registered substantively as a separate registered ownership interest.[28] If for 21 years or less at a rent without taking a fine it is

---

[23] *Industrial Properties (Barton Hill) Ltd.* v. *Associated Electrical Industries Ltd.* [1977] 2 All E.R. 293 (C.A.).

[24] But the contract will, from the start, be an estate contract which is an equitable interest in the land. Or perhaps it can be said that the contract immediately creates an equitable future lease (see above, p. 107). And see *Hasham* v. *Zenab* [1960] A.C. 316; *Skelton* v. *James* [1975] 1 All E.R. 182 at p. 187; and *Property Discount Corp. Ltd.* v. *Lyon Group Ltd.* [1981] 1 All E.R. 379 (C.A.).

[25] See *Brikom Investments* v. *Seaford* [1981] 1 W.L.R. 863 (C.A.).

[26] See Chap. 24, below, for distinction between registered and unregistered land.

[27] See below, p. 528, *et seq.* for registration under L.R.A. 1925.

[28] L.R.A. 1925, s.8; see further, below, p. 544.

an overriding interest enforceable against all the world without registration.[29] Similarly, if the lesee is in occupation his rights may constitute an overriding interest (being the rights of a person in actual occupation of the land).[30] In any other case the lease will be a minor interest and require protection by entry on the register.

(3) There is no privity of estate between a landlord and an assignee of an equitable lease and even those covenants which touch and concern the land will not run with the lease.[31]

(4) A lease is a conveyance for the purpose of section 62 of the Law of Property Act 1925 but a contract is not.[32]

(5) The "usual covenants" are implied into a contract to create a lease. But if they are not expressly included in a lease they will not be implied.[33]

Explanation

The various points (1) to (5) are dealt with elsewhere.

SECTION III.   OBLIGATIONS OF THE PARTIES

Introduction

The requirements essential to the creation of a valid legal or equitable lease have been considered. Assuming that a valid lease does exist, it is then necessary to decide the rights and obligations of the parties who is to be liable for repair; what rent the tenant must pay; and so on. These matters are governed by the covenants[34] contained in the lease which may be:

(1) Implied covenants.
(2) Express covenants.
(3) Usual covenants.

Each of these will be considered in turn.

---

[29] L.R.A. 1925, s.70(1)(*k*). If a fine (premium) is paid, it will be a minor interest.
[30] L.R.A. 1925, s.70(1)(*g*).
[31] But they will run with the reversion. For the running of covenants, see below, p. 419.
[32] See L.P.A. 1925, s.205(1) (ii); *Borman* v. *Griffith* [1930] 1 Ch. 493. See below, p. 375, for s.62.
[33] See below, p. 125.
[34] Strictly a covenant means a promise under seal. In the present context it simply means a term of the lease.

Principle 7.   Implied covenants

In so far as these are not modified or excluded by the express terms of the lease, the position of the parties to a lease is governed by a set of covenants implied by the courts or, in some cases, statute. Some of the covenants implied by statute cannot be excluded.[35]

The following are the most important covenants which may be implied[36]:

(1) By the landlord:

(a) To allow quiet enjoyment.
(b) Not to derogate from grant.
(c) By statute in special cases, an obligation to repair.

(2) By the tenant:

(d) To pay the rent.
(e) (i) In the case of a term of years, to repair.
      (ii) In the case of a periodic tenancy to use the premises in a tenant like manner.
(f) In certain cases to allow the landlord to enter to view.

In general these covenants will be implied whether the lease is legal or equitable and regardless of its duration.

Explanation

Quiet enjoyment.   There is an implied covenant by the landlord that the tenant will be put into and allowed to enjoy quiet possession of the premises.

The covenant is implied into any lease. " . . . In my opinion the law does import this covenant in all cases where the relationship of landlord and tenant is established by instrument under seal, and imports a contract to the same effect where the instrument is not under seal."[37]

Quiet enjoyment means freedom from any substantial physical interference with the enjoyment of the premises. A clear case was *Lavender* v. *Betts*[38] where a landlord tried to force his weekly tenant to vacate by removing doors and windows. The physical interference may result from something done outside the premises. In *Perera* v. *Vandiyar*[39] another landlord seeking to get his

---

[35] For example, the obligation to repair the structure and exterior imposed on a landlord under the Housing Act 1961, ss.32, 33 in the case of a term of less than seven years; see below, p. 119.

[36] See generally Hill and Redman, *Landlord and Tenant* (16th ed.), Chap. III.

[37] Lord Russell C.J. in *Baynes & Co.* v. *Lloyd & Son* [1895] 1 Q.B. 820 at p. 825.

[38] [1942] 2 All E.R. 72.

[39] [1953] 1 W.L.R. 672 (C.A.).

tenants out, cut off their gas and electricity supply. The tenants recovered damages for breach of the covenant.[40] Again, in *Kenny* v. *Preen*[41] the landlord, in addition to writing threatening letters, banged on the tenant's door shouting abuse at her through it. This was held to be a breach. As Donovan L.J. said, " . . . short of battery how more physical can you get. . . . "[42]

On the other hand if there is no physical interference at all, the tenant cannot complain on the basis of this covenant however much he may be affected.[43] In *Browne* v. *Flower*[44] the landlord allowed the tenant of the first floor rooms to build an outside iron staircase which went past the plaintiff tenant's ground floor window. This interfered with her privacy—a right not as such recognised by English law—but there was no physical interference with her enjoyment of the flat and so her claim failed. It is the landlord's positive act of interference which gives rise to liability. He will not be liable under this head for any any disturbance caused by inactivity; for example, non-repair of common lifts and staircases in a block of flats.[45]

The landlord will be liable under this covenant if the act of interference is his own or authorised by him—if it is "by him or through the lawful acts of anyone claiming through or under

---

[40] But not exemplary damages since, so it was held, no trespass was involved; which suggests that there can be a breach of the covenant for quiet enjoyment without any tort being committed against the tenant. Compare *Drane* v. *Evangelou* [1978] 2 All E.R. 437 (C.A.) in which exemplary damages were ordered. For cases in which exemplary damages can still be awarded in tort, see *Rookes* v. *Barnard* [1964] A.C. 1129. In *McCall* v. *Abelesz* [1976] 1 All E.R. 727, Lord Denning suggested that on the basis of *Jarvis* v. *Swan Tours Ltd.* [1973] 1 All E.R. 71, and *Jackson* v. *Horizon Holidays Ltd.* [1975] 3 All E.R. 92, substantially greater damages would be awarded today in a case like *Perera* for loss of enjoyment and mental suffering.

[41] [1963] 1 Q.B. 499 (C.A.).

[42] *Ibid.* p. 515.

[43] In *McCall* v. *Abelesz* [1976] 1 All E.R. 727 at p. 731, Lord Denning suggested a wider definition: "The covenant is not confined to direct, physical interference by the landlord. It extends to any conduct of the landlord or his agents which interferes with the tenant's freedom of action in exercising his rights as a tenant." But this still leaves open the precise extent of the tenant's rights. Note that in *Liverpool City Council* v. *Irwin* [1977] A.C. 239 (H.L.) the county court judge found that there had been breach of the tenant's quiet enjoyment; but in the C.A. and H.L. tenant's counsel conceded that there was no breach of this covenant; see below, p. 120.

[44] [1911] 1 Ch. 219 (Parker J.).

[45] See *Liverpool City Council* v. *Irwin* [1975] 3 All E.R. 658 (C.A.), particularly Lord Denning at p. 663. For the landlord's obligation to repair such common parts, see below, p. 121.

him. . . . "[46] If the act is not authorised,—*e.g.* is the act of an
ordinary trespasser—the tenant will have his claim in tort against
the wrongdoer. The covenant does not cover the acts of those
claiming by title paramount—*i.e.* those whose title is superior to
that of the landlord. Here the tenant may have no remedy at
all—one of the disadvantages of taking a lease as opposed to
purchasing the freehold. For example, in *Jones* v. *Lavington*,[47] L
let the property to T under a lease containing a restrictive
covenant against carrying on business. T sublet to ST who carried
on business for some time in ignorance of the covenant. The
superior landlord, L, then obtained an injunction to enforce the
covenant. It was held that ST had no claim against his sub-lessor,
T, for breach of the covenant for quiet enjoyment. The covenant
did not extend to the acts of those such as L claiming by title
paramount.

In formal leases, the parties will normally include an express
covenant for quiet enjoyment rather than leaving it to be implied
by law. For example[48]:

> "The tenant paying the rent hereby reserved and performing
> and observing the covenants conditions and agreements
> herein contained and on the part of the tenant to be
> performed and observed shall peaceably hold the premises
> (subject to the exceptions and reservations herein contained)
> during the said term without any lawful interruption by the
> Lessor or any person claiming under or in trust for him."[49]

Like the implied covenant this express covenant is invariably
qualified in that it excludes liability for anyone claiming by title
paramount.

Landlord's obligation not to derogate from grant.[50] "The
grantor of land to be used for a particular purpose is under an
obligation to abstain from doing anything on adjoining property
belonging to him which would prevent the land granted from being
used for the purpose for which the grant was made. . . .[51]

In the case from which this quotation is taken, the landlord let
premises to be used for a timber merchant's business. It was *held*

---

[46] Hill and Redman (above n. 36), p. 194. See *Hilton* v. *James Smith & Sons
(Norwood) Ltd.* (1979) 251 E.G. 1063 (C.A.).
[47] [1903] 1 K.B. 253 (C.A.).
[48] Hallett, *Conveyancing Precedents* (1965), 491.
[49] For the use of the word "lawful" and the extent of such an express covenant, see
(1968) 28 Conv.(N.S.) 6 (V.G. Wellings).
[50] See also below, p. 377.
[51] *Aldin* v. *Latimer Clark, Muirhead & Co.* [1894] 2 Ch. 437 (Stirling J.), headnote.

that the assignees of the landlord's adjoining premises could not build it up so as to block the vital flow of air to the stacks of timber.

As this case shows, the obligation not to derogate from grant will run with the adjoining premises.

The obligation is only broken if there is some interference with the envisaged use of the demised premises. In *Browne* v. *Flower*[52] the existence of the staircase past the window made the premises less private but did not interfere with their use. Again, the fact that the use is made less profitable is not a ground for complaint. In the Canadian case of *Clark's Gamble of Canada* v. *Grant Park Plaza*[53] it was held that the lessor of a shop in a shopping centre did not derogate from his grant by letting another shop in the centre to a rival firm.

The two covenants mentioned—quiet enjoyment and non-derogation—overlap to a substantial extent. In principle, the distinction seems to be that the obligation not to derogate limits the use of property adjoining the demised premises; the covenant for quiet enjoyment bars action on the demised premises themselves.[54]

Landlord's obligations as to repair. The general principle at common law is that the landlord is under no implied obligation as to the state of the premises or their suitability for any particular purpose at the start of the tenancy; and under no implied obligation to repair them during the tenancy.

There are, today, important (mostly statutory) exceptions to this principle applicable in certain cases. Some of the more important of these are as follows.

1. At common law, in the case of furnished premises, there is an implied condition that the premises are fit for human habitation at the start of the tenancy.[55]

2. Housing Act 1961, sections 32 and 33.[55a] This important provision applies to any lease of a dwelling-house for a term of less than seven years.[56] Under section 32 a covenant is implied obliging the landlord to keep in repair the structure and exterior of the

---

[52] [1911] 1 Ch. 219 (Parker J.).
[53] (1967) 64 D.L.R., (2nd) 570 (Canadian Supreme Court).
[54] See *e.g.* Woodfall, *Landlord and Tenant* (28th ed.), p. 543.
[55] *Smith* v. *Marrable* (1843) 11 M. & W. 5.
[55a] As amended by Housing Act 1980, s.80.
[56] S.33(1). This includes periodic tenancies. It also includes a term for longer than seven years if the landlord has an unfettered right to determine it within the seven year period; see *Parker* v. *O'Connor* [1974] 3 All E.R. 257. And it includes an equitable lease; see *Brikom Investments* v. *Seaford* [1981] 1 W.L.R. 863 (C.A.).

dwelling-house and to keep in repair and proper working order the installations in the dwelling-house for the supply of water, gas, electricity, sanitation and heating water. Unlike the covenants implied at common law, this covenant cannot, in general, be excluded by agreement.[57]

The covenant has in general been restrictively interpreted by the courts.[58] The landlord will not be liable if he has not had notice of the defect[59]; nor will he be liable if the lack of repair is so bad that the dwelling is not capable of being made fit for human habitation at reasonable expense.[60] What is part of the structure and exterior of a particular dwelling is a question of fact. It does not have to be included in the demise,[61] but the term exterior has been held not to include part of a backyard which was not a necessary means of access to the house.[62]

3. Apart from statute, the courts may be willing to imply terms into a lease (including an obligation to repair) as they will into any contract. Each case depends on its own facts[63]; but, in general terms, they will imply whatever terms are necessary in the light of the circumstances, including the subject matter of the lease and the relationship of landlord and tenant created. In the case of *Liverpool City Council* v. *Irwin*[64] the landlord was a local authority and the tenancy was of a flat in a residential tower block. Local authority tenancies are in general subject to the ordinary rules of landlord and tenant[65]; but here the court considered it relevant that the only tenancy document was a series of unilateral

---

[57] S.32.

[58] See J.I. Reynolds, Statutory Covenants of Fitness and Repair: Social Legislation and the Judges, (1974) 37 M.L.R. 377.

[59] *McCarrick* v. *Liverpool Corporation* [1947] A.C. 219 (H.L.); *O'Brien* v. *Robinson* [1973] 1 All E.R. 583 (H.L). But the duty of care under Defective Premises Act 1972, which appears to extend to tenants as well as visitors, applies where the landlord knows or ought to have known of the defect. See *Winfield and Jolowicz on Tort* (11th ed.), p. 230.

[60] *Buswell* v. *Goodwin* [1971] 1 W.L.R. 92.

[61] *Campden Hill Towers Ltd.* v. *Gardner* [1977] 1 All E.R. 739 (C.A.) Held to apply to horizontal divisions, party walls, exterior walls and supporting structural framework in a block of flats; but not the structure of common parts such as lifts and staircases. See also *Liverpool City Council* v. *Irwin* [1977] A.C. 239 (H.L.).

[62] *Hopwood* v. *Cannock Chase D.C.* [1975] 1 All E.R. 796 (C.A.); compare *Brown* v. *Liverpool Corporation* [1969] 3 All E.R. 1345 (C.A.).

[63] Except where, over a period of time, a general presumption has been developed by the courts in relation to a particular class of case; *e.g.* the rule in *Smith* v. *Marrable* (1843) 11 M. & W. 5.

[64] [1977] A.C. 239 (H.L.) Note judgment of Lord Wilberforce discussing the circumstances in which courts will imply terms in a contract.

[65] Including liability under the Public Health Act 1936, s.99; but not now that under Housing Act 1961, s. 32: see Housing Act 1980, s.80.

obligations imposed on the tenant and contained in the rent book, with no written statement at all of the landlord's obligations. It was, in this sense, a unilateral contract and the court necessarily had to imply some obligations on the landlord's part—*e.g.* a covenant for quiet enjoyment. The House of Lords implied, in favour of the tenants, easements for the use of the lifts, staircases and rubbish chutes and a very limited obligation to take reasonable care to keep the common parts in a reasonable state of repair and useability; with recognition that the tenants had responsibilities in accordance with what a reasonable group of tenants would do for themselves.[66]

4. Public Health Act 1936, s.99. Under this Act, a local authority has powers to take action where the state of the premises constitutes a statutory nuisance; for example, leaking roofs, rats, blocked drains. Under section 99 of the Act, the individual tenant can take enforcement action in the magistrates' courts against the landlord (even where the landlord is a local authority).[67]

Tenant's obligation to pay rent. Even in the absence of any express provision, the mere relationship of landlord and tenant imposes on the tenant an obligation to pay a reasonable sum for the use and occupation of the land.

In most cases the payment of rent is covered by express agreement. For example:

> "The landlord lets and the Tenant takes all those rooms known as Flat No ——etc. for a term of——months commencing on the date of this Agreement and ending on the——day of——At the monthly rent of £——payable in advance the first such payment to be made on the signing of this Agreement and subsequent payments to be made on the——day of each month."[68]

The rent payable under a lease is properly called a rent service; in contrast to a rent reserved out of a fee simple (where the relationship of landlord and tenant does not exist) which is a rent charge.[69]

---

[66] In the event, the L.A. was held not liable for the atrocious state of the building caused by unidentified vandals. For a similar principle in the case of private blocks of flats, see *Miller* v. *Hancock* [1893] 2 Q.B. 177. Compare the principle that there is no general liablity on the grantor of an easement to keep it in repair.

[67] See *Nottingham Corporation* v. *Newton* [1974] 2 All E.R. 760; *Salford City Council* v. *McNally* [1975] 2 All E.R. 860 (H.L.); *R.* v. *Newham Justices, ex p. Hunt* [1976] 1 All E.R. 839.

[68] Hallet (above n. 48), p. 502.

[69] Below, Chap. 22.

Fixed term tenant's obligation to repair. Under the Statute of Marlebridge 1267 a tenant for a fixed term is under an obligation to repair. The statute does not apply to a periodic tenant.

Periodic tenant's obligation to use premises in tenant like manner. Just what can be required of the periodic tenant under this obligation is not certain.[70] The position seems to be as follows:

(a) A periodic tenant, like any tenant, will prima facie be liable for voluntary waste—any positive act which materially changes the premises. And whether he has caused it deliberately or negligently, he must make it good and restore the premises to their original condition. In *Marsden* v. *Edward Heyes Ltd.*[71] the premises consisted of a dwelling-house and shop let to the tenant on an oral tenancy from year to year. The tenant removed a partition wall, a staircase and fireplaces thus converting the whole premises into one large shop. It was held that this was voluntary waste for which the tenant was liable. Of course, the terms of the lease may, expressly or by implication, authorise the waste—" regard must be had to the use of the demised premises which is permissible under the lease."[72]

(b) It is doubtful whether there is any general liability on a periodic tenant for permissive waste[73]; but he can be expected to "take proper care of the place, doing the little jobs which a reasonable tenant would do."[74] In other words he is not obliged to repair but he must use the premises in a tenant like manner. Just what can be expected of a tenant under this very limited obligation may depend on the duration of the lease, whether it is a weekly tenancy, or long term, etc., and on all the other circumstances present. In *Warren* v. *Keen*,[75] a weekly protected tenant was sued by his landlord for the cost of repairs to the premises which the local authority had required to be done. There was no express agreement on the matter but the landlord claimed that the obligation to repair rested on the tenant who should therefore pay the cost. The main trouble was that the outside had not been redecorated, the rendering had cracked and the pointing decayed. As a result of this damp had penetrated a number of the rooms damaging the plaster.

It was held that the tenant was not liable. "If . . . the house falls

---

[70] See Woodfall (above n. 54), p. 629 *et seq.*
[71] [1927] 2 K.B. 1 (C.A.).
[72] *Hyman* v. *Rose* [1912] A.C. 623 (H.L.), Lord Loreburn L.C. at p. 632.
[73] See Woodfall (n. 54 above), at pp. 629, 650.
[74] *Ibid.* p. 629.
[75] [1954] 1 Q.B. 15 (C.A.).

into disrepair through fair wear and tear or lapse of time, or for any reason not caused by him, he is not liable to repair it."[76]

If it is correct that there is no general obligation on a periodic tenant to repair, it means that neither landlord nor tenant is under any implied obligation to keep the premises in repair.[77]

In practice the lease will normally contain express covenants designed to ensure that the premises are kept in a proper state of repair and decoration and allocating the responsibility. For example, a 21-year lease may be found to contain covenants by the lessee to repair the inside and do inside and outside decoration and covenants by the lessor to do outside repairs.[78]

Landlord's right to view. In principle the tenant has exclusive possession and the landlord has no more right of entry than any stranger. But if the landlord is under an obligation to repair there is an implied obligation on the tenant to allow him to enter to view the state of repair. And the lease will normally contain express rights of entry for the landlord.[79]

Principle 8. Express covenants

In general, the parties to a lease can include what express covenants they like. In so far as any matter is governed by an express term there will be no scope for any implied term.

In practice, most formal leases are in more or less standard form and will contain express covenants dealing with, *inter alia,* the following matters:

(1) The payment of rent and the consequences of non payment.
(2) Liability for repair.
(3) Insurance of the demised premises.
(4) Assignment and sub-letting.
(5) Restrictive covenants.

Explanation

In practice the lease is a much more flexible estate than the freehold estates. The parties are more or less free to create what terms and obligations they like and the landlord can use the lease to exercise very detailed control over what the tenant does with

[76] *Ibid.* headnote. This case concerned a weekly tenant but all three judges had doubts as to whether any greater liability rested on a yearly tenant.
[77] Subject to the exceptions mentioned above, p. 119.
[78] See Hallett (above n. 48), for precedent.
[79] See above, p. 93.

the premises. This is particularly significant in the case of positive covenants which can be made to run with leasehold but not with freehold·land.[80]

The express covenants which are included in any particular lease will depend on such things as the intended duration, the type of property and the use to which it is to be put. The matters listed above are only one or two of the more important matters which will be dealt with in most leases.

Payment of rent: Repair. These two matters have already been mentioned. The remedies for non-payment of rent are mentioned below.[81]

Insurance. The landlord will want to protect the value of his reversion in the premises by making sure that they are insured either by himself or the lessee and that he will have the benefit of any insurance moneys.

The following is a clause that might be found in a lease[82]:

> "To keep the Premises during the said term insured against loss or damage by fire explosion storm or tempest in an Insurance Office to be nominated by the Lessor in the joint names of the Lessor and the Tenant to the full value thereof and whenever required produce to the Lessor the policy and receipt for the last premium in respect of such insurance and that in case of destruction or damage of the Premises or any part thereof the moneys received in respect of such insurance shall be laid out in rebuilding or reinstating the same and in case such moneys shall be insufficient for such purpose the deficiency shall be made good by the Tenant and if the Premises cannot be rebuilt or reinstated for any reason the said insurance moneys shall be held in trust for the Lessor beneficially."

In the absence of express provision there is no obligation on either party to insure.

Assignment. In the absence of express provision, a tenant can assign or sub-let his lease in the same way that a fee simple owner can sell his fee simple. It is, however, common to find a covenant in the lease prohibiting assignment and sub-letting either absolutely or without the consent of the landlord. Where there is an absolute prohibition, the tenant cannot assign or sub-let at all

---

[80] But only if they touch and concern the land. See below, p. 419.
[81] See below, Principle 12, for liability on non payment of rent.
[82] Hallett (n. 48 above), p. 485.

(unless he gets the landlord to waive the prohibition). If the prohibition is only against assigning or sub-letting without consent, there is an implied term (which cannot be excluded) that the consent will not be unreasonably withheld.[83] The tenant must seek consent but if it is withheld unreasonably then he can go ahead without it. Whether the landlord has withheld consent unreasonably is a question of fact depending on the circumstances. A common reason (considered to be justified) for refusing consent is where the proposed new tenant's financial references are not satisfactory.[84]

Under section 24 of the Race Relations Act 1976, it is unlawful to discriminate by withholding consent on racial grounds. Under section 31 of the Sex Discrimination Act 1975 there is a similar provision in the case of discrimination against women on the grounds of sex.

Restrictive covenants. These are dealt with elsewhere.[85]

Principle 9. The "usual covenants"

Where there is a contract for a lease which is silent as to the covenants to be included in the lease itself, the parties are entitled to have the "usual covenants" included as express covenants in the lease.

The contract may expressly stipulate that the lease is to include the "usual covenants."

Where a tenant is negotiating for the sale of his lease he must disclose to the prospective purchaser any "unusual covenants" contained in the lease.

Certain covenants are recognised by the courts as always being "usual." Any other covenant may be shown to be "usual" for a particular type of lease.

Explanation

Leases may be, and commonly are, granted without any prior contract. In such case, the parties will be governed by the implied covenants discussed above as modified by any express covenants in the lease itself.

---

[83] Landlord and Tenant Act 1927, s.19.

[84] See *West Layton Ltd.* v. *Ford* [1979] 3 W.L.R. 14 (C.A.); and note *Regan* v. *Regan* [1977] 1 All E.R. 428. For statutory limits on the right to assign, sub-let, etc., see Rent Act 1977, Sched. 15, case 9. (regulated tenancies); Housing Act 1980, ss.36, 37, 54 (secure and protected shorthold tenancies).

[85] Below, Chap. 20.

But in some cases there is a contract to create the lease. And when, in performance of the contract, the lessor draws up the lease, the question may arise as to what covenants he can include. The answer is that in the absence of express provision in the contract, he can include—and only include—the "usual covenants."

The following covenants will be usual for any lease: By the lessee:

    (a) To pay the rent.

    (b) To pay taxes on the land except those which are charged on the landlord by statute.

    (c) To keep and deliver the premises in repair.

    (d) To allow the landlord to enter and view the state of repair.

And:

    (e) The qualified covenant by the landlord for quiet enjoyment.[86]

    (f) A proviso for re-entry on non-payment of the rent.

If a party to a contract for a lease claims to include any covenant other than the above, he will have to prove that it is "usual" for that type of lease. In *Flexman* v. *Corbett*[87] Maugham J. said:

"... the question whether particular covenants are usual covenants is a question of fact, and the decision of the Court on that point must depend upon the admissible evidence given before the Court in relation to that question. I think that it is proper to take the evidence of conveyancers and others familiar with the practice in reference to leases and that it is also permissible to examine books of precedents. It is permissible to obtain evidence with regard to practice in a particular district in which the premises in question are situated. I would add that in my view it is a complete mistake to suppose that the usual covenants in regard to a lease, for instance, of a country house are necessarily usual covenants in regard to the lease of a London residence, and I would add that it seems to me that it may very well be that what is usual in Mayfair or Bayswater, is not usual at all in some parts of London such, for instance, as Whitechapel."[88]

In *Flexman* v. *Corbett*[89] there was a contract to sell a lease and it

---

[86] Above, p. 116.

[87] [1930] 1 Ch. 672 (Maugham J.).

[88] *Ibid.* at p. 678; compare Thesiger L.J. in *Sturges* v. *Bridgeman* (1879) 11 Ch.D. 852, 865; above, p. 42. And see *Chester* v. *Buckingham Travel Ltd.* [1981] 1 All E.R. 386 (Foster J.).

[89] [1930] 1 Ch. 672.

is a general rule that the vendor of a lease must disclose to the prospective purchaser any "unusual covenants" contained in the lease.[90] Here the lease contained a covenant by the tenant not to do "anything which may be to the annoyance, damage or inconvenience of the occupiers of the neighbouring premises." The vendor had not disclosed the existence of this covenant before contract and the purchaser was consequently held entitled to resist the vendor's claim to specific performance.

If the "usual covenants" are not included in a lease when they could be the court has jurisdiction to rectify the lease.

In general it seems that the courts will be very reluctant to recognise as "usual" any covenants other than the ones listed above.[91]

It will be noticed that the "usual covenants" impose a heavier burden on the tenant than the implied covenants.

SECTION IV. DETERMINATION OF LEASES; REMEDIES

Principle 10. Determination[92]

A lease may come to an end in any one of the following ways:
(1) Expiry.
(2) Notice.
(3) By the vesting of the lease and the immediate reversion in the same person. This may be by surrender or merger or under the Leasehold Reform Act 1967.
(4) By becoming a satisfied term.
(5) Enlargement.
(6) Forfeiture.

Explanation

Each of the above will be considered in turn.

Expiry. At common law a lease for a fixed term comes to an end automatically on the expiry of the term and the tenant will have to vacate. There is no need for any notice. If the tenant remains in possession he may become a tenant at sufferance or at will. If the landlord accepts rent from him a new periodic tenancy may arise.[93]

---

[90] Because they are latent defects of title. See below, p. 553 for this duty.
[91] See Woodfall (n. 54 above), at p. 175.
[92] For application of doctrine of frustration to leases, see *National Carriers Ltd.* v. *Panalpina (Northern) Ltd.* [1981] 1 All E.R. 161 (H.L.).
[93] See above, p. 103.

The position on expiry may be affected by the various forms of statutory protection given to tenants. For example, in the case of a business tenancy within Part II of the Landlord and Tenant Act 1954 a tenancy, including a term of years, "shall not come to an end unless terminated in accordance with the provisions"[94] of the Act. Similarly, a tenancy of an agricultural holding subject to the Agricultural Holdings (Notices to Quit) Act 1977 will continue after expiry as a tenancy from year to year unless determined by a notice served and taking effect in accordance with the provisions of that Act.[95] And the tenant of residential premises may be entitled to remain after the expiry of his contractual tenancy as a statutory tenant.[96]

Notice. In the absence of express provision a tenancy for a fixed term cannot be determined by either side before expiry. A periodic tenancy continues from period to period but can be determined at the end of any period by the service of a proper notice. The determination of tenancies at will and sufferance has been considered. The right to serve notice is of course subject to the statutory protection mentioned in the last paragraph.

Vesting of lease and reversion in the same person. (a) *Surrender.* A lease will determine if the lessee surrenders it to his immediate landlord. The estate of the surrenderor will be "drowned"[97] in the landlord's estate. Surrender can only take place with the consent of the landlord. It may be express in which case it must be by deed, though a contract to surrender may be effective in equity. It may also be implied, *i.e.* by operation of law, where the parties between them take some step which is inconsistent with the continuation of the lease. For example, if the tenant gives up and the landlord accepts possession of the premises. Again, if the tenant takes a new lease from the landlord a surrender of the existing one will be implied even if it has longer to run than the new one; or where the terms of an existing lease are varied by extending the term.[98]

(b) *Merger.* If the lessee acquires the immediate reversion the lease will merge with the larger estate, the reversion, and

---

[94] s. 24(1).
[95] s.2. Not more than two and not less than one year's notice must be given.
[96] See below, p. 141.
[97] Woodfall (above, n. 54), p. 821. Even if it is in fact longer than the leasehold reversion into which it merges, the lease will still merge since the reversion is considered in law to be longer.
[98] See *Watney* v. *Boardley* [1975] 2 All E.R. 644 (Golding J.); also *Hoggett* v. *Hoggett* (1979) 39 P. & C.R. 121 (C.A.).

determine.[99] Similarly, if a third person acquires both lease and reversion. But in both cases there will only be a merger if both lease and reversion are acquired in the same capacity and if there is an intention that merger should take place.[1] Both surrender and merger are cases where the lease and the immediate reversion become vested in the same person in the same capacity. They illustrate the general principle of common law that a person cannot hold an interest of himself.[2] A landowner cannot create an interest in his own favour and if he acquires an interest existing over his own land,[3] the interest will merge and disappear; and any interests carved out of the interest which is merged or surrendered will also disappear.[4] But in certain cases in equity, the merger will not take place and the interest will remain alive if such is the intention. For example, in *Snow* v. *Boycott*[5] land was devised to EB for life, remainder to CBW for life, remainder to CBW's son in fee tail, EB was elderly and, wishing to be freed of the burden of managing the estate, she assigned her life interest to CBW in return for which she was to receive an annuity of £400 a year for the rest of her life. CBW died first. The question was whether the assignment caused her life interest to merge in the second and thus disappear. If it did, her annuity could only bind the remaining life interest of CBW and must therefore end on his death. It was held that the intention was clearly that the annuity should continue for the rest of EB's life even if she outlived CBW; and that therefore merger could not have been intended. EB's life interest remained in existence and continued after CBW's death.

(c) *Enfranchisement: Under the Leasehold Reform Act 1967.*[6] A tenant of a house[7] may be entitled to purchase the freehold or an extended lease. He can only exercise the right if the following conditions are satisfied:

    (i) He must be a tenant under a "long tenancy"—that is, one granted for a term exceeding 21 years.[8]

[99] See further *Hill and Redman, Landlord and Tenant* (16th ed.), p. 834.

[1] L.P.A. 1925, s.185.

[2] See *Rye* v. *Rye* [1962] A.C. 496 (H.L.).

[3] For example if he purchases land which enjoys the benefit of an easement over his own land. Below, p. 364.

[4] See, *e.g. Fairweather* v. *St. Marylebone Property Co.* [1962] 2 W.L.R. 1020 (H.L.).

[5] [1892] 3 Ch. 110 (Kekewich J.).

[6] As amended by Leasehold Reform Act 1979.

[7] The Act does not apply to individual flats: s.2(1).

[8] Leasehold Reform Act 1967, ss.1, 3, as amended by Housing Act 1980, s.141 and Sched. 21.

(ii) The tenancy must have been at a "low rent"—that is, generally, not more than two-thirds of the rateable value of the property.[9]

(iii) The rateable value must be within the same limits as fixed by the Rent Act 1977.[10]

(iv) He must have occupied the house as his residence for at least the last three years.[11]

The tenant must pay the "open market" value for the reversion fixed in accordance with section 9 of the Act and the matter is completed by the landlord conveying it to him in accordance with section 8.

Becoming a satisfied term. Where the purpose for which a lease was created is satisfied the lease will automatically cease.

A term of years may be created not to give the lessee occupation of the land but for some other purpose, particularly to secure the payment of money. For example, a mortgage term of 3,000 years may be created in favour of a person who lends money. (This is one of the two possible methods of creating a legal mortgage.)[12] When the money is repaid to the lender (the mortgagee) the purpose of the lease—to act as security—is satisfied and the lease will automatically determine.

Enlargement. This has already been dealt with.[13]

Forfeiture. This is dealt with under remedies.[14]

Principle 11. Right to fixtures on determination[15]

As a general rule fixtures attached by the tenant become part of the land and the property of the landlord.

However, on determination, the tenant will normally be entitled to remove any of the following fixtures, known as tenant's fixtures.

(1) Trade fixtures.

(2) Domestic or ornamental fixtures.

(3) Agricultural fixtures.

Those fixtures which the tenant is not entitled to remove are known as landlord's fixtures.

---

[9] *Ibid.* ss.1, 4.
[10] *Ibid.* s.1(1)(*a*), as amended.
[11] *Ibid.* s.1(1)(*b*), as amended by Housing Act 1980, s.141 and Sched. 21.
[12] See below, Chap. 21.
[13] Above, p. 106.
[14] See below, p. 133.
[15] See above, p. 24 for fixtures.

Explanation

Trade fixtures. If a tenant had no right to remove fixtures he would be unlikely to spend money on them in the first place. It has been said that "the commercial interests of the country might be advanced by the encouragement given to tenants to employ their capital in making improvements for the carrying on of trade, with the certainty of having the benefit of the expenditure secured them at the end of their terms."[16] Trade fixtures are those fixtures attached by the tenant for the purpose of his trade or business. The tenant has a right to remove trade fixtures provided he does so before his tenancy ends[16a] and provided removal does not involve their destruction. In *Webb* v. *Frank Bevis Ltd.*[17] the tenant had laid a concrete foundation and erected on it a shed which could be removed in panels without difficulty. The shed was used for the tenant's trade and it was held that the shed could be removed as a tenant's fixture. The concrete foundation, which could only have been removed by breaking it up, was clearly not a tenant's fixture.

Domestic and ornamental fixtures. "Chattels which have been affixed for ornament or domestic convenience and utility" can similarly be removed before the end of the tenancy—provided they can be removed without any material injury to the land or building to which they are attached.

Agricultural fixtures. At common law agriculture was not regarded as a trade and there was no right of removal. Now, under section 13 of the Agricultural Holdings Act 1948, agricultural fixtures put there by the tenant can be removed within two months after the end of the tenancy, subject to the following conditions:

(a) The tenant must give one month's notice to the landlord.

(b) The tenant must not be in breach of his obligations under the lease.

(c) No avoidable damage must be done and damage that is done must be made good.

(d) The landlord must be given the option to purchase at a fair price.

Principle 12. Landlord's remedies

The following remedies may be available to the landlord to enforce the terms of the lease:

[16a] See *New Zealand Government Property Corp.* v. *H.M. & S. Ltd.* [1982] 1 All E.R. 624 (C.A.).
[16] See Woodfall (above, n. 54), at p. 665.
[17] [1940] 1 All E.R. 247 (C.A.).

(1) The equitable remedies of specific performance and the injunction.

(2) Damages.

(3) Forfeiture.

(4) Distress for non-payment of rent.

A landlord may be entitled to enforce covenants in the lease against:

(a) The original tenant by virtue of privity of contract.

(b) An assignee of the lease by virtue of privity of estate provided the covenant is one which touches and concerns the land and the breach occurs while there is privity of estate.

(c) Any subsequent owner of the land, *e.g.* a sub-tenant, but only if the covenant is restrictive.[18]

Explanation

Between the original landlord and tenant there is privity of contract and all the covenants in the lease (subject to legality, etc.) are enforceable between them throughout the duration of the lease. The tenant may remain liable in contract even after he has assigned the lease and given up all interest in the land.

Between the landlord and a person holding the lease as assignee there is privty of estate, but not between the landlord and sub-tenant. The landlord can use any of the remedies listed above against an assignee but only to enforce those covenants which touch and concern the land. This matter is dealt with in a later chapter,[19] but it can be assumed that the covenant to pay the rent and the other covenants discussed above[20] do touch and concern.

In general, only restrictive covenants can be enforced against a sub-tenant with whom there is privity of neither contract nor estate. But:

(i) the sub-tenant may be liable to his own immediate landlord under the terms of the sub-lease; and

(ii) if a lease is forfeited, any sub-lease carved out of it will automatically disappear.[21]

Thus, for example: Suppose that L leases to T who assigns to A who assigns to B who sub-lets to ST; and that the lease to T includes a covenant by the tenant to keep the premises in repair. ST is now in occupation. If the premises are not repaired, L can sue T (privity of contract); or he can sue B (as there is privity of

---

[18] See below, Chap. 20.

[19] Chap. 19, below.

[20] Principles 7, 8, 9.

[21] Subject to the sub-tenant's right to relief. See below, p. 134.

estate and the covenant touches and concerns the land). He cannot sue A since there is no privity of contract or estate with him; neither can he sue ST (since there is no privity with him and the covenant is not restrictive). B will no doubt have imposed a covenant to repair in the sub-lease to ST in terms similar to the covenant in the head-lease. Therefore, B will be able to sue ST (privity of contract and estate). If L sues T, T will normally have an express or implied right of indemnity against his assignee A,[22] or against the ultimate assignee B[23]; but not against the defaulting sub-tenant ST.[24] Thus, the ultimate burden can, by a somewhat roundabout process, generally be made to fall on ST the person actually responsible.

Equitable remedies and damages. The equitable remedies and the common law remedy of damages are in general subject to the ordinary rules applicable to these remedies. There is one point to note about damages for beach of a repairing covenant. Where a lease is originally for at least seven years of which at least three have still to run, the landlord must serve a notice under section 146 of the Law of Property Act 1925 before claiming damages for breach of any repairing covenant.[24a] The necessary contents of the notice are set out below. It must inform the tenant of his right to serve a counter notice. The landlord must not start action until at least one month after service of the notice and, if the tenant does serve a counter notice, he must obtain the leave of the court before proceeding. The court can only grant leave to proceed if the landlord can prove certain grounds—for example, that the repair is necessary to comply with statute or bye-laws.

Forfeiture. Forfeiture puts an end to the lease forfeited and to any sub-leases carved out of it.

The right of forfeiture for breach by the tenant only exists if either:

(a) it is expressly reserved in the lease; or
(b) the obligation broken is expressed as a condition; or
(c) if the reason for forfeiture is denial of the landlord's title by the tenant.

The normal method of enforcing forfeiture is by issuing a writ (or, in the county court, a summons) for possession—the issue of the writ determining the lease—and obtaining a court order. In the

---

[22] See L.P.A. 1925, s.77 for covenant of indemnity implied on assignment of lease.
[23] Under the rule in *Moule* v. *Garrett* (1872) L.R. 7 Ex. 101.
[24] *Bonner* v. *Tottenham and Edmonton Permanent Investment B.S.* [1899] 1 Q.B. 161.
[24a] See Leasehold Property (Repairs) Act 1938.

case of residential premises this is the only method.[25] In other cases peaceable entry is an alternative but any use of force may be an offence under the Criminal Law Act 1977.

The landlord may expressly or by implication waive his right to forfeit for breach. The procedure to enforce forfeiture depends upon whether the forfeiture is for non-payment of rent or for some other breach.

(a) *Forfeiture for non-payment of rent.* Where a landlord is entitled to forfeit for non-payment of rent then either:

(i) he must first make a proper formal demand for the rent; or
(ii) the lease must expressly excuse the need for a formal demand; or
(iii) the rent must be at least one half-year in arrears and there must be no sufficient distress to be found on the premises to satisfy the arrears.

The tenant may apply to the court for relief and the recovery of his lease within six months of actual re-entry under the judgment.[25a] And the relief will be granted if he pays all arrears of rent, all the landlord's expenses and the court considers it equitable to grant relief. Any sub-tenant has a similar right to claim relief and if he, but not the tenant, obtains relief he will take over the lease.

(b) *Forfeiture for breach of any other covenant.* The landlord, before re-entering or issuing a writ, must serve a notice on the tenant under section 146 of the Law of Property Act 1925. This must:

(i) Specify the breach complained of.
(ii) Require it to be remedied if this is possible.
(iii) Require compensation for the breach if the landlord wants compensation.

The landlord must then allow a reasonable time (generally about three months) to give the tenant a chance to remedy the breach if this is possible[26]; if it is not possible he must give him sufficient time to consider his position. The court has a statutory right to grant relief on such terms as it thinks fit but only if the tenant applies before forfeiture is completed by re-entry. In certain cases there is no need to serve a section 146 notice and the tenant has no right to relief:

(i) For denial of title.
(ii) For beach of a covenant in a mining lease requiring the tenant to produce books and accounts for inspection.

---

[25] Protection from Eviction Act 1977, s.2.
[25a] Note *Thatcher* v. *C.H. Pearce and Sons (Contractors) Ltd.* [1968] 1 W.L.R. 748.
[26] See, *e.g. Scala House Co. Ltd.* v. *Forbes* [1973] 3 W.L.R. 14.

(iii) For breach of a covenant against the bankruptcy of the
lessee or the taking of his lease in execution.

In the case of (iii), section 146 does not apply at all where the
lease is of agricultural land, mines or minerals, a public house or
beershop, a furnished house or where the personal qualifications
of the tenant are important. Any other lease is protected by s.146
for one year from the bankruptcy or taking in execution; or, if the
lease is sold during that year, indefinitely.

Distress. This is the ancient feudal remedy which entitles the
landlord to recover arrears of rent by seizing goods found on the
premises and selling them after a certain time during which the
tenant has the opportunity to recover them by paying off arrears.
In general the goods of third parties are protected; and some even
of the tenant's goods, for example goods in actual use and
perishables, are protected from seizure.[27]

Principle 13. Tenant's remedies

The tenant may enforce the landlord's obligations contained in the
lease in equity by injunction and specific performance[28]; and at
common law by damages.

The convenants in the lease will be enforceable against the
original landlord by virtue of privity of contract; and, if they touch
and concern the land, against an assignee of the reversion by virtue
of privity of estate.[29]

If his possession is interfered with by a third party the tenant will
have the same remedies in tort as a freeholder.

Explanation

The leasehold tenant has an ownership interest in the land; he
has a possession which is protected in the same way as the
possession of the fee simple owner. If I walk across X's field
without authority, he will be able to sue me for the tort of trespass
whether he is freeholder or leaseholder.

However, unlike the fee simple owner for whom tenure has no
practical consequences, the leaseholder is subject to the terms of
his lease. If, for example, I am X's landlord, and the lease gives me

---

[27] The Law Commission has considered distress in *Landlord and Tenant, Interim
Report on Distress for Rent* 1966 (Law Com. Pub. No. 6).
[28] Note Housing Act 1974, s.125, enabliing the court to order specific performance
by the landlord of repairing covenants.
[29] See below, p. 419 *et seq.*

a right of entry onto the land; and if I am exercising such a right I will not be liable in trespass.

Again, in principle, the leaseholder has the same rights of enjoyment as owner of the fee simple; but these rights will be limited by the terms of the lease under which he holds. For example, a fee simple owner does not have to repair his property so long as its state does not constitute a nuisance to neighbours or a breach of planning law. The leaseholder, likewise, must not create a nuisance. But in addition it is likely that his lease will impose some sort of liability to repair on him enforceable by his landlord.

Liability of assignees of the reversion. This is considered below.[30]

Section V. Statutory Protection

Introduction

In the fifteenth and sixteenth centuries equity intervened to protect the mortgagor against the lender of capital, giving him (the mortgagor) a right to redeem and recover his property at any time on repaying the loan with interest—a right which he could not be deprived of even with his own consent.[31]

Somewhat similarly, in the twentieth century, Parliament has intervened to give some protection to the tenant against the capitalist providing accommodation, by giving him security of tenure and controlling his rent.[32]

It has been said that, as a result of parliamentary intervention, the basis of leasehold has shifted from contract to status.[33] Before this intervention, the relationship between landlord and tenant, their respective rights and obligations, was in general governed by the contract made between them. For a tenant with capital this did not matter. In return for a capital payment, a premium, he could obtain a long term of years which gave him security of tenure for a long period as a fixed rent. He was as well off as the freehold tenant.

But for the person without capital who could only afford to pay

---

[30] *Ibid.*
[31] See below, p. 469, *et seq.*; and for history of equity's intervention to protect the mortgagor, see Holdsworth, *History of English Law,* (7th ed.), Vol. 1, p. 458.
[32] To a very limited extent equity did intervene to protect a tenant from forfeiture for non payment of rent, see Hill and Redman, *Landlord and Tenant* (16th ed.), p. 484.
[33] See Megarry and Wade, *Law of Real Property* (4th ed.), p. 1155.

weekly, monthly or yearly and so to get only a weekly or monthly or yearly tenancy, there was no security of tenure or rent.[34] If the landlord demanded a higher rent, the tenant paid or risked getting notice to quit and having to start again somewhere else.

In an age of increasing land shortage, this predominance allowed to freedom of contract put the landlord in a powerful position. As to be expected there is a dispute as to how this power was exercised. One view, for example, suggests that "As the history of the game laws demonstrates too brutally, the landlords never hesitated to coerce their tenants to accept practices which increased the amentities of their estates, and among these good husbandry did not figure prominently."[35]

On November 25, 1915, the Increase of Rent (War Restrictions) Bill, the first of the modern Rent Acts, was introduced into the House of Commons by the President of the Local Government Board. The Bill was the result of high rents being charged particularly in the areas of munitions factories where the influx of workers caused an inflated demand for accommodation. The President felt that they could all "rejoice" because the policy of rent-raising "has not been universal, and has not been what one can call very widespread." But he did go on to say that "The trouble about rent-raising and accommodation has been specially felt in some of our munitions areas . . . it has produced a very deep feeling of bitterness and resentment, and that where the grievance exists you will find masses of people holding tenaciously to the view that the minority who happen to hold houses, are taking advantage of wartime to exploit the war for their own benefit."[36]

This Bill became law and provided a starting point. Today, in a great many cases, the relationship between landlord and tenant is no longer just a matter of contract. The tenant has been given a status, that is a position recognised and protected by law which he himself cannot sign away by agreement. But more important than the new status of the tenant is the principle behind it—that is a recognition, however slight and unwilling to date, that the ownership of property can derive not only from the accumulation of capital but also from agricultural labour, from commercial endeavour and from the sheer necessity of somewhere to live.

However, one point should be made clear. The legislation which is being talked about in this chapter merely protects a tenancy

---

[34] In any case, a landlord might not be willing to grant a fixed term.
[35] O.R. McGregor in Ernle, *English Farming*, p. cxxxi.
[36] Hansard 1915, Vol. LXXVI, cols. 421, 422.

which the parties have chosen to create. It does not impose any sort of obligation on the landowner to grant a tenancy in the first place. Indeed, it is commonly argued that one of the effects of a system of controlling the rent and security of private lettings is that private landowners simply withdraw from the business of letting properties thus causing a shortage of available accommodation.[37] Legislative machinery is of course available which enables and, in some cases obliges, local authorities and others actually to obtain land and provide accommodation.[38] The details of this machinery are beyond the scope of this book.

How far and what sort of protection is necessary or desirable is a matter of much dispute. Protection has been increased and decreased at different times depending on the political situation and the prevailing view. All that the rest of this chapter can attempt to do is to give a very brief survey of the general position. Statutory protection has been introduced in three main fields:

    (a) Residential tenancies.

    (b) Agricultural tenancies.

    (c) Business tenancies.

Each of these will be considered in turn and in each case the two most fundamental aspects of protection, security of tenure and rent control, will be considered. Protection does, of course, extend to other aspects of the landlord-tenant relationship, in some cases to protect the landlord against the tenant.

Principle 14a.   Residential premises: Protected tenancies

Protected tenancies within the Rent Act 1977.[39] Two types of residential letting are given protection by the Rent Act 1977: protected tenancies and restricted contracts.

A contractual tenancy[40] protected by the main part of the Rent Act 1977, is known as a protected tenancy. This is, with exceptions, any tenancy under which a dwelling-house (which may be a house or part of a house) is let as a separate dwelling, whether furnished or unfurnished.[41]

---

[37] See the Report of the Francis Committee on the Rent Acts (1971) Cmnd. 4609; and review of this Report in (1971) 34 M.L.R. 427 (J.E. Trice).

[38] See, for example, Housing (Homeless Persons) Act 1977.

[39] Consolidating earlier legislation; and now as amended by the Housing Act 1980. As to caravan sites, see Mobile Homes Act 1975. See generally, M. Partington, *Landlord and Tenant* (2nd ed.) and P.H.Pettit, *Private Sector Tenancies* (1981).

[40] This part of the Act only applies to tenancies. The protection given to restricted contracts as defined by s.19 is much more limited but does extend to certain occupation licences.

[41] Rent Act 1977, s.1.

The following tenancies, *inter alia*, are excluded from the definition:

(a) Those where the rateable value of the dwelling exceeds £1,500 in Greater London or £750 elsewhere.[42]

(b) Tenancies at low rents, *i.e.* where the rent is less than two thirds of the rateable value.[43]

(c) Lettings where a substantial part of the rent represents payment for board or attendance provided.[44]

(d) Agricultural holdings.[45]

(e) Tenancies granted to their students by specified educational institutions.[46]

(f) Tenancies where the landlord is resident.[47]

(g) Local authority lettings.[48]

(h) Holiday lettings.[49]

Security of tenure. The landlord of a protected tenancy can only recover possession by satisfying *both* the following conditions[50]:

(1) He must determine the protected (contractual) tenancy in accordance with the ordinary rules of landlord and tenant—*e.g.* by giving notice if it is periodic—thus turning the tenancy into a statutory tenancy.[51]

(2) He must apply to the court and either

(a) he must establish one of the grounds set out in Schedule 15, Part II, of the 1977 Act[52] (the mandatory Cases); or

(b) the court must consider it reasonable to order possession and *either*:

(i) the court must be satisfied that suitable alternative accommodation is available for the tenant; *or*

(ii) the landlord must establish one of the grounds set out in Schedules 15, Part I, of the 1977 Act (the discretionary Cases).

---

[42] *Ibid.* s.4.
[43] *Ibid.* s.5. For position of tenants of long leases at low rents, see Landlord and Tenant Act 1954, Part I; and Leasehold Reform Act 1967 as amended by Leasehold Reform Act 1979.
[44] Rent Act 1977, s.7.
[45] *Ibid.* s.10.
[46] *Ibid.* s.8.
[47] *Ibid.* s.12 and Sched. 2, as amended by Housing Act 1980, s.65; (after the decision in *Landau* v. *Sloane* [1981] 1 All E.R. 705 (H.L.)).
[48] *Ibid.* s.9.
[49] *Ibid.* s.14.
[50] *Ibid.* s.98 and Sched. 15, as amended by Housing Act 1980, Pt. II.
[51] *Ibid.* s.2, as amended by Housing Act 1980, s.76.
[52] As amended by Housing Act 1980, ss.55, 66, 67.

Some of the mandatory Cases (*i.e.* the court being obliged to order possession if the Case is established) are as follows[53]:

Case 11.[54] The landlord was an owner-occupier of the dwelling and wants to resume occupation.

Case 12.[55] Where the dwelling was bought by the landlord with a view to retirement and he has retired.

Case 13. The out of season letting of a dwelling, let as a holiday home during the season.

Case 14. The vacation letting of student accommodation.

Case 19. The tenancy was a protected shorthold tenancy which has expired. The protected shorthold was introduced by the Housing Act 1980.[56] It is designed to enable the landlord to let for a fixed, short term (not less than one, not more than five years), whilst being assured of recovering possession at the end of the term.[57]

As will be seen from the above, the mandatory Cases are in general designed to encourage the use of temporarily vacant accommodation. In general, the landlord must have given written notice to the tenant by the start of the tenancy of his intention, eventually, to rely on the specified Case.

Some of the discretionary Cases are as follows:

Case 1. The tenant is in arrears with his rent or in breach of covenant.

Case 2. The tenant has caused a nuisance or been convicted of using the dwelling for an illegal or immoral purpose.

Cases 3 and 4. The tenant has allowed the condition of the dwelling or any furniture provided with it to deteriorate.

Case 5. The tenant has given notice to quit and as a result the landlord has contracted to sell or otherwise prejudiced his position.

---

[53] The Case numbers are as used in the Act.
[54] Rent Act 1977, Sched.15, Pt. II, as amended by Housing Act 1980, s.66.
[55] *Ibid.*
[56] ss.51–55. See, "A Third Alternative," P. F. Smith, [1982] conv. 29.
[57] Whilst, in theory, the protected shorthold could be used universally by landlords to avoid the security provisions of the Rent Act, it is not likely to be particularly popular since it is subject to the fair rent control. In general, a tenant's insecurity is only useful to a landlord if he can use the threat of eviction as a means of raising the rent.

Case 8. The landlord requires the dwelling for another employee.

Case 9. The landlord requires the dwelling for occupation by himself or a member of his family.

Statutory tenancies. Where a tenant's contractual (*i.e.* protected) tenancy has been determined and the tenant retains possesion by virtue of the Act, he has a statutory tenancy which continues so long as the tenant occupies the dwelling as his residence.[58]

Subject to necessary modifications, a statutory tenancy is subject to the same terms and conditions as the contractual tenancy which it replaces. The landlord will only be able to determine a statutory tenancy by applying to court and satisfying the conditions described above.

A statutory tenancy cannot be assigned; nor can it pass on death by will or intestacy; but it can pass to the tenant's spouse living with him or her at his or her at death or, failing such a surviving spouse, to any member of the deceased tenant's family who has lived with him or her for the previous six months. The tenancy of the successor is known as a statutory tenancy by succession. A statutory tenancy can pass twice on death in this way but not more.[59]

Rent control. Either party to a regulated (*i.e.* protected or statutory) tenancy (or the local authority) can apply to the local rent officer for the determination and registration of a fair rent for that dwelling.[60] A landlord cannot charge more for a dwelling than the registered rent (and if less is payable under a contractual tenancy, he can only claim the contractual amount).[61] Where no rent has been registered, then the rent payable during a protected tenancy is, in general, the contractual, *i.e.* the agreed, amount.[62] During a statutory tenancy, the rent limit (in the absence of a registered rent) is, in general, the rent payable during the last contractual period.

In determining a fair rent, the rent officer must take all circumstances into account, in particular, the age, character and

---

[58] Rent Act 1977, s.2. See Catherine Hand, "The Statutory Tenancy: An Unrecognised Proprietary Interest [1980] Conv. 351.

[59] Rent Act 1977, s.2(1)(*b*) and Sched. I, Pt. I, as amended by Housing Act 1980, s.76.

[60] Rent Act 1977, Pt. IV, as amended by Housing Act 1980, ss.59–63.

[61] Rent Act 1977, s.44.

[62] *Ibid.* s.44; and as to rent agreements to increase the rent, see Rent Act 1977, ss.51, 52.

locality of the dwelling and its state of repair. But he must disregard the personal circumstances of the parties, any scarcity value, disrepair due to the tenant's default and voluntary improvements carried out by the tenant.[63] There is a right of appeal to a rent assessment committee.

In general, applications cannot be made to the rent officer at shorter intervals than two years.[64]

Other control. Other control includes, in certain cases, restrictions on the charging of premiums on the creation and transfer of tenancies[65]; the obligation to provide a rent book[66]; and the obligation to repair.[67]

Principle 14b.　　Residential premises:　　Restricted contracts.

A restricted contract is any contract[68] for the occupation of a dwelling as a residence where the rent includes payment for furniture or services.[69]

A tenancy which is not a protected tenancy because there is a resident landlord or because some accommodation is shared with the landlord, is treated as a restricted contract even if no services or furniture are provided.[70]

If a contract is a protected tenancy it cannot be a restricted contract.

Certain other contracts are excluded from the definition; and the following will be outside the Rent Act altogether: holiday accommodation; protected occupancies under the Rent (Agriculture) Act 1976; and contracts under which substantial board is provided.[71]

Historically, the important distinction in the case of private, residential tenancies, was between unfurnished and furnished lettings, the latter having only the limited protection of what are

---

[63] *Ibid.* s.70. It has been said that, "the decisions of rent officers and rent assessment committees are therefore subjective in the sense that in the final analysis there is no external criterion by which a person's conception of fairness can be measured." Hill and Redman, *Landlord and Tenant*, (16th ed.), p. 959.

[64] Rent Act 1977, s.67, as amended by Housing Act 1980, s.60.

[65] See Rent Act 1977, Pt IX, as amended by Housing Act 1980, ss. 78, 79.

[66] Landlord and Tenant Act 1962, s.1.

[67] *e.g.* under Housing Act 1961, ss.32, 33, as amended by Housing Act 1980, s.80; see above, p. 119.

[68] There does not have to be a tenancy but there must be exclusive occupation of at least part of the dwelling.

[69] See Rent Act 1977, s.19.

[70] *Ibid.* ss.20, 21.

[71] *Ibid.* ss.7, 9, 19.

now restricted contracts.[72] As a result of the Rent Act 1974,[73] full protection was extended to furnished tenancies. As a result of that Act, today, the most important distinction is between resident and non-resident landlord tenancies.

Security of tenure.   As in the case of a protected tenancy, the landlord seeking possession must determine the contract in accordance with the ordinary rules of landlord and tenant and he must get a court order.[74] But there is no security of tenure comparable to that given to the regulated tenant. Section 106A of the Rent Act 1977[75] merely enables the court, when making an order for possession, to postpone the giving up of possession for up to three months. This is designed to do no more than give the restricted occupant a chance to try and find somewhere else to live.

Rent control.   Either party to a restricted contract (or the local authority) may apply to a rent tribunal[76] to fix a "reasonable" rent for the dwelling, which will be recorded in a register kept by the local authority.[77] In general, where a rent has been registered for the dwelling, the registered rent is the only recoverable rent; and applications for reconsideration cannot be made at intervals of less than two years.[78]

Principle 14c.   Residential Premises: Local authority tenancies[78a]

Security of tenure.   Local authority tenancies are excluded from the definition of a protected tenancy[79]; and, unless furniture or services are provided, they will not even be able to qualify as restricted contracts. Until the Housing Act 1980, there was no statutory scheme of security of tenure for the local authority tenant. His security depended on the ordinary law of landlord and

---

[72] Under the Rent Act 1968, they were known as Part VI contracts. Furnished accommodation was first given limited protection by the Furnished Houses (Rent Control) Act 1946.

[73] Now consolidated in the Rent Act 1977.

[74] Protection from Eviction Act 1977, s.3, as amended by Housing Act 1980, s.69(1).

[75] Inserted by Housing Act 1980, s.69, which replaces the provisions in ss. 103–106 of the 1977 Act for restricted contracts created after the commencement of s.69 (28/11/80).

[76] The rent assessment committees which hear appeals from rent officers, now constitute the rent tribunals for the purposes of restricted contracts; see Housing Act 1980, s.72.

[77] Rent Act 1977, s.79.

[78] *Ibid.*, s.80, as amended by Housing Act 1980, s.70.

[78a] See M. Partington, *Landlord and Tenant* (2nd ed.), pp. 510–531.

[79] Rent Act 1977, s.14.

tenant and on the control of council policy through the local democratic process.[80]

Under the Housing Act 1980, Part I, Chapter II, a local authority tenant[81] will normally have what is termed a secure tenancy provided he is an individual and occupies the dwelling-house as his only or principal home.[82]

If the landlord authority wishes to regain possession, it must first determine the contractual tenancy in accordance with the ordinary rules of landlord and tenant.[83] Where a fixed term, secure tenancy determines (either by effluxion of time or re-entry) it automatically becomes a periodic tenancy.[84] And no secure periodic tenancy can be determined except by court order.[85] The court can only make an order for possession on one of the Grounds specified in Schedule 4, Part I. These include:

(1) Breach of the tenancy agreement. (2) Nuisance or annoyance to neighbours. (3) and (4) Deterioration of the dwelling or furniture provided with it. (5) Deliberate or reckless misrepresentation to obtain the tenancy. (6) Temporary tenancy granted while work being carried out on the tenant's dwelling. (7) Overcrowding. (8) Intention by the landlord to demolish or reconstruct. (10) Dwelling designed for the physically disabled and no longer being used by the tenant for that purpose. (12) Dwelling used for persons with special needs and no longer being used for that purpose. (13) The tenant succeeded to the tenancy as a member of a deceased tenant's family[86] and the accommodation is larger than reasonably required.[87]

In the case of Grounds 1 to 6 the court must, in addition, consider it reasonable to order possession. In the case of Grounds 7 to 9 it must, again in addition to the Ground being established, be satisfied that suitable alternative accommodation is available. In the case of Grounds 10 to 13 it must, in addition, be satisfied

---

[80] For the very limited possibility of challenging an eviction in the courts on the ground of abuse of power, see *Bristol District Council* v. *Clark* [1975] 3 All E.R. 976; and see *Liverpool City Council* v. *Irwin* [1977] A.C. 239. And see *Cannock Chase District Council* v. *Kelly* [1978] 1 All E.R. 152.

[81] And, in some cases, those housing association tenants who are not protected under the Rent Act 1977; see Housing Act 1980, ss.28(2)(*b*), 56–58. Licences are included in the protection; see Housing Act 1980, s.48.

[82] Housing Act 1980, s.28.

[83] Subject to some modifications; see, *e.g.* Housing Act 1980, ss.32(2), 33(3).

[84] Housing Act 1980, s.29(1).

[85] *Ibid.* s.32(1).

[86] Under Housing Act 1980, s.30(2)(*b*).

[87] Grounds 9 and 11 relate to dwellings owned by charities and housing associations respectively.

both as to reasonableness and the availability of alternative accommodation.

Right of succession to secure tenancies. On the death of a periodic secure tenant there is a right of succession somewhat similar to that given to statutory tenants under the Rent Act 1977. The right to succeed belongs to the deceased tenant's spouse who occupied the dwelling as his (or her) only or principal home at the time of the death. Failing a qualifying spouse, the right belongs to any other member of the deceased tenant's family[88] who resided with the tenant throughout the 12 months prior to the death.[89] Only one such succession is possible.[90]

For the other terms of a secure tenancy dealt with by the Housing Act 1980, (including the right to take lodgers, sub-let and assign, to make improvements and to be consulted), see Sections 35–48 and 80–85.

Under Part I of the same Act, secure tenants of local authority houses (as opposed to flats) are given the right to buy the freehold at a discount, the amount of the discount depending on the length of occupation.

Rent. Under the Housing Act 1957, Sections 111 and 113, housing authorities have a duty to make such reasonable charges for accommodation as they may determine. In general, the courts will not interfere.[91] Under the Housing, Rents and Subsidies Act 1975,[92] authorities have a duty to review their rents from time to time and make such changes as the circumstances require; any balance in the authority's housing revenue account can be used to reduce the rates.[93]

There is a means tested rent rebate scheme for housing authority tenants.[94]

---

[88] As defined by Housing Act 1980, s.50(3).

[89] Failing agreement between two or more qualifying members of the family, the landlord can select the successor; (s.30(3)).

[90] The deceased periodic tenant may himself have been a successor (thus preventing any further right of succession), not only if he himself succeeded under s.30 but also, for example, where the original tenancy was a fixed term which passed to him by assignment under s.37 and then continued on expiry as a periodic tenancy under s.29(1). The basic principle is that anyone (including a surviving joint tenant) other than the original tenant who holds the tenancy will be a successor thus preventing any further succession.

[91] See D. Yates, "Local Authority Rents," (1975) 39 Conv.(N.S.) 387; *Summerfield v. Hampstead B.C.* [1957] 1 W.L.R. 167.

[92] s.1, as amended by Housing Act 1980, s.134.

[93] Housing Act 1980, s.134(2). Today, central government has a large measure of control over the level of rents charged by housing authorities.

[94] And a similar rent allowance scheme for private tenants.

Principle 14d.   Residential premises: Agricultural workers

Protected occupiers. The Rent (Agriculture) Act 1976 was introduced to give security of tenure to agricultural workers in tied accommodation, that is housing provided by the employer. Such workers do not generally have protected tenancies under the Rent Act for one or both of two reasons: first, because they are likely to have licences rather than tenancies[95]; and, secondly, their rents are likely to be less than two thirds of the rateable value.[96] The result was, prior to the 1976 Act, that if such a worker lost or left his job for any reason, he was likely to lose his home at the same time.

The Rent (Agriculture) Act 1976[97] introduced a new category, the protected occupier in his own right. An occupier must satisfy three conditions to qualify as a protected occupier.

First, he must have a relevant tenancy or licence. A relevant tenancy or licence is one that fails to qualify as a protected tenancy under the Rent Act 1977 for one or more of the following reasons[98]: the rent is less than two thirds of the rateable value; it is a licence and not a tenancy; the dwelling is comprised in an agricultural holding and the occupant is responsible for the control of the holding.[99]

Secondly, the occupant must at some time during the tenancy or licence have been a qualifying worker. This means[1] that he must have worked the whole time in agriculture for a period of 91 weeks within a period of 104 weeks.

Thirdly, the dwelling must have been in qualifying ownership at some time during the licence or tenancy.[2] This means that he must have been employed in agriculture by his landlord.[3]

If such a protected occupancy is determined it becomes a statutory tenancy so long as the occupier continues to occupy the dwelling as his residence.[4]

---

[95] See above, p. 97.

[96] The accommodation being, in effect, part of the remuneration for the job.

[97] Now as amended by Rent (Agriculture) Amendment Act 1977. See L.M. Clements, "The 'Demise' of Tied Cottages," [1978] Conv. 259.

[98] Rent (Agriculture) Act 1976, ss.1(4), 2 and Sched.2.

[99] For the position as to board and attendance, see Rent (Agriculture) Act 1976, Sched. 2, paras. 3, 4.

[1] *Ibid.* Sched. 3.

[2] *Ibid.* ss.1(5), 2 and Sched. 3.

[3] Or that his employer has an arrangement with the landlord to provide accommodation for his agricultural workers.

[4] A statutory tenant under this Act should not be confused with a statutory tenant under the Rent Act 1977.

Security. If the landlord wishes to obtain possession he must determine any contract (in accordance with ordinary rules) and establish in court one of the Cases set out in Schedule 4 to the Act. As with the Rent Act 1977, the Cases are divided into two parts: the discretionary cases in Part I to the Schedule in which, in addition to the Case being established, the court must consider it reasonable to order possession; and those (mandatory) Cases in Part II of the Schedule in which the court has no discretion. In general, the Cases are similar to those in the Rent Act 1977, including the provision of suitable alternative accommodation privately or by a housing authority. Sections 27 to 29[5] impose a duty on the local housing authority (where the landlord needs the dwelling for another agricultural worker) to "use their best endeavours" to provide suitable alternative accommodation.

On the death of a protected occupier or statutory tenant there is a right of succession for the spouse residing with him or her at the death; and, failing such a spouse, for a member of his or her family who has resided with him or her for the six months before the death.[6] Only one such succession is possible.

Rent. The rent during the contractual (protected occupancy) period is not controlled by the Act.[7] During a statutory tenancy, the rent, in the first place, will be that payable under the last contractual period. Under Section 13[8] application can be made for registration of a fair rent in which case the registered rent becomes the maximum recoverable. In the absence of a registered rent, the rent can be fixed by agreement between the landlord and statutory tenant under Section 11; or it can be increased unilaterally by the landlord up to a rent based on the rateable value of the dwelling calculated in accordance with Section 12.

The other terms of the statutory tenancy are governed by Section 10 and Schedule 5.

Principle 14e. Residential premises: Protection from Eviction

The Protection from Eviction Act 1977[9] is designed to protect lawful residential possession by making it generally necessary for a landlord to obtain a court order to enforce any right to recover

---

[5] As amended by Rent (Agriculture) Amendment Act 1977.
[6] Rent (Agriculture) Act 1976, ss.3, 4.
[7] Since it will have to be less than ⅔ of the rateable value for the Act to apply.
[8] Which incorporates the relevant provisions of the Rent Act 1977.
[9] As amended by Housing Act 1980, s.69.

possession, and by making unlawful eviction and harassment an offence.

Section 1(2) makes it an offence unlawfully to deprive the residential occupier of his occupation. Section 1(3) makes it an offence to do any act calculated to interfere with the peace or comfort of a residential occupier, or persistently to withdraw or withhold his services. The act must be intended to cause him to give up occupation or not to exercise his rights.[10]

A residential occupier is, broadly, any one in lawful residential occupation.

Section 2 makes it necessary to obtain a court order to enforce a right of re-entry or forfeiture in the case of a dwelling.

Section 3 requires a court order to recover possession on the termination of a residential tenancy.

Under the Criminal Law Act 1977, Section 6, it is an offence to use or threaten violence to secure entry into premises and it is no defence that the defendant had an interest in or right to occupation of the premises. But it is a defence if he is a dipossessed residential occupier.[11]

Principle 15.   Agricultural holdings[11a]

Definition. An agricultural holding within the Agricultural Holdings Act 1948, the main Act, is the land[12] included in a contract of tenancy which is used for agriculture and which is so used for the purpose of a trade or business.[13]

The definition covers a term of years and a yearly tenancy; and a tenancy for less than a year (and a licence to occupy) is treated as a yearly tenancy.

Security of tenure. In general the tenant is entitled to a full year's notice[14] (even on the expiry of a fixed term) and is entitled to serve a counter notice under section 24 of the Act. He is not entitled to serve a counter notice in, *inter alia*, the following

---

[10] See *McCall* v. *Abelez* [1976] 1 All E.R. 727 (C.A.) and *Ex p. Island Records* [1978] 3 All E.R. 824. Contrast *Warder* v. *Cooper* [1970] 1 All E.R. 1112.

[11] As defined in s.12(3).

[11a] See Scammell and Densham, *Law of Agricultural Holdings* (6th ed.).

[12] Including, of course, buildings on the land.

[13] Agricultural Holdings Act 1948, s.1. Thus, in *Rutherford* v. *Maurer* [1962] 1 Q.B. 16 (C.A.) land used by the proprietor of a riding school to graze horses was within the Act. The use was agricultural and the agricultural use was for the purpose of a trade or business. In other words the trade or business does not itself have to be agricultural.

[14] Agricultural Holdings (Notices to Quit) Act 1977, s.1.

cases—so that the notice will take effect and he will have to vacate[15]:

(1) Where the land is required for some purpose other than agriculture for which planning permission has been obtained.

(2) Where the Agricultural Land Tribunal has certified that the land has not been farmed in accordance with the rules of good husbandry.

(3) Where the tenant has failed to pay arrears of rent or remedy a breach of covenant.[16]

(4) Where the tenant has become a bankrupt.

(5) Where the tenant has died within the previous three months.[17]

If the tenant is entitled to and does serve a counter notice within one month of receiving the notice to quit, the notice to quit will not take effect without the consent of the Agricultural Land Tribunal. To obtain the consent of the tribunal the landlord must establish one of the following grounds, *inter alia*[18]:

(a) That the carrying out of the purpose for which the land is required is desirable in the interests of the good husbandry of the land.

(b) That the carrying out of the purpose for which the land is required is desirable in the interests of the management of the estate (of which the land forms part) as a whole.

(c) That the purpose for which the land is required is desirable in the interests of agricultural research, education, experiment, etc.

(d) That greater hardship would be caused by withholding than consenting to the notice taking effect.

Even if the landlord establishes one of these grounds, the tribunal will refuse consent if it is satisfied that a fair and reasonable landlord would not seek possession.

Rent. The rent will in the first place be that agreed in the contract. But at intervals of not less than three years either party can apply to have the rent reviewed by an arbitrator who will decide "the open market rent" for the holding—disregarding any effect of the tenant's own existing occupation. Rent can only be

---

[15] *Ibid.* s.2.

[16] For position where breach is failure to comply with notice to carry out repairs, maintenance or replacement, see Agricultural Holdings (Notices to Quit) Act 1977, ss.4, 5.

[17] Unless an application is made for a new tenancy by a person entitled under Agriculture (Miscellaneous Provisions) Act 1976, s.18.

[18] Agricultural Holdings (Notices to Quit) Act 1977, s.3.

altered in this way from the date when the contractual tenancy could, under the ordinary law, have been determined.[19]

Other statutory provisions. Fixtures have been dealt with above.[20] On the determination of the tenancy, the tenant is entitled to claim compensation in respect of improvements which he has made to the land; for disturbance; and for an increase in its value due to a more beneficial than usual method of farming.[21]

The landlord may be entitled to compensation for dilapidation or deterioration due to the tenant's failure to farm in accordance with the rules of good husbandry.[22]

Right of succession. Under Part II of the Agriculture (Miscellaneous Provisions) Act 1976, there is a right of succession on the death of the tenant of an agricultural holding. The following have the right to apply to the Agricultural Land Tribunal for a new tenancy: the husband or wife, brother or sister, child or child of the family, of the deceased tenant. The applicant must have been working on the holding as his only or principal source of livelihood for a continuous period of five years in the seven years prior to the death.[23] The tribunal will decide whether the applicant (or which if any of them if more than one) is a suitable person to become a tenant; and, if there is a suitable tenant, will make a direction in his favour. He will then be deemed to have a new tenancy of the holding to run, generally, from the end of the year of the tenancy in which the tenant died. In general, only two such successions are possible.

Principle 16. Business premises

Security of tenure. A tenancy protected by Part II of the Landlord and Tenant Act 1954 "shall not come to an end unless terminated in accordance with the provisions of the Act."[24]

The Act applies to premises occupied wholly or in part by the tenant for the purposes of his business.[25] And the term "business" is very widely defined to include any trade or profession or employment and any activity of an incorporated or unincorporated

---

[19] Agricultural Holdings Act 1948, s.8.

[20] At p. 131.

[21] Agricultural Holdings Act 1948, ss.35–56.

[22] *Ibid.* ss.57–59.

[23] See *Littlewood* v. *Rolfe* [1981] 2 All E.R. 51 (Q.B.D.).

[24] Landlord and Tenant Act 1954, s.24. Note that the Act protects tenancies, not occupation licences; see *Shell-Mex and B.P. Ltd.* v. *Manchester Garages Ltd.* [1971] 1 W.L.R. 612.

[25] *Ibid.* s.23(1).

body. Certain business tenancies are excluded, for example, agricultural holdings and mining leases.[26] The landlord can only determine such a tenancy—not before it could have been ended at common law—by serving a notice in accordance with the provisions of the Act. And if he does serve notice the tenant has a right to apply to the court for the grant of a new tenancy. The court must grant an application for a new tenancy unless the landlord establishes one of certain grounds. For example, that the tenant has failed to fulfil his obligations to repair the premises; that he has persistently delayed in paying the rent; that the landlord is willing to provide suitable alternative accommodation; or that the landlord intends to demolish or reconstruct the premises.[27]

The terms of the new tenancy, if granted, including the rent, will be fixed by the court.

Rent control. There is no control on the contractual rent to which the parties can agree; but if a new tenancy is granted on application to the court, the rent will be fixed by the court at that at which the premises "might reasonably be expected to be let on the open market by a willing lessor."[28]

Other control. Under the Landlord and Tenant Act 1927, an outgoing tenant may have a right to claim compensation for improvements which he has carried out.

---

[26] *Ibid.* s.43.
[27] *Ibid.* ss.26 to 31.
[28] *Ibid.* s.34.

PART 3. TRUST OWNERSHIP

CHAPTER 4

TRUST OWNERSHIP: GENERAL

SECTION 1. NATURE AND DEVELOPMENT OF TRUST OWNERSHIP

Principle 1. Definition[1]

Trust ownership exists where the ownership of property is vested in one or more persons (trustees) who hold it for the benefit of others (beneficiaries). Normally, in the case of land, the trustees hold the legal estate[2] while the beneficiaries hold equitable interests.[3]

Explanation

The last Part was concerned with the beneficial owner—the person who owns the whole legal and equitable interest in the land. He can exercise the rights of ownership—the rights of enjoyment, control and disposal—for his own benefit. If, for example, he sells the land he will be entitled to keep the proceeds of sale for himself. If he wants to he can give the land away.

But in some cases a person holds land not as beneficial owner but as trustee. A trust exists wherever the ownership of property is vested in one or more persons (the trustees) who hold it for the benefit of others (the beneficiaries). Generally, in the case of trust ownership of land, the trustees hold the legal estate; the beneficiaries have equitable interests.

Broadly speaking, the object of trust ownership today is, for one reason or another, to put the powers of control, management and disposal in the hands of trustees; but to give the right to enjoy the fruits of ownership—possession, income and the proceeds of sale—to the beneficiaries.

To take a simple example. Suppose that a child of, say, seven, is left a house and a piece of land in a will. Clearly some sort of trust is the only way to deal with the situation. The property will have to be held by trustees who will manage it for the benefit of the infant until he comes of age. When this happens the legal ownership can

---

[1] See Hanbury and Haudsley, *Modern Equity* (11th ed.), p. 154.
[2] *i.e.* either the legal fee simple absolute in possession or the legal term of years.
[3] But an equitable interest, for example, a fee simple remainder can be held in trust. See, *e.g. Re Sharpe's Deed of Release* [1939] Ch. 51; and see *Re Edward's Will Trusts* [1981] 2 All E.R. 941 (C.A.).

be transferred to him[4] and the trust brought to an end. Until then
he has only an equitable interest in the property.

Infancy is just one situation in which the device of trust
ownership is used. The others will be considered later. It will also
be necessary to consider how the trustees' powers of dealing with
the land are limited and controlled; the different types of trust
ownership which can exist; and the precise rights of the beneficiaries.

Before this, however, something must be said about the
distinction between common law and equity and the corresponding distinction between legal and equitable interests in land. As
already stated the trustees normally have the legal estate and the
beneficiaries have the equitable interests. In other words the trust
represents the splitting up of the ownership of land into separate
legal and equitable parts.

The distinction between law and equity is also important in the
field of third party rights and will be considered again in that
context.[5]

The splitting up of both ownership and third party rights in this
way is a result of the way in which English law developed. This
historic development will now be considered briefly.

Principle 2. Development of common law and equity

The common law developed after the Norman Conquest as a
system of law common to the whole land administered by the
common law courts. It gradually absorbed or replaced the local
laws administered by the local customary and feudal courts.

Subsequently, a new system of law, equity, was developed
administered by the court of Chancery.

The two systems, together constituting the bulk of English law,
were administered side by side as two separate but complementary
sets of rules, right up to 1875[6] when they were brought together to
be administered by a single system of courts, the Supreme Court of
Judicature and the House of Lords.[7]

Explanation

Up to the eleventh century there was no common law in the
sense of a law common to the whole land. Each district was
governed for the most part by its own customary rules handed

---

[4] Legal ownership will not pass to him automatically on his coming of age. The
trustees will have to convey it to him by deed.

[5] See, *e.g.* below p. 370, as to distinction between legal and equitable easements.

[6] Supreme Court of Judicature Acts 1873–75.

[7] And the county courts set up by the County Courts Act 1846.

down orally from generation to generation and differing from one area to another. These rules were administered in the local customary courts with little if anything in the way of centralised control. Each local community went its own way. Today, the process of making the law, interpreting, administering and enforcing it is centrally controlled. That is, there is a centralised legislature, judicature and administration. It is true, for example, that local authorities do have a limited power to make local laws (bye-laws), but only under the authority of Act of Parliament. It is true that there are still local courts, for example, the county and magistrates' courts. But the judges of these courts are appointed by the central administration and, more important, there is a centralised appeal system which ensures general uniformity of the law throughout the country. If a county court judge in Manchester decides a dispute one way and a county court judge in Leeds decides an identical dispute in a different way, in a sense there will on this particular point be a divergence between the law of Manchester and the law of Leeds. But sooner or later the point will go to the Court of Appeal or the House of Lords which will decide which is the correct rule to be followed for the future in both Manchester and Leeds.

Apart from the local customary courts, there were the local manorial courts. These developed after the Norman Conquest as part of feudalism. They were based on the allegiance which a tenant owed to his local manorial lord and were very important particularly in the field of land law. But this local allegiance to the lord gave way to the national allegiance owed to the king; and the feudal courts, like the customary courts, gave way to the common law.

By a process which was largely complete in the fourteenth century, these local customary and feudal courts were absorbed into and replaced by the common law administered by the king's judges sitting either at Westminster or as itinerant justices on circuit.

As can be imagined, a great majority of the disputes coming before these judges concerned the ownership of land and rights in land. And it was in the course of deciding such disputes that the common law developed the doctrine of estates and many of the basic principles governing land ownership which are still with us today.

In the course of time the common law became defective. For reasons which cannot be examined here it ceased to be receptive to new ideas and new concepts. People wished to create new property rights and deal with their property in new ways. The common law refused to give its sanction to these innovations. Today, if it is considered necessary to change the law and give legal recognition to new rights, it is possible to turn to the legislature represented by Parliament. For example, in 1967, by the Matrimonial Homes Act, Parliament created a new property right, the spouse's right of occupation of the matrimonial home. Prior to the modern development of Parliament there was no such legislative machinery available.

However, there was one avenue open to the person who wanted some interest protected or some novel transaction recognised and who could get no assistance from the common law. He could turn to the king. From earliest times the king had been recognised as the fountain of justice. If a person could not get justice elsewhere he had a right to turn to the king. Indeed, it was partly by relying on this accepted principle that the king had been able to develop the authority of the common law administered by his own judges at the expense of the local customary and feudal courts. The common law courts had in the course of time achieved an existence independent of the king, and when they proved inadequate, the people again turned to the king himself. If a person did not get justice in the common law courts he could petition the king. And the king dealt with these petitions by giving or refusing a remedy as he saw fit. As such petitions became more numerous the king left them to his Chancellor to deal with. Here was the beginnings of the Court of Chancery. The Chancellor decided the petitions not according to any fixed rules of law but according to equity and conscience, that is according to what he though was fair and just in the particular dispute before him. The justice administered by the Court of Chancery therefore became known as equity. Of course, in the nature of things, many disputes coming before the court were similar to each other; and, of course, there was a tendency for the Chancellor to decide similar disputes in the same way—that is to follow precedent—and to lay down rules and principles of general application. Gradually, the Court of Chancery became more like a court of law, like the common courts, administering a reasonably well defined set of rules; and not just an institution dispensing equity in the sense of the judge's somewhat unpredictable idea of natural justice. Nevertheless, the law administered by the Court of Chancery remained known as equity. And by the time that it had settled down and become largely bound by the rules that it had itself created, the Court of Chancery had made important innovations in the law. It had given legal recognition to important new rights and new modes of dealing with property, new remedies and new procedures.

By the fifteenth century, English law was thus made up of two separate sets of rules, common law and equity, administered by two separate sets of courts, the common law courts and Chancery. It is hardly surprising that for a time there was hostility between them. Equity had been developed to remedy the defects in the common law. The common law judges were naturally jealous of their jurisdiction and resented interference. The situation can be imagined. It was as if, today, French judges boarded the ferry at Calais, came over to Dover, set up courts in the town and started to administer French law to anyone who cared to come before them.

As will be explained below,[8] the two systems sorted out their differences; it will be seen that they came to form two complementary and interdependent parts of a single harmonious[9] English law. There was a final attempt in the seventeenth century, by the victorious Parliamentarians, to abolish Chancery and the rules of equity. But even by then it had to be recognised that equity was as essential to English law as the common law itself.

In 1875,[10] the administration of the two systems was combined in a single set of courts. This is the position today. Each court, today, has jurisdiction to apply both common law and equity and to give both legal and equitable remedies whichever may be appropriate in the circumstances of the particular case.

Principle 3. Relationship between common law and equity

Up to 1875 the relationship between common law and equity was governed by three main principles:
  (a) Equity followed the law wherever possible;
  (b) where it considered necessary, equity modified or added to the common law;
  (c) where there was a conflict between common law and equity, equity prevailed.

As a result of the Supreme Court of Judicature Acts 1873–75, common law and equity have been fused into a single system of law administered by a single hierarchy of courts.

---

[8] At p. 162.
[9] Harmonious, at least, in that there is a single hierarchy of courts with authority to resolve any conflict between the two sets of rules.
[10] Supreme Court of Judicature Acts 1873–75. See Supreme Court of Judicature (Consolidation) Act 1925, ss.18, 44; see further, below, p. 163.

Explanation

Equity followed the law. Equity, like the common law, was from the start involved in disputes relating to land. Where possible, equity followed the law—that is, unless it saw some good reason for departing from it. Thus, in the context of land law, it adopted the common law doctrine of estates; it recognised the fee simple, the fee tail and the life estate as estates which could exist in land. In general, it would recognise the person who was owner at common law as being also the owner in equity; and in general, it would recognise the equitable estate as being subject to the same rules as the corresponding common law estate, for example, the rules of descent on intestacy.

To take an example—and this example would work out in exactly the same way today. Blackacre is conveyed to X in fee simple by deed of conveyance. The effect of this, assuming that X is not an infant, will be to make X the owner of the legal fee simple absolute in possession. This is because a deed is generally necessary and effective to transfer ownership at common law.[11] The deed does not mention equity or equitable ownership. However, equity follows the law. Unless there are special circumstances present equity will follow the law here and also recognise X as being owner. Equity might, of course, give additional protection to X's interest. If, for example, T persistently trespasses on the land, common law will make him pay damages to X as compensation for any damage done. Equity will grant an injunction to prevent any further trespass by T. If necessary X can get both remedies.

Equity modified the law. If equity had invariably followed the law there would have been no need for it as a separate system of law. But in fact in many cases equity considered it equitable to depart from or add to the common law rules. For example, it recognised interests in land which could not exist at common law. A good example of such an interest is the restrictive covenant, a third party right, which will be considered later.[12] More important in connection with the ownership of land it was in some cases prepared to recognise as equitable owner someone who was not owner at common law. Where this happened it did not deny the ownership of the common law owner. It said in effect: "Yes, we recognise that T is the owner of the land at common law; but as far as we are concerned B and C are the owners; and we will compel T to exercise his rights of ownership for the benefit of B and C." In

---

[11] L.P.A. 1925, s. 52.
[12] Chap. 20.

other words, the result was that T held the common law estate in trust for B and C the equitable owners and had to exercise his rights of ownership for their benefit.

This recognition of the trust was one of the most important contributions made by equity to English law. It should be emphasised that in recognising and enforcing the trust, equity was not just imposing some arbitrary solution of its own on the parties. In general it was simply assisting the original owner of the land who had desired to split up the ownership of his land in this way and giving effect to his intentions. The example, often given, is of the landowner who was going off to fight in the Crusades. He gave his property to a friend to administer for the benefit of his family. This worked so long as the friend did not betray the trust thus imposed on him. But if he did, and those intended to benefit from the trust went to court (*i.e.* the common law courts) they were in trouble. The common law recognised the ownership of the friend since it had been transferred to him by the would-be Crusader in the manner recognised by law for transferring ownership. But common law refused to recognise the trust. It refused to recognise the family as having any legally enforceable interest in the land. So far as the common law was concerned the owner could do what he liked with the land and keep all the benefits for himself. It was here that equity stepped in. It was prepared to enforce the intentions of the original owner, the Crusader. It enforced the trust and the equitable interests of the beneficiaries existing behind the trust.

Another example, one which is still relevant today. Suppose that Blackacre is conveyed to X by deed of conveyance. The conveyance makes no mention of equitable ownership. However, on investigation, it is found that X's mother contributed to the purchase price of the property. Here equity will not follow the law and hold X to be the equitable as well as legal owner. In this situation it is likely to recognise both X and his mother as having an interest. In other words X will be the legal owner but he will be deemed to hold in trust for himself and his mother.[13]

The trust was extremely important to landowners from the earliest days of its recognition. It is true that if, before 1926, a landowner wished to settle his land (to carve it up into a succession of interests) he could often do so either in law or equity. He could transfer the legal estate to X and Y in trust for A for life, remainder to B in fee tail. Or he could simply transfer the legal estate to A for life, remainder to B in fee tail, and so on. However, by working in equity behind a trust of the legal estate, the

---

[13] *Bull* v. *Bull* [1955] 1 Q.B. 234, from which this example is taken.

landowner could avoid many of the technical rules which over the years had become attached to the legal estate by the common law courts; and which equity refused to follow. He could create certain types of future interest which could not be created at common law. And he could avoid some of the feudal burdens which affected the legal estate.[14]

Since the modernisation of land law these particular reasons for using the trust no longer exist. But the trust is probably more important now than before. In particular, as will be seen, its use has been extended by Parliament as a means of simplifying conveyancing and the dealing with land; today, whenever a landowner wishes to carve up the ownership of his land by settlement or co-ownership, he no longer has any choice and can only do it in equity behind a trust.

Further, both before and after 1925, the trust has been useful wherever it is wished to give a person some sort of interest in land without giving him managerial control. Infants and spendthrifts[15] are two examples which will have to be mentioned.

Equity prevailed. Where equity recognised one person as owner and the common law another, and indeed in any case where equity was not prepared to follow the law,[16] there was likely to be a conflict between the two systems. This conflict was ultimately resolved by acceptance of the principle that where there is a conflict between common law and equity, equity will prevail. This principle was given statutory recognition by the Judicature Acts 1873–75[17] and still exists to govern the relationship between the two sets of rules. An example will illustrate the situation.

In *Grist* v. *Bailey*,[18] V agreed to sell a house to P. Both parties were under the mistaken impression when they made the contract that the property was occupied by a tenant with statutory security of tenure. On this basis the price was agreed at £2,500. In fact, the tenant had vacated and consequently the house was worth much more. Naturally enough the vendor was reluctant to complete and wanted more money; and the dispute went to court. At common law the rule is that only a common mistake as to the existence of

---

[14] For the history of this matter, see Megarry and Wade, *Law of Real Property* (4th ed.), pp. 110–113; 167–171.

[15] See below, pp. 297, 347.

[16] For example, if equity did, but common law did not, recognise D as having a right of way over S's land.

[17] Supreme Court of Judicature Act 1875, s. 25; now Supreme Court of Judicature (Consolidation) Act 1925, s. 44.

[18] [1967] Ch. 532 (Goff J.); see also *Walsh* v. *Lonsdale* (1882) 21 Ch. D. 9, above, p. 110.

the subject-matter will make a contract void. At common law therefore there was a valid contract and V was obliged to complete or pay damages—the common law remedy. However, equity has jurisdiction in such a situation to set the contract aside on terms. Equity prevailed. The court ordered the contract to be set aside on the terms that V agreed to make a fresh contract to sell to P at a proper vacant possession price.

Relationship today. The Judicature Acts 1873–75[19] created a single hierarchy of courts—the county courts, the High Court, Court of Appeal and the House of Lords. Ever since, there has been debate whether common law and equity have remained separate (two streams running in the same channel) or been fused into a single stream.[20]

The present writer's view is that it is increasingly artificial and even misleading to think in terms of two separate systems of law.[21] If any dispute comes before a court today, it will be decided in accordance with, first any relevant statutes and, secondly, any relevant previous decisions applied in accordance with the doctrine of binding precedent.

However, certain comments on this statement should be noted.

First, the term equity has two meanings: (a) Those rules of law developed by the old court of Chancery; (b) deciding a dispute according to some notion of what is fair and just.[22]

A large part of our law can still be classified as either common law or equity, in the first sense, by reference to its origins. But this is a matter of historical record, not a basis for present decision making. Equally, it can be said that when the courts are deciding any case today, they will, so far as the confines of statute and precedent allow, decide in accordance with their own notions of what is just and fair.

Secondly, since a large part of our law still remains much as developed by the pre-1875 courts, the old relationship is still enmeshed in the law, that is, it still illustrates equity prevailing.[23] But the important point is this: the law has not stood still since 1875. There have been new lines of development and new developments of old doctrines. The courts still exercise an

---

[19] And County Courts Act 1846.
[20] See Megarry and Wade, Law of Real Property, (4th ed.), p. 129.
[21] For support for this view, see *United Scientific Holdings Ltd.* v. *Burnely B.C.* [1977] 2 All E.R. 62 (H.L.). Contrast view of P.V. Baker, "The Future of Equity," (1977) 93 L.Q.R. 529.
[22] And it should be noted that the terms "legal" and "law" are commonly used to refer to the common law as opposed to equity.
[23] See, *e.g. Grist* v. *Bailey* [1967] Ch. 532 (Goff J.); *Walsh* v. *Lonsdale* (1882) 21 Ch. D. 9.

important law creating function.[24] The exercise of this function does not depend on the classification of a rule as common law or equity, but upon the moulding of precedents to fit new situations.[25] One of the significant distinctions between common law and equity was that common law remedies, such as damages were fixed and recoverable as of right; whilst equitable remedies, such as specific performance and the injunction, were discretionary. This distinction is still of some importance; but to use such language today is perhaps misleading. It ascribes too much flexibility to the judicial control of specific performance and the injunction; and too little to its control of damages.

Thirdly, the courts do in certain areas reserve for themselves a judicial discretion, excluding the full rigour of binding precedent and deciding each case "on its own facts." It may be true that more of these areas can be traced back to the old equity than to the common law. But the most significant areas of judicial discretion today are probably those granted to the judiciary by modern statutes.[26] Here the courts will be applying equity but only in the second sense used above.[27]

Fourthly, judicial adherence to the old dual classification may, at times, have stultified the development of the law. For example, there is the judicial failure to recognise the statutory tenant under the Rent Acts as having a proprietary interest in the land.[28]

Fifthly, the 1925 property legislation is built on the distinction between legal and equitable interests in land—as opposed to the distinction between law and equity. This may be mostly a matter of nomenclature, but it is a part of the framework of modern English land law. Further, it should be remembered that, since the 1925 legislation limits the number of possible legal interests in land,[29] any new landed property interests developed by the courts will generally have to be classified as equitable.

---

[24] As shown, *e.g.* in the field of licences, proprietary estoppel and frustration of contracts.

[25] See, *e.g. Wrotham Park Estate Ltd.* v. *Parkside Homes Ltd.* [1974] 1 W.L.R. 798, concerned with the quantification of damages awarded under the Chancery Amendment Act 1858; followed in *Bracewell* v. *Appleby* [1975] 1 All E.R. 993 (Graham J.). And see *Johnson* v. *Agnew* [1980] A.C. 367 (H.L.).

[26] See, *e.g.* L.P.A. 1925, ss. 30, 49: Matrimonial Causes Act 1973, ss. 24, 25; see below, p. 331. On the nature of judicial discretion, see Dworkin, *Taking Rights Seriously* (1977), pp. 31–39, 65–71.

[27] See, *e.g. Martin* v. *Martin* [1977] 3 All E.R. 762 (C.A.), per Ormrod J. at p. 768.

[28] See above, p. 141; and see The Statutory Tenancy: An Unrecognised Proprietary Interest, Catherine Hand, [1980] Conv. 351. A similar attitude has been shown to the spouses right of occupation under the Matrimonial Homes Act 1967.

[29] L.P.A. 1925, s. 1.

Principle 4. Distinction between legal and equitable interests in land before and after the 1925 legislation

(1)**Before 1926.** Before 1926 two of the most important distinctions were as follows:

(a) All legal interests were good against all the world; all equitable interests were good against all the world except a bona fide purchaser for value of a legal estate without notice of the equitable interest and anyone claiming through such a purchaser.

(b) Further, legal interests could in general only be created by deed whereas equitable interests could be created informally.[30]

(2)**Since 1925**

(a) The doctrine of notice still applies but has been modified by the machinery for registering certain third party rights under the Land Charges Act 1925[31]; for registering ownership as well as third party rights under the Land Registration Act 1925; and by the machinery for overreaching beneficial interests.

(b) The distinction as to formalities still generally applies.[32]

Explanation

The doctrine of notice. Suppose that A had a life interest in Blackacre. What difference would it make to him whether his interest was legal or equitable? It might be a matter of interest to lawyers; but did it matter to him? Whether legal or equitable his interest would come to an end when he died; his rights of enjoyment would be the same in both cases.[33] The answer is that it might make a difference—a vital difference. This difference is expressed in the principle stated above and originally it applied to all legal and equitable interests in land whether ownership or third party. Today, as will be seen, its importance is diminished; but it still applies to some legal and equitable interests in unregistered land and it is therefore still important.[34]

The meaning of this distinction is considered later in more detail.[35] But briefly the position is this. If A has a legal interest in Blackacre, for example, a legal right of way—that legal interest will be enforceable against all the world; in particular against any subsequent owner of Blackacre. Whether or not the purchaser

---

[30] Subject to Statute of Frauds 1677.

[31] See now L.C.A. 1972 and Local Land Charges Act 1975.

[32] As to equitable interests, note s.53 of the L.P.A. 1925; below, p. 175.

[33] But both legal and equitable life tenants were subject to the doctrine of equitable waste; see below, p. 244.

[34] See below, p. 517.

[35] Below, p. 513 *et seq.*

knew about it when he bought is not relevant. A legal right of way in unregistered land today would still be governed by the same rule.[36]

On the other hand, an equitable interest will be enforceable against all the world except a bona fide purchaser for value of a legal estate without notice of the equitable interest. Suppose that Blackacre is subject to a restrictive covenant against building, created in 1880, in favour of neighbouring Whiteacre. Suppose that Blackacre is sold to P who, for some reason, does not discover the existence of the covenant until two years later when he starts to build and the owner of Whiteacre objects. If this were a legal interest P would have no defence. But restrictive covenants are always equitable. If P can show that he has purchased a legal estate in the land for value (*i.e.* it wasn't given to him), and that at the time of purchase he did not have notice of it (*i.e.* he did not know and there was no reason why he should have known),[37] then the restrictive covenant will not bind him. Equity considered it not to be equitable to penalise such an innocent purchaser. The bona fide purchaser has been called the darling of equity. It is one of the few cases in which equity allowed the legal estate to prevail.

As with the example of the legal easement, this example of the 1880 restrictive covenant, provided it related to unregistered land, would still be governed by the same rule today.

Position since 1925. The extent to which the doctrine of notice now applies and the modifications made by the registration and overreaching machinery are considered elsewhere.[38]

The present day rules governing formalities for the creation of legal and equitable interests are also considered below.[39]

Principle 5. Trust ownership and conveyancing before 1926

Under pre-1926 land law, the disposal of land might be difficult if not impossible, and conveyancing complex.

Five factors contributed to this situation:

(a) The ownership of land could be split up in both law and equity.

(b) A purchaser of land would have to investigate every legal and equitable interest which might affect the land. If he did not obtain the proper consent of the owner of any legal interest he

---

[36] For the position today if this were registered land, see below, p. 538.
[37] And his agent neither knew nor ought to have known of the interest.
[38] See below, pp. 518, 526.
[39] See below at p. 175.

would take the land subject to that interest. If he did not obtain the proper consent of the owner of any equitable interest he would take subject to that interest unless he could show that he was a bona fide purchaser for value without notice.

(c) In some cases, such as a fee tail held by an infant, there might be no one at the time with power to give consent. In such cases only an expensive private Act of Parliament would enable the land to be sold.[40]

(d) The ownership might be affected by powers of appointment.

(e) The land might be subject to all sorts of legal and equitable third party rights.

Explanation

The splitting up of ownership. To understand the present principle, it is first necessary to be clear about the ways in which the ownership of land could (and still can) be split up. Forgetting about the distinction between law and equity for the time being and dealing only with freehold ownership, let us take Blackacre. There are three possibilities:

(i) The entire freehold ownership may be vested in X. He owns the fee simple absolute in possession—the greatest estate possible. In such a case the ownership has not been split up at all.

(ii) The fee simple may be settled. The ownership may be split up into a succession of estates or interests. For example, it is held by A for life remainder to B in fee tail, remainder to C in fee simple. Each tenant has an interest which gives possession for a certain duration in succession.

(iii) The fee simple may be subject to co-ownership. The ownership may be shared between two or more persons. For example, Blackacre is held by H and W in fee simple. Each tenant shares the same interest and is entitled to possession at the same time—not in succession.[41]

Co-ownership and the settlement represent the two ways (in addition to leases) of splitting up ownership of land in English law. They are the two possible forms of limited ownership. That is, in both cases, each tenant has something less than absolute ownership.

---

[40] See below, p. 194.
[41] Leaseholds can also be created. And leasehold ownership itself can be split up in the same way. A 999-year lease of Blackacre, for example, can be held solely by X; it can be settled, *e.g.* on A for life, remainder to B in fee tail; or it can be held in co-ownership. But it should be noted that (a) before 1926 a fee tail could not be created in leasehold lands; and (b) whatever interest is created will necessarily determine when the lease expires.

Before 1926, this splitting up of ownership was possible both in law and in equity behind a trust. Suppose that G, the fee simple owner of Blackacre, wanted to settle it on A for life remainder to B in fee tail. Generally, he had a choice between doing it in law and equity. He could convey the legal estate to A for life remainder to B in fee tail. Here A would have a legal (and equitable) life interest; B would have a legal (and equitable) fee tail. On the other hand, he could convey the land to X and Y in fee simple in trust for A for life remainder to B in fee tail. Here the interests of A and B would only be equitable. X and Y between them would have absolute ownership at common law although they would be forced by equity to exercise this ownership for the benefit of A and B according to their respective interests.

The reasons why the landowner should choose one rather than the other method have been mentioned[42] and need not be investigated further. What we are concerned with is the way in which this splitting up of ownership could affect a purchaser.

Suppose that Blackacre was on the market and that P was interested in buying. It is important to emphasise, and this is still relevant, that what P would want in return for his money would be absolute beneficial ownership for himself so that he could do with it whatever he wanted. He would want to obtain the whole fee simple in law and equity. To obtain this he would have to obtain the consent of every person with any interest, legal or equitable, in the land. This would include not only those with ownership interests but also those with third party rights. Failing this he might take subject to the interest in question.

To protect himself our prospective purchaser P would have to investigate the ownership of the land very carefully. Whether the settlement suggested above had been created in law or equity, he would have to investigate all the complex details of the settlement itself. The settlement would be on the title. And the settlement would not be a simple matter of two or three interests as in the illustration used here. The ordinary settlement was an extremely complex pattern of rights, interests and powers affecting the land. More will be said about this later. But two further points are relevant here:

(a)*Necessary consents might not be obtainable.*   There might be limited owners whose consent to the sale could not be obtained, either because they were under age, or not yet born or because they just refused to give their consent. In the illustration above (to A for life, remainder to B in fee tail), P could perhaps obtain the consent of A and B. A and B might both be desirous of selling and

---

[42] Above, p. 161.

see the advantage from everyone's point of view. But this would not be enough. The point about the fee tail, indeed the reason for its use by settlors, was that the fee tail tenant could not alienate the interest. If P simply took a conveyance from A and B, he would be in for a surprise on the death of B. The fee tail would take its normal course and pass to B's descendant heir. P would have acquired no more than an interest for the life of A and B. The only way in which the rights of B's descendants could be destroyed would be by B barring the entail and turning it into a fee simple. This is considered later.[43] It is sufficient here to say that it could only be done by B when he came of age (and with the consent of A); and that in practice when he did come of age the land would immediately be resettled on A for life remainder to B for life remainder to B's infant son in fee tail. Once this resettlement had taken place there was once again a consent which could not be obtained. Once again the land could not be sold until the son came of age or a private Act of Parliament had been obtained.

(b)*Powers of appointment.*[44] The existence of powers of appointment might further complicate the settlement and hinder sale of the land. The tenant for life or some other person might be given a power of appointment by the settlement. This meant that he was given power to deal with the land by transferring a beneficial interest from one person to another of his choosing. For example, Blackacre is given "To A for life remainder as he shall appoint." As with all other interests a purchaser would have to investigate any powers contained in the settlement. Such powers were a peculiar difficulty. A purchaser might need to satisfy himself whether any power had been exercised. If it had not, he would need proof that it had not; and of course proof of a negative is always more difficult.

Principle 6. The 1925 legislation and trust ownership

As part of the plan to simplify conveyancing, the 1925 legislation made the following changes affecting trust ownership:

(1) The legal freehold and leasehold ownership of land (*i.e.* the legal fee simple absolute in possession and the legal term of years absolute) cannot now be split up into lesser freehold[45] estates.[46]

---

[43] Below, p. 249.
[44] See below, Chap. 10, for powers of appointment.
[45] But any number of legal leases and sub-leases can still be created. See above, p. 109; below, p. 584. In fact, life interests and fee tails could never be carved out of a legal lease. A life interest, but not a fee tail, could be created out of a lease in equity.
[46] L.P.A. 1925, s. 1 (1).

(2) Not more than four persons at any time can share ownership of the legal estate.[47]

(3) The ownership of land can still be split up into lesser freehold estates by settlement and co-ownership, but only in equity behind a trust. The owners of the legal estate will be trustees holding in trust for the beneficiaries who will have equitable interests.[48]

(4) Most such beneficial interests will be overreached on sale. This means that a purchaser of the legal estate from the trustees will not be concerned with these interests since they will be overreached, that is they will be transferred from the land to the proceeds of sale in the hands of the trustees.[49]

(5) The scope of the old distinction between legal and equitable interests has been restricted by:

(a) The overreaching machinery which applies to beneficial interests under a trust.

(b) The machinery providing for the registration of a large number of third party rights.[50]

(c) The machinery for the registration of title.

Explanation

The 1925 legislation comprises the Acts passed in 1925 incorporating and improving on the piecemeal statutory reforms of the nineteenth century, and designed to put land law on a modern basis, and in particular to simplify the machinery governing the transfer of land (conveyancing). The legislation did not altogether replace the old land law developed by the courts of common law and equity. Parts of it were left alone; parts were incorporated into the legislation. But many fundamental changes were made.

The legislation was not revolutionary. It was not intended to interfere with the recognised forms of land ownership or to limit the ways in which a landowner could distribute his land. It was not an attack on settlements or co-ownership or any other form of ownership. It merely altered the legal machinery by which these interests could be created.

Basically, Parliament was aiming to ensure the free alienability of land.[51] In particular:

---

[47] Trustee Act 1925, s. 34 (2). There can be more than four joint tenants for life under the S.L.A. 1925.

[48] See L.P.A. 1925, s. 1. (3).

[49] See below, p. 280 *et seq.*

[50] See below, at pp. 518, 540.

[51] And this aim was no more than a reflection of its new function as a commodity which industrial and commercial property owners in the nineteenth century expected land to fulfil.

(a) To remove any obstacles which might impede the dealing with land; and to ensure that at any time there would be someone (or a limited number of persons) with the effective power to sell and deal with any piece of land.

(b) To simplify land law and conveyancing, abolishing archaic rules and distinctions and, in general, making the business of selling a piece of land more like that of selling a motor car or stocks and shares.

This aim—the free alienability of land—is examined further in the chapter on settlements. This present Principle is concerned with one aspect, the way in which Parliament used the device of the trust to achieve this aim.

Trust ownership as a conveyancing device. As a result of the changes made in 1925, the position today is this:

A landowner can settle his land—he can make as complex a settlement as he likes. He can create co-ownership. There is no limit on the number of persons who can be given limited beneficial ownership interests in land. But the legislation insists that these limited ownership interests can only exist behind a trust. The legal ownership can no longer be split up—except that it can be held by up to four individuals jointly. The owners of the legal estate—the trustees—will have all the powers of dealing with the land, selling leasing, etc. These powers are not absolute. There are limits which will be considered later; and they exist and must be exercised for the benefit of the beneficiaries entitled in equity. What is important is that, with a few exceptions, any attempt to take these powers away from the trustees or to control their exercise—that is any attempt to restrict the free alienability of the land—will be void.

All this means that at any time there will be up to no more than four persons who have the power of dealing with the land. To discover with whom to deal, a purchaser will simply have to find out who the owners of the legal estate are.

If the legislature had stopped there, the sale and purchase of land would not have been much easier. A purchaser would have had no trouble with the legal estate but he would still have had to concern himself with all the complexities of the equitable interests because of the doctrine of notice. The equities would still have been on the title.

But the legislation is carefully designed to keep the equities off the title, *i.e.* to make sure that a purchaser is not concerned with and cannot be affected by the equitable interests whether or not he has notice of them. The doctrine of notice is no longer generally of relevance in the case of beneficial equitable interests behind a trust. Provided that certain requirements are satisfied, for example, provided there are a least two trustees or a trust corporation to receive the purchase money—the interests of the beneficiaries behind the trust will be overreached; that is they will be transferred from the land to the purchase money. The purchaser will get for his money the legal estate free of any equitable beneficial interests. He will become owner in law and equity, that is, beneficial owner. The beneficiaries will get interests in the money equivalent to the interests which they had in the land.

It will be seen that the legislation has made one fundamental change in the position of the beneficiaries. Their interests can be converted, in general without their consent, from land into money. This sacrifice of the beneficiaries—if it is regarded as such—was necessary if free alienability was to be achieved.

Further, it will be noted that the complexities of settlements have not been made to disappear. It is just that now they do not concern the purchaser. They are left to be sorted out between the trustees and the beneficiaries when dealing with the proceeds of sale.

To illustrate the present position with a very simple example, S, the beneficial fee simple absolute in possession owner of Blackacre wishes to leave it by will to his wife (W) for life remainder equally between his 12 sons. Under modern law the only way to do this is to give the legal fee simple absolute in possession to trustees (say X and Y) in trust for W for life remainder to the 12 sons equally.[52] The trustees will be able to sell; if they do sell, for example to P, P will take a conveyance of the legal estate from them. He will have to make sure that they do own it. But provided he satisfies the overreaching machinery he will not be concerned with the interests of W and the 12 sons. Whereas under the old law he might have had 13 persons to deal with (possibly with further complications arising from infancy, etc.), here he will have only two and cannot have more than four.

W will have her life interest in the land till it is sold. If it is sold her interest will continue in the proceeds of sale. The sons, if the land has been sold, will then share the money between them. (This example assumes that a trust for sale is being employed.)

Principle 7. Present day reasons for using trust ownership

The following are the main reasons for using trust ownership today:

(1) As a device to simplify conveyancing.

---

[52] W herself may be made one of the trustees.

(2) Where, for some reason, it is not wished to give the beneficiaries control of the property.

(3) In the case of constructive trusts, where equity considers it just that the owner should be made to hold his property for someone else's benefit (see below, page 188).

Explanation

(1) **The trust as a conveyancing device.**[53] In some cases the trust serves no other purpose. This is particularly true of co-ownership. In other cases, although the trust does serve this purpose, it also serves some other purpose at the same time.

(2)**Keeping control away from the beneficiaries.** Particularly in the case of complex settlements, it may be convenient from a management point of view as well as desirable from a conveyancing point of view, to have control of the property in the hands of a limited number of trustees rather than the beneficiaries. For example:

(a) Where the intended beneficiary is an infant or a charity.[54]

(b) Where the aim is to relieve the beneficiary of the burden of management. If a husband is making a will and wants to leave his house to his wife for life if she survives him, he will in any case have to use a trust. But his choice between the two possible forms of trust will be based on convenience.[55] If he wants her to have the benefit of the property without the worry of management, he will probably leave it to trustees on trust for sale for her benefit. This is explained later.[56]

(c) Where the intended beneficiaries are not yet ascertained, and perhaps not even born; for example, a gift "To all the sons of my son S who reach the age of 21 in equal shares." It is desirable to have trustees to manage the trust property until all the qualifying sons are ascertained.

(d) In the case of protective and discretionary trusts,[57] the property is kept out of the hands of the intended beneficiary in order to save him from his own extravagance and the property from his creditors and the Inland Revenue.[58]

---

[53] See above, p. 171.
[54] For infants and charities, see below, Chap. 13.
[55] See below, p. 200 for two types of trust which can be used.
[56] See below, Chap. 8.
[57] See further below, p. 297.
[58] But the extent to which such settlements can be used to avoid tax liabilities is now limited.

It needs to be emphasised that under modern law, in most of these cases, some form of trust is compulsory.

(3)**Constructive trusts.** These cases illustrate equity fulfilling its time-honoured function of interfering with the strict legal position in order to do justice.

SECTION II. CREATION OF TRUST OWNERSHIP

Principle 8. Methods of creation

Trust ownership can arise by the following methods:
   (i) express trusts,
   (ii) statute,
   (iii) implied trusts,
   (iv) resulting trusts,
   (v) imposed by equity—constructive trusts.

Principle 9. Express trusts

A landowner can expressly subject his land to a trust provided:
   (a) he complies with the necessary formalities;
   (b) the three certainties are present.

Explanation

Express creation is the normal method by which a trust will come into existence. For one reason or another the landowner will wish to subject his land to a trust and he will execute the necessary documents. In many cases he will have no choice. For example, if he is making his will and wishes to settle his land on his wife for life remainder to his eldest son in fee simple, this can only be done behind a trust.[59] If the will does not create it expressly, the trust will be imposed by statute. In practice in such a situation the landowner will probably create the trust expressly.

The will will probably contain something like the following[60]:

"I give to my trustees in fee simple my property situated at Ashford in the County of Kent and known at Blackacre UPON TRUST with the consent in writing during the life of my said wife to sell the same with full power to postpone the sale for so long as they shall in their absolute discretion think

---

[59] Either a trust for sale or a strict settlement under the S.L.A. 1925; see below, p. 200.
[60] Hallett, *Conveyancing Precedents* (1965), p. 987.

fit and to hold the net proceeds of sale and other moneys
applicable as capital and the net rents and profits until sale IN
TRUST for my said wife during her life And from after the
death of my said wife IN TRUST for my son absolutely.

"AND I EMPOWER my Trustees during the life of my
said wife to permit her to have the use and enjoyment of the
said property for such period or periods as they shall in their
absolute discretion think fit pending postponement of the sale
she paying the rates taxes and other outgoings and keeping
the same in good repair and insured against fire to the full
value thereof in some office of repute nominated by my
Trustees in the joint names of herself and my Trustees."

(a)**Formalities for express creation.** In general a deed is
necessary to create or transfer a legal estate.[61] This does make it
easier for a purchaser to trace legal ownership. In the case of
unregistered land there will be a series of deeds (or at least formal
documents) showing clearly how legal ownership has passed from
one person to another.

The same formality is not required for the creation of equitable
ownership. In the case of trusts arising by operation of law
(implied, resulting and constructive trusts)[62] there may be no
written evidence at all. This may make it more difficult to establish
equitable ownership but it does mean that a person is not denied
his interest for want of a deed or document.

For the *express*[63] creation and transfer of equitable interests
certain formalities must be observed. They are:

(i) The creation of a trust affecting land must be evidenced in
writing and signed by the person creating the trust.[64] This rule
does not affect the creation of a trust of pure personalty[65] nor does
it apply to resulting, implied or constructive trusts of land.[66]

(ii) The transfer of an existing beneficial equitable interest under
a trust must be *in* writing signed by the person transferring the
interest or his agent authorised in writing.[67]

It will be noted that the first rule concerns the creation of a new

[61] L.P.A. 1925, s. 52.
[62] See below, p. 177 *et seq.*
[63] These requirements do not apply to resulting, implied or constructive trusts.
[64] L.P.A. 1925, s. 53(1) *(b)*.
[65] *i.e.* not land.
[66] See *Bannister* v. *Bannister* [1948] 2 All E.R. 133.
[67] L.P.A. 1925, s. 53 (1) *(c)*. But note *D.H.N. Food Distributors* v. *London Borough of Tower Hamlets* [1976] 3 All E.R. 462 (C.A.).

equitable interest. The second rule concerns the transfer of an existing interest.

(b) **Express creation and the three certainties.**[68] Apart from satisfying formalities, a person wishing to create a trust must make sure that it satisfies what are called the three certainties: certainty of words, subject-matter and objects. Otherwise his intention may be defeated.

(i) *Certainty of words.* The words used by the grantor must be imperative. It is not enough to show a hope or a desire that the property be held on trust. They must make it clear that it *must* be so held. There is no essential magic formula that must be used, but the words which are used must show this necessary intention. If they do not then there will be no trust at all and if the property has been transferred the transferee will take it as a gift free of any trust.

In *Re Adams and Kensington Vestry*[69] the testator gave all his real and personal estate unto and to the absolute use of his wife, her heirs, executors and administrators and assigns "in full confidence that she would do what was right as to the disposal thereof between his children, either during her lifetime or by her will at decease." After the death of the testator the widow had sold the land which formed part of the property as absolute owner. The purchaser had now agreed to sell to the plaintiff. And the plaintiff was refusing to complete on the grounds that the widow had held on trust and had therefore had no right to sell as absolute owner. If this was correct, the purchaser had not obtained a good title and the plaintiff was fully justified in refusing to complete with him. It was held that the words used by the testator were merely precatory—they expressed a wish—but did not show an intention to create a trust. Consequently, the widow had been absolute owner and the purchaser could give a good title to the plaintiff.

(ii) *Certainty of subject-matter.* The property held on trust must be identified with certainty. If it cannot be identified the whole transaction will be ineffective. If, for example, a testator makes a will, leaving the "bulk of my property"[70] to trustees to hold on specified trusts, such a provision will have no effect at all.

Further, the interest to be taken by each beneficiary must be specified with certainty.

(iii) *Certainty of objects.* The beneficiaries must be identified or

[68] See Hanbury and Maudsley, *Modern Equity* (11th ed.), p. 206.
[69] (1884) 27 Ch.D. 394.
[70] *Palmer* v. *Simmonds* (1854) 2 Drew, 221.

identifiable with certainty. "With a 'fixed' trust it is, and always has been, that a trust is void unless it is possible to ascertain each and every beneficiary."[71] Where there is uncertainty as to objects, there will be a resulting trust for the settlor.

Principle 10. Trusts imposed by statute

In certain situations, the 1925 legislation insists upon a trust; and if not created expressly by the parties themselves it will be imposed automatically under the legislation.

Explanation

As already explained, co-ownership and settlements[72] can only exist behind a trust. Further, the legislation provides that an infant can only hold an interest in land behind a trust[73], where a person dies intestate his property is held on trust by his personal representatives; and there are other cases.

Some of these trusts imposed by statute are called "statutory trusts" by the relevant legislation; and in these cases the term "statutory trusts" is given a specific meaning[74]; but the term is convenient to refer to all trusts which are created by statute.

The reason why the legislation insists on a trust, to simplify dealings with land and conveyancing, has already been considered.[75]

Principle 11. Implied Trusts

In certain, well recognised situations the courts will imply a trust. What has happened is sufficient to show an intention to create a trust, although no such intention has been stated expressly.[76] Three of the commonest situations are:

---

[71] See Hanbury and Maudsley, Modern Equity, (11th ed.), p. 210. For the position in the case of discretionary trusts and powers, see below, p. 296.

[72] Above, p. 170.

[73] S.L.A. 1925, s. 1 (2).

[74] See L.P.A. 1925, ss. 34, 35, 36 (co-ownership); A.E.A. 1925, s. 47 (trust of proceeds of sale of estate of intestate).

[75] Above, p. 169.

[76] Or, if it has been stated expressly, not in a form which satisfies statutory formalities.

(1) Joint contribution to the purchase price of land.

(2) Enforceable contract to create or dispose of a legal estate in land.

(3) Enforceable contract to create or dispose of an equitable interest in land.

Implied trusts do not have to satisfy the formal requirements of section 53 of the Law of Property Act 1925.

Explanation

Problem of classification. Any trust recognised by the courts, except an express or statutory trust, will be either implied, resulting or constructive. But there is no general agreement as to the distinction between the three; and the courts have sometimes refused to make any distinction.[77] The distinction suggested in this chapter is therefore tentative. What is more important than the terminology is to be able to identify the situations in which the courts will recognise a trust. There is a further problem; that is the relationship between the trust, contractual licences and proprietary estoppel. This is considered below.[78]

Essentials of implied trust. Apart from the lack of certainty, there are two main reasons why it may be impossible to prove an enforceable express trust. First, because there is no express declaration of trust; secondly, because the formalities required by section 53 of the Law of Property Act 1925, have not been complied with. In *Eves* v. *Eves*[79] a man and woman were cohabiting in a house owned by the man; they had a child and another home was purchased, partly out of the proceeds of the sale of the previous one, partly with the aid of a mortgage loan. The evidence showed that the man had made it clear to the woman that he intended her to have a share in the house, and had told her that if she had not been a minor, he would have had it conveyed into their joint names. After purchase, they both laboured to renovate and improve the house. In the present action, the woman was claiming that the man held the legal estate in trust for both of them. What the man had said probably amounted to an express declaration of trust, but it was unenforceable as such for lack of writing.[80] The issue was, therefore, whether a trust could be established on some other basis.[81]

---

[77] See, *e.g. Gissing* v. *Gissing* [1971] A.C. 886, at p. 905, per Lord Diplock. See generally, Hanbury and Maudsley, Modern Equity, (11th ed.), p. 177.
[78] Below, p. 408.
[79] [1975] 3 All E.R. 768 (C.A.).
[80] Compare *Pascoe* v. *Turner* [1979] 2 All E.R. 945 (C.A.).
[81] See further, below, p. 180.

An implied trust does not have to be declared expressly; nor does it have to satisfy section 53 of the Law of Property Act 1925. The following conditions must, however, be satisfied:

(a) The evidence must show a common intention to create a trust. The courts, as always when deciding whether or not to imply any particular intention, will look at all the surrounding circumstances—what the parties have said and done, their relationship, etc. Undertakings, although not in themselves enforceable, may be evidence of intention.[82] And, although the intention must have existed at the moment the trust is alleged to have been created, subsequent conduct may be evidence of what that intention was.[83]

Furthermore, in certain recognised situations,[84] the courts will presume the necessary intention (in the absence of evidence to the contrary) without further evidence. For example, in the case of joint contribution to the purchase price of land. If A and B both contribute to the purchase price of Blackacre which is conveyed into A's sole name, the contribution itself will normally be sufficient for the courts to presume an intention that A should hold the legal estate in trust for A and B as tenants in common in shares in proportion to their respective contributions.[85] Thus, in *Bull* v. *Bull*[86] the property was conveyed to the son, although his mother had contributed to the purchase price. It was held that he held in trust for both of them.

(b) The intention must be embraced in an express or implied contractual agreement. This follows from the principle that equity will not aid a volunteer. Consideration is not necessary to create a valid express trust, but in the case of an implied trust it must be present: though, failing consideration and an implied trust, there may be some sort of proprietary estoppel or constructive trust.[87]

In *Pettitt* v. *Pettitt*[88] a cottage was purchased by the wife and conveyed into her sole name. It was used as a matrimonial home. At that stage there could be no suggestion that the husband had any interest. But he was something of a do it yourself enthusiast and carried out improvements, purchasing the materials and doing the work himself. Among other things, he installed a built in wardrobe, laid a lawn, constructed an ornamental well and a side

---

[82] See *Re Nicholson* [1974] 2 All E.R. 386 (Pennycuick V.-C.).

[83] See, *e.g. Eves* v. *Eves* [1975] 3 All E.R. 768 (C.A.).

[84] See below, p. 181, for more detail as to these situations.

[85] For the possibility of a contrary presumption in favour of an advancement to A, see, below, p. 184; and see p. 324.

[86] [1955] 1 Q.B. 234 (C.A.); see below, p. 311.

[87] See below, pp. 188, 405.

[88] [1970] A.C. 777 (H.L.). For the position now as to improvements made by a spouse, see below, p. 346.

wall to the garden. Perhaps he was enthusiastic about the wrong things, for the marriage ended in divorce. The husband then claimed to be entitled to an interest in the property representing his contribution. His claim failed. If he had contributed to the purchase price, there would have been an implied trust in his favour; but he had made the additions after the purchase had been completed. The ownership of the property had been fixed at the time of purchase. Only an agreement made between them for value could alter it subsequently—if, for example, they had agreed that, if he did the work, he would have an equitable interest in the property in return. There was no evidence of such an agreement. He had in effect made a gift to her of the work and materials.

In *Eves* v. *Eves*[89] a trust could not have been implied on the basis of the defendant's declaration alone. And at first instance, Pennycuick V.-C. found that "the plaintiff's activities were too slight to warrant the inference that when the house was purchased the parties had the common intention to pay the price on the basis of joint contribution in cash or kind."[90] In other words, the work done by the plaintiff (including wielding a fourteen pound sledge hammer) was held to be a subsequent, voluntary act, unrelated to any express or implied promise made by the defendant. In the Court of Appeal, however, reversing Pennycuick V.-C., the court was able to infer that there was such a relationship and a bargain. Brightman J. said[91]: "If, however, it was part of the bargain between the parties, express or to be implied, that the plaintiff should contribute her labour towards the reparation of a house in which she was to have some beneficial interest, then I think that the arrangement becomes one to which the law can give effect. This seems to be consistent with the reasoning in *Gissing* v. *Gissing*.[92] Pennycuick V.-C. was unable to find any such link in the evidence, and I respectfully agree with him that it is not to be found there. But I do not for my own part find much difficulty in inferring that link."

(c) The agreement must be enforceable in equity. Where the agreement is within the Law of Property Act 1925, section 40, this means that there must be a sufficient written memorandum or act of part performance.[93] Otherwise, the person claiming the beneficial interest must have spent money or otherwise acted to his detriment in reliance on the common intention to create a trust.

---

[89] [1975] 3 All E.R. 768 (C.A.).
[90] *Ibid*, at p. 774.
[91] *Ibid*, at p. 774.
[92] [1970] 2 All E.R. 780.
[93] See below, p. 555 for s.40 and part performance.

It is difficult to see why, in some cases such as *Binions* v. *Evans*,[94] the court has not considered the applicability of the Law of Property Act 1925, section 40.[95] Where an equitable interest arises out of (at least an express) contract, section 40 would seem to apply.[96] What does seem clear is that where section 40 and the doctrine of part performance have not been applied, the courts have required the person claiming the benefit of the trust, to show that he has acted to his detriment in reliance on the common intention.[97]

Joint contribution to the purchase price of land.[98] As already mentioned, where A and B both contribute to the acquisition of land which is conveyed into A's sole name, the most usual inference is that the common intention is, in consideration of the contribution, that A is to hold the legal estate in trust for A and B; that in effect B is purchasing a beneficial interest.[99]

In such situations a number of questions may have to be answered. First, has B made a contribution to the *acquisition*? Secondly, if there was a contribution, does the evidence show that something other than a trust was intended? Thirdly, if a trust was intended, what share of the beneficial interest was B intended to acquire?

To take these questions in turn.

First, has there been a contribution? If the full purchase price is paid outright in cash, there is no problem. But, today, most of the purchase price is commonly paid by mortgage instalments over a long period of time subsequent to the actual conveyance. In a matrimonial or cohabitation situation, both partners are likely to be working and bringing money into the home; one partner's wage packet may be used directly to pay the mortgage instalments whilst the other's is used for other household expenses; further, there is some social willingness today to recognise that housework and caring for children has a financial value and can be seen as a contribution to the acquisition of the property.[1] In this context,

---

[94] [1972] Ch. 359 (C.A.).

[95] See below, p. 555, for s. 40.

[96] See, *e.g. Daulia Ltd.* v. *Four Millbank Nominees Ltd.* [1978] 2 W.L.R. 621 (C.A.).

[97] See *Christian* v. *Christian* (1981) 131 N.L.J. 43. It is perhaps arguable that where s.40 has not been satisfied, the court is giving effect not to the common intention but to the equity arising from the act in detriment; in which case the trust is perhaps more appropriately classified as constructive; see below, p. 188.

[98] See Hanbury and Maudsley, *Modern Equity* (11th ed.), p. 324.

[99] For possible presumption of advancement in favour of A, see below, p. 184.

[1] Note Inheritance (Provision For Family and Dependants) Act 1975, s. 3 (2).

the question has to be asked, what today will the courts recognise as a contribution to the purchase price.

In *Hazell* v. *Hazell*[2] a house was purcased in the husband's name with the aid of a mortgage loan. The wife went out to work and used her wage to meet household expenses thus making it easier for the husband to pay the mortgage instalments. The issue was whether the wife had been making a contribution or simply paying household expenses unrelated to the purchase price of the house. There was a specific finding of fact that the wife had gone out to work because otherwise the mortgage payments would have been difficult to meet. On this evidence, the court decided that the wife's payments were referrable to the acquisition and a trust implied.

It is not clear what sort of contribution will be recognised as sufficient to raise a presumption of a trust in such situations. In the leading case of *Gissing* v. *Gissing*[3] Lord Pearson said[4]:

> "Contributions are not limited to those made directly in part payment of the price of the property or to those made at the time when the property is conveyed into the name of one of the spouses. For instance, there can be a contribution if, by arrangement between the spouses, one of them by payment of the household expenses enables the other to pay the mortgage instalments."

The decision in any particular case will depend on the inference drawn by the court from all the evidence surrounding the payments (and perhaps the social attitude of the judge); but, perhaps, certain general points can be made.

First, there is no doctrine of community of assets under English family law; that is, the mere existence of marriage or cohabitation does not by itself entitle a partner to a share in any assets acquired.[5] Nor is there any generally accepted doctrine of joint effort, that is that any effort, financial or labour, put into the maintenance of the home and family, should be reflected in an implied trust of the matrimonial home and assets.[6]

Secondly, if the contribution is a direct financial one to the deposit or mortgage repayments, the courts will readily imply a trust.

[2] [1972] 1 All E.R. 923 (C.A.); and see *Smith* v. *Baker* [1970] 1 W.L.R. 1160.
[3] [1971] A.C. 886 (H.L.).
[4] *Ibid*, at p. 903.
[5] See Jill Martin, s. 70 (1) (*g*) and Vendor's Spouse, [1980] Conv. 361.
[6] But see, *e.g.* language of Lord Denning in *Fribance* v. *Fribance* (No. 2) [1957] 1 W.L.R. 384, at p. 387; and in *Chapman* v. *Chapman* [1969] 3 All E.R. 476, at p. 478; and *Eves* v. *Eves* [1975] 3 All E.R. 768; see below p. 343.

Thirdly, if the contribution is indirect, as in *Hazell* v. *Hazell*,[7] the courts are likely to want further evidence to relate it to the acquisition of the property.

Fourthly, although the relationship between the parties will not, itself, give rise to a trust, that relationship may be a relevant factor in determining the common intention. The courts have stated that the same principles apply between cohabitees as between married couples[8] but where there is a marriage or the intention to marry and set up a home, the courts are probably more likely to imply a trust.[9]

The second question referred to above is, if a contribution is found, whether the intention was to create a trust or some other relationship.

In *Richards* v. *Dove*[10] a man and a woman cohabited in a flat. He paid the rent and electricity. She paid for the gas, cooking and food. Then a house was bought for £3,500 and conveyed into his sole name. £3,150 was raised by a local authority mortgage loan. He provided £50 and the balance of £300 came out of a joint deposit account. When he tried to evict her, she claimed a trust for them both as tenants in common. The court held that the £150 from the joint account had been intended as a loan (which she could of course reclaim) but which gave her no interest in the property.

In *Cooke* v. *Head*,[11] in contrast, a trust was found to exist. Here a man and woman purchased land with a view to building a house and marrying. The claimant woman not only contributed money to the acquisition (to the mortgage payments) but also did a lot of heavy building work on the house. It was this last fact which was held in *Richards* v. *Dove*[12] to justify a distinction; and clearly it is difficult to interpret labour as a loan.

In other cases, the courts have inferred that a licence, not a trust, was intended.[13]

---

[7] [1972] 1 All E.R. 923 (C.A.); and see *Eves* v. *Eves* [1975] 3 All E.R. 768 (C.A.).
[8] See *Cooke* v. *Head* [1972] 2 All E.R. 38 (C.A.); and *Richards* v. *Dove* [1974] 1 All E.R. 888 (Walton J.).
[9] Compare *Eves* v. *Eves* [1975] 3 All E.R. 768 (C.A.) and *Tanner* v. *Tanner* [1975] 3 All E.R. 776 (C.A.). For view that decisive factor is whether the parties constitute a single economic unit, see A.A.S. Zuckerman, (1978) 94 L.Q.R. 26.
[10] [1974] 1 All E.R. 888 (Walton J.).
[11] [1972] 2 All E.R. 38 (C.A.) Compare *Eves* v. *Eves* [1975] 3 All E.R. 768 (C.A.): *Hussey* v. *Palmer* [1972] 1 W.L.R. 1286; and *Re Sharpe* [1980] 1 All E.R. 198 (Browne-Wilkinson J.).
[12] [1974] 1 All E.R. 888 (Walton J.).
[13] See *Tanner* v. *Tanner* [1975] 3 All E.R. 776 (C.A.); and *Re Sharpe* [1980] 1 All E.R. 198. For these cases and the question whether a licence may exist as a proprietary interest behind a trust, see below, p. 409.

Alternatively, the courts may find that a gift of the property was intended by the contributor. In certain relationships, where the contributor is the husband, parent or *in loco parentis* to the person to whom the property is conveyed, the intention to make a gift is presumed in the absence of contrary evidence. This is called the presumption of advancement.[14]

The third and final question mentioned above is, assuming a trust creating contribution, what share in the property it will give rise to. The general rule is clear. The contributor will be entitled to a share in proportion to his contribution. But there may be evidence of a different intention. And in some cases, the courts may apply the principle that equality is equity, particularly where it is difficult to isolate and quantify the respective contributions. In *Re Densham*[15] a house was purchased and conveyed into the husband's sole name. He was subsequently convicted of theft against his employers who took action to recover the amount stolen. This resulted in his bankruptcy. The present action was between the trustee in bankruptcy and the wife who claimed an equal share in the house. It was *held* that the evidence showed a common intention at the time of acquisition that the house should belong to them jointly.[16] Unfortunately, this agreement was void under section 41(1) of the Bankruptcy Act 1914. The court then had to resort to the general principle and held her only to be entitled in proportion to her actual contribution to the acquisition.[17] The court refused to apply the maxim that equality is equity. But, in contrast, in *Gissing* v. *Gissing*[18] Lord Pearson said that if there has been "a very substantial contribution . . . but the proportion borne by the contribution to the total price or cost is difficult to fix," the courts may be prepared to apply the maxim. But he also said[19]: "I think also that the decision of cases of this kind has been made more difficult by excessive application of the maxim 'equality is equity.' "[20]

---

[14] It is doubtful whether this presumption is today very strong in the case of a husband; see *Pettitt* v. *Pettitt* [1970] A.C. 777 at pp. 815, 824; and see *Gross* v. *French* (1976) 238 E.G. 39 (C.A.).

[15] [1975] 3 All E.R. 726 (Goff J.).

[16] For joint tenancies, see below, p. 312.

[17] Goff J. refused to give her credit for the fact that the husband had paid her reduced housekeeping for part of the time so that he could pay the mortgage instalments; or, more remarkably, for the mortgage repayments made by her out of her social security allowance while he was in prison.

[18] [1971] A.C. 886 at p. 903.

[19] *Ibid*, at p. 903.

[20] Contrast Lord Denning in the earlier case of *Chapman* v. *Chapman* [1969] 3 All E.R. 476, at p. 478. See also *Re Nicholson* [1974] 2 All E.R. 386.

Conduct subsequent to the acquisition: The improvement cases.
In the joint purchase cases, for a trust to be implied, the general
rule is that the contribution must be to the acquisition and the
common intention to create a trust must exist at that time.

In general, if subsequent and unrelated to the acquisition, B
puts money or labour into the improvement of land owned by A,
the courts will presume a voluntary gift which will not give rise to
any beneficial interest. The leading case of *Pettitt* v. *Pettitt*[21] has
been mentioned. This general principle needs however to be
qualified.

1. Subsequent conduct may be evidence of the intention at the
time of acquisition.

2. It may be found to be the payment, agreed at the time of
acquisition, in return for which the beneficial interest was to be
granted.

In both these cases there must be evidence from which the
courts can infer a connection between the acquisition and the
subsequent work or payment.[22]

3. There may be evidence from which the courts can find a fresh
bargain to grant a beneficial interest in return for the money or
work.

4. As between husband and wife, the rule in *Pettitt* v. *Pettitt*[23] has
been changed by legislation. Under section 37 of the Matrimonial
Proceedings and Property Act 1970, if a spouse makes a
substantial contribution in money or money's worth to the
improvement of the matrimonial home, a trust will be presumed to
the extent of the contribution.[24]

Contract to create or transfer legal estate. Where there is a
contract to create or transfer a legal estate, the purchaser will not
obtain the legal estate until completion and delivery of the deed of
conveyance.[25] But, provided the contract is specifically
enforceable,[26] equity will recognise the contract as creating not
only contractual rights but also an immediate equitable interest in

---

[21] [1970] A.C. 777 (H.L.); see above, p. 179; and see *Pascoe* v. *Turner* [1979] 2 All
E.R. 945 (C.A.).
[22] See *Hazell* v. *Hazell* [1972] 1 All E.R. 923 (C.A.); *Eves* v. *Eves* [1975] 3 All E.R.
768 (C.A.).
[23] [1970] A.C. 777 (H.L.).
[24] See *Kowalczuk* v. *Kowalczuk* [1973] 2 All E.R. 1042 (C.A.); *Griffiths* v.
Griffiths [1974] 1 All E.R. 932 (C.A.); *Re Nicholson* [1974] 2 All E.R. 386
(Pennycuick J.); *Cann* v. *Ayres* [1977] Fam. Law 47 (C.A.).
[25] L.P.A. 1925, s. 52. In exceptional cases, a deed is not necessary; see, *e.g.* L.P.A.
1925, s. 54 (2).
[26] *i.e.* in general, supported by sufficient written evidence or part performance;
L.P.A. 1925, s.40; see above, p. 180; below, p. 555.

the land. They will imply into the contract an intention, pending completion, to hold the legal estate in trust for the purchaser to the extent of the agreed interest.[27]

This principle applies, for example, to the ordinary contract to transfer the beneficial freehold or leasehold interest. It also applies, under the doctrine in *Walsh* v. *Lonsdale*,[28] to a contract to create a legal lease.[29]

Contract to create or transfer an equitable interest in land. The same doctrine of the implied trust can apply where the contract is to transfer or create something less than a legal estate, an equitable interest, or some other limited occupation right.

In *Binions* v. *Evans*[30] the defendant's husband had worked all his life for the trustees of X estate. He had lived with the defendant, in a house belonging to the trustees. On his death, the trustees made a contract with the defendant allowing her to remain in occupation of the house for the rest of her life rent free. The agreement was in writing and gave the defendant the right to terminate it on four week's notice. It described the agreement as a tenancy at will. Subsequently, the trustees sold the house to the plaintiffs who tried to evict the defendant claiming that she was only a tenant at will. The Court of Appeal held that the term tenancy at will was not a correct description; that, on a proper construction of the agreement, the trustees had shown an intention to allow her to remain there for the rest of her life; that they were therefore trustees and she had an equitable interest in the property.[31]

As already stressed, where the formality requirements of the Law of Property Act 1925, (sections 40 and 53 as the case may be) are not satisfied, the person alleging an implied trust must show that he has acted to his detriment in reliance on the agreement.

---

[27] But it is a limited form of trusteeship; see below, p. 562. For cases in which the presumed intention has been expressly negatived in the contract, see B.M. Hoggett, "Houses on the Never-Never" (1972) 36 Conv. (N.S.) 325; (1975) 39 Conv. (N.S.) 343; T. Shutt and A. Stewart, *Instalment Mortgages in Birmingham*, (1976) 126 N.L.J. 217. See also *Hyde* v. *Pearce* [1982] 1 All E.R. 1029 (C.A.).

[28] (1882) 21 Ch.D. 9; see above, p. 110.

[29] See also, *Daulia Ltd.* v. *Four Millbank Nominees Ltd.* [1978] 2 W.L.R. 621 (C.A.), particularly Buckley L.J. at p. 632; compare *Pritchard* v. *Briggs* [1980] Ch. 338 (C.A.); see also *Mountford* v. *Scott* [1975] 1 All E.R. 198 (C.A.).

[30] [1972] Ch. 359 (C.A.).

[31] There was some disagreement as to the nature of that interest. Megaw and Stephenson L.J.J. held that she had a life tenancy under the S.L.A. 1925; Lord Denning thought she had an irrevocable contractual licence which amounted to an interest in the property; see below, p. 402. It is arguable that *Binions* v. *Evans* was an express trust since it was in writing and although the term "trust" was not used, the intention was clearly expressed.

Principle 12. Trusts not exhaustive: Resulting Trusts[32]

Where a landowner has created a trust of his property but has not disposed of the whole beneficial (equitable) interest, the residue of the beneficial interest will be held in trust for the landowner himself.

Explanation

Suppose that G transfers the legal freehold in Blackacre to X and Y in trust for A for life. Subject to A's life interest, the trustees will hold in trust for G himself; the beneficial interest is said to return or result to G.

The term resulting trust is also sometimes used to describe the situation where A provides the whole or part of the purchase money of land which is conveyed to B. The beneficial interest is said to result to the person who provided the money in proportion to his contribution. This type of situation has already been considered in the context of implied trusts. As already said, there is no generally agreed basis of classification of trusts. But perhaps this can be suggested. Unlike the implied trust (as defined in this book), the resulting trust does not depend on the common, contractual intention of the parties. It operates automatically where there has been no effective disposition of the beneficial interest. When considering the acquisition of land, it is necessary to consider first whether there is any evidence (using the various presumptions, *e.g.* advancement, where relevant) from which an effective disposition of the beneficial interest can be inferred. Failing this, there will be a resulting trust in favour of the person who provided the money or property.[33] If, for example, A has provided the whole of the purchase money of Blackacre, and the only available evidence is a conveyance of the legal estate to B, (and no relationship to raise the presumption of an advancement in favour of B), then it can be said that there can only be a resulting trust in favour of A.[34]

---

[32] On the nature of resulting trusts, see *Re Vandervell's Trusts* [1973] 3 W.L.R. 744 (Megarry J.); and [1974] 3 W.L.R. 256 (C.A.).

[33] See, *e.g. Re Densham* [1975] 3 All E.R. 726 (Goff J.) which can perhaps be analysed by saying that the intention as found was void leaving a resulting trust to the parties in proportion to their contributions; see above, p. 184. See also, *Cantor* v. *Cox* (1975) 239 E.G. 121 (Plowman V.-C.) where intention to make a gift was found.

[34] The definition of the resulting trust used here is perhaps a narrow one, described as an automatic resulting trust in *Re Vandervell's Trusts* (No. 2) [1974] Ch. 269 *per* Megarry J.

It will be appreciated that, in most cases, the same result will be reached whether based on the implied or the resulting trust.

Principle 13. Trusts imposed by equity—Constructive trusts

In some cases the parties have done nothing which shows any intention at all, express or implied, to create a trust. Nevertheless, equity considers that for one reason or another the property should be held in trust for someone else. It therefore imposes a trust.

Explanation

The commonest case is where a trustee uses his position as trustee or uses the trust property to acquire property for himself. He will be forced to hold any property so acquired as part of the trust property. To take an extreme example. Suppose that the trustee of land deposits the deeds with his bank manager as security for a loan. He takes the borrowed money to Newmarket races and "invests" it on a horse. If the horse wins he will hold the winnings as part of the trust property. And if he loses he will have to make good the loss caused by his breach of trust.[35]

In *Protheroe* v. *Protheroe*[36] a husband held the lease of a house which was used as a matrimonial home in trust for himself and his wife in equal shares. After the wife had commenced divorce proceedings against him, he purchased the freehold reversion in the property. It was held that he must hold the reversion as trustee and that his wife was entitled to an equal share in the proceeds of the subsequent sale of the reversion by the husband.[37]

There are other cases in which equity will impose a trust.[38] For example, where a person meddles with trust property he will become trustee of it *de son tort*. Again, a purchaser of a legal estate in unregistered land subject to a trust is bound by the trust if he has notice of it (unless he can claim the benefit of overreaching machinery or some statutory protection).[39] It is said that he has become subject to a constructive trust; but this is perhaps based on a misconception. Once property has become subject to a trust, whether it is express, implied or constructive, that *same* trust and

---

[35] For the powers of trustees to raise money on mortgage and to invest trust funds, see below, pp. 217, 219.
[36] [1968] 1 W.L.R. 519. And see *Keech* v. *Sandford* (1726) Sel. Cas. t. King 61; and *Re Edwards Will Trusts* [1981] 2 All E.R. 941 (C.A.)..
[37] For criticism of this decision, see (1968) 84 L.Q.R. 309.
[38] See Hanbury and Maudsley, Modern Equity (11th ed.), p. 369 *et seq.*
[39] See below, pp. 234, 241.

the same equitable interest will continue to bind the land in the hands of a purchaser (subject to the doctrine of notice, etc.). If it was originally an express trust, it will continue to be the same express trust.

In *Peffer* v. *Rigg*[40] the notion of a *new*, constructive trust arising on sale was applied to registered land.[41] A house was purchased jointly by P and D1. Title was registered in D1's sole name but it was agreed between them that he should hold in trust for himself and P. Subsequently, D1 purported to transfer the house to his wife D2 who was then registered as proprietor. The issue was whether P's equitable interest was binding on D2. In the case of registered land, such an interest as P's is classified as a minor interest, and in general will only bind a purchaser if protected by an appropriate entry on the register. However, such an unprotected interest will bind a transferee who does not take for valuable consideration or (so it was *held*) who does not take in good faith.[42] It was *held* that the consideration (£1) was nominal and so not valuable[43] and that, in any case, D2 did not take in good faith since she knew of P's interest. This part of the decision may be seen as some limit on the basic philosophy of the land registration machinery, *i.e.* that the state of the title should depend on the state of the register.

What is more relevant in the present context, is the other ground for the decision given by Graham J., namely that, even if protected by section 20, D2 knew of P's interest and so became subject to a constructive trust in his favour. Even if the use of the concept of the constructive trust is correct on the sale of unregistered land, its application to registered land is more than doubtful.[44]

A note on the importance of implied, resulting and constructive trusts

These trusts are important today for a number of reasons.

First, the number of legal estates is fixed by the 1925 legislation and the scope for the courts to develop or extend them is limited.

[40] [1978] 3 All E.R. 745 (Graham J.).
[41] See below, p. 528, for registered land.
[42] See L.R.A. 1925, ss. 20 (1), (4), 58 (6) and see (1977) 40 M.L.R. 602.
[43] As defined in L.R.A. 1925, s. 3 (xxxi). Compare *Mountford* v. *Scott* [1974] 1 All E.R. 249 (Brightman J.); and [1975] 1 All E.R. 198 (C.A.).
[44] As made clear in *Williams & Glyn's Bank Ltd.* v. *Boland* [1980] 2 All E.R. 408 (H.L.), the doctrine of notice is not relevant to registered title. For a possible justification for this part of the decision in *Peffer* v. *Rigg*, see (1977) 40 M.L.R. 602, S. Anderson.

There is no such limit on the number of equitable interests. Using the framework of these trusts, the courts have shown a readiness to develop land law and recognise interests (particularly rights of occupation) which do not fit into the mostly, inflexible scheme of traditional freehold and leasehold estates.[45]

Secondly, whilst the general scheme of the 1925 legislation is in favour of writing and registration for the sake of certainty and simplicity for the purchaser, the courts have used these trusts to give effect to what they consider to be legitimate interests which would otherwise have failed for want of statutory formality. Just as the doctrine of part performance was developed to avoid the formality of (what is now) the Law of Property Act 1925, section 40,[46] so these trusts have provided a way of avoiding the formal requirements of section 53 of the same Act.

Similarly, the need to register many third party rights in unregistered land, has been circumvented by developing such non-registrable rights as proprietary estoppel.[47]

It is partly because the law in the area of these trusts is in a stage of development that it is difficult to offer any generally agreed classification of implied, resulting and constructive trusts.

Thirdly, the advantage of such a development is not to allow people's intentions and expectations to be defeated by formality or rigidity in the law. The disadvantage is to increase the purchaser's risk of finding the land unexpectedly burdened.

Principle 14. Machinery governing trust ownership of land

Most cases of trust ownership will fall into one of three categories:
(a) bare trusts;
(b) trusts for sale;
(c) trusts within the Settled Land Act.
Each of these categories is governed by a separate set of rules.

Explanation

When considering any particular case of trust ownership it is important to decide at the start to which of the above categories it belongs. This is because each of these categories is governed by a separate set of rules. The rights of the beneficiaries, the duties and obligations of the trustees and the position of a purchaser may depend on this classification.

---

[45] See further, below, p. 403.
[46] Previously contained in the Statute of Frauds 1677. s. 4.
[47] See further, below, p. 405.

(a)*The bare trust.*   The bare trust is quite distinct from the other two. It exists where the land is held in trust for the benefit of one adult person absolutely. In such a case the beneficiary is absolute owner in equity. He has complete control and the trustees must comply with his instructions as to the disposition of the property. If he wishes he can require the trustees to convey the legal estate to him thus putting an end to the trust. Even if the terms of the trust specify that the property is to be retained by the trustees and the income accumulated for the benefit of the beneficiary, the latter can insist upon the property being conveyed to him at once—provided of course that he is of full age. This is known as the rule in *Saunders* v. *Vautier*.[48]

(b) (c)*The trust for sale and Settled Land Act trust.*   These are dealt with in detail in the following chapters. They cover all cases where ownership is split up either by settlement or co-ownership. They also provide the machinery for giving beneficial interests in land to infants and charities.

In some cases, legislation stipulates which one of the two must be used—*e.g.* in some cases of co-ownership. In other cases, for example, settlements, the landowner can choose which of the two he is going to use. The differences and relative advantages of the two types are also considered below in Chapter 9.

---

[48] (1841) 4 Beav. 115; see also below, p. 309.

CHAPTER 5

SETTLEMENTS: HISTORY

Right up to the end of the eighteenth century and into the nineteenth century the most important form of wealth in this country was land. The most influential and powerful people were the large landowners. It has been estimated that at the end of the eighteenth century there were about four hundred families who could be described as great landowners; that they owned between them some six million acres or about a fifth of the then cultivated area; that their average income was about £10,000 each a year and that the bulk of this income came from the ownership of land. In addition there were the gentry, perhaps some 25,000 families owning between them 50–60 per cent. of the cultivated land.[1]

England was largely agricultural and the income of these landowners came from the rents paid by their tenant farmers[2]; although they might be able to supplement it by exploiting the timber and mineral wealth of their estates.[3]

There were of course sources of income other than the ownership of land. There were the profits of government and judicial office, marriage to wealthy heiresses, and there was even trade. These might help indeed to produce large fortunes but the fortune was seen as a means of becoming a large landowner. (To join the ranks of the large eighteenth century landowners with a large house and 10,000 acres would need at least £100,000 capital.)[4] For the economic, social and political eminence of a family depended on its ownership of land. And once acquired there was rarely any incentive to sell again. Until the end of the eighteenth century and the age of industrialisation and urbanisation, fortunes were not to be made by buying and selling land or by

---

[1] G.E. Mingay, *English Landed Society in the Eighteenth Century* (1963).

[2] At the end of the nineteenth century owner-occupier farmers were rare; by the time of World War II they held 30 per cent. of agricultural land; see N. Harvey, *A History of Farm Buildings in England and Wales* (1970).

[3] Under the feudal system the free and copyhold tenants held their land in return for more or less fixed payments in money or kind to the lord. One of the most important aspects of the transition from feudal to capitalist agriculture was the replacement of this system by a system under which the landlords leased the land to tenant at a rack-rent which could be raised from time to time to keep pace with the depreciation in the value of money and to pass on to the landlord the benefit of increased producitivity. See Tawney, R.H., *The Agrarian Problem in the Sixteenth Century*, particularly Chapter IV.

[4] G.E. Mingay (n. 1, above), p. 26.

developing it for residential or industrial purposes.[5] If a large landowner did sell it was probably as a last resort to pay off his debts.

Thus it was that the large landowners and the gentry, owning between them some 70 per cent. of the cultivated land were primarily concerned to acquire land and having acquired it to keep it. And they were concerned not only to keep it in their own lifetimes but to ensure that it remained in the family from generation to generation, unsold and undivided, and protected from the possible extravagence of any of the younger generation.

The strict settlement was the device, perfected by the lawyers and the courts to serve this desire of the landowners to maintain their land intact from generation to generation, whilst allowing each generation of eldest sons (as head of the family) to occupy and enjoy its income; and also at the same time to make suitable financial provision for widows, daughters and younger sons.

The strict settlement. The essential feature of this settlement was the life interest followed by the fee tail. Land was settled when it was acquired, by purchase or on marriage, on the present head of the family for life with remainder to his eldest son in fee tail . . . remainder to the settlor's next eldest son in fee tail and so on. Thus on the death of the father possession of the land would go to the eldest son and then to the eldest son's eldest son and so on in succession. If the line of descendants of the eldest son died out, the land would pass on through the descendants of the settlor's next eldest son and so on.

The fee tail was first recognised as a separate estate in land as a result of the statute De Donis Conditionalibus 1285. For some 200 years after this the fee tail could be used successfully to tie up the land in the family. But in the fifteenth century the courts began to recognise that the entail could be barred, that is the tenant in tail could turn it into a fee simple. Provided he did it with the consent of the life tenant or when he himself had come into possession, the fee tail tenant could by barring create a fee simple absolute. This destroyed the fee tail and with it the right of the fee tail tenant's descendants to succeed to the land. And it destroyed any subsequent remainders or reversions. The settlement was "broken" and the tenant—now a fee simple absolute tenant—could sell the land or otherwise deal with it as an ordinary owner. In substance this was the legal position right up to the 1925

---

[5] *e.g.* it was largely through the rising income from their London estate that the Grosvenors moved from substantial gentry to become great magnates during the 18th century.

legislation. And it still is. The fee tail can still be barred though today it can only exist in equity behind a trust and is liable to be overreached.

Settlement and resettlement. It might be thought that the ability to bar the entail marked the end of the strict settlement. The father would not bother to tie up the land if it was going to be untied by the son. But the point is that in practice this did not happen. What did normally happen was this: the land was held, for example, by A for life remainder to B in fee tail. B could not in any case bar his entail until he came of age at 21. Even then he could only do it so as to create a marketable fee simple absolute and not just a base fee,[6] if he had the consent of A or if A was dead so that his fee tail was in possession. In practice, when he came of age, he would be persuaded by A to resettle the land. He would bar the entail with A's consent but instead of stopping there and keeping the fee simple absolute he would, as part of the arrangement, resettle the land on A for life, remainder to himself for life, remainder to his (B's) eldest son in fee tail, and so on. B would be persuaded to do this, no doubt, partly out of self interest, probably in the form of a regular immediate cash allowance from his father, and partly out of loyalty to the family and its interests.

The result was that the land was effectively tied up for another generation. B could not enlarge his life interest and B's son could not bar his entail until he in turn came of age when no doubt he would be persuaded to repeat the process of resettlement.

In general, this type of settlement served to keep the land in the family generation after generation; but it could be broken once in each generation when the son came of age. From time to time attempts were made to create settlements which could not be broken. For example, the settlor might give a series of life interests to each succeeding eldest son. A life interest cannot be turned into a fee simple. No son would have a fee tail to bar. All such attempts were thwarted by the courts. The rules against remoteness[7] were developed by the courts "limiting the period for which a settlor can exercise control over his property." As will be seen land as such cannot now be tied up even for a generation; but these rules against remoteness apply to a person's property whatever form it takes. They are therefore still important in limiting the period for which a person can control the destiny of his wealth.

By and large the limited ability to tie up the land for a generation, by using the life interest followed by the fee tail,

---

[6] See below, at p. 250.
[7] See below, Chap. 11.

probably served the needs of landowners very well, at least up to the late eighteenth century. Most of them must have appreciated that it was very useful and indeed necessary to be able to break the settlement once in a generation. For example, it might be desirable to sell off part of the estate to produce capital to invest in the improvement of the rest; it might be desirable to exchange part with another landowner in order to make the estate more compact; or a series of exchanges might enable scattered strips in the open fields to be converted into enclosed fields. It might simply be necessary to sell off part of the estate to pay off the tenant's debts or to pay for the erection of a more lavish mansion. Later, towards the end of the eighteenth century, those landowers who were going to survive and profit from the opportunities of the industrial revolution needed more and more to raise capital to invest in industrial and urban development.

The alienability of land. The nineteenth century saw the end of land as the supremely important form of wealth. With the reform of the electoral system it lost much of its importance as an avenue to Parliament and political power. The industrial revolution represented new opportunities for using capital and making fortunes, and new men came along to take the opportunities. Wealth and with its status came to be founded on an industrial empire rather than a landed estate.

From the point of view of land law, one of the most important consequences of this change was that it was no longer regarded as essential to preserve the family wealth in the form of land. There was still a desire to make and preserve the family fortune. There was still the urge to preserve and control this fortune not only for one but for succeeding generations: that is, to make settlements. But the central feature of the settlement was no longer going to be the tying up of the land itself in the family. Indeed, it was becoming increasingly important, in the interests of the family, that the land was not tied up; important that at any time the land could easily be sold and otherwise dealt with so as to bind all subsequent beneficiaries. In other words, what was wanted was a settlement which allowed the family wealth to be preserved and kept intact for the enjoyment of each succeeding generation; but which gave each generation full control of the wealth, power to decide whether it should be held as land or in some other form; and the power to manage the wealth in the way most profitable and advantageous to the family.

Even in the second half of the eighteenth century the landowners had been moving themselves towards this sort of position. First, it was becoming common for properly drawn settlements to include express powers for the tenant for life to deal with the land so as to bind subsequent beneficiaries by selling, leasing, mortgaging, etc. From a conveyancing point of view the main difficulty here was that a purchaser would have to investigate all the complexities of the settlement to be sure that the powers did exist and were being properly exercised in his favour. And not all settlements included such powers.

Secondly, where such powers were not given by the settlement, the landowner who wanted to deal with the land could obtain a private Act of Parliament giving him the required authority. Obviously, this was an expensive and slow process. But until Parliament passed general legislation in the nineteenth century, it was the only way—apart from waiting until the son came of age that the entail could be barred.

In the nineteenth century Parliament did pass general legislation and this culminated in the Settled Land Act and the other property legislation of 1925. This reformed the legal machinery governing settlements in a way that many landowners themselves had been trying to do. Essentially, it applied two basic principles to the strict settlement. First, there was always to be someone, generally, the tenant for life, with full control over the settled land, the irrevocable right to sell and deal with it so as to bind all beneficiaries. Secondly, the actual mechanics of sale were simplified. In particular, by means of the overreaching machinery it was made possible for a purchaser to deal with the tenant for life without being concerned with or affected by the complexities of the settlement itself.

The trust for sale. The same conditions which led to the increased alienability of settled land also led to the development of an alternative method of creating settlements in the nineteenth century: the trust for sale, sometimes referred to as the "traders' settlement."

From the start the trust for sale embodied the principles which were subsequently to be applied to strict settlements. The settlor never aimed to prevent the land from being sold. As already seen, by the nineteenth century this was no longer a vital consideration. The settlor gave the land (probably together with other property such as stocks and shares) to trustees upon trust to sell it—that is, with express instructions to sell it—and to hold the proceeds of sale and the income until sale in trust for the specified beneficiaries. In practice, the trustees would be given the power to postpone the sale for as long as they saw fit. The proceeds of sale would be invested in suitable trustee investments for the benefit of the beneficiaries; and the wealth would thus be preserved, though not in the form of land, for the settlor's children and grandchildren.

The essential idea behind the trust for sale was that land was just one of a number of possible forms of investment; and that what mattered was not the form of the investment but the income which it produced.

The typical trust for sale probably consisted in essence of life interests to the settlor and his wife followed by a remainder to the children absolutely in equal shares—the children of any deceased child taking his share. The idea was that on the death of the settlor and his wife the property would be shared between the children and grandchildren rather than being preserved primarily for each succeeding eldest son as head of the family. Indeed, before 1926, it was not possible to create an entail in personal property—and a beneficial interest under a trust for sale was classified as personal property.[8] But this hardly mattered. The sort of settlor who used the trust for sale was probably tending to think in terms of "providing for the children and grandchildren" rather than of maintaining the position of the family for generations to come.

Today, the settlement is still widely used by substantial property owners. To some extent the machinery governing settlements of land still differs from that governing settlements of other types of property. But, from the modern settlor's point of view, in most cases, the form in which the property is to be held is not likely to be important. More important will be the preservation and increase of its capital value, the amount of income to be derived from it, and the avoidance of tax. Indeed, the machinery of the modern settlement is geared to the desire of the property owner to maintain his wealth within his family without, so far as possible, attracting tax.

The next chapter sets out some preliminary principles of the modern law. The three following chapters deal in detail with the two types of settlement of land as they exist today; and these in turn are followed by a chapter comparing the two methods from the point of view of the settlor.

[8] See below, p. 275.

CHAPTER 6

SETTLEMENTS: DEFINITION AND CLASSIFICATION

Principle 1. Definition

A settlement of land exists wherever the ownership is carved up into a succession of interests. Each interests in turn carries the right to possession and enjoyment of the land.[1] Both freehold and leasehold property can be settled.

Explanation

The doctrine of estates[2] shows that the ownership of land can be split up into different estates, each estate representing the right to possession—immediately or in the future—for a particular duration. The right to possession will be enjoyed in turn by each estate. Such a succession of estates or interests is a settlement.

This ability of the property owner to settle his property, whether land or some other form, gives him more control over its destiny and enables him to control its distribution among succeeding generations of his family.

To take, by way of example, the sort of situation that might well arise today. X is the beneficial freehold owner of Blackacre. It is occupied by himself and his wife and they have two sons. Suppose that X is making his will and asks your advice. He wants his wife to be able to live in the property for the rest of her life if she should survive him but he wants to ensure on her death it goes to the two sons. In other words, what he wants to do is to settle the land.

These days it is very likely that Blackacre will be jointly owned by X and his wife. This will limit his power to settle it in his will. If they are joint tenants his share will pass to her automatically by right of survivorship when he dies.[3] Even if he does have the right of disposal of an absolute owner, he may prefer to give it to her leaving it to her discretion to make ultimate provision for the sons.

However, if he is sole owner and so wishes he can settle it by will on his wife for life remainder to his two sons (either as joint tenants or tenants in common) in fee simple.

Settlement of leasehold property. Leasehold can be settled in the same way as freehold; though of course any settlement carved

---

[1] See S.L.A. 1925, s.1.
[2] Above, p. 9.
[3] Unless while still alive, he severs his interest, turning it into a tenancy in common; see below, p. 334.

198

out of leasehold must necessarily determine when the lease itself determines. Thus, if X holds a 99-year leasehold interest in Blackacre, he can settle it, for example, on A for life remainder to A's son in fee tail. The same rules govern both freehold and leasehold settlements.

Principle 2. Other cases treated as settlements

In certain other cases land is treated in law as being settled although there is no succession of interests. These are:
  (a) where it is held for an infant absolutely[4];
  (b) where it is held in trust for a person absolutely but contingently on the happening of some event[5];
  (c) where it is held absolutely by a person but subject to family charges.[6]

Explanation

These are cases where it has been considered desirable to insist on the trust machinery of either the Settled Land Act or the trust for sale being employed.

In the case of an infant, the reason is obvious. An infant is considered by the law to be too young to manage his own land.[7] If he is entitled to land it must be held in trust for him. It is convenient to treat the land as settled so that the same legal machinery can be employed.

Normally, an interest in category (b) will be one of a succession of interests in the land. It will in this case be a settlement under Principle 1 above. However, it is possible for land to be held in trust for a person contingently upon the happening of some event without any other person having a beneficial interest. For example, if Blackacre is devised to the testator's first son to reach the age of 21 and the income and profits meanwhile are to be accumulated and added to the gift, the machinery of the Settled Land Act or the trust for sale is applied to such a gift so that the land can be managed and dealt with properly while the beneficial interest is still undecided.

The third category applies where the land is held absolutely by a person but subject to family charges, that is where there are charges "created voluntarily, or in consideration of marriage or by

---

[4] S.L.A. 1925, s.1 (2).
[5] *Ibid.* s.1(1)(iii).
[6] *Ibid.* s.1(1)(v).
[7] An infant cannot hold a legal estate in land; L.P.A. 1925, s.19.

way of family arrangement and whether immediately or after an interval, with the payment of any rentcharge for the life of any person, or any less period, or of any capital, annual, or periodical sums for portions, advancement, maintenance or otherwise for the benefit of any persons, with or without any term of years for securing or raising the same." These are charges found under settlements to secure the payment of jointures, portions, maintenance and advancement and so on.[8] Suppose that Blackacre is limited in favour of A for life remainder to B in fee tail remainder to C absolutely and subject to a charge to secure payment of a jointure for W for life. Here the land is in any case settled under the general definition. But if A dies and then B dies childless C will become absolutely entitled. There will no longer be a succession of interests and if it were not for the provision now being discussed, the land would cease to be settled. However, it is treated as being settled and this means that if the land is sold the outstanding charges can be overreached and cleared off the title.

This third category does not include interests of a commercial nature,[9] those charges granted for money or money's worth, such as mortgages. In the case of a commercial charge, a stranger is only prepared to hand over money because he obtains a charge on the land in return as security. Here it is important that the charge attaches to the land itself and cannot be overreached.[10] Consequently the existence of a commercial charge does not make the land settled.

The inclusion of family charges does mean that if a landowner does no more than create a single charge on his land (for example, an annuity in favour of Aunt Mabel charged on his land by his will), the land becomes settled and all the settlement machinery has to be applied.

Principle 3.   Methods of settling land

There are two alternative methods by which land can be settled:
  (a) the strict settlement governed by the Settled Land Act 1925;
  (b) the settlement created behind a trust for sale.
Wherever land is settled, either *inter vivos* or by will, it will be

---

[8] See below, p. 252.
[9] See below, p. 583, for distinction between commercial and family interests.
[10] But subsequent mortgages may be overreached on sale by a prior mortgagee; see below, p. 458. And a sale of settled land will overreach general equitable charges which are commercial; see below, p. 238.

subject to the Settled Land Act unless it has been made expressly subject to a trust for sale.[11]

Explanation

Note on terminology. The term "settlement" can be used in two different senses.[12] It may refer to any settlement, that is any case where there is a succession of interests in the land. Secondly, it can mean a settlement governed by the Settled Land Act as opposed to one existing behind a trust for sale. It is used in this sense in the 1925 legislation. In this book in general it has seemed convenient to use the word in the first sense; and to use the expression "strict settlement" for a settlement governed by the Settled Land Act.

The principle stated above can be explained by using an illustration. X wishes to settle Blackacre by his will on his wife for life remainder to his two sons. He has a choice. He can use either of the two methods set out above. In many respects it will not matter which he chooses. It is doubtful whether any purpose is served today by retaining two different methods. This is considered below.[13] The most popular method today is the trust for sale. The point is this. If he wishes to use the trust for sale method then he must create an express trust for sale in the will—for example, leaving the land "to X and Y upon trust to sell and to hold the proceeds of sale in trust for W for life remainder to S1 and S2 in fee simple as joint tenants." If he simply leaves that land to W for life remainder to S1 and S2 in fee simple as joint tenants, without mentioning a trust for sale, or if he makes an unsuccessful attempt to create a trust for sale (perhaps by not using the correct language),[14] then the settlement will be governed by the Settled Land Act—whether or not that is what he would have wished.

The difference between the two methods. The main difference between the two methods is as follows:

In the case of a strict settlement, legal ownership and the power of dealing with the land is generally vested in the tenant for life, that is the beneficiary entitled in possession for the time being. He is in the position of being a trustee as well as one of the beneficiaries and must exercise these powers in the best interests

---

[11] S.L.A. 1925, s.1(7). This means that the S.L.A. machinery may be invoked unwittingly; see *Binions* v. *Evans* [1972] Ch. 359 (C.A.); and see P. Smith, Caveat Settled Land, [1978] Conv. 229.

[12] The term is also used to refer to the documents creating the settlement.

[13] Chap. 9.

[14] See below, p. 258.

of all the beneficiaries. Separate trustees, called the trustees of the settlement, have a duty to keep an eye on him and see that he does act properly.[15] If he does sell the land the proceeds of sale are paid to these trustees to be invested by them for the benefit of all the beneficiaries.

In the case of a trust for sale, the legal ownership and the powers of dealing with the land are vested in separate trustees—the trustees for sale—not in the tenant for life. In this case any proceeds of sale are paid to these same trustees to be invested for the benefit of the beneficiaries.

It may by now be appreciated that the distinction is to a great extent one of machinery rather than substance. It is a question not of what can be done with the land but who can do it. Nevertheless, this distinction may be vital for the purchaser of settled land. If he is to get a good title it is essential that he takes a conveyance from the person who does in fact hold the legal estate. It is no good taking a conveyance from the person entitled in possession if in fact the land is subject to a trust for sale. In most cases it will be perfectly clear from the title deeds or land register which method has been used. The wording used will be that established by long precedent as effective to create whichever of the two types of settlement is desired. But in some cases, for example, the home-made will, the matter may not be so clear. The settlor may not have used a recognised form of wording. He may not even have realised that he had a choice between two methods of governing his settlement. Here, where there is ambiguity or doubt the courts will have to decide the true meaning of the words used.

---

[15] But their duties are very nominal; see below, p. 233.

Chapter 7

THE STRICT SETTLEMENT

Section I.   The Tenant for Life and Statutory Owner

Principle 1.   The tenant for life

In the case of a strict settlement the legal estate and the powers of dealing with the land are normally vested in the tenant for life.[1] The tenant for life will hold the legal estate and the statutory powers as trustee for the beneficiaries under the settlement.[2]

The tenant for life is the person who is of full age and for the time being beneficially entitled to possession of the settled land or the whole of the income from it.[3]

Explanation

The tenant for life is the central character of the strict settlement. He is the present beneficiary and owner for the time being; and while his interest continues, he is given the job of administering the land.

The first point to note is that he will not necessarily have a life interest in equity. To take an example: Blackacre is settled on A for life remainder to B in fee tail remainder to C in fee tail remainder to D in fee simple. Here, when the settlement comes into operation, A will be the first tenant for life under the Act. In equity he has a life interest in possession. The settlor will have to transfer the legal estate to him by vesting deed. He will hold this legal estate in trust for himself, B and his descendants, C and his descendants and D. When A dies his life interest will come to an end. The next person entitled in possession, assuming he is still alive, will be B who will then have an equitable fee tail in possession; he will be the next tenant for life under the Act and will be the next person to hold the legal estate and the statutory powers.

A note on terminology: The person beneficially entitled to possession is under the Act called "the tenant for life"; a person with a life interest may properly be referred to as a "tenant for life" or a "life tenant." In order to avoid confusion it is convenient to refer to the latter as a "life tenant."

---

[1] S.L.A. 1925, s.4; and Part II of the Act.
[2] *Ibid.* s.107.
[3] *Ibid.* s.19.

It is important to note that the tenant for life will have two separate interests in the property. First, he will have the legal estated vested in him by virtue of the Act. This he holds as trustee and he can only deal with it in the limited ways permitted by the Act. For example, he has statutory power to sell the legal estate free of the beneficial interests—but only if he gets the best price reasonably possible.[4] Secondly, and quite separately, he has his own beneficial equitable interest. This may be a life interest, a fee tail or something else. It is this which determines what he is entitled to for his own benefit. He can deal with this interest in any way he likes. In the example above, A has a beneficial life interest. He can, for example, sell it for as little as he likes or, for that matter, give it away—thus creating an interest *pur autre vie.*

Even if the tenant for life does part with his entire beneficial interest, he will remain tenant for life under the Act. Indeed, he is not allowed to divest himself of his statutory powers even if he wishes to.[5]

In most cases it will be pretty obvious who is the tenant for life. In the example above: to A for life, remainder to B in fee tail, etc., A will be the tenant for life—assuming that he is not an infant. Next it will be B. When B dies it will be his descendant heir, the next person entitled to the fee tail, and so on.

In some cases the position may not be so clear and indeed in some cases there may not be a tenant for life as defined by the Act. This is illustrated by the case of *Re Gallenga Will Trust, Wood* v. *Gallenga.*[6] This is an interesting case as it involves a discretionary trust, a type of trust that has become popular in modern times.[7] The facts were as follows:

The testatrix, by her will, gave all her freehold property to trustees. *During the life of her son* they were to manage the property and, out of the rents and income, pay the interest on any mortgages charged on the land and pay certain annuities. Subject to these payments, they were given an absolute discretion to apply the balance of the income for "the maintenance or personal support or benefit of all or any one or more to the exclusion of others or other of the following persons, namely, my said son, his wife and his children or remoter issue for the time being in existence whether minors or adults and the other persons for the time being interested in the remainder whether absolutely or

---

[4] See below, p. 213.
[5] But in such a case the court can authorise the trustees of the settlement to exercise the powers if necessary; see S.L.A. 1925, ss.24, 104.
[6] [1938] 1 All E.R. 106 (Bennett J.).
[7] See below, p. 295, for these.

contingently presumptively or otherwise howsoever in my settled freeholds in such manner as my trustees shall in their absolute discretion think proper. . . . "

Any surplus after the exercise of the discretionary trust was to be paid to the person who would be entitled on the death of her son. This person was Count Romeo Gallenga. He was claiming to be tenant for life under the Settled Land Act 1925 as being the person "entitled to the income"[8] of the settled land.

Bennett J. held that he was not tenant for life. The real point was that he was not *"entitled"* to any income at all. He merely had a hope, a possibility, that the trustees would exercise their discretion in such a way that there would be a surplus left for him. Thus there was no tenant for life as defined by the Act; the trustees as statutory owner were the proper persons to control the legal estate.[9]

Similarly, as in *Re Frewen,*[10] a person cannot be said to be entitled to the income if he is only entitled to a fixed part of it. In that case, two-thirds of the income from the settled property was to be paid to Thomas Frewen during his life and the other third was to be accumulated and on his death held in trust for his first and other sons in tail. And so, as in the last case, the trustees were entitled to control the property as statutory owner.

However, a person will still be regarded as being entitled to the income even if the trustees have to make payments out of it before handing it over—even if, as it happens, those payments exhaust the income. The point is that to qualify as tenant for life under this provision he must be entitled to the whole surplus income after any such payments have been made.[11]

Principle 2.   The statutory owner

Where there is no tenant for life as defined by the Act[12] or where the tenant for life is an infant,[13] the legal estate and the statutory powers of dealing with the land will be vested in the statutory owner.

The statutory owner will be the persons expressly nominated as such by the settlement; failing this, the trustees of the settlement will be the statutory owner.[14]

[8] S.L.A. 1925, s.20 (1) (viii).
[9] See below.
[10] [1926] Ch. 580, (Lawrence J).
[11] See, *e.g. Re Jones* (1884) 26 Ch.D. 736 (C.A.).
[12] See S.L.A. 1925, s.23.
[13] *Ibid.* s.26.
[14] *Ibid.* ss.23, 117 (1) (xxvi).

Explanation

The statutory owner has the same powers of dealing with the settled land as the tenant for life; and in general in this book the term tenant for life is used to include the statutory owner.

In accordance with the general policy of the 1925 legislation, to ensure that at all times the land can be dealt with freely, there must always be someone in whom the legal estate and the statutory powers are vested. Normally this person is the tenant for life. But in these two cases, where there is no tenant for life or where he is considered too young, the position is filled by the statutory owner.

SECTION II.   FORMALITIES

Principle 3.   Creation of settlement

A strict settlement can be created *inter vivos* or by will; in both cases there must be two separate documents.

In the case of an *inter vivos* settlement there must be:
  (a) a principal vesting deed transferring the legal ownership to the tenant for life;
  (b) a trust instrument setting out the beneficial interests,[15]

In the case of a settlement by will, the will is treated as the trust instrument and the personal representatives of the deceased settlor will execute a vesting assent in favour of the first tenant for life.[16]

Until these formalities have been complied with the tenant for life will not be able to deal with the land effectively.[17]

Explanation

The vesting deed. The purpose of the vesting deed is to transfer the legal estate to the tenant for life. The settlor himself may be the first tenant for life. Suppose that X the beneficial freehold owner of Blackacre settles it *inter vivos* on himself for life remainder to his son in fee tail. Here the legal estate will already be vested in the tenant for life. Nevertheless, he will have to execute a vesting deed declaring that the legal estate is vested in him as tenant for life.[18] This illustrates the insistence by the legislation on formality for all dealings with settled land; and this

---

[15] *Ibid.* s.4.
[16] *Ibid.* s.6.
[17] *Ibid.* s.13.
[18] A vesting declaration: S.L.A. 1925, s.4(2).

in turn means that ownership of the legal estate—and therefore conveyancing—is kept relatively simple and uncomplicated.

The principal vesting deed must contain certain information.[19] If the tenant for life exercises his statutory power to sell the land he will in fact be selling the legal estate free of the beneficial interests. The vesting deed (together with the earlier title deeds) will be proof to a purchaser that the vendor does in fact hold the legal estate and has power to sell it.[20] The details which are found in the vesting deed are the details and the only details which a purchaser must have.[21]

The vesting deed must, then, contain:

(a) A description of the settled land. When the purchaser is shown the vesting deed it must be clear that it refers to the piece of land which he is buying. Otherwise he will quite rightly refuse to complete.

(b) A declaration that the legal estate is vested in the tenant for life upon the trusts of the settlement.

(c) The names of the trustees of the settlement. A purchaser will need to know the names of the trustees since he must pay the purchase money to them and not to the tenant for life.[22]

(d) The names of any persons authorised by the settlement to appoint new trustees. A purchaser may find that the trustees to whom he is expected to pay his money are not the original trustees named in the vesting deed. A purchaser will need to satisfy himself that they have been properly appointed.

(e) A statement of any additional powers given by the settlement to the tenant for life. The settlement cannot limit the tenant for life's statutory powers. But it can give him additional powers. For example, it might authorise him to create leases of the settled land which do not comply with the statutory requirements. Since an unauthorised lease would not bind the other beneficiaries, the lessee would need to satisfy himself that the lease was authorised by the settlement.

Subsidiary vesting deed.   Where further land is brought into an existing settlement, it is transferred to the tenant for life by means

---

[19] *Ibid.* s.5.
[20] This will be so in the case of unregistered land. When the land is registered the vesting deed will have to be in statutory form; see Land Registration Rules 1925, r. 74 and Sched. The tenant for life will then produce the vesting deed to the Registrar and obtain registration of himself as proprietor; see L.R.A., ss.86, 87.
[21] In the case of registered land the purchaser will learn these details from the register.
[22] S.L.A. 1925, ss.75(1), 94(1).

of a subsidiary vesting deed.[23] This will refer to the principal vesting deed and contain much the same information.

The trust instrument.[24]   The main purpose of this is to declare the trusts of the settlement; that is it sets out all the beneficial interests. It is also the trust instrument which actually appoints the trustees of the settlement and contains any power to appoint new trustees; and it confers any additional powers which are to be given to the tenant for life. As seen, these last three matters are repeated in the vesting deed for the information of purchasers.

Reason for requiring two documents.   The 1925 legislation insists on two separate documents in order to "keep the equities off the title." This is an essential part of the machinery introduced by Parliament, to simplify conveyancing. A purchaser will be buying the legal estate. He will know that the legal estate is held by the tenant for life in trust under the Settled Land Act, and he will have to satisfy certain requirements. But provided he does this he will not be affected by the trusts, *i.e.* the beneficial equitable interests, since they will be overreached. The contents of the trust instrument, all the, possibly complex, provisions of the settlement, concern only the trustees and the beneficiaries. The purchaser is only concerned with the relatively simple matter of the legal title dealt with by the vesting deed and earlier title deeds.

Effect of non-compliance with the above formalities.   In general, the statutory requirements cannot be evaded.

First, the legal estate can only be transferred to the tenant for life if these formalities are observed; and until he has it he cannot deal with it.[25]

Even if the legal estate happens to be already vested in the tenant for life (for example, if he is the settlor), section 13 of the Settled Land Act 1925 ensures that the formalities must be observed before the land is dealt with. This provides:

> "Where a tenant for life or statutory owner has become entitled to have a principal vesting deed or vesting assent executed in his favour, then until a vesting instrument is executed or made pursuant to this Act in respect of the settled land, any purported disposition thereof *inter vivos* by any person, other than a personal representative . . . shall not take effect except in favour of a purchaser of a legal estate without notice of such tenant for life or statutory owner

---

[23] *Ibid.* s.10.
[24] *Ibid.* s.4(3).
[25] *Ibid.* s.4(1).

having become so entitled as aforesaid, but, save as aforesaid, shall operate only as a contract for valuable consideration to carry out the transaction after the requisite vesting instrument has been executed or made, and a purchaser of a legal estate shall not be concerned with such disposition unless the contract is registered as an estate contract."

For example, in *Re Cayley ad Evans' Contract,*[26] the Llannerch estates were subject to compound settlements, including, *inter alia,* an 1882 settlement, and a 1915 resettlement. Under the transitional provisions of the 1925 legislation, the trustees of the settlement for the purposes of the Settled Land Act 1925 were the trustees of the 1882 settlement; and the tenant for life, Sir Kenelm Cayley, was entitled to have a vesting deed in his favour executed by these trustees. A vesting deed was executed but by the trustees of the later settlement and making no mention of the earlier settlement. When Sir Kenelm contracted to sell part of the estate in Colwyn Bay, the purchaser refused to complete on the grounds that the proper vesting deed had not been executed and that therefore the vendor had not shown a good title. The present case was brought by the tenant for life asking for a declaration that good title had been shown. Bennet J. upheld the purchaser's argument. The vesting deed did not satisfy the statute. Therefore, under section 13 if the purchaser completed and took a conveyance it would not give him the legal estate.

This case does illustrate how conveyancing law revolves around "title," that is, ownership of the legal estate. It also illustrates the sort of technical dispute about title that can arise in conveyancing transactions. Has the right document been signed by the right person, etc.? But although these disputes are technical in the sense that they are concerned with the formalities for the transfer of land ownership, they are none the less vital. It is essential to a purchaser to get a good title. Otherwise he will have difficulty in proving title when he himself comes to sell. And it can be as difficult to sell land with a defective title as it can to sell land with defective drains. In both cases the defect must be cured or it will be reflected in a lower price. If the defect is serious the land might be unsaleable. It is for this reason that a purchaser must investigate title so carefully before he hands over his purchase money.

Section 13 of the Settled Land Act 1925 only applies if the land is settled. In *Re Alefounder's Will Trusts, Adams* v. *Alefounder,*[27]

---

[26] [1930] 2 Ch. 143 (Bennett J.).
[27] [1927] 1 Ch. 360 (Astbury J.).

Alefounder was an adult legal tenant in tail in possession. Under the transitional provisions of the 1925 legislation, his fee tail became equitable, the legal fee simple became vested in him and he became entitled to require a vesting deed in his favour. What happened then was that he barred his fee tail,[28] thus becoming absolute fee simple owner in law as well as equity. The court had to decide whether section 13 prevented him from dealing with the land without first getting a vesting instrument. It was held that section 13 did not apply. The land was no longer settled and so no vesting deed was necessary. Of course, if the legal estate had not been vested in Alefounder, he would have had to obtain it before being able to deal with it.

It should be noted that although failure to comply with the formalities "paralyses" the land, it does not invalidate the settlement.[29] For example, the settlor will not be able to change his mind and decide not to settle the land after all. Further, compliance does not prevent a beneficiary from dealing with his own beneficial interest.

Where the correct formalities have not been observed matters can be put right by the trustees of the settlement (not the settlor) executing the vesting deed.[30]

Settlements by will.　The rules discussed above also apply to settlements created by will except that on the death of the settlor the will itself is treated as the trust instrument. The legal estate will have passed on his death to his ordinary personal representatives. After completing the administration of the deceased's estate, they will transfer the legal estate in the settled land to the first tenant for life by vesting assent. This is exactly the same as a vesting deed except that it is under hand (*i.e.* signed) and does not have to be by deed.[31]

Principle 4.　Death of the tenant for life

(1) If the settlement continues on the death of the tenant for life the legal estate will vest in the trustees of the settlement as special personal representatives.[32] After administering the settled land they will vest the legal estate in the next tenant for life by means of a vesting assent.

[28] See below, p. 249.
[29] Assuming the requirements for the creation of a valid trust have been observed.
[30] S.L.A. 1925, s.9 (1) (iii), (2).
[31] *Ibid.* ss.6, 8(1).
[32] A.E.A. 1925, s.22(1); J.A. 1925, s.162(1), as amended by the Administration of Justice Act 1928, s.9.

(2) If the settlement comes to an end with the death of the tenant for life, the legal estate will vest in his ordinary personal representatives. After administration they will vest it in the person finally entitled under the settlement by means of an ordinary assent in writing.[33]

Explanation

An illustration will show what might happen on the death of a tenant for life. Whiteacre is settled on A for life remainder to B for life remainder to C in fee simple. The legal estate will have been vested in A as the first tenant for life. On the death of A his life interest determines and B's life interest falls into possession. There is still a succession of interests and so the settlement continues. The legal estate will vest in the trustees of the settlement as special personal representatives. They will obtain probate limited to the settled land and in due course after payment of capital transfer tax and so on—they will vest the legal estate in the next tenant for life by means of a vesting assent.

When B dies the position is different. The only interest left in the land is the fee simple absolute which has now become a fee simple absolute in possession. There is no longer a succession of interests and so the settlement is at an end. The legal estate in Whiteacre will vest in B's ordinary personal representatives together with the rest of his property. After administration, they will vest it in C (or whoever by that time is holding the fee simple) by means of an ordinary assent in writing. As a result C will become an ordinary beneficial freehold owner.

SECTION III.   DEALINGS WITH THE SETTLED LAND

Principle 5.   The statutory powers of the tenant for life

The tenant for life is given certain powers of dealing with the legal estate in the settled land. Provided he acts in accordance with the statute, the beneficiaries will be bound by his dealings.[34]

The tenant for life can deal with his own beneficial interest as he wishes.

Explanation

It has already been emphasised that the tenant for life has two distinct interests in the land: the legal estate and his own equitable

---

[33] See A.E.A. 1925, s.36.
[34] See generally S.L.A. 1925, Pt.II.

interest.[35] He can do what he likes with his beneficial equitable interest; but whatever he does with it will not, and cannot, affect the other beneficiaries. Blackacre is held under the Settled Land Act 1925 by A for life remainder to B in fee simple. A has an equitable life interest which he can sell, lease, mortgage, etc. But whatever interest he carves out of his life interest will necessarily terminate on his death. If he mortgages it to X to secure a loan to pay for a new car, and shortly afterwards dies; X will be entitled to repayment out of A's personal estate; but X's security will have disappeared and he will have no sort of claim against the land.

On the other hand, the Settled Land Act 1925 confers on A the position of tenant for life and as such gives to him the legal estate. And it not only gives him the legal estate it gives him certain powers to deal with this legal estate free of the interests of the other beneficiaries. If A exercises his statutory power to mortgage the legal estate, for example, to pay for improvements[36]—he would not be able to do it to pay for a new car—this mortgage will bind the land itself, that is the legal estate, and will overreach the interests of the other beneficiaries. In this case, if A dies it will make no difference to the mortgagee. He will be able to enforce his security against the land in the hands of the next tenant.

It is these statutory powers and their limits with which the present section is concerned.

Principle 6.   Notice to trustees

In the case of his powers to sell, exchange, lease, mortgage or charge and to grant options of the settled land, the tenant for life must give at least one month's notice to the trustees of the settlement.[37]

Explanation

The tenant for life does not have to consult or obtain the consent of the other beneficiaries before exercising any of his powers. In a few cases he must obtain the consent of the trustees or, alternatively, an order of the court.[38] But in general all he has to do is to give one month's written notice to each of the trustees of whom there must be at least two or a trust corporation.[39]

---

[35] Above, p. 204.
[36] See below, p. 217.
[37] S.L.A. 1925, s.101.
[38] Below, p. 223.
[39] S.L.A. 1925, s.101(1).

This provision is obviously designed to give some protection to
the other beneficiaries by forcing the tenant for life to keep the
trustees informed of any dealings with the land which he proposes
so that they can if necessary interfere. But it is a weak provision
and does not afford a lot of protection. In particular, a transaction
will not be set aside against a purchaser acting in good faith on the
grounds that notice has not been given.[40] The only remedy here
will be against the tenant for life. Further, except in the case of a
mortgage or charge, a general notice simply stating an intention to
exercise the statutory powers at some time in the future will be
sufficient. The notice does not have to relate to a specific
transaction.[41]

Principle 7. The statutory power of sale

The tenant for life may sell the settled land—that is the legal estate
free of the beneficial interests—or any part of it or any right over
it.

He must obtain the best price reasonably possible and comply
with the other requirements of the Settled Land Act 1925.[42]

Explanation

In *Wheelwright* v. *Walker* (No.2),[43] the tenant for life received
an offer from one of the beneficiaries. Being unwilling to sell to
him he was proposing to sell to a third party for a lower price. This
was clear evidence that he was not obtaining the best price
reasonably possible and the court granted an injunction ordering
him not to sell for less than the price offered by the beneficiary. If
the sale had been completed it would not have been set aside
against a purchaser acting in good faith.

The purchaser will have to pay the purchase price not to the
tenant for life but to the trustees of the settlement.[44] Otherwise he
will not obtain the protection of the overreaching provisions. It is
an essential part of the Settled Land Act machinery that, while the
land is held by the tenant for life, any capital money must be held
by the trustees.

Although he must get the best price reasonably possible, the
tenant for life does not have to sell by auction. And he can sell the

---

[40] *Ibid.* s.101(5).
[41] *Ibid.* s.101(2).
[42] *Ibid.* ss.38, 39, 40.
[43] (1883) 31 W.R. 912.
[44] S.L.A. 1925, ss.75(1), 94(1).

whole or part; he can divide it vertically or horizontally and he can sell rights over it.

He has a similar power to exchange the settled land for other land.

Principle 8.   The statutory power to lease[45]

The tenant for life can make the following leases of the settled land which will bind the other beneficiaries.

(i) building and forestry leases not exceeding 999 years;
(ii) mining leases not exceeding 100 years;
(iii)leases for any other purpose not exceeding 50 years.

In general, any such lease must satisfy the following requirements:

(a) it must be made by deed;
(b) it must be made to take effect either in possession or in reversion on an existing lease with not more than seven years to run;
(c) it must reserve the best rent reasonably obtainable taking into account any fine;
(d) the lease must contain a covenant for the payment of rent and a proviso for re-entry on non-payment for a specified period not exceeding 30 days;
(e) a counterpart of the lease must be executed by the lessee and handed to the tenant for life.

By way of exception to these requirements, if the lease is at the best rent reasonably possible and no fine taken and if the lessee is not exempted from liability for waste, then:

(1) Notice to the trustees is not necessary if the lease does not exceed 21 years.

(2) It can be made in writing instead of by deed if the lease is for not more than three years.

Explanation

Building leases.   A building lease is defined as one made partly in consideration of the erecting, improving, adding to or repairing of buildings.[46]

In the case of a building lease a nominal rent may be reserved for not longer than the first five years (ten in the case of a forestry lease).

[45] *Ibid.* ss.41–48.
[46] *Ibid.* s.117(1) (i).

The rent. The tenant for life must obtain the best rent reasonably possible taking into account any fine. Any fine will be treated as capital.

Where land is let on a long lease the consideration commonly consists partly of a lump sum—a fine or premium—and partly of a rent—generally referred to as a ground rent. In the case of a tenant for life the point is this: any premium represents the capital value of the land converted into money. As such it must be paid to the trustees and held by them. The tenant for life will be entitled to any income earned by investing the money. Any rent will go to the tenant for life as income.

Whether or not any particular payment is a fine or rent or something else may be a difficult question. In *Chandler* v. *Bradley*,[47] the tenant for life of a freehold house granted a lease for seven years at a rent of £25 a year. But in addition the lessee had given the tenant for life £21 as an inducement to grant the lease to him. The action was brought by the other beneficiaries to have the lease set aside as not complying with the statutory requirements. On behalf of the lessee it was argued that the £21 was in the nature of a fine, that it should have been paid to the trustees but that this defect could be cured by handing it over now. However, Stirling J. decided that it was not a fine but a straightforward bribe. "The £21 was never intended either by the defendant or Chandler to be a fine constituting capital money under the Act; it was from first to last intended by both parties to be a payment for the benefit of James Chandler personally, and of no one else."[48] It followed, so the judge decided, that if the lessee was prepared to pay £21 as a bribe he must have been prepared to pay this sum in consideration of the lease. Therefore the best rent reasonably possible had not been obtained, the lessee knew this and the lease must be void.

Mining leases. In the case of mining leases there needs to be special statutory provision.[49] For here, the lessee will gradually be taking out the minerals, that is, he will be removing part of the capital value of the land. There is therefore a capital element in the rent. If he is unimpeachable of waste[50] or if the mine was already opened when he came into possession, the tenant for life is entitled to three-quarters of the rent and only one-quarter is set aside as capital. This is because in such a case he could have

---

[47] [1897] 1 Ch. 315 (Stirling J.). See also *Waite* v. *Jennings* [1906] 2 K.B. 11; *Pumford* v. *Butler & Co.* [1914] 2 Ch. 353; and see above, p. 110.
[48] [1897] 1 Ch. 315 at pp. 323, 324, *per* Stirling J.
[49] S.L.A. 1925, s.47.
[50] See below, p. 244 for waste.

removed minerals himself, sold them and kept all the proceeds for himself. However, if the mine was unopened and if he is liable for waste, the tenant for life can keep only a quarter of the rent as income. In such cases, in the absence of special statutory authority, the tenant for life would not be entitled to touch the mineral wealth which would remain as part of the capital value for the ultimate remainderman.

Possession. *Re Rycroft's Settlement, Rycroft* v. *Rycroft*[51] is a case which illustrates the sort of problem which has arisen in connection with the statutory requirement as to the time when the lease is to take effect in possession.

The facts were as follows: The plaintiff was tenant for life of a number of properties in Clarges Street, London. He was also beneficial owner of other properties in the same street. He entered into a contract with a company, Clarges Street Investments Ltd., for the redevelopment of all the properties. The contract was made subject to the court declaring it valid and the present action was brought by the plaintiff for such a declaration. The contract provided that in consideration of the company agreeing to redevelop the properties, it was, at a future date fixed by reference to the expiry of existing leases of the property, to be granted three separate leases of the property divided into three separate blocks.

The contract could be challenged on the ground, first, that one of the proposed leases was to include both settled and unsettled property. The court held, following *Tolson* v. *Sheard,*[52] that the contract would be invalid on this ground.

Secondly, it was argued that the contract would be void on the grounds that it would contravene section 42(1)(i) of the Settled Land Act 1925. This is the section which requires the lease to take effect in possession or in reversion on a lease with not more than seven years to run. In fact, some of the existing leases affecting the property had more than seven years to run. However, the court decided that the contract would not be void under this section. They drew a distinction: section 42(1)(i) referred to the grant of a lease; the case under consideration concerned a contract to grant a lease in the future. Such a contract was covered by section 90(1)(iii) of the Act. This provides:

> "A tenant for life . . . (iii) may contract to make any lease, and in making the lease may vary the terms, with or without consideration, but so that the lease be in conformity with this Act . . . "

[51] [1962] Ch. 263 (Wilberforce J.).
[52] (1877) 5 Ch.D. 19.

In the present case there was a contract to grant a lease, but no lease. When, in performance of the contract, the lease came to be granted it would be in conformity with the Act; since by that time the existing leases would have expired and the new ones would take effect in possession immediately.[53]

Principle 9.   The statutory power to mortgage the settled land[54]

The tenant for life has a statutory power to raise money by mortgaging the legal estate provided that the money is to be used for one of the specified purposes authorised by the Settled Land Act.

These include:

(a) Raising money which has to be paid out under the provisions of the settlement,[55] *e.g.* portions.

(b) Raising money which is reasonably required to pay for authorised improvements, or to discharge incumbrances affecting the settled land.[56] For example, it might be possible to replace an existing mortgage by a new one at a lower rate of interest.

Principle 10.   The statutory power to carry out improvements[57]

The tenant for life may carry out authorised improvements and have them paid for out of capital either in the hands of the trustees or raised by mortgaging the settled land.

Authorised improvements are divided into three categories: the tenant for life cannot be required to repay money spent on those in the first category; the trustees have a discretion as to whether he should repay money spent on those in the second category; money spent on those in the third category must be repaid by the tenant for life.[58]

Explanation

From time to time it will be necessary to spend money on the settled land. There will be regular outgoings such as rates; and

---

[53] In reaching this conclusion the court had to contend with s.117 of the S.L.A. 1925, which defines a "lease" as including "an agreement for a lease." The court decided that in this context an agreement for a lease meant only an existing equitable lease under the doctrine in *Walsh* v. *Lonsdale* and not a contract to grant a lease in the future. See further above, p. 114.

[54] S.L.A. 1925, s.71.

[55] *Ibid.* s.16(1).

[56] *Ibid.* s.71.

[57] S.L.A. 1925, ss.83–87.

[58] *Ibid.* s.84, and Third Schedule.

repairs may need doing. Both of these matters are concerned with preserving the property in its present state; they maintain but they do not increase its value. They are the recurring expenses which must be paid for by any landowner. Consequently, in the case of settled land they must be paid out of income.

On the other hand, it may be considered desirable to go further and spend money improving the land. If the trustees hold capital improvements may be seen as a good way of investing it; or they may simply be seen as a way of increasing the income from the land. The point is that improvements are likely to increase the capital value of the land; this increase will be to the benefit not only of the present tenant but also of subsequent beneficiaries by producing a larger income for them; and to the ultimate remainderman who will get the land itself or the proceeds of sale if it has been sold. It is therefore reasonable that at least long-term improvements should be paid for out of capital.

It has always been possible for the tenant for life to make improvements at his own expense.[59] But a tenant for life may not wish to spend money on improvements largely for the benefit of subsequent beneficiaries; and even if he is prepared to he may not have capital available. The 1925 legislation, aimed at the more profitable use and development of settled land, has made the following provisions:

The tenant for life can require authorised improvements to be paid for out of capital.[60] This may be capital already held by the trustees; or it may be capital raised by mortgaging the settled land. The Settled Land Act divides authorised improvements into three categories.[61] This classification reflects the degree of permanency of the improvements. Those listed in the first category are long-term improvements; the benefit of them, in terms of increased income and capital value, will continue indefinitely. In respect of these, the tenant for life cannot be required to repay money spent. Improvements in the third category are short-term improvements. The benefit of these is transient and unlikely to outlive the tenant for life himself. In respect of these the tenant for life must repay, possibly by instalments, the money spent.[62] Here, in effect, all he gets is a loan. Improvements in the second category are somewhere in between and in respect of these the trustees have a discretion as to whether the tenant for life should be made to repay the money spent.[63]

---

[59] Improvements constitute ameliorating waste, see below, p. 244.
[60] S.L.A. 1925, ss.73(1) (iv), 71(1) (ii).
[61] *Ibid.* Third Schedule.
[62] *Ibid.* s.84(2).
[63] *Ibid.*

Improvements in the first category, long-term improvements, include for example, "Cottages for labourers, farm servants and artisans, employed on the settled land or not"; also, "Drainage, including the straightening, widening or deepening of drains, streams, and watercourses."[64] In *Re Lord Leconfield's S.E.*[65] it was held that expenditure incurred in the "structural alterations and additions necessary in converting rooms into water closets and sink rooms, including partitions, doors, windows and making good walls" could properly be allowed to the tenant for life under this section. Kekewich J. said that "if the expenditure has been substantially for the making of one complete system of drainage. I think it ought to be allowed."[66]

The list of short-term improvements includes "Heating, hydraulic or electric power apparatus, for buildings, and engines, pumps, lifts, rams, boilers, flues and other works required or used in connection therewith."[67]

Principle 11. Application of capital

Any capital, as opposed to income, arising under the settlement must be paid to the trustees.[68] Such capital must be applied in one of the ways specified in the Settled Land Act 1925.[69] But the tenant for life is entitled to decide in which of the permitted ways the money is to be applied.[70]

Explanation

From time to time the ownership of the settled land will produce money. This will be either capital or income; and the two must be distinguished carefully. All receipts of a capital nature must be treated as capital and paid to the trustees of the settlement or into court. Income will go to the person entitled to the income for the time being, normally the tenant for life. Capital money must be used in one of the ways specified in section 73 of the Settled Land Act 1925. These include investment in trustee securities, the discharge of incumbrances to which the settled land may be subject, the payment for authorised improvements and the

---

[64] *Ibid.* Third Schedule, Pt. I.
[65] [1907] 2 Ch. 340.
[66] *Ibid.* at p. 347.
[67] S.L.A. 1925, Third Schedule, Pt.III.
[68] *Ibid.* ss.75(1), 81, 94(1).
[69] *Ibid.* s.73.
[70] *Ibid.* s.75(2). See *Re Duke of Wellington's Parliamentary Estates, King* v. *Wellesley* [1972] 1 Ch. 374 (Plowman J.).

purchase of freehold land or leasehold with more than 60 years to run.[71] If the capital itself produces income—if, for example, it is invested in trustee securities—the income will be paid to the person entitled to the income under the settlement.

Thus the idea is that although the land can be turned into money and one form of settled property into another, the settled property as a whole, the inheritance, will remain intact.

Definition of capital. The Settled Land Act does not define capital although it does provide how money arising from certain specified transactions is to be treated.[72]

Re Scholfield's Will Trusts, Scholfield v. *Scholfield*,[73] shows how the classification of money arising under the settlement can be vital. In this case leaseholds were settled by will. The testator's children were entitled to the income from the leases for the rest of their lives. The leaseholds would then, if they had not expired, pass to the remainderman. As it happened the properties were damaged in the war and compensation was paid under the War Damage Act 1943. The trustees disclaimed the leases, as they were entitled to, under the Landlord and Tenant (War Damage) Acts 1939 to 1941, and they thus came to a premature end. The issue was how this compensation should be treated. A lease is different from a freehold in that it is more or less a wasting asset. If a leasehold property is purchased for a capital sum, this capital is recovered in the form of income from the sub-letting year by year. The capital value of the lease will diminish as time passes and disappear when the lease expires. In the present case, if the lease had continued in the normal way, the amount which the remainderman would get and the amount which the children would get would have depended on how long the children lived. It was therefore not possible to say how much of the compensation should go to the children as representing lost income from the leases and how much should be put aside for the remainderman as representing the capital value. In the event the court provided a neat solution by treating the compensation money in the same way as the proceeds of sale of a lease under section 79 of the Settled Land Act 1925. It ordered the money to be used to purchase annuities for periods equal to the residue of the leases. This meant that the children would get the annuities until they died or the annuities expired. The remainderman would get the annuities

---

[71] Purchase doesn't have to be for an investment; it may for example be purchased for a house for the tenant for life to occupy; see *Re Wellsted's Will Trusts* [1949] Ch. 296.

[72] See, *e.g.* S.L.A. 1925, ss.79, 80.

[73] [1949] Ch. 341 (Romer J.).

after their deaths if they had not expired—just as he would have got the income from the leases.

Re Pelly's Will Trust,[74] was another case in which money had to be classified. Here the tenant for life occupied and farmed the settled land. He carried out authorised improvements and, as he was entitled to under section 73(1)(iv) of the Settled Land Act 1925, he directed the trustees to pay for the improvements out of capital. So far there was no problem. However, the tenant for life became entitled to certain income tax relief as a result of the improvements. The court had to decide whether the tenant for life was entitled to keep this relief or whether he should pay to the trustees, the amount saved. On the one hand it could be said that the tenant for life was entitled to the whole income from the settled land and that he was therefore entitled to any increase in income due to a reduction in income tax. On the other hand it could be argued that the tax relief was given because of the improvements, and that it therefore represented a reimbursement by the state of the capital cost of the improvements. As such it should be handed over to the trustees. It was held that the tenant for life was entitled to keep the benefit of the relief. Liability to income tax was personal to the tenant for life attaching to his beneficial interest—that is, the income from the land—and that he was entitled to any increase in income due to a reduction in tax just as he would have borne any decrease due to an increase in tax.

These cases show that the distinction between capital and income may be somewhat artificial and difficult to state. Nevertheless, as long as settlements exist, it is a distinction which has to be made. The general idea is quite clear. Each succeeding tenant for life is entitled to have the benefit of the property for his lifetime, but the property itself, the corpus of the inheritance, is to be preserved intact until it is finally taken by the ultimate remainderman—though under the classical strict settlement this was never expected to happen.

But as seen above, difficulties can arise as to what represents the inheritance itself and what represents the profit from it. In the first case above the difficulty arose because the settled property was a wasting asset; in the second case it was a windfall in the form of a tax relief which had to be allocated to capital or income.

Pole v. *Pole*[75] was another "windfall" case. Here the tenant for life received £3,000 from the S.W. Rly. Co. in return for agreeing to support their proposal for a line to Exeter against the rival

---

[74] [1957] Ch. 1.
[75] (1865) 2 Drew. & Sm. 420; 62 E.R. 680.

G.W. Rly Co.'s proposal. It was held that this sum represented capital.

Under section 75 of the Settled Land Act 1925, the tenant for life may direct the trustees in which of the possible ways listed in section 73 the capital is to be used. And this shows that the tenant for life has a wide measure of control over the settled property whether in the form of land or capital.

Principle 12.   Capital money treated as land

Any capital money arising under the Settled Land Act 1925 and any investments representing it is treated as land and subject to the same trusts as the land itself.[76]

Explanation

The main purpose of the statutory machinery now governing strict settlements is to make is as easy as possible to turn land into money and money into land. It is not intended to deprive the beneficiaries of their respective interests. Consequently, although the beneficiaries other than the tenant for life cannot prevent the land from being converted into capital money they will have the same interests in the money that they would have had in the land; further, their interests in the money are *treated* as being interests in the land. This is a sort of reverse of the doctrine of conversion.[77]

The sort of situation in which this principle might be important is seen in the case of *Re Cartwright, Cartwright* v. *Smith*.[78] Here the testator was tenant for life under his marriage settlement. During his life, in exercise of his powers, he had sold most of the land. He died without issue and the settlement provided that in such a circumstance he should become absolutely entitled subject only to certain charges. He was therefore able to dispose of the property by his will. In fact he made a will while living in France which was invalid under the Wills Act 1837, but which was valid as to *personal* property under the Wills Act 1861 (Lord Kingsdown's Act).[79] The result was that his widow was entitled to his personal property under his will; and in this case she was claiming that the

---

[76] S.L.A. 1925, s.75(5).
[77] See below, p. 275, for this.
[78] [1939] Ch. 90.
[79] Repealed and replaced by the Wills Act 1963 which provides that a will shall be treated, both as to moveable and immoveable property, as properly executed if in accordance either with the law of the territory where it is executed; or the law of the domicile or place of habitual residence or nationality of the testator at the time of its execution or his death.

investments made with the proceeds of sale of the settled land were personal property. Those entitled to the property in respect of which he died intestate—his real property—were claiming that the investments must be treated as real property. It was held that under the principle stated above they must be treated as real property and go to those entitled on intestacy.

However, in *Middleton (Earl)* v. *Cottesloe (Baron)*,[80] the House of Lords decided that this section (section 75) did not apply for fiscal purposes. Here part of the settled land, situate in Eire, had been sold and invested in securities worth about £90,000 in England. The case was brought so that the court could decide whether the investments were subject to English estate duty as being property situated in England or whether they were still to be treated as land situate in Eire and therefore subject to Irish estate duty. The House of Lords decided that the section did not affect tax liabilty and that therefore English estate duty was payable. It might be suggested that even if the section were said to apply to make the investments treated as land, this would not prevent them from being treated as land in England where they were.

Principle 13. Powers exercisable with consent

The tenant for life has the following powers which may require the consent of the trustees of the settlement or an order of the court.

(a) to dispose of the principal mansion house[81];

(b) to cut and sell timber[82];

(c) to compromise claims affecting the settled land.[83]

Explanation

In the case of post-1925 settlements consent to dispose of the principal mansion house is only necessary if the settlement expressly requires it. This is a slight concession to the wish of landowners to keep at least the family home in the family. The definition of principal mansion house in the Settled Land Act 1925[84] gives a nice idea of the sort of landowner that the strict settlement was developed to serve.[85] " . . . if the house is usually occupied as a farmhouse, or where the site of any house and the pleasure grounds and parks and lands, if any, usually occupied

[80] [1949] A.C. 418.
[81] See S.L.A. 1925, s.65.
[82] *Ibid.* s.66.
[83] *Ibid.* s.58.
[84] *Ibid.* s.65(2).
[85] And still serves.

therewith do not together exceed 25 acres in extent, the house is *not* to be deemed a principal mansion house . . . "

In *Re Feversham's Settled Estate*,[86] Duncombe Park mansion house, which undoubtedly had been the principal mansion house, had been let on a long lease as a girls' school as the tenant for life could not afford to live there himself.[87] Instead he had moved into a smaller house on the estate and spent £13,000 out of his own pocket in making improvements. In the present case he was claiming to have the cost of these improvements paid for out of capital. The Settled Land Act 1925 provides that improvements to the principle mansion house are long term improvements.[88] The tenant for life is entitled to have them paid for out of capital without having to repay the money spent. In the present case the tenant for life, in order to benefit from this provision was seeking to establish that the "smaller" house had become the principal mansion house. The house had been made into a "not overwhelmingly large, but a reasonable and proper dwelling house for a person who is the owner of an estate such as this."[89] The question which Farwell J. had to decide was "whether a limited owner can, by leasing what is the principal mansion house and moving into another house, or adapting another house for the purpose of his own occupation, change what was the principal mansion house, so that it ceases to be the principal mansion house, and make some other residence the principal mansion house. So far as I can see, there is no authority directly in point on that question. I think, however, that the question of whether or not a particular house is the principal mansion house is a question of fact."[90] He held that as a matter of fact the smaller house had become the principal mansion house.[91]

Timber is dealt with elsewhere.[92]

The compromise of a claim simply means settling a legal action out of court. Any such settlement will be binding and may affect the interests of all the beneficiaries and the requirement as to

---

[86] [1938] 2 All E.R. 210 (Ch.D. Farwell J.).

[87] The estate was over 70,000 acres in extent, the original mansion house had 52 bedrooms and 10 reception rooms.

[88] Third Sched., Pt.I (xxv).

[89] [1938] 2 All E.R. 210, at p. 213.

[90] *Ibid.*

[91] The previous approval of the trustees in writing is also needed for the tenant for life to provide at his own expense "dwellings available for the working classes" on the settled land; but s.107(2) continues to provide that the provision of such houses "shall not be deemed to be an injury to any interest in reversion or remainder in that land."

[92] Below, p. 245.

consent provides a safeguard. Here the consent of the trustees or an order of the court is required whenever the settlement was created. The settlement may dispense with the requirement—since the settlement can always enlarge the tenant for life's statutory powers[93]—but this is unlikely in practice.

Principle 14. The tenant for life as trustee

In exercising his statutory powers the tenant for life is acting as trustee for all the beneficiaries[94]; but he does not have to consult or obtain the consent of the other beneficiaries before acting; and provided that he acts in good faith and complies with the statutory requirements the court will not normally investigate his motives.

Explanation

The tenant for life holds the legal estate and the statutory powers that go with it not just for his own benefit but also as trustee for all the beneficiaries entitled under the settlement. It has been said that, like any trustee, he must "act as an independent and righteous man would act in dealing with the affairs of others."[95] But it has to be accepted that it is a "highly interested trusteeship"[96] in that the tenant for life is himself one of the chief beneficiaries and entitled to consult his own interest to some extent.

It is difficult to state as a principle just when the courts will interfere.

In *Wheelwright* v. *Walker* (No. 1)[97] land was settled on the defendant for life with remainder to his daughter. The daughter sold her remainder to the plaintiff. In this case the plaintiff was asking for an injunction to restrain the defendant as tenant for life from selling the land. The plaintiff had two arguments. First, that he desired to occupy the land on the death of the tenant for life; secondly, that no Settled Land Act trustees had been appointed. Pearson J. refused to interfere on the first ground but granted an injunction on the second. He said:

> "There is nothing that I can see in the Act to enable the court to restrain him from selling, whether he desires to sell because he is in debt, and wishes to increase his income; or

[93] See below, p. 227.
[94] S.L.A. 1925, s.107.
[95] Cheshire, *Modern Law of Real Property* (11th ed., 1972), p. 189.
[96] *Re Earl of Stamford and Warrington* [1916] 1 Ch. 404, at p. 420, *per* Younger J.
[97] (1883) 23 Ch.D. 752.

whether without being in debt, he thinks he can increase his income; or whether he desires to sell from mere unwillingness to take the trouble involved in the management of landed property; or whether he acts from worse motives, as from mere caprice or whim, or because he is desirous of doing that which he knows would be very disagreeable to those who expect to succeed him at his death . . . . So far as I can see, the object of the Act is to enable the tenant for life of real estate comprised in a settlement to take it out of the settlement and to substitute for it *ex mero motu*, the value of it in pounds shillings and pence."[98]

In *Re Hunt's Settled Estates*,[99] Farewell J. expressed a greater willingness to interfere. In this case the tenant for life had gone bankrupt and his interest in the settled land had been assigned by his trustee in bankruptcy to a certain Leppard.[1] Part of the land was sold and the proceeds paid to the trustees of the settlement. The tenant for life and Leppard together contracted to purchase certain leasehold property with more than sixty years to run. Before making the contract they had been advised by the trustees that the latter did not consider it a suitable investment. Nevertheless, they proceeded and then directed the trustees to invest £2,600 of capital in the purchase of the property. They sent the trustees a survey of the property but the trustees obtained their own survey which suggested that he property was "badly planned, badly built, badly drained, and one which would be increasingly expensive to maintain in repair and keep occupied . . . we are of the opinion that the utmost that should be given for the property at the present time for trust purposes is £1,400 but we strongly advise trustees not to buy at any price."[2] On the basis of this report the trustees refused to provide the money. In the present action they were seeking a declaration that they were justified. The court granted them this declaration. Farewell J. found that there was ample evidence of *mala fides,* some sort of collusion between the tenant for life, Leppard and a third person, but he found that even in the absence of *mala fides* the declaration should be granted. A tenant for life, he said, "is neither in a better nor a worse position than an ordinary truste who has a discretionary power to invest in leaseholds."[3]

---

[98] *Ibid.*
[99] [1905] 2 Ch. 418.
[1] Where the tenant for life goes bankrupt he remains tenant for life under the Act, but his beneficial interest passes to his trustee in bankruptcy and, in this case, was sold to Leppard, see S.L.A. 1925, s.103.
[2] [1904–7] All E.R.(Rep.) 736, at p. 738.
[3] *Ibid.* p. 738.

In most cases where the courts have interfered there has been some clear breach of the statutory requirements. In *Wheelwright* v. *Walker* (No. 2)[4] the tenant for life was proposing to sell at one price having been offered a higher price by one of the beneficiaries . . . . Clearly he was not obtaining the best price reasonably possible. In *Chandler* v. *Bradley*,[5] the tenant for life granted a lease at a reduced rent for a bribe. Again, a breach of the statutory requirement as to the best rent reasonably possible.

Perhaps, this can be said: It is for the tenant for life to choose the form of investment, in particular to choose whether the settled property is to remain in the form of land or be converted into some other form. He is, for example, entitled to sell the land and have the proceeds invested in leasehold property. The courts will not interfere even if he makes the change with a view to his own rather than the other beneficiaries' interests. But the tenant for life must comply with the statutory requirements and, subject to the above, he must act like a trustee. For example, as seen in *Re Hunt's S.E.*,[6] if he wishes to invest in leasehold property he is entitled to; but it must not only have more than 60 years to run, it must be leasehold property in which a trustee could properly choose to invest.[7]

Principle 15. Restrictions on statutory powers

The settlement may expressly increase the statutory powers of the tenant for life but any attempt to restrict them or induce him not to exercise them will be void and can be ignored.[8]

Further, the tenant for life cannot assign or contract not to exercise his statutory powers.[9]

Explanation

The settlor can give the tenant for life whatever additional powers of dealing with the settled land he wishes. If he wanted to he could give him all the powers of an absolute owner. It has already been noted that any such additional powers must be set out in the vesting instrument.

---

[4] (1883) 31 W.R. 912.
[5] [1897] 1 Ch. 315, above, p. 215.
[6] Above, n. 99.
[7] As to the right of the tenant for life to be "a selfish trustee" see *Re Duke of Northumberland, decd.* [1951] Ch. 202; *Re Boston's W.T.* [1956] Ch. 395. As to duties of the trustees in selecting investments and to act fairly between those entitled to capital and income, see Hanbury, and Mandsley, Modern Equity, (10th ed.), p. 456 *et seq.*
[8] S.L.A. 1925, s.106.
[9] *Ibid.* s.104.

On the other hand it is obvious that if the settlor could restrict the tenant for life's statutory powers, the whole scheme and purpose of the legislation governing settled land could be defeated. Section 106 of the Settled Land Act 1925, which deals with the matter, is very comprehensive. It provides, *inter alia,* that any provision,

" . . . (*b*) attempting, or tending, or intended, by a limitation, gift, or disposition over of settled land, or by a limitation, gift, or disposition of other real or any personal property, or by the imposition of any condition, or by forfeiture, or in any other manner whatever, to prohibit or prevent him from exercising, or to induce him to abstain from exercising, or to put him into a position inconsistent with his exercising, any power under this Act, or his right to require the settled land to be vested in him; that provision as far as it purports, or attempts, or tends, or is intended to have, or would or might have, the operation aforesaid, shall be deemed to be void."[10]

If a settlement gives a life interest to A with a proviso that he will lose his life interest if he sells, this proviso will clearly be void. A will be able to sell and his life interest will continue in the proceeds of sale.

Again, suppose that the settlement gives X a life interest in Blackacre with a proviso that if he ceases to reside on the property he will forfeit his interest. This proviso will be void to the extent, but only to the extent that it prevents him from exercising any of his statutory powers. He will be able to sell (and consequently cease to reside) without forfeiting his interest. On the other hand if the reason for him ceasing to reside is something other than the exercise of his statutory powers, the proviso will operate and he will lose his life interest: if for example he simply goes to live abroad.

In *Re Ames, Ames* v. *Ames,*[11] the trustees were given the sum of £4,000 on trust to use the income to maintain the settled land and to pay any surplus income to the tenant for life. The settlement included a proviso that if the tenant for life should cease to reside on the land, these trusts should cease and there should be a gift over of the £4,000. The tenant for life sold the land. North J. held that the proviso was void and that the tenant for life should

---

[10] *Ibid.* s.106(1)(*b*); see also the rest of this section. Whilst the section is essential to the scheme of the Act, is probably true that in practice today very few settlors would want to put such restraints on sale.

[11] [1893] 2 Ch. 479 (North J.).

continue to receive the income—now the whole income since there was no longer any land to maintain.

By way of contrast, in *Re Haynes, Kemp* v. *Haynes,*[12] the testator left his house to his wife for life provided "she reside at my said house, and shall not absent herself therefrom for more than three calendar months in any one year or for more than three calendar months continuously at any one time, and also that she shall not entertain or permit to reside at my house her sister Mrs. Burton, or the present or any future husband of the said Mrs. Burton or any children or child of the said Mrs. Burton or of her said husband for more than one week in any one year or more than one week continuously at any one time."

This proviso was held to be effective. If however she had absented herself as a result of selling or leasing the proviso would not have operated.[13]

Assignment of statutory powers. The tenant for life can of course sell, give away or otherwise dispose of his beneficial interest; but he cannot get rid of his statutory powers. If for example Blackacre is held by A for life remainder to B in fee simple under a strict settlement; A can sell his interest to X (who will obtain an interest *pur autre vie*). But A will remain tenant for life of Blackacre under the Settled Land Act. He will not have to obtain X's consent before acting although he will have to give him notice and X will be entitled to the income from the land or proceeds of sale. The same rule applies whatever the reason for the assignment of the beneficial interest—for example the bankruptcy of the tenant for life.

However, in three cases the tenant for life will cease to exercise the statutory powers: First, where his interest is released in favour of the next beneficiary under the settlement[14]; secondly, where the court authorises the trustees of the settlement to exercise the statutory powers—this can happen if the tenant for life has ceased to have any beneficial interest[15]; thirdly, where the tenant for life has become a mental patient.

Further, by section 68 of the Settled Land Act 1925, the trustees

---

[12] (1887) 37 Ch.D. 306.

[13] Where the settlement gives income from some other source to the tenant for life, a provision that he is to lose the income on exercising his statutory powers will be void. This was the position in *Re Ames*; see also *Re Patten* [1929] 2 Ch.276. On the other hand, it has been held that if the settlement provides a fund for the upkeep of the house with a gift over when the tenant ceases to occupy, the gift over will be perfectly valid. See *Re Burden* [1948] Ch. 160; *Re Aberconway's Settlement Trusts* [1953] Ch. 647.

[14] S.L.A. 1925, s.105.

[15] *Ibid.* s.24.

of the settlement will exercise the powers of the tenant for life where the latter is himself purchasing the settled land or otherwise dealing with the settled estate in his personal capacity.

Principle 16. Acts authorised by the court

The court has power under section 64 of the Settled Land Act 1925 to authorise any transaction by the tenant for life which is not otherwise authorised by the Settled Land Act or by the settlement itself provided the transaction is for the benefit of the settled land or the beneficiaries.

Explanation

This provision gives a degree of flexibility to the modern settlement. It enables the land or the beneficial interests to be dealt with in any way that might in the circumstances be desirable; at the same time the exercise of this power is in the responsible and impartial hands of the court.

In *Re Scarisbrick Settled Estates*,[16] the tenant for life found that he was unable to maintain the principal mansion house out of income. He was in the present case applying for authority to use £10,000 out of capital towards maintenance so that he could continue to live there and keep up the house until it could be sold at a better price than could be immediately obtained. The judgment of Cohen J. gives a glimpse into the social conditions of the times:

> "The difficulties of maintaining the estates out of income were no doubt increased by the war and had it not been that the Hall was let to the Red Cross Society under a tenancy agreement dated the 31 December 1940, the sum of £20,000[17] which I have mentioned would no doubt have been exhausted earlier . . . . It may be said that here can be little hope of the applicant being able to continue to live in and maintain the Hall when the war comes to an end."[18]

Cohen J. authorised the expenditure as the continued residence of the applicant at the Hall for the time being was in the interests of all the parties under the settlement.

This section, section 64 of the Settled Land Act 1925, enables

[16] [1944] 1 All E.R. 404.
[17] Which had been appointed to the applicant under a power of appointment in 1931.
[18] [1944] 1 All E.R. 404, at p. 406.

the court to approve transactions on behalf of beneficiaries who are infants or who are not yet born; and the court has even used it to approve a variation of the beneficial interests for the sole purpose of reducing estate duty on the estate. The scheme which the court approved in *Re Downshire Settled Estates*[19] was designed so "that the land should be substantially preserved so as to provide a home or homes for the future holders of the plaintiff's title, by relieving the estate from claims for death duties which would otherwise be liable to cause the properties to be wholly or partly broken up."

Apart from section 64 of the Settled Land Act there are various other statutory provisions which enable the court to authorise variations of settlements.[20]

SECTION IV.   TRUSTEES OF THE SETTLEMENT

Principle 17.   Appointment of trustees

The Settled Land Act 1925 stipulates who will be the trustees of the settlement.[21] In most cases the original trustees will be appointed by the settlor in the trust instrument. There is no minimum number but where capital money arises there must be at least two trustees or a trust corporation to receive it.[22] There cannot be more than four trustees.

Explanation

A strict settlement will be perfectly valid without trustees; but very little can be done with the settled land in their absence and so invariably trustees will be appointed.

The Settled Land Act 1925 gives a list of those entitled to act as trustees of the settlement and their order of priority. For example, the first right to act belongs to any persons to whom the settlement purports to give the power to sell the settled land. They have priority even over persons expressly appointed as trustees by the trust instrument. It is rare to find anyone in this category since any such attempt to give trustees the power to sell under a strict settlement will not be effective. But it may be relevant where a "do-it-yourself" settlor has drawn up his own home-made settle-

---

[19] [1953] Ch. 218 (C.A.).
[20] *e.g.* Variation of Trusts Act 1958; Trustee Act 1925, s.57; S.L.A. 1925, s.46.
[21] s.30.
[22] S.L.A. 1925, s.94. And there must be the same number to receive notice by the tenant for life of his intention to exercise his statutory power, see s.101(1).

ment without appreciating the finer distinctions between strict settlements and trusts for sale.

If there is no one in the above class, then the next persons entitled to act as trustees are the persons expressly appointed to the position by the settlor. This is the normal way of obtaining trustees. If there is no one in this category the Settled Land Act goes on to say who is next entitled and so on. There is no need to continue the list except to say that where a settlement is created by will and there is no one else to act, then the personal representatives of the settlor will be trustees until others are appointed. Further, if all else fails and there is no one to act, then an appointment can be made by the court—exemplifying the principle that "equity never wants for a trustee." No trust will fail merely because there are no trustees to administer it.

The purchaser will only obtain the protection of the over-reaching machinery if he pays the capital money to the trustees of whom there must be for this purpose at least two or a trust corporation. If there is only one trustee, not a trust corporation, a purchaser will need to refuse to complete until another has been appointed. If an attempt is made to appoint more than four the first four named who are of full age and willing to act will be the trustees.[23]

Once the original trustees have been appointed they can be discharged and replaced by new trustees in the same way as any trustees.[24]

There is no rule against the tenant for life being one of the trustees.

Principle 18.   Powers of the trustees

The trustees of the settlement as such *do not* hold the legal estate or have the power to deal with the settled land. They do have the following functions:

(1) The tenant for life must give them notice and in some cases obtain their consent before exercising his statutory powers.[25]

(2) They will receive and hold any capital money.[26]

(3) On the death of the tenant for life, if the settlement continues, they will act as special personal representatives.[27]

---

[23] Trustee Act 1925, ss.34, 39.
[24] See Hanbury and Maudsley, *Modern Equity* (11th ed.), pp. 517-538.
[25] Above, p. 212.
[26] Below, p. 238.
[27] Above, p. 210.

(4) Where there is no tenant for life or he is an infant, they will act as statutory owner.[28]

(5) They will exercise the powers of the tenant for life where he wishes to acquire the land himself or no longer has any substantial interest in it.[29]

(6) In the case of an imperfect settlement they will have to execute a vesting deed.[30]

(7) They will execute a deed of discharge if this is necessary when the settlement determines.[31]

Explanation

These various functions are dealt with separately in more detail elsewhere.

Trustees of the settlement are somewhat peculiar trustees. Unlike ordinary trustees they do not normally hold the trust properly. In certain special cases they do take over from the tenant for life and have the power of dealing with it. But in normal times their function is to "keep an eye" on the tenant for life and check that he is using his powers properly for the benefit of all beneficiaries, not just himself. But the other beneficiaries probably derive little protection. The weakness of the provisions requiring the tenant for life to give notice have already been mentioned; also the fact that the tenant for life has a right to be a somewhat selfish trustee of his statutory powers;[32] further, although capital has to be paid to and held by the trustees (at least the tenant for life cannot run off with it), it is the tenant for life who directs which of the authorised uses is to be made of such capital.[33] Finally, there is section 97 of the Settled Land Act 1925. This provides, *inter alia*, that the trustees will not be liable "for giving any consent, or for not making, bringing, taking or doing any such application, action, proceeding, or thing, as they might make, bring, take or do." The effect of this section has been disputed, but it appears to give the trustees a very wide measure of exemption from liability in respect of anything which they do or fail to do. It certainly seems to mean that the trustees are not under any obligation to investigate the tenant for life's actions to discover whether they are proper. It may mean, further, that they are not obliged to take action even if they

---

[28] Above, p. 205.
[29] Above, p. 229.
[30] Above, p. 210.
[31] Below, p. 254.
[32] Above, p. 225.
[33] Above, p. 219.

discover that they are improper—for example, selling the property for less than he could get for it.

Section V.   The Purchaser of Settled Land

Principle 19.   Overreaching[34]

Provided the statutory requirements are complied with, a purchaser of the settled land will take if free of the beneficial interests which will be overreached; that is they will be transferred from the land to the purchase money. The purchaser will not be concerned to investigate the beneficial interests.[35]

Explanation

A simple illustration will show how overreaching works. Suppose that Blackacre is settled by strict settlement on A for life, remainder to B in fee tail, remainder to C in fee simple. A will be tenant for life and have the statutory power of sale. Suppose that he sells to P. P will take a conveyance of the legal estate held by A. However, whereas A held the legal estate on trust for himself, B and C, P will take it free of all these equitable beneficial interests. He will become owner in law and equity—that is beneficial owner of the land. The interests of A, B and C will be overreached, that is, they will become equivalent interests in the purchase money held by the trustees of the settlement. If, as will normally happen, the money is invested and produces income, then A will receive the income for the rest of his life. When he dies B will receive the income for the rest of his life. When B dies the income will pass to his eldest son (or whoever else is then entitled to the fee tail). If and when the fee tail comes to an end C's fee simple will fall into possession. C will receive the whole capital sum just as he would have become the absolute owner of the land had it not been sold. Of course, by this time the fee simple might have passed from C to someone else on the death of C, by sale or otherwise; it will be necessary to trace it from C to discover who is now entitled. It should also be remembered that B or one of the succeeding fee tail tenants might have barred the fee tail[36] and thus become entitled to the whole sum leaving C without any interest.

Purpose of overreaching machinery.   The overreaching provisions are an essential part of the conveyancing machinery designed

---

[34] See also below, p. 280.
[35] S.L.A. 1925, s.73; L.P.A. 1925, ss.2(1), 205(1) (xxi).
[36] See below, p. 249, for barring the entail.

to simplify conveyancing. The purchaser will not have to[37] investigate the settlement to see what interests might affect him. They will be overreached and not affect him whether or not he happens to have notice of them. Overreaching, together with the provisions simplifying ownership of the legal estate, have made conveyancing a relatively simple matter.

Interests which will be overreached. Not all interests affecting the settled land will be overreached on sale. From a purchaser's point of view it would be the ultimate simplification if they were. He would take the land free of any interests whatsoever. But clearly this is not possible. The importance of some interests is precisely that they are interests in land.[38] They would be meaningless or less valuable if liable to be converted into interests in money.

Suppose that the tenant for life, in exercise of his statutory powers, creates a legal mortgage of the land in order to raise money to pay for improvements. The mortgagee is protected because he has land as his security. If necessary he can enforce payment by going against the land even in the hands of a purchaser. It would hardly be satisfactory if the mortgagee's rights against the land disappeared on sale leaving the mortgagee with the right only to claim repayment out of the money held by trustees. Unlike the land itself, the trustees could "disappear" with the money.[39]

Again, suppose that the tenant for life has created a right of way over the land in favour of a neighbouring landowner. The neighbour needs the right of way to get to and from his property. It would hardly be satisfactory if the neighbour could wake up one morning to find that the land had been sold and that he could no longer use the right of way. It would be little consolation to tell him that he now had a right of way over a sum of money! Or, more realistically, that he was to obtain some sort of compensation out of the proceeds of sale.

Thus, it will be appreciated that the main value of some interests rests largely on the fact that they will be enforceable against the land even in the hands of subsequent owners. On the other hand, some interests can quite conveniently be translated into interests in money without injustice to the holder of the interest.

Overreaching may be to the disadvantage of the remainderman. Blackacre is held for A for life remainder to B in fee simple. If the

---

[37] And will not be entitled to: S.L.A. 1925, s.110(2).

[38] See further below, p. 583, for distinction between commercial and family interests.

[39] But certain mortgages are liable to be overreached; see below, p. 236.

land is sold B will have the prospect, on the death of A, of receiving a sum of money instead of the land itself. He might have preferred the land and the result may be to his financial disadvantage. But he will get his interest, although in a different form; and this is the price which has to be paid for the simplication of conveyancing and the free alienability of land. Further, the beneficiary under a settlement will invariably not have paid for his interest. It will be a gift from the settlor. He can hardly complain if the gift ultimately takes one form rather than another. In contrast, the mortgagee, for example, will have advanced money in return for the mortgage of the land and is more entitled to have the form of his security preserved.

Section 72 of the Settled Land Act 1925 specifies which interests will be overreached. Broadly speaking, the principle is that the beneficial "family interests" created by the settlement will be overreached; whereas any "commercial interests" will not.[40]

In more detail:

A disposition of the legal estate by the tenant for life—that is one which is authorised and complies with the statutory requirements—will overreach the following interests.

(a) All the beneficial interests under the settlement. This includes not only the life interests, fee tails and fee simples, etc. but also any family charges[41] affecting the land. All these interests will invariably be equitable.[42]

(b) Any rights created out of those beneficial interests. For example, if a fee simple remainderman mortgages his fee simple remainder, the mortgage will be overreached. A beneficiary cannot create a greater interest in the land than he has himself.

(c) The following three commercial interests whether or not registered under the Land Charges Act 1972[43]:

   (i) Annuities within Part II of the Land Charges Act 1925.[44]

   (ii) Limited owners' charges.

(iii) General equitable charges.

This class constitutes a limited exception to the general rule that only family interests arising under the settlement—and interests derived out of them—can be overreached. In general, commercial

---

[40] See n. 38 above.

[41] See below, p. 252, for family charges.

[42] But they could be legal interests created by the settlor voluntarily in favour of a beneficiary, *e.g.* a legal rentcharge not created for money or money's worth, or a portions term where the money has not been raised at the date of the conveyance (both unlikely); see S.L.A. 1925, s.72(2) (ii), (iii).

[43] Replacing L.C.A. 1925.

[44] See now L.C.A. 1972, s.1(1)(4).

interests—those created for money or money's worth[45]—will not be affected. Category (i) is not important since it only refers to interests created before 1926. Category (ii) refers to the charge which a limited owner—a tenant for life or statutory owner—has over the land to secure the repayment of money which he has spent and is entitled to recover from the settlement. An example is where the tenant for life has paid capital transfer tax on the settled property out of his own pocket. A limited owner's charge is a commercial interest in that the limited owner has expended money and the charge is his security for its repayment.

Category (iii)—the general equitable charge—is dealt with later on. It includes annuities created after 1925 and equitable mortgages not protected by deposit of title deeds. Like the limited owner's charge, the general equitable charge is a commercial interest.[46]

These three categories will be overreached even if created before the settlement. An important point to note is that these three interests are registrable under the Land Charges Act 1972. As will be seen[47] the purpose of registration is to make the interest enforceable against any subsequent owner of the land. But by way of exception these three interests can be overreached even though registered. The point is that they are interests which, though commercial, Parliament has felt can without injustice be transferred from land to the proceeds of sale. After all, they are charges designed to secure the payment of money—not for example as in the case of restrictive covenants to secure amenities. The holder of the charge is protected by the Settled Land Act machinery. Payment of the money is to two trustees and so he is pretty certain to get what is due to him.

Interests which will not be overreached. The following interests will not be overreached:

(1) Any commercial interests to which the land is subject when the settlement is created.[48] For example, if a landowner leases his land and then settles it for the benefit of his children, the settlement will only take effect subject to the lease. If the tenant for life sells, he will sell subject to the lease.

(2) Any commercial interests affecting the legal estate created by the tenant for life in the exercise of his statutory powers or express powers under the settlement. For example, if the tenant

---

[45] See S.L.A. 1925, s.72(2) (iii).
[46] By definition, it excludes a beneficial interest arising under a settlement, see L.C.A. 1972, s.2(4).
[47] See below, Chaps. 24, 25.
[48] If there are family interests the land must be settled; see S.L.A. 1925, s.1(1) (v).

for life exercises his power to create a legal mortgage of the settled land and then subsequently sells, the purchaser will take subject to the mortgage.

Both these cases are with the exception of the three interests mentioned in C (i), (ii) and (iii) above. As seen these three can be overreached even though commercial interests.

Further, any interest falling in (1) or (2) above which is registrable will only be protected if it is registered. If a registrable interest is not registered then not only will it not be protected from overreaching, it will not be protected at all. It is likely to be void against a purchaser of the land.[49]

Suppose that the tenant for life enters into a contract to sell to P who registers his estate contract under the Land Charges Act 1972. If the tenant for life then sells and conveys the land to Q—in breach of his contract with P—then P will be protected. His interest will not be overreached and he will be able to enforce it against the land in the hands of Q. On the other hand if P has not bothered to register, he will be in trouble. He will not be able to enforce against Q since he has not registered; but neither will he be able to claim against Q's purchase money in the hands of the trustees. His only claim for what it is worth will be against the tenant for life for breach of contract.

(3) Certain voluntary dispositions of the legal estate which the tenant for life is empowered to make. For example, certain gifts of land for public uses. These dispositions though voluntary bind the land and cannot be overreached.

The statutory requirements. In general the overreaching machinery will only operate to protect a purchaser if all the statutory requirements are complied with. The machinery was set up by Parliament to control settled land and a purchaser ignores it at his peril. If he fails to comply with the statutory requirements he will not have the benefit of the overreaching machinery.

Section 18 of the Settled Land Act 1925 provides that:

> "(a) any disposition by the tenant for life or statutory owner of the land, other than a disposition authorised by this Act or any other statute, or made in pursuance of any additional or larger powers mentioned in the vesting instrument, shall be void, except for the purpose of conveying or creating such equitable interests as he has power, in right of his equitable interests and powers under the trust instrument, to convey or create

---

[49] For the effect of registration machinery see below Chap. 24 (Unregistered Land); Chap. 25 (Registered Land).

One of the main requirements of the Act is that any capital money must be paid to the trustees of the settlement or into court and that there must be at least two trustees or a trust corporation for this purpose.[50]

In general, a purchaser will be happy to comply with the statutory requirements since the whole purpose of the legislation is to simplify transactions involving settled land. In the ordinary case the purchaser will get a good title without the trouble and expense of investigating the complex provisions of the settlement; and without having to chase after all the beneficiaries for their consent to the sale.

Where the statutory requirements are not complied with, section 18 makes the disposition void. However, in most cases, a purchaser who is acting in good faith and innocent of the irregularity will be protected.[51]

Transactions to which overreaching applies. Overreaching is not confined to the case of a sale. It applies to any "sale, exchange, lease, mortgage, charge, or other disposition" by the tenant for life.[52]

Principle 20. Sale subject to family charges: Law of Property (Amendment) Act 1926

Where a person holds the legal estate subject only to family charges and where no vesting instrument has been executed, he can deal with the land as a beneficial owner subject to the charges.

Explanation

Prior to 1926, if an estate owner was entitled to land subject only to outstanding family charges, it was *not* deemed to be settled. It could be and was dealt with in the ordinary way subject to the charges. The 1925 legislation, as already explained,[53] treated such land as settled. Overnight it became settled and any dealing would have to comply with the settled land machinery—trustees appointed, a vesting deed executed and so on. And this applied even where the land was no longer held by one of the beneficiaries. Suppose that before 1926 B found himself absolutely entitled to Blackacre subject only to a jointure rentcharge in favour of Aunt Mabel. And suppose that, still before 1926, he sold it to P who sold

[50] See above, p. 231.
[51] See below, p. 241.
[52] S.L.A. 1925, s.72(1).
[53] Above, p. 199.

it to Q who sold it to R in all cases subject to the rentcharge. On January 1, 1926, R who is then the owner suddenly finds that he has been transformed into a tenant for life of settled land.

The Law of Property (Amendment) Act 1926 was passed to remove the hardship caused to a person in R's position who thus found that his land had become settled. It provided that in such a case the estate owner could deal with the land as if it were not settled, that is he could continue to deal with it as a beneficial owner subject to the family charges.

The Act is still available today but is not very important. It can only apply where the person wishing to deal with the land holds the legal estate and no vesting deed has been executed. Once a vesting instrument has been executed—which is likely to be the position today—the land must be dealt with as settled land even if it is held absolutely subject only to family charges. And, apart from exceptions noted later, it will only cease to be subject to the Settled Land Act machinery when a deed of discharge has been executed.[54]

Principle 21.　The "curtain"

Section 110 (2) of the Settled Land Act 1925 provides that in general a purchaser of a legal estate in settled land is entitled to and must assume that the details contained in the vesting instrument are correct; and in general he will not be entitled to investigate the trust instrument.

Explanation

This is the main "curtain" provision of the Settled Land Act 1925. A purchaser deals with the legal estate. All the equitable interests existing under the settlement are kept behind this curtain, that is, they are kept off the title. In the normal sort of transaction the purchaser will be shown the vesting deed or assent.[55] By virtue of section 110(2), he must assume that the details which it shows are correct. It will, for example, no doubt show the vendor as tenant for life; it will name the trustees of the settlement. The purchaser must assume that the persons named as trustees are in fact the present trustees properly appointed and pay his money to them. He cannot call for the production of the trust instrument or other evidence of their authority to act.

In the normal transaction the details contained in the vesting

---

[54] See below, p. 254.

[55] In the case of registered land he will see the register showing the tenant for life registered as proprietor.

instrument will in fact be correct; all will be in order and the overreaching machinery will operate as described above. The purchaser will take the land free of the equitable interests.

But it is possible and obviously going to happen from time to time that the vesting instrument conceals some irregularity. For example, the trustees named are not in fact the real trustees appointed by the trust instrument. What is the purchaser's position in the case of such—or indeed any—irregularity which has occurred in the transaction?

The general principle is that any transaction which is irregular in any respect, that is, which does not comply with all the requirements of the Act, will be void.[56] The overreaching machinery will not operate and the purchaser will not be protected.

If this were the end of the matter it would not be fair to the purchaser. His title would depend upon matters which he was not allowed to investigate. In fact, the machinery of the Act is designed to protect the honest purchaser from such irregularities which he is precluded from discovering. This protection is dealt with in the next Principle.

Principle 22. Protection of purchaser in case of irregularities

Section 110(1) of the Settled Land Act 1925 provides:

> "On sale, exchange, lease, mortgage, charge, or other disposition, a purchaser dealing in good faith with a tenant for life or statutory owner shall, as against all other parties entitled under the settlement, be conclusively taken to have given the best price, consideration, or rent, as the case may require, that could reasonably be obtained by the tenant for life or statutory owner, and to have complied with all the requisitions of this Act."

Explanation

As already explained the general principle is that a purchaser will only be entitled to the benefit of the overreaching provisions if all the statutory requirements have been complied with.

However, in certain cases, the legislation protects the purchaser even if there has been some irregularity. The most important of these protective provisions is section 110 (1).

Where there has been some irregularity two separate questions have to be distinguished. First, does the irregularity entitle an

[56] S.L.A. 1925, s.18, see above, p. 238.

injured beneficiary to a remedy against the guilty tenant for life? Secondly, does it affect the purchaser and impair his title, that is can the injured beneficiary enforce his remedy against the land in the hands of the purchaser or a subsequent owner? An example will perhaps make this clearer. Suppose that the tenant for life agrees to sell to P for £5,000 subject to contract. An agreement "subject to contract" is not binding on either side but it is sometimes felt that such an agreement is morally binding and that the vendor should not back out at this stage merely because he has been offered a higher price for the property. Suppose, however, that before a binding contract is made the tenant for life gets a substantially higher offer from Q. It has been held that the duty of the tenant for life in such a situation will normally be to accept the higher offer if it is a serious one likely to result in a contract. If, therefore, our tenant for life proceeds to contract with P at the lower price he will probably be liable to the other beneficiaries for breach of his duty to get the best price reasonably possible. They will be able to sue him for the difference between the price which he did get and the price which he could have got. That is the answer to the first question. But can the beneficiaries pursue their claim against the purchaser? The answer to this question might be vital, if for example the tenant for life is not worth suing. And the answer is probably no. Section 110 (1) protects a bona fide purchaser in such a case even though the best price has not in fact been obtained.[57]

Again, the same section will protect a purchaser if the proper notice has not been given to the trustees.[58]

Thus, it can be said that, in general, if the purchaser deals with the tenant for life in good faith, he will be protected and obtain a good title even if there has been some failure to comply with the Settled Land Act 1925. In *Re Morgan's Lease*[59] the tenant for life let part of the settled property to the plaintiffs for a 10-year term. The lease, which was not under seal, gave the plaintiffs an option to renew for a further seven years at a yearly rent of £475. The plaintiffs did not know that the landlord held the property as tenant for life. The tenant for life died and when, subsequently, the plaintiffs claimed to exercise the option, the defendants as his successors in title resisted. The plaintiffs claimed specific performance of the executory contract which arose on the exercise of the option.

The main argument of the defence was that £475 was not the

---

[57] See *Re Morgan's Lease* [1972] Ch. 1 (Ungoed-Thomas J.).
[58] *Ibid.* pp. 4, 5.
[59] Above, n. 57.

best rent reasonably obtainable. Ungoed-Thomas J. held that whether or not it was, the plaintiffs were acting in good faith and protected by section 110(1); and that the option was therefore valid and specifically enforceable.

In reaching this conclusion, the judge decided, *inter alia,* that the section applied to a contract for a lease and not just to a completed transaction[60]; and that it applied even where the purchaser did not know that he was dealing with a tenant for life.[61]

There are situations in which a purchaser will not be protected. In particular, he will not be protected if he is not in good faith and knows of the irregularity.[62] And there may be cases where even a purchaser in good faith will not be protected.[63]

Other protective provisions. There are a number of other provisions which give protection to a purchaser, in addition to section 110 (1), for example, section 152 of the Law of Property Act 1925 which applies to leases of the property, and sections 13, 39 (4) (iii) and 112 (2) of the Settled Land Act 1925.

SECTION VI.   RIGHTS OF ENJOYMENT OF THE BENEFICIARIES

Principle 23.   Liability of the life tenant for waste

In the absence of provision to the contrary in the settlement, a life tenant in possession will be impeachable of waste; that is, he will not be liable for ameliorating or permissive waste, but he will be liable for voluntary waste.

If the settlement makes him unimpeachable of waste, he will not be liable for ameliorating, permissive or voluntary waste, but he will still be liable for equitable waste.

Explanation

We have seen that it is the machinery set up by the Settled Land Act which controls the way in which the tenant for life can deal with the land, sell it and so on.

On the other hand, his rights of enjoyment, that is what he can do on the land while he is in possession, are still largely governed by the doctrine of waste developed by common law and equity.

---

[60] *Ibid.* pp. 4, 5.
[61] Disagreeing on this point with Dankwerts J. in *Weston* v. *Henshaw* [1950] Ch. 510.
[62] See S.L.A. 1925, s.110(1).
[63] See, for example, Megarry and Wade, *Law of Real Property* (4th ed.), p. 307.

Before explaining the doctrine of waste, there are two points to note.

First, the life tenant will naturally have more limited rights of enjoyment than the beneficial fee simple owner. The basic principle of the strict settlement has always been to allow the present beneficiary to enjoy the inheritance for his lifetime but not to dissipate it. Under modern legislation he has the right to turn it from one form of property into another. But he is not allowed to appropriate it for himself. If the property is in the form of money or investments, he is allowed the income, but cannot touch the capital. If it is in the form of land he has possession and enjoyment, but the doctrine of waste is designed to pevent him from taking anything which is part of the land itself. A beneficial owner can sell the minerals and timber on his land; he can if he likes knock down the buildings and sell the materials.[64] For a life tenant to do this would be voluntary waste and not allowed unless authorised by the settlement or statute.

Secondly, the precise rights of enjoyment of the tenant for life depend upon the extent of his equitable beneficial interest. A fee tail tenant's rights of enjoyment are far wider than those of a life tenant. In most cases in practice the tenant for life is likely to have a life interest in equity.

The doctrine of waste.   Waste is any act which alters the nature of the land for better or worse. There are four types of waste:

(a) *Ameliorating waste.*   This is any act which improves the land. In general a life tenant will not be liable for ameliorating waste. *Meux* v. *Cobley*[65] was a case of a leasehold tenant but the same principle applies. There the tenant of an arable and pasture farm converted part of it into a market garden erecting glass houses for the production of "such known agricultural produce as tomatoes, grapes, mushrooms and other vegetables." The landlord—for reasons not given in the report—objected. Kekewich J., after considering all the evidence, came to the conclusion that the alterations were an improvement and as such could not be challenged. He said[66] that, "so far from being an injury to the inheritance, [they were] of the greatest possible advantage and that the addition of these [green] houses, if they are substantially built, and if they are kept in good order, is a most advantageous addition to a farm of this kind, in the neighbourhood of London."

---

[64] Subject, of course, to planning law.
[65] [1892] 2 Ch. 253 (Kekewich J.).
[66] *Ibid.* p. 264. The judge also decided that, in any case, on a proper construction the lease entitled the tenant to make these alterations.

(b) *Permissive waste.* This is damage due to neglect, that is failure to repair. The general rule is that a life tenant is not liable for permissive waste[67]; but the settlement may expressly make him liable.

(c) *Voluntary waste.* This means some positive act of damage to the property; it includes not only damage in the ordinary sense, such as pulling down buildings, but also any act which diminishes the value of the inheritance. To open a mine and sell the minerals may be a perfectly normal way of exploiting land, but it will leave less for succeeding tenants and is regarded as voluntary waste. The rules of waste in relation both to minerals and timber are particularly important and are considered separately below.

In the absence of special provision in the settlement, a life tenant is not allowed to commit voluntary waste, that is he is said to be impeachable of waste. However, it has always been common practice in settlements to make the life tenant "unimpeachable of waste"—that is not liable for voluntary waste.

(d) *Equitable waste.* This is "wanton destruction"[68] of the property. It is the same as voluntary waste only done with some improper or malicious motive—the sort of act that even an absolute owner would not do. The point is that even if the life tenant is unimpeachable of waste, equity will step in and protect the remainderman if he is acting unreasonably. In *Vane* v. *Lord Barnard,*[69] "the defendant, the Lord Barnard, having taken some displeasure against his son, got 200 workmen together, and of a sudden, in a few days, stript the castle of lead, iron, glass doors, and boards, etc., to the value of £3,000." The castle was Raby Castle and it had been settled by the defendant on himself for life without impeachment of waste, remainder to his son (the plaintiff) for life, remainder to the son's first and other sons in fee tail. The court granted an injunction ordering the defendant not to do any further damage and to make good damage already done.

The settlement could expressly make the tenant unimpeachable even of equitable waste, but this is not likely to be done in practice.

Principle 24.   Rights of the life tenant in respect of timber

If a life tenant is unimpeachable of waste, he may cut and sell timber for his own benefit.

---

[67] The principle that a person does not incur liability by inaction is found in several branches of common law; see Kenny's Outline of Criminal Law, (19th ed.), p. 19.

[68] Megarry and Wade, *Law of Real Property* (4th ed.), p. 105.

[69] (1716) 2 Vern. 738; 23 E.R. 1082.

If he is impeachable of waste, the general rule is that he may not cut and sell timber. However, there are a number of important exceptions.

In certain circumstances the cutting of trees may be equitable waste.

Explanation

The strict settlement was developed by landowners with the help of the courts to serve an agricultural society. Apart from letting land to farmers, two of the most important ways of exploiting land ownership were to cut and sell timber and to extract minerals. This could be done either by letting the timber and mineral rights or by the landowner working them himself through managers. "In 1791, the Myddelton family drew as much as £796 from their collieries, limekilns and slate quarries. Six coal mines let on 21-year leases—some paying rents others a royalty of a sixth of the coal—brought in £656; two limekilns paid a royalty of sixpence on each cartload burnt and brought in £120, and two slate quarries produced £20 each."[70]

It is for this reason that timber and mineral rights received detailed consideration by the courts. But, unlike the letting of land for agriculture, the removal of timber and minerals was waste. It did reduce the inheritance; and the interests of future as well as present tenants had to be considered.

In general, whether or not a life tenant can remove timber depends on whether he is impeachable of waste. If he is unimpeachable he can cut it for his own benefit; but even if he is impeachable, he can, in certain cases, remove timber. For example, if the timber is part of a timber estate, he can cut it in accordance with the rules of proper estate management. This is because timber from a timber estate is regarded as part of the income from the land to which the tenant in possession is entitled. It can be regarded like any other agricultural crop.

Again, the life tenant can cut any wood which is not classified as timber unless to do so would be equitable waste. And according to the common law the only trees regarded as timber are oak, ash and elm; although, by local custom recognised as binding by the courts, additional trees may be included in various parts of the country. In *Re Harker's Will Trusts*,[71] Simonds J. decided that larch was not timber either by common law or the custom of Cumberland and Westmorland. In that case the tenant for life was

---

[70] G.E. Mingay, *English Landed Society in the Eighteenth Century*.
[71] [1938] Ch. 323.

impeachable of waste. He had sold certain larch plantations on the estate for £1,407. The court decided that since larch was not timber he could properly sell it and keep the proceeds. If larch had been timber then the proceeds would have represented capital and would have had to be paid to the trustees.

But circumstances may make it waste to cut trees which are not timber, *e.g.* trees planted for ornament or shelter.

The most important case in which the tenant can cut timber even if impeachable of waste is under the Settled Land Act 1925.[72] This gives him a statutory right—which cannot be taken away by the settlement—to cut and sell any timber which is ripe for cutting provided the consent of the trustees or an order of the court is first obtained and provided that three-quarters of the proceeds are set aside as capital. The tenant for life is entitled to keep the other quarter.

Where trees, whether or not timber, have been planted, for example, for ornament or shelter, the courts are likely to restrain any attempt to cut them as equitable waste.

Principle 25.   The life tenant and minerals

If the life tenant is unimpeachable of waste he can open and work mines and keep any profit. If he is impeachable of waste he cannot open mines, but he can continue to work for his own benefit mines already opened at the start of his possession. Under the Settled Land Act 1925 the tenant for life has a statutory right to grant certain mining leases.

Explanation

The tenant can continue to work a mine that is already lawfully opened, even if he is impeachable. The opening of the mine (either by the settlor himself or with his authorisation under the settlement) is enough to show an intention that the minerals in the mine are to be exploited as a source of present income and not to be preserved intact as part of the inheritance. In such circumstances the extraction of minerals is not really waste at all since it is what can properly be classified as income. The case is similar to that of timber on the timber estate.

The statutory right of the tenant for life to grant mining leases has been considered.[73] It is, of course, to be remembered that the right of the tenant himself to take minerals and cut timber can only

[72] s.66.
[73] Above, p. 215.

continue for his lifetime; whereas a mining lease, if properly granted under the statute, will continue for its full course regardless of his death and will bind all the other beneficiaries.

Principle 26.   The life tenant and fixtures

In general, any fixtures added by the life tenant pass with the settled land. But when the life interest determines his personal representatives (or he himself if it is an interest *pur autre vie*) have a right to enter and remove trade fixtures and ornamental and domestic fixtures put there by the life tenant.

Explanation

The subject of fixtures has already been considered.[74]

Principle 27.   Emblements

On the determination of the life interest, the personal representatives (or the life tenant himself if it is an interest *pur autre vie*) have a right to enter to remove emblements.

Explanation

The term emblements refers to cultivated crops ("annual profits") which are sown and harvested within one year and which the tenant himself has sown.[75] It includes such crops as corn, roots, hops and potatoes. It does not include permanent crops ("natural profits") such as timber, fruit on fruit trees, clover, grass, etc. because grass is the natural profit of the earth even if the tenant "by good husbandry and industry, either by overflowing, or trenching, or compassing of the meadows, or digging up of bushes and such like, makes the grass to grow in more abundance."[76]

"Natural profits" become part of the land and on the death of the life tenant, they pass with the settled land even if planted by the tenant himself.

Emblements do not become part of the land but in the absence of the present rule there would be no right to enter the land to harvest them once the tenancy had ended. And it has been said that since a life tenant does not know when his tenancy might end, he would be discouraged from sowing in the first place. "And it is

---

[74] Above, p. 24.
[75] See *Graves* v. *Weld* (1833) 5 B. & A. 105; 110 E.R. 731.
[76] Co.Litt. 55b.

for the good of commonwealth that the ground be sown."[77] The
life tenant might die but at least he can control the distribution of
the final crops which he has sown.

The distinction between emblements and other crops is perhaps
becoming increasingly artificial with modern agricultural
methods.[78] A farmer might not appreciate the distinction between
sowing a field with potatoes on the one hand and pruning,
spraying, etc., an apple orchard on the other. But if he were a life
tenant of the land and died before harvest the distinction might be
important.

Principle 28.   Tenant in tail: Rights of enjoyment

In the absence of provision to the contrary in the settlement, a
tenant in tail in possession will not be liable for any type of waste.

Explanation

Under the traditional practice of settlement and resettlement
the tenant in possession usually had a life interest rather than a fee
tail. The fee tail was more likely to be in remainder.

Today it is probably unusual to find property being entailed at
all—though a number of old settlements still no doubt continue.
However, today, entails are still possible both in remainder and in
possession—though of course they must be equitable. And the
rights of enjoyment of a tenant in tail in possession need to be
mentioned.

The position is quite simply that in the absence of special
provision in the settlement, a tenant in tail is not liable for
waste—not even equitable waste. In other words, the rights of
enjoyment of a fee tail tenant are much the same as those of a
beneficial fee simple owner. This is understandable since a tenant
in tail in possession can quite simply bar his entail and turn it into a
fee simple absolute.

Principle 29.   Tenant in tail: Barring the entail

A tenant in tail may turn his entail into a fee simple by barring it.
If he bars either when himself in possession or with the consent

---

[77] Co.Litt. 55b.
[78] Compare the distinction between *fructus naturales* which are, and *fructus
industriales* which are not, part of the land; see above, p. 21 ("industrial growing
crops" may have a wider meaning than emblements; see Sale of Goods Act 1979,
s.61).

of the protector of the settlement (the tenant entitled in possession), he will create a fee simple absolute.

If he bars when not in possession and without the consent of the protector of the settlement, he will create only a base fee: that is, a fee simple which will determine if and when the entail from which it has been created would have determined had it not been barred.

The tenant in tail can bar by either of the following methods:

(a) an assurance (conveyance) of the property by deed;

(b) by will if he is in possession.

Explanation

Since the fifteenth century the courts have allowed the tenant in tail to bar his entail. Indeed, it has long been the rule that it is not possible to create an unbarrable entail.

The effect of barring the entail. The effect of barring can be explained by an illustration. Blackacre is settled on A for life remainder to B in fee tail remainder to C in fee simple. A is the protector of the settlement.[79] (He will also be tenant for life under the Settled Land Act.) B—provided he is of full age—can bar his entail. If he does it with the consent of A he will create a fee simple absolute in remainder which will fall into possession when A dies. The rights of his descendants will be destroyed; and so will any subsequent interests—in this case C's fee simple remainder. It is important to realise that C has no way at all of preventing this from happening and receives no sort of compensation for the loss of his interest. This means that the fee simple remainder after the entail is hardly of commercial value. But this hardly matters. The strict settlement was and still is a family affair. The final remainder is not really expected to fall into possession, since it is hoped that the settlement will continue to keep the property in the family for ever. It is merely a sort of long stop to provide what is to happen to it if ever there are no more direct descendants of the settlor to take.

To return to the illustration. If B cannot get the consent of A, he can wait until A is dead and his fee tail is in possession; if he does this he will again obtain a fee simple absolute and destroy all subsequent interests.

On the other hand, if he bars without A's consent and while A is still alive, he can create only a base fee.

A base fee is a type of fee simple. It has all the attributes of a fee simple and like it can be sold, left by will or pass on intestacy. The interest of B's descendants will be destroyed. However, unlike the

---

[79] See Fines and Recoveries Act 1833; L.P.A. 1925, Sched. 7.

fee simple, it suffers from one serious defect. It will determine when the fee tail from which it has been created would have determined. It does not destroy any subsequent interests.

Suppose that, in the above example, B creates a base fee in remainder on A's interest. And suppose that he transfers it to P who dies leaving it to Q. At this point A dies; this leaves Q with a base fee in possession and all the rights of enjoyment of a fee simple[80] beneficial owner. But tragedy strikes. At this point B dies a bachelor. At this point the fee tail would have come to an end. The base fee will come to an end. No doubt Q will find a solicitor's letter dropping through the letter-box asking him whether he will kindly arrange to move since C is now entitled to the land.

Two final points to note: First, the base fee is even less likely to arise today than the fee tail. Secondly, under the modern law, all this barring of entails can only take place in equity and is subject to the overreaching provisions. It may be in fact an interest in money rather than land which is being barred.

Methods of barring. There are two methods of barring an entail.

(1) *By disentailing assurance.* The tenant in tail can bar the entail by executing a deed conveying the land to another person. The grantee will receive a fee simple. If the fee tail tenant is selling the fee simple which he is creating, then the conveyance will be in favour of the purchaser. If he wishes to keep the fee simple himself, then the conveyance will be in favour of a trustee for the tenant who is barring. The trustee can then transfer the new fee simple back to him.

(2) *By will.*[81] A tenant in tail can bar by will provided the following requirements are satisfied. He must be in possession and of full age; and the will must specifically refer to the property or the instrument under which it was acquired or to entailed property generally. For example, a general devise of all a testator's property by will would not be sufficient to bar any entails which he held.

Principle 30. Enlarging a base fee

A base fee can be enlarged into a fee simple absolute in the following ways:

[80] And Q is now in a position to enlarge his base fee into a fee simple absolute; below, p. 252.
[81] L.P.A. 1925, s.176.

(a) If the former tenant in tail executes a fresh disentailing assurance either when in possession or with the necessary consent.[82]

(b) By the owner of the base fee acquiring the immediate fee simple remainder or reversion.[83]

(c) By the owner of the base fee being in possession of the land for 12 years after the end of the protectorship.[84]

(d) By will by the person who was the fee tail tenant; but only if he still holds the base fee and only if it is in possession.[85]

Principle 31. Family charges

The settlement may include provision for the payment of pin money, jointures and portions.

Explanation

As already explained, traditionally the central feature of the strict settlement is the entail providing for the land to pass from the eldest son to eldest son. But where the settlement is designed to keep the land intact and in the hands of one member of the family in this way, it is necessary somehow to make financial provision for the other members of the family. In general there are three types of provision to be made:

(a) *Pin money for the wife.* This is a regular income for the wife during the life of the life tenant for her personal expenditure (to purchase her clothes, pins (brooches), etc.).

(b) *Jointures.* A jointure is a regular income for the wife if she should survive her husband. If he dies the land will go to the eldest son but she will have to be provided with a substantial income— not just pin money—on which to live (no doubt in the style to which she was accustomed in her husband's lifetime).

(c) *Portions for younger sons and daughters.* A portion is a lump sum of money paid to each of the younger sons and the daughters to give them a start in life—set the sons up in the law or some other profession suitable to the dignity of a younger son of a

---

[82] Fines and Recoveries Act 1833, ss.19, 35.
[83] See *ibid.* s.39.
[84] Limitation Act 1980, s.27.
[85] L.P.A. 1925, s.176.

landed family. And a daughter had to have a portion large enough to attract a sufficiently wealthy husband.

Two factors affect the provision of these payments. First, it has to be possible to raise them without selling off any of the land. Secondly, they need to be secured, that is they have to be charged on the land so that the widow or other beneficiary can enforce payment by going against the land if the money is not duly paid.

Today, the normal procedure is that the settlor will include provision for these payments in the trust instrument together with the entails and other beneficial interests. They will be charged on the land and like other beneficial interests under the settlement will constitute equitable interests in the land.

A provision for a regular payment to the widow, as pin money or a jointure, will constitute an equitable rentcharge and in the trust instrument it will be given priority to the other beneficial interests. In the normal way it will be paid by the tenant for life out of the regular income derived from the property; but if it is not paid the widow will have all the remedies of a rentcharge owner against the land to enforce payment.[86]

Similarly, the provision for the payment of a lump sum as a portion will constitute an equitable charge on the land. Again it will be given priority over the beneficial disposition of the land itself. If the trustees are holding sufficient capital money it will be possible to pay portions out of this. If a beneficiary is entitled to land subject only to portions, he may pay the money out of his own pocket in order to clear the land. If necessary the trustees can require the tenant for life to raise the capital to pay portions by creating a legal mortgage of the land. If this is done the interest payments on the mortgage will have to be paid out of the income from the land. If the land is sold the capital will be repaid to the mortgagees out of the proceeds of sale. If the land cannot be mortgaged (if for example it is not of sufficient value or already fully mortgaged to secure other portions) and if the money cannot be raised in some other way, it may be necessary to sell off part of the land to raise the money. This is one of the ways in which the settled land might be dissipated—large families and too many portions. But, today, the cause of a break up is perhaps more likely to be capital transfer tax and too many deaths.

One final point, these family charges are not registrable[87]; and they will be overreached on sale.

---

[86] See below, Chap. 22, as to these.
[87] Being equitable charges arising under a trust for sale or settlement; see below, p. 520.

SECTION VII. DETERMINATION OF THE SETTLEMENT

Principle 32. Deed of discharge

Subject to exceptions, when a settlement comes to an end the trustees must execute a deed of discharge declaring that they are discharged.[88]

In certain exceptional cases a deed of discharge will not be required.

Explanation

It is the vesting instrument which brings all the machinery of the Settled Land Act 1925 into operation; once this has happened a purchaser will only be protected if he complies with the statutory requirements.[89]

The deed of discharge is the deed which formally terminates the settlement. The settlement may have ended in fact but the person finally entitled to the land cannot deal with it as a beneficial owner until a proper deed of discharge has been executed.

If, for example, Blackacre is settled on A for life remainder to B in fee simple and A purchases B's fee simple the settlement will come to an end. At this point, A will hold the legal estate (vested in him as tenant for life) and he will also be absolutely entitled in equity. Nevertheless, if he sells the land, the purchaser will have to insist on either production of a deed of discharge or compliance with the statutory requirements—payment of the purchase money to the trustees, etc. In this example the purchaser would as it happens get a good title since the vendor, A, does in fact hold the legal and equitable ownership. Section 18 does not avoid the conveyance since it is not a "disposition by the tenant for life or statutory owner." But the point is that in the absence of a deed of discharge, the purchaser will have no *proof* that the settlement has come to an end and that A is beneficially entitled. This means that if the title were not in fact in order (*e.g.* if the settlement had not come to an end) the purchaser would not be protected by s.110(1).

In two cases a deed of discharge is not required:

(a) Where no vesting instrument has been executed.[90] This is a rather unlikely situation since once land has become settled it cannot be dealt with until a vesting instrument has been executed. It might happen if, for example, the beneficial owner of Blackacre

---

[88] S.L.A. 1925, s.17.
[89] Subject to protection given by s.110(1), etc., see above, p. 241.
[90] See *Re Alefounder's W.T.* [1927] 1 Ch. 360.

created a rentcharge *inter vivos* in favour of his wife for life, paid the rentcharge but never executed a vesting deed in his own favour as tenant for life. If his wife died, he could deal with the land beneficially without any deed of discharge.

(b) Where personal representatives have made an assent of the land without stating in it who are the trustees of the settlement.

For example, if land is settled on A for life remainder to B in fee simple and A dies, the settlement will come to an end. The legal estate will pass to A's ordinary personal representatives—and they will transfer it to B by ordinary assent in writing—not by vesting assent. B will then be able to deal with the land as beneficial owner and he will not need any deed of discharge.[91]

---

[91] s.18 of the S.L.A. 1925 (requiring a deed of discharge) does not apply to personal representatives; and under s.110(5) a purchaser will be bound and entiled to accept an ordinary assent as evidence that the settlement has come to an end, see *Emmett on Title* (17th ed.), pp. 751–755.

CHAPTER 8

THE TRUST FOR SALE

General introduction

As already explained,[1] the basic principle of the trust for sale is that the land (the legal estate) is held by the trustees who are under an obligation to sell it and to hold the proceeds of sale in trust for the specified beneficiaries. If and when the land is sold—the trustees invariably have a power to postpone sale—the interests of the beneficiaries will be satisfied out of the proceeds of sale.

The trust for sale is the most important of the three types of trust ownership that can exist under modern law. Since the early nineteenth century it has been used as one of the two methods by which land can be settled. But its use is not confined to settlements. Parliament has extended its use to most cases of co-ownership and to intestacy.

The present chapter is concerned with the trust for sale with particular reference to settlements. Its application in the case of co-ownership and intestacy is dealt with in other chapters.[2]

The trust for sale and settlements. The trust for sale means no more than giving the land to trustees with an instruction to sell it and use the proceeds for some specified purpose.

In its simplest form it can be traced back over 500 years when testators are found giving land to trustees on trust to sell and to use the proceeds to discharge the testator's debts. This is still found. If real or personal property is left by a testator on trust for sale the trustees will be instructed to pay the debts and funeral expenses out of the proceeds before anything else.

It was in the nineteenth century that it became popular as a means of settling land. The essence of the strict settlement was the fee tail to ensure that the land passed intact from eldest son to eldest son, from generation to generation. Even where personal property was settled it was generally given to trustees with instructions to use it to purchase land and to settle the land on the beneficiaries by strict settlement.

The trust for sale was designed by lawyers to serve a different class of clients with a different attitude to land as a form of wealth. Such a would-be settlor no doubt had property which might

---

[1] Above, p. 202.
[2] See below, Chap. 12 (co-ownership), p. 578 (intestacy).

256

include land and also other investments. His general aim was that this wealth should be invested in safe investments producing a reasonable income for himself and his wife for life and that on their deaths it should still be there to be divided between the children and grandchildren. Such a settlor—who had perhaps accumulated his wealth from trade or industry—attached no special significance to land as a form of wealth. The important thing was not that the land should be retained at all costs but that at any time the trustees should be in a position to convert the property into whichever form was most advantageous from an investment point of view. Further, he was not interested in entails—and until 1925 land subject to a trust for sale could not be entailed.[3] All he wanted to do was to make certain that the children were provided for, not to preserve the wealth itself in any particular form for generation after generation.

The trust for sale was ideal for this purpose largely because it was (and still is) subject to the doctrine of conversion. Under this doctrine land which is subject to a trust for sale is treated as if it had been sold. This means that from the moment when the trust for sale is created the land is deemed to be, and is subject to all the same rules as money—that is personal property. It means further that from the start the beneficiaries are regarded as having interests in the proceeds of sale and not in the land itself. This doctrine gave the trust for sale a number of advantages.

(a) There was no difficulty in settling real and personal property together. All the property, real and personal, was held by the trustees as personalty—generally referred to as the "trust fund," as it still is—and made subject to a common set of beneficial interests set out in a single document.

(b) The sale of the land was as simple as possible. The legal ownership and control of the land was vested in a limited number of trustees. By dealing with them and them alone a purchaser would get a good title. Under the doctrine of conversion the beneficiaries did not have interests in the land and so the purchaser did not need to concern himself with these at all.

(c) The obligation on the trustees to sell could be qualified in two useful ways. They could be given a power to postpone sale and they could be required not to sell without the consent of specified persons. It was obviously desirable that trustees should be able to decide the best moment to sell. Further, the settlor might wish that he or his wife should have the choice of occupying the land themselves for their lives. The courts recognised this sort of need,

[3] See L.P.A. 1925, s.130.

and allowed these qualifications without the advantages of conversion being lost.

It is this type of settlement which is the commonest type of settlement today; frequently with property including land and other forms being held for the benefit of the settlor and his wife for life and then to be distributed equally between their children; and the whole thing operated behind a trust for sale.

The strict settlement is, of course, still available but what has happened is that most of the advantages and features which belonged to the trust for sale have now also been applied to the strict settlement as well.

SECTION I. DEFINITION

Principle 1.   Express creation of trust for sale

The term trust for sale under the 1925 legislation means an immediate binding trust for sale.[4]

To create an express trust for sale the following requirements must be satisfied:

  (a) There must be an obligation on the trustees to sell—not just a power of sale.
  (b) The obligation must be to sell immediately.
  (c) The trust must be binding.

Explanation

The obligation to sell.   The essence of a trust is that the trustees are put under an obligation to use the property for the benefit of beneficiaries. This has been considered already.[5] If for example property is given to "trustees" merely in the hope that they will use it in a particular way, but without imposing any obligation on them, there will be no trust at all; and the "trustees" will take it as a gift.

The trust for sale requires something more. There must be an obligation to deal with the property in a particular way, that is, to sell it and to hold the proceeds for the specified beneficiaries.

Generally, in a properly drawn conveyance on trust for sale, the obligation to sell will be clear. The property will be conveyed to the trustees with words such as "upon trust to sell and hold the proceeds of sale in trust for" the specified beneficiaries; and there

---

[4] L.P.A. 1925, s.205(1) (xxix).
[5] Above, p. 176.

will be nothing in the rest of the document to conflict with or limit this trust.

On the other hand, it might be equally clear that no obligation to sell is intended and that the trustees are merely intended to have a power of sale.

But where the matter is not clear the court must read the whole document and decide what the settlor intended. In *Re Newbould, Carter* v. *Newbould*[6] the testator gave his real property to his trustees to sell "as and when they think proper." They were told to hold the trust property in trust for his widow for life and then for his daughter absolutely. The daughter died intestate before the widow so that when the widow died it was necessary to decide who had become entitled to the daughter's interest in the land. The dispute was between the daughter's heir-at-law and her next-of-kin. And the issue turned on whether or not the testator had created a trust for sale. If he had then the doctrine of conversion applied. This meant that, although the land had not been sold, it would be treated as if it had been; that is, it would be treated as money and go to the next-of-kin; on the other hand, if there were not a trust for sale there would be no conversion, the land would be treated as land; it would therefore still be real property and the heir would be entitled.[7]

It was held that the trustee had merely been given a power of sale. There was no trust to sell and so the heir was entitled.

If a settlor creating a settlement does not impose a trust to sell on the trustees, the settlement will necessarily be governed by the Settled Land Act machinery.[8] Whatever the settlement says, the trustees will not have a power of sale since under the Settled Land Act 1925 the powers of sale must be in the tenant for life.

Obligation to sell immediately. It is possible to have a valid trust to sell at some time in the future. But if a trust for sale is created today which is not immediate, it will not be a trust for sale within the meaning of the 1925 legislation; and until it becomes immediate the settlement will be governed by the Settled Land Act and not the trust for sale machinery.

For example: If Blackacre is left by will to A for life remainder to X and Y upon trust to sell and to hold the proceeds in trust for B for life remainder to C, the Settled Land Act will apply until the

---

[6] (1913) 110 L.T. 6 (C.A.).
[7] The same rules now govern the descent of both real and personal property on intestacy. A.E.A. 1925, s.34(1).
[8] S.L.A. 1925, ss.1, 4. Before the S.L.A. 1882, a power of sale could be given to the trustees under a strict settlement but a trust for sale was preferable.

death of A. Until then the legal estate and powers of dealing with
the land will be with A. If it has not by then been sold it will be
conveyed to X and Y upon trust to sell.

In *Re Horne's Settled Estate*,[9] real property was devised to
trustees upon trust to sell; but the will went on to stipulate that the
M estate was not to be sold until 21 years after the testator's death.
It was held that his did not create an immediate trust for sale.

The trust must be binding. There is argument as to the
meaning of this term. It may have been included in the statutory
definition merely to emphasise that there must be an obligation
and not merely a power of sale.

There are, however, cases which suggest that it means that the
trust will only be binding if it applies to the whole legal and
equitable interests. Thus, in *Re Sharpe's Deed of Release*,[10] the
Hoxton estates were subject to a strict settlement under the
Settled Land Act 1925. The legal estate was held by trustees.
Under this settlement the land was held in trust for J.W.S.
absolutely subject only to certain equitable annuities which were
payable under the settlement. In his will J.W.S. purported to leave
his land to his trustees upon trust for sale and to hold the proceeds
of sale in trust to pay certain further annuities and subject to these
in trust for W.H.S.S. absolutely. On the death of J.W.S. the court
had to decide whether the land then became subject to this trust
for sale or whether (in spite of the obvious intention of the will to
set up a trust for sale) it continued subject to the Settled Land Act.

It was held that the land remained subject to the Settled Land
Act. The "trust for sale" set up by the will was not binding because
it did not bind the whole legal and equitable interest in the land.
J.W.S. did not have the legal estate at all since this was held by
trustees of the earlier strict settlement. And he could not even
bind the whole equitable interest since it was still subject to the
annuities under the earlier settlement.

If this and other similar decisions are correct, it means that land
cannot be made subject to a trust for sale so long as it is still
subject to any outstanding interests created by an earlier
settlement.[11] In other words if a beneficiary under a strict
settlement wishes to settle his beneficial interest, he can only do so
using the Settled Land Act machinery .

The validity of beneficial interests will not be affected by

⁹ (1888) 39 Ch.D. 84.
¹⁰ [1939] Ch. 51 (Morton J.).
¹¹ See, in support of this, S.L.A. 1925, s.3(*a*).

whatever meaning is given to the word "binding." But as seen, its meaning may determine whether the land is subject to the Settled Land Act or a trust for sale—and therefore determine the vital question of who can convey a good title to a purchaser.

Principle 2. Power to postpone sale

The trustees may be given a power to postpone the sale; and in the absence of any express provision to the contrary such a power to postpone is implied.[12]

Explanation

The 1925 legislation accepted the practice which developed in the nineteenth century of allowing trustees for sale the power to postpone sale. The result is that the trust for sale is something of a self-contradictory creature. There will only be a trust for sale within the 1925 legislation if there is an obligation to sell immediately. But once this obligation has been imposed, the trustees can validly be told that they need not sell at once.

Nevertheless, the distinction between a trust for sale with a power of postponement and a mere power of sale—though largely dependent on the wording used—is vital.

If land is given to trustees on trust to retain or sell, this is now treated as a trust to sell with a power to postpone.[13]

In general, the sale can only be postponed if all the trustees agree to postpone. If just one trustee favours sale then the general rule is that the obligation to sell prevails and the property must be sold. However, each trustee will have to join in the conveyance to give a good title to the purchaser; and if any trustee refuses to co-operate an application to the court will be necessary. In such a case the court has jurisdiction under section 30 of the Law of Property Act 1925 to make "such order as it thinks fit." This section has proved important in the case of disputes between husband and wife over the matrimonial property.[14]

Principle 3. Consents to sale

The trustees may be required not to sell or to exercise their other powers without the consent of the one or more specified persons.[15]

[12] L.P.A. 1925 s.25.
[13] *Ibid.* s.25(4).
[14] See further, below, p. 331.
[15] L.P.A. 1925, ss.26, 205(1) (xxix).

Explanation

The settlor can use this power to give the present beneficiary the right to have the land retained. This means that the beneficiary is able to occupy the property rather than have it sold and receive the income from the investment of the proceeds of sale.[16] By way of comparison, it will be remembered that, in the case of a strict settlement, the tenant for life has the same choice since he has the actual power of sale vested in him. But in the case of a trust for sale, the settlor can specify any person; it does not have to be the present beneficiary. It can be a subsequent beneficiary or it can be an independent third person. This means that to some extent the settlor can prevent the land from being sold by specifying someone who is not likely to give his consent.

If the settlor stipulates that the trustees are to obtain specified consents before selling they will have to obtain the same consents before exercising any of their statutory powers.

The consent of an infant or mental patient may be given by the parent or receiver as the case may be[17]; and if any necessary consent cannot be obtained, the court has jurisdiction under the Law of Property Act 1925, section 30, to dispense with it.

The settlor can specify any number of consents but, if more than two consents are required, a purchaser for value will be protected provided at least two of them have been obtained[18]; but the trustees may still be liable to beneficiaries if they have not obtained all the necessary consents.

Re Herklots' Will Trusts, Temple v. *Scorer,*[19] illustrates how the machinery of the trust for sale with a provision requiring consent before sale can be useful.

The dispute concerned the provisions in the will of the testatrix dealing with residue. These provisions started off by creating an express trust for sale of the residue and giving the income until sale and the proceeds of sale to Miss G. for life and on her death equally between three named persons one of whom was the plaintiff. This residue included a house known as No. 8, Cannon Place, Hampstead, London; and the will went on to stipulate that the trustees "shall permit her (Miss G.) to reside in my said house, No. 8, Cannon Place, aforesaid, during her lifetime for so long as she wishes." A subsequent codicil provided that the trustees

---

[16] Subject to L.P.A. 1925, s.30; see below, p. 331.
[17] *ibid.* s.26(2).
[18] *Ibid.* s.26(1).
[19] [1964] 1 W.L.R. 583 (Ungoed-Thomas J.).

should on the death of Miss G. transfer the house to the plaintiff if he should so wish in satisfaction of his third share.

The present dispute arose because Miss G. wanted to sell whilst the plaintiff wanted the house to be retained. The crux of the dispute was this: Did the will and codicil impose an obligation on the trustees not to sell during Miss G.'s lifetime? If this was the correct construction then there would be no trust for sale, the property would be subject to the Settled Land Act and Miss G. as tenant for life could sell without anyone's consent. On the other hand, could it be said that the will merely imposed an obligation not to sell without the consent of Miss G. and the plaintiff? If this were the true meaning then there was a valid trust for sale and the house could not be sold without the plaintiff's consent.

As already pointed out, the distinction is largely a question of the wording used; but in this case the testatrix had not made herself very clear. The court came to the conclusion that the intention to be gathered from the will and codicil as a whole was that the plaintiff was intended to have the chance to enjoy the house itself. The intention could only be effected by a trust for sale requiring his consent before sale. The court therefore concluded that on a proper construction the will showed an intention to create a trust for sale requiring the consent of Miss G. and the plaintiff before sale.

By way of contrast, in *Re Hanson, Hanson* v. *Eastwood*,[20] the court was faced with somewhat similar facts and came to the opposite conclusion. In this case the trustees of a personalty settlement created by will, were instructed by the testator to purchase a house for his wife as a residence for herself until his son David should attain the age of 25 "if she should so long continue the testator's widow." When the first of these events happened the house was to be held on trust for sale. The issue was whether the house purchased in compliance with this provision was subject to the Settled Land Act or a trust for sale.

Unlike *Re Herklots' Will Trusts*, the testator had not here started by creating an express trust for sale. But section 32(1) of the Law of Property Act 1925 provides that where trustees of a personalty settlement invest money in land, the land shall be deemed to be held on trust for sale "unless the settlement otherwise provides." The court held that the provision as to residence followed by an express trust for sale did otherwise provide since it showed an intention that the land was not to be sold until a later date. It did not, as did the provision in *Re*

Herklots' W.T., simply mean that the property was not to be sold until a later date without the consent of specified persons. Thus, whilst the wife's interest continued, the house was subject to the Settled Land Act. Then the express trust for sale would become immediate and the Settled Land Act ousted.

It is worth noting that in *Re Hanson* the dispute did not affect the interest of any beneficiary as it did in *Re Herklot's W.T.* It was concerned with the more technical question of who was the proper person to make title to a purchaser of the land. It did not matter to anyone whether the Settled Land Act or a trust for sale applied—so long as it was certain which applied.

These cases do illustrate that if a settlor wishes to prevent the land from being sold, his best method is to create a trust for sale requiring consents before sale—and to specify persons who are not likely to give consent. In *Re Inns*,[21] the testator left his house on trust for sale for the benefit of his wife for life, remainder to Stevenage U.D.C. The will specified that it was not to be sold without the consent of both the widow and the U.D.C. and this made it unlikely that the house would be sold before the death of the widow.[22]

Principle 4. Formalities

Where a trust for sale is created *inter vivos* the settlor will convey the legal estate by deed of conveyance to the trustees upon trust to sell and to hold the proceeds of sale for whatever beneficial interests are to be created. It is usual but not essential to set out the beneficial interests in a separate document.

Where the trust for sale is created by will, the personal representatives of the settlor, after administration, will make an assent in writing vesting the legal state in the trustees for sale.[23]

Explanation

Unlike a strict settlement, a trust for sale can validly be created by one document. The beneficial interests can be set out in the conveyance on trust for sale. In the case of co-ownership this is what normally happens. In the case of a settlement the practice is

[21] [1947] Ch. 576 (Wynn-Parry J.).
[22] A sale would be even less likely if the interest of the remainderman was made contingent on the property not being sold. But it might then be argued that there was no trust for sale at all. In any case the court could authorise sale under L.P.A. 1925, s.30.
[23] A.E.A. 1925, s.36(4).

to use two separate documents: a conveyance of the legal estate to the trustees and a trust instrument setting out the beneficial interests.

In the case of creation by will, the will is treated as the trust instrument. The assent transfers the legal estate to the trustees. Even if, as is common, the executors are also the trustees for sale, they must execute an assent vesting the legal estate in themselves in their trustee capacity.[24]

Principle 5. Importance of definition of trust for sale

It is important to be able to recognise a trust for sale for at least two reasons:

(a) any settlement will be governed by the Settled Land Act 1925 if it is not expressly made subject to a trust for sale;

(b) the doctrine of conversion applies to a trust for sale.

Explanation

The first of these two reasons has been dealt with. The second, the doctrine of conversion, is dealt with below.[25]

Principle 6. Statutory trusts for sale

In the following cases a trust for sale is imposed by statute:

(a) in most cases where there is equitable co-ownership[26];

(b) land passing on intestacy[27];

(c) land acquired by trustees for sale and trustees of pure personalty[28];

(d) land vested in trustee mortgagees free of the equity of redemption[29];

(e) land purchased in breach of trust.[30]

---

[24] *Re King's Will Trusts* [1964] Ch. 542 (Pennycuick J.); and see *Re Edward's Will Trusts* [1981] 2 All E.R. 941 (C.A.).

[25] Below, p. 275.

[26] See below, p. 319.

[27] See below, p. 578.

[28] L.P.A. 1925, s.32, see *Re Hanson* [1928] Ch. 96, above, p. 263.

[29] L.P.A. 1925, s.31, see below, pp. 463, 464 for determination of equity of redemption by limitation and foreclosure.

[30] See *Emmett on Title* (17th ed.), p. 794.

Explanation

(a) *Co-ownership.* As already explained, the modern trust for sale developed in the nineteenth century as an alternative method of settling land. It is still available for this purpose; but the 1925 legislation has extended its use. The legislators appreciated that it provided a convenient device, already tried and tested, whereby dealings with land could be simplified without prejudice to the beneficial interests. These interests could be hidden behind the trust "curtain" and overreached on sale; and the purchaser did not have to concern himself with them. It was for this reason that the strict settlement—although not abolished—was modified to make it more like the trust for sale. It was for the same reason that the trust for sale was extended to co-ownership.

In these cases of co-ownership, the co-owners do not have any choice in the matter. If the trust for sale is not created expressly it is imposed by statute.

(b) *Intestacy.* Here again the trust for sale is imposed for the same reasons; although of course here there is no possibility of express creation. Intestacy and co-ownership are dealt with in separate chapters.

SECTION II.   THE POWERS OF TRUSTEES FOR SALE

Principle 7.   Statutory powers

In general, until the land is sold, the trustees for sale have the same powers of managing and dealing with the land as the Settled Land Act 1925 confers on the tenant for life and the trustees of the settlement.

Explanation

Dealings.   The above principle is contained in section 28 of the Law of Property Act 1925 which has been described as the charter of trustees for sale as it is the source of most of their powers.

The essential difference between a trust for sale and a strict settlement lies not in what can be done with the land but in who can do it. The principle governing the strict settlement is that control of the land is given to the tenant for life whilst in the case of a trust for sale it is given to the trustees.

Thus, the trustees for sale have the same statutory powers of selling, leasing, mortgaging, etc., the land as a tenant for life. And the exercise of these powers is subject to the same restrictions—for example, when selling they must obtain the best price reasonably possible. Any capital arising from the exercise of their powers must be applied in the same way as capital arising under a strict settlement (or in the same way as the trust instrument stipulates that the proceeds of sale are to be applied).[31] Like a tenant for life, the trustees can ask the court to authorise transactions not otherwise authorised.

If the trust instrument requires the trustees to obtain any specified consents before sale then the same consents must be obtained before the exercise of any of the statutory powers.[32]

The trust instrument may increase the powers of the trustees for sale just as the powers of a tenant for life may be increased.

In certain cases, statute expressly permits the powers of the trustees to be limited. For example, the power to postpone sale given by section 25 of the Law of Property Act 1925 may be limited or excluded.[33] And, of course, exercise of the powers can be made subject to consents.[34] But apart from such express authorisation by statute, it is probably correct to say that section 106 of the Settled Land Act applies to a trust for sale—as it applies to a strict settlement—so that any unauthorised attempt to limit or reduce the statutory powers will be void.[35]

Management. Section 28 of the Law of Property Act 1925 makes specific mention of the powers of day to day management contained in section 102 of the Settled Land Act 1925. Section 102 of the Settled Land Act 1925 gives these powers to the trustees of a strict settlement to exercise when the tenant for life is an infant or where there is no tenant for life. At other times, of course, the management of the land is in the hands of the tenant for life and he will bear the cost of management out of the income. In the case of a trust for sale it is the trustees who are in control of the land; so section 28 gives the section 102 management powers to them to exercise throughout the trust.

These section 102 powers which are conferred subject to any provision to the contrary,[36] include the following:

---

[31] L.P.A. 1925, s.28(1).
[32] *Ibid.*
[33] Compare the tenant for life who could not be put under an obligation to sell at once (since he would then be a trustee for sale).
[34] The powers of management derived from section 102 of the S.L.A. 1925 can be limited, see S.L.A. 1925, s.102(6).
[35] See Megarry and Wade, *Law of Real Property* (4th ed.), p. 368.
[36] See n. 34, above.

to fell timber and cut underwood in the usual course for sale or
  repairs;
to erect, pull down, repair and rebuild houses and other
  buildings and erections;
to continue the working of mines, minerals and quarries which
  have usually been worked;
to insure against loss by fire;
generally, to deal with the land in a proper and due course of
  management.

The transactions, such as the sale of property, specifically
authorised in other parts of the Settled Land Act 1925 are major
transactions affecting the settled land. Section 102 is a general
authorisation covering the day to day administration of the
property; it enables the trustees to manage it without having to
make constant applications to the court under section 64 of the
Settled Land Act 1925.

Capital and income. It has already been mentioned that any
capital arising from the exercise of the statutory powers must be
applied by the trustees either in one of the ways specified in section
73 of the Settled Land Act 1925, or in the same way as the trust
requires the proceeds of sale to be applied. Any income arising
from the property must be treated in the same way as income
arising from the proper investment of the proceeds of sale. In
other words, after discharge of outgoings it will normally be
payable to the beneficiary entitled for the time being under the
settlement.[37]

By way of example: Suppose that Blackacre is conveyed to
trustees on trust to sell and to hold the proceeds of sale in trust for
A for life remainder to B in fee simple. If and when they do sell
they will have to invest the proceeds of sale in authorised
securities; A will be entitled to the income from the investments
and when he dies the trustees will hold the investments in trust for
B absolutely. Of course, if they continue to exercise the power to
postpone they may not sell at all in A's lifetime and when he dies
they will hold the land (still subject to the trust to sell) for the
benefit of B absolutely.

Until they sell they can exercise the statutory powers. If, say,
they lease the property any rent will be income[38] and will go to A
as being entitled to the income from the proceeds of sale. If a
premium is paid for the lease this will be capital. The trustees will

---

[37] L.P.A. 1925, s.28(2).
[38] Unless it is a mining lease; see above, p. 215.

be able to apply it in one of the ways specified in section 73 of the Settled Land Act 1925—for example, they may invest it in authorised securities or they may pay for any of the improvements authorised by Schedule 3 to the Settled Land Act 1925. If the trustees sell all the land, they automatically cease to be trustees for sale.[39] Section 73 and the other statutory powers of trustees for sale of land no longer are applicable. They will then simply be in the position of ordinary trustees of pure personalty holding the investments and proceeds of sale in trust for the various beneficiaries with the ordinary powers of investment of all trustees.

Outgoings. There is also the question of whether any authorised expenditure on the property by the trustees is to be charged to income or capital: a question of great importance to the beneficiaries. Suppose that the trust property is held for the benefit of A for life remainder to B in fee simple; and that it is let, producing £1,000 a year; and that the trustees are proposing to spend £1,000 on repairs. If they pay for repairs out of income that is A's income gone for a year; if they are paid for out of capital—for example, by borrowing on a mortgage of the property—that is to B's disadvantage.[40]

The general principles for allocating expenditure between income and capital are as follows:

The legislation specifies which expenses may be paid out of capital and which out of income. For example, section 28 of the Law of Property Act 1925 provides that trustees can deduct from income "the cost of repairs and insurance and other outgoings." All expenses incurred in the exercise of the management powers under section 102 of the Settled Land Act 1925 can be charged to income.[41] On the other hand, long-term improvements listed in Part I of the Third Schedule may be paid for out of capital.[42]

In some cases these provisions overlap so that the trustees have a discretion whether to meet an expense out of capital or income. For example, one of the expenses which can be met out of capital under section 73 of the Settled Land Act 1925 is: "Repairs to fixed equipment, being equipment reasonably required for the proper farming of the holding, other than repairs which the tenant is

---

[39] *Re Wakeman, National Provincial Bank Ltd.* v. *Wakeman* [1945] Ch. 177 (Uthwatt J.). But see the comment of Cohen L.J. in *Re Wellsted's W.T.* [1949] Ch. 296, p. 319.
[40] See *Emmett on Title* (17th ed.), pp. 806, 807.
[41] S.L.A. 1925, s.102(3).
[42] S.L.A. 1925, s.84.

under an obligation to carry out."[43] Yet the same expense can alternatively be paid for out of income as a repair within section 102 of the Settled Land Act 1925.

In such cases the trustees must exercise their discretion in the manner that is fairest in all the circumstances as between those entitled to income and those entitled to capital, bearing in mind their duty so far as possible to preserve the settlor's capital intact. But, in general, the courts will not interfere with their desision.

The case of *Re Wynn, Public Trustee* v. *Newborough (No.2)*[44] illustrates these principles.

The testator, who died in 1932, left his landed property on trust for sale (with power to postpone). The trustees were to divide the income equally between his two nephews for their joint lives and then pay all the income to the survivor for his life. On the death of the survivor they were to hold the proceeds of sale and any land not then sold in trust for certain remaindermen. The will directed that repairs were to be paid for out of income. Between 1946 and 1952, the Public Trustee—the trustee for sale—had spent considerable sums on repairs to agricultural properties which formed part of the estate; and he had paid for these repairs out of income. In this action, the two nephews as tenant for life, were claiming to have these repairs paid for out of capital.

It was *held* that they were not entitled to recover from capital what had been spent out of income on the repairs. The trustee did have a statutory authority to pay for these repairs out of capital under section 73(1)(iv) of the Settled Land Act 1925. And this statutory authority could not be restricted by the direction in the will to pay repairs out of income. He also had express authority in the will to pay for the repairs out of income. The trustee thus had a discretion which he had exercised against income and the court would not interfere.

Principle 8. Power to purchase land

Trustees for sale of land have a statutory authority to purchase land either as an investment or for some other purpose.[45]

But once they have parted with all the land, they cease to be trustees for sale and can only purchase land if expressly authorised by the trust instrument.

---

[43] S.L.A. 1925, s.73(1) (iv) and Agricultural Holdings Act 1948, Sched. 3, Pt. II.
[44] [1955] 1 W.L.R. 940 (Harman J.).
[45] L.P.A. 1925, s.28(1), and S.L.A. 1925, s.73(1) (xi).

Explanation

Trustees may want to purchase land, either as an investment or for some other purpose—commonly as a residence for one of the beneficiaries.

Under section 73 of the Settled Land Act 1925 trustees for sale of land can use any capital in their hands to purchase other land. In *Re Wellsted's Will Trusts, Wellsted* v. *Hanson,*[46] the testator had left his residuary property, which included both land and personalty, on trust for sale. The trustees had sold part of the land and invested the proceeds. What they now wanted to do was to sell more land, to realise some of the investments representing earlier sales and use the money raised, together with some cash in hand, to purchase other land. The court held that they were entitled to do this. Section 73 of the Settled Land Act 1925 authorised trustees for sale to apply the proceeds of sale in the purchase of either freehold land or leasehold land with at least 60 years to run. And the proceeds of sale remained the proceeds of sale even if converted into investments—so long as they could be traced, that is, distinguished from other money or property.

However, in *Re Wakeman, National Provincial Bank* v. *Wakeman,*[47] it was held by Uthwatt J. that once the trustees had sold all the land held by them they ceased to be trustees for sale of land within the definition of section 205 of the Law of Property Act 1925. It followed, so it was decided, that they no longer had the statutory powers enjoyed by trustees for sale of land under section 73. They merely had the ordinary powers of trustees of pure personalty: that is, to invest capital in authorised investments together with any additional powers given by the trust instrument. Since the purchase of lands is not an authorised investment they must rely on any express authority given by the settlor. In *Re Wakeman,* there was no express power and so the trustees were not able to purchase a house for occupation by the testator's daughter who was life tenant under his will.

If trustees are given an express power to "invest" in the purchase of land, this does not include buying a house solely for the sake of providing a beneficiary with somewhere to live; since this is not an investment. But if they buy a house as an investment, it does not matter that it is incidentally intended to provide a beneficiary with somewhere to live.[48]

Where trustees do purchase land either under section 73 of the

---

[46] [1949] Ch. 291 (C.A.).
[47] [1945] Ch. 177.
[48] But see *per* Cohen L.J. in *Re Wellsted's W.T.* [1949] Ch. 296 at p. 319.

Settled Land Act 1925 or under express authority they will hold
such land on trust for sale unless in the latter case the settlement
expressly provides otherwise.[49]

Principle 9. Investment of capital money

The authorised use of capital money includes investment in trustee
securities. Trustee securities are those authorised by the Trustee
Investment Act 1961 (known as "authorised investments") and
any additional investments expressly permitted by the trust
instrument.[50]

Explanation

Where trustees are going to invest capital money under the
Settled Land Act 1925, s.73(1)(i) they must choose investments
from those specified in the trust instrument or in the Trustee
Investment Act 1961.

Three main considerations affect the choice of investments:

(a) *The security of capital.* Some people might well consider
backing a "certain winner" at the Newmarket races to be a good
investment. It might be, if the horse wins! It is hardly the surest
way of preserving capital intact.

(b) *The real value of capital in purchasing power.* If £2,500 had
been invested in gilt edged securities in 1900 it would still be worth
£2,500—nominally. But everyone knows that £2,500 would have
been worth much more in 1900 than it would be worth today. If
that £2,500 had been used to purchase land it would probably have
maintained its real value in terms of purchasing power.

(c) *The need to obtain the best possible income.* If money is
invested in ordinary shares, "equities," the income will depend on
the success of the company whose shares have been purchased. If
it is invested in wasting assets such as a lease with a short term to
run or a mine, it might produce a high income for a number of
years. But in the course of time the asset and with it the capital will
disappear; the lease will expire or the mine will be exhausted.

The choice of investment may involve a conflict between the
interests of the present beneficiaries concerned only with income
and the remaindermen concerned only to maintain capital. A

---

[49] L.P.A. 1925, ss.28(1), 32(1); below, p. 277.
[50] S.L.A. 1925, s.73(1) (i).

wasting asset, for example, will produce a high income for the present beneficiary but leave no capital for the remaindermen.

When investing trust money, the trustees must not only choose from permitted investments; they must also act fairly as between those entitled to income and those entitled to capital.

Permitted investments. Broadly speaking investments can be divided into two categories: loans and ordinary shares.

The essence of the first type is that money is lent and the borrower agrees to repay the money at some future date and meanwhile to pay interest on it at an agreed rate. This category includes gilt-edged securities.

The essence of the second type is that the investor purchases a share in the fortunes of the company. The value of the share varies according to the worth in assets and prospects of the company; and the income (the dividend) each year will depend on how much profit the company has made that year.

The Trustee Investment Act 1961 divides authorised investments into two main categories.

(a) *Narrower-range investments.* The investments specified here are of the first type, loans to bodies whose solvency is pretty well guaranteed. It includes fixed interest securities issued by the government, by the nationalised industries, debenture stock of United Kingdom companies. These investments give more or less complete security for capital, a guaranteed but fixed and not very high income and no protection against inflation. Prior to 1961, these were the only type of authorised investment unless the trust instrument expressly increased the investment powers of the trustees.

(b) *Wider range investments.* The investments specified here are ordinary shares in any United Kingdom company which satisfies certain requirements, for example, it must be quoted on the stock exchange and must have a paid-up capital of at least £1,000,000. The object of introducing these wider ranger investments in the 1961 Act was to preserve a reasonable degree of security for capital but to allow trustees to provide for capital growth (and thus counter-inflation) and a higher income for the present beneficiary.

Under the 1961 Act trustees are allowed to invest half the trust fund in the narrower range and half in the wider range investments.

The investment powers of trustees and the range of possible investments can be extended by the trust instrument. Indeed if he so wishes there is nothing to stop a settlor expressly giving the trustees authority to take the trust fund to Newmarket.

Principle 10.   Control of trustees by beneficiaries

(a) The trustees may allow the beneficiary entitled to the income from the land for the time being to occupy the land itself instead of receiving the income.

(b) They may revocably delegate to him their powers of leasing, accepting the surrender of leases and management of the property whether granted by statute or otherwise.[51]

(c) In the case of a statutory trust for sale or where the trust instrument expressly requires it, the trustees must consult him and so far as is consistent with the general interests of the trust give effect to his wishes.[52]

Explanation

Control and management of the land pending sale lies with the trustees—though in some cases they may have to obtain consents before acting.[53] In general, the only part which a beneficiary is able to play is to receive whatever is due to him from income or proceeds of sale. His interest is not in the land but in the money which it may earn. And no doubt in most cases he will be happy enough with this arrangement.

However, if they wish, the trustees can transfer some measure of control to the beneficiary entitled to income for the time being. They can let him occupy the land instead of, for example, letting it and paying him the rent. Indeed, one of the reasons for settling the land may have been to provide a home for a beneficiary. If a man makes a will leaving his house on trust for sale for the benefit of his widow for life, remainder to his children, it will no doubt be his wish that she should be allowed to live there so long as she wishes. And in the case of co-ownership the whole object of purchasing is in the vast majority of cases, to provide a home in which to live.[54]

Further, the trustees can transfer the management of the property to the present beneficiary. And this includes the power of leasing and accepting the surrender of leases. The delegation must be made in writing and it can be revoked at any time—though this will not invalidate anything done before revocation. A lessee is

---

[51] L.P.A. 1925, s.29.
[52] L.P.A. 1925, s.26(3).
[53] See above, p. 267.
[54] For the question how far a beneficiary has a right to occupy, see below, p. 326.

entitled to rely on the written delegation as sufficient evidence that the powers have been delegated and not revoked.

Under these above provisions, the beneficiary can to some extent attain the position of a tenant for life under a strict settlement—but only to a limited extent. Most of the important powers, including the power to sell and mortgage, must remain with the trustees. And the beneficiary has no absolute right to either occupation[55] or management of the property.

There is a further provision[56] which requires the trustees to consult the present beneficiary before exercising any of their powers. But this only applies if the trust for sale is statutory or expressly requires such consultation. And the trustees only have to comply with the wishes of the beneficiary if consistent with the interests of the trust as a whole. Further, a purchaser does not have to check that there has been consultation.

Two final points. First, trustees are, of course, subject to the general principles of equity governing the conduct of trustees, and these can be enforced at the instance of a beneficiary.[57] Secondly, a beneficiary may himself be a trustee.[58] In the common case, for example of a beneficial joint tenancy of a matrimonial home, the husband and wife will hold the legal estate upon trust for sale for the benefit of themselves as joint tenants in equity. Here the trustees and beneficiaries will be the same persons.

SECTION III. CONVERSION AND RECONVERSION

Principle 11. Conversion

By the doctrine of conversion, the interests of beneficiaries under a trust for sale are from the beginning classified as interests in the proceeds of sale and not in the land itself.

Explanation

The whole point of the trust for sale, originally at least, was that the trustees should convert the land into money by selling it, and

---

[55] See below, p. 326.
[56] L.P.A. 1925, s.26(3).
[57] See, *e.g. Peffer* v. *Rigg* [1978] 3 All E.R. 745 (Graham J.).
[58] For limits on this, see Hanbury and Maudsley, *Modern Equity* (11th ed.), p. 532 *et seq.*

use the money either to pay debts, to invest or to distribute among various beneficiaries. Equity of course enforced this obligation to sell. But equity went further. It applied the important equitable principle that equity treats as done that which ought to be done. Right from the moment of the trust's creation it gave notional effect to the settlor's intention by treating the land as having been sold and converted into money. This means that the interests of beneficiaries under a trust for sale are classified as interests in money (personal property) and not as interests in land (which if freehold is real property).[59] This doctrine applies even though there is power to postpone the sale and the trustees are acting quite properly in not selling.

Before 1926, the doctrine of conversion was of great importance because the rules relating to real and personal property were so often different. For example, personal property could not be entailed. If freehold land was given to trustees on trust to sell and to hold the proceeds for A in fee tail, conversion applied so that this was treated as a gift of personal property. An attempt to give a person a fee tail in personal property took effect as an absolute gift. So the trustees would hold for A absolutely.

Again before 1926, the rules of inheritance for real and personal property were different. Who was to take on a person's death might depend on the doctrine of conversion. In *Fletcher* v. *Ashburner*,[60] "John Fletcher, by his will devised his burgage houses and free rents in Kendall, and all his personal estate to trustees and the survivor and the heirs, executors and administrators of such survivor, in trust to sell so much as should be sufficient to pay his debts, and then to permit his wife Agnes to enjoy the residue during her life, if she so long continued his chaste widow; and after her decease to sell and dispose thereof, and the money arising thereby, after deducting charges and half a guinea each to the trustees for their trouble, to pay to and between his son William and his daughter Mary, share and share alike." The will also provided that if either child died in the lifetime of the widow his share was to go to the other child. In the event, the daughter died followed by the son followed by the widow. Thus the son took the daughter's share and thus became entitled absolutely subject only to the widow's life interest. The dispute was between those entitled to the son William's property on his death. His heir claimed the land as real property. His personal representatives claimed it as personal property. Sir Thomas Sewell M.R. held that

[59] See below, p. 581.
[60] (1799) 1 Bro.C.C. 497; 28 E.R. 1259.

the doctrine of conversion applied. There was a binding trust for sale—even though the trustees were not to sell till the death of the widow which had not yet happened. And therefore the land passed to the personal representatives as personal property.

Importance of conversion since 1925. Since 1925 it has been possible to create entails in personal property; and the same rules of inheritance apply to real and personal property. The doctrine of conversion is therefore no longer important for these reasons. However, it is still part of the law and may still be of importance. In general, wherever the term "real property" is used, in a will or elsewhere, it will not include an interest under a trust for sale of freehold land. For example, if A chooses to make a will leaving all his "real property" to X and all his "personal property" to Y, any interests which he may have under a trust for sale of land will go to Y.

The doctrine of conversion also applies in situations other than the trust for sale.[61]

Principle 12. Land acquired by trustees

Land acquired by trustees for sale of land or trustees of pure personalty will in the absence of stipulation to the contrary be held by the trustees on trust for sale.[62]

Explanation

Trustees may in some cases purchase land. Trustees for sale of land have statutory power to purchase land with capital money; trustees of pure personalty may be expressly authorised or directed to purchase land with trust funds.

In all such cases, in the absence of express provision to the contrary in the trust instrument, the land will be held by the trustees on trust for sale; and thus be subject to the doctrine of conversion. The settlor has either settled pure personalty in the first place, or by using the trust for sale he has shown an intention that the land should be treated as pure personalty. In both cases the application of the present principle preserves this original character of the trust property—unless the settlor has declared his intention to the contrary.

---

[61] *e.g.* to an enforceable contract for the sale of land, the land in the vendor's hands is treated as money (personalty); see Hanbury and Maudsley, *Modern Equity* (11th ed.), p. 335.

[62] L.P.A. 1925, ss.29(1), 32.

Trustees for sale of land and trustees of pure personalty may also lend money on the security of mortgages of land. This land may become vested in the mortgagees free of the equity of redemption—either by foreclosure or under the Limitation Act 1980. As in the case of purchased land, the trustees will hold the land on trust for sale.[63] This again is simply a provision designed to preserve the original character of the trust property, so that the rights of beneficiaries do not depend on the chance of what particular form the trust property takes at any particular moment.

To give a simple example: Land is held on trust for sale for the benefit of A for life remainder to B in fee simple. B makes his will leaving his real property to X and his personal property to Y. By the time B dies, the trustees may have sold the land or they may still hold it. Or they may have sold part of it and bought other land with the proceeds or sale; and so on. It makes no difference. Whatever form the property happens to take when B dies, it will pass as personal property to Y (in remainder if A is still alive).

The above provisions do not apply to land acquired by trustees of a strict settlement under the Settled Land Act. Here again the original character of the property—in this case as land—is preserved. Any capital and any land purchased with capital is treated as land and subject to the Settled Land Act machinery.[64]

Principle 13.   Reconversion

When the trust for sale comes to an end the interests of beneficiaries will automatically be reconverted and once again treated as land.

Explanation

The doctrine of conversion applies because there is an obligation to sell. Once, for any reason, this obligation ceases, so must the conversion. The beneficial interests are reconverted into interests in land.

Reconversion can occur in a number of situations. For example:

(a) If the legal and equitable ownership becomes vested in one person. This is because a single person cannot hold property in trust for himself. In *Re Cook, Beck* v. *Grant,*[65] a freehold house was held by husband and wife as beneficial joint tenants. Under

[63] L.P.A. 1925, s.31(1).
[64] S.L.A. 1925, s.75(5).
[65] [1948] Ch. 212 (Harman J.).

section 36 of the Law of Property Act 1925 they held it on the statutory trust for sale for the benefit of themselves. The husband died first. When the wife died she had made a will leaving all her personal estate to her nephews. In the present case they were claiming the house. It was held by Harman J. that they were not entitled. On the death of the husband the wife became—by right of survivorship—the sole owner of the house both in law and equity. This made her an ordinary beneficial owner and automatically put an end to the trust for sale. Her interest was reconverted into an interest in freehold land and so did not pass with a gift of her "personal estate."

It is to be noted that if she had made it clear in her will that she meant to include the house in the term "personal estate," the courts would have given effect to this intention.[66] The courts will always give expressions used in a will the meaning which the testator intended them to have. But in the absence of a clear indication to the contrary, they must assume that technical expressions such as "personal estate" are intended to have their ordinary technical meaning. If a testator wishes to include a freehold house in a gift of "personal estate," he must make this sufficiently clear in the will.

(b) Where all the beneficiaries—provided they are of full age and between them absolutely entitled to the property—unanimously elect to terminate the trust for sale. Beneficiaries under a trust for sale cannot in general tell the trustees how to exercise their powers. But they can put an end to the trust altogether.[67] If, for example, Blackacre is held by X and Y on trust for sale for A and B as joint tenants and B dies, this leaves A as the sole owner in equity. Provided he is of full age he can terminate the trust for sale and direct the trustees to convey the legal estate to him. The moment he makes his election clear, his interest is reconverted into land. Similarly, if Whiteacre is held on trust for sale for the benefit of A, B and C as tenants in common in equal shares; A, B and C—again assuming them to be of full age—could all get together and agree to partition the land allotting a separate part to each one. And they could then terminate the trust for sale directing the trustees to convey to each tenant his allotted part of the land.

---

[66] And if the house had been leasehold it would in any case have been personal property.

[67] See *Re Kipping* [1914] 1 Ch. 62.

SECTION IV.   THE PURCHASER OF LAND HELD ON TRUST FOR SALE

Principle 14.   Overreaching

Provided that all the statutory requirements are complied with the interests of beneficiaries will be overreached on sale.

Explanation

Trustees for sale do not of course have unlimited powers of dealing with the land. However, provided they act within their powers—get the best price reasonably possible when selling, etc.—and proceed in a regular manner, the interests of the beneficiaries will be overreached. A purchaser—including a mortgagee, lessee, etc.—will take free of the beneficial interests while the interests themselves will be satisfied out of the purchase money held by the trustees.

The purchaser will take free of the interests even if he has notice of them. Section 27 of the Law of Property Act 1925 provides that he will not be concerned with the trusts affecting the proceeds of sale or income until sale even if declared in the same instrument.

Payment of capital money.   The main requirement which a purchaser must satisfy in order to obtain the protection of the overreaching provisions is that he must pay any capital, *e.g.* the purchase money on sale, to the trustees of whom there must be at least two or a trust corporation. If necessary a second trustee must be appointed before the transaction is completed.[68]

Overreaching and conversion.   It has been suggested that in strictness the doctrine of overreaching does not apply to a trust for sale.[69] The argument is that under the doctrine of conversion the beneficiaries have interests in the proceeds of sale and not the land from the start. Thus, it can be argued, there are no interests in land to be overreached.

However, this may be to mistake the nature of conversion. The doctrine of conversion is merely concerned with the classification of interests. It does not say that the beneficiaries do not have interests in land—merely that their interests in the land shall be treated as if they were interests in money. It is land—not money—which the trustees hold and it is the land which is subject to a trust in favour of the beneficiaries. This gives the beneficiaries

---

[68] L.P.A. 1925, s.27(2).
[69] See, *e.g.* Megarry and Wade, *Law of Real Property* (4th ed.), p. 377.

an interest in the land (deemed to be money) enforceable against purchasers like any other equitable interest.

Suppose that Blackacre is given to trustees on trust to sell and hold the proceeds of sale in trust for A for life. . . . Certainly, A's life interest will be classified as money, that is pure personalty, wherever a classification has to be made. And perhaps it is true to say that indeed A does not have a *life interest* in the land; but only a life interest in the income and proceeds of sale. But the trustees for sale are under an obligation, owed to the beneficiaries, to deal with the land in a certain way; that is to collect the income, to sell the land, etc., for the benefit of these beneficiaries. It is these obligations which are enforceable by the beneficiaries and together constitute their equitable interest in the land.[70]

If the trustees act improperly when selling, the purchaser will take subject to this interest and these obligations.[71] In other words, the purchaser will take the land subject not to a life interest but subject to the trust for sale. If on the other hand the trustees do act properly when selling, the purchaser will take the land free of the trust. In a sense it might be agreed that this is not overreaching. The interest in the land is not *transferred* to the purchase money. Rather it simply comes to an end since the trust has, so far as the land is concerned, been properly performed by the trustees.

In any case, the term overreaching is conveniently used to indicate that the purchaser takes free of the trust and that the beneficiaries are left with interests in the proceeds of sale instead of the land.

Principle 15. Irregularities

In certain cases a purchaser may be protected even where there have been irregularities.

Explanation

As a general principle, overreaching is designed to operate only where the trustees and purchaser are acting properly and complying with all the statutory requirements. Thus, in principle, where there has been any irregularity, the purchaser will take subject to the trust.

---

[70] See further, below, p. 326.
[71] Unless he can claim protection under one of the rules mentioned in the next Principle.

However, and this is what we are concerned with here, in certain cases a purchaser is given special statutory protection so that he will take free of the trust even where there has been some irregularity. Further, failing statutory protection, he may be able to fall back on the doctrine of notice.[72]

Statutory protection. The statutory protection given to a purchaser from a trustee for sale is not so wide as that given to a purchaser from the tenant for life under the Settled Land Act 1925. It will be remembered[73] that under section 110(1) of the Settled Land Act 1925 a bona fide purchaser provided he deals with the tenant for life will conclusively be presumed to have complied with the statutory requirements; in general he will be protected. On the other hand where the statutory protection does not apply, the transaction is void. The purchaser cannot fall back on the doctrine of notice since this is excluded by section 18 of the Settled Land Act 1925.[74]

In the case of a trust for sale the statutory protection given to the purchaser is more piecemeal and limited; but here the doctrine of notice is still available and may give a purchaser a defence where there has been some irregularity.

The purchaser will be able to rely on statutory protection in the following cases:

(a) *Consents.* Where the trust is exercisable only with more than two specified consents, the purchaser will be protected provided any two of the necessary consents have been obtained. And he does not have to concern himself with the consents of infants or persons under disability.[75]

(b) *Consultation and delegation.* A purchaser is not concerned with any requirement that the trustees must consult beneficiaries before acting.[76]

The trustees may delegate certain of their powers to the present beneficiary. A purchaser must accept the written delegation as sufficient evidence that there has been a valid delegation to the person named and that the delegation has not been revoked.[77]

---

[72] See below, p. 284, for the doctrine of notice.

[73] Above, p. 241.

[74] But the protection given under s.110(1) to the purchaser dealing in good faith with the tenant for life is very analogous to that given by the doctrine of notice.

[75] L.P.A. 1925, s.26(1), (2).

[76] L.P.A. 1925, s.26(3), as amended by L.P.(A.)A. 1926, s.7, Sched.

[77] L.P.A. 1925, s.29(1).

(c) In favour of a purchaser the trust for sale is deemed to continue until the property has been conveyed by the trustees: it has already been explained that the trust for sale may come to an end while the property is still vested in the trustees. If this happens the trustees no longer have either obligation or indeed the right to sell without the consent of the beneficiaries. Under this provision the purchaser is entitled to assume that the trust for sale does in fact still exist as long as the legal estate is vested in the trustees; and he does not have to check with the equitable beneficiaries that it has not been terminated.[78]

(d) Under the Law of Property (Joint Tenants) Act 1964 a purchaser from the survivor of joint tenants is entitled to assume that the trust has ceased and that the survivor is the beneficial owner. This is dealt with under co-ownership.[79]

The general effect of the overreaching machinery and these statutory provisions is that a purchaser need concern himself only with the legal estate. There is a curtain between himself and the equitable interests which he need not and cannot penetrate. He is not affected by what goes on behind the curtain. Where the trustees are acting properly in every respect the ordinary over-reaching machinery applies. Even where there has been some irregularity or breach of trust behind the curtain he will generally be protected by one of the statutory provisions mentioned above.

However, there are occasions when a purchaser cannot rely on any statutory protection. In such cases, he is entitled to and, to protect himself, must investigate behind the curtain just in case there has been any irregularity. To give an example. Suppose that P is buying Blackacre with unregistered title from A. He starts to investigate A's title in the normal way tracing ownership of the legal estate back 15 years.[80] But the first thing that he discovers is that the property was conveyed to A last year by trustees for sale and that it appears from the conveyance that it was conveyed to A not on sale but as a beneficiary who had become absolutely entitled to the property. No doubt everything is in order and A was in fact entitled to the property. And so he will be able to give P a good title. But what if the conveyance to A was in breach of trust? A's title will be bad. He will have taken subject to the trust since he was not a purchaser for value. And P in turn will also take subject to the trust. There is no relevant statutory protection

---

[78] L.P.A. 1925, s.23.
[79] Below, p. 340.
[80] See below, p. 563, for proof of title.

available to P in such a case.[81] And so P will be entitled to and will
have to check the equitable ownership and satisfy himself that A
had in fact become entitled to the land outright.[82] It should be
noted that this problem will not generally arise if the land is
registered, since section 74 of the Land Registration Act 1925
provides: "Subject to the provisions of this Act as to settled land,
neither the registrar nor any person dealing with a registered
estate or charge shall be affected with notice of a trust express,
implied or constructive, and references to trusts shall, so far as
possible be excluded from the register."[83]

Principle 16.   The doctrine of notice

The doctrine of notice applies to a trust for sale. Therefore if a
purchaser takes without notice that the land is subject to a trust for
sale, he may obtain the legal estate free of the trust.

Explanation

If a purchaser knows that the land is subject to a trust for sale,
he will normally have notice of all the equitable interests behind
the trust. If he has not acquired actual notice by investigation of
the trust he will be fixed with constructive notice—since a prudent
purchaser in his position would investigate the trust.[84] In practice
of course, as already explained, he will not be affected and will not
need to investigate the terms of the trust. He will be able to rely on
taking free of equitable interests either under the overreaching
machinery or the statutory protection mentioned above. But, as
explained, there may be cases where there is no statutory
protection available and the purchaser will be driven to investigate
the equities or run the risk of being affected if there has been some
irregularity.

It is possible, however, that the purchaser may not know that
the land is subject to a trust for sale at all. If, in such a case, he can
show that he took the legal estate for value and without notice of
the trust he will take free of it. If A and B contribute to the
purchase price of land which is conveyed into A's sole name, the
result is likely to be that A will hold in trust for himself and B.[85] If

---

[81] And he would not be protected by the doctrine of notice because he has notice of
     the trust; see below.
[82] See *Emmett on Title* (17th ed.), p. 800.
[83] See below, Chap. 25, for registered land.
[84] See below, p. 513, for notice.
[85] See above, p. 181.

A then deals with the legal estate (*e.g.* by sale or mortgage), the purchaser will not have the benefit of the overreaching machinery since he has taken title from only one trustee.[86] But if the purchaser can show that he took without notice of B's equitable interest he will take free of it.[87] B's only remedy will be a personal one against A for a share of the proceeds.

SECTION V. THE BENEFICIAL INTERESTS

Principle 17. Dealing with the beneficial interest

A beneficiary under a trust for sale may deal with his beneficial interest in any way permitted by law.

Explanation

A beneficiary under a trust for sale has a property interest of value. And although a limited interest he holds it for himself, not as trustee, and he can deal with it as he pleases.

Suppose that X and Y hold Blackacre upon trust to sell and to hold the proceeds of sale in trust for A for life remainder to B in fee tail remainder to C in fee simple. The ways in which the legal estate held by X and Y can be dealt with have already been considered. They are limited by statute and their position as trustees. But A, for example, can do what he likes with his life interest. He can sell it, give it away, mortgage it, and so on, remembering all the time that as a life interest it will come to an end when he dies and any interest which he has carved out of it must also come to an end when he dies. For example, if he mortgages it to secure a loan and then dies, the loan will still be owing and can be claimed by the mortgagee from his personal representatives. But the life interest and with it the security will have disappeared. The mortgagee will not be able to go against the land to enforce repayment of the loan.

The position is the same with B's fee tail and C's fee simple; and

---

[86] See above, p. 280.

[87] See, *e.g. Caunce* v. *Caunce* [1969] 1 W.L.R. 286 (Stamp. J.) in which occupation by the contributing wife was held not to amount to notice; but on the issue of what amounts to notice this decision was disapproved by the House of Lords in *Williams & Glyn's Bank Ltd.* v. *Boland* [1980] 2 All E.R. 408 (H.L.), and is now of doubtful authority.

[88] For a discussion of this issue in the case of registered and unregistered land—see (1973) 36 M.L.R. 25 (R.H. Maudsley); and see n. 74, above.

the rights going with these interests in equity—to bar the entail, and so on—have already been considered in the context of strict settlements.[89]

CHAPTER 9

COMPARISON OF THE STRICT SETTLEMENT AND TRUST FOR SALE

The choice of settlement. The detailed rules governing the two methods of settling land have been considered. This chapter is merely intended, by way of summary, to make some comparison between the two methods and to mention some of the factors that might influence an intending settlor today when choosing which method to use.

A settlement may comprise a large landed estate of thousands of acres or just a farm with a few hundred acres; it may be no more than a semi-detached house in the suburbs together with a few stocks and shares. It may be complex or it may be simple. It may contain all the paraphernalia of the classical settlement with life interest followed by life interest followed by successive fee tails the whole embellished with portions, jointures and the rest; or it may be a few lines in a home-made will leaving the family house to the widow for life and then to the children equally.

Naturally, the smaller the size and value of the land, the simpler will be the provisions of the settlement. There is nothing to stop you entailing your back garden and indeed charging it with the payment of a jointure to your widow when you die. It would be perfectly valid in law and would give you something in common with what is left of the landed aristocracy. But the legal costs would probably amount to more than the value of the land and the jointure would have to be a peppercorn—or a cabbage.

However, complex or simple, the settlement will have to be governed either by the Settled Land Act 1925 or the trust for sale machinery. When the intending settlor is instructing his solicitor, he will have to consider a number of matters in making his choice between the two methods. Some of these will now be mentioned.

Control. In the case of the strict settlement the benefit and burden of control of the land are normally with the tenant for life, that is the present beneficiary. The legal estate is vested in him as also the statutory powers of dealing with, and the day to day management of, the property. This means that it is for him to decide what is to happen to the land; if and when it is to be sold; and of course it means that he can choose to occupy it himself if he wishes. As already seen, his powers are not unfettered. He is a trustee for all the beneficiaries and is to some extent subject to control by the trustees of the settlement.

In the case of a trust for sale—and this is the fundamental distinction between the two types—the legal estate and all these powers of control over the land are vested in the trustees. The present beneficiary is not without some influence. The trustees may have to consult him.[1] They may, if they wish, delegate the day-to-day management to him and let him occupy the property. They may have to obtain his consent before dealing with the land under their statutory powers. And since they are trustees they must generally act in the best interests of him and all the other beneficiaries. Nevertheless, it is still essentially true to say that control rests with them and not the present beneficiary.

If the property consists of a large farm which is expected to be occupied and worked by the tenant for life, a strict settlement may be more suitable. On the other hand, suppose that it consists of a landed estate comprising many farms all occupied by tenant farmers; and suppose that the tenant for life is interested only in receiving a steady income without much responsibility. No doubt he would be happy to see the whole estate in the hands of professional trustees for sale who—for a fee—would manage the estate, shoulder the responsibility of decision making and send him a cheque half-yearly in payment of his income.

Beneficial interests.   Traditionally, the beneficial interests behind a strict settlement and a trust for sale were quite different. The strict settlement designed to keep the land in the family represented by the line of eldest sons, was based on the fee tail. The eldest son of each generation was intended to hold the entire land. Financial provision was made for other members of the family by means of jointures, portions, etc., as charges on the land. And in the absence of misfortune there was no need to sell the land or split it up to meet these payments.

In the case of a trust for sale, the intention was generally that, after the death of the settlor and his wife, the property should be sold and the proceeds divided up between the children and grandchildren. There was no desire either to keep the land in the family or to favour eldest sons.

Today, this tradition probably continues to some extent. A family which has traditionally used the strict settlement with its typical limitations will continue to do so. On the other hand, where a person wants to settle land on himself and his wife for life followed by division between the children the natural thing is to use the trust for sale which has always been used for this sort of settlement.

---

[1] And he may possibly be one of the trustees.

But it is important to realise that today, with one exception, all the possible beneficial interests can be created under either a strict settlement or a trust for sale. For example, the entail—in so far as it is used any longer—can be created under a trust for sale. Before 1926, it could only be created under a strict settlement since personal property could not be entailed.

The exception is this: A tenancy in common can only exist behind a trust for sale.[2] It is for this reason that where a settlement is to include a tenancy in common, there is some advantage in using the trust for sale—since when the tenancy in common falls into possession it will in any case have to be governed by the trust for sale machinery.

Restrictions on sale. Historically, the strict settlement was developed as the legal device by which landowners could ensure that their lands remained in the family. The policy of modern legislators had been to ensure that in general one generation cannot tie up the land and limit the freedom of the next generation to deal with it. Broadly speaking, the position today is this: A person can settle his land just as he can settle the rest of his property, stocks and shares and so on. Subject to the rules against remoteness,[3] and revenue law, he can ensure that his wealth will be preserved intact for his family for many years after his death. But if it is land which he settles, whichever method he uses he cannot guarantee that the land will not be sold and converted into some other form of wealth. The only point is that if he uses the trust for sale he can stipulate consents before sale.

Formalities. Two separate documents must be employed in the case of a strict settlement. This is not essential in the case of a trust for sale.

It has been suggested that "a trust for sale is usually less complicated and expensive than settled land"[4] (*i.e.* a strict settlement). It is true that two documents are not essential in the case of a trust for sale. But in practice where the trust for sale is being used to settle land, two documents—a conveyance to the trustees and a trust instrument—will be employed. Whichever method is used there will have to be further documents executed when an estate owner dies. A trustee is no more immortal than a tenant for life—unless the trustee is a trust corporation, in which

---

[2] A joint tenancy can exist under a strict settlement in which case there will be joint tenants for life. See S.L.A. 1925, s.19(2).
[3] Below, Chap. 11.
[4] Megarry and Wade, *Law of Real Property* (3rd ed.), p. 393.

case the trust for sale probably does have a significant advantage. But in general it is difficult to see that a strict settlement is greatly more complicated and expensive than a trust for sale.

And a trust for sale does have this disadvantage: it hardly means what it says. It is important that a client should understand the bits of paper which his lawyer gets him to sign. It may well be disturbing to a surviving widow—anxious that she should be able to remain in the home for the rest of her life—to read that it has been transferred to trustees with instructions to sell at once. Her lawyer might find it difficult—without enrolling her for a course of study in land law—to explain to her that this does not really mean what it says; that it is merely a nineteenth century device put to twentieth century use.

A strict settlement is surely more comprehensible. It says that A is to have the land for life and he has it—vested in him by vesting deed—for life.

Capital money.   In both types of settlement any capital money must be paid to the trustees and looked after by them; and the use which can be made of it is much the same in both cases.

However, in the case of a strict settlement it is the tenant for life who can choose between the various permitted ways of applying capital. In the case of a trust for sale it is the trustees. Thus, the distinction which exists while the land is unsold, continues after sale. In the case of a strict settlement managerial control of the trust property—whether in the form of land or capital—rests with the tenant for life. In the case of the trust for sale it rests with the trustees.

The purchaser.   From the point of view of a purchaser it does not normally matter whether the land is subject to the Settled Land Act or a trust for sale—provided he knows *which* it is. So long as he deals with the estate owner, makes a proper investigation of title and complies with all the formalities required of him, he will obtain the property free of any possible claims by beneficiaries. And in neither case will he have to go behind the curtain and investigate the beneficial equitable interests. In most cases, under both types of settlement, he will be protected even if there has been some irregularity.

Taxation.   Probably the most important factor influencing the development of modern settlements has been the desire of property owners to avoid estate duty. The subject of capital transfer and other taxation is beyond the scope of this book but, today, the choice between a strict settlement and a trust for sale will not affect liability to capital transfer tax.[5]

In conclusion. In conclusion this may be said. Which machinery an intending settlor adopts will depend very much on whom he wishes to control the property. Subject to this, and to the fact that a tenancy in common can only exist behind a trust for sale, it probably matters very little which method is used. Indeed, it could well be concluded that the existence of two alternative methods serves little purpose and is the result of historical development rather than modern need.

The essential features of the modern settlement are common to both. The legal estate is vested in no more than four individuals who have the control and disposition of the land; and in general their control cannot be limited. Further, a purchaser is not in general concerned with the beneficial interests which are kept behind a curtain.

There is perhaps much to be said for replacing the Settled Land Act settlement and the trust for sale with a single form of trust ownership incorporating these basic principles. Such a trust could be governed by a single set of rules whilst yet allowing the settlor to choose who was going to manage the property. The advantages of the present trust for sale could be incorporated—for example the right to specify consents before sale—but it would no longer be necessary to give the land to trustees with instructions to sell when the whole intention was that they should not sell.[6]

---

[5] See Cheshire, *Modern Law of Real Property* (12th ed.), pp. 204–207; see generally on capital transfer tax, Mellows, *Taxation for Executors and Trustees* (4th ed.).

[6] See Law.Com.W.P. 42, at para. 108, which proposes a "matrimonial home trust," in the case of the matrimonial home.

CHAPTER 10

POWERS

Principle 1. Definition and classification

A power is usually defined as the authority vested in a person (the "donee" of the power) to deal with or dispose of property not his own.[1]

A power will fall into one of the following categories:

(1) The power of a trustee estate owner to deal with his legal estate free of the beneficial interests.

(2) The power to deal with a legal estate vested in someone else.

(3) Power to deal with an equitable interest vested in someone else.

Explanation

Definition. A trust imposes an *obligation* to deal with property in a particular way. A power merely gives the donee *authority* to deal with the property. He is not in general under any obligation to exercise the power.

Power of the estate owner to deal with his legal estate. Under the 1925 legislation trustee estate owners, such as trustees for sale and tenants for life, are given statutory powers of dealing with the legal estate free of the beneficial interests. These powers have already been dealt with.

Power to deal with legal estate vested in someone else. In a very few cases since 1925 it is still possible for a person to deal with a legal estate which he himself does not hold. Thus a mortgagee has a statutory power to sell the legal estate vested in the mortgagor.[2] And under a strict settlement, in a few special cases, the trustees can deal with the legal estate when it is vested in the tenant for life.[3] Finally, any person can give another authority to deal with his property (including legal estates in land) by power of attorney.

Equitable powers. With the above exceptions, since 1925, all powers can exist only in equity.

In the case of land these equitable powers must operate behind a

---

[1] See *Words and Phrases Legally Defined*, ed. John B. Saunders, 1969.

[2] See below, p. 456.

[3] *e.g.* where the tenant for life is going to purchase the land himself: S.L.A. 1925, s.68.

trust for sale or a strict settlement. They will operate only on the equitable interests and will not affect the legal estate. A purchaser of the legal estate should not therefore normally be concerned with them, providing he complies with the overreaching requirements.

The commonest type of equitable power is the power of appointment. A power of appointment entitles the donee of the power (who becomes the appointor when he exercises the power) to appoint the property to one or more persons. For example, the beneficial freehold owner of Blackacre makes an *inter vivos* settlement of it on A for life and then to whomever A shall by deed or will appoint. This has created a strict settlement. A will be the tenant for life and have the legal estate vested in him. A purchaser of the land from A, will not be concerned with the power of appointment. He will not even know of its existence. He will be concerned only with the title to the legal estate including the vesting deed in favour of A.[4] If A has already made an appointment, for example, in favour of B for life remainder to C absolutely, the interests of B and C will be transferred to the purchase money.

Today, powers of appointment are likely to be found under discretionary settlements of both land and other property. In the case of land, if a trust for sale is used, the legal estate will be transferred to the trustees upon trust to sell; and the trust instrument will instruct them to hold the "trust fund" (*i.e.* the proceeds of sale and the investments for the time being representing the proceeds of sale), for example, " . . . for the benefit of all or any one or more exclusively of the others or other of the Beneficiaries as the Trustees . . . in their absolute discretion shall at any time or times during the Specified Period[5] by any deed or deeds revocable or irrevocable appoint. . . . "[6]

Principle 2. Powers of appointment

A power of appointment may be general or special. A general power entitles the donee to appoint any one including himself.[7] A special power entitles him to appoint only from among a specified class (the "objects" of the power).

In general, any appointment must comply exactly with the terms

---

[4] Or his registration as proprietor in the case of registered land.
[5] *i.e.* the perpetuity period; see below, p. 302.
[6] Hallett, *Conveyancing Precedents* (1965), pp. 804, 805.
[7] See Perpetuities and Accumulations Act 1964, s.7.

of the power. However, regardless of what the power stipulates, the appointment will be valid as to formalities if, in the case of appointment by will, it complies with the requirements for a valid will; and, in the case of an *inter vivos* appointment, it is by deed and signed in the presence of and attested by two witnesses.[8]

If a special power is exercised in favour of a non-object, this is an excessive execution, and the appointment will be void as to the excess; but if the good cannot be severed from the bad the whole appointment will be bad.

If a special power is exercised in favour of an object but in fraud on the power, the appointment will generally be void. But it may be valid in favour of a purchaser under section 157 of the Law of Property Act 1925.

Explanation

General and special powers.   If a testator leaves Blackacre to his son for life and then to whichever of the grandsons A should appoint, A has a special power.

The main importance of the distinction is in the application of the rules against remoteness.[9]

Excessive execution.   If in the above example, A were to appoint Blackacre to one of the testator's grandsons for life with remainder to a granddaughter, the appointment in favour of the grandson would be valid; but the appointment in favour of the granddaughter, a non-object, would be excessive and void. Where there is default of appointment because no valid appointment has been made, the property will be held on a resulting trust for the donor of the power—unless he has provided for what is to happen in default of appointment.

Fraud on power.   There is a fraud where the donee of a special power exercises it with the intention of achieving some purpose not intended by the power. For example, where the appointment is made in pursuance of an agreement to benefit a non-object. There would be a fraud in the above example, if A appointed to the grandson absolutely but on the understanding that the grandson would transfer property of equal value to the granddaughter.

Whereas an excessive appointment will be apparent, a fraudulent exercise of the power may not be discovered immediately.

---

[8] L.P.A. 1925, s.159.
[9] See below, p. 306.

And where a fraudulent exercise makes the appointment void, this may prove fatal to the title of an innocent purchaser. It was for this reason that section 157 of the Law of Property Act 1925 was passed to give some possibility of protection. The purchaser will be protected and his title to the property upheld, but only to the extent of the share which the appointee would have taken in default of appointment; and only if:

(a) he bought for money or money's worth without notice of the fraud; and

(b) the appointee was at least 25 years of age.

The distinction between a power of appointment and a trust[10]

There are a number of important differences, including the following:

(a) Certainty: In the case of a fixed trust the beneficiaries must be identified with certainty.[11] In the case of a power it is sufficient if it can be stated "with certainty that any given individual is or is not a member of the class."[12]

(b) In the case of a trust each beneficiary has an enforceable interest in the property. In the case of a power, the potential beneficiary merely has a hope that the power will be exercised in his favour.

Principle 3. Discretionary trusts

A trust, known as a discretionary trust, may confer powers of appointment on the trustees without ceasing to be a trust.

Explanation

The distinction between a trust and a power is "complicated by the fact that a trust may give to the trustees considerable discretion. A trustee may be given a discretion to select the beneficiaries from a specified class, or to determine the proportions in which specified beneficiaries are to take. This is the basis of the discretionary trust."[13]

As already seen,[14] a trust for sale can contain a power to

---

[10] See Hanbury and Maudsley, *Modern Equity* (11th ed.), at p. 165 *et seq.*
[11] See above, p. 176.
[12] Hanbury and Maudsley, *Modern Equity* (11th ed.), at p. 170, quoting Lord Wilberforce in *McPhail* v. *Doulton* [1971] A.C. 424, at p. 456. For meaning of "fixed" trust (in contrast to discretionary trust) see Hanbury and Maudsley at p. 210.
[13] Hanbury and Maudsley, *Modern Equity* (11th ed.) at p. 167.
[14] Above, p. 261.

postpone sale without ceasing to be a trust for sale. Similarly, a trust may contain a power of appointment without ceasing to be a trust. A court may have to decide, on a proper construction of the words used, whether a settlor has created a mere power or a trust containing a power of appointment, *i.e.* a discretionary trust.[15]

In the case of a mere power, if the power is not exercised, the potential beneficiaries will take nothing; and, in the absence of a gift over, there will be a resulting trust for the settlor. Further, as already mentioned, in the case of a power, the potential beneficiary (the postulant) has no enforceable interest in the trust property. In the case of a discretionary trust, no beneficiary has an interest in any specified part of the trust property until the discretion has been exercised in his favour. But, and this is the crucial point, between them they are entitled to the trust property. It follows that if the power is not exercised, the beneficiaries will be entitled to share it between them[16] and, further, if they are all of full age and not under disability, they will be able to combine and put an end to the trust and direct the distribution of the property.

The rule as to certainty of objects is the same for discretionary trusts as it is for mere powers.[17]

The use of the discretionary trust. Until the Finance Act 1969,[18] discretionary trusts were widely used to avoid estate duty.[19] The duty was payable when property passed on death. Since the beneficiaries were not regarded as owning any property, none passed on their deaths.[20] Under the legislation now imposing capital transfer tax, discretionary trusts "have moved from the top of the fiscal league to the bottom."[21]

Today, discretionary trusts are more commonly found as elements in superannuation schemes and trusts for the benefit of employees.

Another use is dealt with in the next Principle.

---

[15] Discretionary trusts will normally give trustees other, incidental powers, *e.g.* power to accumulate income and necessary administrative powers.

[16] As to the shares in which they will be entitled, see *McPhail* v. *Doulton* [1971] A.C. 424 (H.L.).

[17] *McPhail* v. *Doulton* [1971] A.C. 424.

[18] s.36. And see now Finance Act 1975, Sched. 5; and Hanbury and Maudsley, *Modern Equity* (11th ed.), at p. 289.

[19] Now replaced by capital transfer tax; see Finance Act 1975, Sched. 5.

[20] See *Gartside* v. *I.R.C.* [1968] A.C. 553 (H.L.).

[21] Hanbury and Maudsley, *Modern Equity*, (11th ed.), at p. 299.

Land held under discretionary trusts. Any land included in the property held on such trusts will, of course, have to be subject to a trust for sale or the strict settlement machinery.

Where a strict settlement is used and the discretionary trusts are in operation, the legal estate will have to be vested in the trustees of the settlement as statutory owner since there will be no tenant for life as defined by the Settled Land Act.

Principle 4. Protective and discretionary trusts

The protective and discretionary trust is the device commonly used to protect a beneficiary from the consequences of his bankruptcy or improvidence.

The intended beneficiary is given a life interest determinable[22] on his bankruptcy or any other event which would deprive him of the income from the property.

There is then a gift over of the property, in such an event, to trustees on discretionary trusts for the remainder of the trust period; that is, giving the trustees absolute discretion to appoint the income to whichever of the specified beneficiaries they think fit. The beneficiaries specified will usually include the intended beneficiary (who had the life interest), his spouse and issue.

Explanation

The basis of this device is the determinable interest and the power of appointment.

The beneficiary has a determinable life interest which determines if he goes bankrupt, etc. He will be entitled to the income to start with, but if the determining event happens his interest in the property will cease. It will no longer be his to be taken by his creditors. Instead, the right to the income will pass to the trustees named by the settlor with power to appoint it among the specified class of which the principal beneficiary will be a member. If the trustees exercise their discretion by making an appointment in his favour, then the income appointed may become available to his creditors. It may, therefore, be better from this point of view, if instead of giving him the price of a meal, they "pay a hotel keeper to give him a dinner,"[23] since the right to eat a dinner "is not property which could pass by assignment or bankruptcy."[24]

---

[22] For determinable interests, see further, above, at p. 18.
[23] Hanbury and Maudsley, *Modern Equity* (11th ed.), at p. 275.
[24] *Re Coleman* (1888) 39 Ch.D. 443, at p. 451.

Trustee Act 1925, s.33

The Trustee Act 1925, s.33, sets out a form of protective and discretionary trust which a settlor can if he wishes incorporate by reference, with or without modification, into his settlement.
Section 33 provides:

33.—(1) Where any income, including an annuity or other periodical income payment, is directed to be held on protective trusts for the benefit of any person (in this section called "the principal beneficiary") for the period of his life or for any less period, then, during that period (in this section called the "trust period") the said income shall, without prejudice to any prior interest, be held on the following trusts, namely:—

(i) Upon trust for the principal beneficiary during the trust period or until he, whether before or after the termination of any prior interest, does or attempts to do or suffers any act or thing, or until any event happens, other than an advance under any statutory or express power, whereby, if the said income were payable during the trust period to the principal beneficiary absolutely during that period, he would be deprived of the right to receive the same or any part thereof, in any of which cases, as well as on the termination of the trust period, whichever first happens, this trust of the said income shall fail or determine;

(ii) If the trust aforesaid fails or determines during the subsistence of the trust period, then, during the residue of that period, the said income shall be held upon trust for the application thereof for the maintenance or support, or otherwise, for the benefit, of all or any one or more exclusively of the other or others of the following persons (that is to say)—

(*a*) the principal beneficiary and his or her wife or husband, if any, and his or her children or more remote issue, if any; or

(*b*) if there is no wife or husband or issue of the principal beneficiary in existence, the principal beneficiary and the persons who would, if he were actually dead, be entitled to the trust property or the income thereof or to the annuity fund, if any, or arrears of the annuity, as the case may be;

as the trustees in their absolute discretion, without being liable to account for the exercise of such discretion, think fit.

(2) This section does not apply to trusts coming into operation before the commencement of this Act, and has effect subject to any variation of the implied trusts aforesaid contained in the instrument creating the trust.

(3) Nothing in this section operates to validate any trust which would, if contained in the instrument creating the trust, be liable to be set aside.

CHAPTER 11

SETTLEMENTS AND ALIENABILITY

Principle 1. Alienability

Today, the free alienability of property is protected by the following rules:

(1) In general, it is not possible to control the form which settled property will take. In the case of land, with minor exceptions, there will always be an estate owner with the power to sell the land, thus converting it into money or some other form of investment.

(2) It is not possible to create an unbarrable entail.

(3) Any condition against alienation attached to a gift will generally be void.[1]

(4) The rule against perpetuities (sometimes known as the rule against the remoteness of vesting). This provides that any contingent gift will be void if the contingency does not happen and the gift vest withn the perpetuity period.

(5) The rule against accumulations: Any direction to accumulate the income of property must be limited to the accumulation period.

Explanation

The history of the settlement has been the history of the attempts by the landowner to control the destination of his property after his death. These attempts have been met by "the general policy of the law against the withdrawal of property from commerce."[2]

As a result of common law and statute law, the position today is broadly speaking that:

(a) the settlor cannot control the form in which his property will be maintained; and

(b) the period for which he can ensure that it will remain intact in any form after his death and determine its devolution is strictly limited by rules (2)–(5) above.

Suppose that S settles Blackacre by a strict settlement on A for life remainder to B in fee simple on condition that B does not attempt to alienate. In the first place, A—assuming that he is the

---

[1] Compare *Re Buchanan-Wollaston's Conveyance* [1939] Ch. 738. Also *Caldy Manor Estate Ltd.* v. *Farrell* [1974] 3 All E.R. 753 (C.A.).

[2] Morris and Leach, *The Rule against Perpetuities* (2nd ed., 1962), p. 2.

tenant for life—cannot be prevented from selling the land free of the equitable interests. In other words, the condition against alienation cannot prevent the conversion of the settled property into a different form. In the second place, such a condition against alienation will be void; B will be absolutely entitled to his interest, subject to A's life interest, but free of the condition; whether it happens to be in the form of land or money or other investments, B will be entitled to dispose of it as he wishes.

Similarly, if B has a fee tail in remainder. Again it may be converted from land into money; but in either case B can bar the entail and thus acquire an absolute interest which he can then dispose of as he wishes.[3]

But what if S has settled Blackacre by will on A for life remainder in fee tail to the first son of A to reach the age of 21? It might be many years after the death of S before any son of A reaches the required age. Until this happens there is no one entitled to the fee tail and therefore no one entitled to bar it and dispose of the property.

This illustration shows a way in which a settlor might be able to prevent the settled property from being disposed of for a long time. What he has to do is to give the property to a beneficiary who will not be ascertained until the happening of some event; until this event happens and the beneficiary is ascertained there is no one with power to dispose of the property. The further in the future the event the longer must the property be held. If I were allowed to create a valid settlement in favour of "whoever is my eldest surviving descendant in A.D. 2100," this would ensure the retention of the property until that date when the person entitled could be ascertained.[4]

The rule against perpetuities has been developed to prevent this sort of restriction on the free disposal of property. The rule does not avoid all future interests made to depend on some contingency; the example first given above of the gift to the first son of A to reach 21 would be valid. But it does limit the period for which property can be preserved in this way for a future beneficiary.

The rule against perpetuities will be considered next. The rule against accumulations will then be dealt with.

It needs to be emphasised that this Chapter is concerned with the rules designed to maintain the free alienability of property, rules which reflect the capitalist basis of English property law,

---

[3] But he will need A's consent or have to await A's death: see above, p. 249.
[4] For the rule governing the right to have the income accumulated whilst the property is retained, see rule against accumulations, below, p. 309.

ensuring that in each generation capital is at the free disposal of its owners to be used in private industry and commerce. It is not concerned with rules designed to *prevent* the private accumulation of property by one and its voluntary transfer to succeeding generations. Such rules as there are designed to prevent the accumulation of private property and enforce its redistribution or public use are found in the province of tax law (capital gains and capital transfer tax, etc.) and the law relating to public enterprises and are beyond the scope of this book.

Principle 2. The rule against perpetuities[5]

Any limitation of property will be void unless it vests during the perpetuity period.

The perpetuity period is either:
  (a) a life or lives in being plus a further period of 21 years; or alternatively,
  (b) any period not exceeding 80 years expressly stipulated by the settlor.[6]

Where a gift is void only because vesting is by reference to an age greater than 21, the specified age will be reduced so far as necessary to save the gift.[7]

Explanation

The rule applies to the vesting in interest of contingent interests: the distinction between vested and contingent interests.

An interest will be vested in possession where the beneficiary is entitled to immediate possession. Otherwise it will be a future interest. A future interest may be vested in interest or contingent. It is vested in interest if the beneficiary is ascertained and the only things which delays his right to possession is the existence of prior interests. It is contingent if the beneficiary is not yet ascertained or if the right to possession depends on some contingency other than the determination of prior interests.

If property is given to A for life remainder to B absolutely, B has a vested interest (although not in possession). There is an

---

[5] This Principle sets out the rules as modified by the Perpetuities and Accumulations Act 1964 which governs instruments taking effect after July 15, 1964. For the unamended rules governing earlier instruments, see Megarry and Wade, *Law of Real Property* (4th ed.), Chap. 5, at p. 199 *et seq.*
[6] Perpetuities and Accumulations Act 1964, s.1(1).
[7] *Ibid.* s.4, (as amended by Children Act 1975, Sched. 3.) repealing the less flexible provisions of the L.P.A. 1925, s.163.

existing beneficiary entitled to deal with the property immediately and no question of the rule against perpetuities applying. The right to possession depends only on the determination of the prior interest.

On the other hand, if property is given by will to A for life remainder to the first son of A to reach 21, this creates a contingent interest in remainder. Even if A has a son of 20 when the testator dies, that son might die before his 21st birthday. Until the contingency occurs it is not possible to say who, if anyone, will obtain a vested interest. Until then there will be no one in a position to deal with the property. If a son of A does reach the required age, his interest will become vested.

The rule against perpetuities is applied to limit this possible method of using contingent gifts to suspend the free alienability of property. The rule specifies a limited period within which the gift must vest. If it fails to vest in that period it will be void. This means that any intending settlor will have to confine his instructions for the future of the property within the perpetuity period.

The perpetuity period. The period allowed at common law is a life or lives in being plus an extra 21 years. A life in being is the life of any person who is alive when the instrument creating the gift takes effect and is referred to in the instrument as a life in being either expressly or by implication. There can be any number of lives in being; but, however many there are, the period cannot extend beyond the death of the survivor (plus 21 years). The advantage of specifying a large number of lives—as is done in the once commonly used "royal lives" clause—is that one of them is likely to be a long one.

Suppose that T leaves this property by will to the first of his grandchildren to reach the age of 21. Any children of T will be counted as lives in being. This is because when the will takes effect, on the death of T, any of his children must then be alive (or at least conceived; and the rule allows a relevant period of gestation to be added at the beginning or end of the period). Although they are not expressly named as lives in being, they are necessarily implied by the limitation; reference to the grandchildren implies the existence of the children.

Thus, suppose that when he dies T leaves two children, S1 and S2, and that five months after his death his widow gives birth to a third child, S3. All three children will be lives in being. Any son of S1, S2 or S3 to reach the age of 21 must do so within 21 years—plus possibly a period of gestation—of his father's death. It is therefore possible to say, even at the time of T's death, that if the gift vests at all it will necessarily do so during the perpetuity period; that is within the period of 21 years of the death of the survivor of the lives in being, S1, S2 and S3.

Where no life in being is stipulated expressly or by implication, the period is 21 years.

The statutory period. Under the Perpetuities and Accumulations Act 1964 the settlor can specify a fixed period not exceeding 80 years. This enables him to ensure a relatively long perpetuity period without having to specify a large number of lives.

The wait-and-see rule. At common law the rule was that a gift was void if, considered at the time the instrument creating it came into operation, there was any possibility however remote of it vesting outside the perpetuity period. And at common law no man or woman was considered too old or too young to have children.

For instruments taking effect after July 15, 1964,[8] if there is a possibility of the gift vesting outside the period, the rule "wait-and-see" applies. This means that it will be saved if it does in the event vest within the period.

Further, there is presumption that a male cannot have a child under the age of 14; and that a female cannot have a child under the age of 12 or over the age of 55.

Suppose that T leaves property by will to the first of his great-grandchildren to reach the age of 21. This would have been void at common law because of the possibility that the first great-grandson to reach this age would do so more than 21 years after the death of the last surviving son of T. Under the Act it is possible to "wait-and-see" whether any great-grandson reaches the required age within this period. If he does he will take the gift.

Where the wait-and-see rule is being applied to a gift, the lives of any of the following who are in existence and ascertained at the time of the instrument will be treated as lives in being:

(a) The donor.

(b) Any donee or potential donee.

(c) Any donee or potential donee's parents or grandparents.

(d) The owner of any prior interest.

Vesting expedited under section 4 of the Perpetuities and Accumulations Act 1964.[9] Where a gift is void only because it depends on some person reaching a specified age greater than 21, it will be saved by section 4 of the 1964 Act. This provides that the

---

[8] *i.e.* those governed by the Perpetuities and Accumulations Act 1964.
[9] As amended by Children Act 1975, Sched. 3.

specified age will be reduced to the age necessary to save the gift. But it cannot be reduced to less than 21 under this provision.

For example, if property is given by will to A for life, remainder to his first son to reach the age of 35, this would be void at common law.[10] Under the 1964 Act the position will be as follows:

(a) The "wait-and-see" rule will apply and this will save the gift if a son does reach 35 within 21 years of A's death.

(b) If not saved under the above rule, it will be rescued by section 4. For example, if A dies survived by an only son aged 5 years, section 4 will reduce the 35 years to 26—the least reduction necessary to save the gift. The son will obtain a vested interest if and when he reaches the age of 26.

Application of the rule to contracts.   The rule only applies to interests in property. It does not apply to personal contractual obligations. However, a contract creating an interest in land which is void for perpetuity will itself be void even between the contracting parties.[11] If V sells P an option to purchase the freehold of Blackacre, this creates both a personal contractual relationship between V and P and also an interest in the land which P can assign. But it is subject to a perpetuity period of 21 years,[12] and once this has expired the option will not be enforceable either by an assignee as a property interest or by P as a contractual obligation.

Principle 3.   The rule against perpetuities: Special cases

1.   **Options.**   The rule does not apply to an option to renew contained in a lease.

It does not apply to an option contained in a lease to purchase either the freehold or a superior leasehold so long as the option is exercisable only by the lessee or his successors in title not later than one year after the expiry of the lease.[13]

In the case of any other option to acquire an interest in property, there is a fixed perpetuity period of 21 years.

2.   **Conditional and determinable interests.**   The rule applies in the ordinary way to an interest subject to a condition precedent.

It applies to a right of re-entry to enforce a condition subsequent

---

[10] Unless A was already dead or he already had a son aged 35.
[11] Perpetuities and Accumulations Act 1964, s.10.
[12] *Ibid.* s.9(2); apart from some special cases, the perpetuity period for an option to acquire an interest in land is 21 years.
[13] *Ibid.* s.9(1).

attached to property. If the right of re-entry is not exercised within the perpetuity period, the condition will be void and the interest will become absolute.[14]

It also applies to the possibility of reverter attached to a determinable interest. If the interest does not determine within the period it will become absolute.[15]

3. **Class gifts.** The rule does apply to class gifts. Those members of the class who have obtained vested interests when the period closes will take to the exclusion of all others.[16]

4. **Entails.** The rule does not apply to a gift limited to take effect during or at the moment of determination of a fee tail.

5. **Charities.** In general the rule applies in the normal way to gifts to charities except that a gift over from one charity to another in some event is not subject to the rule.

6. **Mortgages.** The rule does not apply to the right of redemption contained in a mortgage.

7. **Powers of appointment.** (a) *Validity of the power.* A special power will be valid if it is *exercised* during the perpetuity period; the period being calculated from the time when the instrument creating the power takes effect. A general power is valid provided it is *acquired* during the perpetuity period again calculated from the date of the instrument by which it is created even if it is exercised outside the period.

(b) *Validity of an appointment made under the power.* Any interest appointed will be void if it vests outside the perpetuity period. In the case of a special power the period is calculated from the date of the instrument creating the power. In the case of a general power the period is calculated from the date of exercise of the power.

Explanation

Some of the above cases need some explanation.

---

[14] By way of exception the rule does not apply to a right of entry to enforce payment of a rentcharge; L.P.A. 1925, s.121(6); nor does it apply to a right of entry reserved to a lessor in a lease to enforce the terms of the lease: *Re Tyrrell's Estate* [1907] 1 I.R. 292, at p. 298.

[15] Perpetuities and Accumulations Act 1964, s.12.

[16] *Ibid.* s.4(3) (4).

Conditional and determinable gifts. An interest in land may be made either subject to a condition precedent, to a condition subsequent, or determinable.

An interest subject to a condition precedent does not vest at all unless and until the condition is satisfied. For example, a gift "to X when he marries."An interest subject to a condition precedent is just another name for a contingent interest and the rule against perpetuities applies as already described.

An interest subject to a condition subsequent, on the other hand, is a vested interest which is liable to be divested if and when a certain event happens. If the event does happen it does not terminate automatically; but the person next entitled has a right to enter and terminate it. This right of entry, since it is contingent on the event, is subject to the perpetuities rule; and if it does not become exercisable within the perpetuity period it will be void and the interest will become absolute. For example, a gift "to A on condition that he never sells out of the family" creates an interest subject to a condition subsequent. If he does not sell out of the family during he perpetuity period, the condition can no longer be enforced and the gift becomes absolute.

A determinable interest is a vested interest which will determine automatically if and when the specified event happens. Whether a gift is determinable or subject to a condition subsequent depends entirely on the wording used to create it. A gift "to A until he sells out of the family" creates a determinable interest. Where an absolute or fee simple gift is determinable the grantor is said to have a possibility of reverter—a possibility that the land will come back to him if the interest does determine. At common law the rule against perpetuities did not apply to such a possibility of reverter. Under the Perpetuities and Accumulations Act 1964, it does apply. If the gift does not determine during the period the gift becomes absolute.

Class gifts. A class gift is "a gift of property to all who come within some description, the property being divided in shares varying according to the number of persons in the class."[17]

The share of each person depends on the number in the class. If it is fixed independently it is an individual not a class gift. Thus, a gift of property "to all my children who reach the age of 21" is a class gift. On the other hand, a gift of property "to each of my five children" is not. In the first case it is not possible to say what each

---

[17] See Megarry, *Manual of the Law of Real Property* (5th ed.), p. 113.

beneficiary will take until the class closes. In the second case, each child is given a distinct pre-fixed one-fifth share.

At common law, if the interest of any member of the class could possibly vest outside the perpetuity period, the whole gift failed. Now under the 1964 Act, the rule is that any member of the class who does in fact qualify and obtain a vested interest within the perpetuity period will share the property to the exclusion of any who may qualify outside the period.

Powers of appointment. A general power is tantamount to making an absolute gift to the donee, since he is entitled to appoint to himself. Consequently, the rule is applied to general powers in much the same way as it applies to an absolute gift. The power must vest in the donee within the perpetuity period calculated from the date of the instrument creating the power; any appointment made by the donee must vest within the period calculated from the date of the appointment.

On the other hand, an appointment made under a special power is somewhat different. The appointment is made in part by the *donor,* of the power when he specifies the objects—*i.e.* the possible beneficiaries. Thus, the perpetuity period runs from the date of the instrument creating the power—not from the date of its exercise. The power must be exercised within that period and any appointment must vest within the same period. In other words, an appointment under a special power is treated in the same way as a gift by the donor himself.

To give a very simple example. T makes a will giving property to D for life, remainder as D should appoint among his (D's) children. The power given to D can only be exercised within D's lifetime and is therefore valid. D appoints *inter vivos* to his son S "when he reaches 35." Unless S already is 35 this is a contingent gift and the rule must be applied. As it is a special power the period is calculated from the death of T. D is therefore the only life in being and the perpetuity period, his life plus 21 years. The validity of the appointment depends on the age of S when D dies. If for example, D dies when S is four, then S will only be 25 when the period ends. In this situation, the 1964 Act[18] will operate to save the gift by reducing the specified age of 35 to 25. If, another possibility, D dies when S is 30, the gift will vest in S at 35 since this will be within 21 years of D's death.

[18] s.4.

Principle 4.   The rule against accumulations

Any direction to accumulate the income of property for a period exceeding the perpetuity period will be altogether void.

Any direction to accumulate for a period exceeding the accumulation period will be void as to the excessive period.

The accumulation period is whichever of the following periods is most appropriate to the particular direction:

1. The life of the grantor or settlor.
2. 21 years from the death of the grantor, settlor or testator.
3. The minority of any person living at the death of the grantor, settlor or testator.
4. The minority or respective minorities of any person or persons who would be entitled absolutely to the income if of full age.
5. 21 years from the making of the disposition.
6. The minority of any person in being at the date of the disposition.[19]

Under the rule in *Saunders* v. *Vautier*[20] where a beneficiary is of full age and absolutely entitled he has the right to require any accumulation to stop and the property transferred to him.

Explanation

By his will made on April 2, 1796, Mr. Thellusson directed that his property should be accumulated during the lives of his sons, grandsons and their issue who were living at his death and that on the death of the survivor, the accumulated fund should be divided among certain of his descendants.[21] The property together with the accumulated income would therefore finally vest on the ending of a life in being and the direction was therefore quite valid under the perpetuity rule. What was unusual about this direction was that not only was the capital to remain undistributed for this period; so was the income from the investment of the capital; and the income as it arose would itself be invested producing more income and increasing the capital all the time. It was calculated that the accumulated fund could have amounted to many millions of pounds.[22] Parliament considered the accumulation of property in this way to be undesirable and passed the Accumulations Act

[19] Perpetuities and Accumulations Act 1964, s.13, amending L.P.A. 1925, s.164.
  Note that under the Family Law Reform Act 1969, the age of majority is 18.
[20] (1841) 4 Beav. 115; 49 E.R. 282.
[21] *Thellusson* v. *Woodford* (1799) 4 Ves. 227; 31 E.R. 117.
[22] Partly because of legal fees, it never did.

1800 imposing a further limit on the permissible period of accumulation. The rules are now contained in the Law of Property Act 1925, s.164, and the Perpetuities and Accumulations Act 1964, s.13.

Any income arising during an excessive period of accumulation will go to the person who would have been entitled if there had been no direction to make the excessive accumulation.

CHAPTER 12

CO-OWNERSHIP (CONCURRENT INTERESTS)

SECTION I. DEFINITION AND CLASSIFICATION

Principle 1. Definition

If at any one time only one person is entitled to possession of a piece of land, he is said to be a several owner. Where two or more persons are entitled to possession[1] at the same time it is called co-ownership (or concurrent ownership).

Explanation

Co-ownership is concerned with the sharing of the right of enjoyment. Suppose that John is told to share his book with Mary. He might feel inclined to do this by tearing it down the middle and giving her half. Or he may offer to let her have it when he has finished with it. Probably what is expected of him is that he sits beside her and lets her read it with him. The same sort of possibilities exist in the case of land.

Suppose that Jack and Jill are told to share Blackacre. They could divide it into two equal plots, put a fence down the middle and take a plot each. Each would become absolute or "several" owner of his own plot. If Jack climbed over into Jill's plot he would be committing trespass.

Alternatively they might agree that they should take it in turns to enjoy the whole of Blackacre. This would be to create some sort of successive ownership, a settlement. But if they decided to enjoy it together at the same time, this would be co-ownership.

In *Bull* v. *Bull*,[2] a mother and her son had both contributed to the purchase of a house for their joint occupation. The legal estate was conveyed to the son alone; but the court held that in equity they were co-owners since they had both contributed to the purchase price. Thus, although the son was sole owner at law—as the property had been conveyed to him alone—he held the legal

---

[1] Two or more persons may share ownership of the same estate or, unusually, two or more estates may be granted to take effect in possession at the same time. In this context, possession means only physical possession and does not have the extended meaning given to it by L.P.A. 1925, s.205(1)(xix).

[2] [1955] 1 Q.B. 234.

estate in trust for himself and his mother as equitable co-owners. Trouble started when the son got married. At first it was agreed that the mother should occupy two rooms at the top and that the son and his bride should occupy the rest of the house. Even this did not work for long and in this case the son was claiming possession of the whole house. He failed. The essence of co-ownership is that each co-owner is equally entitled to possession of the whole property. And therefore neither mother nor son was entitled to exclude the other from the house or indeed from any part of it.[3]

Principle 2. Types of co-ownership: Joint tenancy and tenancy in common

English law recognises two main types of co-ownership: joint tenancy and tenancy in common. The main distinction between the two is that a joint tenancy is subject to the right of survivorship.

Explanation

The right of survivorship means that if a joint tenant dies his interest passes automatically to the other joint tenants.[4] Whilst he lives each joint tenant is equally entitled to possession and enjoyment of the property; but a joint tenant does not have any separate share in the property which he can leave by will or which can pass on his intestacy. When he dies he simply drops out of the ownership. In contrast, each tenant in common has what is called a separate but undivided share in the land. It is important to understand what this means. He cannot point to any part of the land, or to one of the rooms in the house, and say that it represents his share and exclude the other tenants from that part. As already stated, each tenant is equally entitled to possession of the whole. But he does have a separate share in the whole ownership—maybe a half-share or some other sized share—and if a tenant in common dies this share will not automatically pass to the other tenants. He

---

[3] But since, in general, co-ownership can today only exist behind a trust for sale, the mother's interest was, in one sense at least, only an interest in the proceeds of sale; it is arguable that she did not have any right to occupy the land itself at all and that the co-ownership was in the proceeds of sale. See further, below, p. 326.

[4] Or rather, it ceases to exist. But note that under the Inheritance (Provision for Family and Dependants) Act 1975, s.9, a claim can be made against a deceased joint tenant's beneficial interest.

can leave it by will to whom he likes; or it will pass according to the ordinary rules of intestacy.

Suppose that H and W (husband and wife) are joint tenants of Blackacre; if H dies W will become absolute owner of the property. Whether or not H has left a will is not relevant.

Suppose, however, that X, Y and Z are tenants in common of Whiteacre. Perhaps they are partners in a business and have bought Whiteacre to use as an office. If Z dies the other two will not automatically benefit. Z's share will pass to whoever is named in his will and failing that, to the person entitled on his intestacy. If he has left all his property to B then B, X and Y will now be tenants in common.[5]

The share of a tenant in common can be likened to the share of a shareholder in a company. A shareholder cannot say that he owns some specific part of the company's assets. He cannot say that he owns two windows and the front door of the company's head office. But he can say that he owns so many shares representing a portion of the company as a whole.

As will be explained later,[6] a joint tenant can quite easily change his joint tenancy into a tenancy in common if he wishes and thus avoid the consequences of the right of survivorship; but he can only do it while he is still alive and not by will to take effect when he dies.

Principle 3.   The four unities

A joint tenancy can only exist if the four unities are present: namely, the unity of possession, unity of interest, unity of title and unity of time. The only unity essential to a tenancy in common is the unity of possession.

Explanation

The essence of joint tenancy is that the joint tenants do not have separate interests in the property; rather they are all together entitled to the same interest. They form a sort of single composite owner. The necessity of the four unities follows from this basic idea.

Unity of possession has been mentioned. Each tenant is equally

---

[5] But, of course, B will not automatically become a partner in the business. This will depend on the partnership agreement.
[6] Below, p. 334.

entitled to possession of the whole property and can sue if he is excluded from any part of it by one of the other joint tenants.

Unity of interest means that the interest of each tenant is precisely the same in extent nature and duration. Indeed, as already stated, in theory they hold the same interest.

Unity of title means that the interest of each tenant must have been derived from the same deed oř document.

Finally, unity of time means that the interest of each tenant must have begun at the same time.

Suppose that H and W purchase the freehold of Blackacre from V. There is unity of possession. This is implied from the fact that the whole property is conveyed to both of them without any suggestion that it is to be physically divided. There is unity of interest because the same interest, the fee simple, is conveyed to both of them. There is unity of title because it is conveyed to both of them by the same document. And unity of time because the interest of both will begin at the same moment—that is the delivery of the conveyance. Where there is this complete unity of ownership, as in the above common case of a conveyance to two purchasers, there is nothing to prevent joint tenancy arising. But this does not mean that they *must* be joint tenants in equity— (tenancy in common is no longer possible at law). They can be joint tenants if they wish. But they may alternatively agree to take separate shares in the common fee simple—that is, to hold as tenants in common in equity.

Where unity of possession is absent there is no co-ownership at all. Where one or more of the other unities is absent then it can only be a case of tenancy in common. Suppose, for example, that X and Y are joint tenants in fee simple of Blackacre; and suppose that X sells and conveys his interest to P. (It might be argued that logically he has no separate interest to sell; but the law has always allowed him to do this.) The effect of such a conveyance is to destroy the unity of title. Y still traces his interest from the original conveyance to him and X. But P traces his interest from the conveyance to him from X. The two titles have taken different roads and become separated. The complete unity essential to joint tenancy has been destroyed. P and Y can only be tenants in common.[7]

---

[7] In equity. Only X and Y together could effectively transfer the legal estate. A joint tenancy of the legal estate cannot be severed (L.P.A. 1925, s.36(2)).

SECTION II. CO-OWNERSHIP OF THE LEGAL ESTATE

Principle 4.   Distinction between legal and equitable co-ownership

Since 1925 the only possible form of co-ownership of the legal estate is joint tenancy. A legal tenancy in common cannot now arise.[8] The maximum number of legal joint tenants is four.[9]

Both joint tenancy and tenancy in common can still be created in equity; and there is no limit on the number of co-owners in equity.

Equitable co-ownership can only exist behind a trust for sale; that is, wherever there is co-ownership in equity the legal estate will necessarily be held by trustees upon trust to sell and to hold the proceeds in trust for the equitable co-owners.[10]

Explanation

The importance of the distinction between legal and equitable ownership in general has already been considered, but it cannot be over emphasised It is not sufficient to talk about joint tenancy or tenancy in common. It is essential to say whether it is the legal or equitable interest that is being discussed. The rights attached to the legal and equitable ownership are not the same; and the rules governing the co-ownership of the two are different.

As already explained,[11] legal ownership carries with it all the rights of dealing with the land, the managerial control. On the other hand, equitable ownership represents the beneficial interest, the right to enjoyment and the fruits of ownership. The legal owner as trustee must deal with the land for the benefit of the equitable beneficiaries. In the case of *Bull* v. *Bull*,[12] the son held the legal estate. This meant that he could sell the land and otherwise deal with it—although as trustee there were important limits on his powers; but the equitable ownership was held to be shared between him and his mother. Therefore the right to possession was shared[13]; and any income and the proceeds of sale would have to be shared.

---

[8] L.P.A. 1925, s.34(1).
[9] See T.A. 1925, s.34. Under the S.L.A. 1925, there can be more than four joint tenants for life.
[10] L.P.A. 1925, ss.34–36. But see n.23 below. And it is possible to have joint tenants for life under the S.L.A. 1925.
[11] Above, p. 155.
[12] Above, n.2.
[13] But see n.3, above.

This separation of ownership of land into the two aspects of managerial control and beneficial enjoyment, was used by the 1925 legislature as part of its overall plan to simplify conveyancing. All this has already been considered in the context of settlements. Here we are concerned with it in the context of co-ownership.

The legislature had no wish to restrict the varieties of co-ownership which could be created; they did not wish to stop a man from sharing his land between his 129 children and grandchildren if that was what he wanted to do. At the same time it did want to prevent the complexities of co-ownership from restricting alienability and complicating conveyancing. What it did to reconcile these two aims was to permit only the simplest type of co-ownership of the legal estate to exist. But in equity no restrictions were imposed on the types of co-ownership which could be created or on the number of co-owners.

An illustration will perhaps show the legislative plan at work. Suppose that you as purchaser are shown the title deeds of Blackacre.[14] Looking through them you find that the most recent transaction is a conveyance to X, Y and Z upon trust to sell and to hold the proceeds of sale in trust for A, B, C, D and E as tenants in common in equal shares. You will first of all need to know with whom to deal; that is, who will be the correct persons to convey Blackacre to you at completion. The answer is X, Y and Z as owners of the legal estate. In this case there are three of them; it is more common for there to be only two trustee owners; but in any case there can never be more than four for a purchaser to deal with. Suppose now that you discover that Z has died since the date of the last conveyance. What difference does this make? Very little. Since co-owners of the legal estate can only be joint tenants the right of survivorship will apply. X and Y will now hold the legal estate between them, and they will be able to convey it to a purchaser. But imagine the position if X, Y and Z had been tenants in common at law. You, as purchaser, would have had to trace the descent of Z's share; and taken a conveyance from X, Y and the new owner (or owners) of Z's shares. Obviously, all this would have been much more complicated.

What of the equitable ownership? In our example we have kept it quite simple. But it could be infinitely more complicated.[15] Suppose that A has died leaving his share in Blackacre by will to his six sons in equal shares; and suppose that B has given his share *inter vivos* to his three children in equal shares. There will by now

---

[14] Assuming it to be unregistered.
[15] See, *e.g. Barclay* v. *Barclay* [1970] 2 Q.B. 677.

be 12 persons with equitable interests of varying sizes in the property.

However, the equitable interests simple or complex do not concern a purchaser. They will be overreached and there will be no need for a purchaser to chase to the ends of the earth to get the consent of each equitable co-owner.

Three points should be noted:

First, why was co-ownership of the legal estate not abolished altogether? This would have been a further simplification, but the answer is that it is often desirable to have more than one person sharing the responsibility and power of trusteeship.[16]

Secondly, the complexities of co-ownership have not disappeared. But now they only concern the trustees and the beneficiaries. They do not affect a purchaser or stand in the way of simple conveyancing and the free alienability of land.

Thirdly, the change has to some extent reduced the control of the beneficiaries over what happens to the land. They cannot be deprived of their interests; but they can find them changed from land into money. In the majority of cases of co-ownership this does not cause problems. The legal estate is held by the beneficiaries themselves. H and W hold as joint tenants upon trust for themselves as joint tenants (or tenants in common). The consent of each legal owner—and therefore each beneficiary—is necessary before any dealing with the land takes place in such cases.[17]

Principle 5. Creation of legal joint tenancy

Wherever the legal estate is conveyed to or held by more than one person they will hold as joint tenants in trust for whoever is entitled in equity. There cannot be more than four legal joint tenants at any one time.[18]

Explanation

Suppose that X is the beneficial freehold owner of Blackacre. He conveys it (*i.e.* the legal estate) to A, B, C and D by deed of conveyance. These four will as a result hold the legal estate as joint tenants. Normally, the conveyance will expressly declare them to be joint tenants; but in any case they cannot be anything else. And

---

[16] In general, there must be at least two if the land is to be dealt with; see above, p. 280.
[17] See further, above, p. 261; below, p. 330.
[18] L.P.A. 1925, s.34(1)(2); T.A. 1925, s.34(2); J.A. 1925, s.160(1) (personal representatives).

joint tenants they must remain. A legal joint tenancy cannot be turned into a tenancy in common. If it could then legal ownership could again be split up between innumerable persons and the whole aim of the legislation, to simplify conveyancing, could be defeated.

Further, not more than four persons at any one time can hold the legal estate. This again is to simplify conveyancing and again the rule cannot be avoided. Suppose that X has attempted to convey it to five partners, A, B, C, D and E as tenants in common. The legislation provides that in such a case the first four named who are of full age will take the legal estate as joint tenants.[19] Assuming that in this case they are, then E will not receive any *legal* interest in the land.

Of course there can be a change of joint tenants of the legal estate. If one of them dies survivorship applies. If, in the present example, A dies, this will leave B, C and D as legal joint tenants. If by subsequent deaths only B is left, he will then be the sole (several) legal owner. There will no longer be co-ownership at all in law. Equally, the number can be increased. If B is holding the legal estate it will probably be necessary to appoint a new trustee of the legal estate to act with him. If E is appointed then B will have to execute the necessary deed of conveyance transferring the legal estate from himself to himself and E jointly. Notice that the fifth partner does not automatically become one of the legal owners when the number is reduced below four by the death of A. If he is, as we have suggested, subsequently appointed, there will have to be a new conveyance to vest the legal estate in him.[20] This illustrates one of the basic principles of English land law: that in general a deed (or at least a document) is necessary to transfer the legal estate *inter vivos*. The transfer of legal ownership is a formal matter carried out by properly drawn documents. For this reason the ownership of the legal estate is normally a fairly simple matter to trace.

If the legal estate is held by joint tenants they must all join in any conveyance disposing of it. Any attempt by less than all the joint tenants to deal with the legal estate will be without any effect.

It needs to be emphasised again that the rules governing ownership of the legal estate do not affect the position in equity. To return to the above illustration—the original conveyance to A, B, C, D and E. Normally, the equitable interests will be declared

---

[19] L.P.A. 1925, s.34(2).
[20] Under T.A. 1925, s.40, the legal estate can be vested in the new trustee by a declaration contained in the deed of appointment, but it must be a deed.

in the conveyance. If they are not equity will normally follow the law and assume that the grantees A, B, C, D and E are intended to take in equity as well as law. The special statutory rule limiting the legal ownership to the first four will not affect the position in equity. The result then will be that A, B, C and D will hold the legal estate as joint tenants upon trust (a trust for sale) for the benefit of A, B, C, D and E, as tenants in common. Assuming that they are tenants in common in equity, then if A dies leaving all his property to S the result will be that B, C and D will now hold the legal estate upon trust for sale for the benefit of S, B, C, D and E as tenants in common in equal shares. And so on.

What difference does it make to S and E that they do not hold the legal estate? It does not affect their right to share possession with the others[21]; or their right to share any income or profits from the land and to share the proceeds of sale when it is sold. It does mean that, to a great extent, control of the land lies with B, C and D.

SECTION III.   CO-OWNERSHIP IN EQUITY

Principle 6.   The creation of the trust for sale

Beneficial co-ownership can only exist behind a trust for sale.[22] This trust for sale may be created expressly or implied by statute.[23]

Explanation

The reason why co-ownership can only exist behind a trust for sale—to simplify conveyancing—has already been considered. We are here concerned with the methods by which the trust for sale comes into existence.

---

[21] See below, p.326.

[22] An exception to this is that a beneficial joint tenancy can exist under the S.L.A. 1925.

[23] The general intention of the legislation is fairly clearly that a trust for sale should be implied in all cases where it is not created expressly. Unfortunately, the relevant sections do not clearly cover all possible cases of equitable co-ownership. For example, L.P.A. 1925, s.36(1), imposes a trust for sale in all cases of *beneficial* joint tenancy; s.34(2) of the Act covers the case where land is expressed to be conveyed to tenants in common, *e.g.* "To A, B and C as tenants in common." But, *e.g.* there is no provision clearly applicable where the legal estate is conveyed "To X and Y upon trust for A and B." It is generally assumed that the courts would interpret the legislation so as to impose the trust for sale in all cases; see *Re House* [1929] 2 Ch. 166; *Bull* v. *Bull* (below) and *Re Rayleigh Weir Stadium* [1954] 1 W.L.R. 786. An equitable joint tenancy can also exist under the S.L.A. 1925.

In the normal case the conveyance of the legal estate will expressly create the trust for sale and also declare the trusts on which the property is to be held—that is declare the beneficial interests. For example, take the common case of a conveyance to husband and wife. The conveyance will contain words something like the following[24]:

> NOW THIS DEED WITNESSETH as follows:
>   1. In pursuance of the said agreement and in consideration of the sum of £—— paid by the Purchasers to the Vendor (the receipt whereof the Vendor hereby acknowledges) the Vendor as beneficial owner HEREBY CONVEYS unto the Purchasers ALL——(parcels) TO HOLD unto the Purchasers in fee simple.
>   2. The Purchasers shall hold the property hereby conveyed upon trust to sell the same and to stand possessed of the net proceeds of any such sale upon trust for the Purchasers as joint tenants.

In the case of a conveyance to partners in a business the following wording might be found:

> . . . Upon trust to sell the same and to stand possessed of the net proceeds of any such sale upon the trusts and with and subject to the powers and provisions applicable thereto as part of their partnership property.

In some cases however there will be no express declaration of a trust for sale. For example, suppose that a conveyance provides:

> . . . the Vendor as beneficial owner HEREBY CONVEYS unto the Purchasers ALL that piece or parcel of land known as Blackacre TO HOLD unto the Purchasers in fee simple as beneficial joint tenants.

Here the conveyance has expressly declared that the purchasers are to be joint tenants in equity as well as at law (*i.e.* beneficial jóint tenants); but it has made no mention of a trust for sale.[25]

In other cases there may be no mention of the trust for sale or even of the co-ownership in equity. *Bull* v. *Bull*[26] was such a case. On the face of the conveyance there was no indication of any co-ownership in equity at all.

In such cases, that is wherever there is co-ownership in equity

---

[24] Hallett, *Conveyancing Precedents* (1965), p. 300.
[25] Here L.P.A. 1925, s.36(1) would impose the trust for sale.
[26] [1955] 1 Q.B. 234 (C.A.). Here Denning L.J. relied on the S.L.A. 1925, s.36(4), as imposing the trust for sale.

but no express trust for sale, a trust for sale is imposed by statute.[27] The legal estate will be held on the statutory trusts which are defined by section 35 of the Law of Property Act 1925 as meaning upon trust to sell and to hold the proceeds of sale and the rents and profits until sale in trust for the equitable co-owners according to their respective interests. Thus, in *Bull* v. *Bull*[28] the son held upon trust for sale for the benefit of himself and his mother.

Principle 7. Creation of joint tenancy and tenancy in common in equity

1. Where co-ownership is held to exist in equity, the intention of the parties will normally determine whether they are joint tenants or tenants in common; and if they are tenants in common, the size of their respective shares.

2. Where there is an express declaration of intention in favour of either joint tenancy or tenancy in common, the express declaration will normally prevail. Words of severance are words which show an express intention to create a tenancy in common.

3. In the absence of an effective expression of intention the courts apply certain presumptions.

4. Normally they will presume an intention to create a joint tenancy, but:

5. By way of exception, in three cases they will presume a tenancy in common:
   (a) where the purchasers have contributed the purchase money in unequal shares;
   (b) where mortgagees have together lent money on mortgage;
   (c) where partners have together purchased property as part of their partnership assets.

6. Where one of the unities of time, title or interest is absent, there can only be a tenancy in common.

Explanation

Express declaration. The question of how the courts decide who owns the property in equity has already been considered.[29] Wherever the conclusion is that two or more persons share the interest in equity, this will be a case of equitable co-ownership. In such a case, it may be necessary to go further and decide whether

---

[27] But see n. 23, above.
[28] n. 26, above.
[29] Above, p. 174 *et seq.*

the co-owners are joint tenants or tenants in common and, if they are tenants in common, to decide whether they hold in equal or some other shares.

If there is an effective[30] declaration of intention this will normally decide the issue.[31] As in the precedents quoted above,[32] an ordinary conveyance will usually contain a clear declaration as to the beneficial interests and this will prevail. In *Bedson* v. *Bedson* [33] the matrimonial home had been conveyed into the joint names of the husband and wife on an express trust for sale and the conveyance declared that they were to hold the proceeds of sale in trust for themselves as beneficial joint tenants. In fact, the purchase money had been provided entirely by the husband and he had been advised to put the house in their joint names in order to lessen possible estate duty. The house consisted of a residence over a shop which the husband ran. The wife deserted the husband and in the present case she was seeking a declaration that she was entitled to a half share in the proceeds of sale and an order for sale under section 30 of the Law of Property Act 1925. The court held that in accordance with the express declaration, she was entitled to a half share in the proceeds but refused to order a sale under section 30.[34]

Occasionally, the express declaration may be ambiguous and the courts have to decide what the words used intended. In *Joyce* v. *Barker (Bros.)*[35] the court had to decide what was intended by a conveyance to J and his wife "in fee simple as beneficial joint tenants in common in equal shares." Or the express declaration may fail, like any declaration of trust, for some reason like non-compliance with the statutory formalities,[36] fraud or mistake. In *Re Colebrook's Conveyances*[37] the court ordered rectification of an express declaration of a joint tenancy. In *Burgess* v. *Rawnsley*[38] Lord Denning (dissenting on this point) held that the express declaration of a joint tenancy failed (the purposes for which it had

---

[30] *i.e.* effective according to the rules for creating trusts; see above, p. 174 *et seq.*
[31] See *Pettitt* v. *Pettitt* [1970] A.C. 777, at p. 813, per Lord Upjohn; and see *Leake (formerly Bruzzi)* v. *Bruzzi* [1974] 2 All E.R. 1196 (C.A.).
[32] P. 320.
[33] [1965] 2 Q.B. 666 (C.A.); contrast *Gross* v. *French* (1976) 238 E.G. 39 (C.A.).
[34] See below, p. 330, for s.30.
[35] *The Times*, February 26, 1980.
[36] L.P.A. 1925, s.53.
[37] [1972] 1 W.L.R. 1397 (Graham J.).
[38] [1975] 3 All E.R. 142; and see *Re Densham* [1975] 3 All E.R. 726 (Goff J.); above p. 184.

been created having failed) leaving a resulting trust for the contributors as tenants in common.

Words of severance. Words of severance are any words which show an intention to create a tenancy in common and not a joint tenancy. The term comes from the common law which favoured the unity of joint tenancy and always presumed that a joint tenancy was intended unless there were express words which showed an intention by the parties to sever that unity, *i.e.* to create the separate shares of a tenancy in common.

The normal conveyancing practice today, where two or more purchasers have agreed to hold the property as tenants in common, is for the conveyance to contain a declaration that they are to hold upon trust (trust for sale) for the benefit of themselves "as tenants in common in equal shares" or whatever shares have been agreed.

But the words "tenants in common" do not have to be used. Any words which show this intention to create a tenancy in common are effective as words of severance. If T makes a will leaving Blackacre to A and B "share and share alike," A and B will take as equitable tenants in common; or "To A and B equally"; "To be divided between A, B and C"; and so on.

The presumptions. In the majority of cases there will be an express declaration creating either a joint tenancy or a tenancy in common. In such cases the express words normally prevail and there is no room for the presumptions. These presumptions become relevant where there is no express declaration. Suppose that John dies having made a will leaving his property Blackacre "to my daughters Jill and Janet." He has not stipulated whether they are to take as joint tenants or tenants in common. And it is too late to ask him what he intended. If there is no other admissible evidence[39] of what he intended the courts will have to get an answer by applying the relevant presumption.

The courts have developed these various presumptions as the solution to a problem which has also faced them in other fields. It is a problem which arises wherever the courts have a duty to give effect to the intentions of the parties but cannot ascertain their actual intentions from their words or conduct. In dealing with this problem in the case of co-ownership the courts have developed the presumptions set out in the Principle above. In contract law the same sort of problem has produced, *inter alia*, the doctrine of *The*

---

[39] See Theobald, *Wills* (13th ed.), p. 157 *et seq.*

Moorcock[40] and the doctrine of frustration[41]; in land law, the implied easement[42]; and so on.

The presumption is a sort of judicial guess at what most people would decide to do in a particular situation; it is then assumed that the parties in question would have made the same decision had they considered the matter.[43]

The use of presumptions in such cases can be criticised. Take the case of John above. Here the general presumption in favour of a joint tenancy is likely to be applicable. But the courts have not derived this presumption from any expert statistical evidence as to whether testators prefer joint tenancy or tenancy in common when leaving their property. Even if there were evidence that most testators favoured joint tenancy this does not mean that John did or would have done so had he considered the matter at all. Indeed this particular presumption in favour of joint tenancy was developed by the old common law courts for the convenience of feudal lords and conveyancers rather than as an attempt to give effect to the intentions of the parties concerned.

Further, the common attitudes of people change and it may be that the presumptions that were once considered valid no longer reflect present day attitudes. In this context, it is fair to say that the courts are not incapable of replacing old presumptions by new ones more nearly reflecting contemporary attitudes. For example, in *Pettitt* v. *Pettitt*,[44] Lord Diplock said: "It would in my view be an abuse of the legal technique for ascertaining or implying intention to apply to transactions between the post-war generations of married couples presumptions . . . based on inferences of fact which an earlier generation of judges drew as the most likely intentions of earlier generations of spouses belonging to the propertied classes of a different social era. . . . The old presumptions of advancement and resulting trust are inappropriate to these kinds of transaction (*i.e.* where a matrimonial home is acquired on mortgage as a result of concerted action between husband and wife) and the fact that the legal estate is conveyed to the wife or to the husband or to both jointly though it may be significant in indicating their actual common intention is not necessarily decisive

---

[40] (1889) 14 P.D. 64.

[41] See Cheshire and Fifoot, *Law of Contract* (10th ed.), p. 512 *et seq.*

[42] See below, p. 371 *et seq.*

[43] In *Pettitt* v. *Pettitt* (below, n. 44), Lord Diplock said (p. 825): "In applying the general technique (for imputing intention to the parties) the court is directing its attention to what would have been the common intention of the spouses as fair and reasonable husband and wife at the time of the relevant transaction."

[44] [1970] A.C. 777 at p. 824; above, pp. 179, 185.

since it is often influenced by the requirements of the building society which provides the mortgage."

At times, in some situations, the courts have abandoned the attempt to fathom the unexpressed and probably non-existent intentions of the parties; instead they have imposed what they considered to be a just and fair solution. For example, when deciding on the equitable ownership of property as between two or more claimants the courts have sometimes arrived at a solution by applying the principle that equality is equity.[45]

To summarise: where the courts are faced with this problem of deciding something which the parties could have, but have not decided for themselves, they can solve it by applying presumptions as to the parties' intentions; or instead they can simply impose their own just and fair solution. Both approaches have been adopted at different times. In most cases at least both approaches are likely to lead to the same result.[46]

In the case of co-ownership the courts have developed certain more or less fixed presumptions. These will be considered next.

Particular presumptions used in the case of co-ownership. The presumption normally applied in the absence of any express declaration or other admissible evidence of intention is the presumption in favour of joint tenancy. This presumption was developed by the old common law courts and followed by equity. But the presumption is unfair in the sense that it benefits the tenant who happens to live longest; and in three cases equity has applied the opposite presumption in favour of a tenancy in common. These cases are listed above.

Partnership. Most people will probably agree that a tenancy in common is more likely to represent the wishes of partners. A partnership is invariably a business relationship. If you ask a partner what he expects to happen to his share in the land owned by the business when he dies, he is more likely to say that he expects it to go to his family or friends—not that he expects it to go to his partners. A tenancy in common implements this probable wish. Consequently, in the absence of express provision to the contrary, equity presumes a tenancy in common in such a case.

---

[45] See above, p. 184.
[46] See *Liverpool City Council* v. *Irwin* [1975] 3 All E.R. 658 (C.A.) and [1977] A.C. 239 (H.L.); particularly the speech of Lord Wilberforce in the House of Lords analysing the nature of implied terms and criticising the reasonable solution approach of Lord Denning in the Court of Appeal.

Mortgages.   The same applies to co-mortgagees.

Purchase money in unequal shares.[47]   The other case where a tenancy in common is presumed is perhaps more debatable. This is the case of co-purchasers of land. If the contributions are equal a joint tenancy is presumed; but if unequal, a tenancy in common with shares in proportion to the amounts contributed. Most cases of co-purchase today must be husband and wife where they both contribute to the purchase of the matrimonial home. In the vast majority of these cases the conveyance will declare them to be equitable joint tenants whether their contributions are equal or not. Further, one imagines that in most cases of husband and wife, each will make a will leaving his property to the other on death or allow it to pass in the same way on intestacy. It is arguable that in the case of a domestic arrangement such as husband and wife the presumption should be in favour of a joint tenancy regardless of the amount of each contribution. Indeed, at least in some cases, the courts have been prepared to disregard the difference in the amounts of the respective contributions and to hold the parties to be entitled in equal shares[48]; although they have not made it clear in these cases whether they regarded them as joint tenants or tenants in common in equal shares. However, (as already indicated) in general, the courts have maintained the ordinary rules when dealing with spouses and cohabitees. Moreover, where a joint tenancy does exist, it may be that the courts are developing an increasing readiness to find that severance has taken place.[49]

Principle 7a.   The nature of the equitable interests

Under the doctrine of conversion, the interests of the beneficiaries will be classified as interests in personalty. But, nevertheless, the courts will recognise them as having interests in the land itself and as having a limited right of occupation prior to sale.

Explanation

As already explained,[50] under the 1925 legislation, beneficial co-ownership can today generally only exist behind a trust for sale.

The trust for sale was developed in the nineteenth century as a convenient   conveyancing   device   for   settling   investment

---

[47] See further, above, p. 181.
[48] *e.g. Chapman* v. *Chapman* [1969] 3 All E.R. 476 (C.A.).
[49] See below, p. 337 *et seq.*
[50] See above, p. 319.

properties.[51] The beneficiaries were concerned only to receive their share of the income until sale and of the proceeds of sale. The doctrine of conversion accurately reflected this, deeming them to have interests in the proceeds of sale (personalty) from the start, and not in the land itself. The trust for sale was convenient because the purchaser did not have to concern himself with the complex equitable interests; the land was marketable and conveyancing (in an age of complex family settlements) was relatively simple.

For this reason, the 1925 legislation, dedicated to the free alienability of land, extended the use of the trust for sale, in particular to most cases of co-ownership. However, increasingly today, the traditional principles relating to the trust for sale do not reflect the real purpose for which the land has been bought. To take the case of the matrimonial home conveyed in law to the husband but held by him on trust (for sale) for himself and his wife as equitable joint tenants or tenants in common. On the one hand, traditional principle says that he, as trustee, has managerial control (subject to appointing a second trustee to act with him where capital money arises), including the right to mortgage, sell, etc.; she has an interest only in the proceeds of sale, no control over sale, no interest in the land[52] and so no enforceable right to occupy.

On the other hand, the reality is likely to be that the property has been bought to provide a home for both of them and any children, that the purpose is occupation, not income, and that sale is only contemplated to purchase a new home or, possibly, if the relationship breaks up.

This dichotomy has forced the courts to make some attempt to adapt traditional principles to meet their perception of modern reality. In this area it is particularly important to remember that equity is not "past the age of child bearing"[53] but that, at the same time, one decision does not necessarily indicate a healthy child. In other words, the law in this area is somewhat uncertain.

The following principles can, perhaps, be derived from the authorities:

1. The beneficiary *does* have an interest in the land[54] (although it is classified as personalty). There are some cases which suggest the

---

[51] See, further, above p. 256.

[52] Her position will be even weaker if she does not even have an equitable interest.

[53] See (1952) 68 L.Q.R. 237 (H.W.R. Wade); and see H. Forrest, Trusts for Sale and Co-ownership—A Case for Reform, [1978] Conv. 194.

[54] See further, above p. 280. See also A.E. Boyle, Trusts for Sale and the Doctrine of Conversion, [1981] Conv. 108.

contrary. One of the latest is *Cedar Holdings Ltd.* v. *Green*.[55]
Here, husband and wife held the matrimonial home as beneficial
joint tenants. The husband and another woman, purporting to be
his wife, executed a legal charge of the legal freehold to a bank as
security. This was clearly void as to the legal estate. The bank
claimed, *inter alia*, that it was effective under the Law of Property
Act 1925, s.63, to charge his equitable interest as being "all the
estate, right, title, interest, and claim and demand which the
conveying parties respectively have in, to, or on, the property
conveyed." The Court of Appeal held that his interest was in the
proceeds of sale and so did not pass under the section.

However, in *Williams & Glyn's Bank Ltd.* v. *Boland*[56] the
House of Lords considered that *Cedar Holdings* had been wrongly
decided.

In *Boland's* case the legal estate was held by the husband in trust
for himself and (by her contribution to the purchase price) his
wife. He charged it to the bank and the issue was whether the wife
had an overriding interest as the right of a person in actual
occupation.[57] It was held that she did. Similarly, in the case of
unregistered land it is beyond doubt that the interest of the
beneficiary is capable of binding a purchaser if the sale is in breach
of trust. The necessary implication of these cases is that, until an
effective overreaching conveyance, the beneficiary has an interest
in the land.

It seems to be clear now that the beneficiary has an interest in
the land for the purpose of the Law of Property Act 1925, s.40.[58]
In *Burgess* v. *Rawnsley*[59] it was assumed that the agreement by one
joint tenant to sell his interest to the other, was unenforceable as
such for lack of written evidence. It is also noteworthy that in this
case the majority of the court thought that if there had been a

---

[55] [1979] 3 All E.R. 117 (C.A.). See also *Irani Finance Ltd.* v. *Singh* [1971] Ch. 59;
equitable interest of beneficial joint tenant held not to be "land or interest in
land" so as to be subject to a charging order under Administration of Justice Act
1956, s.35(1); compare *National Westminster Bank Ltd.* v. *Stockman* [1981] 1
W.L.R. 67 (Russell J.) decided under Charging Orders Act 1979, s.2, which
replaces s.35 and enables any beneficial interest held by debtors under a trust to
be charged. See also *National Westminster Bank Ltd.* v. *Allen* [1971] 2 Q.B. 718
(Waller J.) distinguishing *Singh*. See also *Re No. 39 Carr Lane, Acomb* [1953] 1
All E.R. 699 and *Elias* v. *Mitchell* [1972] Ch. 652.
[56] [1980] 2 All E.R. 408 (H.L.).
[57] Which would bind the bank without protection on the register; see below,
p. 537. See also *Hodgson* v. *Marks* [1971] Ch. 892.
[58] See below, p. 558.
[59] [1975] 3 All E.R. 142 (C.A.); see below, p. 336; and see *Cooper* v. *Critchley*
[1955] Ch. 341.

common intention by both joint tenants to purchase the house as a matrimonial home, the failure of that purpose would have given rise to a resulting trust for them as tenants in common with shares in proportion to their contributions.[60] In other words, the court was prepared to look behind the formal declaration, in the conveyance, of a joint tenancy in the income and proceeds of sale, and to recognise their occupational purpose as an element in their beneficial interest.[61]

2. Until sale the equitable beneficiary has a limited right to possession (*i.e.* occupation) of the land.[62] This right to possession is subject to the discretion of the court. In exercising its discretion, the court will apply principles similar to those applied in deciding whether to order sale.

It has been argued that as a result of the imposition of a trust for sale and the doctrine of conversion, the beneficiaries have no right to possession. The authorities seem clearly to show otherwise.[63] Section 30 of the Law of Property Act 1925, provides that "If the trustees for sale refuse to sell or to exercise any of the powers conferred by the last two sections . . . the court can make such order as it thinks fit." It has been decided that, in dealing with an application for a sale order, the court can deal with any incidental issue as to possession. Moreover, it is arguable that the right of the trustees to delegate to the beneficiary under the Law of Property Act, s.29, includes the power to allow the beneficiary into actual occupation. On this basis, an application can be made by a beneficiary under section 30, asking for possession, without any question of sale being in issue.

A claim by a beneficiary to possession frequently does arise in connection with a section 30 application for sale. In *Re McCarthy*[64] the matrimonial home was held by the husband and wife as beneficial joint tenants. The husband went bankrupt and the trustee in bankruptcy was applying for an order for possession and

---

[60] Only the man envisaged marriage. Lord Denning decided that there *was* a resulting trust as both parties' purposes failed. It is arguable that it was because there *was no* initial common purpose that the express trust failed leaving a resulting trust for them as tenants in common from the start.

[61] Under the L.P.A. 1925, s.30, the court looks at the occupational purpose of acquisition as one factor in deciding how to exercise its discretion, (see below, p. 330); but here it was looking at it as an element in defining the beneficial interest.

[62] As to liability of one co-owner to pay occupation rent to another, see *Dennis* v. *McDonald* [1981] 1 W.L.R. 810 (Purchas J.); on appeal, [1982] 1 All E.R. 590.

[63] Section 9 of the Matrimonial Homes Act 1967 was added by the Matrimonial Proceedings and Property Act 1970, s.38 because of doubts on the point.

[64] [1975] 2 All E.R. 857 (C.A.); and see *Re Turner* [1975] 1 All E.R. 5 (Goff J.).

sale. The court held that, although there was jurisdiction under section 30 to order possession, it should only be granted against a beneficiary when the facts necessitated it. On the facts before them (the husband and wife both being willing to co-operate in selling and there being a disabled child) the court considered it sufficient to make an order that they concur in the sale of the house. In *Re Densham*,[65] another bankruptcy case, an order for possession postponed for six months, was made.[66]

In deciding a claim to possession, the court will, as in the case of sale, look at the particular purpose for which the property was acquired (*i.e.* the trust created); whether that purpose can still be achieved and any other factors which exist to effect the equities between the respective claimants. In *Bull* v. *Bull*[67] the purpose was clearly to provide a home. In contrast, in *Barclay* v. *Barclay*,[68] where the trustees were granted possession against one of the beneficiaries, it can be said that the property had been left by the testator with a view to actual sale and division of the proceeds.

3. If the property is in fact conveyed by a valid overreaching conveyance,[69] any right of occupation will cease.

4. There are certain statutory rights of occupation independent of ownership of a legal or equitable interest in the land. These are dealt with below.[70]

Principle 7b. Sale of the property

Where a necessary consent to sale cannot be obtained, any person interested can apply to court under the Law of Property Act 1925, s.30, or (in the case of husband and wife) the Married Women's Property Act 1882, s.17.

On an application the court has a discretion to make "such order as it thinks fit."

---

[65] [1975] 3 All E.R. 726 (Goff J.).
[66] Note view of Purchas J. in *Dennis* v. *McDonald* [1981] 1 W.L.R. 810, that the section does not entitle court to make any other order where no order for sale is made.
[67] [1955] 1 Q.B. 234. In this case Lord Denning derived authority for the beneficiary's right to possession from L.P.A. 1925, ss.14 and 35, and from the principle that equity follows the law; see above, p. 311.
[68] [1970] 2 Q.B. 677 (C.A.).
[69] Or where the purchaser's title is otherwise protected.
[70] See below, p. 344.

Explanation

Need for consent. The general machinery governing land subject to a trust for sale has already been explained.[71] It is the trustees of the legal estate who have the power of sale and who must all join in any conveyance if it is to be valid. In addition, the trust may stipulate one or more additional, specified consents to sale.[72] Where any necessary consent is refused an application can be made to the court by "any person interested."

In general, the consent of beneficiaries to a sale is not necessary (unless of course the beneficiary happens to be a trustee or his consent is stipulated in the trust instrument). A sale without their consent will be valid provided it complies with the overreaching machinery of the Law of Property Act 1925.[73] Nevertheless, it is submitted that if a beneficiary applied in time the court would, in a proper case,[74] grant an injunction against sale; and a sale even though valid in favour of a purchaser, might (as between trustee and beneficiary) constitute breach of trust. Further, if the beneficiary is in occupation, the trustees will need to get possession if they are to sell with vacant possession. The right to occupation has already been considered.[75]

Discretion under s.30 and s.17. The court has a discretion under these sections to make "such order as it thinks fit." Each case will be considered on its facts and the courts will not allow this sort of discretion to become fettered by precedent.[76] This fact must be kept in mind when reading the reports of these and any decisions where the courts are exercising a statutory discretion. Nevertheless, in applying sections 30 and 17, two limiting factors do exist.

First, the sections do not entitle the courts to redistribute the

---

[71] Above, p. 256.

[72] See above, p. 261.

[73] And the Land Registration Act 1925, in the case of registered land; see, *e.g. Peffer* v. *Rigg* [1978] 3 All E.R. 745 (Graham J.); *Williams & Glyn's Bank Ltd.* v. *Boland* [1980] 2 All E.R. 408 (H.L.); and note L.R.A. 1925, ss.58, 74.

[74] *i.e.* applying the principles to be applied under s.30.

[75] Above, p. 329. In *Burke* v. *Burke* [1974] 2 All E.R. 944 (C.A.) the legal ownership was vested in the husband's sole name whilst the wife and children remained in occupation. The court granted the husband's application for possession and sale. Compare *Re Bailey* [1977] 1 W.L.R. 278; contrast *Williams (J.W.)* v. *Williams (M.A.)* [1976] Ch. 278 (C.A.). In the last two cases the wife was joint owner of the legal estate as well as having an equitable interest.

[76] See, *e.g. Jones* v. *Challenger* [1961] 1 Q.B. 176, at p. 000, per Donovan J.; and *Chamberlain* v. *Chamberlain* [1974] 1 All E.R. 33 at p. 38, per Scarman L.J.

existing beneficial interests between the parties.[77] They can ascertain what share in the land each party is entitled to and then order (or refuse to order) the conversion of that share into money by ordering sale. In other words, the discretion lies in deciding whether to order sale; not in deciding what to do with the proceeds of sale. In contrast, under its divorce jurisdiction,[78] the Family Division has a very wide jurisdiction to transfer property rights between spouses. It is for this reason that the courts have frequently stated that where divorce is involved, disputes relating to matrimonial property should be dealt with in the Family Division under the divorce legislation. In *Williams (J.W.)* v. *Williams (M.A.)*[79] the parties divorced in 1970. The wife remained in occupation of the matrimonial home with the four children. In 1973, the husband applied for sale under section 30 which was granted by Foster J. On appeal, the Court of Appeal ordered the matter to be transferred to the Family Division on the wife undertaking to make an application there under the Matrimonial Causes Act 1973, s.24.[80]

Secondly, in practice, certain broad principles to be applied when deciding whether or not to order sale, do emerge. These principles will now be considered.

The basic principle can perhaps be stated as follows: The courts will consider all relevant factors, but so long as the purpose for which the property was acquired, can still be achieved, the court will not order sale unless there is some overriding equitable reason for doing so. Conversely, if that purpose is at an end, the court *will* order sale in the absence of an overriding equitable reason requiring retention.

In *Re Buchanan-Wollaston's Conveyance*[81] the court refused to order a sale where land had been purchased by four persons in order to preserve the amenities and they had covenanted between

---

[77] On s.17, see *Pettitt* v. *Pettitt* [1970] A.C. 777 (H.L.); and *Gissing* v. *Gissing* [1971] A.C. 886 (H.L.).

[78] See Matrimonial Causes Act 1973, ss.23–25.

[79] [1976] Ch. 276 (C.A.).

[80] Compare *Jackson* v. *Jackson* [1971] 3 All E.R. 774, a case between husband and wife in which there was no prospect of divorce proceedings. See also *Griffiths* v. *Griffiths* [1974] 1 All E.R. 932 (C.A.) and *Leake (formerly Bruzzi)* v. *Bruzzi* [1974] 2 All E.R. 1196 in which Ormrod L.J. expressed the hope that it would be the last case in which parties to matrimonial proceedings would be content to leave their interests to be determined without invoking the Matrimonial Causes Act 1973. Contrast *Re Holliday* [1980] 3 All E.R. 385 (C.A.) in which the dispute was between the wife and the husband's trustee in bankruptcy. See J.G. Miller, Sale of the Matrimonial Home, [1978] Conv. 301.

[81] [1939] Ch. 783.

themselves not to sell. In *Bedson* v. *Bedson*[82] the property had been bought partly as a home but also partly as premises for the business which the husband was still running. The court refused to order sale on the application of the wife who had deserted. In *Re Evers Trust*,[83] a case of cohabitees, P and D were living together. D already had two children by her previous marriage. She and P had another one. They subsequently purchased a home which was conveyed to them jointly. When the relationship broke up and D remained in the house with the three children, P's application for sale under section 30 was refused by the Court of Appeal.

As these cases illustrate, the courts have moved away from the old, narrow view that in the absence of bad faith the trust for sale must prevail.[84] But it does leave the court with the task of identifying the underlying purpose. In matrimonial cases, the more limited view is that the purpose is to provide a joint home for the man and woman, and that when this relationship breaks down, the purpose is at an end. On this view, the interests of the children are not (at least directly) relevant.[85] The wider view, which is perhaps likely to prevail, is that the purpose is to provide a family home and that even after break up, the needs of the respective parties and any children to have a home should be taken into account.[86]

Re Holliday[87] suggests, perhaps, a judicial view somewhere between the above two. Here the dispute was between the husband's trustee in bankruptcy and the wife who remained in the home with the three children. It was held that as the children were not beneficiaries under the trust, they were not entitled to consideration as needing a home. Nevertheless, in balancing the respective claims of the creditors and the wife, the fact that she was burdened with the obligation of providing the children with a home (on social security) was a relevant factor; and the court

---

[82] [1965] 2 Q.B. 666 (C.A.); see above, p. 000.
[83] [1980] 3 All E.R. 399 (C.A.). Note that in this case the husband had no particular need to realise his investment. And see *Dennis* v. *McDonald* [1981] 2 All E.R. 632 (Purchas J.).
[84] See, *e.g. Re Mayo* [1943] 1 Ch. 303 (Simmonds J.).
[85] See *Jones* v. *Challenger* [1961] 1 Q.B. 176 (C.A.), criticised by Lord Denning in *Williams (J.W.)* v. *Williams (M.A.)* [1976] Ch. 278 (C.A.). And see *Burke* v. *Burke* [1974] 2 All E.R. 944 (C.A.), considered in *Re Bailey* [1977] 1 W.L.R. 278.
[86] See *Williams (J.W.)* v. *Williams (M.A.)* [1976] Ch. 278 (C.A.), particularly the judgment of Lord Denning; also *Re Evers* [1980] 3 All E.R. 399 (C.A.); and *Dennis* v. *McDonald* [1981] 1 W.L.R. 810 (Purchas J.).
[87] [1980] 3 All E.R. 385 (C.A.). Distinguished in *Re Lowrie (a bankrupt)* [1981] 3 All E.R. 353.

ordered that the house should not be sold without the wife's consent until the two eldest children reached 17 years of age.

Where a third party has a legitimate interest in the property, this will be a weighty factor in favour of sale; particularly where one of the beneficiaries is bankrupt and the property is his only substantial asset.[88]

SECTION IV.   DETERMINATION OF CO-OWNERSHIP

Principle 8.   Severance[89]

A legal joint tenancy cannot be severed.[90]

An equitable joint tenant can sever his interest turning it into an equitable tenancy in common. He can only do it *inter vivos* and not by will.

There are five recognised methods of severance:
  (a) By acquisition of another interest in the land;
  (b) by alienation;
  (c) by an enforceable contract to do (a) or (b);
  (d) by mutual agreement between all the joint tenants;
  (e) by a notice in writing served on the other joint tenants; this method is only available to a beneficial joint tenant.[91]

Explanation

Severance is the method by which a joint tenancy is turned into a tenancy in common. Of course a legal joint tenancy cannot be severed since a legal tenancy in common cannot now exist.[92]

A joint tenant will sever his interest, for example, where he does not wish it to pass to the other joint tenants by survivorship on his death. It equally means that he himself will not benefit if the other joint tenants happen to die first. In *Re Draper's Conveyance*[93] the divorced wife severed and then shortly afterwards the husband died. If she had not severed she would have become entitled to the whole by survivorship. As it was, she had her half-share but his passed elsewhere.

Once severance has taken place the separate share can be left by

---

[88] See *Re Bailey* [1977] 1 W.L.R. 278; *Re Turner* [1975] 1 All E.R. 5 (Goff J.). Contrast *Re Holliday* [1980] 3 All E.R. 385. And see *Re Lowrie (a bankrupt)* [1981] 3 All E.R. 353.
[89] See J.F. Garner, "Severence of a Joint Tenancy," (1976) 40 Conv. (N.S.) 77.
[90] L.P.A. 1925, s.36(2).
[91] *Ibid.*
[92] Note *Re McCarthy* [1975] 2 All E.R. 857 (Goff J.)—legal interest of bankrupt joint tenant cannot automatically pass to his trustee in bankruptcy.
[93] [1969] 1 Ch. 486 (Plowman J.).

will or pass on intestacy. But a joint tenancy cannot be severed to take effect on death; if it is going to be done it must be done *inter vivos*. And once it has been done it is irrevocable.[94] A tenant in common cannot unilaterally turn his interest back into a joint tenancy.

Methods of severance. Severance can be effected by destroying either the unity of title or the unity of interest both of which are essential to a joint tenancy. Unity of possession can be destroyed but this is partition and puts an end to the co-ownership altogether. The other unity, unity of time, cannot be destroyed. If the interests were created at the same time, that is a historical fact which cannot be changed.

Unity of title is destroyed if a joint tenant alienates his interest. The title of the other joint tenants derives from the original conveyance to all of them; the title of the grantee is derived from the conveyance to him by the severing joint tenant.

If there are more than two joint tenants, severance does not affect the interests of the others *inter se*. Suppose that A, B and C are equitable joint tenants. If A severs by conveying his interest to P, the result will be that P will become a tenant in common of a one-third share. B and C will remain joint tenants of a two-thirds share. If B were then to die, P would remain a tenant in common of a one-third share; C would become entitled by survivorship to a two-thirds share which, as against P, he would hold as tenant in common.

If the joint tenant wishes to keep the severed interest for himself he severs by alienating to a trustee to hold in trust for him. The trustee can then transfer the newly created tenancy in common back to him.

Unity of interest is destroyed if a joint tenant acquires another interest in the land. Suppose that A and B are joint tenants for life of Blackacre with remainder in fee simple to X; if A acquires, for example by purchase, X's remainder then the unity of interest is destroyed. A's life interest merges with the fee simple; B retains his life interest. During the life of B, A and B will be tenants in common in equal shares. On the death of B, A or his successor in title will be absolutely entitled in fee simple in possession.

But in the case of either acquisition or alienation, the act must be irrevocable. In *Re Wilkes*[95] a fund was held in trust for three

---

[94] Except of course by agreement between all the parties.
[95] [1891] 3 Ch. 59. But see doubts cast on this case in *Burgess* v. *Rawnsley* below, n.98.
Note that *Re Wilkes* was decided before the enactment of L.P.A. 1925, s.36(2).

infants as joint tenants. One of them, on reaching his majority, made an application in court to have his share paid out to him. He gave evidence, the hearing was adjourned and he then died. It was held that there had been no severance. The point was that, up to the time that the court made an order, he could have withdrawn his application. If an order had been made the act would have been irrevocable and severance effected.

A specifically enforceable contract either to alienate or to acquire another interest will be effective to sever.[96]

In the light of recent authorities, it is not clear what additional methods of severance are available, today, to a joint tenant.[97] The following principles can, perhaps, be supported from the authorities.

1. A mutual agreement between all joint tenants to sever will be effective. Such an agreement may be specifically to sever (*e.g.* we hereby agree henceforth to hold as tenants in common); or it may be inferred from an agreement to deal with the property in a way that is inconsistent with a joint tenancy; or (even without any finalised agreement) the conduct of the parties may show a common intention to sever.

The commonest situation in which the issue arises today is in relation to a jointly owned home. In *Burgess* v. *Rawnsley*[98] a chance encounter at a bible meeting in Trafalgar Square led to the joint purchase of a house. He had marriage in mind; she had separate flats in mind. Eventually, so it was held on the evidence, she orally agreed to sell her share in the house to him; nothing was done to give effect to the agreement and he died. The Court of Appeal held that the mutual agreement (even though not itself enforceable under the Law of Property Act 1925, s.40),[99] was sufficient to sever the equitable joint tenancy. Clearly, a mutual agreement under which one joint tenant is going to transfer his interest to the other, is inconsistent with an intention to preserve the joint tenancy. Section 40 was not relevant because the court was giving effect not to the contract, but to the common intention

---

[96] See Megarry and Wade, *The Law of Real Property*, (4th ed.), at p. 406; and *Burgess* v. *Rawnsley* [1975] 3 All E.R. 142 at p. 151.

[97] See in particular, *Hawksley* v. *May* [1956] 1 Q.B. 304; *Re Draper's Conveyance* [1969] 1 Ch. 486; and *Burgess* v. *Rawnsley* [1975] 3 All E.R. 142 (C.A.) Contrast *Re Wilkes* [1891] 3 Ch. 59; and *Nielson-Jones* v. *Fedden* [1974] 3 All E.R. 38 (Walton J.).

[98] [1975] 3 All E.R. 142 (C.A.).

[99] Implying that an interest under a trust for sale is an interest in land; see above, p. 328.

to sever. It is always (and only) this common intention to sever, express or implied, by words or conduct, that is crucial and must be found to have existed if there is to be a severance.[1]

The mere fact that the beneficial joint tenants decide to sell the property does not *necessarily* involve an intention to sever. In the common case, where a married couple sell the matrimonial home with a view to purchasing another, the common intention will probably be to retain the joint tenancy throughout, transferring it from one house into money and then into another house. The first part of the judgment in *Nielson-Jones* v. *Fedden*[2] can perhaps be justified on this basis.[3] The marriage had broken down and there was no intention of buying another joint home; but there was an agreement that the proceeds of sale should be used to provide a home for the husband. A contract to sell was made, £200 paid out to each of them out of the purchaser's deposit, and then the husband died. It was held that there had not been a severance. However, it is probably true today that the policy of the law leans in favour of severance and that, in future, where steps have been taken to sell the matrimonial home on breakdown of a relationship, the courts will be inclined to find a common intention to sever even before actual sale has taken place.

2. Before 1926, a *unilateral* declaration of intention to sever, whether or not in writing, and whether or not communicated to the other joint tenants, was not itself sufficient. The Law of Property Act 1925, s.36 (2)[4] has introduced a new method of severance available to beneficial joint tenants—that is, a notice in writing served on the other joint tenants.[5] Such a notice does not have to be in any particular form so long a it shows what amounts to an intention to sever. In *Re Draper's Conveyance*[6] an application to court by the wife under section 17 of the Married Women's Property Act 1882 for an order for sale and distribution of the proceeds between herself and the husband, was held to have

---

[1] Consider the old case of *Partriche* v. *Powlett* (1740) 2 Atk. 54 in which one of two joint tenants made a marriage settlement dealing with her property. It was held that this did not contain an enforceable alienation of her share and, further, since the other joint tenant was not a party to the settlement, there was no severance by mutual agreement
[2] [1974] 3 All E.R. 38 (Walton J.).
[3] Though hardly the decision that there had been no severance under L.P.A. 1925, s.36(2).
[4] There is doubt as to the correct interpretation of this proviso to s.36(2). See *Re Draper's Conveyance* [1969] 1 Ch. 486 and *Burgess* v. *Rawnsley* [1975] 3 All E.R. 142.
[5] See, *e.g. Re 88 Berkeley Road* [1971] 1 All E.R. 254.
[6] Above.

severed the joint tenancy under section 36 (2).[7] The decision in *Nielson-Jones* v. *Fedden*[8] that the notice must in some way be irrevocable, is, it would seem, incorrect.

3. Apart from section 36 (2), it still cannot be said that a unilateral declaration will sever.[9] But it should be remembered that the trend seems to be in favour of recognising severance, that the courts are increasingly likely to find a common intention to sever, and that a general right to sever by unilateral declaration might emerge.

It is to be emphasised that severance as such has no effect on the legal ownership. If A and B are beneficial joint tenants and B severs his interest transferring it to P, then A and B will remain joint tenants of the legal estate. A and B will now hold the legal estate upon trust for sale for the benefit of A and P as tenants in common. In practice, in such a situation, arrangements will also be made to transfer the legal estate; A and B will join in to convey it to A and P. B will not wish to remain a trustee of the legal estate when he no longer has any beneficial interest in the land.

One final point: If a joint tenant does sever his interest, he will normally need to have a memorandum of severance endorsed on the conveyance to the trustees.[10]

Principle 9.   Determination of co-ownership

Co-ownership ends by union in a sole tenant or partition of the land.

Explanation

These two methods of determination apply to both legal and equitable co-ownership. Whereas severance merely turns joint tenancy into tenancy in common, these two end co-ownership altogether. The rules are perhaps best explained by some illustrations.

Union in a sole tenant.   The commonest case of co-ownership is probably where husband and wife hold the legal estate upon trust for themselves as joint tenants. If, for example, the wife dies then the husband will become sole owner by survivorship in both law

---

[7] The judicial order for sale that was made was not sufficient because under s.17 there is no jurisdiction to alter existing property rights.
[8] [1974] 3 All E.R. 38.
[9] But see, *e.g.* Lord Denning in *Burgess* v. *Rawnsley* [1975] 3 All E.R. 142 at p. 147.
[10] L.P. (Joint Tenants) Act 1964, s.1. See below, p. 340.

and equity. A person cannot hold in trust for himself. He will therefore automatically become beneficial owner.

This sort of situation arose in *Re Cook*.[11] In 1924 freehold land had been conveyed to husband and wife "in fee simple as joint tenants." The effect of the transitional provisions of the 1925 legislation was to impose a trust for sale on the land; so that they held the legal estate upon trust for sale for the benefit of themselves as joint tenants. In 1944 the husband died. Later that year the widow made her will providing, *inter alia*, "I give and bequeath unto my nieces and nephews . . . all my personal estate whatsoever to be equally divided." She died not long afterwards. The court had to decide whether the nieces and nephews were entitled to the land. The point was that if there was a trust for sale, conversion operated to turn the land notionally into money—that is personal estate.[12] The court held that on the death of the husband, the wife became entitled absolutely in law and equity. The trust for sale automatically terminated and so did the conversion. The land was land and, being freehold, did not pass with the personal estate.

The mere fact that the legal co-ownership determines does not in itself affect the position in equity—and vice versa. If X and Y hold upon trust for sale for the benefit of A and B as tenants in common, and X dies, this does not affect the beneficial position of A and B at all. It simply means that Y is now sole trustee and a new one will probably have to be appointed. Similarly if A sells his interest to B, this will determine the co-ownership in equity; but X and Y will continue to hold the legal estate as joint tenant trustees upon trust for sale for B absolutely.

Partition. Partition means that the land is physically divided between the equitable co-owners. If all the equitable co-owners are of full age and agree they can divide the land between themselves as they wish. The trustees will then have to convey the legal estate of each part to the tenant to whom it has been allotted by the agreement.[13]

Section V. Special Cases

Principle 10. Beneficial joint tenancy

A puchaser from the survivor of two or more joint tenants must normally assume that the survivor is absolutely entitled in equity.

[11] [1948] Ch. 212 (Harman J.).
[12] See above, p. 275.
[13] See L.P.A. 1925, s.28(3), as to the statutory right to apply for partition.

Provided the survivor conveys as beneficial owner the purchaser
will be protected from any adverse equitable interests unless either
a memorandum of severance has been endorsed on the conveyance to the joint tenants or a bankruptcy petition or order has
been registered against any of them under the Land Charges Act
1972.

Explanation

A beneficial joint tennancy exists, *inter alia*, where two or more
persons hold the legal estate in trust for themselves as joint
tenants. This is commonly the way in which the matrimonial home
is held by husband and wife. Using the example of husband and
wife, what is normally going to happen is that one of them is going
to die leaving the other, by right of survivorship, absolutely
entitled in law and equity. The trust will be at an end and the
survivor will be entitled to deal with the property as beneficial
owner.

But suppose that, before she died, W severed her equitable
interest. She could do this, for example, by mortgaging it; H might
not even know that she had severed it and might honestly believe
himself to be absolutely entitled on her death. If the equitable
joint tenancy has been severed, the trust for sale will continue and
the surviving joint tenant will hold in trust for himself and whoever
is entitled to the deceased's share as tenants in common. In this
case it will be necessary to appoint a new trustee to join in any
conveyance of the legal estate; and the purchaser will take subject
to the equitable interests if he does not protect himself by paying
the purchase money to at least two trustees.[14]

The difficulty is—or rather was until 1964—this: how was a
purchaser to know whether or not a surviving joint tenant was
absolutely entitled in equity as well as law? He could only find out
by investigating the equitable interests or, by assuming the worst
and insisting on the appointment of a new trustee just to be on the
safe side.

Now, however, by the Law of Property (Joint Tenants) Act
1964, if the survivor conveys as beneficial owner,[15] then the
purchaser is protected unless a memorandum of severance has
been endorsed on the conveyance to the joint tenants. Thus, the
purchaser will see that the land has been conveyed to, say, H and

---

[14] He will not be able to claim protection as a bona fide purchaser without notice
since he will have notice of the trust.

[15] Or if the conveyance contains a statement that he is beneficial owner.

W as beneficial joint tenants; he will be given proof that W has died and check that no memorandum has been endorsed on the conveyance to H and W; and get a clear search from the Land Charges Registry. If he does this he will be safe to take a conveyance from and pay his money to H as the survivor. The same protection is available to the personal representatives of a surviving joint tenant if the latter dies.

This provision of the 1964 Act is interesting in that it illustrates the basic aim of the property legislation to keep equities off the title and to hang a curtain between the purchaser and the equitable interests. The 1964 Act covered up one of the gaps in the curtain left by the 1925 legislation.

Registered land.[16] The 1964 Act does not apply to registered land. In general, co-ownership law does apply to registered land as it does to unregistered. But the right to deal with the land and the effect of interests on a purchaser depends on the state of the register. In particular, section 74 of the Land Registration Act 1925 provides that a person dealing with the registered estate will not be affected by notice of any trust. Thus, a purchaser can safely deal with a survivor of joint registered proprietors. He will only be affected by any severance of the joint interest in equity which is properly protected on the register.

Principle 11. Coparceny

Coparceny arises where two or more persons inherit an entailed interest. In general, it is subject to the same rules as a tenancy in common.

Explanation

A fee tail passes on death according to the old common law rules of descent on intestacy. Where two or more persons are entitled as heir under these rules they take as coparceners.

Today, in almost all respects coparceny is like a tenancy in common. Each coparcener has a separate undivided share in the land and there is no right of survivorship. As with a tenancy in common it can only exist behind a trust for sale. If a coparcener alienates his share the grantee takes as tenant in common.

To give an illustration of coparceny. Blackacre is settled on A for life, remainder to B in fee tail. B dies leaving no sons but two

---

[16] For the distinction between registered and unregistered land see below, Chap. 24.

daughters, D1 and D2. They will take as coparceners—in
remainder so long as A is alive. If D1 then dies leaving only a son,
then the son will inherit her share in the coparceny. D2 and the son
will now be coparceners. When A dies their interest will fall into
possession. But like a tenancy in common coparceny can only exist
behind a trust for sale. Even if A was holding under the Settled
Land Act, the strict settlement will cease and the land become
subject to a trust for sale for the benefit of D2 and the son as
coparceners in tail. Suppose that the son then dies leaving no
issue. His share in the coparceny—since it is a fee tail—will cease.
This will leave D2 solely entitled in tail in possession. And that is
the end of the coparceny. Suppose further—for the sake of a tragic
end to the story—that D2 subsequently also dies without issue.
The fee tail will be at an end and the next interest will fall into
possession. It will be remembered that the fee tail can be barred at
any time subject to the rules set out earlier.

Principle 12.   Co-ownership of settled land

Where land is subject to the Settled Land Act 1925 and two or
more joint tenants become entitled in possession they together
constitute the tenant for life under the Act.[17]

Where two or more tenants in common become entitled in
possession to such land, the Settled Land Act ceases to apply and
the land becomes subject to the trust for sale machinery.[18]

Explanation

Co-ownership is not confined to the fee simple. Any of the
recognised estates and interests can be held by co-owners. For
example, Blackacre is left by will to A and B for life, remainder to
C in fee simple. In such cases there is both co-ownership and a
settlement.

As explained in a previous chapter, a settlement can in general
be operated under the Settled Land Act or the trust for sale
machinery. Normally, the presence of co-ownership does not
make any difference. If Blackacre is settled under the Settled Land
Act on A and B as joint tenants for life they will together
constitute the tenant for life for the purposes of the Act. And
apparently there is no restriction on the number of joint tenants
for life under the Act. This is an exception to the rule that there
cannot be more than four persons holding the legal estate.

[17] S.L.A. 1925, s.19(2).
[18] S.L.A. 1925, s.36(1); L.P.A. 1925, Sched. 1, Pt. IV, para. 2.

But where the beneficiaries entitled in possession are tenants in common, then the Settled Land Act cannot apply. There can only be a trust for sale. If it is not created expressly it will be imposed by statute. If the land is already being governed by the Settled Land Act machinery this will cease to apply and will be replaced by the trust for sale machinery. Suppose that Blackacre is settled by strict settlement on A for life, remainder to B and C for life as tenants in common; the legal estate is vested in A as the first tenant for life. On the death of A the Settled Land Act ceases to apply—whatever the settlor may have stipulated—and the legal estate will vest in A's ordinary personal representatives. They will have to transfer it to the trustees of the settlement who will hold it on the statutory trusts, *i.e.* on trust for sale for the benefit of B and C as tenants in common for life.[19]

As noted elsewhere, it is for this reason that where a settlor wishes to include a tenancy in common in the settlement—*e.g.* to my wife for life, remainder to my children in equal shares—there is some advantage in using the trust for sale from the beginning since it must apply eventually.

Principle 13.   Spouses and cohabitees

Subject to some important (mainly statutory) qualifications, the ordinary principles of land law apply between spouses and cohabitees.[20]

Explanation

As should be appreciated by now, a great number of the disputes which come before the courts today, relating to trust ownership, the trust for sale and co-ownership of land, concern either spouses or cohabitees.

Whilst it is true that there have been important judicial developments in these areas of land law, in general the same principles apply regardless of the relationship between the parties. There have been some judicial modifications of this rule—for

---

[19] S.L.A. 1925, s.36(1)(2).
[20] See *Dennis* v. *McDonald* [1981] 2 All E.R. 632 (Purchas J.). For the recommendations of the Law Commission, see Third Report on Family Property: The Matrimonial Home (Co-ownership and Occupation Rights) and Household Goods, Law Com. No. 86. For commentary on this Report, see O. Stone, (1979) 42 M.L.R. 192. For the view that no fundamental change in the law is needed, see A.A.S. Zuckerman, Ownership of the Matrimonial Home, "Commonsense and Reformist Nonsense," (1978) 94 L.Q.R. 26.

example, in relation to the presumption of advancement[21]; and the relationship between the parties viewed in its comtemporary social context may be relevant in the actual application of the principles—for example, in inferring the intention of the parties where an implied trust is alleged.[22]

More important, there are a number of statutory provisions affecting spouses and cohabitees.

Right of occupation of the matrimonial home. Under the Matrimonial Homes Act 1967,[23] a spouse has a statutory right to occupy the matrimonial home where a beneficial estate or interest is vested in the other spouse. The right exists where the non-owning spouse has only an equitable interest or no beneficial interest at all in the home. It exists in relation to any home which is or has been the matrimonial home.[24] The right entitles the non-owning spouse to remain in occupation or to be put back into occupation. Either spouse can apply at any time to the court which has a wide discretion to make such order as it thinks "just and reasonable," including an order excluding the owning spouse from occupation.[25]

The right is registrable against the legal estate as a class F land charge[26] or, in the case of registered land, can be protected by notice.[27]

In *Wroth* v. *Tyler*[28] the wife registered her right of occupation the day after the husband had entered into a contract to sell. She refused to remove it with the result that the husband had to pay substantial damages.

It should be emphasised that the Act does not give the spouse a

---

[21] See above, p. 324. Compare *Williams & Glyn's Bank Ltd.* v. *Boland* [1980] 2 All E.R. 408, where Lord Wilberforce recognised (at p. 415) "the widespread development of shared interests of ownership" between husband and wife in recognising that a wife can have her own distinct actual occupation of the matrimonial home. And see *Dyson Holdings Ltd.* v. *Fox* [1975] 3 W.L.R. 744 (C.A.).

[22] See above, p. 183.

[23] As amended by Matrimonial Proceedings and Property Act 1970, s.38; and Domestic Violence and Matrimonial Proceedings Act 1976, s.3; and Matrimonial Homes and Property Act 1981.

[24] But it can only be registered in respect of one home at a time; see s.3.

[25] See Domestic Violence and Matrimonial Proceedings Act 1976, s.3, passed as a result of the decision in *Tarr* v. *Tarr* [1973] A.C. 154.

[26] Where the legal estate is vested in trustees the right is registrable provided there are no beneficiaries other than the spouses; Matrimonial Homes and Property Act 1981, s.(1)(4). And see *Barnett* v. *Hassett* [1982] 1 All E.R. 80.

[27] See Matrimonial Homes and Property Act 1981, s.4.

[28] [1974] Ch. 30; see (1974) 38 Conv. 110 (D.J. Hayton).

share in the beneficial interest in the property; but it does create a right of occupation which has proprietary effect like any other registrable land charge; and it means that an owning spouse will be wise to get the proper consent of a non-owning spouse to any dealing with the land.

Under the Domestic Violence and Matrimonial Proceedings Act 1976, s.4, the court is given discretion to control the right of occupation where the legal estate is vested in both spouses.

Where violence against a spouse or child of the family is involved, an application can be made to the magistrates court for an order controlling occupation of the matrimonial home.[29]

Under the Domestic Violence and Matrimonial Proceedings Act 1976, the jurisdiction of the courts to control occupation is extended to the home of cohabitees living with each other in the same household[30] as man and wife.[31] Here again, a non-owning cohabitee can be given occupation to the exclusion of an owning cohabitee.[32]

In the case of cohabitees, under the 1976 Act, there is (presumably) no property right, registrable or otherwise, at least until a court order has been made. But, maybe, once proceedings have been started, the claim could be registered as a pending land action.[33]

It has been suggested by the Court of Appeal that the 1976 Act is designed only to provide a short term remedy and that injunctions made under it should be limited in time to allow the claimant time to find somewhere else to live or (in the case of a spouse) to start divorce proceedings.[34]

---

[29] Domestic Proceedings and Magistrates Courts Act 1978, ss.16–18. See *McCartney* v. *McCartney* [1981] 1 All E.R. 597 (D.C.). A "child of the family" is either a child of both parties or any child (with certain exceptions) who has been treated by both parties as a child of the family. Compare Inheritance (Provision for Family and Dependants) Act 1975, s.1(1)(*d*). See generally on the Act, A. Samuels, [1981] 11 Fam. Law, pp. 13, 60.

[30] See *Adeoso* v. *Adeoso* [1981] 1 All E.R. 107 (C.A.).

[31] S.1 of this Act also applies to spouses in relation to the matrimonial home; but the view in *Davis* v. *Johnson* [1978] 1 All E.R. 1132 (H.L.) was that it does not add to the existing rights between spouses but merely extends the better procedures and remedies of the 1976 Act to them. See J.M. Masson, The Mistress's Limited Rights of Occupancy [1979] Conv. 184; and see, on the Act, J.G. Miller, (1977) 41 Conv. (N.s.) 330.

[32] See *Davis* v. *Johnson* [1978] 1 All E.R. 1132 (H.L.).

[33] See Megarry & Wade, *Law of Real Property*, (4th ed.), at p. 1037; *Calgary and Edmonton Land Co. Ltd.* v. *Dobinson* [1974] 1 All E.R. 484; and *Whittingham* v. *Whittingham* [1978] 3 All E.R. 813 (C.A.).

[34] *Hopper* v. *Hopper* [1979] 1 All E.R. 181 (C.A.); and see *Spindlow* v. *Spindlow* [1979] 1 All E.R. 169 (C.A.).

Statutory provisions affecting the beneficial interest.   (a) Under the Matrimonial Proceedings and Property Act 1970, s.37, a spouse making a substantial contribution to the improvement of property owned by both or solely by the other, will be presumed to have acquired a beneficial interest in proportion to the contribution.[35]

(b) In matrimonial proceedings the court has a wide jurisdiction to alter existing property rights in both the matrimonial home and other property.[36]

(c) Under the Inheritance (Provision for Family and Dependants) Act 1975, a claim can be made for financial assistance against a deceased's estate by, *inter alia*, the spouse, child or child of the family of the deceased or by a person maintained wholly or partly by the deceased.[37]

Principle 14.   Party walls[38]

Where a wall divides two properties, the ownership will have to be decided like any other question of property ownership by evidence and proof from the title deeds, etc. In general, as with any building or fixture, ownership of the wall is presumed to belong to the owner of the soil. There is no precise definition of the term party wall but in general it can be said to mean a dividing wall in which each adjoining owner has either a share in the ownership or easements in respect of the wall. The situation is likely to fall into one of the two following categories:

(1) The wall is owned solely by one property in which case there may be an easement entitling the other to have it maintained.

(2) The ownership of the wall is divided vertically, in which case each owner will probably enjoy the benefit of easements of support from the other's part of the wall.[39]

---

[35] See above, p. 185.
[36] See, in particular, Matrimonial Causes Act 1973, ss.23–25. See, *e.g. Griffiths* v. *Griffiths* [1974] 1 All E.R. 932 (C.A.); *Martin* v. *Martin* [1977] 3 All E.R. 762 (C.A.); *Backhouse* v. *Backhouse* [1978] 1 All E.R. 1158 (Balcombe J.).
[37] See below, p. 574.
[38] See, generally, V. Powell-Smith, *The Law of Boundaries and Fences* (2nd ed.).
[39] Before 1926, it was quite common for a party wall to be subject to a tenancy in common. By L.P.A. 1925, s.38, the ownership of such a party wall is deemed to be divided vertically, each owner having rights of support and user over the other's half.

CHAPTER 13

DISABILITIES: INFANTS; BANKRUPTS; CHARITIES; MENTAL PATIENTS

Principle 1.   Infants

A legal estate cannot be conveyed to or held by an infant.[1]

There is no restriction on his right to receive or hold an equitable interest in land.

Where an infant is beneficially entitled (*i.e.* in equity) to an interest in land, the legal estate must be held for his benefit either under a trust for sale or the Settled Land Act 1925.[2]

An attempt to convey a legal estate beneficially to an infant will operate as a contract by the grantor to make a proper settlement in his favour.[3]

An attempted conveyance of the legal estate beneficially to an infant jointly with an adult, will transfer the legal estate to the adult to hold on trust for sale; but the infant will take the interest intended in equity.[4]

An infant cannot be a personal representative until he comes of age.

An infant cannot be a trustee. If an attempted conveyance is made to an infant as trustee, it will operate as a declaration of trust.[5] If an attempted conveyance is made to an infant jointly with an adult as trustees, the legal estate will vest in the adult.[6]

Principle 2.   Bankrupts[7]

There are four main stages leading to bankruptcy:

(1) An act of bankruptcy, *e.g.* non-compliance with a bankruptcy notice.[8]

(2) A bankruptcy petition to the court asking for a receiving order. A petition must be founded on an act of bankruptcy

---

[1] L.P.A. 1925, s.1(6).
[2] S.L.A. 1925, s.1(2).
[3] L.P.A. 1925, s.19(1); S.L.A. 1925, s.27(1).
[4] L.P.A. 1925, s.19(2).
[5] *Ibid.*, s.19(4).
[6] *Ibid.*, s.19(5).
[7] See Williams and Muir Hunter, *The Law and Practice in Bankruptcy* (19th ed., 1979).
[8] See Bankruptcy Act 1914, s.1, as amended by Insolvency Act 1976, s.4.

committed within the previous three months[9]: "an available act of bankruptcy."

(3) A receiving order, placing the debtor's property under the custody and control of the official receiver.

(4) An adjudication order making the debtor a bankrupt and automatically vesting his property in the trustee in bankruptcy for the benefit of his creditors.[10]

Bankruptcy petitions and receiving orders must both be registered (as pending actions and writs or orders respectively) in the Land Charges Registry.[11]

In the case of registered land,[12] the Chief Land Registrar is under an obligation to register a creditor's notice or (in the case of a receiving order) a bankruptcy inhibition against the title of any land which appears to be affected.[13]

The title of the trustee in bankruptcy relates back to the first available act of bankruptcy within the last three months before the presentation of the petition.[14] However, in the case of unregistered land, a purchaser dealing with a person who has committed such an act of bankruptcy will normally be protected if he is a purchaser for value provided[15]:

(a) no petition or receiving order has been registered; and
(b) he does not otherwise have notice of any available act of bankruptcy.[16]

Similar protection is given to the purchaser of registered land.[17]

Principle 3. Charities

Under the Charities Act 1960, all restrictions on gifts of land to charities have been abolished.

Where land is vested in trustees for "charitable, ecclesiastical or public purposes," it is deemed to be settled land and the trustees are given all the powers of the tenant for life and the trustees of a settlement.[18] But the conveyancing machinery of the Settled Land Act 1925 does not apply.

---

[9] *Ibid.*, s.4, as amended by Insolvency Act 1976, s.1.
[10] *Ibid.*, ss.18, 38, 53; L.P.A. 1925, s.61(5).
[11] L.C.A. 1972, ss.5(1), 6(1)(c).
[12] See below, Chap. 25 for registered land.
[13] He will obtain information as to petitions and receiving orders by checking the Land Charges Register.
[14] Bankruptcy Act 1914, s.37.
[15] See *ibid.*, s.45.
[16] L.C.A. 1972, s.6(5).
[17] See L.R.A. 1925, s.61(6).
[18] S.L.A. 1925, s.29.

In some cases special restrictions apply to the disposition of its land by a charity.[19]

Principle 4. Mental patients

Under the Mental Health Act 1959, where a person is found by a judge[20] to be a "patient"—that is "a person incapable by reason of mental disorder, of managing and administering his property and affairs,"[21] his property comes under the control of the court acting through a receiver when one has been appointed.[22]

In general, once his property has come under the control of the court, the patient has no power to deal with it. But he can make a valid will during a lucid interval.[23]

---

[19] See Charities Act 1960, s.29.

[20] *i.e.* one of the judges nominated by the Lord Chancellor to administer this part of the Act: s.100.

[21] *Ibid.*, s.101.

[22] *Ibid.*, s.105; and L.P.A. 1925, s.22(1). For the position if a trustee for sale becomes a mental patient see L.P.A. 1925, s.22(2), substituted by the Mental Health Act 1959, s.149(1), Sched. 7, Pt. I.

[23] Subject to the Mental Health Act 1959, s.102; see *Emmett on Title* (17th ed.), p. 474; for the position where the court has not intervened, see *Emmett on Title* (17th ed.), pp. 471, 472; and Megarry and Wade, *Law of Real Property* (4th ed.), p. 999.

PART 4.   THIRD PARTY RIGHTS

CHAPTER 14

GENERAL INTRODUCTION

Nature of third party rights. A third party right is a right over another person's land binding on successive owners of that land but giving something less than exclusive possession of it. It may be a right to use or restrict the use of the land in a particular way; or it may be a right to require the performance of some positive obligation by its owner.

Third party rights are sometimes referred to as incorporeal hereditaments or interests, rights *in alieno solo* or *servitudes*. In general this book will use the term third party rights—"third party" in the sense of rights which are enforceable by and against third parties, that is, persons other than the original grantor and grantee of the right.

Important third party rights. The following are some of the more important third party rights.

(1) Easements. An easement entitles a landowner to use or restrict the use of his neighbour's land in some particular way. Only certain uses and restrictions on land are recognised by the courts as capable of forming easements; for example, various rights of way, the right of light to a window, the right of support for a building from another building or the soil.

(2) Profits *à prendre*. A profit is the right to take something from the land. For example, the right to fish or hunt, the right to extract minerals, and the right to graze animals.

(3) Rentcharges. A rentcharge is the right to a periodic payment of money charged (*i.e.* secured) on freehold land.[1]

(4) Restrictive covenants. A restrictive covenant is an agreement by which an owner of a property, for the benefit of a neighbouring property, agrees to restrict in some way the use to which his own land will be put. Common examples are restrictive covenants against building, or against building in a particular way, restrictive covenants against carrying on any or some particular trade.

(5) Mortgages. A mortgage is an interest in land which a lender can be given as security for the repayment of his loan with interest. A mortgagee might—at least according to the scheme of this book—be regarded as having an ownershp rather than a third party interest, since he does have a right to possession. But this

[1] More correctly, where the relationship of landlord and tenant does not exist; see below, p. 497.

353

right to possession is limited to recovering what is due to him and it is more realistic to treat him as having a third party right.

The burden and benefit of third party rights. Any third party right has a benefit and a burden. It is thus an obligation as well as a right and it is always important to be clear which of these one is talking about. To take a simple example: Albert buys Blackacre which enjoys a right of way on foot (an easement) over neighbouring Whiteacre. The burden of that right of way rests on Whiteacre—the servient property—the property that will be walked over. The benefit is attached to Blackacre, referred to as the dominant property.

The burden of third party rights runs with the land. The most significant feature of all third party rights in land is that their burden runs with the servient property. And this is the most important distinction between third party rights (and indeed any property right) and mere personal rights such as personal licences.[2] Suppose that I give D a right of way[3] (an easement) over my land and that at the same time I give him a licence to play cricket on it. D can enforce his right of way and his licence to play cricket (at least if it is a contractual licence) against me; but suppose that I subsequently sell my land. The distinction now becomes vital. The right of way will bind the purchaser. The licence, being only a personal right against me, will not.

The benefit may be appurtenant to and run with a dominant property or it may be in gross. An easement can only exist if it is appurtenant—that is, if its benefit is attached—to a dominant property. The same is true of restrictive covenants. Where the benefit is appurtenant it will run with the dominant land so as to be enforceable by any subsequent owner.

A profit on the other hand may be appurtenant or it may be in gross—that is, held by a person independently of the ownership of land. Where it is in gross its benefit is not connected with and does not run with the ownership of any piece of land. The benefit is enforceable by the person to whom it is first granted, his personal representatives and assigns.

Distinction between third party rights and some other rights. Third party rights should be distinguished from the following:

---

[2] Some licences may have proprietary effect; see below, Chapter 17.
[3] "Right of way" may be used to indicate a public or customary right of way, or even a right of way by licence; but commonly it refers to the easement.

(1) *Ownership interests.* In this book the word ownership is in general used to indicate those interests which give possession of the land, for a longer or shorter period, and either immediately or at some time in the future. A third party right is a limit on the landowner subject to it but it does not deprive him of possession.

(2) *Natural rights.* Natural rights are those which all landowners are entitled to exercise automatically by virtue of their ownership of the land. Third party rights have to be acquired.[4]

(3) *Licences and personal rights.* A third party right in land, like an ownership interest is a property right, a right *in rem.* This means that it is a right in the thing itself (the *res*) enforceable against anyone who interferes with it including a subsequent owner.

A personal right such as a licence,[5] on the other hand, is enforceable only against the person who created it.

This important distinction can be illustrated by the case of *Hill* v. *Tupper.*[6] The owner of both land on the bank of a canal and of the bed of the canal leased the land to Hill and gave him the exclusive right to put his pleasure boats on the canal. As owner of the bed he was certainly entitled to do this. Subsequently, the defendant Tupper put rival pleasure boats on the same stretch of water. Hill sued him. The question which the court had to decide was whether Hill had an easement or only a personal licence. And they decided that he had only a licence.

An easement would, as a property interest, have entitled him to sue Tupper. As it was he had only a licence which at best only entitled him to sue the owner of the canal bed as licensor for allowing the interference with the enjoyment of his licence.[7] Of course, the owner of the canal bed could himself have sued Tupper in trespass.

The distinction could again have become important had the owner sold the land and the canal bed. The purchaser would have taken subject to Hill's lease of the land—a property interest. If there had been an easement to put boats on the canal he would have been bound by that too. But he could have ignored a mere licence with impunity and ordered Hill to remove his boats from the canal.

---

[4] See above, p. 57.
[5] See n. 2 above.
[6] (1863) 2 H. & C. 121.
[7] But possession, without any proprietary interest, is sufficient to maintain trespass against all but someone with a better right to possession.

(4) *Public rights.* A public right is one enjoyed by every member of the public. The commonest public right is the public right of way—the highway; another example is the public right to fish and navigate in tidal waters.

(5) *Community rights.* These are dealt with below.[8]

Legal and equitable third party rights. The Law of Property Act 1925 states which third party right can be legal. All others can only be equitable.[9]

Third party rights and the doctrine of estates. The doctrine of estates applies to third party rights to determine their duration.[10]

---

[8] See below, at p. 393.
[9] s.1(2); see below at p. 512.
[10] See above, p. 15.

CHAPTER 15

EASEMENTS[1]

SECTION I. DEFINITION AND REQUIREMENTS

Principle 1. Definition

An esement is an interest in land which entitles a landowner to use
or restrict the use of his neighbour's land in a particular way
without giving him possession of it.

The courts recognise a limited number of rights which can exist
as easements; and will not normally allow the addition of new
easements to this number. Occasionally, they will recognise a new
species of easement provided it is sufficiently certain and similar to
existing easements and provided it satisfies the other requirements
of a valid easement.

Explanation

A right less than possession. This is not peculiar to easements.
It is the essence of ownership interests, as that term is generally
used in this book, that they give exclusive possession of the land
for a longer or shorter period; whilst a third party right is an
interest in land which falls short of possession.

If the claimant is enjoying exclusive possession of the servient
property he cannot have an easement over it.

It is not easy to say when the courts will regard a person as
having the exclusive possession[1a] which is incompatible with an
easement. In *Copeland* v. *Greenhalf*[2] the plaintiff owned a house
and orchard. Access to the orchard was by means of a strip of land
varying in width from 15 to 35 feet which led from the road. The
defendant, who was a wheelwright with premises on the opposite
side of the road, was claiming an easement to store his vehicles on
the strip of land, where he and his father before him had been
storing them for many years.[3] He failed, because what he was
claiming in effect was the whole beneficial use of this strip, more
than possible under any easement.

---

[1] See generally, P. Jackson, *The Law of Easements* (1978); and Gale, *Easements*
(14th ed.).
[1a] For further reading on the nature of possession as seen by English courts see
above, p. 4, n. 2.
[2] [1952] Ch. 488 (Upjohn J.).
[3] *i.e.* long enough to create an easement by prescription; see below, p. 379 *et seq.*

On the other hand, in *Miller* v. *Emcer Products*,[4] it was held that the right to use a neighbour's lavatory could exist as an easement. Although this right involved the exclusive, though intermittent, occupation of this part of the servient property, it did not amount to "such an ouster of the servient owner's rights as was held by Upjohn J. to be incompatible with a legal easement in *Copeland* v. *Greenhalf*."[5]

If a person does have exclusive possession, although he cannot have an easement, he may have a lease or some other ownership interest. In *Selby* v. *Greaves*[6] it was held that an agreement giving exclusive use of part of a room for working lace machinery gave sufficient exclusive possession to constitute a lease, and not just a licence of that part.[7]

Negative and positive easements. Most easements are positive in that they entitle the dominant owner to do something on the servient owner's land. A right of way on foot entitles him to walk across it along the specified route; similarly there can be an easement to take water from a stream or river on the servient property; to discharge water onto it; to enter the land of another to open sluice gates; to fix a sign board onto a neighbour's building; and so on. With one exception easements are never positive in the sense of requiring the servient owner to do something.[8]

Some easements are negative requiring the servient owner to refrain from doing something. An easement of light to a window prevents the servient owner from building so as to obstruct the light. Similarly, an easement of support for a building from the servient owner's building means that the servient owner must not remove the supporting building (although it does not oblige him to keep it in repair).

New easements. Some of the rights which can exist in the form of easements have been mentioned above. There are many others;

---

[4] [1956] Ch. 304 (C.A.).

[5] *Per* Romer L.J., at p. 316. In *Wright* v. *Macadam* [1949] 2 K.B. 744 (C.A.) apparently not referred to in *Copeland* v. *Greenhalf*, the use of a coal shed to store coal was recognised as "a right or easement of a kind which could readily be included in a lease or conveyance by the insertion of appropriate words in the parcels" (p. 752). It was therefore included by virtue of L.P.A. 1925, s.62, in a lease of the flat enjoying the use. For s.62 see below, at p. 375. And see *Grigsby* v. *Melville* [1973] 1 All E.R. 385.

[6] (1868) L.R. 2 C.P. 594.

[7] But today exclusive possession does not necessarily indicate a lease rather than a licence, see above, p. 96; below, p. 398.

[8] An easement obligating a neighbour to maintain a fence; see Megarry and Wade, *Law of Real Property* (4th ed.), p. 879.

but the list of possible easements is more or less fixed and will not normally be added to by the courts. Suppose that it would be convenient for my neighbour to use a clothes line on my land; I am willing to oblige him. I could, of course, give him a licence. But can I give him an easement with all the advantages—to him—of an easement over a mere licence? The answer is, yes. It is hardly the commonest easement found in practice, but it has been recognised by the courts and included in the list of possible easements.[9]

On the other hand, suppose that the wall of my neighbour's house stands very close to the wall of my house. It does not support my house but it does protect it from the weather. My neighbour may be co-operative and willing to execute a deed purporting to grant me an easement. It will make no difference. The right to have a building protected from the weather by another building cannot exist as an easement. The courts have specifically refused to add it to the list.[10] My neighbour himself may be bound by his agreement under the ordinary rules of contract law; but if he sells there will be nothing to stop the purchaser pulling down the house and taking away the protection.[11]

In *Hill* v. *Tupper*,[12] Pollock C.B. said[13]: "A new species of incorporeal hereditament cannot be created at the will and pleasure of the owner of property, but he must be content to accept the estate and the right to dispose of it, subject to the law as settled by decisions or controlled by Act of Parliament." This statement applies to all third party rights (and, indeed, all property interests). It means two things: First the landowner is not at liberty himself to create new property interests. He can only create those recognised by the law. Secondly, as a general rule, the courts will not create new property interests for him.[14]

At various times the courts have been urged but have refused to recognise the following rights as easements: the right to have a building protected from the weather by another building; the right to a view[15]; the right to the general flow of air across the dominant

---

[9] *Drewell* v. *Towler* (1832) B. & Ad. 735.
[10] *Phipps* v. *Pears* [1965] 1 Q.B. 76 (C.A.).
[11] A restrictive covenant could be created by a willing servient owner preventing the house giving protection from being demolished.
[12] (1863) 2 H. & C. 121.
[13] At p. 127.
[14] See *Anderson* v. *Bostock* [1976] 1 All E.R. 560 (Blackett-Ord. V.-C.).
[15] *Browne* v. *Flower* [1911] 1 Ch. 219, at p. 225.

land to a mill,[16] or to a shed for storing timber,[17] or to a chimney.[18]

The courts have given different reasons for refusing to recognise rights such as these as possible easements. In *Phipps* v. *Pears*,[19] Denning L.J. said that the right claimed had not previously been recognised as an easement and that if it were to be permitted, "it would unduly restrict your neighbour in his enjoyment of his own land. It would hamper legitimate development. . . . "

The courts have often been influenced by the fact that easements can be acquired by prescription—that is, by long enjoyment.[20] At any time easements may be maturing against a landowner by the prescriptive enjoyment of his neighbour. For example, if the neighbour's window enjoys light from his land for a period of 20 years, this will probably be enough to create an easement of light and limit his right to build. To stop this happening he will normally have to interrupt the flow of light to the window before the 20-year period expires. In view of this, it is reasonable that the courts should only recognise as easements those rights which are certain in that they affect the servient land in a fairly defined, limited and apparent way. The servient owner then has a fair chance to see what easements are threatening to mature against him and to protect himself without having to take unreasonable steps. If, for example, the right to a view were a possible easement, he might only be able to protect himself by immediately building so as to block all possible views across his land.

In *Bryant* v. *Lefever*, in which the flow of air to a windmill was rejected as an easement, Barnwell J. said[21]: "But here the claim is of such a character that its enjoyment could only be prevented by surrounding the land with erections as high as it might at any time be wanted to be built on the land. . . . The claim is not one the law allows, being too vague and uncertain; one the acquisition of which the adjoining owner could not defend himself against."

From time to time the courts have recognised new easements. And no doubt will do so again. "The categories of servitudes and easements must alter and expand with the changes that take place in the circumstances of mankind."[22]

---

[16] *Webb* v. *Bird* (1862) 13 C.B.(N.S.) 841; 143 E.R. 332.
[17] *Harris* v. *De Pinna* (1888) 33 Ch.D. 238.
[18] *Bryant* v. *Lefever* (1879) 4 C.P.D. 172.
[19] [1965] 1 Q.B. 76, at p. 83.
[20] See below, p. 379.
[21] Above, n. 18, at p. 178.
[22] *Dyce* v. *Lady James Hay* (1852) 1 Macq. 305, at p. 312 *per* Lord St. Leonards. But it is unlikely that the courts will recognise new negative easements (see Gale, *Easements* (14th ed.), p. 34).

If a right is sufficiently definite and limited in extent; and sufficiently similar to existing recognised easements, the courts may be prepared to add it to the list.[23] An easement already mentioned,[24] the right to use a neighbour's lavatory, was first recognised as a possible easement in 1955. Romer J., deciding the case, thought it sufficiently similar to the previous recognised easement to wash in a neighbour's kitchen. Because it is easier for the servient owner to be aware of and resist their arising by prescription, the courts may well be more willing to recognise new positive than negative easements.

Principle 2. Requirements of a valid easement

A right can only exist as an easement if the following requirements are satisfied:

(1) It must belong to the list of recognised easements.

(2) There must be a dominant and a servient property (tene ment).

(3) The right must accommodate (*i.e.* be for the benefit of) the dominant property, and not merely a personal benefit for the dominant owner.

(4) The dominant and servient properties must be separately owned.

Explanation

The right must belong to the list of recognised easements. This has already been dealt with. But if a person wishes to claim an easement, it is not enough for him just to satisfy this requirement. He must in addition satisfy the other three listed above.

There must be a dominant and a servient property. Like all third party rights in land, an easement is a burden on and is capable of running with a piece of land known as the servient land. Like some but not all third party rights in land, the benefit of an easement must be attached to another piece of land, *i.e.* it must be appurtenant to a dominant property—and the benefit of it can only pass with the dominant property.

In *Re Ellenborough Park*[25] the owners of Ellenborough Park

---

[23] In *Dowty Boulton Paul Ltd.* v. *Wolverhampton Corporation (No. 2)* [1973] 2 W.L.R. 618 (C.A.), Russell L.J. said (at p. 624): "A tendency in the past to freeze the categories of easements has been overtaken by the defrosting operation of *Re Ellenborough Park, Re Davies (decd.), Powell* v. *Maddison.*"

[24] *Miller* v. *Emcer Products*, above, p. 305.

[25] [1956] Ch. 131 (Danckwerts J. and C.A.).

and the surrounding land, in 1855 developed the surrounding land for residential purposes and sold it off in plots to individual purchasers. Each conveyance included a grant to the purchaser of "the full enjoyment . . . at all times hereafter in common with other persons to whom such easements may be granted of the pleasure ground set out and made in front of the said plot of land . . . but subject to the payment of a fair and just proportion of the costs charges and expenses of keeping in good order and condition the said pleasure ground." The plot taken by the purchaser represented the dominant property. The "pleasure ground" (a large private garden laid out in lawns and walks, etc.—not a fun fair) retained by the developer was the servient property.[26]

In *Hill* v. *Tupper*[27] the land held by the plaintiff under the lease was the dominant property. The bed of the adjoining canal retained by the lessor was the servient property. The plaintiff had been granted by the lessor the exclusive right to put pleasure boats on the canal and he was claiming that this right was an easement appurtenant to the leasehold land.[28]

The easement must accommodate the dominant property. The basic idea of this requirement is that the easement must be a benefit to the dominant owner in his use and occupation of that particular piece of land; not just a benefit to him personally without reference to the ownership of the land. The position has been stated as follows: " . . . One of the fundamental principles concerning easements is that they must be not only appurtenant to a dominant tenement but also connected with the normal enjoyment of the dominant tenement. . . . " The easement must be "reasonably necessary for the better enjoyment of that tenement, for if it has no necessary connection therewith, although it confers an advantage on the owner and renders his ownership of the land more valuable, it is not an easement at all but a mere contractual right personal to and only enforceable between the contracting parties."[29]

As always the distinction is easier to state than apply. In *Re Ellenborough Park*,[30] Lord Evershed M.R. agreed[31] with counsel

---

[26] See below, for the point at issue in this case.
[27] (1863) 2 H. & C. 121. See below, p. 363, for the issue in this case.
[28] His claim failed on other grounds. See below, p. 363.
[29] Chesire, *Modern Law of Real Property* (7th ed.), p. 457, cited with approval in *Re Ellenborough Park* (n. 25, above), at p. 168.
[30] Above, n. 25.
[31] *Ibid.* at p. 174.

for the plaintiff (opposing the easement) that the right given to the purchaser of a house to use the Zoological Gardens free of charge or to attend Lord's Cricket Ground without payment would not accommodate the dominant property. On the other hand, in that case, it was held that the right to use the private garden in the middle of the square did accommodate the surrounding residential properties and could exist as an easement.

Two of the factors which are relevant in deciding whether the alleged easement accommodates the dominant property are, first, the proximity of the two properties; and, secondly, the use to which the dominant property is put.

First, proximity: The two properties do not have to be contiguous, but they must be close. As it has been judicially suggested, a right of way over land in Northumberland cannot be considered of any benefit to land in Kent[32]; though it might be a personal benefit to the owner of land in Kent, if, for example, he spends weekends walking in Northumberland.

Secondly, the use of the dominant property: In *Re Ellenborough Park* Lord Evershed noted that the use of the dominant property was residential and that the right to use the garden was a benefit to that user. Whilst the courts have always been ready to recognise that something which benefits the residential or agricultural use of land accommodates the land, they have at times shown a reluctance to recognise something which benefits a particular commercial or trade use as being a benefit to the land; showing a tendency to regard a business as having no connection with the land on which it is carried on. In *Hill* v. *Tupper*,[33] the court refused to recognise the right to put pleasure boats on a canal as an easement. " . . . it is not competent to create rights unconnected with the use and enjoyment of land, and annex them to it so as to become a property in the grantee."

However, there is little doubt that an easement will be recognised if its benefit is confined to a business pursued on the dominant property.

If the dominant property is used as an inn, the right to fix the inn sign to the neighbouring property will be recognised as an easement.[34] In *Clapman* v. *Edwards*[35] a lease of a garage gave the lessee the right "to use the flank walls of the adjoining premises

---

[32] *Bailey* v. *Stephens* (1862) 12 C.B.(N.S.) 91, at p. 115; 142 E.R. 1077, at p. 1086 *per* Willes J.
[33] (1863) 2 H. & C. 121, at p. 127; 159 E.R. 51, at p. 53 (Pollock C.B.).
[34] *Moody* v. *Steggles* (1879) 12 Ch. D. 261.
[35] [1938] 2 All E.R. 507 (Bennett J.).

marked A, B . . . for advertising purposes." It was held that this did not create an easement since the user was not limited to the requirements of the dominant property. On the other hand the right limited to advertising business carried on on the dominant property could be a valid easement.[36]

The dominant and servient properties must be separately owned. A landowner cannot have an easement over his own land. If D owns Whiteacre and Blackacre he may find it convenient to use a pathway across Blackacre to get to and from Whiteacre. But he cannot be exercising any easement over Blackacre; simply his natural rights as beneficial owner of Blackacre. On the other hand, if he then leases Whiteacre to T he could include in the lease the grant of an easement of way over Blackacre which would continue for the duration of the lease.

This rule is not peculiar to easements. A third party right is by definition a right over someone else's land. However, the rule does have some special significance in the context of easements. A right in the nature of an easement which a landowner is in the habit of exercising over one part of his land for the benefit of another is called a quasi-easement. And quasi-easements are important because if the landowner sells the quasi-dominant property any quasi-easements may automatically become proper easements in favour of the purchaser over the land retained. The landowner may find that he has given the purchaser a little more than he realised.[37]

SECTION II.   CREATION AND EXTINGUISHMENT OF EASEMENTS

Principle 3.   Creation: General

Apart from statute, the law recognises the following methods by which easements can be created:
  (1) Express grant or reservation.
  (2) Implied grant or reservation.
  (3) Presumed grant (prescription) which may be:
      (a) common law prescription;
      (b) lost modern grant; or
      (c) prescription under the Prescription Act 1832.

---

[36] For the same problem in connection with covenants see below, pp. 423, 428.
[37] See below, p. 373.

Explanation

Easements lie in grant. Easements are said to lie in grant. This means that, in theory, apart from statute, they can only be created by means of a deed of grant. The normal method is express grant. A deed will be executed by the servient owner expressly creating the easement in favour of the dominant owner.[38] However, in certain cases the courts may be prepared to imply a grant. They will do this where there has been a conveyance of land without any express grant of the easement in question to the purchaser. The surrounding circumstances suggest that an easement must have been intended. To give effect to this presumed intention the courts will imply the easement—that is, in effect, write it into the conveyance for the parties.

In the case of prescription there is no deed expressly creating the easement; and there is no conveyance of the land into which it can be implied. There is merely long enjoyment of the right claimed by the dominant owner[39] without objection from the servient owner. The court is anxious to legalise this enjoyment by recognising an easement. Faced with the principle that easements can only be created by deed of grant, it simply presumes that originally there was such a deed untroubled by the fact that the claimant cannot produce it and that almost certainly there never was one. This presumption is a typical example of legal fiction—a bit of judicial make-believe—useful to circumvent an inconvenient but binding common law rule.

Principle 4. Creation: Express grant and reservation

To create an express legal easement a deed of grant must be executed by a capable grantor in favour of a capable grantee. This deed must:

(1) Identify the dominant property and show an intention to annex the benefit of the easement to it.

(2) Identify and show an intention to burden the servient property.

Explanation

Satisfaction of the requirements of a valid easement set out in the last section[40] means that an easement can exist—not that it

---

[38] If a deed is not used there may still be an equitable easement.
[39] Or his predecessors in title.
[40] Above, p. 361.

does. Suppose that my neighbour is found using a footpath across my land. He may have an easement. He may; but not necessarily. He may only have a licence from me. The distinction may be vital if, for example, I sell the land and the purchaser wishes to block off the footpath. Again he may be exercising a public or even a customary right of way.[41] He will only be able to establish an easement if he can show that it has been properly created at some time in the past by one of the recognised legal methods listed in the last Principle. And even if my neighbour produces a deed purporting to make him an express grant, it will still be necessary to examine the deed to see that it satisfies the requirements of an express grant set out in the present Principle.

Grant and reservation. The normal method of creating an easement is by grant in favour of neighbouring land. But if a landowner sells off part of his land he may stipulate in the contract for an easement over the land sold for the benefit of land which he is retaining. This is a reservation. In practice most easements arise where a person sells off part of his land and either grants easements over the land retained or reserves them over the land sold. A reservation is technically regarded as a grant of the easement by the purchaser of the servient property back to the vendor[42]; and in general a reservation is subject to exactly the same rules as a grant. Unless otherwise indicated the term grant is used here to include reservation.

Identification of and annexation to dominant property. Whether a deed creates an easement or some lesser right such as a licence is essentially one of intention as shown by the words used. No particular form of words is essential. Neither the word "grant" nor the word "easement" must be used.[43] But the dominant property must be identified and an intention to benefit that property must be shown. In other words, an intention must be shown to connect and limit the enjoyment to the ownership of a specific piece of land (the dominant property).

A typical formula is as follows:

> The Vendor hereby conveys unto the Purchaser all that piece or parcel of land known as Blackacre and for the

---

[41] See below, p. 393, for these.

[42] And so prior to L.P.A. 1925, s.65, the conveyance had to be executed by the purchaser. On the effect of s.65, see *St. Edmundsbury & Ipswich Diocesan Board of Finance* v. *Clark (No. 2)* [1975] 1 All E.R. 772 (C.A.).

[43] And, conversely, use of the word "easement" will not create an easement if the rest of the document shows that an easement was not intended.

purpose of identification only shown on the plan drawn hereon and thereon edged in red together with full free right and liberty at all times hereafter and for all purposes connected with the existing use of the said property of the Purchaser but on foot only to go pass and repass along the passageway leading from the back of the property hereby conveyed into Valley Road which passageway is hatched black on the said plan to hold the same unto the purchaser in fee simple.[44]

This precedent clearly identifies the dominant property (*i.e.* "the said property" which is being conveyed to the purchaser and which has just been identified by description and plan). The words "and for all purposes connected with the existing use of the said property," show that the right of way is intended to be annexed to the dominant property.

Extrinsic evidence, that is, evidence from outside the deed itself, is allowed to show the identity of the property intended to be benefited. In *Johnstone* v. *Holdway*,[45] a company sold off part of its land. It retained adjoining land which included a quarry. The conveyance reserved to "the company and its successors in title or their servants and workmen . . . " a right of way across the land sold "at all times and for all purposes (including quarrying) with or without horses carts and vehicles of all types and description between the points marked A and B on the said plan." The quarry was in fact marked on the plan and the earlier title deeds showed that the vendors owned this quarry land. But the conveyance did not state expressly that the benefit of the right of way was intended to be limited to this land. Nevertheless the Court of Appeal held that extrinsic evidence could be admitted to show that it was this quarry land which was intended to be benefited. A valid easement appurtenant to this quarry had therefore been created. Upjohn L.J. said (giving the judgment of the court)[46]: "In our judgment it is a question of the construction of the deed creating a right of way as to what is the dominant tenement for the benefit of which the right of way is granted and to which the right of way is appurtenant. . . . In construing the deed, the court is entitled to have evidence of all material facts at the time the execution of the deed, so as to place the court in the situation of the parties."

In *Thorpe* v. *Brumfitt*[47] the grant of a right of way "for all

---

[44] See Hallett, *Conveyancing Precedents* (1965), p. 216.
[45] [1963] 1 Q.B. 601 (C.A.).
[46] At p. 612.
[47] (1873) 8 Ch.App. 650 (C.A.).

purposes . . . between the piece of land hereinbefore conveyed and a street called the Tyrrels" was held to mean "for all purposes which make it necessary to pass between that piece of ground and the street."[48] On this interpretation, the benefit of the right of way was limited to the use of the dominant land and there was therefore sufficient annexation to the land conveyed.

It follows from the same general principle that the dominant owner cannot extend the use of an existing easement to serve some additional property which he may own or acquire.[49]

Identification of and annexation of burden to the servient land. The deed should identify the servient property intended to be burdened and the nature and extent of the burden. In the case, for example, of a right of way it should make clear the route of the way and the extent of user to be permitted—whether on foot only; or "with or without motor vehicles and horses and other animals of every respective description and whether laden or unladen to go pass and repass . . . "[50]; and so on. In *Woodman* v. *Pwllbach Colliery Co. Ltd.*[51] the defendants claimed that under a lease they obtained an easement to discharge coal dust from the land leased onto the lessor's adjoining land. This adjoining land was not identified at all in the lease. Swinfen Eady L.J. said[52] "There is no reference to any other land than the land coloured pink on the plan (the land leased). It may well be that the grantor has no other land. It is necessary for an easement that there should be a servient tenement that can be defined and pointed out. Here there is no reference to any such tenement."

Possibly today, provided the intention to create an easement was clear, the courts would allow extrinsic evidence of the circumstances at the time of the grant to identify the servient property and the user intended.

In addition to identifying it, the deed must show an intention to create a burden on the servient property and not just a licence binding the licensor personally. The precedent set out above satisfies these requirements.[53] It defines the route of the way and

---

[48] *Per* Mellish L.J. at p. 657. Note that in the precedent set out above the right granted is expressly limited to purposes "connected with the existing use" of the property, thus making the annexation clear.

[49] See *Bracewell* v. *Appleby* [1975] 1 All E.R. 993 (Graham J.); and see *Nickerson* v. *Barraclough* [1981] 2 All E.R. 369 (C.A.).

[50] See *Hallett* (n. 44, above), p. 220.

[51] (1914) 111 L.T. 169; affirmed in H.L., *sub nom. Pwllbach Colliery Co. Ltd.* v. *Woodman* [1915] A.C. 634.

[52] At p. 174.

[53] At p. 366, above.

the extent of user to be allowed; the use of the words "at all times hereafter" and the fact that the grant is in fee simple clearly indicate an intention to burden the servient land and not just create a licence.

By way of contrast the following is a form of wording which could be used to create a licence to convey water through pipes on the servient property[54]:

" . . . the said A to the intent that the liberty and the licence hereby granted may for the time being until revoked be annexed to Y house aforesaid, hereby grants unto the said B full and free liberty and licence at all times hereafter, until the same shall be revoked under the provision in that behalf hereinafter contained, to take and convey water by means of any pipes and tanks already laid down . . . from the said X estate to the use of Y house aforesaid."

There must be a capable grantor and grantee. This follows from the principle that easements lie in grant and applies to implied grant and prescription as well as express grant. There can be no easement if for any reason the grantor lacks the capacity to create the easement; or if the grantee lacks the capacity to receive an easement.

This principle applies to the creation of all property interests, not just easements. A person can neither create a property interest nor have one created in his favour if he lacks the necessary legal capacity. In *Paine Co. Ltd.* v. *St. Neots Gas and Coke Co.*[55] the plaintiffs had a malt extract business which required a supply of pure water. Four of the commoners of the adjoining land purported to grant them an easement for a term of years to sink a well and take water. The well was subsequently polluted by ammonia from the defendant's works. It was held that the common rights did not include the right to take water far less to grant an easement to others to take it: and that in any case the four did not have power to bind the other commoners. Therefore, the grantors had no capacity and there could be no easement. Consequently the plaintiffs had no title to sue the defendants.

For the same reason, the grantee must have capacity. It is said, for example, that a fluctuating body of persons cannot acquire an easement; because a deed of grant can only be made in favour of

---

[54] Key and Elphinstone, *Precedents* (15th ed.), Vol. 1, p. 1260.
[55] [1939] 3 All E.R. 812 (Goddard L.J.).

recognised legal persons—that is, either specified individuals or corporations.[56]

Need for a deed: Legal and equitable easements. A legal easement can only be created if (a) it is for an interest equivalent to a fee simple absolute in possession or a term of years absolute.[57] In addition (b) it must be created by deed, implied into a deed or by prescription (or statute).[58] Any easement which fails to satisfy these requirements can only be an equitable easement; if, for example, an easement is granted for life or for an indefinite period until a specified notice is given; or if there is a specifically enforceable contract to create a legal easement but no deed. In *E. R. Ives Investment* v. *High*,[59] there was such a contract.[60] The defendant bought a bombed site on which to build a house. W. bought the adjoining site and started to build a block of flats. Unfortunately, his foundations were just over the boundary—a trespass against the defendant. The parties met and an amicable solution was reached. The foundations would be allowed to stay and in return W. agreed to give the defendant a right of way through the yard at the back of the flats. Subsequently, the flats were sold to a purchaser who made no objection when the defendant built a garage on his own land the access of which was through the yard. And later the purchaser persuaded the defendant to resurface the yard he himself paying one-fifth of the cost. In 1962 the purchaser sold the flats to the plaintiffs who had notice of the agreement. Two of their Lordships considered that there was an enforceable contract to create an easement which was in itself effective as a valid equitable easement.[61]

The term equitable easement has been defined, by the Law of Property Act 1925, s.2(3)(iii), to mean "Any easement, liberty or privilege over or affecting land created or arising after the commencement of this Act and being merely an equitable interest."

It has been suggested that this definition may include not only

---

[56] But a fluctuating body can have a customary right which does not depend on a grant. See below, p. 393.

[57] L.P.A. 1925, s.1(2)(*a*).

[58] L.P.A. 1925, s.52. An assent can be used when this is allowed as an alternative to a deed, *e.g.* by a personal representative.

[59] [1967] 2 Q.B. 379 (C.A.).

[60] But Lord Denning M.R. did not agree; see next note.

[61] *Ibid., per* Danckwerts L.J., at p. 399; *per* Winn L.J., at p. 403. Denning L.J. held, somewhat surprisingly, that it was not because "The right of Mr. High to cross this yard was not a right such as could ever have been created or conveyed at law" (at p. 396).

those rights which are equitable because they fail to satisfy the two requirements mentioned above, but also certain rights which are not capable of being legal easements.[62]

Principle 5.   Implied grant (not including implied reservation)

Where a landowner conveys part of his land the court may, in the absence of express grant, be prepared to imply the grant of an eaesment over the land retained in favour of the purchaser.

In recognising an implied easement the courts are giving effect to the intention of the parties as shown by the circumstances surrounding the transaction.

Implied easements can be classified as follows[63]:
(1) Rights of way of necessity.
(2) Ancillary easements.
(3) Quasi-easements within the rule in *Wheeldon* v. *Burrows*.
(4) Easements implied in other special circumstances.
(5) Easements arising under section 62 of the Law of Property Act 1925.

In addition a right in the nature of an easement may arise from the obligation of a grantor not to derogate from his grant.

Explanation

Implied easements have been classified in various ways. But they are all governed by the same general principle which is that by looking at the circumstances surrounding the transaction the courts are able to gather the unexpressed intention of the parties and make it express. In the oft-quoted words of Lord Parker in *Pwllbach Colliery Co.* v. *Woodman*[64]: "The law will readily imply the grant or reservation of such easements as may be necessary to give effect to the common intention of the parties to a grant of real property, with reference to the manner or purposes in and for which the land granted or some land retained by the grantor is to be used."

In *Lyttelton Times Co. Ltd.* v. *Warners Ltd.*[65] Lord Loreburn said[66]: "When it is a question of what shall be implied from the contract, it is proper to ascertain what in fact was the purpose, or what were the purposes, to which both intended the land to be put,

---

[62] See below, p. 522. And see (1969) 33 Conv. (N.S.) 135 (Paul Jackson).
[63] There is no generally agreed classification.
[64] [1915] A.C. 634 (H.L.).
[65] [1907] A.C. 476 (P.C.).
[66] *Ibid.*, at p. 481.

and, having found that, both should be held to all that was implied in this common intention."

In *Sovmots Investments Ltd.* v. *Secretary of State for the Environment*[67] which concerned the notorious Centre Point tower block in London, the local authority made a compulsory purchase order on a group of flats which formed part of the whole tower complex, since they had been kept empty for a long time. The flats could only be used if they had the benefit of easements of access and services over the rest of the complex. The House of Lords held that under the relevant legislation, a local authority had no power to compulsorily acquire such new (as opposed to already existing) ancillary rights. They held, further, that they did not pass by implied grant since "There is no common intention between an acquiring authority and the party whose property is compulsorily taken from him and the very basis of implied grants of easements is accordingly absent."[68]

Rights of way of necessity. In *Bolton* v. *Bolton*[69] Fry J. said: "Where a man grants a close which is land locked, and is also the owner of an adjoining close, the grantee shall have a right of way over the adjoining close, as incident to the grant, for otherwise the grantee cannot have any benefit from the grant."

In *Nickerson* v. *Barraclough*[70] it was held at first instance that any attempt in a conveyance to exclude a right of way of necessity would be void as being against public policy on the grounds that land should not be rendered unuseable.

Ancillary easements. Where a property interest is granted expressly the courts will be prepared to imply the grant of any incidental easements necessary to its reasonable enjoyment. It is, as it were, no good giving the horse a right to drink if he cannot get

---

[67] [1977] 2 All E.R. 385 (H.L.).

[68] *Per* Lord Edmund-Davies, at p. 397. But this is to apply private law principles to what is in effect a field of public law; and at the same time to fail to develop appropriate principles for the interpretation and application of such law. See above, p. 88. Compare the judicial attitude to the Housing Act 1961, s.32; see J. I. Reynolds, "Statutory Covenants of Fitness and Repair," (1974) 37 M.L.R. 377. Note that under the Local Government (Miscellaneous Provisions) Act 1976, s.13, local authorities are given compulsory purchase powers to acquire new rights over land.

[69] [1949] 2 All E.R. 908.

[70] [1979] 3 All E.R. 312. See P. Jackson, (1981) 34 C.L.P. 133. The decision of Megarry V.-C. was reversed in the Court of Appeal [1981] 2 All E.R. 369, on the grounds, *inter alia*, that the land in question was not landlocked at the time of conveyance; therefore no way of necessity could be implied, and so the question of public policy did not arise.

to the water. In *White* v. *Taylor (No. 2)*[71] in which the plaintiffs successfully claimed that they had common sheepgrazing rights over the defendant's downs, the court held that they were entitled to an ancillary right to go onto the downland to water the sheep. Buckley J. said[72]: "Anyone having a right to depasture sheep on the down must also incidentally be entitled to go onto the down, either himself, or by his servants or agents—for instance by his shepherd—to do anything necessary for the proper care and management of his sheep; but this does not mean that an owner of sheep rights can drive anywhere on the downs in a vehicle."

Quasi-easements within the rule in Wheeldon v. Burrows.[73] The rule is as follows: Where a landowner contracts to sell or lease part of his land, any quasi-easements which he has enjoyed over the land retained for the benefit of the land sold may become proper easements in favour of the purchaser. For the rule to operate the following requirements must be satisfied[74]:

(a) The landowner must sell or lease the quasi-dominant land.

(b) The right must be continuous and apparent.

(c) It must be reasonably necessary for the enjoyment of the land sold.

(d) It must be in use at the time of disposition.

The principle behind this rule is the same as the principle behind all implied grants—the intention of the parties to be inferred from the circumstances. In *Borman* v. *Griffith*,[75] Maugham J. said (dealing with a right of way): "But the authorities are sufficient to show that a grantor of property, in circumstances where an obvious, *i.e.* visible and made road, is necessary for the reasonable enjoyment of the property by the grantee, must be taken prima facie to have intended to grant a right to use it."[76] If a prospective purchaser is viewing the property and sees that some right is clearly being enjoyed with it over the vendor's neighbouring land, it is reasonable to assume that this right is included in the sale.

"Continuous and apparent" seems to mean that there is some feature which is permanently present and which, on inspection of the land, will indicate the existence of the quasi-easement. In

---

[71] [1968] 2 W.L.R. 1402 (Buckley J.). And see *Liverpool City Council* v. *Irwin* [1977] A.C. 239 (H.L.).

[72] *Ibid.*, at p. 199.

[73] (1879) 12 Ch.D. 31.

[74] As to requirements to be satisfied, and particularly as to whether (b) and (c) are alternative requirements, see Gale, *Easements* (14th ed.), p. 93.

[75] [1930] 1 Ch. 493.

[76] *Ibid.*, at p. 499.

Ward v. *Kirkland*[77] the plaintiff was claiming the right to go onto the defendant's property to maintain the wall of his cottage which was on the boundary. This was the only means of maintaining the wall. He claimed that a grant could be implied into the 1928 conveyance by which the common owner of the cottage and the defendant's farm had sold off the cottage to the plaintiff's predecessor in title. Ungoed-Thomas J. held that there was "no continuous and apparent feature designed or appropriate for the exercise of the easement on the servient property."[78]

In *Borman* v. *Griffith*,[79] on the other hand, the owner of a private park containing two residences made an agreement under hand to lease one of them to the plaintiff for seven years. A drive went from the public road through the park to the plaintiff's premises and then on to the other premises. In 1926 the defendant, who had subsequently taken a lease of the park and other premises, obstructed the plaintiff's use of the drive. It was held that the right to use the drive passed under *Wheeldon* v. *Burrows*. The driveway was a feature permanently there and clearly suggesting that it was in use as a means of access from the road across the servient property (the park) to the property which was being leased.[80]

Other continuous and apparent features would be a window on the quasi-dominant property; and the support given by a building on the quasi-servient property to one on the quasi-dominant property.

Even if the right is continuous and apparent, it will not pass if it is not reasonably necessary to the enjoyment of the land purchased. In *Goldberg* v. *Edwards*[81] the defendant leased an annexe at the rear of her house to the plaintiffs. This annexe could be reached either by an outside passage or by a covered passage entered through the house. It was held that the passage through the house was not necessary for the reasonable enjoyment of the annexe.[82]

Other special circumstances. There are other cases which do not fall conveniently into any particular category, in which the courts have found sufficient evidence of intention to justify the

---

[77] [1967] Ch. 194.
[78] *Ibid.*, at p. 226.
[79] Above, n. 75.
[80] s.62, of the L.P.A. 1925, did not operate to create an easement in the plaintiff's favour because there had been no "conveyance" see below, p. 375.
[81] [1950] Ch. 247 (C.A.).
[82] But the plaintiff succeeded under the L.P.A. 1925, s.62; below, p. 375.

creation of an implied easement. *Lyttelton Times Co. Ltd.* v.
Warners Ltd.[83] is an example. The appellants and respondents
agreed that the appellants should rebuild their premises on the
understanding that they were to have a printing works on the
ground floor whilst the respondents would lease the upper floors as
extra bedrooms for their adjoining hotel. After this agreement had
been implemented it was held that the respondents could not
complain of excessive noise from the printing machinery even if it
did constitute a nuisance;[84]; the appellants were merely using the
premises for the purpose contemplated by both parties to the
transaction. To stop them would be to frustrate that purpose.

Section 62 (1) of the Law of Property Act 1925. This provides:

> "A conveyance of land shall be deemed to include and shall
> by virtue of this Act operate to convey, with the land, all
> buildings, erections, fixtures, commons, hedges, ditches,
> fences, ways, waters, watercourses, liberties, privileges,
> easements, rights, and advantages whatsoever, appertaining
> or reputed to appertain to the land, or any part thereof, or, at
> the time of the conveyance, demised, occupied, or enjoyed
> with, or reputed or known as part or parcel of or appurtenant
> to the land or any part thereof."

In *Ward* v. *Kirkland*,[85] the facts of which have already been
given, the plaintiff was held to be entitled to a right of entry (as an
easement) on to the defendant's land to repair the boundary wall
of his cottage. The right was in fact being enjoyed at the time of
the conveyance by the common owner to the plaintiff's predecessor in title in 1928. It therefore passed with the conveyance thus
being converted into a proper easement.

Section 62 overlaps the rule in *Wheeldon* v. *Burrows*. Suppose
that V owns Whiteacre and Blackacre and that a house on
Whiteacre occupied by P as a tenant enjoys light from Blackacre.
V sells Whiteacre to P. The rule in *Wheeldon* v. *Burrows* will apply
entitling the purchaser, P, to an easement of light. So will section
62. Under this section the conveyance of Whiteacre will automatically include an easement of light in favour of the purchaser.[86]

The following points should be noted about the doctrine of
Wheeldon v. *Burrows* and section 62:

---

[83] [1907] A.C. 476 (P.C.). Note that this was in fact a case of an implied
reservation.
[84] The right to commit a nuisance being a possible easement.
[85] [1967] Ch. 194 (Ungoed-Thomas J.); above, p. 374.
[86] Compare *Wright* v. *Macadam* [1949] 2 K.B. 744.

(a) Both operate to create *new* third party rights in favour of a purchaser. There is an important distinction between:

(i) Those existing third party rights which are already appurtenant to the property at the time of sale. If these are capable of running they will pass to a purchaser automatically at the time of sale.

(ii) Those third party rights which are *created* in the purchaser's favour at the time of sale either expressly, impliedly, or under section 62. To continue the above illustration. P now holds Whiteacre together with the benefit of an easement of light over Blackacre. He then sells Whiteacre to Q. This right of light will pass automatically to Q without reference to *Wheeldon* v. *Burrows* or section 62.[87]

(b) Section 62 only applies to a conveyance. *Wheeldon* v. *Burrows* applies to a contract as well as a grant by conveyance. In *Borman* v. *Griffith*[88] there was an agreement under hand to lease the premises to the plaintiff for seven years but no lease was executed—that is there was an equitable lease but no conveyance as defined by section 205 (1) (ii) of the Law of Property Act 1925. He was therefore not able to rely on section 62; but he was able to claim an easement under *Wheeldon* v. *Burrows*.

This distinction may be important on the sale of land. In the normal sale of land transaction there is a contract (which creates the binding obligations) followed subsequently by a conveyance which actually transfers the legal ownership.[89] It is the contract which determines what the purchaser is entitled to have conveyed to him by the conveyance. If, for example, the contract expressly excludes all quasi-easements then the vendor will be entitled to insist on them being expressly excluded in the conveyance. If they are not and section 62 operates to create easements in the purchaser's favour, he will be getting more than he is entitled to under the contract and the vendor will be entitled to ask the court to rectify[90] the conveyance to make it conform to the terms of the contract.

(c) Section 62 is much wider in its operation in that:

(i) It is not confined to easements.

---

[87] But see *Anderson* v. *Bostock* [1976] 1 All E.R. 560 (Blackett-Ord. V.-C.), and *Re Yateley Common* [1977] 1 All E.R. 505 (Foster J.), suggesting that s.62 is relied on to pass the benefit of existing rights.

[88] See above, n. 75.

[89] See below, p. 555.

[90] But rectification is an equitable discretionary remedy. The vendor is clearly advised to make sure that the conveyance is confined to the terms of the contract.

(ii) The only requirement is that the right must have been enjoyed at the time of conveyance.[91] There is no need for it to have been continuous and apparent or reasonably necessary for the enjoyment of the land granted. Thus, in *Goldberg* v. *Edwards*,[92] the plaintiff failed under *Wheeldon* v. *Burrows* but succeeded under section 62. Similarly, in *Ward* v. *Kirkland*[93] the right of entry was not continuous and apparent but it was being enjoyed and so passed by the conveyance under section 62.

(d) Section 62 is narrower in one respect at least. For it to operate there must have been separate occupation of the two properties[94]; *Wheeldon* v. *Burrows* can apply even where the vendor has been in actual occupation of both quasi-dominant and quasi-servient properties.

Derogation from grant. There is a general principle that a grantor must not derogate from his grant; that is he must not do anything to interfere with the purpose for which the grant was made. The doctrine of implied easements is sometimes said to be a branch of this principle. The importance in the present context is that it goes beyond the doctrine of implied easements. It may impose on the grantor an obligation which is not an easement but which nevertheless runs with the grantor's land as a property interest. It has been said that,[95] " . . . though possibly there may not be known to the law any easement of light for special purposes,[96] still the lease of a building to be used for a special purpose requiring an extraordinary amount of light, might well be held to preclude the grantor from diminishing the light passing to the grantee's windows. . . . "

In *Cable* v. *Bryant*[97] the owner of a stable and adjoining yard let the stable which enjoyed light and ventilation through two

---

[91] See, e.g. *Nickerson* v. *Barrachough* [1981] 2 All E.R. 369 (C.A.). In *Re Yateley Common* (above), Foster J. thought there was no need for a right of common to be in actual use at the time of conveyance; but this was a case of an already existing right.

[92] Above, p. 374. As to the nature of the right created in this case see *Gale* (above, n. 74), at p. 127.

[93] Above, p. 374.

[94] But see *Gale* (above, n. 74), p. 125, and (1966) 30 *Conveyancer* 340 *et seq.* And see *Sovmots Investments Ltd.* v. *Sec. of State for Environment* [1977] 2 All E.R. 381 (H.L.). Compare P. Smith, [1978] Conv. 449.

[95] *Browne* v. *Flower* [1911] 1 Ch. 219, at p. 226 *per* Parker J.

[96] On this point, see *Allen* v. *Greenwood* [1979] 1 All E.R. 819 (C.A.).

[97] [1908] 1 Ch. 259 (Neville J.). Neville J. did not decide the point but possibly an easement could not have been implied because the servient property was in the possession of a tenant at the time of the grant; see *Gale* (above, n. 74), at p. 91.

windows looking onto the yard. Subsequently he sold the yard and the purchaser erected a hoarding which blocked the windows. It was held that, although possibly there was no easement, the owner could not derogate from his grant by doing something in the yard which interfered with the use of the building as a stable; and that this obligation bound the purchaser of the yard.

Principle 6.   Implied reservation *

If a grantor wishes to reserve any easement over the land granted he must normally do so expressly.

The courts will not generally be prepared to imply the reservation of an easement in favour of the grantor. They will only do so in the case of easements of necessity and support and in other cases where there is the clearest evidence that the grantee consented to the reservation.

Explanation

It is the vendor who drafts the agreement and decides what he wants to sell and what he wants to reserve. The purchaser is entitled to rely on the agreement as showing exactly what the vendor is offering. If the vendor wishes to reserve rights over the property sold he must make this clear in the agreement. There are, of course, exceptions.

Easements of necessity.   If a right of way over the land sold is essential to the continued use of the land retained the courts will imply the necessary reservation.

The reservation of a right of support for a building on the land retained by a building on the land sold will also be implied by the courts.

In any other case, the circumstances must "be such as to raise a necessary inference that the common intention of the parties must have been to reserve some easement to the grantor, or such as to preclude the grantee from denying the right consistently with good faith."[98]

In contrast to *Wheeldon* v. *Burrows* previous user is not enough—even if it was with the consent of the grantee. The court must be "able to draw the necessary inference from the evidence that the grantee consented to the user continuing after the grant." In *Re Webb's Lease, Sandom* v. *Webb*,[99] the landlord let the first

---

[98] *Re Webb's Lease* [1951] Ch. 808 (C.A.), at p. 823 *per* Jenkins L.J.
[99] Above, n. 98.

and second floors of his premises to the defendant in 1939. In 1949 he granted the defendant a new lease for 22 years. At the time of the 1939 lease and from then on to the grant of the new lease in 1949, the landlord was using the outside walls of the first and second floors to advertise the butcher's business which he was carrying on on the ground floor, and also to advertise "a certain brand of matches."

During the years 1939 to 1949 the defendant was of course aware of the advertisements and had not raised any objection. After the grant of the 1949 lease he did object and required the removal of the advertisements. It was held that the reservation of an easement to affix the advertisements could not be implied. The facts did not "raise a necessary inference of an intention common to both parties at the date of the 1949 lease that the landlord should have reserved to him the right to maintain these advertisements throughout the 21 years' term thereby granted."[1]

Principle 7. Prescription (or presumed grant): nature and requirements

Even in the absence of proof of any express or implied grant, a person may be able to claim an easement by prescription over his neighbour's land provided he can prove:

(1) That the essential requirements of a valid easement are present.

(2) That he has been in actual enjoyment of the right claimed for a sufficient length of time.

(3) That his enjoyment has been:

    (a) as of right—that is, *nec vi, nec clam, nec precario*;

    (b) continuous;

    (c) in fee simple.

Only a legal fee simple easement can be acquired by prescription.

Explanation

Basis of prescription. There is a presumption in English law that the actual enjoyment of property derives from a lawful origin.[2] "Where there has been long continued possession in assertion of a right, it is a well settled principle of English law, that

---

[1] *Ibid., per* Jenkins L.J., at p. 829.
[2] See further below, p. 503 *et seq.*

the right should be presumed to have had a legal origin if such a
legal origin was possible."[3]

This chapter is only concerned with the application of this
principle to easements. To illustrate the sort of situation that may
arise[4]: Jack is in the habit of using a drive across his neighbour's
land to get to the main road from his garage. The neighbour's land
changes hands and the purchaser tries to stop Jack's user suing him
in trespass. What is the position? Jack's only possible defence is
that he has an easement of way. He *could* have such an easement;
all the essential requirements of a valid easement are present. But
he cannot produce any express grant in favour of his property. If
there ever was one it has been lost. And there has been no
conveyance in the past splitting up the ownership of the two
properties into which the grant of an easement could be implied.
There is no evidence of how the user started. All that Jack can
prove is that he has been using the way regularly for the last 10
years, his father for the 30 years before that, and that the
neighbouring owner never complained or objected to the user.
Prescription is simply legal acceptance of the argument that such
long unopposed enjoyment is in itself sufficient reason for
recognising a right.

The fiction of the presumed grant. Prescription is then the
legalisation of long uninterrupted enjoyment. But in developing
this doctrine the courts were faced with a difficulty, a principle of
their own creation, the principle that an easement can only be
created by deed of grant. The courts could not ignore their own
rule. They therefore resorted to a legal fiction. They presume that
there was a grant creating the alleged easement but that for some
reason it cannot now be produced. And they simply do not allow
the defendant to prove that there never was any grant.[5]

The requirements of a valid easement must be present. Prescription does no more than avoid the need to produce the deed of
grant. The requirements essential to the existence of any easement
must still be present.[6]

Enjoyment for sufficient length of time. The length of enjoyment which must be shown depends on which of the three types of

---

[3] *Per* Lord Herschell, *Philipps* v. *Halliday* [1891] A.C. 228, at p. 231.
[4] See *Healey* v. *Hawkins* [1968] 1 W.L.R. 1967 for a typical set of facts.
[5] As to whether the defendant to the claim will be allowed to challenge whether
there ever was a grant, see *Dalton* v. *Angus* (1877–1881) 3 Q.B.D. 85; 4 Q.B.D.
162; 6 App.Cas. 740; and *Gale* (above, n. 74), at p. 138. And see below, p. 384.
[6] The requirements set out in Principle 2, above, p. 361.

prescription is being claimed. This is dealt with in the next Principle. But, in general, the claimant will have to show at least 20 years' enjoyment by himself or his predecessors in title.

Requirements of prescription. The enjoyment must satisfy certain requirements.

(a) *User as of right; nec vi, nec clam, nec precario.* I can hardly expect to cross my neighbour's land secretly each night for 20 years in order to poach rabbits from his wood and then, as it were, pop up one morning and claim a right of way by prescription. Prescription is only recognised where the dominant owner has behaved throughout the period as if he had an easement; and where the servient owner, having had every opportuniy to challenge this assertion of right, has tacitly accepted it. Therefore the dominant owner's user must have been as of right, that is, *nec vi, nec clam, nec precario* (not by force, not secretly, and not under licence from the servient owner).

For example, in *Liverpool Corporation* v. *Coghill (H.) & Son,*[7] the plaintiffs were the sanitary authority for Liverpool; in conjunction with the disposal of sewage they ran a sewage farm where they grew "the usual sewage farm crops," such as rye, grass, turnips, mangolds, etc. For more than 20 years the defendants had discharged waste liquid containing borax from their borax works into the plaintiffs' sewers and this "noxious effluent had injuriously affected their farm and the crops thereon."[8] The defendants claimed a prescriptive right to discharge into the sewer. But it was held that the discharge had been secret and unknown to the plaintiffs[9] and therefore did not entitle them to an easement.[10]

Again, if the enjoyment is under licence from the servient owner there can be no easement. In *Gardner* v. *Hodgson's Kingston Brewery Co.*[11] for more than 40 years without interruption the owner of a house used a cartway from his stables through the yard of an adjoining inn to the public road, paying 15 shillings (75 pence) each year to the owner of the inn-yard for permission to use it. His enjoyment derived from the licence, it was therefore not as of right and could not give rise to an easement. Of course, a person with a licence does have a right; but it is a different right from an

---

[7] [1918] 1 Ch. 307, Eve J.
[8] *Ibid.* headnote.
[9] At least until 1908 which meant that the user had been known to the plaintiff for less than 20 years—not long enough to create a prescriptive easement.
[10] See also, *Diment* v. *N.H. Foot Ltd.* [1974] 2 All E.R. 785 (Pennycuick V.-C.), and *Allen* v. *Greenwood* [1979] 1 All E.R. 819 (C.A.).
[11] [1903] A.C. 229 (H.L.).

easement. And the court cannot presume that the right has been exercised as an easement when there is positive evidence that it has been enjoyed only as a licence.[12]

(b) *The user must have been continuous.* This means that the right must have been in regular use for the full period. The actual frequency of the use required must depend on the nature of the easement claimed. " . . . It cannot be necessary to prove an actual continuous user of the way day and night for 20 years without cessation whatever."[13] In *Hollins* v. *Verney*,[14] decided on section 2 of the Prescription Act 1832 which requires actual enjoyment as of right without a break (meaning the same as "continuous") for 20 years, the defendant was claiming an easement of way to cart timber cut from his wood across the plaintiff's land. It was shown that the last cutting was the year before the action, the cutting before that 12 years earlier, and the one before that 12 years earlier again. It was held that this user "confined to rare occasions" was not continuous enough to come within section 2.

(c) *The user must be in fee simple.* This means that it must be:
    (i) by or on behalf of the fee simple owner of the dominant property;
    (ii) against the fee simple owner of the servient property.

An easement, like any other third party right, can be created expressly in fee simple, for a term of years, or any other recognised estate. But only a legal fee simple easement can be acquired by prescription.[15] The person enjoying the user may well only be a tenant of the dominant property. But his enjoyment will be deemed to be on behalf of his landlord. This means that, if an easement is acquired, it will attach to the fee simple in the dominant property, not just to his leasehold interest; and will continue even after expiry of his lease.

Similarly, the enjoyment must be against the fee simple owner of the servient property. Prescription may continue even while the servient property is subject to a tenancy but the enjoyment, to be effective, must be against the servient landlord in the sense that he knows of the user and is in a position to resist it. If an easement is then acquired it will be a burden on the landlord's fee simple and continue after expiry of the lease of the servient property. In *Pugh*

---

[12] Consider *Davis* v. *Whitby* [1974] 1 All E.R. 806 (C.A.), (change of route of way by agreement during period of prescription).
[13] *Per* Lindley L.J. in *Hollins* v. *Verney* (1884) 13 Q.B.D. 304, at pp. 307, 308.
[14] See n. 13, above.
[15] For reasons given for the rule, see *Gale* (above, n. 74), at p. 161.

v. *Savage*[16] the servient property had been subject to a tenancy between about 1940 and 1950. Cross L.J. said[17]: "If a tenancy is in existence at the beginning of a period of user, it may well be unreasonable to imply a lost grant by the owner at the beginning of the user. He might not have been able to stop the user, even if he knew about it. If, on the other hand, you get a period of user against an owner or owners without any evidence that they did not know about it when they were in possession, and then afterwards the grant of a tenancy, though undoubtedly such a tenancy during the period of user is a matter to be considered, it would be quite wrong to hold that it is a fatal objection to presuming a grant or to a claim under the Prescription Act 1832."[18]

Where the fee simple ownership of both properties is in the same person, there cannot be prescription (even if one or both properties are let to separate tenants) for this would involve the fee simple owner prescribing against himself.

Where a claim is made under the Prescription Act 1932, the requirements that have just been discussed are subject to some modifications.[19]

Principle 8.   Prescription: The three methods

There are three methods of prescription:
(1) Prescription at common law.
(2) Prescription under the doctrine of lost modern grant.
(3) Prescription under the Prescription Act 1832.

A claimant may be able to establish his claim under any one or more of these methods.

The main distinction between the three lies in period of enjoyment which must be shown to establish the claim.

Explanation

Prescription at common law. This refers to the method of prescription first recognised by the courts. The claimant must in

---

[16] [1970] 2 Q.B. 373 (C.A.).
[17] *Ibid.* at p. 383.
[18] It is arguable that a claim to prescription based on 40 years (60 years in the case of profits) under the Prescription Act 1832 does not require the presumption of a grant; and that therefore the ability of the fee simple owner to resist is not relevant. But this view is not supported by *Davies* v. *Du Paver* [1953] 1 Q.B. 184 (C.A.); see Megarry and Wade, *Law of Real Property* (4th ed.), p. 860. (In *Pugh* v. *Savage*, above, the claim was based on the shorter, 20-year period under the Act). See also *Diment* v. *N.H. Foot Ltd.* [1974] 2 All E.R. 785 (Pennycuick V.-C.).
[19] See below, p. 385 *et seq.*

principle show that his enjoyment, in accordance with the prescription requirements, has continued by him and his predecessors in title since before 1189.[20] This would be impossible in virtually every case. And so if the claimant can show enjoyment for a long time—generally at least 20 years—the court will presume that it has continued since 1189. But the claim can be defeated by showing that the easement could not have existed at any time since 1189; for example if it is shown that there was unity of ownership of the two properties; or if it is shown that a building to which a right of light is claimed was not built.

Lost modern grant.[21]   In the case of common law prescription the court presumes that the grant was made before 1189. The difficulties to which this gives rise have just been mentioned. In the case of lost modern grant the court avoids these difficulties by presuming that the grant was made in modern times—that is just before the relevant period of enjoyment began—but that it has been lost.

Generally, 20 years' enjoyment will be sufficient. The enjoyment during this period must satisfy the prescription requirements. But the claim cannot be defeated by anything which happened before this period, that is, since before the presumed grant.

Thus, suppose that B the owner of Blackacre claims a right of way over Whiteacre on the basis of 30 years' enjoyment. Proof that there was unity of ownership in 1900 will defeat a claim based on common law prescription but not if it is based on lost modern grant. Proof that there was unity of ownership five years ago would defeat the claim under both heads.

The claimant does not have to produce the presumed grant— since it is irrebuttably presumed to have been lost—but he will be defeated if it can be shown that no valid grant could have been made during the relevant period. In *Neaverson* v. *Peterborough Rural Council*[22] under an Inclosure Act of 1812, the council had statutory authority to let the verges of certain roads for the grazing of sheep. Since 1846 they had let them for the grazing of cattle and horses as well. On complaint by the plaintiff (whose costs of performing his liability to maintain the verges was increased by this additional user), it was claimed that the council had acquired the right to pasture horses and cattle, which they could therefore let, by prescription. It was held that by virtue of the provisions of

[20] See *Gale on Easements*, (above, n. 74), for a reason for this rule.
[21] Like common law prescription, this method was also developed by the common law courts.
[22] [1902] 1 Ch. 557 (C.A.).

the Act such a grant could not properly have been made to the council by the owners of the soil of the road. A grant could not therefore be presumed.[23]

The Prescription Act 1832: the statutory periods. The Act divides easements into two categories.

(a) *Easements other than easements of light*.[24] The Act lays down alternative periods of enjoyment for these easements, 20 years and 40 years. Enjoyment for the 20-year period which satisfies the common law prescription requirements will create a valid easement. As at common law the user must be *nec vi, nec clam* and *nec precario*; it must be continuous[25]; and in fee simple. Thus, for example, if oral consent is given at the beginning of the period it will defeat the claim. But the evidence may show that an oral consent has been withdrawn and, once that has happened, user becomes as of right and the statutory period can start to run.[26]

Enjoyment for the 40-year period will similarly give rise to an easement. And here again enjoyment must in general satisfy the prescription requirements. But the 40-year period has at least one advantage over the 20-year period. Oral consent given at the beginning of the period but not renewed, will defeat a claim based on the 20-year period but not one based on the 40-year period.

(b) *Easements of light*.[27] In this case all that is required is 20 years' "actual enjoyment"[28] of the light. Only consent in writing will defeat the claim. Oral consent, whether given at the beginning or during that period, will not defeat the claim.

Prescription Act 1832: General points

(a) The enjoyment must be for the period next before the start of the action in which the easement is claimed. This means that

---

[23] And see *Tehidy Minerals Ltd.* v. *Norman* [1971] 2 All E.R. 475 (C.A.).

[24] Prescription Act 1832, s.2.

[25] The wording of the Act is that it must have been "actually enjoyed by any person claiming right thereto without interruption for the full period of twenty years . . ." (s.2).

[26] See *Healey* v. *Hawkins* [1968] 1 W.L.R. 1967, at p. 1973: "In principle it seems to me that once permission has been given, the user must remain permissive and not be capable of ripening into a right save where the permission is oral and the user had continued for 40 or 60 years unless and until, having been given for a limited period only, it expires or, being general, it is revoked or there is a change in circumstances from which revocation may fairly be implied."

[27] Prescription Act 1832, s.3.

[28] Note Rights of Light Act 1959, as amended by Local Land Charges Act 1975, Sched. 1., under which the owner of the servient property can register notice instead of actually obstructing the light in order to prevent the easement arising by prescription. The notice is registrable as a local land charge.

there will be no proper easement under the Act until it has been confirmed by the courts in some action. Thus, however long the enjoyment has been, it will be no use if it is interrupted for a year or more during the relevant period immediately before the start of action in which it is claimed.

(b) Under the Act an interruption will only stop time running if it is "submitted to or acquiesced in" for one year.[29] Thus enjoyment which is interrupted during the 20th year may form the basis of a successful claim since the period of interruption can be added on so long as it has not continued for a full year.

Interruption means some hostile obstruction. Whether or not the dominant owner has acquiesced in the obstruction is a question of fact. In one case[30] where the dominant owner protested when a fence barring the way was erected but not again during the ensuing year, nevertheless his protest was held to be effective and prevent acquiescence throughout the whole year.

(c) Any period during which the servient owner is an infant, lunatic or tenant for life is deducted from the shorter period.[31]

(d) Any period during which the servient property is held for a term of more than three years is deducted from the 40-year period[32] provided the reversioner brings his claim within three years of the determination of the term.[33]

The disabilities in (c) and (d) do not apply to an easement of light.

Principle 9.   Extinguishment of easements

Easements may be extinguished:

(1) By express or implied release by the dominant owner.

(2) By union of ownership of the dominant and servient properties.

(3) By statute.

Explanation

Release.   A release may be expess or implied. It will be implied where the dominant owner's actions show an intention to abandon the easement. For example, if a mill enjoying an easement of

---

[29] Prescription Act 1832, s.4.

[30] *Davies* v. *Du Paver* [1953] 1 Q.B. 184 (C.A.).

[31] Prescription Act 1832, s.7.

[32] *Ibid.* s.8. This section does not apply to profits.

[33] For a possible case where a claim based on the shorter period might succeed but one based on the longer period of enjoyment fail, see Megarry and Wade, *Law of Real Property* (4th ed.), p. 858.

water is demolished with no intention of replacing it, a release will be implied.

Mere non-user does not imply a release; nor does demolition of a building which enjoys an easement. There must be an intention to abandon. But both non-user and the demolition are evidence from which the intention to release may be inferred.[34]

Union of ownership. As already explained a man cannot have an easement over his own land. Where ownership of the dominant and servient properties become vested in the same person the easement will disappear automatically.

But of course, union of the fees simple will not destroy an easement so far as it is attached to a leasehold interest so long as the leasehold continues. Suppose that D owns the fee simple in Dominant Property to which belongs the benefit of an easement over neighbouring Servient Property held by S in fee simple; D leases Dominant Property to T who thereby as part of his leasehold interest becomes entitled to the benefit of the easement. Suppose that D then sells the fee to S. There is now unity of the fees simple in S. But in so far as the benefit of the easement is attached to the leasehold interest it will continue for the duration of the lease. On this happening, it will disappear altogether.[35]

---

[34] See *Tehidy Minerals Ltd.* v. *Norman* [1971] 2 All E.R. 475 (C.A.); *Re Yateley Common* [1977] 1 All E.R. 505 (Foster J.).
[35] See *Richardson* v. *Graham* [1908] 1 K.B. 39 (C.A.).

CHAPTER 16

PROFITS A PRENDRE

Principle 1. Definition and classification

A profit à prendre (a "profit" for short) is a right to remove something capable of ownership from the land of another person—either part of the soil itself or some part of the natural produce of the soil.[1]

Profits are either appurtenant to a dominant property or in gross.

They are also either several (sole profits) or profits in common (frequently referred to as "common rights" or just "commons").

Explanation

Definition. There does not seem to be any limit to what can be the subject-matter of a profit so long as it is something naturally part of the servient property and capable of ownership.

A list of some of the profits recognised by the courts gives an idea of the diversity; it also shows the ancient origins of this branch of the law, a revealing picture of the life of the mediaeval agricultural community which the common law (together with local customary and feudal law) was called on to regulate. The list includes the right to take acorns and beechmasts; brakes, fern, heather and litter; thorns; turf and peat; boughs and branches of growing trees; rushes; freshwater fish; stone, sand, shingle from the seashore; ice from a canal; also the right to pasture animals and shoot pheasants. But whilst of ancient origin, the subject is not dead. Some of the rights which can, and still do, exist as profits are still of great economic value.

In *White* v. *Taylor*[2] decided in 1968, the plaintiffs were claiming[3] between them the right to depasture nearly 2,000 sheep on Martin Down in Hampshire. It may no longer be the practice to feed pigs on acorns and beechmasts, but sheep are still fed on grass.

Profits may be appurtenant or in gross. A profit may be appurtenant (attached to and passing with a dominant property). If it is then its enjoyment must be limited to the needs of the dominant property. In *Lord Chesterfield* v. *Harris*[4] the defendants

---

[1] See Halsbury, *Laws of England* (4th ed.), Vol. 14, p. 115.
[2] [1968] 2 W.L.R. 1402 (Buckley J.).
[3] By prescription and express grant.
[4] [1908] 2 Ch. 397 (C.A.). And see *Anderson* v. *Bostock* [1976] 1 All E.R. 560.

were fishermen and freeholders in the hundreds or manors of Wormelow, Herefordshire. They were claiming as a profit appurtenant to their freeholds the right to catch salmon in the River Wye and sell it off. It was held that their claim must fail since it was not limited to the needs of the dominant properties.[5]

However, in contrast to easements and restrictive covenants, profits can exist in gross without any dominant property. If A has a profit in gross it belongs to him personally, not to any particular piece of land. He may not own any land. He can sell the profit and it will pass under his will or intestacy in the ordinary way.

But a profit in gross is of course an interest in land. The burden of it will be attached to and run with a servient property.

If a profit exists in gross, its enjoyment is not limited to the needs of any land and may validly authorise the taking of the subject-matter for sale. In *Lord Chesterfield* v. *Harris*[6] the fishermen had no chance of claiming a profit in gross. The only evidence which they could produce of the profit was evidence of 300 years' enjoyment by the successive owners of their freehold properties. The profit was either appurtenant to those properties or it did not exist at all.

Several profits and commons.   A several profit is one enjoyed by one person to the exclusion of others. A profit in common is a profit enjoyed by two or more persons in common over the land of a third.

It would seem that a profit is several (not in common) where it is enjoyed by one person together only with the servient owner— because the servient owner is merely exercising his natural rights of ownership and not a profit at all.[7]

In general, common rights are subject to the same rules as several profits; some special points about them are noted below.

Any profit will be either appurtenant or in gross; and at the same time it will be either several or a common. Thus, for example, the right to fish, the profit of piscary, in S's river may be appurtenant exclusively to neighbouring Blackacre—a several profit appurtenant. Or it may be appurtenant to the ownership of neighbouring Blackacre, Whiteacre and Greenacre—a profit

---

[5] See also *Davies* v. *Davies* [1975] Q.B. 172 (C.A.), where it was held that the appurtenant owner could licence someone else to exercise his common rights of grazing; but note that the licensee was enjoying the right in conjunction with his farming of the dominant holding.

[6] Above, n. 4.

[7] See *White* v. *Taylor (No. 2)* [1968] 2 W.L.R. 1402, at p. 1414. On the express grant of a profit there is a presumption that the owner of the land is intended to be excluded. A profit which does exclude the owner is called a right of sole vesture.

appurtenant in common (sometimes called a free fishery). Or, again, it may belong exclusively to John—a several profit in gross; and so on.

Principle 2.   Creation of profits

A profit may have been created in any one of the following ways[8]:
(1) Privilege.
(2) Statute.
(3) Express grant.
(4) Prescription.
Today, new profits can be created only in the last three ways.

Explanation

Privilege.   A profit in common (chiefly and possibly exclusively of pasture) arose by operation of law on the sub-infeudation of arable land by the lord to a freehold tenant. The grant automatically entitled the tenant to pasture his sheep on the manorial waste. Commons which have arisen in this way are generally known as commons appendant. Since sub-infeudation was abolished in 1290 such a common can only exist today if it was created before that date.

Statute, grant and prescription.   Subject to the points mentioned below,[9] the rules here are exactly the same as for easements.

Principle 3.   Commons

In general profits in common are subject to the same rules as several profits. However, the following points should be noted:
(1) Any common rights created before January 2, 1970, must have been registered in the register kept by local authorities, before that date. Otherwise it will no longer be exercisable.[10]

---

[8] There may also be a profit by custom in the case of land formerly copyhold. See Harris and Ryan, *Law Relating to Common Land* (1967), p. 52. And also a common *pur cause de vicinage*; see *Newman* v. *Bennett* [1980] 3 All E.R. 449 (Q.B.D.).

[9] p. 392.

[10] Commons Registration Act 1965, s.1(2); Commons Registration Act (Commencement) Order 1966, S.I. 1966 No. 971. See *Central Electricity Generating Board* v. *Clwyd County Council* [1976] 1 All E.R. 251 (Goff J.); *Re Turnworth Down* [1977] 2 All E.R. 105 (Oliver J.); and *Box Parish Council* v. *Lacey* [1979] 1 All E.R. 113 (C.A.).

Any common rights created after January 2, 1970, must be registered and will not be exercisable until registered.

(2) Common land is not publicly owned.[11] At common law the public have no rights in common land. It is private land subject to profits in common. However, under section 193 of the Law of Property Act 1925, and other statutes, the public may have a right of access to common land.

Explanation

The same benefits can exist either as several profits or as commons. But there are six usually found common rights. These are the common of pasture; of pannage; of estovers; turbary; common in the soil; and piscary.

The term "common" originally meant the right although today it usually refers to the land over which common rights are exercisable.

Common land is privately owned land, different from other privately owned land only in that it is subject to common rights.[12] At common law the public have no rights of access. But, in practice, since the owner is prevented from cultivating or enclosing it because of the common rights, it is likely to have the distinctive appearance generally associated with "common land." And in this situation there is not a lot to stop the public using it, even though technically they are trespassing.

In the past the ownership of the soil in common land was vested in the lord of the manor; today it is more likely to be in other private hands or owned by a local authority.

Registration. The Commons Registration Act 1965 introduced a system of registration of all common rights as defined by the Act. And it is now too late to register such rights created before January 2, 1970. There is no time limit for registering those created subsequently but they will not be enforceable until registered.

Booker v. *James*[13] illustrates one aspect of registration and a typical history of common rights. Prior to 1817 there was certain commonable and wasteland in Hampshire. And it appears that among other rights the commoners had the right to collect fuel on the common. In that year the land was inclosed under an inclosure

---

[11] See s.13 of the 1965 Act; and Commons Registration (New Land) Regulations 1969, S.I. 1969 No. 1843, Art. 3. Note the definition of common land in the 1965 Act, s.22(1).

[12] Tawney, *Agrarian Problems in the Sixteenth Century*, at p. 237 *et seq.*

[13] (1968) 19 P. & C.R. 525 (Pennycuick J.).

award, and an allotment of 40 acres was made to trustees to "produce fuel for the consumption of the poor inhabitants of the said tything of Hawley, who may be legally settled therein and may not respectively occupy messuages lands and tenements of more than the yearly value of six pounds." This was of course intended as some sort of compensation for the common rights which they were losing by the inclosure. In 1902 this allotment was vested in charity trustees as a charity. By the 1960s the land had become of great value and the trustees wished to sell it with the benefit of planning permission for housing development. The defendant, a member of the Cove Residents' Association which opposed the development, got the land provisionally registered under the 1965 Act. But registration cannot create a common which does not exist. It was held that the inclosure award had not left ownership of the land in the lord of the manor subject to the rights of the trustees to take fuel. What it had done was to take the ownership and vest it in the trustees of the charity. The land was therefore no longer common land and there were no common rights to register.[14]

Public access. Section 193 of the Law of Property Act 1925[15] gives members of the public a right of access "for air and recreation" to any metropolitan common or manorial waste or common within a borough or urban district; and "the lord of the manor or other person entitled to the soil of any land subject to rights of common" can extend this right of access to his own land.

Common rights may be legal. Under section 187 (2) of the Law of Property Act 1925, the fact that a profit is held in common with others does not prevent it from being legal.[16]

Principle 4. Comparison of profits and easements

Subject to the following points profits are subject to the same rules as easements:

(1) A profit is the right to take something from the land. An easement is the right to use or restrict the use of the land.

(2) An easement can only exist appurtenant to a dominant land. A profit may be appurtenant or in gross.

[14] As to duty of a purchaser's solicitor to search the commons' register see *G.L.K. Ladenbau (U.K.) Ltd.* v. *Crawley & De Reya* [1978] 1 W.L.R. 266 (Mocatta J.).
[15] Amended by Local Government Act 1972, s.189 and Sched. 30.
[16] But this means where there are several dominant properties enjoying the same profit; it should not be confused with the holding of a profit in undivided shares (*i.e.* tenancy in common) which cannot be legal, see Halsbury's *Statutes* (3rd ed.), Vol. 27, p. 605.

(3) The Prescription Act 1832 applies to profits as to easements except that:
    (a) the relevant periods are 30 years and 60 years.[17]
    (b) A profit in gross cannot be prescribed for either under the Act or otherwise.

(4) Profits in common are subject to registration under the Commons Registration Act 1965.

(5) Profits will not be implied under the rule in *Wheeldon* v. *Burrows* but section 62 of the Law of Property Act 1925 applies equally to both easements and profits.

Principle 5.   Local community rights

A local community cannot as such acquire easements or profits.

It may establish a customary right similar to an easement.

It cannot acquire a customary right similar to a profit. However, where there has been long enjoyment of such a right the court may recognise its validity by either,
    (a) presuming a grant from the Crown incorporating the community for the purpose of holding the profit; or
    (b) presuming a grant to an existing corporation in trust for the community.

Explanation

Easements and profits lie in grant and a grant can only be made in favour of legal persons, either individuals or incorporated bodies. A local community such as the inhabitants of a parish, or a village, or a community of local fishermen, is neither and cannot acquire easements or profits as such.

Customary rights. Where, however, such a community has been enjoying such a right with every appearance of legality for a long time, the court will seek to recognise its validity. In the case of rights similar to easements there is no problem. A customary right in favour of such a group can exist—it requires neither identified individuals nor a corporation; nor does it require dominant properties.

For the custom to be recognised by the courts, it must be ancient, certain, reasonable and continuous.[18]

Profits. The courts have decided that there can be no customary right for a fluctuating body of persons to take a profit[19]

---

[17] And s.8 does not apply to profits.
[18] See, *e.g.*, *New Windsor Corporation* v. *Mellor* [1975] 3 W.L.R. 25 (C.A.).
[19] *Gateward's Case* (1607) 6 Co.Rep. 59b.

because such a claim might exhaust the subject-matter and leave nothing for the owner of the soil. However, where there has been long and peaceful enjoyment, the court may discover a legal basis for it in one of two possible ways:

(a) Where the right claimed derives from the Crown, and those claiming it have always behaved as if they were a corporation, the court may feel able to presume a grant from the Crown (now lost of course) making the community a corporation for the purpose of holding and enjoying the right. The Crown has always had the power to grant a charter incorporating any body of persons.[20]

(b) Where the enjoyment of the right has been shared with an existing, undoubted, corporation, the court may presume a grant of the right to the corporation in trust for the local community.[21]

---

[20] See, *e.g. Re Free Fishermen of Faversham* (1887) 36 Ch.D. 329.
[21] See, *e.g. Goodman* v. *Mayor of Saltash* (1882) 7 App.Cas. 633.

CHAPTER 17

LICENCES[1]

Principle 1. Definition

A licence is a permission given by one person (the licensor) allowing another person (the licensee) to enter upon land.

It makes lawful what would otherwise be trespass or other tort but in general it gives the licensee only a personal right against the licensor, not any property interest in the land.

A licence may give exclusive possession of the licensor's land or some lesser benefit.

If certain conditions are satisfied it may have proprietary effect.

Explanation

Distinction between property and personal rights relating to land. The distinction between property rights such as easements and personal rights such as licences has already been mentioned.[1a] In general, there are a certain limited number of property interests that can exist in land, and if a person wishes to prove that he has a particular property interest he must satisfy the requirements appropriate to that interest. For example, if he wishes to establish his position as a tenant, he will have to convince the court that he has been allowed into exclusive possession in the capacity of tenant for one of the recognised leasehold interests.[2] If he is trying to claim an easement he will have to prove dominant and servient properties, etc.[3]

In addition he will have to prove that the interest claimed has been created in one of the recognised ways.

But all he has to prove to establish a licence is the permission of the landowner, nothing else.

The differences between licences and property interests can be summarised by contrasting licences with easements; but the same points distinguish licences from other property rights.

1. An easement can only exist if it satisfies the essential requirements of a valid easement and has been created in one of the permitted ways, and for one of the recognised estates.

---

[1] See I.J. Dawson and R.A. Pearce, *Licenses Relating to the Occupation or Use of Land* (1979).
[1a] See above, p. 355.
[2] For requirements necessary to create a tenancy see above, p. 91 *et seq.*
[3] Above, p. 361 *et seq.*

Mere permission, however informally given, is sufficient to create a licence.

2. An easement is a property right, a right *in rem*. As such:
  (a) the benefit will run with the dominant land;
  (b) the burden will run with the servient land;
  (c) it will be enforceable against any third party who interferes with it[4];
  (d) it cannot be revoked by the grantor.

A licence is a personal right, a right *in personam*. As such:
  (a) the benefit can generally be assigned[5] but it will not run automatically with any land;
  (b) the burden will not run and it cannot be assigned;
  (c) it cannot be enforced against a third party but only, if at all, against the licensor;
  (d) it may be possible for a licensor to revoke it.

Because of point (1) licences are wider in scope. Many uses of land which cannot exist as easements (or as any other property interest) can be sanctioned by licence. Indeed, the only real limit to what can be permitted by licence is legality.

Because of point (2) a licence is of course much more precarious than an easement. Suppose that a purchaser is buying a house that can only be reached along a private road. He will be unwise to buy without making sure that there is a sufficient easement of way and not just a licence from its owner to use the road.

If, again, a person is going to build a house on someone else's land, he will be wise to make sure that he has a proper interest—for example, a long lease or a contract to purchase—and not just an occupation licence.[6]

A licence may permit exclusive possession of the licensor's land, in which case it will resemble a lease[7]; or it may permit some use less than possession, in which case it will most probably resemble an easement. But the distinction is essentially the same in both cases.

For this reason, licences cannot be classified as either ownership or third party rights in accordance with the scheme of this book. In so far as they are mere personal rights they do not properly belong to either. It is however convenient to deal with them here. The more important question, considered below, is the extent to which, today, licences can acquire proprietary attributes.

---

[4] Provided, where necessary, it has been registered.

[5] See below, p. 411, as to the assignment of benefits of covenants; and see, generally, books on contract law.

[6] See *Inwards* v. *Baker,* below, p. 406, for case where proprietary estoppel gave protection.

[7] See above, p. 96; and below, p. 398.

Inadequacy of two-fold classification. The above two-fold classification into personal and property rights, rights *in personam* and rights *in rem,* although important, is, however, an oversimplification for at least three reasons.

First, some property rights are less *in rem* than others. Indeed, study of the subject shows that there are many stages between the pure personal right enforceable against one person and the complete property right enforceable against all the world. To take the easement as an example. A legal easement in unregistered land will be enforceable against all the world. Before 1926, an equitable easement would have been enforceable against all the world except a *bona fide* purchaser for value of a legal state without notice. (Indeed, in the past, equitable interests in land were classified as rights *in personam*).[8] Today, such an easement will be void against a purchaser for money or money's worth (regardless of notice) if it is not registered. In the case of registered land, if a registered proprietor grants an express easement over his land it must be completed by registration to be enforceable.[9] Again, a positive covenant is a property interest to the extent that the benefit can be made to run with the dominant land, but not the burden with the servient land though—a further variation—there are conveyancing devices by which the burden can be made to run. A tenancy by estoppel is enforceable only against the landlord and his successors in title.[10] And an equitable lease may not be as good as a legal lease.[11]

Today, the distinction has become even more blurred with the creation of various statutory rights of occupation which have some but not all the characteristics of conventional property rights. For example, the statutory tenancy under the Rent Act 1977[12]; a purchaser of the land will be bound by it but it only continues so long as the tenant "occupies the dwellinghouse as his residence."[13] And there is only a very limited possibility of succession to such a tenancy.[14]

The same sort of comments can be made about a spouse's right of occupation under the Matrimonial Homes Act 1967, the duration and terms of which is subject to the discretion of the

---

[8] And commonly still are.
[9] See below, p. 538.
[10] See above, p. 106.
[11] See above, p. 114.
[12] See Catherine Hand, The Statutory Tenancy: An Unrecognised Proprietary Interest. [1980] Conv. 351.
[13] Rent Act 1977, s.2.
[14] See Rent Act 1977, ss.2, 3 and Sched 1, Part I. And yet it is more desirable than, say, an unprotected weekly tenancy which can be determined by notice.

Courts.[15] Again, under the Domestic Violence and Matrimonial Proceedings Act 1976, the Court can authorise a non-owning cohabitee to occupy the common home to the exclusion of the other owning cohabitee.[16] The above comments are important, for one reason, because they suggest that there might be no simple yes or no answer to the often argued question whether the contractual occupation licence is a property interest and so capable of binding third parties.[17]

Secondly, in the context of occupation, the distinction between personal and property rights has been blurred by the judicial recognition that a licence may give exclusive possession. Traditionally, the law was that once a person was given exclusive possession he must have some sort of leasehold or freehold tenancy.[18] It has been suggested that exclusive possession may have two meanings, namely, the right to exclude and mere *de facto*, unshared occupation; and that in those modern cases where a licence rather than a tenancy has been found to exist, there has only been exclusive possession in the second sense.[19] But the better view is probably that a licence can confer exclusive possession in the sense of the right to exclude.[20]

Thirdly, the Courts are still capable, by moulding precedent, of gradually developing a personal right into a property right. This once happened to the restrictive covenant. Today, it may be happening to the contractual occupation licence. Not only has it been recognised that such a licence can give exclusive possession yet remain distinct from any traditional tenancy; it now seems that such a licence may itself be recognised as having at least some of the attributes of a fully fledged property interest. This is considered further below.

Principle 2. Types of licence

Licences may be classified as follows:
(1) Bare licences.
(2) Contractual licences.
(3) Licences coupled with interests.

[15] See *Wroth* v. *Tyler* [1973] 1 All E.R., particularly at p. 918.
[16] See *Davis* v. *Johnson* [1978] 1 All E.R. 1132 (H.L.); above, p. 345.
[17] See, further, below, p. 401.
[18] See above, p. 96.
[19] See, *e.g.* discussion in *Cobb* v. *Lane* [1952] 1 All E.R. 1199 (C.A.); and *Heslop* v. *Burns* [1974] 3 All E.R. 406 (C.A.).
[20] This still leaves the question whether it is a right to exclude the licensor or others as well, such as purchasers of the land.

Explanation

This, traditional, classification is based on the extent to which the licence is enforceable as a property interest. In this context, two distinct questions need to be kept in mind. First, how far is the licence enforceable against the licensor; secondly, how far is it enforceable against third parties?

The bare licence. A bare licence is a gratuitous permission. So long as it continues it saves the licensed act from constituting trespass. But it has neither contractual nor proprietary force; it is revocable at will and if the licensee does not then remove himself within a reasonable time he will become a trespasser.

The common, everyday example of the licensee is the visitor to one's house. In these cases the permission is normally implied. Again such licences are commonly granted between neighbours for one reason or another (*e.g.* "Please Mr. can I get my ball back?"). In *Armstrong* v. *Sheppard & Short Ltd.*[21] the plaintiff gave the defendant permission to lay a sewer under his land. For reasons not relevant here the defendant did not acquire an easement, the benefit of proprietary estoppel or any other interest in the land. Neither was the licence supported by any contract. The plaintiff was therefore at liberty to revoke the licence and force the defendant to remove his sewer.

The contractual licence. If the licence to enter land for some purpose is created by contract, then it is at least as enforceable as the contract. If the licence is wrongfully revoked, the licensee will certainly have a claim for damages for breach of contract. But there is a further question which has been discussed at length both in and out of court: Will the court treat an attempted wrongful revocation as invalid and enforce the licence by specific performance or injunction as appropriate?

The old judicial view was that even a contractual licence could always be revoked (making the licensee a trespasser) though wrongful revocation might give rise to a claim for damages for breach of contract.[22]

Today, there is no doubt that the Courts will protect a contractual licence *at least against the licensor* with the aid of equitable remedies.[23] They will treat any purported (wrongful) revocation as invalid and grant specific performance or an injunction to prevent eviction. And if for any reason the contract is

---

[21] [1959] 2 Q.B. 384 (C.A.).
[22] See, *e.g. Wood* v. *Leadbitter* (1845) 13 M. & W. 838; 153 E.R. 351.
[23] See, *e.g. Chandler* v. *Kerly* [1978] 2 All E.R. 942 (C.A.), particularly judgment of Lord Scarman.

not specifically enforceable the Courts will at least refuse to recognise or assist a wrongful eviction. Thus, in *Hurst* v. *Picture Theatres Ltd.*[24] the plaintiff obtained a ticket to see a cinema performance; he was wrongfully ejected by the management and sued them for the tort of assault and battery. The defence was that the licence to view had been effectively revoked, whether rightfully or wrongfully, that the plaintiff had therefore become a trespasser and could be ejected like any other trespasser. This argument was rejected. The management were not in a position to treat the defendant as a trespasser.[25] But two qualifications to this principle should be noted.

1. The courts will, as with any contract, have to decide in the first place, the express or implied terms of the licence. In *Chandler* v. *Kerly*[26] a husband and wife had jointly purchased a home. They separated and the wife became the mistress of the plaintiff who purchased the house. When the relationship broke up he claimed possession. In defence, she claimed to be, *inter alia*, a life tenant, or the beneficiary under a trust on the terms that she could stay there so long as she wished, or a licensee for life. The court decided that the only arrangement that could be inferred from the facts was that she should have a licence to occupy terminable on reasonable (12 months) notice.

2. As with other equitable interests, the licensee's position depends on the usual limits which apply to equitable remedies.[27] For example, the contract may not be of a type that is specifically enforceable,[28] or there may, on the particular facts, be some bar to equitable relief. In *Tanner* v. *Tanner*[29] the plaintiff purchased, in his own name, a home for his mistress. She gave up her own rent controlled flat and moved in to part of the house with her child and managed the letting of the rest of the house for the plaintiff. Subsequently, the plaintiff tried to evict her. It was held by the Court of Appeal that she had an implied contractual licence to

[24] [1915] 1 K.B. 1 (C.A.); and see *Verrall* v. *Great Yarmouth Borough Council* [1980] 1 All E.R. 839 (C.A.).
[25] And see also, *Hounslow London Borough* v. *Twickenham Garden Developments Ltd.* [1971] Ch. 233 (Megarry, J.).
[26] [1978] 2 All E.R. 942 (C.A.); and see *Horrocks* v. *Forray* [1976] 1 All E.R. 737 (C.A.) distinguishing *Tanner* v. *Tanner* [1975] 3 All E.R. 776.
[27] Compare doctrine of *Walsh* v. *Lonsdale* (1882) 21 Ch.D 9 (C.A.); above, p. 110.
[28] See, *e.g. Hurst* v. *Picture Theatres Ltd.* [1915] 1 K.B. 1 (C.A.) and *Hounslow London Borough* v. *Twickenham Garden Developments Ltd.* [1971] Ch. 233 (Megarry, J.). In *Mountford* v. *Scott* [1974] 1 All E.R. 249, Brightman J. appears to have missed this point, that a gratuitous promise is not specifically enforceable and so cannot create an equitable interest; compare, on appeal, [1975] 1 All E.R. 198.
[29] [1975] 3 All E.R. 776 (C.A.). See also *R. Sharpe* (1980) 1 All E.R. 198.

occupy the house so long as the child was of school age and the accommodation reasonably required. Unfortunately, by the date of the appeal hearing she (having lost the case in the lower court) had moved out and been rehoused by the local authority. The court decided that it was no longer practicable to enforce the licence specifically and that the appropriate remedy was to order her compensation for the loss of her right of occupation.[30] In *Williams* v. *Staite*[31] the court made the point that in deciding whether to grant equitable relief the court will take into consideration the conduct of the licensee. If he does not have clean hand he will not obtain the help of equity. But in the case before them, the plaintiff (a purchaser from the licensor), had pleaded in the wrong way. He had, in effect, admitted the existence of the licence but claimed that it had been revoked or forfeited as a result of the licensee's misconduct. The court decided that such a licence cannot be revoked.[32] The remedy for misconduct by the licensee in the case of such a licence (as with any interference with a property interest) lies in an action in tort for nuisance, trespass, etc.

The contractual occupation licence as a proprietary interest. The question whether a contractual licence is proprietary has generally arisen in the context of occupation licences, and will be discussed in that context; but the same arguments apply to a licence to enter land for a more limited purpose.

So far it has been suggested that the courts will recognise a contractual occupation licence as having a proprietary character at least as against the licensor. But as already noted,[33] the generally accepted hallmark of a proprietary interest in land is its enforceability against third parties and in particular against subsequent owners of the land. The legal position is not clear, but a number of points can be suggested.

1. The language of the judges is confusing. In *Errington* v. *Errington*[34] Lord Denning said[35]: "The difference between a

---

[30] Note that compensation was based on the value of her occupation right rather than the financial loss resulting from the eviction, suggesting a proprietary rather than a personal right.

[31] [1978] 2 All E.R. 928 (C.A.).

[32] Lord Denning thought that extreme misconduct might justify revocation; and, of course, the right to revoke could be reserved expressly. For a criticism of this case, see S. Anderson, (1978) 42 M.L.R. 203. Compare *Taylor Fashions Ltd.* v. *Liverpool Victoria Trustees Co. Ltd.* [1981] 1 All E.R. 897 in which Oliver J. considered that the defendant's ignorance of the legal position might make it unconscionable to enforce a proprietary estoppel against him.

[33] Above, p. 355.

[34] [1952] 1 K.B. 290.

[35] At p. 297.

tenancy and a licence is, therefore, that, in a tenancy, an interest passes in the land, whereas in a licence, it does not." And later he said[36] that the defendants "had a mere personal privilege to remain there, with no right to assign or sub-let." And yet he went on to state that such a licence would be protected in equity against revocation and to suggest that "neither the licensor nor anyone who claims through him can disregard the contract except a purchaser for value without notice." In *Tanner* v. *Tanner*,[37] Browne, L.J. said[38]: "I agree that this is not a case like *Cooke* v. *Head*[39] or *Eves* v. *Eves*[40] where the defendant has any sort of proprietary interest in the property. But I agree that there was here a licence by the plaintiff to the defendant for good consideration; it could not be revoked at will."

This confusion can perhaps be explained. A distinction has to be made between, on the one hand, an interest, such as a tenancy in common, which represents a share in the value of the property as well as consequentially the right to occupy; and on the other hand, an interest, such as the occupation licence, which carries no more than the right to occupy. This is the distinction between *Eves* v. *Eves*[41] and *Tanner* v. *Tanner*.[42]

To say that an occupation licence is a personal privilege is to emphasise that it is in the latter category; and that it is personal in the sense that the benefit of it cannot be transferred. It is personal to its proprietor.

2. This still leaves the question whether such an occupation licence will bind subsequent owners of the land. It may be that many if not all the cases which suggest that it can have this proprietary effect can be justified on more conventional grounds. For example, the majority in *Binions* v. *Evans*[43] held there to be a life interest under the Settled Land Act 1925. In *Errington* v. *Errington*[44] the action for possession was brought by the personal representatives of the licensor, and under ordinary contract law a contract is in general, enforceable against the estate of the

---

[36] At p. 299.
[37] [1975] 3 All E.R. 776 (C.A.).
[38] At p. 780.
[39] [1972] 2 All E.R. 38 (C.A.).
[40] [1975] 3 All E.R. 768 (C.A.).
[41] [1975] 3 All E.R. 768 (C.A.).
[42] [1975] 3 All E.R. 776 (C.A.); but as shown by *Tanner* a value can be put on such a licence.
[43] [1972] Ch. 359 (C.A.). But such a life interest did not match the arrangement made by the parties as closely as the contractual licence propounded by Lord Denning.
[44] [1952] 1 K.B. 290.

contractor.[45] Again, cases like *Williams* v. *Staite*[46] can perhaps be justified on the basis of proprietary estoppel.

Nevertheless, it is probably true to say that the judicial trend is towards recognising the contractual occupation licence as a proprietary interest which, subject to the limits referred to above, will enable a personal right of occupation to be made binding on subsequent owners of the land.[45a]

3. The cases raise a further point of difficulty; that is the relationship between the contractual occupation licence and the trust (constructive and implied).[47] The best analysis may be as follows. The occupation licence arises from and depends on the existence of an express or implied contract. The importance of the contract is that it defines the terms and conditions of the licence; and it provides the consideration (value) which is essential since equity will not in general aid a volunteer.[48] But it is probably true that, as with the implied trust, it is the essential fact that the licensee has taken occupation or otherwise acted to his detriment that brings equity into operation.

If these two essential elements (the contract and the acting upon it) are present two consequences follow. First, the right of occupation will be enforceable against subsequent owners of the land except (in the case of unregistered land) a bona fide purchaser for value of the legal estate without notice).[49] Secondly, the licensor will become a trustee for the licensee to the extent of the licensee's interest.

Two further points follow from the above. First, the term contractual licence (and equitable licence) is misleading, and where a licence is to be recognised as having this proprietary effect it should be referred to as a proprietary (occupation) licence. Secondly, such a licence gives rise to a trust and is a class of implied trust.[50]

4. The significance of the proprietary occupation licence is that it does not fall into the traditional pattern of equitable interests

[45] It is not clear from the report whether she was suing in this capacity or as a beneficiary of the deceased.
[45a] See *Midland Bank Ltd.* v. *Farmpride Hatcheries Ltd.* (1981) 260 E.G. 493 (C.A.).
[46] [1978] 2 All E.R. 928 (C.A.). The County Court judge in this case applied *Inwards* v. *Baker*, [1965] 2 Q.B. 29, one of the classic applications of proprietary estoppel.
[47] And also between these and proprietary estoppel; see below, p. 408.
[48] Proprietary estoppel is an exception; see below, p. 408.
[49] In the case of registered land the actual occupation would make the licence an overriding interest.
[50] See *Re Sharpe* [1980] 1 All E.R. 198; *D.H.N. Food Distributors* v. *London Borough of Tower Hamlets* [1976] 3 All E.R. 462 (C.A.).

governed by the doctrine of estates. For example, in *Tanner* v. *Tanner*[51] there was a right to occupy (without any share in the value of the house as such) as long as a child was of school age and the accommodation reasonably required. In *Chandler* v. *Kerly*[52] there was a right to occupy determinable on reasonable notice.

This means that the proprietary licence is an interest of great flexibility in the duration and conditions to which it can be made subject. It also means (which may or may not be desirable), that it is contrary to the philosophy which favours the free alienability, registration[53] and the certainty of interests in land.

It must be emphasised that the law on contractual licences is not certain and that what has been said above in the present author's own view of the trend to be found in the cases.

The licence coupled with an interest. Any licence coupled with an interest in land will be enforceable to the same extent as the interest itself. Thus, it has been said[54] that if a landowner gives another the right to enter and cut down trees, this involves the grant of a proprietary interest in the trees coupled with a licence to enter to cut and remove them. And the licence will be irrevocable, assignable and enforceable against the landowner's successors in title.

It is arguable, however, that this is not a case of a separate licence somehow acquiring the enforceability of a proprietary interest, but that the right to enter is included in and part of the grant of the proprietary interest in the trees. If a landowner grants an easement to his neighbour to take water from a spring, the easement will expressly or by implication include the right to enter for the purpose. It is artificial and unnecessary to say that there is a licence to enter which is quite separate from but enforceable to exactly the same extent as the easement to abstract water.

Similarly, suppose that a person enters another's land to build a house induced by a promise that he will be allowed to live there. The landowner will be prevented by proprietary estoppel from evicting him. It is not the licence to enter but the property interest, the proprietary estoppel which protects the house builder. The licence (together with other factors) has given rise to the property interest but itself has no proprietary force.[55]

---

[51] [1975] 3 All E.R. 776 (C.A.).
[52] [1978] 2 All E.R. 942 (C.A.).
[53] See, *e.g.*, *Taylor Fashions Ltd.* v. *Liverpool Victoria Trustees Co. Ltd.* [1981] 1 All E. R. 897 (Oliver J.).
[54] *Thomas* v. *Sorrell* (1673) Vaughan 330, 351; 124 E.R. 1098.
[55] See (1953) 69 L.Q.R. 466 (A.D. Hargreaves), for a similar view.

CHAPTER 18

PROPRIETARY ESTOPPEL

Principle 1. Definition

Proprietary estoppel will arise where:

(a) A person has spent money or otherwise acted to his detriment[1] in reliance upon an expectation that the landowner will give him an interest or some other beneficial use of the land[2]; and

(b) the landowner has knowingly created that expectation by his words, conduct or silence.[3]

The court will give effect to this proprietary estoppel in whatever way they think appropriate and it will be enforceable as an equitable interest in the land.

Explanation

In general, if I spend money improving B's land, then I have made him a gift. If I build a house on my neighbour's land in the mistaken belief that it is mine, then the house, as a fixture, becomes part of his land and his property.

In *Pettitt* v. *Pettitt*,[4] the husband spent money and time improving the house owned by his wife. His subsequent claim to a share in the proceeds when the house was sold failed. Lord Upjohn said[5]: "It has been well settled in your Lordships' House . . . that if A spends money on the property of B, prima facie he has no claim on such property."

If a person is going to spend money in this way, and he is wise, he will make sure that the necessary interest is properly granted to him before starting work. But where he has failed to take this precaution, equity may consider it equitable to help him.

The essence of proprietary estoppel is that the landowner has led another to spend money or to alter his position in the belief

---

[1] See *Greasley* v. *Cooke* [1980] 3 All E.R. 710 (C.A.).

[2] But see *Western Fish Products Ltd.* v. *Penwith D.C.* [1981] 2 All E.R. 204 (C.A.).

[3] It will arise by silence where the landowner stands by while knowing that the other is acting in reliance on the expectation. The ignorance of the landowner as to his legal position will not prevent the estoppel arising, but it is a factor which may be taken into account by the court in deciding whether to grant relief; see *Taylor Fashions Ltd.* v. *Liverpool Victoria Trustee Co. Ltd.* [1981] 1 All E.R. 897.

[4] [1970] A.C. 777 (H.L.). But see now the Matrimonial Proceedings and Property Act 1970, s.37; see above, p. 346.

[5] At p. 818.

that he would be allowed the benefit of his expenditure. In such circumstances it would be inequitable to allow the landowner to return to his strict legal rights, which he is therefore estopped from asserting.

In *Inwards* v. *Baker*[6] the son was looking for somewhere to build a bungalow as a home. His father owned land and said: "Why don't you build the bungalow on my land and make it a bit bigger?" which the son did and went into occupation in the expectation that he would be allowed to live there for his life or for so long as he wished. Subsequently the father died having by his will, made long before the bungalow was built, left all his property to the woman he was living with. The trustees of the will were now suing for possession claiming that the son had no more than a licence which they could revoke. It was held that there was an estoppel in favour of the son and that the estoppel—or perhaps the interest in the property which it created—was enforceable against the trustees as successors in title to the father.

In *E.R. Ives Investment Ltd.* v. *High*[7] there was an agreement between the defendant and an adjoining property owner that the defendant should have a right of way over the adjoining property behind the block of flats being built there. Both properties were unregistered land and the agreement was not registered as an equitable easement as it should have been under the Land Charges Act 1925 to make it enforceable against subsequent owners of the flats.[8]

Without objection from the adjoining owner, the defendant used the way and built a garage on his own land with access onto the way. And he also resurfaced it, the adjoining owner contributing to the cost. Subsequently, the adjoining owner sold to the plaintiffs who bought with notice of the use of the way. They claimed to terminate the use of the way and in the present case were suing the defendant in trespass. It was held that they failed; that there was a proprietary estoppel in favour of the defendant which bound the purchaser with notice. And although the equitable easement should have been registered, the proprietary estoppel was a distinct interest from the easement and not subject to registration.

In general the money will have been expended on the landowner's land; but it may have been on the claimant's own land. In *Rochdale Canal Co.* v. *King*[9] the defendant had built a

---

[6] [1965] 2 Q.B. 29 (C.A.).
[7] [1967] 2 Q.B. 379.
[8] Lord Denning M.R. considered that there was not an equitable easement.
[9] (1853) 16 Beav. 630; 51 E.R. 924.

steam-driven mill in reliance on the plaintiff's promise to let him supply the mill with water from their canal. It was held that they were not entitled to an injunction to stop the use. Sir John Romilly M.R. said that: "If one man stands by and encourages another, though but passively, to lay out money, under an erroneous opinion of title, or under the obvious expectation that no obstacle will afterwards be interposed in the way of his enjoyment, the court will not permit any subsequent interference with it, by him who formerly promoted and encouraged those acts of which he now either complains or seeks to obtain the advantage."[10]

In *Crabb* v. *Arun District Council*[11] the plaintiff indicated to the defendants that he was dividing his land into two and would need an additional access to their road. The defendants agreed to this and constructed the access; subsequently, the plaintiff sold the part which depended on the new access.[12] Over a year later the defendants closed off the access. The court held that the principle of proprietary estoppel operated in favour of the plaintiff to protect his right of way.

In *Pascoe* v. *Turner*[13] the plaintiff owned a house and the defendant went to live with him. Eventually, he went to live with another woman telling the defendant: "The house is yours and everything in it." She spent money on improvements and subsequently, the plaintiff sought to evict her, claiming that she was only a licensee. It was held in the Court of Appeal that she had the benefit of a proprietary estoppel and ordered the fee simple to be vested in her.[14]

Giving effect to the equity. In the case of the contractual licence as described above[15] the courts are giving effect to the express or implied agreement between the parties; though they will only do so if it has been acted upon.[16] They will therefore be limited by the terms of that agreement.[17]

[10] 51 E.R. 924, at p. 925.

[11] [1975] 3 All E.R. 865 (C.A.).

[12] Although the defendants did not know of the actual sale, it was held sufficient that they knew of the *intention* to sell, that is to act in reliance on the expectation of having access.

[13] [1979] 2 All E.R. 945 (C.A.); and see *Williams* v. *Staite* [1978] 2 All E.R. 928 (C.A.) and *Re Sharpe* [1980] 1 All E.R. 198 (Browne-Wilkinson, J.).

[14] Compare *Tanner* v. *Tanner* [1975] 3 All E.R. 776 (C.A.).

[15] Above, p. 403.

[16] See above, p. 403.

[17] But even here the court will have a measure of flexibility if it has to decide what terms to imply; further, it will have the flexibility always available when deciding a claim for equitable relief; see *Tanner* v. *Tanner* [1975] 3 All E.R. 776; *Chandler* v. *Kerly* [1978] 2 All E.R. 942; *Taylor Fashions Ltd.* v. *Liverpool Victoria Trustee Co. Ltd.* [1981] 1 All E.R. 897.

In contrast, proprietary estoppel does not depend on the existence of any contractual agreement.[18] The court is therefore not giving effect to an agreement but, as it is said, satisfying the equity which has arisen as a result of the claimant altering his position. This means that it can consider the position in which he finds himself at the time of the action.[19] More important, it means that the court has a wider discretion in deciding what interest or remedy justice requires them to give to the claimant. Thus, in *Pascoe* v. *Turner*[20] the court considered granting a licence for life as an alternative and decided that a fee simple would be more appropriate. In *Inwards* v. *Baker*[21] the equity was satisfied by giving the son the right to live in the bungalow for life or so long as he wished.[22]

Relationship between proprietary estoppel, the proprietary contractual licence and the implied trust. As already suggested,[23] (partly because they are developing areas of the law) the relationship is far from clear.[24]

It may be that there is a common principle underlying all three—what has been called betrayal of faith and prejudicial reliance.[25] It is also true that many of the cases could be decided on the basis of either, *e.g.* proprietary contractual licence or proprietary estoppel. By way of summary, it is suggested that the position is as follows:

1. The implied trust (as defined in this book) and the proprietary contractual licence both depend on a preceding implied or express contract; though, in both cases, the beneficiary must have acted on

---

[18] See, *e.g. Pascoe* v. *Turner* [1979] 2 All E.R. 945 (C.A.); and *Crabb* v. *Arun District Council* [1975] 3 All E.R. 865 (C.A.).

[19] See judgment of Goff, L.J. in *Williams* v. *Staite* [1978] 2 All E.R. 928 (C.A.).

[20] [1979] 2 All E.R. 945 (C.A.).

[21] [1965] 2 Q.B. 29 (C.A.).

[22] And see *E.R. Ives Investment Ltd.* v. *High* [1967] 2 Q.B. 379; *Dillwyn* v. *Llewellyn* 45 E.R. 1285. In *Crabb* v. *Arun D.C.* (above n.11), the court considered subjecting the right of access to payment of a charge.

[23] Above, p. 404.

[24] See S. Anderson, (1978) 42 M.L.R. 203.

[25] See A. Everton, Betrayal of Faith and Prejudicial Reliance, (1974) 38 Conv. (N.S.) 25. And see (1981) 44 M.L.R. 461. For what may be seen as a judicial attempt to move towards a common principle, see the broad formulation of proprietary estoppel by Oliver J. (in *Taylor Fashions Ltd.* v. *Liverpool Victoria Trustee Co. Ltd.* [1981] 1 All E.R. 897) in terms of what would be "conscionable." This formulation was adopted in *Amalgamated Investment & Property Co. Ltd.* v. *Texas Commerce International Bank Ltd.* [1981] 2 W.L.R. 554 (Goff. J.); and see *Habib Bank Ltd.* v. *Habib Bank AG Zurich* [1981] 2 All E.R. 650 (C.A.); and (1981) 97 L.Q.R. 513.

the contract to which the court is giving effect. Proprietary estoppel does not depend on the existence of any contract.[26]

2. By virtue of 1. above, the courts have more flexibility in deciding the terms on which to give effect to a proprietary estoppel.[27]

3. All three give rise (if the necessary conditions are satisfied) to equitable, proprietary interests, capable of binding subsequent owners of the land.

4. The proprietary contractual licence should be seen as a class of implied trust, making the landowner a trustee of the legal estate for the licensee to the extent of his interest. Equally, it might be said that proprietary estoppel (at least where it protects occupation) makes the landowner a constructive trustee.[28]

5. The licence is different from the conventional implied trust in that the latter relates to the creation of the traditional property interests governed by the doctrine of estates. The licence can give proprietary protection to a mere personal right of occupation and is not subject to the usual confines of the doctrine of estates. In this respect, proprietary estoppel is like the licence.[29]

6. All three are important because they can operate outside the formality requirements of the 1925 legislation as to creation, registration and overreaching.[30]

Finally, it must be emphasised once again, that there is no general accepted analysis of the nature of or relationship between the three; and that the above is no more than a tentative attempt to rationalise what is in the cases.

---

[26] If Professor Atiyah's view of consideration is accepted this basis of distinction becomes difficult if not impossible to make; see P.S. Atiyah, *An Introduction to the Law of Contract* (3rd ed.), particularly pp. 125–128. The act in expectation will constitute consideration and the interest expected in return for the act will define the terms of the contract.

[27] But see above, p. 407, n.17.

[28] See *Re Sharpe* [1980] 1 All E.R. 198 (Browne-Wilkinson J.); and above p. 183

[29] See *Jones A.E.* v. *Jones F.W.* [1977] 2 All E.R. 231 (C.A.).

[30] See, *e.g.*, *Peffer* v. *Rigg* [1978] 3 All E.R. 745, above p. 189; also *Taylor Fashions Ltd.* v. *Liverpool Victoria Trustee Co. Ltd.* [1981] 1 All E.R. 897—unregistered option held to be enforceable by virtue of proprietary estoppel.

CHAPTER 19

COVENANTS RELATING TO LAND: POSITIVE COVENANTS

General Introduction

A covenant simply means an agreement under seal.

The parties to a covenant are the covenantor who assumes an obligation, and the covenantee in whose favour the covenant is made.

Covenants relating to land may be:

(a) Positive, the covenantor undertaking that something will be done, *e.g.* that the premises will be kept in repair.

(b) Restrictive or negative, the covenantor undertaking that something will not be done, *e.g.* that the land will not be built on.

As with other third party rights a covenant consists of a benefit and a burden.

A restrictive covenant is a fully fledged property interest. The burden runs with a servient property. The benefit is appurtenant to and runs with a dominant property. It is, however, useful to remember that before its recognition by equity as a property interest, a restrictive covenant was simply a contract between two persons. Even today it is regarded by the courts as both a property interest and, at the same time, a contract. And contract law has left its impression not only on the terminology but also on the substantive rules governing restrictive covenants.[1]

Positive covenants stand somewhere between property and personal rights, between restrictive covenants and licences. The benefit can be made to run—a feature of appurtenant property rights. The burden can be made to run with leasehold,[2] but not—subject to certain exceptions—with freehold land.

Principle 1. The benefit of positive freehold covenants

Positive covenants relating to freehold land are enforceable between covenantor and covenantee[3] in accordance with the ordinary rules of contract law.

The benefit of a positive covenant can be assigned expressly as a

---

[1] For example, the benefit of a restrictive covenant can be assigned with the land, see below, p. 436.
[2] See below, p. 419, for leasehold covenants.
[3] And their respective personal representatives.

chose in action.[4] And in some cases assignment may be implied.

If certain requirements are satisfied the benefit of a positive covenant will run automatically with the land[5] without express assignment.

Under section 56 of the Law of Property Act 1925, a covenant relating to land can be made enforceable by a person specified in but not a party to the covenant.

Explanation

Enforcement under contract law. There are two general rules of contract law which are relevant here. First, a covenant creates a contractual relationship binding between the parties to it in accordance with the ordinary rules of contract law. Secondly, the benefit of a covenant, like the benefit of most contracts, can be assigned to a third party as a chose in action.[6] In *Griffith* v. *Pelton*,[7] a lease contained an option giving the lessee the right to purchase the freehold reversion. In 1948, the lessee assigned the lease to the plaintiff. This assignment made no reference to the option. In 1956, no doubt to clarify the position, the lessee expressly assigned the benefit of the option to the plaintiff in so far as it was not already his. The court held that the benefit of the covenant passed on the assignment of the lease but that—just in case they were wrong on that point—it passed in any case by the express assignment.[8]

Three other minor points about assignment can be mentioned here:

(a) The terms of the original contract may modify the right to assign. For example, it is a common provision of leases that the lease is not to be assigned either at all or without the consent of the landlord. Again, an option contained in a lease to purchase the freehold can generally be assigned to anyone. The lease can be assigned to A and the option to B. But the lease might provide that the option is only to be assignable to an assignee of the lease.[9]

(b) Where the covenant relates to a particular piece of land, the courts may be prepared to imply an assignment of the benefit with the transfer of the land. In *Griffith* v. *Pelton*,[10] the court

---

[4] See (1954) 18 Conv.(N.S.) 546, at p. 552.
[5] As to whether it runs with the estate or the land, see below, p. 414.
[6] See n. 4, above.
[7] [1958] Ch. 205 (C.A.).
[8] See also *Shayler* v. *Woolf* [1946] Ch. 320.
[9] See *Re Button's Lease* [1964] Ch. 263, where Plowman J. thought that such was the proper construction of the lease before him.
[10] Above, n. 7.

considered that a transfer of the lease implied an assignment of the option to purchase the freehold reversion which was contained in the lease.[11]

(c) Even after assignment the original covenantee may still be able to sue the original covenantor by virtue of the privity of contract between them.[12] In *Smith & Snipes Hall Farm* v. *River Douglas Catchment Board*,[13] Denning L.J. suggested[14] in passing that an original covenantee could have sued the Board on its covenant to maintain the river banks even though he had parted with the land which the covenant was intended to protect from flooding; and even though he had expressly assigned the benefit of the covenant to the new owner. But of course, not having suffered any loss, he would only have recovered nominal damages.

Benefit of positive covenants running with the land. The above are rules of contract law and do not depend on the relationship of the covenant to any piece of land. However, if the covenant does relate to land and if certain conditions are satisfied, the *benefit* will run with the land without the need for assignment express or implied.

These conditions are as follows:

(a) *The covenant must touch and concern ascertained*[15] *land of the covenantee.*[16] The exact meaning of this requirement and the dividing line between what does and what does not touch and concern the land is not easy to trace.

It has been said that the covenant must "either affect the land as regards its mode of occupation or it must be such as *per se,* and not

---

[11] Note that implied assignment is not the same as the benefit of a covenant running without any assignment (see below, as to the benefit running). In *Griffith* v. *Pelton* the option would not have run with the lease without assignment because such an option does not "touch and concern"; *Woodall* v. *Clifton* [1905] 2 Ch. 257.

[12] But see (1971) 87 L.Q.R. 539, at p. 543 (D.J. Hayton), dealing with restrictive covenants: and *Re King* [1963] Ch. 459, dealing with the right of assignor of a reversion on a lease to sue the lessee for breach of a covenant to repair; held that on wording of s.141 of the L.P.A. 1925, the assignment of the reversion implied an assignment of the right to sue thus depriving the assignor of any right to sue.

[13] [1949] 2 K.B. 500.

[14] *Ibid.* at p. 516.

[15] See below, p. 414, for need to identify benefited land.

[16] The same requirement exists for restrictive covenants (below, p. 426) and leasehold covenants (below, p. 421) to run with the land. Similarly, easements must accommodate the dominant land.

merely from collateral circumstances, affects the value of the land. . . . "[17]

Suppose, for the sake of an illustration, that I, being a manufacturer of these articles, covenant to supply X, the owner of Blackacre, with all his requirements of red and blue biros, writing paper and other stationery over the next five years. His ownership of Blackacre is irrelevant. No one will suggest that his covenant touches and concerns the land.[18] He can assign the benefit of the covenant but it will not pass automatically on the sale of Blackacre.

Decided cases naturally tend to be borderline. Otherwise they would not get to court. But *Sharp* v. *Waterhouse*[19] provides a clear example. W was the owner of a mill and he covenanted with S "to supply S with pure water sufficient to supply his cattle on certain closes . . . and convey it to a reservoir made by S for the purpose. . . . " It was admitted by counsel for the defendant that the benefit of the covenant ran with the land so as to be enforceable by the devisee of the closes.

On the other hand, in *Austerberry* v. *Oldham Corporation*[20] there was a covenant with the plaintiff's predecessor in title to maintain and repair a road which ran through both the plaintiff's and other properties. Cotton and Lindley L.JJ. considered that the covenant was not "pointedly with reference to his land." It was "a mere covenant with him, as with all the adjoining owners, to make this road, a small portion of which only abuts on his land, and there is nothing specially relating to his land at all."[21] This view is perhaps a little surprising, since there is no doubt that covenants can be made to benefit more than one property. Indeed, one of the other judges, Fry L.J., was "rather inclined to think that the road [that is the road in issue] connecting the land with the public highway was so far incident to the use and occupation of the remainder of Mr. Elliott's land, that it might be conceivable that it came within the principle of covenants relating to things incident to the land."[22]

---

[17] *Smith & Snipes Hall Farm* v. *River Douglas Catchment Board* [1949] 2 K.B. 500, at p. 506 *per* Tucker L.J.
[18] Unless possibly he runs a stationer's business on Blackacre. See below, p. 428, as to restrictive covenants designed to benefit a business.
[19] (1857) 7 El. & Bl. 816; 119 E.R. 1449.
[20] (1885) 29 Ch.D. 750. For other cases on the meaning of "touch and concern" see below, pp. 421, 426.
[21] (1885) 29 Ch.D. 750, at p. 781, *per* Lindley L.JJ.
[22] *Ibid.* at p. 784. The plaintiff lost in any case because all three judges agreed that the burden of a positive covenant could not run.

The land intended to be benefited must be identified clearly either from the terms of the covenant or from extrinsic evidence.[23]

(b) *The wording of the covenant must show that the benefit of the covenant is intended to run with the land and not merely to give the covenantee a personal right.*[24]   In other words the covenant must be annexed to the land intended to be benefited.

If a covenant does touch and concern the land of the covenantee this means that it can be made to—not that it necessarily does—run with the land. If I covenant with my neighbour to supply his household with fresh water from my pump, this will certainly touch and concern his land.[25] But the wording of the covenant might make it clear that a benefit to him personally only is intended and that I will be under no obligation to any subsequent owner of the land. For example, the wording might be "It is hereby agreed that the benefit of the foregoing covenant shall belong only to C.D. and his personal representatives and shall not be assignable."[26]

On the other hand, a covenant intended to run might specify that it is made with the covenantee "to the intent that the benefit thereof may be annexed to and run with the land of the covenantee coloured pink on the plan drawn hereon and every part thereof."[27]

Section 78(1) of the Law of Property Act 1925 provides that:

> "A covenant relating to any land of the covenantee shall be deemed to be made with the covenantee and his successors in title and the persons deriving title under him and shall have effect as if such successors and other persons were expressed."

The effect of this is that provided the other requirements are satisfied the intention to make the covenant run will be presumed in the absence of express provision to the contrary.[28]

(c) *The benefit can only be enforced by a subsequent owner of the land who has the same legal estate as the original covenantee.*

It is commonly said that the benefit of a covenant is attached to the legal estate rather than the land itself. This means the original covenantee must have had a legal estate in the land benefited and

---

[23] See *Smith & Snipes Hall Farm* v. *River Douglas Catchment Board* (above, n. 13).
[24] For the similar requirement in the case of restrictive covenants, see below, p. 429.
[25] See *Shayler* v. *Woolf* [1946] Ch. 320.
[26] See Hallett, *Conveyancing Precedents* (1965), p. 355.
[27] See *ibid.* p. 357.
[28] On the effect of s.78 see further, below, p. 432.

the plaintiff must have the same legal estate. Equity has not stepped in, as it has done in the case of restrictive covenants, to allow the benefit to pass with the land itself so that *any* subsequent owner of the benefited land can enforce.[29]

However, in *Smith & Snipes Hall Farm* v. *River Douglas Catchment Board,*[30] this rule seems to have been extended if not lost altogether. The Board had covenanted with eleven landowners to maintain the bank of a river which passed through their properties. In 1940 the first plaintiff purchased one of the properties from one of the original 11 covenantees and the conveyance contained an express assignment of the benefit of the covenant. In 1944 he let the property to the second plaintiff on a yearly tenancy. Subsequently, as a result of the Board's failure to maintain, the river burst its banks flooding the plaintiffs' meadows. It was held that the covenant touched and concerned the land. "It affects the value of the land *per se* and converts it from flooded meadow to land suitable for agriculture. . . ."[31] And it was held that by virtue of section 78(1) it could be enforced not only by the purchaser but also by his lessee even though the latter had a lesser estate than the original covenantee.[32]

Section 56 of the Law of Property Act 1925: Benefit to third parties. This sections provides that:

> "A person may take an immediate or other interest in land or other property, or the benefit of any condition, right of entry, covenant or agreement, over or respecting land or other property, although he may not be named as a party to the conveyance or other instrument."

The effect of this section is that an interest in land can be created in favour of a person who is not a party to the transaction by which the interest is created. This section is not confined to covenants but it only applies to recognised interests in land.[33]

When the developer of a block of flats sells off each separate flat to a purchaser, the conveyance—made only between the developer and that particular purchaser—will probably contain a covenant in something like the following terms[34]:

---

[29] See L.P.A. 1925, s.78(1), where this distinction is recognised.
[30] [1949] 2 K.B. 500 (C.A.).
[31] *Ibid.* at p. 506 *per* Tucker L.J.
[32] Denning L.J. considered that s.78(1) had changed the law on this point. George and George, *The Sale of Flats* (4th ed.), p. 71, suggest that the decision can be supported on the basis of s.62 of the L.P.A. 1925; see above, p. 375, for s.62.
[33] See *Beswick* v. *Beswick* [1968] A.C. 58.
[34] See *George and George* (above, n. 32), p. 272.

"The Purchaser hereby covenants with the Vendor and with the owners of the other flats comprised in the said block, that the Purchaser will at all times hereafter:

(1) Keep the flat and all walls party walls sewers drains pipes cable wires and appurtenances thereto belonging in good and tenantable repair and condition and in particular (but without prejudice to the generality of the foregoing) so as to support shelter and protect the parts of the building other than the flat. . . . "

By a combination of section 56 and section 78(1) of the Law of Property Act 1925 not only can other flat owners enforce; so can their successors in title. This principle is illustrated in *Forster* v. *Elvet Colliery Co. Ltd.*[35] which concerned support for the surface. Here the surface and the subjacent minerals were in separate ownership. The owner of the minerals leased the coal to be worked by the lessee who covenanted to pay compensation for any damage caused by the working. This covenant was made with the lessor but was also expressed to be for the benefit of the various surface owners. In 1906 serious subsidence took place. An action was brought against the lessee[36] by several surface owners. One of the plaintiffs had held his land at the time of the original covenants. The others were successors in title of the original owners. It was held that under section 5 of the Real Property Act 1845 (the predecessor of section 56), the original surface owners were entitled to claim the benefit of the covenant. And under section 58 of the Conveyancing and Law of Property Act 1881 (the predecessor of section 78) the covenants ran with their lands. So all the plaintiffs succeeded.

A final point about section 56. The third party must be in existence and identified when the covenant is made for his benefit.[37]

Principle 2.   The burden of positive freehold covenants

The burden of positive freehold covenants cannot be assigned and cannot be made to run with the burdened land.

However, there are a number of methods by which the burden can be made enforceable against subsequent owners. These include the following:

---

[35] [1908] 1 K.B. 629 (C.A.); affd. *sub nom. Dyson* v. *Forster* [1909] A.C. 98.
[36] Actually against his executors as he was dead.
[37] *Westhoughton Urban Council* v. *Wigan Coal and Iron Co.* [1919] 1 Ch. 159.

(1) Where the benefit of an interest in land is made conditional on the performance of positive obligations.

(2) The use of the estate rentcharge with a right of entry annexed.

Explanation

The running of the burden as a distinguishing feature of property interests. One of the most important features which distinguishes an interest in land from a merely personal right[38] (and, more generally, a right *in rem* from a right *in personam*) is the fact that the burden of an interest runs with the land. The common and distinctive feature of easements, profits, restrictive covenants and other third party rights in land, is that the burden of them is attached to the land and enforceable against successive owners. A personal right is essentially enforceable only against the person who created it.

Positive covenants are by no means ordinary personal contractual interests. As we have seen their benefit can be attached to the land and this is an important and essential feature of some property interests[39] such as easements and restrictive covenants. But the burden of a positive covenant can only be enforced against the covenantor himself. It does not run with the land. And in this sense it cannot be classified as a property interest.

This defect of positive covenants relating to land can create practical problems, for example, in the development of blocks of residential flats. And both the Wilberforce Committee[40] and the Law Commission[41] have recommended legislation to make positive covenants run with the land in the same way as restrictive ones. Two of the methods used to avoid the rule will now be mentioned.[42]

(1) Obligations incidental to the enjoyment of a benefit. " . . . it is an ancient law that a man cannot take a benefit under a deed without subscribing to the obligations thereunder."[43]

---

[38] But note comments above, p. 397.

[39] But not all, *e.g.* profits in gross.

[40] Report of the Committee on Positive Covenants affecting Land (Wilberforce Report) (1965 Cmnd. 2719).

[41] Law Com. No. 11. In this report the Law Commission recommend a single "land obligation" to include both positive and restrictive covenants which would run with the land if satisfying certain requirements: see *ibid.* para. 30.

[42] For other methods, see George and George, *The Sale of Flats* (4th ed.), p. 73; also Law Com. W.P. No. 24 (Rentcharges); the Wilberforce Report (n. 40 above), at para. 8; and (1973) 37 Conv.(N.S.) 194.

[43] *Halsall* v. *Brizell* [1957] Ch. 169, at p. 182, *per* Upjohn J. See also *Ives* (*E.R.*) *Investment* v. *High* [1967] 2 Q.B. 379.

If a person wishes to enjoy the benefit of a right over another's land he must be prepared to perform any obligations incidental to that benefit. *Halsall* v. *Brizell*[44] concerned a nineteenth century residential development known as Cressington Park in Liverpool. The roads and sewers remained vested in the developers but by a deed of covenant between them and the various plot purchasers they declared themselves trustees of these roads and sewers for the benefit of all the plot owners whilst for their part the plot owners agreed to contribute to the cost of upkeep and maintenance. In 1950 the then trustees supported by a meeting of owners sought to charge a higher contribution to those properties which had been converted into multi-occupation. Upjohn J. held that the covenant to contribute was positive and as such did not bind a present owner. Nevertheless an owner could only claim the benefit of the deed allowing him to use the roads and sewers if he was willing to comply with the obligation to contribute to the cost of maintenance. Upjohn J. did in fact however go on to decide that the present levy in question was *ultra vires* in that the deed provided for assessment on the basis of plots not dwelling units.

(2) **Estate Rentcharges.** An estate rentcharge is one which either reserves a nominal rent and is created to secure the performance of covenants by the landowner for the time being or is created to secure contribution by the landowner to the cost of maintenance, repairs, etc., to the land to be carried out by the rentcharge owner. In this latter case, the amount secured must be reasonable.[45] Such estate rentcharges can be used, for example, where a developer sells off individual flats freehold. Each conveyance will contain the necessary covenants by the purchaser, *e.g.* to repair,[46] and will reserve an estate rentcharge in favour of the developer. The rentcharge will have annexed to it a right of re-entry[47] (*i.e.* to forfeit the purchaser's interest in the land) exercisable on non-payment of the rentcharge or breach of any of the covenants. Since the rentcharge (and with it the right of re-entry) is a proprietary burden which runs with the purchaser's

---

[44] n. 43, above.

[45] Rentcharges Act 1977, s.2(4). For rentcharges generally and the 1977 Act, see below, Chapter 22.

[46] Under L.P.A. 1925, s.79, in the absence of provision to the contrary, the covenant will cover the acts of the purchaser and his successors in title.

[47] See L.P.A. 1925, s.1(2)(*e*). Such a right of re-entry (termed a right of entry in the section) could presumably be legal; see n. 49 below. Compare *Shiloh Spinners Ltd.* v. *Harding* [1973] A.C. 691 (H.L.).

estate, it will be exercisable on any breach by a subsequent owner. There is no statutory right to redeem such estate rentcharges.[48] It seems that land can be made subject to a right of re-entry on breach of covenant without it being annexed to a rentcharge.[49]

Principle 3.   Leasehold Covenants: Privity of estate

The benefit and burden of covenants contained in leases will run with the land (*i.e.* run with the lease and the reversion) provided the following requirements are satisfied:

(1) The covenant must touch and concern the demised land—in other words have reference to the subject-matter of the lease.

(2) There must be privity of estate between the plaintiff and the defendant.

Explanation

The distinction between leasehold and freehold covenants. The main difference between freehold and leasehold covenants is that in the case of leasehold, since there is privity of estate, the relationship of landlord and tenant, the burden as well as the benefit of covenants can run. This difference is one of the most important remaining distinctions between freehold and leasehold ownership.[50] In all other respects there can be little if anything to choose between freehold ownership of a property and a long lease for, say, 999 years. This disadvantage of freehold is particularly apparent in the case of flat developments. The Wilberforce Report[51] stated that, "The inconveniences of the present law are accentuated in the case of divided buildings and blocks of flats because of the large extent to which each owner of a flat depends for the comfort and enjoyment of his home on the maintenance and repair of the rest of the building, the continuance of any service provided for his flat and the upkeep of any amenities included in the development. . . . Any failure to repair and

---

[48] Rentcharges Act 1977, ss.8(4), 17(2) and Sched. 2 (repealing L.P.A. 1925, s.191). One of the weaknesses in using the rentcharge device before the 1977 Act was that there was a statutory right to redeem the rentcharge and redemption would destroy the right of re-entry. Such already existing rentcharges (if they come within the definition in s.2(4)) will no longer be redeemable.

[49] See *Shiloh Spinners Ltd.* v. *Harding* [1973] A.C. 691 (H.L.). Such a right of re-entry would necessarily be equitable; see L.P.A. 1925, s.1(2)(*e*). Indeed, it is difficult to see how a rentcharge of nominal amount can be said to have been created for the purpose of enforcing covenants by the landowner as required by the 1977 Act, s.2(4), for its validity.

[50] See further below, p. 586, *et seq.*

maintain the common parts, or to afford the necessary shelter or support, may seriously affect not only the comfort of the flat dwellers, but also the value of any unit in the building. The evidence before us shows that, because under the present law it is not always possible to impose effective obligations to do these things, freehold flats are not generally considered to be a satisfactory security for a mortgage. . . . Many building societies we understand will not make loans on the security of freehold flats at all."[51a]

Turning to leases, the same Report concluded[52]:

"If the land which is to be burdened with the obligation can be leased instead of being sold outright, the direct legal relationship of landlord and tenant will continue to subsist between successive owners of the leasehold and of the reversion. In consequence of this privity of estate, positive covenants will continue to be enforceable by the owner for the time being of the freehold against the current owner of the leasehold. The creation of a leasehold interest cannot normally be used for the purpose of creating enforceable obligations between adjoining owners of land but it is extensively used to safeguard the position of vendors of land who, like local authorities, have a substantial interest in the performance of the covenants and for developments like blocks of flats which involve numerous inter-locking covenants. In the case of such subdivided buildings the common parts of the building can be vested in the landlord, who can then enter into covenants for their maintenance and repair and for the provision of services, while the leaseholders of each of the units covenant to contribute to the cost of the maintenance and repair and enter into obligations to maintain their own units in so far as it is necessary to do so in order to provide shelter or support for other units or common parts. Provided the reversion is vested in a person or body whose continuing existence is assured and who can be relied upon to meet his own obligations and to take effective action to enforce the leaseholders' covenants, the leasehold method works satisfactorily,[53] and it has the added advantage that planned redevelopment can take place when the life of the

---

[51] Above, n. 40, at para. 5.
[51a] There is probably less reluctance today.
[52] *Ibid.* para. 8 (1).
[53] It does not in itself enable one flat owner to enforce positive covenants against another flat owner.

building ends. For these reasons some professional bodies have expressed a preference for leasehold as opposed to freehold ownership of divided buildings; and one of them, the Royal Institution of Chartered Surveyors, has recommended that the use of the leasehold system should be made obligatory whenever a severance of ownership in land and parts of buildings erected on it takes place in such a way that the owner of each part depends for the proper enjoyment of his property on continuing and positive action on the part of the owners of other units. There is no doubt, however, that many purchasers prefer freeholds. The suggestion that they should be prevented from acquiring them raises issues of social policy with which we are not concerned. In any event the leasehold system, which works well where there is a reliable and permanent landlord and is probably the simplest solution to the problems inherent in a building divided into a number of flats, may not provide the most suitable machinery in all cases, and we think that, quite apart from questions of social policy, the results would not be satisfactory if purchasers who prefer freeholds were prevented from acquiring them. At the same time, it must be appreciated that ownership of flats cannot be enjoyed with the degree of freedom of action normally associated with freehold ownership; it must involve the acceptance of many burdens and obligations at present more commonly attributed to leasehold tenure."[54]

(1) **The covenant must touch and concern the demised land.** The rule here is the same as for positive freehold covenants. But there is this point to note. In the case of positive freehold covenants it is the land of the covenantee which must be benefited. The benefit may result from doing something on the covenantee's land or, less usual, from doing something on the covenantor's own adjoining land. In the case of leasehold covenants it is the demised land which must be touched and concerned. And the interests of covenantor and covenantee, the landlord's reversion and the tenant's lease, both reside in this single piece of land. The covenant may be a benefit to the reversion and a burden on the leasehold interest (in the case of a covenant by the tenant) or a burden on the reversion and a benefit to the leasehold interest (in the case of a covenant by the landlord).

---

[54] The leasehold cannot be used to make positive covenants enforceable directly between neighbours since the relationship of landlord and tenant will be lacking.

To give some idea of what covenants touch and concern.[55] The following lessees' covenants have been held to touch and concern the land: The covenant to pay the rent; all the covenants implied by law into a lease[56]; covenants to repair and insure the demised premises; to reside on them; to pay compensation for damage to the property; covenants not to assign without consent or not to assign at all; to carry on a particular trade. In one case,[57] a covenant by the lessee of licensed premises that a certain person S should not be concerned in any way in the conduct of the business was held to touch and concern. Scott L.J. said[58]: " . . . where the premises are let for the purpose of some business occupation, the way in which the premises are to be used is an essential feature, and, as the rent depends on that user, the covenant dealing with the user runs with the land."

Covenants by the lessor held to run with the land include covenants to repair; to pay for improvements; and a covenant by the lessor to provide a housekeeper for the premises.

The following covenants have been held not to run: A covenant by the tenant to replace chattels on the premises which became worn out; an option to purchase the freehold given to the tenant[59]; and a right of pre-emption of adjoining land given to the tenant.

One of the best known cases dealing with the question of whether a covenant touched and concerned was *Congleton Corporation* v. *Pattison*.[60] This was a 300-year building lease and the lessees covenanted to build a silk mill. Amongst other things they covenanted to give the landlords, the Corporation, notice of every intended employee and not to employ anyone who did not have a settlement[61] in Congleton. Assignees of the lease broke this covenant and the plaintiff corporation were complaining that as a result "the township of Congleton had become liable to relieve them and their families; and had expended a large sum in the

---

[55] See above, p. 412. See also Woodfall, *Landlord and Tenant* (28th ed.) p. 457 *et seq.*

[56] See above, p. 116 *et seq.*

[57] *Lewin* v. *American & Colonial Distributors Ltd.* [1945] Ch. 225 (C.A.).

[58] *Ibid.* p. 237.

[59] But an option to purchase the freehold is an interest in and a burden on the freehold which, if registered under the L.C.A. 1925, will run with the freehold. And the benefit of the option can be assigned with the lease, see above, p. 411 *et seq.* An option to renew the lease does run though this has been described as a somewhat anomalous case.

[60] (1808) 10 East 130; 103 E.R. 725.

[61] The point was that outsiders employed by the lessees might thereby acquire a settlement in the township and thus become its responsibility under the Poor Laws in the event of unemployment.

same; and continued liable to the burden; and that the plaintiffs had also incurred great expense . . . and their estates and property in the township had been lessened in value."

But Lord Ellenborough was not to be impressed by this horror story of immigrant labour[62]:

> "But this covenant does not affect the thing demised, in one way or the other. It may indeed collaterally affect the lessors as to other lands they may have in possession in the same parish, by increasing the poor's rate upon them; but it cannot affect them even collaterally in respect of the demised premises during the term. How then can it affect the nature, quality or value of the thing demised? Can it make any difference to the mills whether they are worked by persons of one parish or another?"

A covenant which is to be performed on other land may nevertheless touch and concern the demised land. In *Ricketts* v. *Churchwardens of the Parish of Enfield*[63] the lessor covenanted not to erect buildings on a neighbouring plot in front of the building line. This was held to touch and concern. And in *Easterby* v. *Sampson*[64] a covenant by the lessee to build a new smelting mill on nearby property was held to touch and concern since it was to be used for the more effective working of the mines and minerals on the demised premises.

On the other hand, in *Thomas* v. *Hayward*[65] a covenant by the lessor of a public house not to open a rival house within half a mile of the demised premises was held not to touch and concern. Bramwell B. made the distinction[66] that "the covenant touches and concerns the beneficial occupation of the thing but not the thing itself"—a distinction which it is perhaps a little difficult to follow.[67]

---

[62] 10 East 130, at p. 135.

[63] [1909] 1 Ch. 544 (Neville J.).

[64] (1830) 6 Bing. 644; 130 E.R. 1429. Distinguished in *Dewar* v. *Goodman* [1909] A.C. 72.

[65] (1867) L.R. 4 Ex. 311. See also *Dewar* v. *Goodman* [1909] A.C. 72, where a covenant to repair adjoining premises by the sublessor was held not to touch and concern although repair was necessary to save the sublease from forfeiture.

[66] (1867) L.R. 4 Ex. 311, at p. 311. See also above, at p. 363.

[67] Contrast *Lewin's* case, above, p. 422, n.57. In *Lewin's* case Vaisey J. said of the licensed premises (p. 231): "This was not merely a lease of so much of land and so much of bricks and mortar, but . . . it was a lease of business premises. . . . " In other words it is arguable that a distinction cannot properly be made between the land and the use to which it is put. And see above, n. 18.

(2) **There must be privity of estate.**   Privity of estate means the relationship of landlord and tenant. If freehold owner L1 leases Blackacre to T1 for a 21-year term, this creates privity of estate between them. (There is also privity of contract). If the landlord assigns his reversion to L2, and the tenant assigns the residue of his lease to T2, the privity of estate has now shifted. The only privity of estate is now between L2 and T2.

Where the tenant assigns his lease the benefit and burden of any covenants which touch and concern the demised premises will run with the land (*i.e.* the lease) at common law.[68] Similarly (in this case by statute) where the landlord assigns his reversion, the benefit and burden of any covenants which have reference to the subject-matter of the lease—the statutory expression which means the same as touch and concern—will run with the reversion.[69]

If the tenant sublets, there will be no privity of estate between the head lessor and the subtenant. The covenants in the head lease will not be enforceable by or against the subtenant. However, any covenants which do satisfy the rules governing restrictive covenants which do not depend on privity will be enforceable.

There will be privity of estate between the sublessor and his subtenant and this privity of estate can support its own covenants contained in the sublease.

The benefit and burden can run with the reversion even if the lease is not by deed (*e.g.* an oral tenancy of up to three years); and even if the lease is only valid in equity under *Walsh* v. *Lonsdale.*

The benefit and burden can run with the lease provided the lease is by deed or a valid legal lease without a deed. However, it seems that if the lease is only equitable the benefit, but not the burden, can run with it.[70]

---

[68] *Spencer's Case* (1583) 5 Co.Rep. 16a; 77 E.R. 72.
[69] L.P.A. 1925, ss.141, 142. See *Re King* [1963] Ch. 459. Note that under L.P.A. 1925, s.80(4), the expression "runs with the land" includes running with the lease and with the reversion.
[70] See Hill and Redman, *Law of Landlord and Tenant* (16th ed.), p. 574.

CHAPTER 20

RESTRICTIVE COVENANTS

Principle 1. Definition

A restrictive covenant is an agreement under seal by which one landowner undertakes, for the benefit of neighbouring land, that the use of his own land will be restricted in some specified way.

Explanation

The various aspects of this definition will be clearer when the requirements of a valid restrictive covenant are considered.

Restrictive covenants are very similar to negative easements[1]; but a restrictive covenant can only be created by express agreement; it will not be implied and cannot arise by prescription.

Restrictive covenants are important and distinct from positive covenants because, although called covenants, they are not just personal agreements binding in contract. They are fully fledged property interests the burden and benefit of which can run with the land.

Principle 2. Requirements I

To create a valid restrictive covenant the following requirements must be satisfied:

(1) The covenant must be restrictive.

(2) There must be a dominant and a servient property.

(3) The covenant must touch and concern the dominant property.

Explanation

(1) **The covenant must be restrictive or negative.** A covenant is restrictive if its observance requires the servient owner to abstain from doing something. It is positive if it requires him to do something. Whether it is expressed in a positive or restrictive form is immaterial; it is the substance which matters. In the case which really gave birth to restrictive covenants, *Tulk* v. *Moxhay*,[2] the owner of Leicester Square Gardens in London sold off the Gardens retaining the surrounding land. The purchaser cove-

---

[1] Above, p. 358.
[2] (1848) 2 Ph. 774; 41 E.R. 1143.

nanted, *inter alia,* that he "his heirs and assigns should and would . . . at all times thereafter . . . keep and maintain the said piece of ground and square garden . . . in an open state, uncovered with any buildings. . . . " In form this is a positive covenant, requiring the covenantor to do something. But in substance it is negative, a covenant not to build. A covenant not to let a building fall into disrepair may sound negative. In substance, it is positive. A covenant requiring the property to be used for residential purposes only is negative. In substance it simply means that it must not be used for any other purpose.

Equity, which gave recognition to restrictive covenants as property interests, refused the same recognition to positive covenants. The reason was no doubt that the equitable remedies of specific performance and the injunction were not suitable. An ordinary injunction tells the defendant to stop doing something which he should not have started doing. Specific performance, which does order the performance of a contractual obligation, will not be granted where enforcement would require the "constant superintendence of the court."[3]

(2) **The need for a dominant and a servient property.** Like easements restrictive covenants can only exist if they are appurtenant to a dominant property. Normally, the dominant land will be a neighbouring property but it may be a different interest in the same property. A mortgagee has an interest in the property mortgaged which "he is entitled to protect by covenants restrictive of the user of it."[4] In *Regent Oil Co. Ltd.* v. *J.A. Gregory (Hatch End) Ltd.*[5] a mortgage by way of charge of leasehold premises included a covenant by the mortgagor to sell only the mortgagee's oils, etc. It was held that the covenant was enforceable against an assignee of the premises subject to the charge.[6]

And it seems also that a landlord's reversion is a sufficient dominant property to support restrictive covenants contained in the lease. This means that such covenants will be enforceable not only against the tenant but also against one such as a sub-tenant with whom there is neither privity of contract nor estate.

(3) **The covenant must touch and concern the dominant property.** This is the same as the requirement for making the

[3] *Ryan* v. *Mutual Tontine Westminster Chambers Association* [1893] 1 Ch. 116 (C.A.), at p. 123 *per* Lord Esher M.R.

[4] *Regent Oil Co. Ltd.* v. *J.A. Gregory (Hatch End) Ltd.* [1966] Ch. 402 (C.A.), at p. 433 *per* Harman L.J.

[5] n. 4, above.

[6] But this was not the main ground for the decision in the case.

benefit of positive covenants run.[7] It is also essentially the same as the requirement that an easement must accommodate the dominant property.

In the case already mentioned, *Regent Oil Co. Ltd.* v. *J.A. Gregory (Hatch End) Ltd.*[8] Salmon L.J. said[9] of the clause containing the covenant to sell only the plaintiffs' fuels, etc. (this especially for our motoring readers!):

> "I agree also that clause 1(9) does not relate solely to the promotion of the plaintiffs' business interests, but that it is in reality related to their security. . . . Moreover, the plaintiffs' petrol is known to the public as a very high class product. No doubt a number of the plaintiffs' competitors sell equally good petrol. Some however, do not. In stipulating that only a high class product (albeit the plaintiffs' exclusively) should be sold on the premises, the plaintiffs were protecting their security, although no doubt also obtaining an advantage over their competitors."

In *Re Gadd's Land Transfer*[10] there was a residential development abutting onto a private lane called Bridle Lane which gave access to the public highway. In 1955 the developers sold off another block of land (the "pink land"), for which planning permission had been refused, part of which also abutted onto Bridle Lane. The purchaser of this land covenanted that development would be limited to one dwelling-house. In 1964 there was some prospect of planning permission being obtained for 60 or so houses on the pink land and the owners applied for a declaration under the Law of Property Act 1925, s.84(2), as to whether the covenant would be binding on subsequent purchasers of the pink land. By this time the developers had sold off all the plots abutting on Bridle Lane leaving them with only the soil of the lane itself subject to all the rights of way in favour of all the plots. Finally, they had sold off the lane itself to the defendant company (whose members were residents of the various plots), and expressly assigned the benefit of the covenant to them. The real beneficiaries of the covenant to build only one dwelling-house on the pink land were the plots' owners; but there were reasons why they could not sue. This left only the defendant company and the only possible dominant property was the lane. To succeed the defendants had to

---

[7] See above, p. 412.
[8] Above, n. 4.
[9] *Ibid.* at p. 436.
[10] [1966] Ch. 56 (Buckley J.).

prove that the covenant touched and concerned their interest in Bridle Lane.

Buckley J. decided that it did touch and concern. He cited the well known statement of Farwell J. in *Rogers* v. *Hosegood*[11]: "The covenant must either affect the land as regards its mode of occupation, or it must be such as *per se,* and not merely from collateral circumstances, affects the value of the land." It was true that here the dominant property consisted of no more than ownership of the soil subject to innumerable rights of way which made it more or less valueless and unmarketable. But the building of more houses in breach of covenant would mean more people using the land and increased repair costs—and if the defendants didn't repair they ran the risk of incurring liability under the Occupiers Liability Act 1957. Further, the increased burden might make it more difficult to sell the land, for example to the residents.[12]

In *Newton Abbot Co-operative Society* v. *Williamson & Treadgold Ltd.*[13] it was held that the dominant property which was used as an ironmongers was sufficiently touched and concerned by a covenant, intended to prevent competition, not to carry on a similar business in the premises of the covenantor across the road.

This last case is authority for saying that a covenant can be regarded as touching and concerning if it is designed to benefit a business carried on on the dominant property.[14] If restrictive covenants benefit the residential use or value of property, they certainly will be accepted as touching and concerning. Most commonly used restrictive covenants come into this category—not to build; to build only in a particular way; not to carry on any business (in a residential area); or not to carry on specified trades (covenants on properties in residential developments commonly allow only those professions, such as the law, which are not considered to lower the tone and value of the neighbourhood).

The following is a typical set of restrictions which might be found included in the sale of a flat in a freehold block[15]:

> "The Purchaser so as to bind the owner for the time being of the Flat and so that this covenant shall be for the benefit and protection of the Mansion and the other flats therein and

[11] [1900] 2 Ch. 388, at p. 395.
[12] Note *Wrotham Park Estate Co.* v. *Parkside Homes Ltd.* [1974] 2 All E.R. 321 in which Brightman J. took the broad view that it was sufficient if reasonable men could believe that the land was benefited.
[13] [1952] Ch. 286 (Upjohn J.).
[14] See above, p. 413, n. 18.
[15] George and George, *Sale of Flats* (4th ed.), at pp. 272, 279.

every part thereof HEREBY COVENANTS with the Vendors and with the owners of the other flats comprised in the Mansion that the Purchaser and the persons deriving title under him will at all times hereafter observe the restrictions set forth in the First Schedule hereto.

The First Schedule above referred to

1. Not to use the Flat or permit the same to be used for any purpose whatsoever other than as a private dwelling-house in the occupation of one family only or for any purpose from which a nuisance can arise to the owners lessees and occupiers of the other Flats comprised in the Mansion or in the neighbourhood or for any illegal or immoral purpose.

2. Not to do or permit to be done any act or thing which may render void or voidable any policy of insurance on any flat in or part of the Mansion or may cause an increased premium to be payable in respect thereof.

3. Not to throw dirt rubbish rags or other refuse or permit the same to be thrown into the sinks, baths, lavatories, cisterns or waste or soil pipes in the Flat.

4. The exterior of the Flat shall not be decorated otherwise than in a manner agreed to by a majority of the owners or lessees of the flats comprised in the Mansion or (failing such agreement) in the manner (as near as may be) in which the same was previously decorated."

The above are only illustrations. In practice a number of other restrictions would also be included

Principle 3.   Requirements II

(4) For the burden of a restrictive covenant to run, the covenant must identify and show an intention to annex the burden to the servient property.

(5) For the benefit to run either,

(i) the covenant must identify and show an intention to annex the benefit to the dominant property; or,

(ii) there must be a scheme of development (a building scheme) including the dominant and servient properties (Principle 4, below).

Even if the benefit has not been annexed under (i) or (ii) it may still be assigned with the property (Principle 5, below).

Explanation

A valid restrictive covenant must satisfy the requirements set out in both this and the last Principles if the benefit and the burden are to run. It is convenient, however, to deal with these requirements in two separate parts.

If the three requirements (1), (2) and (3) are satisfied, then a covenant is *capable* of being made to run. Whether or not it does in fact run depends on the intention of the covenantor which will normally have to be gathered from the wording of the covenant.

In origin and in form a restrictive covenant is simply a contractual agreement. Equity has intervened to allow this agreement to be stamped with the character of a property interest. But the covenantor must make it clear that this is his intention; otherwise, however much it benefits a dominant property, the covenant will remain within the confines of contract law enforceable only between covenantor and covenantee as a right *in personam*.

If the covenant shows an intention to annex the burden to the servient land (requirement (4)), then the burden will run; if it shows an intention to annex the benefit to the dominant land (requirement (5)), then the benefit will run.

Annexation of the burden. The covenant must identify the servient property and show the covenantor's intention to bind the property and not just himself personally. This requirement does not normally cause problems. It is difficult to formulate a restrictive covenant without saying what land it is to affect. And in most cases it is the property which is being purchased (and therefore defined in the conveyance) which is subject to restrictive covenants. In the precedent given above,[16] the words " . . . so as to bind the owner for the time being of the Flat. . . ." show a clear intention to annex the burden to an identified property.

Even without such express words, section 79(1) of the Law of Property Act 1925 provides:

> "A covenant relating to any land of a covenantor or capable of being bound by him, shall, unless a contrary intention is expressed, be deemed to be made by the covenantor on behalf of himself his successors in title and the persons deriving title under him or them, and subject as aforesaid, shall have effect as if such successors and other persons were expressed."

[16] p. 428.

Section 79(2) provides:

> "For the purposes of this section in connexion with covenants restrictive of the user of land 'successors in title' shall be deemed to include the owners and occupiers for the time being of such land."

Provided that the burdened land is identified as the one to which the covenant relates the words implied by this section will be sufficient to make the burden of the covenant run.[17]

But the words of a covenant might, in contrast, show an intention to create a personal obligation only. In *Re Royal Victoria Pavilion Ramsgate*[18] the covenantor owned the leasehold of the pavilion in Ramsgate. He sold off other theatres which he owned there and covenanted with the purchaser that he would "procure" that until March 5, 1969, the pavilion would not be open to the public between September 30 and Whit Saturday each year. It was held that on a proper construction all this amounted to was a covenant that he himself, the covenantor, would procure, etc.—a personal covenant not intended to bind any successors in title. This was sufficient to exclude section 79.[19]

Annexation of the benefit. The covenant must identify and annex the benefit to the dominant land. This requirement has given rise to more litigation than the last. The usual formula is for the covenantor to identify and say that the covenant is for the benefit of the identified dominant land; or that it is made with the present and future owners of the land. The precedent given above is sufficient.[20] It identifies the dominant land—the Mansion and the other flats therein and every part thereof—and the words "so that this covenant shall be for the benefit and protection of the Mansion and the other flats therein and every part thereof . . . " shows a clear intention to annex.

The case of *Miles* v. *Easter*[21] illustrates the distinction between words which are and those which are not sufficient to annex the benefit. In this case, the purchasers of land by a conveyance dated

---

[17] But see the views of Lords Upjohn and Wilberforce in *Tophams Ltd.* v. *Earl of Sefton* [1966] 2 W.L.R. 814, at pp. 829, 836; contrast decision of Stamp J. at first instance, [1964] 1 W.L.R. 1408, at p. 1421.

[18] [1961] Ch. 581 (Pennycuick J.).

[19] A personal covenant may be intended to make the covenantor personally liable only for his own acts or also for the acts of subsequent owners of the land; see Megarry and Wade, *Law of Real Property* (4th ed.), pp. 724, 753, 757.

[20] p. 428.

[21] *Re Union of London and Smiths Bank Limited's Conveyance, Miles* v. *Easter* [1933] Ch. 611 (C.A.).

October 23, 1908, had made a covenant with the vendors who retained land referred to in the conveyance as the "green land." The relevant part of the covenant was that the purchasers would not do anything on the land conveyed which might be or grow to be a nuisance and that they would not erect any hotel, public house, beer house or beer shop on the property. The court had to decide whether this covenant was binding on subsequent owners of the land. Before turning to this covenant Bennett J. looked at another restrictive covenant in the same conveyance but given by the vendors to the purchasers. And he said[22]: "The phrase, 'The Vendors for themselves and their successors and assigns as owners of the land coloured green,' indicates, in my judgment, the intention to throw the burden of the negative and restrictive covenant which follows upon and to annex it to the green land, whilst the fact that the covenant is given to 'the purchasers their heirs and assigns or other the owners or owner for the time being of the land coloured pink or any part or parts thereof' is, in my judgment, a clear indication of the intention to annex the benefit of the covenant to each and every part of the pink land. Therefore the draftsman has shown that when he desires to annex the benefit and burden respectively of restrictive covenants to different parcels of land he knows the appropriate language to use in order to do so."

Bennett J. then turned to the covenant in dispute, and said[23]: "The covenant now under consideration is given to the vendors, their successors and assigns. . . . It is not given to the owner or owners for the time being of the land coloured green or any part thereof . . . and yet a reference to it is, in my judgment, necessary if the defendant's construction is to prevail. I cannot imply a reference to it."

Section 78(1) of the Law of Property Act 1925 provides that:

> "A covenant relating to any land of the covenantee shall be deemed to be made with the covenantee and his successors in title and the persons deriving title under him or them, and shall have effect as if such successors and other persons were expressed."

And the subsection goes on to provide that in connection with restrictive covenants the expression "successors in title" is to include owners and occupiers for the time being of the land.

There has been dispute about the effect of this provision; in

[22] At first instance, *ibid.* p. 623.
[23] *Ibid.* p. 624.

particular, whether it merely means that the benefit of the covenant is not confined to the covenantee personally and so can be assigned by him, or whether it means that the benefit of the covenant is (in the absence of contrary intention) annexed to the land.

It is submitted that the latter view is correct and this is supported by the decision in *Federated Homes Ltd.* v. *Mill Lodge Ltd.*[24] Here the conveyance contained a covenant that the "Purchaser shall not build at a greater density than a total of 300 dwellings so as not to reduce the number of units which the Vendor might eventually erect on the retained land under existing planning consents." The court held that the "retained land" was sufficiently identified elsewhere in the conveyance as referring to "any adjoining or adjacent property retained by the vendor." The court then went on to hold that the effect of section 78 was to give the benefit of the covenant to the vendor, his successors in title, owners and occupiers for the time being of this land, *i.e.* to annex the benefit to the retained land.

Section 78 shows that the benefit is not to be confined to the covenantee personally, and is annexed to the land, but it is still necessary for the document creating the covenant to identify the land to which it relates.

In the *Newton Abbot* case Upjohn J. said that "in order to annex the benefit of a restrictive covenant to land, so that it runs with the land without express assignment on a subsequent assignment of the land, the land for the benefit of which it is taken must be clearly identified in the conveyance creating the covenant."[25] In that case the dominant owner had to rely on express assignment because the premises for the benefit of which the covenant was taken were not even mentioned in the conveyance.

A covenant may be annexed to the whole of the dominant property or to the whole and every part of it. If it is simply annexed to the land as a whole, then it will only be enforceable by a subsequent owner of the whole; and only then if it does in fact benefit the whole. On the other hand, if, as in the normal practice,

---

[24] [1980] 1 All E.R. 371 (C.A.); and see Megarry and Wade, *Law of Real Property*, (4th ed.), at p. 764. Contrast view of G.H. Newsom, Universal Annexation, (1981) 97 L.Q.R. 32. And see D.J. Hurst, (1982) 2 Legal Studies 53.

[25] [1952] Ch. 286, at p. 289; see above, p. 428 and see *Miles* v. *Easter* n. 21 above; and see *Wrotham Park Estate Co.* v. *Parkside Homes Ltd.* [1974] 2 All E.R. 321. In *Smith and Snipes Hall Farm* v. *River Douglas Catchment Board* [1949] 2 K.B. 500 (C.A.) extrinsic evidence was allowed to identify the dominant property in the case of a positive covenant. In the *Federated Homes* case (n. 24, above) Brightman J. left the question open. For the position in the case of easements, see above, p. 367.

it is annexed to the whole and to each and every part of the specified property,[26] it will be enforceable by a subsequent owner of any part so long as it does benefit that part. In *Re Ballard's Conveyance*[27] on the sale of a piece of land, the purchaser made a covenant to erect only private dwelling-houses on the land. The covenant was expressed to be for the benefit of the land retained by the vendor known as the *Childwickby Estate* which was about 17,000 acres. Most of this land was too far away for it possibly to be affected by any breach of the covenant. The annexation therefore failed altogether.

Under section 56 of the Law of Property Act 1925, dealt with above,[28] the benefit can be annexed to land owned by someone who is not a party to the covenant.

The other method by which the benefit can be annexed, the building scheme, is dealt with in the next Principle.

Principle 4. Implied annexation of the benefit under a scheme of development (building scheme)

Where there is a scheme of development (sometimes referred to as a building scheme), the annexation of the benefit of the covenant to every property within the scheme will be implied. Express annexation will not be necessary. The owner of each property will be able to enforce the covenants against the owner of every other property within the scheme.

For a scheme of development to exist the following conditions must be satisfied:

(1) The original owner or owners[29] of the land within the scheme must have formed the intention to create a scheme, that is:

(a) To sell off a defined area of land in individual plots[30]; and
(b) to impose a common set of restrictions at the time of sale on each plot for the benefit of every other plot.

(2) The purchaser of each plot, in order to come within the scheme, must have agreed to this common set of restrictions appreciating that they were intended for the benefit of the other plots within the scheme, *i.e.* he must have appreciated that he was subjecting himself to a scheme as defined in (1) (a) and (b) above.

---

[26] See precedent, above, p. 428.
[27] [1937] Ch. 473 (Clauson J.).
[28] p. 415.
[29] See *Re Dolphin's Conveyance* [1970] 1 Ch. 654 (Stamp J.).
[30] They need not necessarily have actually laid it out beforehand in individual plots: *Baxter* v. *Four Oaks Properties* [1965] Ch. 816 (Cross J.).

Explanation

Whenever a site is divided up into plots to be developed as a single residential or other estate, it may be desirable to impose common standards on each plot in the best interests of all to preserve their value and amenities.

To some extent such common standards are achieved today through planning law and local byelaws. But even today there is scope for the more detailed control of privately created restrictions using the machinery of the restrictive covenant. And indeed such privately created restrictions may be used to thwart the public purposes of local authorities! In *Re Dolphin's Conveyance,*[31] a private scheme restricting development to one house per quarter of an acre was held to be binding on Birmingham Corporation which wanted to build several dwelling-houses and lock up garages on 0.71 of an acre which it had acquired.

Where a scheme of development is held to exist, the position is as follows: There are a number of properties forming a single estate. There is a common set of restrictions binding each property on the estate. The owner of each property has the benefit of and can enforce these restrictions against the owner of any other property on the estate.

In general, the ordinary restrictive covenant rules apply to such schemes and all the requirements must be satisfied. The one exception is that where a scheme is proved to exist, the courts do not require proof of express annexation of the benefit of the covenants to every other plot within the scheme. An intention to annex the benefit is sufficiently implied from the purchaser becoming part of the scheme when he buys his plot. "The view taken by the courts has been . . . that the common vendor imposed a common law on a defined area of land and that whenever he sold a piece of it to a purchaser who knew of the common law, that piece of land automatically became entitled to the benefit of, and subject to the burden of, the common law."[32]

The requirements, as set out in this Principle, are all essentially aimed at ensuring that the extent of the burden on each plot is defined and known to the purchaser of each plot which is to become part of the scheme. This is important because in the absence of express annexation, this extent will not be indicated by the wording of the covenant itself.

If the requirements (1) (a) and (b) are satisfied it means that there is sufficient evidence of an intention to apply a common set

---

[31] Above, n. 29.
[32] *Baxter* v. *Four Oaks Properties* (above, n. 30), at p. 826 *per* Cross J.

of restrictions to a defined area consisting of a number of individual plots and that the intention is that these restrictions are to be for the benefit of each plot and not just for the developer's personal benefit. Provided that there is sufficient evidence of this intention, it does not matter that the site was not laid out in plots on an estate plan before any sales took place.[33] Further, it does not matter that there are separate owners of different parts of the land when the scheme is set up—so long as there is proof that these different owners had a common intention to apply the scheme to the whole area.[34]

Once it is shown that a scheme has been set up in this way, it is then necessary to show that the purchaser of a plot—if the plot is to be affected—has brought his property within the scheme. This is done by showing that he has agreed to the covenants (which will be contained in the conveyance of the plot to him) in the knowledge that the vendor intends these covenants as part of a scheme. In *Re Dolphin's Conveyance*,[35] for example, the conveyance to each purchaser (except the last)[36] contained a covenant by the vendor to take a similar set of covenants from all other purchasers.

This was evidence that the purchaser knew that the vendor's intention was to create the covenants for the benefit of all plots within the defined area (Selly Hill Estate) as part of a scheme.

Principle 5.   Assignment of the benefit

In the absence of express annexation or implied annexation under a scheme of development, the benefit of a restrictive covenant may be expressly assigned with the dominant land or any part of it.

Explanation

Where there has been no annexation either express or implied under a building scheme, the benefit of a restrictive covenant cannot run with the dominant land.

It will still have validity as a contract. The original covenantee will be able to enforce against the original covenantor in contract. Again, under ordinary contract rules, he can assign the benefit as a chose in action so that the assignee can sue the original covenantor.

It will also have some effect as a property interest. Provided the

---

[33] *Baxter* v. *Four Oaks Properties*, above, n. 30.
[34] *Re Dolphin's Conveyance*, above n. 29.
[35] Above, n. 29.
[36] As to this see (1971) 87 L.Q.R. at p. 551.

other requirements or a valid restrictive covenant are satisfied the burden will run; so that the original covenantee, so long as he retains the dominant land,[37] will be able to enforce against a subsequent owner of the servient land.

But the benefit will not be attached to the dominant land so as to pass with it automatically on sale. The covenantee will in effect have two separate disconnected things—the land, and the benefit of the covenant. However, equity allows them to be assigned together so that the assignee takes the land and the benefit of the covenant and can use the benefit to protect the purchased land. And he will be able to sue not only the covenantor but any subsequent owner of the servient land.

It is important to emphasise that express assignment does no more than cure a defect in the form in which the covenant has been expressed in the first place—that is, the omission of any proper words of annexation. The dominant owner is allowed to cure this failure by showing—by extrinsic evidence[38]—that the covenant was in fact intended as a benefit for that land and that the benefit has been expressly assigned with the land.

The benefit can only be assigned with the land. The reason for allowing assignment is to enable the sale value of the property to be maintained. Once all the land has been disposed of this reason no longer applies.

The benefit can be assigned expressly to a purchaser of the whole or any part of the dominant land.[39] Thus, as with a covenant expressly annexed to each and every part, one dominant property may be split up into several.

Normally, the benefit must be assigned each time that the property changes hands.[40] However, where the benefit is held on a bare trust (*e.g.* by an executor), for the dominant owner, he has a sufficient interest in it to enable him to assign it with the land; and the absence of any express assignment from the trustee to him will not be fatal.[41]

---

[37] *Chambers* v. *Randall* [1923] 1 Ch. 149.

[38] *Newton Abbot Co-operative Society Ltd.* v. *Williamson & Treadgold* [1952] Ch. 286.

[39] See (1971) 87 L.Q.R. at p. 560.

[40] But see Megarry and Wade, *Law of Real Property* (4th ed.), at p. 768, for a possible view to the contrary.

[41] *Newton Abbot* case (n. 38, above) and *Marten* v. *Flight Refuelling* [1962] Ch. 115 (Wilberforce J.); also *Earl of Leicester* v. *Wells-next-the-Sea U.D.C.* [1972] 3 W.L.R. 486 (Plowman J.).

Principle 6.   Restrictive covenants and planning law

All property is subject to planning law. Any particular piece of property may or may not be subject to restrictive covenants.

Planning permission to develop does not entitle a landowner to ignore restrictive covenants; nor does the absence of restrictive covenants entitle him to ignore planning requirements.

Explanation

Restrictive covenants were worked out by developers in the nineteenth century and recognised by the courts at a time of rapid urban growth when there was no public planning law. They provided a method—particularly important in the middle class residential areas—whereby owners could ensure that the character, amenities and value of their properties would not deteriorate through the incursion of industry, high density building or back-to-back housing for the working classes.

As to their present position, in its Report on Restrictive Covenants, the Law Commission says[42]:

> "16. . . . it is clear that the role of restrictive covenants has, to some extent, been taken over by the planning control which Parliament has entrusted to local authorities. It is, therefore, instructive to note that, despite this, the number of registrations has been increasing in recent years and that in the period of ten years to the end of 1965 more than 600,000 new sets of restrictive covenants were entered in the Land Charges Registry alone. In addition to these, substantial numbers of new sets were noted against registered land.

> 17. These new registrations include many arising from small transactions in which, for example, a house-owner sells part of his garden for the building of one or two houses: but the majority are imposed in the laying out of new building estates for residential or industrial use. It is the invariable practice of estate developers to impose by means of restrictive covenants quite elaborate restrictions designed to give the estate a particular character which will attract purchasers and maintain the value of their unsold plots. The result is to create what has been judicially described as a kind of 'local law' for each estate. Many development companies use their own standard forms of covenant, which may vary in content according to the locality of the estate.

[42] Law Com. No. 11, para. 16 *et seq.*

18. In principle we can see no objection to the creation of 'local law' in that way, nor have we found evidence that the practice is regarded either as oppressive to the purchasers of the plots (although particular restrictions can be irksome) or as inconvenient to the planning authorities. From the individual's point of view control by private covenant has obvious advantages over planning control, in that it can cover matters of important detail with which a planning authority would not be concerned and the procedure of enforcement is available to a person who is entitled to the benefit of a covenant and is aggrieved by a breach, instead of depending on the planning authority's decision to act.

19. We conclude that, notwithstanding the broad control now exercised by planning authorities in matters such as density of building and the use of land, privately imposed restrictions will continue to have a useful part to play, complementary to that of planning controls."

Principle 7. Extinguishment of restrictive covenants

A restrictive covenant may be extinguished in any one of the following ways:

(1) Express or implied release by the dominant owner.

(2) Union of ownership of the dominant and servient properties.

(3) By statute; in particular on application to the Lands Tribunal under section 84(1) of the Law of Property Act 1925 as amended by the Law of Property Act 1969.

Explanation

Release. The dominant owner may expressly release the benefit of the covenant. In the absence of express release, a release may be implied where the acts or omissions of the dominant owner show an intention to abandon the right to the benefit of the covenant.

Such a release may be implied, for example, where the dominant owner has stood by without intervening while the servient owner spends money in breach of the covenant; or where he has released the covenant on so many neighbouring servient properties and allowed the character of the neighbourhood to change so completely that the covenant can no longer have any purpose or value. It is common to have a set of covenants affecting a particular area and it is not unusual for the dominant owner (*e.g.* an estate company) to release the covenants in particular cases.

But such an individual release will not necessarily imply a general release. In *Chatsworth Estate Company* v. *Fewell*[43] houses in a residential area were each subject to a covenant not to use the house otherwise than as a private dwelling-house. The estate company had licensed a number of the properties on the estate to be used as schools, some as blocks of flats, one as an hotel and three as boarding houses. The defendant had started to use his house on the estate as a guest house without any licence and, when challenged, claimed that all the licences previously granted had brought about a change in the residential character of the neighbourhood from which a general abandonment of the covenant could be implied. It was held that the facts did not justify this conclusion. Farwell J. put the principle like this[44]: "In some cases it is said that the plaintiffs by their acts and omissions have impliedly waived performance of the covenants. In other cases it is said that the plaintiffs, having acquiesced in past breaches, cannot now enforce the covenants. It is in all cases a question of degree. It is in many ways analogous to the doctrine of estoppel, and I think it is a fair test to treat it in that way and ask, 'Have the plaintiffs by their acts and omissions represented to the defendant that the covenants are no longer enforceable and that he is therefore entitled to use his house as a guest house?' "

A release by one dominant owner does not imply a release by another.

Unity of ownership. This follows from the principle that a man cannot have a third party right over his own land.[45]

Statute. There are a number of statutes under which there is authority by which restrictive covenants can be discharged in various circumstances. The most important is the general jurisdiction to discharge or modify given to the Lands Tribunal by section 84(1) of the Law of Property Act 1925 as amended by section 28 of the Law of Property Act 1969.

Section 84(1) as amended entitles the servient owner to apply for a discharge or modification of the restrictive covenant or any one of the following grounds:

(1) The restriction is obsolete as a result of changes in the

---

[43] [1931] 1 Ch. 224 (Farwell J.).
[44] *Ibid.*, p. 231.
[45] See above, p. 364. And see *Re Tiltwood, Sussex* [1978] 3 W.L.R. 474 (Foster J.). If both properties are part of a building scheme, unity will not destroy the covenants; see *Brunner* v. *Greenslade* [1971] Ch. 993 (Megarry J.); and *Texaco Antilles Ltd.* v. *Dorothy Kernochan* [1973] A.C. 609 (H.L.).

character of the property or neighbourhood or some other circumstance.

(2) The dominant owners have agreed expressly or by implication to the discharge or modification sought.

(3) The dominant owners will not be injured by the discharge or modification sought.

(4) The covenant is impeding the reasonable use of the land either (a) without any substantial benefit to any dominant owner; or (b) contrary to the public interest.

The discharge of a restrictive covenant can be looked at from three different points of view: the effect of the covenant on the servient land; its effect on the dominant land; and its effect on the public interest. Broadly speaking, section 84(1) allows the covenant to be discharged where the dominant owner can no longer properly claim to be protected either because his land no longer derives any substantial benefit from the covenant or because he has released it. But even where the covenant is still benefiting a dominant property it can be discharged if its continuance is not in the public interest. The main purpose of section 28 of the Law of Property Act 1969 was to widen the grounds on which the Lands Tribunal could discharge a covenant and in particular to enable them to consider the public interest as expressed in an established planning policy.[46]

The case of *Re Henman's Application*[47] was one of the earliest cases decided by the Lands Tribunal subsequent to the 1969 Act. The application concerned a plot on Wentworth's Estate at Virginia Water in Surrey. It was a three-quarter acre plot subject to a restrictive covenant against building more than one house together with a servant's lodge. The owner, Henman, sold the house with 0.405 of an acre leaving him with 0.34 of an acre for which he obtained planning permission. His application to the Lands Tribunal to discharge the restrictive covenant was rejected. As to the public interest, Sir Michael Rowe, the chairman, said[48]: "Unless it is to be said that it is against the public interest that there should be any really high class exclusive . . . estates near London, a proposition which I do not accept, then I have no doubt that it is in the public interest that the high quality should be

---

[46] L.P.A. 1925, s.84(1B), as amended by L.P.A. 1969, s.28: " . . . the Lands Tribunal shall take into account the development plan and any declared or ascertainable pattern for the grant or refusal of planning permission in the relevant areas."

[47] *Estates Gazette Digest of Cases* (1971), p. 14 (Lands Tribunal).

[48] *Ibid.* p. 17.

preserved . . . consent to modification would be breaching the fortifications of a fine estate. . . . "

Further, the covenant did still secure practical benefits both to the estates company (which still had plots to sell) and neighbouring dominant property which would have its view spoilt.

Conclusion

Restrictive and positive covenants. The main distinction between restrictive and positive covenants relating to land is that the burden of positive covenants (except in a lease) cannot normally be made to run with the servient land. Both the Law Commission and the Wilberforce Committee on Positive Covenants have recommended that the two should be assimilated and the burden of both allowed to run with the servient land.[49]

As to the problem of actually enforcing positive covenants, the Wilberforce Committee suggested that the dominant owner should be given a right of entry on to the servient property to carry out the covenant himself with a right to recover the expense as a charge on the servient property.[50]

Contractual aspects of covenants. If a restrictive covenant satisfies the necessary requirements it constitutes a fully fledged property interest, a third party right *in rem* with the burden running with the servient property and the benefit appurtenant to a dominant property. At the same time even a restrictive covenant is also a contract retaining many purely contractual characteristics. For example, the convenantee can sue the covenantor even after he has parted with the dominant land. More important the benefit can be annexed without the burden being annexed and vice versa.

Both the Law Commission and the Wilberforce Committee have recommended that a clearer distinction should be drawn between contractual and property covenants and that the latter should lose their contractual features becoming straightforward property interests. Thus, the Wilberforce Committee recommends that a clear distinction should be made between "covenants *in rem*" and "personal covenants" and that covenants *in rem* should only be enforceable between the owners for the time being of the dominant and servient properties.[51] It would not be possible to

---

[49] See above, p. 417.
[50] (1965), Cmnd. 2719, para. 22. Compare Housing Act 1974, s.125, allowing specific performance of landlord's repairing covenant.
[51] *Ibid.* paras. 16, 18, 19, and Law Com. No. 11, Proposition 6.

cure an original failure to annex by the subsequent assignment of the benefit.[52]

Covenants and easements. Restrictive covenants are very similar to negative easements, such as the right of light. Both require the servient owner to abstain from doing something on his land; both can only exist appurtenant to a dominant property and must touch and concern (or "accommodate") this dominant property. Both require separate ownership of the two properties and a capable covenantor and covenantee (grantor and grantee). The rules governing the express creation of easements and the express annexation of restrictive covenants are similar.

There are differences: There is now a more or less limited list of possible easements. There is virtually no limit to the restrictions which can be imposed on land by a properly worded restrictive covenant. Restrictive covenants can only arise from express agreement, whereas easements can also arise by implication and prescription. As already mentioned restrictive covenants still reflect their origins in contract.

If the proposals of the Law Commission and the Wilberforce Committee are accepted both positive and restrictive covenants will become more like easements, that is more purely property interests.

Registration of restrictive covenants. The need to register a restrictive covenant if the burden is to run with the land is considered later.[53]

Enforcement. Being an equitable interest, only equitable remedies are available[54]; and being a negative covenant, the only appropriate remedy is the injunction, either ordering the defendant not to breach the covenant or (by means of the mandatory injunction) ordering him to undo the wrong. As an equitable remedy, the injunction is subject to the usual equitable bars to relief; for example, where the plaintiff has delayed taking action.[55]

Under the Chancery Amendment Act 1858, the court can order damages in lieu of an injunction.[56] In *Wrotham Park Estate Co.* v.

---

[52] Law Com. No. 11, Proposition 6.

[53] Below, pp. 521, 542.

[54] Unless there is privity of contract, as between the original parties to the covenant, in which case common law damages will be available. For possibility of an action in tort for inducing breach of contract, see *Sefton* v. *Tophams Ltd.* [1965] Ch. 1140 (C.A.).

[55] See, *e.g. Bracewell* v. *Appleby* [1975] Ch. 408 (an easements case).

[56] See further, below, p. 568; and see generally, Hanbury and Maudsley, *Modern Equity*, (11th ed.), at p. 72 *et seq.*

Parkside Homes Ltd.[57] Brightman J. refused to order houses, built in breach of covenant, to be pulled down on the social ground that it would be "an unpardonable waste of much needed houses;"[58] and went on to decide that, although the usual measure of damages would be the actual loss flowing from the breach (which in this case would have led to nominal damages), he was entitled to apply the "price or hire" principle—*i.e.* ordering the payment of a reasonable sum that might have been expected for waiver of the covenant.

---

[57] [1974] 2 All E.R. 321.
[58] *Ibid.* at p. 327; and see *Bracewell* v. *Appleby* [1975] Ch. 408.

CHAPTER 21

MORTGAGES OF LAND

SECTION I. DEFINITION AND CLASSIFICATION

Principle 1.   Definition

A mortgage is a form of real security for a loan. It should be distinguished from other forms of real security such as a pledge or pawn, a lien and a charge. Both land and chattels can be mortgaged.[1] The main features of a mortgage are as follows:

(1) It arises from agreement not by operation of law.

(2) The borrower (mortgagor) transfers a proprietary interest in the property to the lender (mortgagee) but normally retains possession.

(3) The mortgagor has a right of redemption, *i.e.* a right to repay the loan (with interest at the agreed rate and incidental costs), and so to put an end to the mortgage.

(4) If the mortgagor defaults the mortgagee will be entitled to enforce his security, *i.e.* to recover what is due to him, by proceeding against the mortgaged property and, for example, selling it.[2]

(5) The mortgagee will be entitled to the satisfaction of his claim in full out of the security, to the exclusion of all other creditors except any with a prior claim to the same security.

Explanation

Secured and unsecured loans.   If I lend a friend £5 (or £500) that, without more, is an unsecured loan. There is a simple debt. I am the creditor and he is the debtor. No doubt he will repay me. If he fails to do so I can sue him, prove the debt in court and get judgment against him for the amount owing. But by the time that I get the case to court he may have disappeared or he may have gone bankrupt. If a debtor goes bankrupt, his unsecured creditors have to share what available assets he does have between them in proportion to their debts. An unsecured creditor, if he is lucky, may get, for example, 50p in the pound—that is half of what is due to him. A secured creditor will obtain payment in full, provided the security is sufficient in value.

---

[1] This chapter is concerned with land but mortgages of chattels are subject to similar rules.

[2] In addition to suing the mortgagor personally for debt.

Most lenders will therefore want some form of security. Go to your bank manager and ask him to lend you £10,000. He will explain to you what security is! It simply means some guarantee that the debt will be repaid even if the debtor himself fails to repay.

There are two types of security: personal and real.[3]

Personal security means the guarantee given by another person. It gives the creditor another personal claim for the debt against an extra person. But just as payment by the debtor depends on the continued solvency of the debtor, so payment by the guarantor depends on the continued solvency of the guarantor. Neither gives any preference over other creditors.

Real security means that there is some specified property against which the creditor can enforce payment; and that the other creditors (except those with a prior interest)[4] cannot touch the security until he has been satisfied in full. "A right protected by a real security entitles the creditor to take the security for the discharge of his own secured debt even to the extent of exhausting the whole security and of withdrawing it altogether from the general creditors."[5]

Some of the advantages of the real security—in this case the mortgage—can be shown by an illustration. Suppose the following to be the sad story of one Spendthrift.

1974. He mortgages Blackacre to X to secure a loan of £5,000.

1975. He borrows a further £2,000 this time from Y on a further mortgage of Blackacre.

1976. His bank account is £500 overdrawn. The bank has no security.

1977. Spendthrift goes bankrupt.

His assets consist of Blackacre, which is sold for £6,000, and £500 in premium bonds. Three worried creditors are between them owed £7,500 with only £6,500 to meet it. X has his security; he is entitled to his £5,000 in full. Y has his security too; but X's mortgage cannot be affected by Y's subsequent interest.[6] Y will have to wait his turn and there will be only £1,000[7] for him from the proceeds of Blackacre. This leaves him an unsecured creditor for £1,000, with the bank an unsecured creditor for £500 and total

[3] See Fisher and Lightwood, *Law of Mortgages* (9th ed.), p. 3.
[4] See below, p. 484, for priority.
[5] Waldock, *Mortgages*, p. 2.
[6] Assuming that the priority is the same as the order of creation. See below, p. 484, for priority.
[7] Ignoring the costs of sale which would have to be paid first, before X and Y, out of the proceeds of sale.

assets of only £500. Y and the bank will each get one-third of his debt.

A mortgage of land has a particular advantage. Unlike chattels, land cannot in general be moved; so that the mortgagee will always be able to find his security without having to retain possession of it.[8] Further, land is not in general likely to depreciate in value and become insufficient to satisfy the loan.

A mortgage arises from agreement. Unlike a lien, a mortgage arises as a result of an agreement between the parties. A legal lien[9] is the right of a creditor to retain possession of the debtor's property until his claim is satisfied. If you take your car to a garage to be repaired, the garage will be entitled to retain possession until their bill has been paid. This lien does not arise from an agreement between the parties; it is given to the creditor by law.

A mortgage depends on a property interst, not possession. Like a mortgage, a pledge or pawn is created as a result of an agreement. But here the essence of the security is that possession of the security is given to the pledgee to retain until the debt and interest is paid. A mortgagee is entitled to possession of the property; but his security depends upon his mortgage interest and not on possession. Indeed, this is one of the advantages of the mortgage. If you mortgage your house you will invariably be allowed to go on living there so long as you do not default. If you pawn your watch you will not be able to tell the time by it until you redeem.

The mortgage and the charge. A charge is the appropriation of real or personal property for the discharge of a debt or other obligation.[10] In its legal effect is is very similar to a mortgage; but the chargee, unlike the mortgagee, does not obtain any ownership interest in the security or possesion of it. But he does of course have an interest in the property (*i.e.* his charge) which is enforceable by the appropriate legal action.

One form of charge is the charge by deed expressed to be by way of legal mortgage (commonly referred to as the "legal charge"). Under section 85 (1) of the Law of Property Act 1925, this is one of the two methods by which a legal mortgage of land can be

---

[8] But to realise it he will actually have to take possession which might give some difficulty in practice, see below, p. 459.

[9] See Crossley Vaines, *Personal Property* (5th ed.), p. 137. An equitable lien is a charge given to a person by equity in certan situations, to secure a claim. See Halsbury, *Laws of England* (4th ed.), Vol. 28, p. 245. For the equitable lien given to vendors and purchasers of land, see below, p. 566.

[10] *Fisher and Lightwood* (n. 3, above), p. 4.

created. And section 87 (1) of the Law of Property Act 1925 provides that a mortgagee will have the same "protection, powers and remedies" whichever method is used. This particular type of charge is therefore now indistinguishable in its effect from a mortgage.

Any other charge will be an equitable charge[11] of which there are different categories—for example, the limited owner's charge; and the general equitable charge. Equitable charges are enforceable, *inter alia,* by applying to court for an order for the sale of the land.[12]

Principle 2. Types of mortgages

The following mortgages of either freehold or leasehold land can be created:
1. Mortgages of the legal estate. These may be either:
    (a) legal mortgages, or
    (b) equitable mortgages ("informal" mortgages).
2. Equitable mortgages of an equitable interest.

Explanation

Both freehold and leasehold may be mortgaged. Any ownership interest in land can be mortgaged. But the value of it as a security and consequently the amount that a lender will be prepared to advance must depend in part on the extent of the borrower's interest. A two-year lease of a small house can be mortgaged; but the security will disappear when the lease expires, and so if anyone is prepared to lend on such a security it is likely to be a small amount repayable over a short period.

Legal and equitable mortgages of the legal estate. The estate owner—the person who holds the legal estate—can create either a legal or equitable mortgage of that estate. His mortgage will be equitable either because he has chosen an equitable mortgage by preference or because he has failed to comply with the formalities necessary to create a legal mortgage. The distinction between the two is considered further below.[13] It is important because an equitable mortgagee may not have the same remedies as a legal mortgagee.

Only an equitable mortgage can be created from an equitable

---

[11] L.P.A. 1925, s. 1.
[12] See *Supreme Court Practice* (1979), O. 88 (p. 1321).
[13] p. 479.

interest. It is a general principle of English property law that an interest created out of a legal estate may be legal or equitable but that only an equitable interest can be created out of another equitable interest.

Capacity. The beneficial freeholder or leaseholder can borrow money for whatever purpose he likes on the security of his land—so long as he can find a willing lender. On the other hand, trustee owners—trustees for sale, tenants for life, personal representatives, etc.—are empowered to borrow money for certain purposes on the security of the trust property.[14]

Principle 3. Classification by method of repayment

Mortgages may be:
(a) instalment; or
(b) standing; or
(c) fluctuating.[15]

Explanation

Any mortgage involves the mortgagor in repaying the loan (referred to as "the capital") together with interest on that capital at the agreed rate and also generally the mortgagee's costs incurred in creating and discharging the mortgage. The mortgage will be the security for the repayment of all these sums (the "mortgage money"). The distinction between an instalment and a standing mortgage lies in the method by which the mortgage money is repaid. The choice between the two methods affects the borrower's finances rather than his legal rights.

Instalment mortgages. The majority of mortgage loans today are made by building societies to assist with the purchase of homes. And generally such loans are repayable by instalments. The usual instalment method is that the borrower makes equal monthly payments for an agreed number of years (often 20 or 25). Each payment represents a part repayment of capital together with interest on the amount outstanding. The payments are so calculated that at the end of the agreed period the capital and all interest will have been repaid in full.

Standing mortgages. Before the advent of building societies and similar financial institutions, if an individual wanted to borrow

---

[14] See above, p. 217.
[15] For a more detailed classification, see *Fisher and Lightwood* (n. 3, above), p. 30.

money for any purpose he would normally have to find another private individual with money to lend. And if a private individual had surplus capital one of the best, indeed one of the few, forms of investment was to lend it on the security of land.

Such a mortgage would normally be a standing mortgage. The borrower would be required to pay interest on the sum borrowed regularly—perhaps every six months—but he would not be required to repay any part of the capital. The lender would not want repayment in small amounts, or at all, so long as the investment was satisfactory. The capital would only be repaid—in one lump sum—if the lender decided that he needed the money for some other purpose and called in the loan,[16] or if the borrower decided for any reason to redeem.

In the relatively few cases where private individuals still lend on the security of mortgages, this method is likely to be used. It is also used—but in a rather special way—by insurance companies and building societies when repayment is to be provided for by an endowment policy. What happens here is that the borrower makes regular payments which represent interest only. Instead of paying instalments of the capital debt, he pays regular premiums on a life endowment insurance policy on his own life. The result is that when the policy matures after an agreed number of years or on his prior death, the insurance money will become available to repay the capital in one lump-sum. In substance, therefore, this really amounts to repayment by instalments.[17]

Fluctuating mortgages. This term is used in this book to refer to bank mortgages where land is mortgaged to the bank to secure an overdraft on current account. Here the amount of the loan fluctuates. Each time that the customer pays into the account he is making a repayment; each time that he draws a cheque on the account he is taking a further loan (a "further advance"). Such mortgages give rise to special rules considered below.[18]

---

[16] The mortgagee can, subject to agreement to the contrary in the mortgage, enforce repayment by threatening foreclosure or by giving 3 months' notice to repay with sale in default (see below, p. 456). The same methods may be used to get the mortgagor to agree to pay a higher rate of interest.

[17] Mortgage law will only be understood if it is remembered that most of the common law and equity on the subject was developed in relation to standing mortgages.

[18] p. 495.

SECTION II. LEGAL FREEHOLD AND LEASEHOLD MORTGAGES

Principle 4.   Creation of legal mortgages

A legal mortgage of freehold land can be created by either of the following two methods:

(a) A demise for a term of years absolute (generally 3,000) with a proviso for cesser on redemption.

(b) A charge by deed expressed to be by way of legal mortgage.[19]

A legal mortgage of leasehold land can be created by either:

(a) A sub-demise for a term of years absolute, at least one day (generally it is made about 10 days) less that the mortgaged lease with a proviso for cessor on redemption.

(b) A charge by deed expressed to be by way of legal mortgage.[20]

The choice of method will make no difference to the rights of the parties.[21]

Explanation

Only a legal estate can be subject to a legal mortgage. In addition the mortgage must be created by deed and must employ one of the two methods referred to above—a term of years granted to the mortgagee or a charge by deed expressed to be by way of legal mortgage.

Demise method. The demise method was available before 1926; but the commonest method then—abolished in 1925[22]—was an outright conveyance of the fee simple to the mortgagee with a proviso for reconveyance on redemption. The demise method conforms to the 1925 legislation principle of keeping legal ownership in the real owner who will be dealing with the land—that is the mortgagor.[23] The mortgagor will retain the legal reversion on the term of years granted.

The real demerit of the demise method is that to a layman, untutored in the legal mysteries, what is supposed to be a

---

[19] L.P.A. 1925, s. 85 (1).
[20] *Ibid.* s. 86 (1).
[21] *Ibid.* s. 87.
[22] *Ibid.* ss. 85 (2), 86 (2).
[23] Under the old conveyance method the mortgagor had only an equity of redemption. See for example *Millett* v. *Davey* (1863) 31 Beav. 470; 54 E.R. 1221; see below, p. 478.

mortgage looks to him very much like a 3,000-year lease. The vital clause will be something like this:

> "The Borrower as beneficial owner Hereby Demises unto the Lender All That the mortgaged property (which will be described) To Hold the same unto the Lender for a term of 3,000 years from the date hereof without impeachment of waste and subject to the proviso for redemption hereinafter contained."

Technically there *is* a lease. The mortgagee *does* have a 3,000-year term. And from time to time the judges have had to consider whether they should apply various leasehold rules to mortgages.[24] But, although certain leasehold rules apply, the transaction is a mortgage in substance and a lease in form only; and the rights and liabilities of the parties are those of mortgagor and mortgagee, not landlord and tenant.

In the case of a mortgage of leasehold property, the mortgagee will technically be given a sub-lease due to expire a few days before the lease which is being mortgaged. This leaves the mortgagor with the legal leasehold reversion vested in him. Again, despite the form, the rights and liabilities of the parties are essentially those of mortgagor and mortgagee, not tenant and sub-tenant.

The charge method. As this method avoids the leasehold form it avoids the possible confusion between two quite different transactions. A typical formula will be:

> "In consideration of the advance, the Borrower as Beneficial Owner charges the property, short particulars of which appear in the First Schedule, by way of legal mortgage, with the repayment to the Society of the advance interest and other moneys covenanted to be paid by the Borrower or otherwise secured by the Mortgage."

Two points should be noted. First, as with the demise method,

---

[24] See for example *Regent Oil Co. Ltd.* v. *J.A. Gregory (Hatch End) Ltd.* [1966] Ch. 402 (C.A.). The attornment clause by which a mortgagor acknowledges himself as a tenant of the mortgagee does not give the mortgagor protection under the Rent Acts (*Steyning & Littlehampton Building Society* v. *Wilson* [1951] Ch. 1018; *Fisher and Lightwood* (n. 3, above), p. 32). And see *Portman Building Society* v. *Young* [1951] 1 All E.R. 191, 193, *per* Sir R. Evershed M.R. on the relationship between mortgagor and mortgagee.

the mortgage must be by deed. Secondly, the mortgage deed must state expressly that it is by way of legal mortgage.[25]

The other main advantage of the charge method is that, with a single formula for freehold and leasehold property, both types can be included in a single mortgage deed using a single charging clause as in the precedent above. With the demise method, the document will be complicated by the fact that there will have to be a demise of the freehold property and a sub-demise of the leasehold. The vast majority of mortgages today use the charge method.

The legal position of all parties is exactly the same whichever of the two methods is used. Section 87 of the Law of Property Act 1925 provides that in the case of a legal charge, the mortgagee shall have "the same protection, powers and remedies (including the right to take proceedings to obtain possession . . .)" as if the mortgage had been created by demise.

If the above requirements for the creation of a legal mortgage are not satisfied, the transaction may still be effective as an equitable mortgage.[26]

Legal mortgages of registered land.[27] In general, mortgages of registered and unregistered land are created in exactly the same way. The real difference lies in the way in which the mortgagee's interest is protected against subsequent owners and incumbrancers.

Thus the charge or the demise method may be used. As with unregistered land the charge is the method usually used. Building societies commonly use a single standard form for registered and unregistered land.

The normal method of protecting a legal mortgage of registered land is to register it as a "registered charge." The mortgagee will be registered as proprietor of the charge in the Charges Register of the Register of Title of the property in question. The land certificate will be held at the Land Registry and the mortgagee will receive a charge certificate. Any number of legal mortgages of registered land can be created and protected in this way.

---

[25] In the case of registered land the deed does not need to state expressly that it is by way of legal mortgage. *Cityland & Property (Holdings) Ltd.* v. *Dabrah* [1968] Ch. 166.

[26] See below, p. 479.

[27] See further, below, p. 546 for mortgages of registered land.

## Principle 5.	Mortgagee's rights: General

The mortgagee has certain rights to enable him both to enforce and to protect his security. Whilst these rights exist for the benefit of the mortgagee, when exercising them he owes a duty of care to the mortgagor not unnecessarily to damage the latter's interest in the property.

His more important rights are:

(1) To sue the mortgagor personally on the covenants in the mortgage deed.
(2) To take possession.
(3) To sell.
(4) To foreclose.
(5) To appoint a receiver.
(6) To lease.
(7) To insure.
(8) To hold the title deeds.

Explanation

The mortgagor's interest in the property is commonly referred to as his equity of redemption (or just his "equity").[28] The property is his subject only to the mortgage.

The mortgagee is not, so it has been said,[29] a trustee for the mortgagor. Each holds his own separate interest in the property. The mortgagee has his mortgage; the mortgagor his equity. Nevertheless, many of the mortgagee's powers—especially his power to take possession and his power of sale—do put him in a position to damage the mortgagor's interest. If, for example, he exercises his power of sale and obtains no more than the amount due to him under his mortgage, then the mortgagor's equity will have disappeared realising nothing.

Chancery, in controlling the mortgagee, has always taken the view that the purpose of a mortgage is to secure repayment of the loan with interest and costs. The mortgagee has no right to speculate with or make an additional profit for himself out of the property. Further, whilst the mortgagee is entitled to prefer his own interest where there is a conflict, he does owe a duty of care when handling the property to preserve the mortgagor's equity. The following Principles will now deal with the specific rights of the mortgagee.

---

[28] For explanation of equity of redemption, see below, at p. 478.
[29] *Cuckmere Brick Co. Ltd.* v. *Mutual Finance Ltd.* [1971] Ch. 949, 969, *per* Cross L.J. But the decision in this case shows that he is very much in the position of a trustee in so far as he is in control of the mortgagor's interest in the property.

Principle 5a. Mortgagee's rights: (i) To sue on the covenants

The mortgagee has a personal action against the mortgagor on the covenant to repay and on any other covenant contained in the mortgage deed.

Explanation

The main purpose of the mortgage deed, whether by charge or demise, is to give the mortgagee his mortgage interest in the property. In addition, however, every mortgage deed will contain a number of express covenants by the mortgagor. In general, these will be purely personal covenants ' enforceable only by the mortgagee against the mortgagor himself.[30] And in general they will be designed to protect the security in some way.

Invariably there will be a covenant to repay the moneys secured by the mortgage. For example[31]:

> "The Borrower will pay to the Society the monthly payments referred to in this Mortgage on the day specified so long as they are payable together with all such fines fees and other moneys as may become payable by him in respect of the Advance."

In addition there will be a number of other covenants to keep in repair, insure, not to alter the property without consent and so on. A mortgagor can always sell the property subject to the mortgage[32]—that is sell the equity of redemption—but he will remain liable on these covenants.[33] In practice, the mortgagor will obtain his release either by discharging the mortgage (leaving the purchaser to obtain his own mortgage loan) or by getting the mortgagee to accept covenants from the purchaser in substitution for his own.

The personal covenant to repay may be important where for any reason the realisation of the security does not raise sufficient money to discharge the mortgage debt in full.

---

[30] But see *Regent Oil Co. Ltd.* v. *J A. Gregory (Hatch End) Ltd.* [1966] Ch. 402 (C.A.) which suggests that, at least where there is an attornment clause, covenants may run by virtue of privity of estate so as to bind a person who purchases the land subject to the mortgage. For covenants running by virtue of privity of estate, see above, p. 419 *et seq.*

[31] Halifax B.S. Form L.M. 18. Even in the absence of an express covenant, there is a personal debt.

[32] As to risk from consolidation when buying a property subject to a mortgage, see below, p. 492.

[33] The purchaser may also be liable; see n. 30, above.

Principle 5b.   Mortgagee's rights: (ii) Sale

The mortgagee has a statutory right to sell the legal estate vested in the mortgagor free of the mortgagor's equity of redemption provided that:

    (a)the mortgage was by deed;
    (b)the mortgage money is due.[34]

He cannot exercise this right to sell unless, in addition, one of the following events specified in section 103 of the Law of Property Act 1925 has occurred:

  (i) the mortgagor has failed to repay the loan after being given at least three months' notice to do so; or

  (ii) the mortgagor is at least two months in arrears with the payment of interest; or

  (iii) the mortgagor is in breach of any covenant in the mortgage deed (other than those for the payment of money).[35]

When selling, the mortgagee must take reasonable care to obtain "the true market value" of the property.[36]

The interests of the mortgagor and any subsequent mortgagees will be overreached[37] and the mortgagee will hold any surplus proceeds of sale in trust for the subsequent mortgagees and the mortgagor in accordance with their priority.[38]

Explanation

If a mortgagor defaults—fails to keep up with his payments—the mortgagee may allow the mortgage to continue and take steps to recover arrears by taking possession, appointing a receiver or suing on the personal covenants. Alternatively, he may decide to put an end to the mortgage altogether and obtain repayment of the full loan. To do this, he can again sue on the personal covenant or start foreclosure proceedings; but the method normally adopted today is to obtain possession and sell.[39]

Protection of the purchaser.   A purchaser from a mortgagee

---

[34] L.P.A. 1925, s. 101 (1) (i); see further, below, p. 470.

[35] The mortgage may expressly alter or extend the circumstances in which the mortgagee can exercise the power of sale. And see the Consumer Credit Act 1974, ss. 87, 126.

[36] *Cuckmere Brick Co. Ltd.* v. *Mutual Finance Ltd.* [1971] Ch. 949 (C.A.) p. 968, *per* Salmon L.J.

[37] L.P.A. 1925, s. 104 (1).

[38] *Ibid.* s. 105.

[39] The mortgagee can also use the threat of sale to persuade the mortgagor to repay the loan (L.P.A. 1925, s. 103 (1)) or to agree to a higher rate of interest (by threatening to call in the loan if it is not agreed).

must always check that the power of sale has arisen; he must check that the mortgage is by deed and that under the terms of the mortgage the mortgage money is in fact due.[40] If the power of sale has not arisen, the purchaser can only take subject to the mortgagor's right to redeem.

The purchaser does *not* need to check whether one of default events specified in section 103 has occurred. If the power of sale has not become exercisable in accordance with section 103 or the provisions of the mortgage, the mortgagee will be personally liable to the mortgagor for any loss, but the title of the purchaser will not be invalidated. Section 104 of the Law of Property Act 1925, designed to facilitate the transfer of land in such a situation, provides that "the title of the purchaser shall not be impeachable on the ground:

(a) that no case has arisen to authorise the sale; or
(b) that due notice was not given; or
(c) . . . that leave of the court, when so required, was not obtained; or
(d) . . . that the power was otherwise improperly or irregularly exercised."

The section goes on to provide that the purchaser is not concerned to investigate these matters. This section means that the purchaser bona fide[41] need not investigate the propriety of the sale.[42] His mere failure to investigate will not fix him with constructive notice[43] of any irregularity. But it has been held that if he does happen to discover some irregularity then he will not be acting in good faith and will not be protected.[44]

Duty of mortgagee as to price. A building society exercising its statutory power of sale is under a statutory obligation to obtain the

---

[40] See further, below, p. 470.

[41] See L.P.A. 1925, s. 205 (1) (xxi).

[42] s. 104 protection extends to any irregularity under the Consumer Credit Act 1974; see s. 177 (2) of that Act. For the application of the Consumer Credit Act 1974 to Mortgages, see J. Adams, Mortgages and the Consumer Credit Act 1974, (1975) 39 Conv. (N.S.) 94; Fisher and Lightwood, *Law of Mortgages* (9th ed.), Ch. 9.

[43] See below, p. 514 *et seq.*, for constructive notice.

[44] It has been suggested that the sale may be set aside against a purchaser who had only constructive notice of the irregularity: see *Fisher and Lightwood* (n. 3, above), at p. 367. But the cases cited there are all cases of actual notice by the purchaser. *Bailey* v. *Barnes* [1894] 1 Ch. 25 was concerned with the title of a purchaser from a purchaser. The predecessor to s. 104 was therefore not strictly relevant.

best price reasonably possible.[45] Any other mortgagee is under a similar, if not identical, obligation to get what has been described as the "true market value."

In *Cuckmere Brick Co. Ltd.* v. *Mutual Finance Ltd.*[46] the mortgagees sold the mortgaged land by auction but failed to advertise that it had the benefit of planning permission for 100 flats with garages; and when informed of the omission by the mortgagors they refused to postpone sale to allow further advertising. It was held that they must account to the mortgagors for the extra price that could have been obtained.

In conducting the sale, choosing the method, the time, etc., the mortgagee is entitled to give preference to his own proper interest. But subject to this, he owes a duty of care to the mortgagor. And he cannot sell to himself.[47]

Overreaching effect of the conveyance. Provided the sale is regular (or, if irregular, is protected under section 104), the purchaser will take the legal estate—until then vested in the mortgagor—free of the mortgagor's equity of redemption and free of any subsequent mortgages. The mortgagee will receive the purchase money and hold it in trust for the mortgagor and subsequent mortgagees in accordance with their respective interests.[48]

The sale by a mortgagee is one of the few cases under modern land law where a legal estate can be transferred by a person other than the estate owner. A mortgagee has a long term of years (or the equivalent if the mortgage is by way of legal charge). He can at any time sell or otherwise dispose of his rights as a mortgagee. This is called a transfer of the mortgage and merely transfers the interest and rights held by the mortgagee. The mortgagor's equity is not affected. On the other hand, if the mortgagee exercises the power of sale, what he transfers to the purchaser is the legal freehold (or leasehold) vested in the mortgagor.

The proceeds of sale. As trustee of the purchase money, the mortgagee must distribute it as follows[49]:

(a) To discharge any prior mortgages if they have joined in the sale. A sale by one mortgagee cannot affect the interest of any *prior* mortgagee but commonly the prior mortgagees will agree, in

---

[45] Building Societies Act 1962, s. 36. Compare the duty of the trustee for sale and the tenant for life.
[46] [1971] Ch. 949 (C.A.).
[47] *Williams* v. *Wellingborough B.C.* [1975] 3 All E.R. 462.
[48] L.P.A. 1925, ss. 104, 105. And see :Duke v. *Robson* [1973] 1 W.L.R. 267.
[49] *Ibid.* s. 105.

order to get a better sale, to release their mortgages on condition that they are satisfied out of the proceeds.[50]

(b) To pay the expenses of the sale.

(c) To pay what is due to himself.

(d) To pay any balance to the mortgagee next in order of priority or, if there is none, to the mortgagor. For this purpose the mortgagee will have to search the appropriate register for subsequent mortgages. If there is a subsequent mortgagee to whom the balance is paid, he will satisfy his own claim and hand on the surplus in the same way. Ultimately, at the end of the queue, the mortgagor will receive any money left over as representing his equity.

Principle 5c. Mortgagee's rights: (iii) Possession

Subject to the terms of the mortgage deed and the Administration of Justice Act 1970, the mortgagee is entitled to possession of the mortgaged property at any time.

If he takes possession he must account not only for the actual income from the property but also for the income which, but for his gross mismanagement, it could have produced.[51]

Whilst in possession he must take reasonable steps to preserve the property.[52]

If he remains in possession for 12 years without acknowledging the mortgagor's title and without any payment, the mortgagor's right to redeem will be barred.[53]

Explanation

The right to possession,[54] Unlike sale, taking possession does not put an end to the mortgage. The general principle is that the mortgagee is entitled to take possession as soon as the mortgage has been created—before the ink on the mortgage is dry, as one judge put it. He does not have to show any default by the mortgagor or even that the mortgage money is due.

There are two possible limitations to the right to possession. First, it may be limited by the express or implied terms of the

---

[50] See below, p. 484.

[51] See *Fisher and Lightwood* (n.3, above), pp. 293, 294, 295; Coote, *Mortgages* (9th ed.), Vol. 1, p. 830.

[52] *Fisher and Lightwood* (n. 3, above), p. 296 *et seq.*

[53] Limitation Act 1980, ss. 16, 29 (4), 31 (3) (4).

[54] As to what amounts to taking possession, see *Mexborough U.D.C.* v. *Harrison* [1964] 1 W.L.R. 733 (Pennycuick J.).

mortgage deed.[55] Building society mortgages commonly provide that the society will not take possession unless there has been some specified default by the mortgagor. Secondly, under the Administration of Justice Act 1970, s. 36,[56] where the mortgagee of a dwelling-house is claiming possession, the court has a wide discretion to delay his entry on such terms as it thinks fit. For example, it may suspend execution of the order for possession whilst the mortgagor is given a chance to pay off arrears of instalments or to repay the whole loan.[57] And if the mortgage provides (as is common in instalment mortgages) for the whole mortgage loan to become due immediately on default, the court may ignore such a provision. The court must be satisfied that the mortgagor is likely to be able not only to pay off arrears, but also to maintain future instalments.[58] Apart from these two possibilities the court has no jurisdiction to refuse the mortgagee's claim to possession.[59]

To the mortgagee his mortgage is an investment and, as long as he is receiving the agreed payments, he is not likely to want possession. Possession would only be an embarrassment, and indeed because of the liability to account strictly, a burden. If the mortgagee is seeking to recover arrears he is better advised to appoint a receiver. And in practice today a mortgagee will normally only seek possession if the situation is hopeless and he wants to exercise the power of sale with vacant possession.

Liability to account strictly. If the mortgagee does take

---

[55] See *Esso Petroleum Co. Ltd.* v. *Alstonbridge Properties Ltd.* [1975] 3 All E.R. 358 (Walton J.); and *Western Bank Ltd.* v. *Schindler* [1976] 2 All E.R. 393 (C.A.).

[56] As amended by the Administration of Justice Act 1973, s. 8. Under the 1973 Act the power is extended to foreclosure proceedings. See R.J. Smith "The Mortgagee's Right to Possession," [1979] Conv. 266.

[57] See *Royal Trust Co. of Canada* v. *Markham* [1975] 3 All E.R. 433 (C.A.); and *Western Bank Ltd.* v. *Schindler* (above).

[58] Administration of Justice Act 1973, s. 8, amending the courts' interpretation of the 1970 Act in *Halifax B.S.* v. *Clark* [1973] Ch. 307. On application of s. 8 to a traditional standing mortgage, see *Centrax Trustees Ltd.* v. *Ross* [1979] 2 All E.R. 952 (Goulding J.). For suggestion that there might be a wider judicial power to refuse possession if not sought to protect the value of, or enforce, the security, see *Quennell* v. *Maltby* [1979] 1 All E.R. 569. See A. Nicol, Outflanking Protective Legislation—Shams and Beyond, (1981) 44 M.L.R. 21, at p. 35. For position of a spouse of the mortgagor in possession cases, see Matrimonial Homes Act 1967, ss. 1(5), 7A, as amended by Matrimonial Homes and Property Act 1981.

[59] But only jurisdiction to grant a limited adjournment to give the mortgagor a chance to redeem; *Birmingham Citizens Permanent B.S.* v. *Caunt* [1962] Ch. 883.

possession an account will evenutally have to be prepared.[60] On the one hand this account will debit him with sums that he has or should have received from the property; on the other hand it will credit him with sums due to him under the mortgage and any expenses which he has properly incurred in respect of the property. If all the items on the account cannot be agreed between the parties, the court will have to adjudicate.

If it can be shown that the mortgagee could reasonably have obtained a greater income he will be charged with this in the accounts and so the loss will fall on him. In *White v. City of London Brewery Co.*,[61] the plaintiff was a small publican who "took a public house in the Isle of Dogs, and having no money with which to carry on business, he was obliged to borrow. In such a case it is usual to borrow from brewers, and the plaintiff borrowed from the defendants, the brewery company, to whom he gave a mortgage of his public house to secure £700 advanced at once, and such further sums of money as they might advance, with a proviso that the sum recoverable under the security should not exceed £900. The business turned out a total failure."[62]

The defendants took possession and subsequently let the premises. This lease contained a tie clause by which the lessee agreed to take all his "ale, beer and porter" from the defendants. Eventually the property was sold by the defendants as mortgagees and an account taken. The issue was whether they must account to the plaintiff for the extra income which they would have received had they let the premises as a free house. It was held that they must. "Now they are bound to account to him after the sale—for the proceeds of the sale for any rents which they have received, or but for their wilful default or neglect might have received from the property while they were in possession; and for any profits which during that period they made out of and by the mortgaged property. They have not to account for anything more, and as against that they are entitled to set the expenses which they have fairly incurred in consequence of having been obliged to take possession, and keep possession and to sell. They have a right to set off against the sale the expenses of the sale. They have a right to set off against the rents and profits they have recieved, any rents which they have been obliged to pay [it was leasehold property] and any insurance they were obliged to pay, and anything else

---

[60] For the practice on taking of accounts, see *Supreme Court Practice* (1979), O. 43, p. 674.

[61] (1889) 42 Ch.D. 237 (C.A.).

[62] *Ibid.* headnote.

which was an expense put upon them by reason of their being obliged to take and keep possession."[63]

Duty to preserve the property. Usually, the mortgagee will be "without impeachment of waste."[64] But in the case of a mortgagee this does not mean that he can indulge in what voluntary or permissive waste he likes. It really means that he can commit waste but only so long as it is justified by his position as mortgagee.[65]

The mortgagee in possession must keep the premises in reasonable repair so long as there is income available from the property[66] to meet the cost; and this expenditure will be allowed to him in the accounts. If he wrongfully fails to repair he will be charged with any resulting deterioration in the accounts.[67]

He may also be allowed the cost of reasonable improvements which increase the value of the premises.

In general, he must not commit voluntary waste. The court, in such a case, "would interfere by injunction to prevent him from destroying any part of the inheritance: it would say, you are in possession of a property sufficient to keep down the interest on your mortgage and to pay all that is due to you on your mortgage, you, if you please, may file a bill to foreclose, but you are not entitled to destroy any part of the inheritance, and if you do so, it is at your risk and peril, and you must make that good to the mortgagor in taking the account."[68] For example, he must not open mines. If he does so, he will have to account for the value of the minerals taken and any profit on them without being allowed his expenses. However, if the security is insufficient, he may as it were "dig into" the capital and, for example, open mines, and cut timber. In this case he will only have to account for the profit after deduction of his expenses; but if he makes a loss it seems that it will fall entirely on him and cannot be charged to the mortgagor.[69] Further, he has a statutory right, in the absence of provision to the contrary, to cut and sell timber which is ripe for cutting.[70]

---

[63] *Ibid.* p. 243, *per* Lord Esher M.R.

[64] See L.P.A. 1925. s. 87 (1), which applies where the charge method is used. Where the leasehold method is used it will invariably be made expressly without impeachment of waste.

[65] See generally *Fisher and Lightwood* (n. 3, above), p. 350 *et seq.*

[66] He need not spend his own money.

[67] See Coote (n. 51, above), p. 830.

[68] *Millett* v. *Davey* (1863) 31 Beav. 470, 475, *per* Sir John Romilly M.R. (54 E.R. 1221, 1223).

[69] See *Millett* v. *Davey* (n. 68, above); *Thorneycroft* v. *Crockett* (1848) 16 Sim. 445; 60 E.R. 946.

[70] L.P.A. 1925, s. 101 (1) (iv).

Application of income.   The balance of income as shown by the accounts must be used to pay the interest due under the mortgage. He may, but is not obliged to, use any surplus towards repaying capital. Otherwise any balance must be paid to the mortgagor.

Limitation.   If the mortgagee remains in possession, in his capacity as mortgagee, for 12 years without accepting any payment of any part of the mortgage moneys and without making any written acknowledgment of the mortgagor's title then the mortgagor's title will be barred; and the mortgagee will become absolute beneficial owner of the mortgagor's interest.[71]

In the case of unregistered land, he can execute a vesting deed vesting the mortgagor's ownership in himself.[72] In the case of registered land, he will become entitled to have his name entered on the register as registered proprietor in place of the mortgagor.[73]

Principle 5d.   Mortgagee's rights: (iv) To appoint a receiver

The mortgagee has a statutory power to appoint a receiver. This power arises and is exercisable in the same circumstances as the statutory power of sale.[74]

The receiver has full powers to recover the income of the property and in addition the mortgagee may delegate his powers of leasing to the receiver.[75]

The receiver must use the income, first, to discharge outgoings including payments due under prior mortgages; secondly, to pay his own commission; and, thirdly, to pay the interest due to the mortgagee appointing him. The mortgagee may take any surplus towards repayment of capital. Otherwise it will be handed over to the mortgagor.[76]

The receiver is deemed to be agent for the mortgagor who will be liable for his acts and defaults.[77]

Explanation

As with taking possession, the appointment of a receiver does not put an end to the mortgage. Where a mortgagee is not intending to sell but merely wishes to get control of the income,

---

[71] Limitation Act 1980, ss. 16, 29 (4), 31 (3) (4).
[72] L.P.A. 1925, ss. 88, 89.
[73] L.R.A. 1925, ss. 34 (2), 75.
[74] L.P.A. 1925, s. 101 (1) (iii).
[75] *Ibid.* ss. 99 (19), 100 (13), 109 (3).
[76] *Ibid.* s. 109 (8).
[77] *Ibid.* s. 109 (2).

appointment of a receiver has this great advantage over the mortgagee taking possession himself: the receiver is deemed to be agent for the mortgagor. This means that the mortgagee will only be liable to account for income which he does in fact receive from the receiver; not, as in the case of possession, for income which the property might have earned. The mortgagee will not be liable for any default of the receiver.

Principle 5e. Mortgagee's rights: (v) Foreclosure

Foreclosure is an order of the court which puts an end to the mortgagor's right to redeem and vests the mortgaged property absolutely and beneficially in the mortgagee.[78]

The mortgagee can start foreclosure proceedings at any time after the legal date for redemption has passed.

The court may either:
- (a) make a foreclosure order nisi to be made absolute if the mortgagor does not redeem within a specified time;
- (b) on the application of any interested party, order a judicial sale of the property.[79]

Explanation

Like sale, foreclosure is one the methods by which the mortgagee is allowed to put to an end to the mortgagor's right of redemption. But with foreclosure there is no section 103 requirement to be satisfied and the mortgage does not have to be by deed. The mortgagee can start foreclosure proceedings as soon as the legal date for redemption has passed.[80]

The result of foreclosure is very different from the result of sale. In the case of sale, the money is used to pay outstanding mortgages, but any surplus is paid to the mortgagor. So he does not lose the value of his equity. In the case of foreclosure, the property vests in the foreclosing mortgagee subject only to prior mortgages. The mortgagor loses his equity and gets nothing for it; similarly, any subsequent mortgagees lose their security without being repaid.[81]

It is not quite as bad as this sounds. The court will first make an

---

[78] *Ibid.* s. 88 (2).
[79] *Ibid.* s. 91. Or, in the case of a dwelling-house, the court may order an adjournment on terms under A.J.A. 1973, s. 8.
[80] See *Twentieth Century Banking Corp. Ltd.* v. *Wilkinson* [1976] 3 All E.R. 361 (Templeman J.); and below, p. 469.
[81] They still have a right to sue the mortgagor personally.

order nisi which gives the mortgagor and any subsequent mortgagees[82] a specified time within which to find the money due and redeem the foreclosing mortgagee. It is only failing this that the order is made absolute. And even then the court does have jurisdiction to re-open the foreclosure and allow a further chance to redeem.[83] More important, under section 91 of the Law of Property Act 1925, the court can on the application of any interested party order a sale instead of foreclosure. If this happens each mortgagee will receive what is due to him and the mortgagor will get the balance. The court will always be prepared to order sale unless there are special circumstances present. For example, in *Silsby* v. *Holiman*,[84] the court refused to order sale because the property could only have been sold subject to a statutory tenancy and as such would not have raised enough to discharge the mortgage.

Since a foreclosure action is in any case likely to end in sale, the latter is today the usual method of enforcing repayment of a mortgage loan.

Principle 5f. Mortgagee's rights: (vi) Leases of mortgaged property

A mortgagee who is in possession or who has appointed a receiver, has a statutory power to grant leases binding on the mortgagor provided the following conditions are satisfied[85]:

1. (a) In the case of a building lease, the term must not exceed 999 years.

   (b) In the case of an agricultural or occupation[86] lease it must not exceed 50 years.

2. In all cases the lease must satisfy the following requirements:

   (a) It must be made to take effect in possession within 12 months.

   (b) It must reserve the best rent reasonably possible and must not include a fine.

   (c) It must include a covenant by the lessee to pay the rent and a proviso for re-entry on non-payment.

---

[82] See below, p. 489, for effects of foreclosure on subsequent mortgagees.
[83] See *e.g. Lancashire & Yorkshire Reversionary Interest Co.* v. *Crowe* (1970) 114 S.J. 435 (Foster J.) where the judge took into consideration the fact that the property was worth much more than the amount of the debt.
[84] [1955] 1 Ch. 522 (Upjohn J.).
[85] L.P.A. 1925, s. 99.
[86] As to the meaning of "occupation" see *Brown* v. *Peto* [1900] 2 Q.B. 653 (C.A.) (mining leases are not included in the statutory power).

(d) A counterpart of the lease must be executed by the lessee and delivered to the lessor.

Any lease not authorised by the statute or by the terms of the mortgage will bind the mortgagee by estoppel but not the mortgagor.

The statutory power of leasing can be delegated to a receiver.

Explanation

If the mortgagee takes possession or appoints a receiver he needs to be able to lease the property if it is not already let so that it will produce an income. The difficulty is that in the absence of his consent or some statutory power, the mortgagor would not be bound by any lease created by the mortgagee. The mortgagee can always bind himself but he has no general power unilaterally to impose a burden on the mortgagor's equity of redemption. If the mortgagor redeems he can recover possession from the mortgagee or any tenant put in by the mortgagee. It is for this reason that either a statutory or an express power in the mortgage deed is necessary. In practice the statutory power is generally considered sufficient.

Principle 5g.   Morgagee's rights: (vii) Right to insure

The property may be insured in one (or more) of the following four ways:

(a) The mortgagee has an insurable interest in the property and may insure it in his own name and at his own expense.

(b) Under sections 101, 108 of the Law of Property Act 1925, the mortgagee has a statutory power to insure against loss or damage by fire for up to two-thirds of the cost of reinstatement.[87] In this case the premiums will be payable by the mortgagor as part of the mortgage debt. This statutory power may be increased by an express power contained in the mortgage deed—and usually is.

(c) There may be an express covenant in the mortgage deed imposing an obligation on the mortgagor to keep the premises insured or authorising the mortgagee to insure at the mortgagor's expense.

(d) Subject to the terms of the mortgage deed, the mortgagor may independently take out his own insurance in his own name. Usually either under the statute or an express power in the

---

[87] Or any greater sum provided for in the mortgage deed.

mortgage, the mortgagee will be entitled to use any insurance money to reinstate or to discharge the mortgage debt.

Explanation

Where the mortgaged property includes any sort of buildings, the mortgagee will need to be certain that they are properly insured—otherwise he may see his security turn into smoke.

Insurance of the property raises two main questions. First, who is going to pay the premiums? Secondly, what is going to happen to any insurance money which becomes payable?

(a) If the mortgagee takes out his own insurance policy, he will be entitled to any insurance moneys but he himself will have to pay the premiums.

(b) Alternatively, the mortgagee may rely on the statutory power. This makes the premiums a charge on the property[88] and gives the mortgagee control over the application of the insurance money.[89] But the statutory power is considered inadequate in many respects and the usual practice is for the mortgage deed expressly to give the mortgagee a more extensive power to insure.

The express power might for example entitle the mortgagee to insure for what amount and against what contingencies he thinks fit. The mortgagor will covenant expressly to pay the premiums; that any unpaid premiums will be part of the mortgage debt and a charge on the property. The mortgagor will further covenant not to take out his own separate insurance on the property,[90] and that any insurance moneys can be applied by the mortgagee towards the discharge of the mortgage debt or reinstatement.

(c) A similar result can be obtained if the mortgage contains a covenant by the mortgagor to maintain the necessary insurance and to produce the premium receipts for inspection if required. In this case the mortgagee is entitled to direct any insurance moneys to be used towards discharge of the mortgage debt or reinstatement.[91]

(d) If the mortgagor, independently of any obligation in the mortgage deed,[92] takes out his own insurance policy at his own

---

[88] L.P.A. 1925, s. 101 (1) (ii).
[89] To be used either for reinstatemet of the property or towards discharge of the mortgage debt. L.P.A. 1925, s. 108 (3) (4).
[90] For the possible danger of allowing a separate insurance to be held on the property by the mortgagor, see *Halifax Building Society* v. *Keighley* [1931] 2 K.B. 248.
[91] L.P.A. 1925, s. 108 (3) (4).
[92] Or in breach of a covenant not to take out insurance himself.

expense, he will (subject to any term of the mortgage to the contrary) be absolutely entitled to any insurance moneys. However, under the Fires Prevention (Metropolis) Act 1774, any interested party can always require any insurance money payable in the event of fire to be used for reinstatement. And, in any case, the mortgage will normally provide for any insurance money received by the mortgagor either to be used for reinstatement or to be held in trust for the mortgagee.[93]

Principle 5h. Mortgagee's rights: (viii) Right to the title deeds

Unregistered land. A first mortgagee, whether legal or equitable, is entitled to have the title deeds deposited with him. A mortgage not so protected will be registrable.[94]

Registered land. Any first or subsequent legal mortgage of registered land must generally be registered substantively as a registered charge.[95] The land certificate will be held at the Land Registry and the mortgagee will receive a charge certificate.[96]

Explanation

The deposit of title deeds is important in relation to priority[97] and protection against third parties[98] and is considered below under these headings.

Principle 6a. Mortgagor's rights: Right to redeem

The right to redeem is the right of the mortgagor to repay the outstanding loan, interest and costs secured by the mortgage and so to put an end to the mortgage.

The mortgagor has a right to redeem on the date stipulated in the mortgage deed for repayment (known as the legal or contractual right to redeem). He cannot be required and is not entitled to redeem before this date.

Even after this date has passed, he still has a right to redeem—his equitable right to redeem—which will continue

---

[93] For possible result of not including such a clause see *Halifax B.S.* v. *Keighley* (n. 90, above).
[94] See below, p. 520.
[95] L.R.A. 1925, ss. 25, 26.
[96] See below, p. 546.
[97] Below, p. 484.
[98] Below, p. 523.

indefinitely until it is determined either by redemption or by the mortgagee foreclosing or exercising his power of sale.[99]

Any provision imposed by the mortgage deed (or as part of the mortgage transaction) which makes the right to redeem illusory or imposes a harsh or oppressive burden on the mortgagor will be void as a clog or fetter on the equity of redemption. This principle cannot be avoided by disguising the mortgage as some other transaction.[1]

Explanation

The legal and equitable right to redeem. One of the most important contributions of equity to the development of land law was its intervention to protect the mortgagor against the harsh terms which lenders of money were allowed to impose at common law.

The traditional standing mortgage contains a proviso for cesser on redemption that the mortgage will be discharged *provided* that the loan is repaid on the date specified in the mortgage deed. This date is the legal date of redemption and is generally put at six months after the date of the mortgage. Until this date neither party can insist on redemption.

At common law this proviso meant what it said—which made it harsh but at least intelligible. Failure to comply with the terms of the proviso and repay on the specified date[2] meant that the property became the mortgagee's absolutely, free of the right to redeem.[3]

Equity took a different view. It regarded the mortgage as solely a security for a loan with interest and the loan-seeking mortgagor as being in need of its protection. It therefore developed the following three principles:

(a) That the mortgagor is allowed to redeem even after the legal date has passed so long as he repays all money outstanding under the mortgage. Unlike the legal right to redeem, this equitable right to redeem is given by equity and does not depend on the terms of the mortgage agreement made between the parties. The next two points follow from this.

---

[99] Or under the Limitation Act 1980; see above, p. 463.

[1] See below, at p. 474.

[2] Or breach of any other condition of the agreement; see *Twentieth Century Banking Corp. Ltd.* v. *Wilkinson* [1976] 3 All E.R. 361 (Templeman J.).

[3] And the borrower was still liable to repay the debt; see *Littleton on Tenures*, para. 332.

(b) That any term of the mortgage which is a clog on the equity of redemption will be void and can be ignored by the mortgagor.

(c) That equity will apply the above two principles to any transaction which is in substance a mortgage whatever outward form the transaction takes.

The equitable right to redeem. Now that there is an equitable right to redeem the traditional form of standing mortgage is fairer but less intelligible.[3a] On the face of it, failure by the mortgagor to repay only six months after the date of the loan is fatal; in fact neither he nor the lender will expect the money to be repaid then. The private lender would no doubt be embarrassed if it was offered since he would have to find another investment for his money.

The only purpose for specifying a legal date for redemption which neither side expects to be honoured, is that under the present day rules the right to start foreclosure proceedings (and in general the statutory power to sell and appoint a receiver) does not arise until after the legal right has been lost by non-compliance with the proviso.

Instalment mortgages and the right to redeem. The essence of the instalment mortgage is that the mortgagor agrees to repay the capital loan by instalments over a fixed number of years. In addition, it is commonly a feature of the bargain contained in such a mortgage today, that (a) the borrower will be allowed to redeem at an earlier date if he wishes; and (b) the mortgagee will not take action to enforce his security so long as the borrower complies with the terms of the mortgage and pays the instalments when due. At the same time, the mortgagee will want to be sure that he will have the right to enforce his security at any time when necessary throughout the life of the mortgage.

The law, developed by the common law and equity to suit the traditional standing mortgage, has had to be adapted by the courts to suit this type of bargain. This has given rise to problems and tended to make the law of mortgages even more difficult to analyse and explain. Two aspects will now be considered.

First, the mortgagee's power of sale. A purchaser from a mortgagee exercising his power of sale is concerned to check that the mortgage money is due.[4] In the traditional mortgage form

---

[3a] For a discussion of the artificiality of the modern mortgage form and areas of mortgage law that need reforming, see P. Jackson. "The Need to Reform the English Law of Mortgages," (1978) 94 L.Q.R. 571.

[4] L.P.A. 1925, s. 101 (1) (i).

there is no problem. The conventional proviso for redemption provides that there will be a legal right to redeem provided the money is repaid on a specified date six months after the mortgage deed. This means the money becomes due on that date and thereafter a purchaser is protected.

If an instalment mortgage contains no provision other than an agreement to pay by certain instalments, the money becomes due and the power of sale arises, so it has been held,[5] when any instalment is outstanding. But this is not satisfactory since, so it seems, only outstanding instalments—not future instalments can be recovered out of the proceeds of sale. It is therefore possible for such a mortgage to provide that the whole amount outstanding will become immediately due in certain specified events—for example, a default in payment of two months' instalments or upon the mortgagee giving a specified notice to repay. The difficulty with such a provision is that the purchaser has to examine facts outside the mortgage deed to be certain of his title. Alternatively, therefore, such mortgages may include a clause like the following:

> "The legal right of redemption shall cease one month after the advance date specified below and in favour of a purchaser the mortgage money shall be due and the power of sale shall arise on that date."[6]

Such a mortgage may go on to provide that the power of sale will only be *exercised* in one of the section 103 or other specified events; and a sale in breach of such a restriction will give the mortgagor a personal cause of action against the mortgagee, but it will not affect the title of a purchaser.

Secondly, the right to redeem and foreclose. In the absence of special provision, the mortgagor would only be able to pay by the agreed instalments. He would have no legal right to redeem earlier by paying off the full amount outstanding if, for example, he wanted to sell the property. It is usual, therefore, to provide an express right to redeem at any time, possibly on giving a specified short period of notice.[7]

As to foreclosure; until the legal right to redeem has arisen and

---

[5] *Payne* v. *Cardiff R.D.C.* [1932] 1 K.B. 241 (C.A.).

[6] Contrast the mortgage terms in *Twentieth Century Banking Corp. Ltd.* v. *Wilkinson* [1976] 3 All E.R. 361 (Templeman J.).

[7] Absence of such an express right would be likely to be a clog on the equity of redemption; and the mortgagor would be allowed *in equity* to redeem at any time during the life of the mortgage; see below, p. 472.

been lost, the mortgagee has no right to foreclose (since foreclosure can operate only to destroy the equitable right to redeem). Thus, if there is an express (*i.e.* legal) right to redeem throughout the life of the mortgage, the right to foreclosure will never arise. Again, therefore, it is common to make express provision (as in the form quoted above) stipulating that the legal right to redeem will be lost at a date soon after the date of the mortgage.

Some of the problems created by a badly drawn instalment mortgage are illustrated in *Twentieth Century Banking Corporation Ltd.* v. *Wilkinson.*[8] There, in a fifteen-year instalment mortgage, it was expressly provided that for the purposes of the Law of Property Act 1925, section 101, the mortgage money was not to be due until the last day of the 15-year term. There was no express proviso for redemption stating when or how the legal right to redeem would be lost. After only a few years, the mortgagor defaulted in his payments of interest. The mortgagee was claiming sale and foreclosure. The court held that the statutory power of sale had been expressly excluded for the fifteen-year period[9]; that where there is an express proviso for redemption, the legal right to redeem is lost when the terms of that proviso have been broken; that where, as in the mortgage before them, there is no express proviso, it is a question of construction whether any breach is sufficient to destroy the legal right to redeem. The court went on to hold that on a proper construction of the mortgage before them, the continued right to redeem was conditional on compliance with the covenant to pay interest. The court held, therefore, that the legal right to redeem had been lost and so the right to foreclose had arisen. In the event, in the exercise of its discretion under the Law of Property Act 1925, section 91, the court ordered a judicial sale in lieu of foreclosure.[10]

Clogs or fetters on the equity of redemption. Where equity holds a mortgage provision to be void as a clog on the equity of redemption, it is assisting the mortgagor to escape the contractual obligations which he has—on the face of it at least—freely accepted. And in modern times the courts have shown an

---

[8] Above, n. 6.
[9] Note that under the L.P.A. 1925, s. 101 (3), the statutory power of sale can be varied or extended.
[10] This case illustrates that the money does not necessarily become due on the same date that the legal right to redeem is lost. Note the suggestion in this case that the court may be able to order sale under the section even where a right to foreclose has not been established.

increased reluctance to interfere. In *Knightsbridge Estates Trusts Ltd.* v. *Byrne*,[11] Sir Wilfrid Greene M.R. said of the argument by counsel for the mortgagor that a postponement of the right to redeem must be reasonable: "Now an argument such as this requires the closest scrutiny for, if is is correct, it means that an agreement made between two competent parties, acting under expert advice and presumably knowing their own business best, is one which the law forbids them to make upon the ground that it is not 'reasonable.' If we were satisfied that the rule of equity were what it is said to be, we should be bound to give effect to it. But in the absence of compelling authority we are not prepared to say that such an agreement cannot lawfully be made. A decision to that effect would, in our view, involve an unjustified interference with the freedom of business men to enter into agreements best suited to their interests and would impose upon them a test of 'reasonableness' laid down by the courts without reference to the business realities of the case."

On the whole, equity has tended to retreat from the field leaving the mortgagor and the mortgagee bound by whatever terms they can or will negotiate.

It is difficult to state any general principle as to just when equity will intervene. In the *Knightsbridge* case the court thought that to be void the provision must render the right to redeem illusory or be harsh or oppressive to the mortgagor.[12] It was not enough, they thought, for a provision to be "unreasonable."

If the validity of a provision is challenged, the courts will look at all the relevant circumstances—the relevant bargaining strength of the parties; whether the borrower is a private individual in need of a loan or a commercial undertaking raising capital; whether there is a mutuality[13]; whether the proviso imposes an additional burden on the property or just a personal obligation on the mortgagor; whether the burden is to cease on or continue after redemption.

The following statements attempt to reflect the modern judicial attitude:

(1) A postponement of the right to redeem will not of itself be regarded as a clog, unless it imposes a harsh or oppressive burden on the mortgagor.[14] In the *Knightsbridge* case, a loan of £310,000

---

[11] [1939] Ch. 441 (C.A.). And see *Multiservice Bookbinding Ltd.* v. *Marden* [1978] 2 All E.R. 489.

[12] [1939] Ch. 441, at p. 457.

[13] *i.e.* whether a postponement of the right to redeem is matched by a postponement of the right to call in the loan.

[14] See, *e.g. Fairclough* v. *Swan Brewery Co. Ltd.* [1912] A.C. 565—mortgage of lease not to be redeemed till lease had only 6 weeks to run.

made to a company by an institutional lender, was made repayable by 80 half-yearly instalments and not otherwise. The mortgagees for their part covenanted not to call in the loan during that period. This was held not to be a clog.[15]

(2) A proviso, including a postponement of the right to redeem, which takes away the right to redeem or makes it illusory will be void.

In *Salt* v. *Marquess of Northampton*[16] a loan secured on a life assurance policy provided that if the mortgagor died before redemption, the whole policy money should belong to the mortgagees. This was a clog and the mortgagor's personal representatives were held entitled to recover the balance of the insurance moneys after payment of the loan.

(3) The rule forbidding clogs cannot be avoided by disguising the mortgage as some other transaction. It is said that "Once a mortgage, always a mortgage."[17]

However, there is perhaps a present tendency to take the view that if a mortgage is part of a complex commercial transaction it cannot be treated simply as a mortgage, and the ordinary rules against clogs will not apply. In *Rosemex Service Station* v. *Shell-Mex & B.P.*[18] Ungoed-Thomas J. took the view that "If I were driven to it, [I] would conclude that the contract comprehending the sales agreement and the agreement to lend on the legal charge was not in its 'real nature and substance,' as a whole, a mortgage transaction, nor, to use Lord Haldane's words, 'a mere mortgage,' and so falls outside the doctrine of once a mortgage always a mortgage, of which the clog on the equity of redemption is an emanation. I again quote Lord Haldane, where he said:

> 'That the substance of the transaction must be looked to in applying this doctrine and that it did not apply to cases which were only apparently or technically within it but were in reality something more than cases of mortgage.'

If there were the one contract, as the plaintiffs say, then it was 'something more than' a mortgage—it was a commercial transaction of which the mortgage formed part."[19]

(4) A collateral advantage—some additional advantage given to the mortgage over and above his interest—will only be void if it is

---

[15] [1939] Ch. 441.
[16] [1892] A.C. 1 (H.L.).
[17] See *Danby* v. *Read* (1675) Rep. Temp. Finch. 226.
[18] (1968) 20 P. & C.R. 1. For facts see below, p. 475.
[19] At p. 12; see also *Thomas* v. *Rose* [1968] 1 W.L.R. 1797.

to continue after redemption and if, in the circumstances, it is harsh or oppressive to the mortgagor.[20] The typical collateral advantage is the tied clause binding the mortgagor for the period of the mortgage or longer to obtain his supplies of petrol, beer or whatever it is that he retails, exclusively from the mortgagee. The big petrol companies for example often obtain tied agreements from garage proprietors, sometimes as part of a mortgage loan to the garage, sometimes independently of any loan. The main purpose of such an agreement is that the garage gets a rebate on the wholesale price of the petrol which it buys; the petrol company has an assured and exclusive outlet for the period of the agreement. In *Rosemex Service Station* v. *Shell-Mex & B.P.*[21] the plaintiff entered into a tie agreement with Shell-Mex. A mortgage loan was granted at a later date to finance improvements to the forecourt, but the plaintiff had not, so it was held, been obliged to accept the tie in order to get the loan. The tie agreement was held valid. One of the main principles behind the doctrine of clogs has always been to protect the person who is in a peculiarly weak bargaining position because he needs to borrow money. In the present case the mortgagor was not asking for a loan when he agreed to the tie; and so the doctrine really had no application. The tie agreement would remain valid after redemption.

Collateral advantages were attacked by equity on two main grounds. First, because they were an attempt by lenders to avoid the usury laws which limited permissible rates of interest. This view led the judiciary to develop the general principle that all collateral advantages were void.[22] The present attitude of the courts to this idea was neatly summed up by Viscount Haldane L.C. in *Kreglinger* v. *New Patagonia Meat & Cold Storage Company Limited*[23]: "But equity went beyond the limits of the statutes which limited the interest and was ready to interfere with any usurious stipulation in a mortgage. In doing so it was influenced by the public policy of the time. The policy has now changed, and the Acts which limited the rate of interest have now been repealed."[24]

The second ground, already mentioned, was to protect the vulnerable individual from the oppressive moneylender. A classic

---

[20] A collateral advantage which is to cease on redemption cannot normally be challenged.
[21] See above, n.18.
[22] See *Jennings* v. *Ward* (1705) 2 Vern. 520; 23 E.R. 935.
[23] [1914] A.C. 25 (H.L.).
[24] *Ibid.* p. 37.

example, is the case of *James* v. *Kerr*.[25] James needed money in order to pursue his claim to his inheritance in the courts. A certain solicitor lent him money on the security of the property which he hoped to recover. Apart from interest at five per cent, the mortgage provided for the payment of an extra "bonus" of £225 for the solicitor if James was successful. Kay J. held that James was not bound to pay the bonus "the ground for relief in equity arising from the position of poverty and necessity in which the plaintiff was, put him practically at the mercy of the money lenders, whatever terms they chose to exact." It is still possible for a collateral advantage to be attacked successfully on this ground; but even here the picture is changing. On the one hand the majority of individuals who borrow money borrow it from building societies to assist with the purchase of a home. Oppressive collateral advantages are not likely to be found in building society mortgages. On the other hand, today, the collateral advantage is likely to be found in a mortgage which is part of a complex business arrangement between sometimes large commercial undertakings. In such cases the courts will be reluctant to find any reason for intervening.

Nevertheless, individuals and small business concerns do still find the need to borrow money from powerful trading companies and financial institutions; in doing so they are likely to be in a weak bargaining position, forced either to accept the lenders' terms without question or do without the money. However one-sided such agreements may be, they are not likely to come within the now rather restricted scope of clogs on the equity of redemption. Further, equity has never used the doctrine of clogs to control the rate of interest. Since the abolition of usury laws, there is in general[26] no limit to the rate which a borrower may be required to pay.[27]

---

[25] (1889) 40 Ch.D. 449.

[26] See Moneylenders Acts 1900–27.

[27] But see *Cityland Property (Holdings) Ltd.* v. *Dabrah* [1968] Ch. 166, Goff J.; there a loan on mortgage contained no provision for the payment of interest, but instead, provision for the payment of a premium the whole of which became immediately payable on default. It was held that in view of its amount the premium was a clog, the mortgagor was entitled to redeem on repaying the loan with interest at a reasonable rate; see notes on this case in Fisher and Lightwood, *Law of Mortgage* (9th ed.), p. 528. Compare *Multiservice Bookbinding Ltd.* v. *Marden* [1978] 2 All E.R. 489. And see further the Consumer Credit Act 1974 which applies to certain mortgage loans; especially ss. 16, 58, 59.

Principle 6aa.   Restraint of trade and mortgages

Any term in a mortgage which is in unreasonable restraint of trade will be void.

Explanation

The doctrine of clogs is concerned to protect the mortgagor's equity of redemption. The doctrine of restraint of trade is concerned to protect the public's interest, as seen by the courts, in freedom of trade. Further, the doctrine is not confined to mortgages. Nevertheless, it is convenient to mention it in the present context since the same term in a mortgage—such as a collateral advantage may be open to attack both as a clog and as an unreasonable restraint.

In *Esso Petroleum Co. Ltd.* v. *Harper's Garage (Stourport) Ltd.*[28] the court had to consider the terms contained in a mortgage by a garage proprietor to Esso which tied the garage to Esso. The mortgage was not to be redeemable for 21 years and during that period the mortgagor was to sell only Esso's motor fuels. The House of Lords held that the doctrine of restraint applied to such agreements and that the restraint in question was, on the facts, void as being in unreasonable restraint of trade.[29]

Principle 6b.   Mortgagor's rights: Right to possession

Subject to the mortgagee's right to possession and to enforce his security, the mortgagor is entitled to:
(a) possession of the property;
(b) receive the income and profits;
(c) commit waste.

Explanation

The mortgagor remains the real beneficial owner of the property subject only to the payment of the mortgage debt; and he can continue to exercise all the rights of the ordinary beneficial owner subject only to the rights of the mortgagee.

It follows that the mortgagor can retain possession and that the only person who can oust him is the mortgagee exercising his rights under the mortgage.

---

[28] [1968] A.C. 269. See also *Petrofina (G.B.) Ltd.* v. *Martin* [1966] 1 Ch. 146 and *Robinson* v. *Golden Chips (Wholesale) Ltd.* [1971] N.Z.L.R. 257.

[29] In the same case, the court held that a similar restraint (not contained in a mortgage) which was to continue for only 5 years was valid.

Whilst the mortgagor is in possession he is entitled to take the rents and profits. If the mortgagee takes possession or appoints a receiver he can only retain what is due to him. Any surplus belongs to the mortgagor. Similarly, if the mortgagee sells, any surplus will be held for the mortgagor.

Whilst he remains in possession the mortgagor can in general do what he likes. He will not be liable for waste. However, he will be restrained by injunction if his actions—for example, cutting timber or removing fixtures—threaten to leave insufficient security.[30] Further, the mortgage deed will invariably contain express covenants controlling the mortgagor's use of the property. For example, he will probably covenant to keep the premises in good and substantial repair; and 'not without the written consent of the mortgagee to make any structural or material alteration to the property or to institute any change of use," and so on.

Principle 6c. Mortgagor's right to lease

The mortgagor has a statutory right to create leases binding on the mortgagee subject to the same conditions as the mortgagee's statutory right to lease.[31]

He can exercise this right so long as he is in possession and there is no receiver appointed by the mortgagee.

In practice the mortgagor's statutory right to lease is usually excluded by the mortgage deed; and in such case any lease created subsequent to the mortgage by the mortgagee will bind him by estoppel, but not bind the mortgagee.[32]

Any lease created by the mortgagor *before* the creation of the mortgage will bind both the mortgagor and the mortgagee.[33]

Principle 6d. Mortgagor's equity of redemption

The mortgagor's interest in the property (representing all his rights including the equitable right to redeem) is known as his equity of redemption.

Explanation

As explained above, the mortgagor is owner of the property subject only to the mortgage. This ownership is commonly

---

[30] See, *e.g. Harper* v. *Alpin* (1886) 54 L.T. 383.
[31] L.P.A. 1925, s. 99.
[32] But note *Quennell* v. *Maltby* [1979] 1 All E.R. 569 (C.A.).
[33] Subject to any registration requirements being satisfied where necessary. See below, Chaps. 24 and 25.

referred to as his equity of redemption—a term which is somewhat misleading under post 1925 law since the mortgagor now retains a legal reversion in the property.

The equity of redemption comprises the aggregate of all his rights in the land; and, of course, the mortgagor is free to sell or otherwise dispose of his "equity" as he wishes. In other words he is free to deal with the property subject to the mortgage. If he does dispose of the equity he will remain *personally* liable on the covenants in the mortgage unless released by the mortgagee.

Principle 6e.   Limitation of mortgagee's rights

The mortgagee's right to sue for capital will be barred after 12 years from when it becomes due. His right to sue for interest will be barred after six years from when it becomes due.[34]

His right to foreclose or take possession will be barred after 12 years from when the right accrues.[35]

Time will start to run afresh if the mortgagor makes any part payment of capital or interest or any written acknowledgment of the mortgagee's title.[36] But no more than six years' arrears of interest be claimed.[37]

SECTION III. EQUITABLE MORTGAGES

Principle 7.   Equitable mortgages of the legal estate (informal mortgages): Creation[38]

An equitable mortgage of a legal freehold or leasehold estate can be created provided the following conditions are satisfied:

(1) There must be a contract to create a mortgage of the land.

(2) This contract must be evidenced in writing or supported by a sufficient act of part performance.[39]

(3) The loan must in fact have been advanced.

Explanation

A legal mortgage can only be created by a deed using either the demise or the charge method.

---

[34] Limitation Act 1980, s. 20 (1) (5).
[35] *Ibid.* ss. 15, 20 (4) and Sched. 1.
[36] *Ibid.* s. 29.
[37] *Ibid.* s. 20 (5) (6) (7).
[38] See Fisher and Lightwood, *Law of Mortgage* (9th ed.), p. 11 *et seq.* Snell's *Equity* (27th ed.), p. 425 *et seq.*.
[39] L.P.A. 1925, s. 40.

An equitable mortgage can be created without these formalities. It may arise either because there has been some failure to comply with the formalities—failure to use a deed for example—or, more commonly, because the parties have preferred an equitable mortgage.

A mere deposit of the title deed's with the mortgagee is sufficient to create an equitable mortgage. This method is commonly used to secure a bank overdraft. No writing of any sort is necessary[40] but commonly there will be a memorandum of deposit either under the hand or seal of the mortgagor. The use of a memorandum under seal (*i.e.* by deed) gives the mortgagee the same statutory remedies as a legal mortgagee[41]; but it largely negates the main advantage of the equitable mortgage which is simplicity and informality.

There must be a contract to create a mortgage. This means that there must be sufficient evidence of an intention to create a mortgage in consideration for a loan. In *Thomas* v. *Rose*,[42] there was an agreement between the landowner and R by which R paid the landowner £500 and later another £1,000; and agreed to discharge all outgoings on the property and prepare it as a building site. It would then be sold and the proceeds of sale divided. This agreement was registered[43] in the Land Charges Registry as an equitable mortgage (as a Class C III land charge, a general equitable charge). Megarry J. held that there was no loan in existence that could stand charged on the land and that the agreement was no more than a contract to divide the proceeds of sale. Consequently it could not be an equitable mortgage and the landowner was entitled to have the register vacated.

If there is a memorandum of deposit this will be clear evidence of the necessary intention; and even the mere deposit will generally be sufficient. But in *Dixon* v. *Muckleston*,[44] Lord Selborne L.C. said: "The mere possession of deeds without evidence of the contract upon which the possession originated or at least of the manner in which that possession originated, so that a contact may be inferred, will not be enough to create an equitable security."

If there is sufficient evidence of an enforceable contract to create a mortgage, then equity will do two things: First, it will

---

[40] Since the deposit is a sufficient act of part performance by both parties.
[41] L.P.A. 1925, s. 101.
[42] [1968] 1 W.L.R. 1797 (Megarry J.).
[43] See below, p. 518.
[44] (1872) L.R. 8 Ch. App. 155, 162.

grant specific performance of the contract ordering the mortgagor to execute a legal mortgage in proper form. Secondly, in accordance with the principle that equity treats as done that which ought to be done, the contract itself will be treated as actually creating a valid equitable mortgage. In the majority of cases, the parties are quite satisfied to know that their agreement constitutes a valid equitable mortgage and never in fact intend to proceed to a formal legal mortgage.

Written evidence or part performance. A contract to create a mortgage of land is within section 40 of the Law of Property Act 1925 and to be enforceable must be evidenced in writing or supported by a sufficient act of part performance.[45] Where, as is commonly the case, the mortgage is created by deposit of title deeds, the actual deposit is regarded as a sufficient act of part performance by both the mortgagor and the mortgagee.

The loan must have been advanced. If the lender has not yet advanced the money he has not yet been put at risk and there is no reason why equity should assist him.

An equitable mortgage of a legal estate in unregistered land is registrable under the Land Charges Act 1972 as a general equitable charge unless it is protected by the deposit of title deeds with the mortgagee.[46]

Registered land. These rules as to the creation of equitable mortgages apply to registered as well as unregistered land except that, where the mortgage is created by deposit, it will be the land certificate that is deposited. In all cases, the mortgage will need to be protected on the register.[47]

Principle 8. The rights of the equitable mortgagee

If an equitable mortgage is made by deed—for example, by a memorandum of deposit under seal—the mortgagee has in general the same rights as a legal mortgagee.

Where an equitable mortgage is created without a deed—for example, by a simple deposit of title deeds—the mortgagee cannot exercise the statutory powers given by section 101 of the Law of Property Act 1925, to sell, appoint a receiver, cut timber and insure without first obtaining a court order. However, apart from

---

[45] See below, p. 555.
[46] See below, p. 520.
[47] See below, p. 546.

the power of sale, these powers can be given to the mortgagee expressly.

An equitable mortgagee will only have a power of sale out of court if the mortgage is by deed *and* the power is given expressly.

Explanation

The reason for deliberately choosing the equitable rather than legal mortgage is likely to be cheapness ad simplicity of creation. The easiest and cheapest method is simply to deposit the title deeds with the lender.[48] The disadvantage of this is that without anything in writing, it may subsequently be difficult to prove that a mortgage was intended and, further, the mortgagee will have to apply to court to enforce his security. These difficulties can be avoided by having something under hand or better still under seal; but then the advantages of using the equitable mortgage are largely lost.[49]

To give the equitable mortgagee the most important remedy of all, sale, without him having to go to court, it is not enough to use a deed and rely on the statutory power since the statutory power of sale is only available to a legal mortgagee. It is necessary for the deed to contain a suitable express power of sale.[50]

Principle 9.   Equitable mortgages of an equitable interest

A mortgage of an equitable interest can only be equitable.

Such a mortgage is created by an absolute assignment (or by an enforceable contract to assign it, or an express declaration of trust by the mortgagor) of the interest to the mortgagee with a proviso for reassignment on redemption.

The mortgage must be in writing and signed by the mortgagor or by his agent authorised in writing.[51]

Explanation

The ordinary case of these mortgages is where the beneficiary under a trust for sale or a strict settlement mortgages his beneficial equitable interest. Such a beneficiary can in general deal with his beneficial interest as he pleases, but he cannot give the mortgagee

---

[48] But in the case of registered land, registration of a notice of deposit will normally be necessary to preserve priority; see below, p. 547.

[49] There is the advantage that, in the case of unregistered land, an equitable mortgage is kept off the title.

[50] See Fisher and Lightwood, *Mortgages* (9th ed.), p. 379.

[51] L.P.A. 1925, s. 53 (1) (c).

more than he himself has. If, for example, a life interest is mortgaged the security will last only as long as the life. In practice it will be necessary to have an insurance policy on the life as an additional security.

The remedies of a mortgagee of an equitable interest are the same as those of an equitable mortgagee of a legal estate; though of course his enforcement can only be against the equitable interest mortgaged. He cannot, even with the assistance of the court, touch the legal estate.

SECTION IV. SUBSEQUENT MORTGAGES

Principle 10.   Nature of subsequent mortgages

A subsequent mortgage is a second or further mortgage by the mortgagor[52] of the same interest in the same property.

There is no limit in law to the number of subsequent mortgages that can be created.

A subsequent mortgage is created in the same way as a first mortgage; and, like a first mortgage, a subsequent mortgage may be legal or equitable.

Explanation

Suppose that B the beneficial freehold owner of Blackacre borrows £5,000 from X giving him a legal first mortgage on the property as security. He then needs to borrow more money and finds Y who is willing to lend him £1,000 on the security of the same property. B creates a second mortgage in favour of Y. Again, he borrows a further £1,000 from Z on yet another mortgage—a third mortgage—of the same property.

Each of these mortgages may be legal or equitable according to the rules already set out.

In law, there is no limit to the amount which B can borrow on the security of each mortgage or on the number of mortgages which he can create of the same property. In practice, the amount which he can borrow will be limited by the value of the property and his ability to find a willing lender. If his property is worth £20,000, he is not likely to get a mortgage loan on it of £40,000. At least half the £40,000 would in effect not be secured.

Creation of subsequent mortgages. In general the rules are exactly the same as for first mortgages. As with a first mortgage,

---

[52] Or a transferee of the equity of redemption.

either the charge or the demise method can be used to create a legal mortgage. If the demise method is used the term (in the case of leasehold, the sub-term) vested in the mortgagee will be one day longer than the term vested in the previous mortgagee.

Principle 11. Priority

The order or priority is the order in which various mortgagees of the same interest are entitled to enforce their rights against the property. In particular, it determines the order in which they are entitled to be satisfied out of the proceeds of sale if the security has to be realised.

The order of priority is not necessarily the order of creation.

The rules which determine the order of priority are as follows:

A. *Unregistered land*: mortgages (whether legal or equitable) of the legal estate:
  (a) If the mortgage is protected by the deposit of title deeds, the mortgagee is generally entitled to priority from the date of creation of the mortgage. The mortgage will not be registrable.
  (b) If the mortgage is not protected by the deposit of the deeds, it will be registrable and priority will be fixed by the date of registration.

B. *Unregistered land*: mortgages of an equitable interest: Priority is governed, under the rule in *Dearle* v. *Hall*,[53] by the order in which notice of the mortgage is given to the trustees of the legal estate.

C. *Registered land*: In the case of registered land priority is governed by the date of protection by entry on the register.[54]

Explanation

Priority is rather like getting a place in a bus queue. If the bus comes along and there are seats for all then no problem arises. If, on the other hand, there is room for only two and there are twenty people in the queue, it is going to make all the difference in the world whether you are second or third in the queue.

Similarly with mortgages. Suppose that X is owed £5,000 and Y is owed £1,000, both debts secured by mortgages of the freehold of Blackacre. And suppose that the mortgagor goes bankrupt and

---

[53] (1823–28) 3 Russ. 1; 38 E.R. 475.
[54] See further, below, p. 546.

payments to X and Y stop. The property is sold for £5,000. If X is first in priority he will get his full £5,000[55] and Y will get nothing. If the order of priority is Y, X, Y will get £1,000 and X will get only £4,000.

Mortgages of a legal estate in unregistered land. The rules can be illustrated as follows:

1965	B	First mortgage protected by deposit	X
		————————————————————————>	
1966	B	Second legal mortgage not protected	Y
		————————————————————————>	
1966	Y registers		
1968	B	Third equitable mortgage not protected	Z
		————————————————————————>	
1968	Z registers		

The order of priority here will normally be X, Y, Z (which is also the order of creation).

The mortgagee protected by the deposit of title deeds (X in this illustration) may lose this protection and thus his priority to a subsequent mortgagee if he is guilty of fraud or gross negligence or (where his mortgage is equitable) if the subsequent mortgagee is a bona fide purchaser for value of a legal estate without notice of his mortgage.

In *Briggs* v. *Jones*,[56] the owner of a leasehold property mortgaged it to the plaintiff as security for a loan of £250 with interest and deposited the lease with the plaintiff. Subsequently, the mortgagor persuaded the plaintiff, against the advice of the latter's solicitors, to let him have the return of the lease to raise a further loan. The plaintiff told him that he must warn any other lender of the existing mortgage. The mortgagor deposited the lease with his bank as security for a loan without, of course, mentioning the plaintiff's existing mortgage. It was held when the plaintiff started foreclosure proceedings that he must be postponed to the bank. Lord Romilly M.R. said: "A person who puts it in the power of another to deceive and to raise money must take the consequences."[57]

Thus, in the above illustration, if X through such gross negligence allowed B to have the title deeds back and so to deceive Y, the order of priority might become Y, X, Z. And if his negligence resulted in Z being deceived a well, it might become Y, Z, X.

---

[55] Ignoring the costs of sale.
[56] (1870) L.R. 10 Eq. 92.
[57] *Ibid.* p. 98.

As to registration: section 97 of the Law of Property Act 1925 provides that a mortgage not protected by deposit "shall rank according to its date of registration as a land charge pursuant to the Land Charges Act 1972."[58]

Mortgages of equitable interests in unregistered land. Mortgages of the legal estate and of the equitable interest are completely separate. There can be no question of priority between them.

If a tenant for life exercising his statutory power under the Settled Land Act 1925 mortgages his legal estate to X, Y and Z, priority between X, Y and Z will be governed by the rules discussed above. If he mortgages his equitable beneficial interest to A and B, priority between A and B is governed by the rule in *Dearle* v. *Hall*. This states that priority depends upon the order in which notice in writing is given to the trustees of the legal estate. In the case of a strict settlement notice is given to the trustees of the settlement. A mortgagee cannot gain priority by giving notice under the rule, if he has actual notice of a prior mortgage when he takes his security.

Registered land. Mortgages of registered land need to be protected by one of the possible methods of registration. In general, priority will be governed by the date of registration.[59]

Mortgages of equitable interests in registered land are protected by registration in the minor interests index which is quite separate from the title register.

Principle 12.   Tacking of further advances

If a further advance—that is, a further loan, generally provided for in the original mortgage[60]—can be tacked to an earlier mortgage, it will gain the same priority as the earlier one, thus postponing any intervening mortgages.

A further advance can be tacked provided *any one* of the following three conditions is satisfied:

(1) The intervening mortgagee agrees.

---

[58] As amended by the L.C.A. 1972, s. 18 (6). There is a possibility of a conflict in some cases (which has not yet been resolved judicially) between s. 97 and s. 4 of the L.C.A. 1972 which provides that a mortgage which is not, but should be, registered will be void against a subsequent purchaser (which includes a mortgagee). If the section is applied it is too late to gain priority against a subsequent mortgage by registering once that mortgage has been created.

[59] See further above, p. 468; below, p. 546.

[60] See *Burnes* v. *Trade Credits Ltd.* [1981] 2 All E.R. 123 (P.C.).

(2) The earlier mortgage is expressly made security for the further advance (as well as the original loan) and the further advance is made without notice of the intervening mortgage. In this case registration does not constitute notice of a subsequent mortgage.

(3) The earlier mortgage imposes an obligation to make further advances.[61]

Explanation

Tacking is a method of jumping the priority queue.
B mortgages Blackacre as follows:

1966	B	1st mortgage—£5,000	X

>

1967	B	2nd mortgage—£1,000	Y

>

1968	B	Further advance—£1,000	X

>

Assuming that the first mortgage is protected and the second and third registered on creation, the ordinary order of priority will be X, Y, X. The fact that the third is a further advance from the first mortgagee and possibly secured by the original mortgage deed, does not of itself entitle X to any special priority for the further advance. However, if X can establish the right to tack the further advance, the order of priority will be X, X, Y. Clearly such queue jumping must be carefully limited.

Consent of intervening mortgagee. This needs no comment.

Earlier mortgage expressed to be security for further advances-
This is the most important category. A typical building society mortgage provides: "This mortgage is made for securing also further advances." But its main importance is in the case of the mortgage to a bank to secure an overdraft on a current account. Emma mortgages Blackacre to her bank to secure the overdraft on her current account. This means that the mortgage is security not only for the original overdraft but also for any subsequent loans. And each time that the bank honours one of Emma's cheques on the account it is making her a further advance.

The bank can safely honour Emma's cheques so long as it does not have notice of any intervening mortgage. Each advance will have the same priority as the original overdraft. It is in this context that the provision as to notice is important. If registration were notice—as it is for most purposes—the bank would have to make a

[61] L.P.A. 1925, s. 94.

search in the register before honouring each cheque drawn on the account, an impossible state of affairs. By section 94 (2) of the Law of Property Act 1925 the mere registration of a subsequent mortgage will not affect the bank which will be safe to continue honouring cheques in the ordinary course of business without searching so long as it has not received actual notice of any intervening mortgage.[62]

This tacking is not unfair to a subsequent lender. Before lending money he will investigate the mortgagor's title including any outstanding mortgages. He can thus discover whether any earlier mortgage was made for securing further advances. He can discover, as it were, whether anyone ahead in the queue has reserved a place. And if he makes the loan he will be able to protect himself from the danger of tacking by giving express notice of his mortgage to the earlier mortgagee.

In the case of registered land, section 30 (1) of the Land Registration Act 1925 provides for notice of a subsequent mortgage sent for registration to be served by the registrar on the earlier mortgagee; the earlier mortgagee can tack further advances made before such notices "ought to have been received in due course of post."

Obligation to make further advances. In such a case a subsequent mortgagee cannot prevent tacking even by giving express notice; but, again, he should have been warned by his investigation of the mortgagor's title.

Principle 13. Rights of a subsequent mortgagee

A subsequent mortgagee has the same rights as a first mortgagee. However, his rights are subject to those of any prior mortgagee.[63]

Explanation

A first mortgagee's rights cannot in any way be limited or adversely affected by the creation of any second or subsequent mortgage (or by any other subsequent dealing with the land).[64]

Similarly, the second mortgagee will hold his interest and exercise his remedies subject to the first mortgage but will not be affected by any subsequent mortgage or dealing with the land.

---

[62] For effect of registration generally see below, p. 523.
[63] See also below, p. 493.
[64] Provided he has taken any necessay steps such as registration to protect his mortgage.

This is just part of the general principle that a landowner can only deal with his property subject to existing interests (protected if necessary by registration and subject to the doctrine of notice).

The position of a subsequent mortgagee exercising his right of sale, foreclosure and redemption merits further consideration. Suppose that B mortgages Blackacre to, in order of priority, W, X, Y and Z.

Sale. If, for example, X exercises the power of sale he can only sell subject to W's prior mortgage—unless, as is likely to happen, W agrees to join in the sale to release his mortgage on the understanding that he is paid first out of the proceeds of sale. Y and Z will have no choice in the matter. Their interests, being subsequent to W's, will be overreached and transferred to the balance of the proceeds of sale, if any, left after payment of W (if he has joined) and X.[65]

Foreclosure. If X starts foreclosure proceedings this cannot affect prior mortgagee W. But if the foreclosure is made absolute it will destroy any subsequent mortgages as well as the equity of redemption. This is because a subsequent mortgage cannot be any more durable than the equity of redemption out of which it has been carved. This makes a subsequent mortgage more precarious than a first mortgage. But a subsequent mortgagee is given reasonable protection by the rule "foreclose down" which applies to all foreclosure proceedings. This rule is that if a mortgagee starts foreclosure proceedings he must make all subsequent mortgagees (*i.e.* all those at risk) parties to the action as well as the mortgagor. The court will then make a foreclosure order nisi providing that each subsequent mortgagee in turn and finally the mortgagor is to be given a chance to save himself by redeeming those above him.

Thus, in the above illustration, Y, Z and B will each in turn have the chance to be foreclosed and lose his security or to save himself by redeeming and taking a transfer of the prior mortgages involved in the action. Y, for example: if he fails to redeem X, his security will disappear. If he finds the money and redeems, he will pay whatever is due to X and take a transfer of his mortgage. If Y fails to redeem, Z will next be given the chance to redeem X. If Y has redeemed X, then Z will need to redeem the two mortgages now held by Y. If he does this the borrower, B, will have to redeem all three mortgages now held by Z in order to save himself. If, for example, he fails to do so the result will then be that Z will hold

---

[65] L.P.A. 1925, ss. 2 (1) (iii), 104 (1).

the property absolutely subject only to the mortgage in favour of W which has not been affected by any of these proceedings.

Redemption. If the mortgagor, or a subsequent owner of the equity of redemption, redeems, the result will be to discharge the mortgage altogether.

A subsequent mortgagee also has a right to redeem any prior mortgage. In this case the effect will normally be a transfer of the mortgage. The redeeming mortgagee will take over the security which he redeems. Normally no problem will arise. Suppose, using the same example that Y wishes to redeem W. He will pay to W whatever is owing under his mortgage and take a transfer of the mortgage. The position will now be Y, X, Y and Z, with B still holding the equity.

It may however be necessary for Y to start a redemption action—for example, if there is a dispute as to the outstanding amount due to W. Where a redemption action in court is necessary, the principle "Redeem up, foreclose down" applies.

This states that where a mortgagee starts an action to redeem a prior mortgagee he must

(a) also redeem any mortgages standing between himself and that prior mortgage ("redeem up"); and

(b) he must foreclose all subsequent mortgages and the mortgagor ("foreclose down"). The reason for this rule is as follows: An account will have to be taken of the amount due to the prior mortgagee. The amount held to be due to this prior mortgagee will, of course, affect the value of the security available for subsequent mortgagees. Suppose that the property is worth £10,000. If the court decides that £6,000 is due to W this leaves £4,000 to satisfy X, Y and Z. If only £5,000 is held to be due, there will be another £1,000 available for the subsequent mortgagees and the mortgagor.

The court therefore considers it desirable that all affected parties (*i.e.* all those "interested in the proper taking of accounts")[66] should be before the court so that their rights can be finally determined, their respective interests cleared from the property and the possibility of further expensive litigation and accounts avoided. The court will order an account to be taken of the amount due to each intervening mortgagee and his mortgage redeemed. Y will have to pay the amount found to be due to X as well as W. Further, each subsequent mortgagee and the mortgagor will have to have the amount due to him decided and be foreclosed, *i.e.* each will have the chance to redeem all those

---

[66] Coote, *Mortgages* (9th ed.), Vol. 1, p. 746.

mortgagees prior to himself involved in the action or lose his security. The final result will be that one person will hold the property free of all the involved mortgages.

It is to be remembered that in the case of a foreclosure or a redemption action, any interested party can ask for a judicial sale.[67]

SECTION V. SUB-MORTGAGES; CONSOLIDATION; AND SOME SPECIAL TYPES OF MORTGAGES

Principle 14.   Sub-mortgages

A sub-mortgage is a mortgage of a mortgage. It will normally consist of:

(1) A covenant by the sub-mortgagor to pay the amount due under the sub-mortgage.

(2) A transfer to the sub-mortgagee of the mortgage and the mortgage debt with a proviso for re-transfer on redemption.

The sub-mortgagee will be in a position to exercise all the rights and remedies of the mortgagee against the land and the mortgagor. In addition he will be able to sue the mortgagee on the covenant to pay contained in the sub-mortgage.

Explanation

Suppose that B has mortgaged Blackacre to L to secure a loan of £1,000 and that he now wants to raise a loan of £500. He can, unless prevented from doing so by the terms of the mortgage deed, call in the £1,000. But a mortgagor cannot be called on to repay only part of a mortgage debt. If the mortgagee can find a person (call him SL), willing to lend the needed £500, what he can do is to offer him the mortgage as security. This will be a sub-mortgage. L will now be both mortgagee under the main mortgage and sub-mortgagor under the sub mortgage. SL will be sub-mortgagee.

What the sub-mortgagor does in effect is to transfer all his rights as mortgagee to the sub-mortgagee. In addition he personally covenants to repay the £500 borrowed from SL. The sub-mortgagee steps into his shoes. The original mortgagor will be required to make payments to the sub-mortgagee. If the original mortgagor defaults it will be the sub-mortgagee who will take steps to enforce the security. The sub-mortgagee will be able to recover all moneys due under the principle mortgage; but of course he will only be able to retain what is due to him. If for example B defaults

---

[67] L.P.A. 1925, s. 91 (2).

and SL exercises the power of sale over Blackacre he will deduct
from the proceeds of sale the £1,000 with interest and costs due
under the mortgage. The balance will go to the mortgagor (or
subsequent mortgagee) in the usual way. Out of the £1,000 SL will
deduct his £500 with costs. The balance will be handed to L.

Since arrears of interest and costs may accumulate in addition to
the original loan, a sub-mortgagee will not lend as much as the
loan under the principal mortgage; because however much is due
to him, he will not be able to recover—except by suing the
sub-mortgagor personally—more than is due under the principal
mortgage. Subject to this the sub-mortgage is better security than
the mortgage itself since the sub-mortgagee has all the remedies of
the mortgagee and in addition the personal action against the
mortgagee.

Principle 15. Consolidation

If a mortgagee holds two separate mortgages on two separate
properties he may be entitled to consolidate and treat them as one
mortgage, thus making each property security for both debts.

This means in particular that:

(1) He can refuse to allow one mortgage to be redeemed unless
the other is redeemed at the same time.

(2) If he exercises the power of sale against one property he can
use any surplus towards discharging the debt secured on the other
property.

The right to consolidate, which is a permitted restriction on the
equity of redemption, only arises if the following conditions are
satisfied:

(a) The legal date of redemption of both mortgages must have
passed.

(b) The right to consolidate must have been reserved in at least
one of the mortgages.[68]

(c) Both mortgages must have been created by the same
mortgagor.

(d) There must have been some point in time when both equities
of redemption were vested in one person and both mortgages
vested in one other person.

Explanation

Consolidation is likely to become important to a mortgagee
holding mortgages on separate properties where one of the

[68] L.P.A. 1925, s. 93 (1).

properties has become insufficient security. Suppose that B owns Blackacre and Whiteacre both worth £10,000. He mortgages Blackacre to L to secure a loan of £5,000 and Whiteacre to L to secure a loan of £1,000. All seems to be well; but if a motorway unexpectedly appears at the backdoor of Blackacre making it unsaleable, L is in some difficulty. Consolidation is designed to prevent the mortgagor taking advantage of such a situation to redeem Whiteacre on payment of only £1,000 thus recovering for himself the property worth £10,000; leaving L with the possibly worthless property and a personal claim against B as the only security for his debt of £5,000. In such a situation, if L can consolidate he has no worry. To obtain the release of Whiteacre, B will have to pay the full £6,000 owing.

Consolidation is a principle of equity. The same person (condition (c)) has incurred two debts. Both are owed to the same creditor[69]—either the original mortgagee or someone who has acquired both mortgages. It is true that technically they are separate debts secured on distinct properties. But the debtor is responsible for them both and it would be inequitable to allow him to insist on the separation to the disadvantage of the creditor.

However, consolidation can work harshly against a purchaser of the equity of redemption or a subsequent mortgagee. Once the right to consolidate has arisen it becomes a burden on the equity of redemption. If the mortgagor sells one (or both) of the two properties subject to a mortgage, the purchaser will take it subject to any right to consolidate. Similarly, a second mortgagee may find the first mortgagee entitled to priority not only for the amount due under the first mortgage but also under some other mortgage on a different property. The possibility of a right to consolidate is one of the drawbacks of accepting a subsequent mortgage as security or purchasing property subject to a mortgage.

Principle 16.   Special types of mortgage

The following mortgages are to some extent subject to special rules:

(1) building society mortgages;
(2) mortgages to secure bank overdrafts;
(3) mortgages to trustees.

[69] The right to consolidate may not arise until after the original mortgagor has parted with both properties. For example: B mortgages Blackacre to X and Whiteacre to Z. He sells both properties to C and then X and Y both transfer their mortgages to Z. At that moment the right to consolidate attaches to the equities in both properties.

Explanation

Building societies constitute one of the most important, probably the most important, sources of finance for the purchase of homes for owner occupation. The money which they lend comes entirely from the money which members of the public invest in building societies as a method of saving. The rate of interest which they charge borrowing members is governed by the rate of interest which they have to pay saving members in order to attract sufficient funds. Clearly the building society system plays a central rôle in determining the spread of owner occupation and the extent to which each family is able to purchase "a *small* freehold or leasehold"[70] stake in the nation's wealth.

Most money which is lent on mortgage today passes through the channels of the financial institutions, such as the building societies, the insurance companies and the banks. There is little direct lending as there was up into the nineteenth century, between individual and individual.

In general the building society mortgage is an ordinary mortgage governed by the age-old mortgage laws; although rules designed for the traditional standing mortgage have had to be adapted to the instalment mortgage commonly used by building societies. However, there are some special rules—chiefly contained in the Building Societies Act 1962—designed in general to protect the money of the countless investing members, but also to give added protection to the borrowers.

Some of these special rules are as follows:

1. The borrower will be not only a mortgagor but a member of the society from which he borrows.[71] His express rights and obligations will be contained partly in the mortgage deed and partly in the rules of the society.

2. There are a number of limits on the lending powers of building societies. For example, they cannot in general lend more than a certain amount to each borrower.[72] They cannot lend on the security of a second or subsequent mortgage unless they also hold the prior mortgages.[73] If the building society exercises its power of sale it is under a statutory obligation to get the best price reasonably possible.[74]

---

[70] Preamble to Building Societies Act 1836. (Italics mine).
[71] Building Societies Act 1962, s. 1 (1).
[72] *Ibid*. ss. 21, 22.
[73] *Ibid*. s. 32; see *Nash* v. *Halifax B.S.* [1979] 2 W.L.R. 184 (Browne-Wilkinson J.).
[74] *Ibid*. s. 36.

Bank mortgages. Two main types of mortgage are made to banks. First, there is the mortgage to secure a single lump sum loan. This is an ordinary mortgage subject to the ordinary rules. Secondly, there is the mortgage to secure an overdraft on current account. As explained before,[75] the essence of such a mortgage is that each time a cheque drawn on the account is honoured, there is a further loan; each time that money is paid into the account there is a repayment.

Such mortgages are subject to the ordinary rules, but a number of points need to be noted:

(a) *Continuing security clause*: The mortgage will stipulate that it is security not only for any existing overdraft, but also for all subsequent advances, that is, all subsequent drawings on the account.

(b) *Tacking*: Tacking has already been dealt with.[76] As long as the bank has not received express notice of another mortgage it will be able to tack each advance onto the original mortgage debt. It is in connection with tacking that the next point is relevant.

(c) *The Rule in Clayton's Case*[77]: This states that in the case of a current account each payment in will be credited to the earliest payment out of the account. An illustration will perhaps explain this and its importance in connection with tacking. B has an overdraft on current account at his bank secured by a mortgage. The following events happen:

1 June B withdraws £100
2 June B withdraws £200
3 June B withdraws £100
6 June Bank received express notice of second mortgage to X
7 June B withdraws £300
8 June B withdraws £100
10 June B pays in £400

B then goes bankrupt. The mortgage security is realised and realises £400 less than is needed to satisfy both X and the bank in full. What is the bank's position? First, the £400 advanced on June 7 and 8 cannot be tacked onto the original mortgage. Secondly, under the rule in *Clayton's Case* the £400 paid in on June 10 must be appropriated to the earliest undischarged payment out—in this

---

[75] Above, p. 450.
[76] Above, p. 486.
[77] *De Vaynes* v. *Noble* (1816) 1 Mer. 529, 572; 35 E.R. 767.

case the £400 withdrawn on June 1, 2 and 3. The result is that the £400 shortfall in the proceeds is borne by the bank.

To prevent this happening the bank will need to stop lending once it has received notice of another mortgage. If it does allow further drawings without fresh security it will need to rule off the existing account and start a fresh one. In the illustration it will rule off the account on June 6. Any payments in can then be appropriated with withdrawals on the new account. The £400 paid in on June 10 would satisfy the £400 drawn on June 7 and 8 and the other mortgagee, X, would bear the loss.

Trustees.[78] One of the ways in which trustees can invest trust moneys is to lend it on mortgage. But whereas the ordinary beneficial owner of money can lend it on what security he likes, or no security at all, trustees, must comply with certain rules. They may lend on the security of freehold land or leasehold with at least 60 years to run.[79] Provided the trustees select a person whom they reasonably believe to be an able practical surveyor or valuer and act on the advice of his report and do not lend more than two-thirds of the value of the property as shown in his report, they will not be liable merely because the security proves insufficient. Apart from this, the trustees must exercise the standard of care required of trustees on all occasions.

Principle 17.　Discharge

A receipt endorsed on or annexed to the mortgage, providing it is signed by the mortgagee and names the person paying the money, will normally be effective to discharge the mortgage.

However, if the receipt shows that the person paying the money was not entitled to the immediate equity of redemption, then (unless it provides to the contrary) the receipt will operate as a transfer of the mortgage to the payer.[80]

If a building society mortgage is receipted using the special statutory form (which does not state who paid the money), it cannot operate as a transfer.[81]

---

[78] For powers of trustees to borrow on security of trust property, see above, p. 217.
[79] Trustees Investment Act 1961, Sched. I, Pt. II, para. 13.
[80] L.P.A. 1925, s. 115.
[81] Building Societies Act 1962, s. 37 and Sched. 6.

CHAPTER 22

RENTCHARGES

Principle 1.   Definition and creation[1]

A rentcharge is a periodic payment charged on land where the
relationship of landlord and tenant does not exist.
It may be legal if:
   (a) in possession;
   (b) either perpetual or for a term of years absolute; and
   (c) created by deed (or assent).[2]
Any other rentcharge must be equitable.
A rentcharge may be created:
   (1) By statute.
   (2) Expressly, either *inter vivos* or by will.

Explanation

There are two types of rent and they should not be confused.
First, there is the rent service. This is a periodic payment made by
a tenant to his landlord. In theory such a rent could be reserved on
the grant of a life interest or fee tail[3]; but in practice it is only
found today on the grant of a leasehold interest.

Secondly, there is the rentcharge. This is a periodic payment
charged on a fee simple.[4] This chapter is concerned with the
rentcharge. Any rent by whatever name it is known will fall into
one of these two categories.

Whereas the rent service (commonly referred to simply as rent,
or a ground rent) is a feature of almost every lease, the rentcharge
is not often found in practice except in the areas of Manchester
and Bristol. And as a result of the Rent charges Act 1977, which
provides for their eventual abolition, they will be of decreasing
importance.

Unlike the landlord who has his reversion, the rentcharge owner
has no interest in the land except his rentcharge.

The rentcharge as an interest in land.   The rentcharge is a third
party interest in land. The burden of it is attached to and runs with

---

[1] See generally Law Com.(W.P.), No.24, "Transfer of Land: Rentcharges." Also
Law Com.(W.P.), No. 49. Compare definition in Rentcharges Act 1977, s.1.
[2] L.P.A. 1925, ss.1(2), 52.
[3] For position as to leases for lives see below, p. 585.
[4] A rentcharge can be charged on a leasehold interest (in favour of someone other
than the landlord) but these are rare (Law Com.(W.P.), No. 24, para. 7).

the land charged. The benefit of it is not attached to any dominant land. It is held by the rentcharge owner and, like a profit in gross, can be dealt with by him regardless of the ownership of any land.

Creation. Rentcharges can only be created by statute or expressly. Only those rentcharges permitted by the Rentcharges Act 1977, can be created today.[5] For a (permitted) rentcharge to be legal it must be created by statute or deed or, if created by will, a written assent in favour of the beneficiary; moreover, it will have to be in possession and either perpetual or for a term of years absolute.

Principle 2.   Enforcement

A rentcharge can be enforced by the following methods:
(1) Action for money.
(2) Distress.
(3) Entry into possession.
(4) Demise to a trustee.

Explanation

Action for money.   The rentcharge owner can sue the terre-tenant (that is the freehold tenant in possession of the land on which the rent is charged).

If the land has been divided the terre-tenant of each part will be liable for the whole rent unless released by the rentcharge owner, or unless an apportionment has been made under the Rentcharges Act 1977, ss.4–7.

Distress.   If any rent is 21 days in arrears the rentcharge owner has a right of distress.[6]

Entry into possession.   If any rent is 40 days in arrears the rentcharge owner can take possession without impeachment of waste and collect the income until all rent has been paid.[7]

Demise to a trustee.   If any part of the rent is 40 days in arrears, the rentcharge owner can demise the land to a trustee for a term of years on trust to raise the money due by mortgaging the land, collecting the income, or by any other reasonable means.[8]

---

[5] See below, p. 499.
[6] L.P.A. 1925, s.121(2).
[7] *Ibid.* s.121(3).
[8] *Ibid.* s.121(4).

Principle 3.   Extinguishment

Under the Rentcharges Act 1977, subject to exceptions:
   (a) No new rentcharge can be created;
   (b) all existing rentcharges will automatically be extinguished at the end of 60 years from the passing of the Act;
   (c) there is a statutory right to redeem existing rentcharges.

In addition, rentcharges can be extinguished by
   (i) release;
   (ii) merger;
   (iii) lapse of time.

Explanation

The Rentcharge Act 1977.   This Act is designed to put an end to the rentcharge as an interest in land, except in certain exceptional cases.

Under the Act,[9] the only new rentcharges that can be created are:–
   (1) Those which arise under settlements.
   (2) Estate rentcharges.[10]
   (3) Statutory rentcharges for securing work to be done on land.
   (4) Those created under court order.

By section 3 of the Act, all existing rentcharges (with the same exceptions)[11] will automatically cease after sixty years from the passing of the Act.[12]

By sections 8–10,[13] (again with the same exceptions) the owner of land subject to a rentcharge has a statutory right to redeem it on paying the amount specified by the appropriate minister and calculated in accordance with the formula contained in the Act.

Release.   The rentcharge owner may release the land charged wholly or in part. A partial release may release part of the land of the whole rent, or the whole land of part of the rent. The owner of the land charged of course has no right to release it himself.

Merger.   Where the rentcharge and the land on which is is charged become vested in the same person in the same capacity, the rentcharge will generally be extinguished by merger.[14]

---

[9] s.2(3).
[10] See above, p. 418.
[11] And those mentioned in s.3(3), (4).
[12] Or the date on which it first becomes payable, if later.
[13] Replacing the L.P.A. 1925, s.191.
[14] See L.P.A. 1925, s.185.

Lapse of time.   If no payment of the rentcharge is made for 12 years without any written acknowledgment by the owner of the land charged, the rentcharge will be extinguished.[15]

[15] Limitation Act 1980, ss.15(1), 38(7) (8).

PART 5. TRANSFER OF OWNERSHIP (CONVEYANCING)

General Introduction

Distinction between land law and conveyancing. This distinction which is sometimes made is entirely a matter of convenience of exposition. A look at the list of contents of a standard work on conveyancing will give an idea of the topics usually included under this head. Broadly speaking, land law deals with what interests in land can exist; conveyancing deals with the transfer of interests and, in particular, with the rights and obligations of the parties to a transfer, the forms of wording and the documents necessary to carry it out.

The main conveyancing transactions. Ownership may be created or transferred either

(a) *inter vivos, i.e.* between living persons; or

(b) on death, by will or intestacy.

The transactions commonly giving rise to a transfer or creation of ownership are the following:

(i) Sale.

(ii) Gift.

(iii) Lease.

(iv) Mortgage.

(v) Settlement.

(vi) Adverse possession.

(vii) Bankruptcy.

Most of these have already been considered in sufficient detail, but something will be said below on adverse possession, sale, wills and intestacy.

Enforceability of ownership and third party rights against a transferee. One of the most important questions in land law is, how far is any interest in land (whether an ownership interest or a third party right) enforceable against a purchaser or some other transferee of the land. It is not enough to say that A has a restrictive covenant over Blackacre; or that B has a legal right of way over Blackacre. It is necessary to go on and ask how far that restrictive covenant or that right of way, assuming they exist at all, will be enforceable against a subsequent owner of Blackacre.

Although the essence of a property interest in land is that it runs with the burdened land and is enforceable against subsequent owners, examination shows that not all property interests are enforceable to the same extent against subsequent owners.

Suppose that A's restrictive covenant was created in 1936. And suppose that Blackacre is unregistered land. Such a restrictive covenant is registrable under the Land Charges Act 1925; and the extent to which it is enforceable depends on whether it has been registered. If it has been registered it will be enforceable against any subsequent owner; if it has not, it will be void, not altogether, but against a purchaser for money or money's worth of a legal estate in the land.[1]

If, on the other hand, B's easement is legal and the land is unregistered, it will not require registration and will in any event be enforceable against a subsequent owner of the land.[2]

It follows from what has been said that a transferee may take land free of rights which bound the transferor. Another example of this, already considered, is where a subsequent mortgagee gains priority over an earlier mortgagee because the earlier one has not been protected by deposit of title deeds or registration. The mortgagor himself will remain bound by both mortgages.[3]

Conversely, a transferee may sometimes take subject to rights which did *not* bind the transferor.

The problem of enforceability can be looked at from two points of view. First, the transferee will be concerned to know what interests in the land are going to bind him. This will be particularly important if he is giving value as, for example, a purchaser or mortgagee. He will not wish to pay his money and then subsequently discover the existence of binding interests, existing mortgages which reduce its value, rights of way or covenants which prevent him from using the land as he intended, and so on. Secondly, the problem can be looked at from the point of view of the owner of the interest, the mortgagee, the dominant owner entitled to the benefit of the restrictive covenant or right of way. From his point of view, the question is, what must he do to protect his interest?

Unregistered and registered land. The enforceability of interests against a purchaser or other transferee depends in the first place on whether the land is unregistered or registered under the Land Registration Act 1925.

The next chapter deals with the transfer of ownership by adverse possession, and the subsequent two chapters deal with the enforceability of interests on the transfer of unregistered and registered land respectively.

---

[1] L.C.A. 1972, s.4, and see above, p. 397.
[2] See below, p. 511 *et seq.*
[3] For example, see *Gordon* v. *Holland* (1913) 82 L.J.P.C. 81.

CHAPTER 23

TRANSFER OF OWNERSHIP: ADVERSE POSSESSION

Introduction

Possession is a state of affairs. Whether or not a person is in possession is a question of fact.[1]

But the law protects possession which thereby becomes a right as well as a fact.[2] For example, it is possession (not ownership) which the law of trespass to land protects.[3] It is in general an offence to take possession by force without a proper court order regardless of the wrongfulness of the possession.[4]

The law recognises that this right to possession can continue even after possession has been lost. Thus, under the old possessory assizes, if the person in possession was dispossessed he would be restored. Today, he can bring an action to recover land.

This raises the problem of competing claims to possession. We have just mentioned the simple case of one person in possession and another person whom he has dispossessed. Which of two conflicting possessions is to be protected by the law and therefore give the better right to possession? The answer of English law is essentially that the earlier possession has the better right.

Suppose the following events:

1920 A is in possession of Blackacre.
1921 A sells and conveys as to B.
1922 C wrongfully takes possession from B; *i.e.* he takes adverse possession.
1940 C, still in possession, sells and conveys to D.
1972 D sells and conveys to E.

Suppose that A and B now both come forward and claim possession from E. Ignoring the Limitation Act 1980 for the moment, who is entitled to possession; or rather and this is how English law looks at the matter—which of the claimants before the court has the better right to possession? Starting with A, he was in possession. This gives him a right to possession which he does not lose merely because he has lost possession—he can be restored.

---

[1] But not every legal system will recognise the same set of facts as constituting possession; and the same legal system may define possession differently for different purposes. For further reading on possession see n. 2 to p. 4, above. And see *Parker* v. *British Airways Board* [1982] 1 All E.R. 834.
[2] See *Asher* v. *Whitlock* (1865) L.R. 1 Q.B. 1.
[3] See above, p. 47.
[4] See Protection from Eviction Act 1977 and Criminal Law Act 1977.

503

But he has of course transferred his right to possession, however good or bad it might have been, to B in one of the ways recognised by law—conveyance on sale. Next B: He has lost possession to C, but not in a way recognised by law for the transfer of the right to possession. Therefore B has retained his right to possession. It is true that C has a right to possession arising from the fact of his possession. But B's right is earlier and therefore has preference over C's right, and C's right cannot be improved by transfer to D and later to E. Prima facie, B is entitled to recover from E.

That is the essence of what English law means by the ownership of land. The owner is the claimant who now has that right to possession which can be shown to have the earliest origin and which has not been extinguished—for example by the determination of the fee tail estate from which it arose.

It is here that adverse possession becomes relevant. Adverse possession is one of the recognised ways by which the right to possession can be lost.

A line has to be drawn somewhere. In the above illustration both purchasers, D and E, would have to investigate the title back to 1921 to discover the flaw in the title and the claim of B. And of course investigation further back might reveal earlier flaws. This means that in theory any right to possession, no matter how ancient, would be liable to be defeated by the discovery of an earlier right. A purchaser would have to trace title back indefinitely.

However, it has always been the practice of conveyancers to limit the period of investigation. It is now fixed by statute at a minimum period of 15 years.[5] Under the rules as to adverse possession, this gives a purchaser reasonable protection without having to trace the ownership of the land back indefinitely.[6]

The principle of adverse possession is that if a person has a right to recover possession of land from someone else he must either assert that right without delay or lose it. Thus, the law not only protects possession; it recognises that peaceful possession for a sufficient period can defeat an earlier and, prima facie, better right to possession. Wrongful possession becomes rightful possession.

---

[5] L.P.A. 1969, s.23. It is necessary to go back to the first good root of title which is at least 15 years old. See also below, p. 563.

[6] In the case of registered land, registration of a person as proprietor is (subject to the possibility of rectification) sufficient to guarantee title.

Principle 1. Adverse possession[7]

A right of action to recover possession of land is generally extinguished 12 years from the date on which the right of action accrues.[8]

In general, time does not begin to run until:
(a) the claimant is entitled in possession; and
(b) there is someone in adverse possession (the squatter or adverse possessor).

In certain cases the relevant period is other than 12 years.

In certain cases the running of time will be suspended.

When all claims have been barred by time the adverse possessor will have acquired title by adverse possession (a possessory title).[9] In the case of registered land he may apply to be registered as proprietor.[10]

Explanation

Essentials. There are two requirements both of which must be satisfied before time will start to run under the Limitation Act 1980. First, (a), there must be someone in adverse possession. A landowner does not sacrifice his title merely by leaving his property unoccupied for 12 years. Secondly, (b), the owner whose title is to be barred must be entitled to immediate possession.

(a) *Adverse possession.* There must be possession and it must be adverse to (*i.e.* incompatible with) the title of the owner. For example, a tenant cannot begin to bar the title of his landlord so long as the tenancy continues, because, although he has possession, it is not adverse to his landlord's possession. Similarly, time will not begin to run against a licensor until the licence has been determined.[10a]

Whether or not there is adverse possession is a question of fact. Exclusive occupation and use of the land is generally sufficient. In *Rains* v. *Buxton*[11] the plaintiff occupied a cellar under the defendant's property and made use of it for sixty years. This was held to give him title by adverse possession. In *Philpot* v. *Bath*[12] the defendant's predecessor had placed rocks and piles on the land

---

[7] For limitation in case of mortgages, see above, pp. 396, 463/479; as to tenancies at will and sufferance see above, pp. 95, 105.

[8] Limitation Act 1980, s.15 and Sched.1.

[9] For whether this is a new title or the old title transferred, see (1973) 37 Conv. (N.S.) 85 (J.A. Omotolo).

[10] L.R.A. 1925, s.75.

[10a] See *Hyde* v. *Pearce* [1982] 1 All E.R. 1029 (C.A.).

[11] (1880) 14 Ch.D. 537.

[12] (1905) 21 T.L.R. 634.

to protect a house on his own land from encroachment by the sea. It was held that this did not amount to possession of the land and so did not give the defendant title—but it was held sufficient to create an easement by prescription.[13]

If the owner does not take steps to regain possession, within the limitation period, his title will be barred. It is no excuse for inaction that he does not know of the possession; or that he does not know that it is adverse.[14] Nor is it any excuse that he has no immediate use for the land and that the possession is not inconveniencing him. As Sir John Pennycuick said in *Treloar* v. *Nute,*[15] "if inconvenience to the owner had to be established, it would be difficult ever to acquire a possessory title, since the owner, if inconvenienced, would be likely to take proceedings."

In *Treloar* v. *Nute*[16] the disputed land was derelict and there was no evidence that the plaintiff owner was intending to put it to any particular use. In 1961, the defendant's father purchased the adjoining land and the conveyance included the disputed land. In 1962, the defendant and his father placed soil in a gully running across the disputed land with a view to levelling it and building. They also grazed cattle on it. In 1963, they erected a fence along the western (outer) boundary, at which the plaintiff protested and removed the fence. The defendant's father replaced the fence and it was not removed again. In 1965, the father conveyed the disputed land to the defendant by way of gift. In 1966, the plaintiff complained when the defendant dumped soil on the land, in reply to which the defendant claimed to be owner. In 1974, the defendant started to erect a bungalow and the plaintiff started proceedings. It was held that the defendant had acquired title by adverse possession.

In one line of cases,[17] it was decided that where the possession did not interfere with any present or intended future use of the land by the owner, time did not start to run against him. This line

---

[13] See also *Marshall* v. *Taylor* [1895] 1 Ch. 641 (C.A.); and *Redhouse Farms (Thorndon) Ltd.* v. *Catchpole* (1976) 244 E.G. 295 (C.A.).
[14] For example, if he does not know that he owns the land.
[15] [1977] 1 All E.R. 230 (C.A.), at p. 236.
[16] Above, n. 15.
[17] See *Leigh* v. *Jack* (1879) 5 Ex.D. 264 (C.A.); *Williams Brothers Direct Supplies Ltd.* v. *Raftery* [1958] 1 Q.B. 159 (C.A.); *Wallis's Cayton Bay Holiday Camp Ltd.* v. *Shell-Mex & B.P. Ltd.* [1974] 3 All E.R. 575 (C.A.); and *Powell* v. *McFarlane* (1977) 38 P. & C.R. 452; contrast *Treloar* v. *Nute* [1977] 1 All E.R. 230 (C.A.). See also *McPhail* v. *Persons Unknown* [1973] 3 W.L.R. 71 in which Lord Denning was of the opinion that a squatter is not in possession but a mere trespasser until the owner has acquiesced in the occupation in some way.

of cases has, however, been overruled by statute. The Limitation Act 1980[18] provides that:

> "For the purpose of determining whether a person occupying land is in adverse possession of the land it shall not be assumed by implication of law that his occupation is by permission of the person entitled to the land merely by virtue of the fact that his occupation is not inconsistent with the latter's present or future enjoyment of the land.
>
> This provision shall not be taken as prejudicing a finding to the effect that a person's occupation of any land is by implied permission of the person entitled to the land in any case where such a finding is justified on the actual facts of the case."

In other words, to prevent time running, there must be positive evidence from the words or conduct of the parties or surrounding circumstances, which justifies the courts in finding that the possessor was occupying as licensee (or tenant) and not asserting the rights of an owner.

(b) *Time will not start to run against the owner until he is entitled in possession.* The basis of adverse possession is that the owner has failed to assert his right to possession against an adverse claimant. But until he is entitled to possession he is not in a position to assert it. For example, where a tenant has been dispossessed, this will not affect the title of the landlord. Time will only begin to run against the landlord from when the lease determines by, for example, expiry or surrender.[19]

Special periods. In some cases special periods apply. For example, a claim by the Crown is only barred after 30 years from when the claim accrues.[20] Two other special cases, trust property and disabilty, will now be dealt with.

Trust property. In the case of land subject to a trust special rules apply as to the relevant time.

(a) Where a stranger takes possession the owner of a future interest is not barred until 12 years from when the preceding beneficiary was dispossessed or six years from when he himself became entitled in possession, whichever gives him the longer

---

[18] s.15 and Sched. 1, consolidating Limitation (Amendment) Act 1980, s.4.

[19] See *e.g. Fairweather* v. *St.Marylebone Property Co. Ltd.* [1963] A.C. 510 (H.L.). Compare *Spectrum Investment Co.* v. *Holmes* [1981] 1 All E.R. 6 (Browne-Wilkinson J.); below, p. 536.

[20] Limitation Act 1980, Sched. 1, paras 10, 11.

period.[21] And the legal estate cannot be barred until the last beneficial interest has been barred.[22]

(b) Where a trustee is in possession of trust property time for recovering the trust property does not run against a beneficiary.[23]

(c) Where a beneficiary is in possession the general rule, under Sched.1, para. 9 of the Limitation Act 1980, is that, unless the beneficiary is solely and beneficially entitled, time will not run in his favour against the trustees or his fellow beneficiaries.

In *Re Landi*[24] there were two tenants in common of land. Since 1923 one of them had been in possession of all the rents and profits from the land. In other words, prima facie, he was in adverse possession and by the date of the action would have acquired a good title against his fellow tenant in common.

However, the effect of the 1925 legislation was to impose a statutory trust for sale. Each tenant in common became a joint trustee of the legal estate as well as a beneficiary. As a trustee time could not run in his favour against a beneficiary. If the 1980 Act had been in force sched.1, para. 9[25] would have been a further reason preventing him as a beneficiary claiming by adverse possession against his fellow beneficiary.

Disability.[26]   If the person entitled is under a disability when the right of action accrues,[27] he has whichever of the following two periods gives him longest:

(i) The ordinary period of 12 years from the accrual of the action.
(ii) Six years from the ending of the disability or death, whichever happens first.

But in any case there is a maximum period of 30 years from the accrual of the action.

Disability means infancy and being of unsound mind.[28]

Suspension of time running: Fraud and mistake.   Where the action is concealed by the fraud of the defendant or by mistake, time does not start to run until the fraud or mistake is, or could with reasonable diligence have been, discovered.[29]

---

[21] *Ibid.* s.15(2), Sched.1, para. 4.
[22] *Ibid.* s.28(2), (3).
[23] *Ibid.* s.21(1), (2).
[24] [1939] Ch. 828 (C.A.).
[25] Previously, Limitation Act 1939, s.7(5).
[26] Limitation Act 1980, s.28.
[27] Disability arising subsequently has no effect.
[28] See Limitation Act 1980, s.38(2).
[29] Limitation Act 1980, s.32.

Acknowledgment. Any acknowledgment (in writing signed by the person in possession) of the claimant's title made during the period will start time running afresh.[30] But once the title has been barred by adverse possession, it cannot be revived by a subsequent acknowledgment.[31]

[30] *Ibid.* ss.29, 30.
[31] *Nicholson* v. *England* [1926] 2 K.B. 93 (Sankey J.).

CHAPTER 24

ENFORCEABILITY OF INTERESTS: ON THE TRANSFER OF UNREGISTERED LAND

General introduction

Unregistered land is land which has not been registered under the Land Registration Act 1925.

Any interest in unregistered land will fall into one of the following categories:

(1) Those legal interests which are not registrable and which are good against all the world.

(2) Those equitable interests which are not registrable and which are good against all the world except a bona fide purchaser for value of a legal estate without notice of the equitable interest ("bona fide purchaser" for short).

(3) Those interests, chiefly equitable, which are registrable under the Land Charges Act 1972.

The enforceability of any interest in unregistered land against a transferee depends on:

(a) which of the above three categories it belongs to; and

(b) whether or not it can be overreached.

Position before 1926. Before the statutory reforms culminating in the 1925 legislation, all land was unregistered. Neither the ownership nor third party interests were registrable in any sort of official register.

The enforceability of any interest (whether ownership or third party right) in land depended solely on whether it was legal or equitable. If it was legal it was good against all the world. If it was equitable it was good against all the world except a bona fide purchaser.

The 1925 legislation. The 1925 legislation reformed this system in two quite distinct ways. First, it modified the existing system of unregistered conveyancing by the introduction of overreaching and the machinery for registration of certain third party rights under the 1925 Lands Charges Act.[1] Secondly, it introduced a completely new system—the registered land system—to replace the existing unregistered system.[2] At the moment the two still exist side by side; but ultimately the plan is that all land will be

---

[1] And by reducing the number of possible legal interests.
[2] For the statutory history of registration of title see Ruoff and Roper, *Registered Conveyancing* (4th ed.).

registered, and unregistered conveyancing will disappear. Meanwhile, the rest of this chapter is concerned with unregistered land in its modified form. The next three Principles will deal with the three categories listed above. The Principle after that will deal with the effect of overreaching.

Principle 1.   Legal interests good against all the world

Those legal interests in unregistered land which have not been made registrable and which are not overreached are still good against all the world.

Explanation

An example will illustrate: V is the legal fee simple owner of Blackacre. He grants a legal right of way over it in favour of neighbouring Whiteacre. He then sells to P. P may discover the existence of the right of way before he completes, that is before he pays the balance of his purchase money and takes a conveyance of the legal estate. Probably, V was under a duty to and did warn him about the right of way before contract.[3] Failing this, P may discover its existence for himself before completion either from his examination of the title deeds or from an inspection of the land. If he does, he may be entitled to refuse to complete and have other remedies against V for not disclosing its existence.

But the point is this: if he does complete, he will necessarily be bound by the right of way since it is legal and good against all the world. Whether or not he knew about it or should have known about it is not relevant. His only remedy, if any, will be to sue V for non-disclosure.

The same principle applies to the legal ownership. Suppose that, in the above illustration, V is not in fact the real fee simple owner but has forged a set of title deeds which make it appear that he is the owner. The real owner is X. X's legal ownership is good against all the world. Even if the purchaser, P, has a conveyance in his favour executed by V, it will not help him. The conveyance will not be effective; and the real legal owner, X, will be entitled to come along and claim the land.[4]

Reduction in number of legal estates and interests. Before 1926, most interests in land could exist either at law or in equity, depending in general on the method of creation. For example, the

---

[3] As to vendor's duty of disclosure, see below, p. 553.
[4] Unless his ownership has been extinguished under the Limitation Act 1980.

beneficial interests under a settlement could be legal or equitable. This made conveyancing complicated and somewhat hazardous for a purchaser. He had to make absolutely[5] sure that the vendor did own the legal estate which he had agreed to sell and that there were no adverse legal rights which would bind him whether or not he knew about them.

As part of its policy of simplifying conveyancing, the 1925 legislation has therefore reduced the number of legal estates and interests.

Section 1 of the Law of Property Act 1925 provides:

(1)   The only estates in land which are capable of subsisting or of being created at law are:

    (a) An estate in fee simple absolute in possession;

    (b) A term of years absolute.

(2)   The only interests or charges in or over land which are capable of subsisting or of being conveyed or created at law are:

    (a) An easement, right, or privilege in or over land for an interest equivalent to an estate in fee simple absolute in possession or a term of years absolute;

    (b) A rentcharge in possession, issuing out of or charged on land, being either perpetual or for a term of years absolute;

    (c) A charge by way of legal mortgage;

    (d) Any charge on land (similar to land tax or tithe rentcharge) which is not created by an instrument;[6]

    (e) Rights of entry exercisable over or in respect of a legal term of years absolute, or annexed, for any purpose, to a legal rentcharge.[7]

(3)   All other estates, interests, and charges in or over land take effect as equitable interests.

Apart from those few which have been made registrable,[8] all these legal estates and interests are still good against all the world.[9] A purchaser no longer faces the possibility of an undiscovered legal life interest but he must still watch out for, for

---

[5] See below, p. 564, for how absolute proof was.

[6] Land tax and tithe rent charge referred to in this section were abolished by Finance Act 1963, s.14, and Tithe Act 1936, s.47(1), respectively.

[7] As to the meaning of this see *Shiloh Spinners Ltd.* v. *Harding* [1973] A.C. 691. And see above, p. 418.

[8] See below, p. 518 *et seq.*

[9] Unless overreached. Only rarely will a legal interest be overreached on sale. See above, p. 236, n. 42.

example, legal easements; and be certain that the vendor does in fact own the legal fee simple or term of years which he has agreed to sell.[10]

Principle 2.   Equitable interests subject to notice

Those equitable interests in unregistered land which are not registrable and which are not overreached, will be good against all the world except a bona fide purchaser for value of a legal estate without notice of the equitable interest.

Explanation

The doctrine of notice.   Before 1926, all equitable interests were good against all the world except a bona fide purchaser for value of a legal estate in the land without notice of the equitable interest.

This doctrine of notice still applies to those interests which have not been made registrable and which are not overreached.[11] It must therefore be explained.

The bona fide purchaser has been called "the darling of equity." It is one of the few cases in which equity allowed the legal estate to prevail over the equitable. Take an example of an interest which has not been made registrable. Suppose that Blackacre is subject to a restrictive covenant created in 1920 against building on the land. P purchases Blackacre. In general he will be bound by the covenant, but if he can show that he has purchased a legal estate in Blackacre for value and that at the time of completion he had no notice of the covenant, then it will not be enforceable against him. There will be nothing, apart from planning permission, to stop him building.

In order to take free of such an equitable interest, a purchaser must satisfy the following conditions[12]:

(a) *He must be a bona fide purchaser.*   At law the meaning of the word purchaser is not confined to the ordinary everyday meaning of a person who buys the land. It means anyone who

---

[10] See below, p. 563, for proof of title.

[11] The doctrine has been excluded in the case of land held under the S.L.A. 1925, since a sale which does not comply with the Act will be "void" (S.L.A. 1925, s.18(1) (a)) unless the purchaser can rely on some specific statutory protection (*e.g.* S.L.A. 1925, s.110(1)). But see above, p. 282, n. 74.

[12] The doctrine of notice is given statutory expression in L.P.A. 1925, s. 199, but this is stated not to impose notice where it would not have been imposed in equity (s. 199(4)).

takes the land otherwise than by descent on intestacy. It thus includes a beneficiary under a will, though such a beneficiary will not normally be a purchaser for value. It does include, more important, a lessee and a mortgagee[13] of the land.

Bona fide means good faith; but since any absence of good faith would imply constructive notice, the expression does not add anything to the rest of the expression.[14]

(b) *He must be a purchaser for value.*   Value means in general the same as value in contract law. It does not include a transfer in consideration of natural love and affection. The requirement as to value is most important. It means that a person who receives land as a gift by will or *inter vivos* (or on intestacy) will be bound by these existing equitable interests regardless of notice.[15]

(c) *He must have obtained a legal estate.*   The purchaser of an equitable interest normally takes subject to any equitable interests. The general rule is that: "Where the equities are equal the first in time prevails." But even the purchaser of an equitable interest may take free of "mere equities"[16] of which he does not have notice.

(d) *He must have purchased without notice of the equitable interest.*   If a purchaser does have notice there is no reason why equity should protect him and he will not escape the burden of the interest. The whole justification for the development was that it was fair to protect the purchaser from an interest which he neither knew nor had any reason to know about.

Notice.   A purchaser may be fixed with actual, constructive or imputed notice of the interest in question. Each will be considered in turn.

Actual notice.   This is where he actually knows of the interest. It does not matter how he acquired his knowledge.

Constructive notice.   The purchaser has constructive notice if the interest "would have come to his knowledge if such inquiries

---

[13] See, *e.g. Caunce* v. *Caunce* [1969] 1 W.L.R. 286 (C.A.).

[14] But see view of Lord Wilberforce in *Midland Bank Trust Co. Ltd.* v. *Green* [1981] 1 All E.R. 153, at p. 157. For the significance of good faith in registered conveyancing, see *Peffer* v. *Rigg* [1978] 3 All E.R. 745 (Graham J.).

[15] Under L.P.A. 1925, ss. 199, 205 (1) (xxi), "value" includes marriage but not a nominal consideration in money. For the position under L.R.A. 1925 and L.C.A. 1972, see cases cited in n. 14 above.

[16] For the nature of mere equities see Hanbury and Maudsley, *Modern Equity* (11th ed.), p. 753 *et seq.*

and inspections had been made as ought reasonably to have been made by him."[17]

The question is, what inquiries can a reasonable purchaser be expected to make? Investigation of title by a purchaser is considered further below,[18] but it is convenient to explain here that there are three main ways in which constructive notice may arise.

(i) Constructive notice resulting from failure to investigate title for the statutory period: Under section 44(1) of the Law of Property Act 1925, as amended by section 23 of the Law of Property Act 1969, in the absence of agreement to the contrary, a purchaser is entitled to investigate the vendor's title for a period of 15 years. This means that the vendor must produce evidence—the title deeds and documents—of the ownership of the property starting with a deed at least 15 years old and tracing it down to his own ownership. The purchaser will examine this title to satisfy himself of the vendor's ownership and that there are no adverse third party rights. A purchaser is not entitled to call for any earlier title, but he is protected in that he will not be deemed to have constructive notice of equitable interests which such earlier investigation would have revealed.[19]

He will, however, have constructive notice of interests which a proper investigation for the 15-year period would have revealed. In *Re Nisbet and Potts' Contract*[20] Nisbet had purchased land from a squatter who had acquired ownership by 12 years' adverse possession.[21] Title by adverse possession is perfectly valid ownership, but it meant that the squatter had not obtained the title deeds from the previous owner or a conveyance to himself, as a normal purchaser would have done. The only evidence of his ownership was his actual possession for more than 12 years; and when he bought Nisbet had accepted this as sufficient proof of title. Nisbet had now agreed to sell to Potts who had somehow discovered that before the squatter took possession the land had been subject to a restrictive covenant and he refused to complete the purchase from Nisbet. It was held that if Nisbet when he bought had insisted on proof of title for the statutory period (then 40 years) he would have discovered the existence of the restrictive covenant. He was therefore fixed with constructive notice of and

---

[17] L.P.A. 1925, s.199(1) (ii) (*a*).
[18] pp. 563 *et seq.*
[19] L.P.A. 1925, ss.44(8).
[20] [1906] 1 Ch. 386 (C.A.).
[21] Above, Chap. 23.

bound by it. Potts had actual notice of the covenant and if he went ahead and completed he in turn would be bound by it.[22] Therefore since it had not been disclosed to him by the vendor Nisbet he was entitled to refuse to complete.

The purchaser of leasehold is not, in the absence of agreement to the contrary, entitled to call for title to the freehold reversion. This is a serious drawback for the purchaser of leasehold at a premium; but he is protected to the extent that he is not deemed to have constructive notice of equitable interests which investigation of the freehold would have revealed.[23]

It needs to be emphasised that the absence of notice only protects a purchaser from equitable interests. In practice the investigation of title will reveal any legal interests affecting the land; but if there are any they will bind the purchaser whether or not he did, or could have, discovered their existence.

(ii) Constructive notice arising from failure to investigate a known incumbrance[24]: If a purchaser has actual knowledge, however gained, of any incumbrance, he must investigate that incumbrance fully; and he will be fixed with constructive notice of any further interest which a proper investigation would have revealed.

(iii) Constructive notice arising from failure to inspect the land: Adverse interests which are not mentioned elsewhere may be apparent from an inspection of the land. A purchaser will have constructive notice of any equitable interests which such inspection would have revealed. Generally, if a person is in occupation the purchaser will be fixed with notice of the occupier's interest.

Where the legal owner is himself in occupation, the question may arise whether a purchaser is fixed with notice of the interest of a joint occupier—such as a spouse or other relation. There has been some difference of judicial opinion. In *Caunce* v. *Caunce*[25] the legal title was vested in the husband. By virtue of her contribution to the purchase price, he held in trust for himself and the wife. Whilst she was still in occupation with him, he charged the legal estate to the bank. Stamp J. held that the bank did not have constructive notice of the wife's interest, so the bank's charge had priority. But this case was disapproved in *Williams & Glyn's*

---

[22] If Nisbet had been a purchaser without notice, Potts would have been protected as a subsequent transferee; see below, p. 517.

[23] But it may transpire that the lessor had no legal title to grant a lease.

[24] There is some doubt as to the meaning of the word "incumbrance"; but it is used here in the widest sense of a defect in title, see Emmett, *Title* (17th ed.), p. 502.

[25] [1969] 1 W.L.R. 286 (C.A.).

Bank Ltd. v. *Boland.*[26] It is a question of fact in each case what a reasonable purchaser would infer from his inspection of the land and the facts known to him; but it is perhaps now likely, in general, that knowledge of the fact of marriage and the spouse's occupation will be held to be constructive notice of any interest of the spouse.

Imputed notice. Imputed notice is the actual or constructive notice of the purchaser's solicitor or agent acquired whilst acting in that particular transaction.[27]

Subsequent transferees. Once an equitable interest has become unenforceable under the doctrine of notice, it cannot in general be revived even against a subsequent transferee who does have notice. However, a person subject to an interest who parts with and subsequently re-acquires the land will be bound, even if there is an intervening bona fide purchaser.

Interests to which the doctrine of notice applies. The doctrine does not apply to those interests which are registrable under the Land Charges Act 1972. These are dealt with in the next Principle.

It may apply to interests under a trust for sale in so far as they are not overreached. If such an interest is overreached it does not concern a purchaser whether or not he knows about it, but if for any reason the overreaching machinery fails to operate, he may still be able to claim protection as a bona fide purchaser. This may happen, for example, where, on the face of the title deeds, the vendor is the sole beneficial owner when in fact he is a trustee for sale.

There are not many third party rights still subject to this old doctrine of notice. An example commonly given is the restrictive covenant created before 1926 and the restrictive covenant contained in a lease. Others are proprietary estoppel[28] and an equitable right of entry.[29]

Any new interest in land which the courts may recognise from time to time must be subject to this doctrine since they must be equitable[30] and they cannot be made registrable without Parlia-

---

[26] [1981] 1 All E.R. 153 (H.L.). For a suggestion that the mortgages in both this case and *Caunce* v. *Caunce* were void, see S.M. Clayton, [1981] Conv. 19.
[27] See L.P.A. 1925, s.199(1) (ii) (*b*).
[28] See above, Chap. 18. What interests are registrable depends partly on the interpretation given to the term "equitable easement": s.2(5) (Class D (iii)) of the Land Charges Act 1972.
[29] See *Shiloh Spinners Ltd.* v. *Harding* [1973] A.C. 691 (H.L.). But it is a little difficult to see why the right was not considered legal.
[30] L.P.A. 1925, s.1.

ment. This is illustrated by the case of the deserted wife's right of occupation—the case of the interest that never was! Until it was rejected altogether as an interest in land by the House of Lords it was regarded as an equitable interest subject to notice. Now of course an equivalent registrable interest has been created by statute.[31]

The beneficial interests under a strict settlement will not be affected by the doctrine since a conveyance of land subject to a strict settlement either operates under the Settled Land Act 1925 or not at all.[32]

Principle 3. Interests registrable under the Land Charges Act 1972

The following third party rights are registrable under the Land Charges Act 1972 at the Land Charges Registry against the name of the estate owner of the land affected:

(i) Pending Actions.

(ii) Annuities.

(iii) Writs and Orders affecting land.

(iv) Deeds of Arrangement affecting land.

(v) Land Charges.

Further, any charge acquired by a local authority is registrable against the property, as a local land charge, in the register of local land charges kept by each authority.

If a land charge is registered it will be valid against any subsequent owner of the land.

If it is not registered it will, in general, be void against any purchaser for value of any interest in the land. In the case of any Class D land charge or an estate contract, it will only be void for non-registration against a purchaser for money or money's worth of a legal estate in the land.[33]

If a purchaser is adversely affected by a charge registered prior to a 15 year root of title he may be able to claim compensation from a public fund under the Law of Property Act 1969.

---

[31] See *National Provincial Bank Ltd.* v. *Ainsworth* [1965] A.C. 1175; and Matrimonial Homes Act 1967, as amended by Matrimonial Homes and Property Act 1981.

[32] See S.L.A. 1925, s.18(1). But a purchaser is given statutory protection very similar to that given by the doctrine of notice by s.110(1) of the S.L.A. 1925; see above, p. 282 *et seq.*

[33] L.C.A. 1972, s.4. See *Midland Bank Trust Co. Ltd.* v. *Green* [1981] 1 All E.R. 153 (H.L.).

Explanation

Register of Pending Actions. A pending action is any action proceeding in court relating to land or any interest in land. Such an action is a challenge in some way to the present owner's title and is therefore something which concerns a purchaser of the land.[34]

Register of Annuities. This includes only annuities created and registered before 1926 under earlier legislation. It cannot be added to and is of diminishing importance.

Register of Writs and Orders affecting land. This includes any writ or order made by a court to enforce a judgment against land.

The registration of a pending action or a writ or order only remains effective for five years from the date of registration, though if necessary it can be renewed.

Register of Deeds of Arrangement affecting land. A deed of arrangement is in general a document by which a debtor assigns his property for the benefit of his creditors.

Register of Land Charges. This is the most frequently used register. It consists of any charge or obligation affecting land within the following six categories.

Class A Land Charges.[35] This class includes any charge on land arising on the application of some person under an Act of Parliament to secure the payment of money. There are many statutes entitling a person to claim a charge on land, generally to recover money which he has spent. For example, under section 49 of the Agricultural Holdings Act 1948, a tenant of an agricultural holding may be entitled to compensation from his landlord in respect of long term improvements which he has made. Under section 72 of the same Act, where the landlord fails to discharge his liability to pay within one month, the tenant is entitled to obtain from the Minister an order charging the holding with payment of the amount due.

Class B Land Charges. This includes any charge on the land arising under a statute to secure the payment of money, as in Class

---

[34] See *Calgary and Edmonton Land Co. Ltd.* v. *Dobinson* [1974] 1 All E.R. 484, Megarry J. Compare *Whittingham* v. *Whittingham* [1978] 3 All E.R. 805 (Balcombe J.); *Allen* v. *Greenhi Builders Ltd.* [1978] 3 All E.R. 1163 (Browne-Wilkinson J.); and *Selim Ltd.* v. *Bickenhall Engineering Ltd.* [1981] 3 All E.R. 210 (Megarry V.—C).

[35] The lettering used is that used by the L.C.A. 1972 and in practice to refer to the various land charges.

A, but where the charge arises automatically without any application having to be made. Since local land charges are excluded, being registrable in the local land charges registries, there are few charges in this class. The only common one is the charge arising in favour of the Law Society on land which has been recovered in an action supported by legal aid. Here the Law Society has a charge to recover its contribution.[36]

Class C Land Charges. This class includes the following charges created or transferred since 1925:

C (i) Puisne Mortgages.
C (ii) Limited Owners' Charges.
C (iii) General Equitable Charges.
C (iv) Estate Contracts.

C (i) *Puisne mortgages.* A puisne mortgage is any legal mortgage not protected by the deposit of title deeds with the mortgagee.[37]

C (ii) *Limited Owners' Charges.* A limited owner's charge is an equitable charge arising under statute in favour of a tenant for life or statutory owner to secure the repayment to him of money which he has paid out of his own pocket and is entitled to recover. The commonest example arises under section 28(4) of the Finance Act 1975 where the tenant for life pays capital transfer tax on the settled land out of his own pocket.

C (iii) *General Equitable Charges.* A general equitable charge is any equitable charge which is not protected by deposit of title deeds with the chargee, which does not arise under a trust for sale or a settlement and which is not registrable in any other class of land charge. This is a residual class for equitable charges not registrable elsewhere. It includes annuities created after 1925 and equitable mortgages not protected by deposit of title deeds with the mortgagee. It also includes vendors' and purchasers' liens.

On the conveyance of land subject to a strict settlement both limited owners' charges and general equitable charges will be overreached even though registered.[38]

C (iv) *Estate Contracts.* An estate contract is any contract by an estate owner[39] (or any person entitled to have a legal estate conveyed to him) to convey or create a legal estate in the land. It

---

[36] See Legal Aid Act 1974, s.9(6).
[37] See above, p. 468.
[38] See above, p. 236.
[39] *i.e.* the owner of a legal estate.

includes not only the ordinary contract to purchase but also, for example, an option or right of pre-emption in respect of the legal estate, a contract to create a legal mortgage and possibly a contract to create a legal easement.

In *Re Rayleigh Weir Stadium*.[40] M owned the fee simple of a greyhound racing stadium and entered into a partnership with R. Subsequently M and R were adjudicated bankrupt and the trustee in brankruptcy (the applicant in the proceedings) wished to sell the premises. He was not able to do so because the respondent had registered an estate contract and a general equitable charge against the premises both relating to an alleged contract by which the respondent claimed that he had paid £10,000 to M and R in return for a one-eighth share in the premises. It was held that the creation of the partnership made M a trustee for sale of the premises for himself and R,[41] that the alleged contract therefore related to the proceeds of sale and not the legal estate in the land.[42] It was therefore not an estate contract. Further, it was held that the contract could not have created a general equitable charge since the definition of these under the Land Charges Act excluded interests arising under a trust for sale.

A right of pre-emption is only exercisable if the landowner *chooses* to sell in which event the holder of the right must be given first refusal on the agreed terms. In *Pritchard* v. *Briggs*[43] it was held, somewhat remarkably, that a right of pre-emption only becomes an interest in land when it becomes exercisable on the landowner deciding to sell; so that, until then, registration cannot be effective.[44]

Class D Land Charges. This class is also sub-divided.

D (i) *Inland Revenue Charges.* This includes any charge in favour of the Inland Revenue to secure the payment of death duties.

D (ii) *Restrictive Covenants.* This includes only restrictive

---

[40] [1954] 1 W.L.R. 786 (Harman J.).
[41] As a result of L.P.A. 1925, ss.1(6), 34(1). See above, p. 319, n. 23.
[42] L.P.A. 1925, s.42(6).
[43] [1980] Ch. 338 (C.A.). Compare *Greene* v. *Church Commissioners* [1974] 3 All E.R. 609 (C.A.); and *First National Securities Ltd.* v. *Chiltern D.C.* [1975] 2 All E.R. 766. For support for the view taken by the C.A. in *Pritchard* v. *Briggs*, see D.G. Barnsley, Land Options (1975), p. 157. On the distinction between options and rights of pre-emption, see D.G. Barnsley, *Land Options*, pp. 1–7; and see, Jill Martin, The Right of Pre-emption: A Potential Proprietary Interest, [1980] Conv. 433. See also C. Harpur (1980) 39 C.L.J. 35.
[44] Goff L.J. considered that it was never an interest in land.

covenants created since 1925 and not made between lessor and lessee. These have been fully dealt with, above in Chapter 20.[45]

D (iii) *Equitable easements.* This includes "any easement right or privilege over or affecting land" created after 1925 "and being merely an equitable interest."[46]

There is uncertainty as to the scope of this definition.[47] It certainly includes those rights which are easements in the sense defined in the chapter on easements and which could be legal if created by deed for an interest equivalent to a fee simple absolute in possession or a term of years absolute. But it is arguable that it includes a wider range of interests which, however created, could not be legal. In *Ives (E.R.) Investments* v. *High*[48] Lord Denning M.R. applied the narrower view deciding that the right in question was "not such as could ever have been created . . . at law" and could therefore not be an equitable easement. Danckwerts and Winn L.JJ. did not accept the narrower view. Acceptance of the narrower view increases the number of equitable interests subject to the doctrine of notice.

Class E Land Charges. This includes annuities created before 1926 and registered subsequently.

Class F Land Charges. This includes the spouse's right of occupation of the matrimonial home owned by the other spouse. It is a new class created by the Matrimonial Homes Act 1967.[49]

Local Land Charges.[50] Whilst there is a single national register of land charges kept at Plymouth, Devon each local authority has its own register of local land charges affecting land within its area.

Local land charges include[51] not only charges to secure the payment of money due to the local authority, but also a whole host of conditions and restrictions relating to land which can be imposed by local authorities and are registrable as local land

---

[45] The Law Commission (Law Com.(W.P.), No. 18), rejected the suggestion that restrictive covenants should revert to the old doctrine of notice.

[46] L.C.A. 1972, s.2(5).

[47] The same question may arise in the case of registered land; see L.R.A. 1925, s.70(1) (a): and (1969) 33 Conv.(N.S.) 135 (Paul Jackson).

[48] [1967] 2 Q.B. 379 (C.A.); see above, p. 317. See also *Shiloh Spinners Ltd.* v. *Harding* [1973] A.C. 691; also *Lewisham B.C.* v. *Maloney* [1948] 1 K.B. 50.

[49] As amended by the Matrimonial Proceedings and Property Act 1970, s.38, and Domestic Violence and Matrimonial Proceedings Act 1976; and Matrimonial Homes and Property Act 1981.

[50] See generally, J.F. Garner, *Local Land Charges* (8th ed., 1977); and Local Land Charges Act 1975.

[51] See Local Land Charges Act 1975, ss.1, 2.

charges. Examples of financial charges include charges to recover money spent for various purposes under the Public Health Act 1936—for example, half the total expense incurred by the authority in replacing earth closets by water closets under section 47; the cost of removing or pulling down work erected in contravention of the building regulations, on default by the owner in complying with a notice to do the work himself.[52]

The commonest type of charge restricting or prohibiting use is the planning charge. These planning charges include any restrictions or prohibitions arising under the Town and Country Planning Acts. For example, an enforcement notice served under section 87 of the Town and Country Planning Act 1971[52a] in respect of a contravention of planning control, tree preservation orders, building preservation notices, etc.[53]

Effect of failure to register land charges and local land charges.[54] Section 198(1) of the Law of Property Act 1925 provides that registration under the Land Charges Act "shall be deemed to constitute actual notice" to all persons and for all purposes. The effect of this is that if a registrable interest is registered it will bind any subsequent owner of the land (unless it is overreached). The old doctrine of notice becomes irrelevant. This means, in principle at least, that the owner of the interest has a simple method of protecting it; whilst the purchaser of land has an equally simple method of checking for adverse interests before completing and handing over his money.

If a registrable interest is not registered it will generally be void against a purchaser of any interest in the land for value (which includes marriage). In a number of cases however it will only be void against a purchaser for money or money's worth of a legal estate.[55]

This means that an unregistered interest is not void against every subsequent owner. If Blackacre is left to me as a gift by will, or given to me *inter vivos*, I will take it subject to equitable interests whether or not they are registered. Also, of course, a donee will have no claim against the donor if there are adverse interests.

A local land charge is binding whether or not registered and whether or not revealed on a search; but if not registered or not

[52] See *Garner* (n. 50, above), pp. 27, 28.
[52a] As amended by Local Government and Planning (Amendment) Act 1981.
[53] Garner (n. 50 above), p. 42.
[54] Note *Wroth* v. *Tyler* [1973] 2 W.L.R. 405 (Megarry J.).
[55] See above, p. 518; L.C.A. 1972, s.4.

shown on an official search, a purchaser may have a right of compensation.[56]

The search procedure. Local land charges are registered against the property. The purchaser will simply search against the property in the registers kept by the local authorties for the areas where the land is situate. The registers are public.

In the case of the central Land Charges Register, the system is more complicated and less satisfactory because interests are registrable against the estate owner whose interest is intended to be affected.[57] The only way of discovering all registered interests which might affect the land is therefore to search against the name of every estate owner of the land since 1925. However, in practice this is neither possible nor necessary for the following reasons:

(a) In practice searches will have been made on previous purchases and there will in general be with the title deeds an official certificate of search against each previous owner, showing any entries against his name at the time he parted with the land. This will leave a search against the present vendor only to be made. If, for any reason, an official certificate is not available against any previous owner a search will have to be made against him too.

(b) Assuming that section 198 of the Law of Property Act 1925 prevails over section 44(8) of the same Act, a purchaser is bound by any adverse interests even though registered before the root of title against estate owners whose names he will not be entitled to ask for when investigating title before completion. However, under section 25 of the Law of Property Act 1969, he may be able to claim compensation from a public fund in respect of any such "old" land charge which is subsequently discovered to affect his land. To claim compensation he must prove that at the time of completion he did not in fact know about the charge, and that it was registered against an estate owner not revealed by the 15–year title to the property.

There is a further problem arising from registration against names and not against the land itself. A person can change his name or may be known by different names at the same time. A registration may be made against one name and a subsequent search against a different name. In *Oak Co-operative Building Society* v. *Blackburn*,[58] an estate agent, whose full and correct name was apparently Francis David Blackburn, agreed to sell a

[56] Local Land Charges Act 1975, s.10.
[57] See *Barrett* v. *Hilton Developments Ltd.* [1974] 3 All E.R. 944 (C.A.).
[58] [1968] Ch. 730 (C.A.).

house to a purchaser. The agreement was somewhat informal, there being nothing in writing and no conveyance, and the price was to be paid by instalments over 15 years. The purchaser did eventually register an estate contract but against the name of *Frank* David Blackburn by which name the estate agent was commonly known in business. Subsequently, the respondent building society agreed to grant Blackburn a mortgage loan on the property and they made an official search—but against the name of Francis *Davis* Blackburn[59] and received an official certificate of search which did not reveal the estate contract.

If a purchaser makes an official search and obtains an official certificate of search, that certificate is conclusive. If due to a mistake on the part of the registry in searching (or due to the interest having been registered against the wrong name) a registered interest is not shown the purchaser will take free of it under section 10(4) of the Land Charges Act 1972. But as the *Oak Co-operative Building Society* case shows, to obtain the protection of an official certificate of search, the purchaser must search against the correct name. Since the Building Society searched against the wrong name, they were not protected and took subject to the estate contract.

If a registrar negligently fails to show an adverse interest on an official certificate an incumbrancer who suffers loss (by having his interest barred under section 10(4) may have a claim in negligence against the registrar.

An official search is the method invariably used today by purchasers. A personal search by attendance at the registry can be made but this does not have the benefit of section 10(4). There is a further advantage in making an official search. If a purchaser completes his purchase within 15 days of the date of the official search, he will not be affected by any entry put on the register during the intervening period unless put there in pursuance of a registered priority notice (which his search will have revealed to warn him of the impending registration). The official search machinery therefore protects the purchaser during the interval which is bound to elapse between the search being made and completion of the transaction.[60]

---

[59] Apparently a slip on the part of the building society's solicitor.
[60] Land Charges Act 1972, s.11.

Principle 4. Overreaching

A purchaser will take free of any interest which is overreached.
    The following are overreaching conveyances[61]:
    (1) Conveyance of settled land by a tenant for life or statutory owner.[62]
    (2) Conveyance by trustees for sale.[63]
    (3) Conveyance by a mortgagee exercising his power of sale.[64]
    (4) Conveyance by personal representatives.[65]
    (5) Conveyance under an order of the court.[66]
    If, on a transfer of land, an interest is capable of being, but is not, overreached, its enforceability against the transferee will depend in general on whether it is legal, equitable or registrable according to the rules covered in the last three Principles.

Explanation

Whether an interest is overreached depends on
    (a) whether the interest in question is capable of being overreached by that particular conveyance; and
    (b) whether the required formalities have been complied with.
    The various overreaching conveyances and the interests which they can overreach have been dealt with elsewhere. However, one or two general points may conveniently be mentioned here.
    First, some interests may, in certain cases, be overreached even though they are registered. For example, on the sale of settled land by a tenant for life or statutory owner. Part II annuities, limited owners' charges and general equitable charges affecting the land will be overreached.[67] Again, on the sale by a mortgagee, subsequent puisne mortgages and equitable mortgages will be overreached even though registered.
    Secondly, the purchaser must in general comply with the appropriate statutory requirements in order to obtain the benefit of the overreaching machinery. But even if there has been some irregularity, there may be some statutory protection available to

---

[61] L.P.A. 1925, s.2(1).
[62] See above, p. 234 *et seq.*
[63] See above, p. 280 *et seq.*
[64] Above, p. 458.
[65] See Emmett, *Title* (17th ed.), pp. 207–209.
[66] *Ibid.* p. 211.
[67] Above, p. 236.

him. Indeed in most cases, the overreaching machinery protects the purchaser so long as he is acting in good faith.[68]

Thirdly, if a conveyance fails to overreach an interest the enforceability of the interest will generally[69] depend on the rules set out in the last three Principles. The example of a conveyance by a single trustee for sale has already been given.[70]

Fourthly, the failure which prevents overreaching from operating may vitiate the whole sale. Here the purchaser will get nothing. For example, if a first mortgagee exercises his statutory power of sale, the normal result will be to overreach the interests of any subsequent mortgagee. If, however, he sells when the power of sale has not arisen—if for example the money was not due, or the mortgage was not by deed—the conveyance will not be valid and the purchaser will get nothing at all. Similarly, under the Settled Land Act 1925, s.18(1), any disposition which is not authorised by the Act will be "void"; and again the purchaser will get nothing.[71]

---

[68] See, *e.g.* S.L.A. 1925, s.110(1) as to settled land. As to sale by mortgagee, see L.P.A. 1925, ss. 104(2), 205(1) (xxi), the latter section defining purchaser as a "purchaser in good faith . . . ." As to a purchaser from trustees for sale, see p. 281.

[69] Unless the irregularity vitiates the whole transaction; see next paragraph.

[70] Above, p. 517.

[71] Unless protected, *e.g.* by s.110(1).

CHAPTER 25

ENFORCEABILITY OF INTERESTS: ON THE TRANSFER OF REGISTERED LAND

Introduction

The modern system of registration of land (more correctly registration of title) was introduced in this country over a century ago in 1862.[1] Between 1898 and 1902 it was made compulsory throughout the old London County Council area. In December 1970 the areas of compulsory registration comprised 22,700,000 people.

Today, registration is mainly governed by the Land Registration Act 1925[2] and the rules made thereunder.

The following are the general principles which govern registered land:

(a) It is the title (*e.g.* the ownership or interest) to a piece of land which is registered, not the land itself. Each registered title is given an individual title number by which it can be identified. Since there can be more than one legal owner of a piece of land, it follows that there can be more than one registered title. For example, if X is registered as the legal freehold owner (proprietor) of Blackacre and then grants a 99-year lease to Y, then Y's title will be registered on a separate register[3] with its own title number—although it will also be noted on the register of X's title.

(b) It is intended that ultimately all areas will be subject to compulsory registration. This means that on the first occasion on which freehold or leasehold land is sold after the introduction of compulsory registration to the area, the purchaser must apply to have his title registered.

At the moment certain areas are compulsory. New areas can be made compulsory by Order in Council.

(c) Ownership of registered land depends on the register. This means that in general it is not the validity of the transfer which confers ownership on the transferee of registered land, but the fact

---

[1] "An Act to facilitate the Proof of Title and the Conveyance of Real Estate."

[2] See also Land Registration Act 1966. And see A. Offer. The Origins of the Law of Property Acts 1910–1925, (1977) 40 M.L.R. 505. And see D. Hayton, "Registered Land" (3rd ed. 1981).

[3] The term "register" is used in a number of different senses in the context of registered land. Here, it means "the official typewritten record of one estate owner's title to a particular property described by reference to an official plan kept at the Land Registry, each separate register bearing its individual title number." See Ruoff and Roper, *Registered Conveyancing* (4th ed.), at p. 13 for this and the other possible meanings.

that he has been registered as proprietor at the Land Registry.[4] It follows from this that:

(i) A transferee must take the necessary steps to get his transfer registered.

(ii) Once a person has been registered as proprietor, his ownership cannot, in general, be challenged. In the few cases where the register can be rectified, the proprietor may have a claim to compensation out of a public fund.[5]

(iii) Where a registered proprietor is selling, all he has to do to prove his title to the purchaser is to show that he is registered as proprietor of the interest which he is selling.

(d) In general, the rules governing the existence and creation of interests in registered land are the same as those governing unregistered land. However, the rules which govern enforceability are quite distinct and the classification set out in the last chapter has in general no relevance to registered land.[6] The enforceability of interests in registered land is dealt with in the present chapter.

(e) The register of each title has an identifying number and consists of three parts (each part also being called a register)[7]:

(i) The property register: This contains a description of the land in the title with a reference to the plan filed wih the register. It will also contain a note of easements, covenants and other rights enjoyed with the land.

(ii) The proprietorship register: This states the nature of the title (whether absolute, etc.), and contains the name, address and description of the proprietor. It also contains any cautions, inhibitions or restrictions affecting his right to deal with the land in one way or another.[8]

(iii) The charges register: This contains details of adverse interests affecting the land and in particular charges and notices of adverse interests other than charges.

(f) The general principle behind land registration is to simplify conveyancing by requiring not only the registration of third party rights (as under the Land Charges Act 1972) but also of the ownership of the land itself. Conveyancing is simplified because,

---

[4] Nevertheless, if the transfer is not in order, the registrar will not register the purchaser as proprietor.

[5] See generally as to rectification and indemnity, Ruoff and Roper (n. 3, above), Chap. 40. See also *Epps* v. *Esso Petroleum Co. Ltd.* [1973] 2 All E.R. 465 (Templeman J.); and see below, p. 547.

[6] The distinction between legal and equitable interests may on occasion still be important, see, *e.g. Barclays Bank Ltd.* v. *Taylor* [1973] 2 W.L.R. 293.

[7] See n. 3, above.

[8] See below, p. 541 *et seq.*

subject to some qualifications, all that is required is inspection of the register; it is less risky because, again subject to exceptions, a purchaser can only be affected by adverse interests which are shown in one way or another on the register; and interests in registered land are more secure because they can be protected by registration.

However, there are interests which are not registrable and yet which will still bind a purchaser—overriding interests. These present a hazard for the purchaser of registered land.

Principle 1.   Classification of interests in registered land

Any interest (ownership or third party) in registered land will fall into one of the following three categories:

(1) Registered interests.

(2) Overriding interests.

(3) Minor interests.

The enforceability of an interest against a transferee of the land depends in the first place on the category to which it belongs.[9]

The following Principles will deal with each of these categories in turn with particular reference to freehold land. Something will then be said about leasehold and mortgages.

Principle 2.   Registered interests[10]

A registered interest is an interest which has been registered substantively under the Land Registration Act 1925.

The only ownership interests which can be registered are[11]:

(a) the fee simple absolute in possession;

(b) the term of years absolute with more than 21 years to run at the time of registration.

The only third party rights which can be registered are those which under section 1(2) of the Law of Property Act 1925 can exist as legal interests.

The person who is registered as owner of a registered interest is the proprietor of that interest.[12]

In general, only the forms of legal ownership, the fee simple absolute in possession and the long term of years, and legal

---

[9] An interest may be a minor interest and an overriding interest at the same time; see below, p. 538.

[10] See L.R.A. 1925, s.3 (xxiii). It is convenient though not strictly correct to use the term to include registered charges which are also registered substantively.

[11] L.R.A. 1925, s.2.

[12] *Ibid.* s.3 (xx).

rentcharges, are registered under separate titles. The legal third party rights are normally registered on the register of the freehold or leasehold title which they affect.

Until a registrable interest has been registered it is only a minor interest.[13]

Explanation

The registrable interests. Under modern law, the legal estate is the basis of registered and unregistered conveyancing. Two of the basic principles of unregistered conveyancing are that only the legal estate owner can deal with the land; and, secondly, that legal ownership and legal third party rights are in general good against all the world. The same two principles are fundamental to registered conveyancing except that they only apply if the legal ownership and legal third party rights are properly registered.[14] Until they are registered they are only minor interests and so liable to be void against a transferee for value[15] unless protected on the register as minor interests.

In general only the two types of legal ownership[16]—the fee simple absolute in possession and the term of years absolute—are normally registered under separate titles.

A legal rentcharge is also[17] likely to be registered separately with its own register and title number and a rentcharge certificate issued to the proprietor. But most other third party rights will be registered on the register of the title which they affect. Legal easements cannot be registered apart from the dominant land.[18] Similarly, mortgages must be registered on the register of the land mortgaged.[19]

To give an example: X is the registered proprietor of the fee simple interest in Blackacre. His ownership will have a title number and a register at the land registry. He grants by deed a legal rentcharge to R, charged on Blackacre. R will have to

---

[13] *Ibid.* s.3 (xv).
[14] It is arguable that an equitable mortgage by deed can be registered substantively under the Administration of Justice Act 1977, s.26.
[15] *Ibid.* ss.3(xv), 20, 23.
[16] A transferee does not have a legal title until his interest has been registered; L.R.A. 1925, s.20(1).
[17] In addition, notice of the rentcharge will have to be entered on the register of the burdened land; Land Registration Rules 1925, r. 107 (2).
[18] Land Registration Rules 1925, r. 257. In practice they will also be noted on the register of the servient land, but this is not essential since legal easements, provided they are substantively registered when necessary, are overriding interests.
[19] L.R.A. 1925, ss.4, 8(1)(*a*), 26.

register his rentcharge and on application to the proper land registry for the district in which the land is situated, he will be registered as proprietor of this rentcharge which, like the fee simple, will have its own title number and register. A note of it will also be entered on the register of X's title so that a purchaser of the land will be able to discover its existence.[20] Suppose further that the neighbouring freehold owner of Whiteacre, W, has a legal easement over Blackacre. W will be the registered proprietor of the freehold title to Whiteacre; he will also be proprietor of the easement which will be registered on the register of W's freehold title. In practice a note of the easement will be made on the title to the servient property, that is on the register of X's title. But even if this is not done the easement will bind the purchaser as an overriding interest.[21]

Similarly, if the registered proprietor of a leasehold estate in Greenacre mortgages it, the mortgage will be registered (as a registered charge) on the register of the leasehold title.[22]

Principle 2a.   First registration of freehold land

The title to freehold land must be registered upon the first conveyance on sale made after the area becomes one of compulsory registration.

Application must be made by the transferee to the appropriate district land registry within two months after the date of the conveyance.[23]

Failure to apply for registration makes the conveyance void in respect of the legal estate.

The effect of registration depends on whether the land is registered with:

(i) absolute title; or
(ii) qualified title; or
(iii) possessory title.[24]

Explanation

Application. A purchaser of freehold land in an area of compulsory registration, must apply for registration of his title. It

---

[20] Land Registration Rules 1925, r. 107 (2).
[21] See below, at p. 538 *et seq.*
[22] L.R.A. 1925, s. 8(1) (*a*).
[23] The registrar can allow an extension.
[24] For good leasehold title, see below, p. 545.

is by this means that the freehold title to all land will eventually be registered, and unregistered conveyancing will disappear.

The application is made on the prescribed form and accompanied by the conveyance to the applicant, all the other deeds and documents relating to the title and the appropriate fee. The registrar then investigates the title in the same way as in the case of unregistered conveyancing and, if satisfied, registers the applicant as proprietor of the freehold with one of the three classes of title discussed below. A separate title with its own title number will be opened for the freehold and a land certificate prepared and sent to the proprietor.

The land certificate contains a replica of the entries on the register; but, although in some ways it is the equivalent of the title deeds of unregistered conveyancing, it must be emphasised that the proprietor's title depends on the state of the register, not the land certificate. Legal ownership of unregistered land is created or transferred by an appropriate deed of conveyance between the parties. Similarly, an appropriate deed of transfer is necessary in the case of registered conveyancing; but it is fundamental that, here, the transaction will only be effective if completed by the registration of the transferee as proprietor at the land registry. This principle is enforced in the case of first registration by the Land Registration Act 1925, s.123, which makes the conveyance void as to the legal estate if registration is not applied for within the two months from completion (plus any extension allowed by the registrar).[25]

The same principle means that registration may cure a defective title.

The effect of first registration. The general principle is that registration of a registrable interest protects the proprietor of the interest registered from any possibility of adverse claims. However, apart from the question of third party rights dealt with below, this principle is not unqualified. In particular, the effectiveness of registration as a guarantee of title depends on which of the three categories of registration it enjoys.

(a) *Absolute title.*[26] Where the owner of unregistered freehold land applies for registration, he may apply for registration with either absolute or possessory title. The registrar will grant an application to be registered with absolute title if he approves the

---

[25] See D.G. Barnsley, *Conveyancing Law and Practice*, p. 403 for the effect of this provision.

[26] L.R.A. 1925, s.5.

title.[27] This means that the applicant has proved his title to the satisfaction of the registrar as he would to a purchaser of the unregistered land. Where a proprietor is registered with absolute title it means that his interest is state guaranteed subject only to:

(i) any entries on the register[28];

(ii) overriding interests.

In other words, absolute title is an absolute guarantee of ownership subject only to those third party rights which are protected by entry on the register or as overriding interests.[29] Where the registered proprietor is a trustee owner, the title will in addition be subject to minor interests of which he has notice even though not protected on the register.

(b) *Possessory title.* A proprietor will be registered with possessory title when, on application for first registration, he cannot prove his ownership—for example, where the title deeds have been lost. Registration with possessory title has the same force as registration with absolute title except—an important exception—that the title is subject to "any estate, right or interest adverse to or in derogation of the title of the first proprietor, and subsisting or capable of arising at the time of registration of that proprietor."[30] At the time of first registration this is no guarantee of title at all. If the applicant for registration has no title, registration with possessory title will not give him one. However, it does guarantee the title against any subsequent adverse interests except those created and protected in accordance with the Land Registration Act 1925. And in due course it can be converted into absolute title.[31]

(c) *Qualified title.* This lies somewhere between the previous two in its enforceability. An applicant for first registration cannot ask for registration with qualified title; but the registrar will use it if appropriate. It is the same as absolute title—subject to entries on the register and overriding interests—but it is subject also to some particular defect which is noted on the register. For example, the registrar may not be satisfied with the title before a certain date and so the registration will be specified to be subject to any adverse interests arising before that date. As with possessory title,

---

[27] *Ibid.* s.4.

[28] L.R.A. 1925, s.5; but only in so far as those interests are subsisting and valid when entered on the register; see *Kitney* v. *M.E.P.C. Ltd.* [1978] 1 All E.R. 595.

[29] See below, at p. 537, for overriding interests. The register is also subject to the possibility of rectification.

[30] L.R.A. 1925, s.6.

[31] *Ibid.* s.77.

if no adverse interests appear, it can in due course be converted into absolute title.[32]

Principle 2b. Dealings with registered freehold

A transfer of registered land must be in a form approved by the registrar in accordance with the Land Registration Rules. The transferee must apply to the appropriate district registry for registration of his title. The application must be in the specified form, accompanied by the transfer itself and other relevant documents.

Registration of a transfer for value[33] of an absolute freehold title vests the legal title in the transferee together with appurtenant rights[34] subject only to minor interests protected on the register in so far as they are valid and subsisting,[35] and overriding interests. A transferee not for value will in addition take subject to any minor interests which bound the transferor even though not protected on the register.

Explanation

It needs to be stressed that, in general, the same rules of land law govern the existence, creation and transfer of interests in both registered and unregistered land. Thus, on the sale of freehold registered land, the transaction will in general follow the same course as on the sale of unregistered land and will be completed by delivery of a deed of transfer. This transfer, although it has to comply with the requirements of the Land Registration Rules, is very much the same as a conveyance of unregistered land. However, there are two vital differences in the case of registered land. First, the vendor will prove his title simply by showing that he is registered as proprietor. Secondly, the purchaser will not acquire the legal ownership until he has produced the transfer to the land registry and been registered as proprietor in place of the vendor.[36]

Two cases[37] are worth mentioning to illustrate dealings in

---

[32] *Ibid.* s.77.
[33] And in good faith, see *Peffer* v. *Rigg* [1978] 3 All E.R. 745.
[34] Including those which arise in favour of a purchaser under L.P.A. 1925, s.62; see above, p. 375, for s.62.
[35] See *Kitney* v. *M.E.P.C. Ltd.* [1978] 1 All E.R. 595 (C.A.).
[36] But if he went into occupation his interest would be protected as an overriding interest and any subsequent transferee, even if registered, would take subject to it.
[37] And see *Williams & Glyn's Bank Ltd.* v. *Boland* [1980] 2 All E.R. 408 (H.L.).

registered land and the differences between registered and unregistered conveyancing; and to show that registration of title does not (and in justice cannot) reduce the ownership of land altogether to the one simple proposition that what is on the register is protected, what is not on is not protected.

Peffer v. *Rigg*[38] has already been considered, and shows that a transferee will only take free of interests not protected on the register (in this case the beneficial interest under a trust) if he takes for value and in good faith.

In *Spectrum Investment Co.* v. *Holmes*[39] D was registered as proprietor of the long leasehold interest in a house. T, who held as sub-tenant of D, paid no rent for over 12 years and so acquired title to the leasehold by adverse possession. T was thereupon entitled to and did get himself registered as proprietor of the leasehold interest in place of D.[40] Subsequently, D purported to surrender the lease to the freeholder who then claimed possession against T. His claim failed. If this had been a case of unregistered land, it would have succeeded.[41] But it was registered land and only the registered proprietor (which D no longer was) can deal with the registered interest.[42] The case shows that registration can give the proprietor's interest a validity that it would not have in the case of unregistered land; and that a registered title can be upset by events (in this case adverse possession)[43] which occur off the register.

It should be emphasised that the vast majority of registered land transactions take place without legal difficulty or dispute.[44]

After registration of the disposition of the freehold, the new proprietor will be sent the land certificate made up to date by the land registry.[45]

---

[38] [1978] 3 All E.R. 745; above, p. 189. Compare *Midland Bank Trust Co. Ltd.* v. *Green* [1981] 1 All E.R. 153 (H.L.), a case of a land charge affecting unregistered land.

[39] [1981] 1 All E.R. 6 (Browne-Wilkinson J.).

[40] See L.R.A. 1925, s.75.

[41] See *Fairweather* v. *St. Marylebone Property Co. Ltd.* [1963] A.C. 510; see above, p. 507. But see criticism of this case in Megarry and Wade, *Law of Real Property*, (4th ed.), at p. 1029. And compare *Jessamine Investment Co.* v. *Schwarz* [1976] 3 All E.R. 521 (C.A.).

[42] See L.R.A. 1925, s.69(4).

[43] Being an overriding interest; L.R.A. s.70(1)(*f*).

[44] As do the vast majority of unregistered transactions.

[45] Where the land is mortgaged by the new proprietor, the land certificate will be retained in the registry and a charge certificate issued to the chargee.

Principle 3. Overriding interests

Overriding interests are those third party rights which do not require protection on the register and which are binding on any transferee whether or not he has notice of them.[46]

The overriding interests are set out in section 70(1) of the Land Registration Act 1925 and include, *inter alia,* the following[47]:

(a) Rights of common, drainage rights, customary rights (until extinguished), public rights, profits *à prendre,* rights of sheepwalk, rights of way, watercourses, rights of water, and other easements not being equitable easements required to be protected by notice on the register.

(f) Rights acquired or in the course of being acquired under the Limitation Acts.

(g) The rights of every person in actual occupation of the land or in receipt of the rents and profits thereof, save where inquiry is made of such person and the rights are not disclosed.

(h) In the case of a possessory, qualified or good leasehold title, all estates, rights, interests and powers excepted from the effect of registration.

(i) Rights under local land charges unless and until protected on the register in the prescribed manner.

(j) Leases for any term or interest not exceeding 21 years granted at a rent without taking a fine.

Explanation

It is probably true that under any system of conveyancing there will need to be some interests which are enforceable even though not protected on any register.

It has been said that "overriding interests consist of a miscellany of liabilities which are not usually, or at any rate not invariably, shown in title deeds, nor mentioned in abstracts of title, and as to which, therefore, it is impracticable to form a trustworthy record and entirely impossible to form a complete record on the register. They are an essential feature in registration of title if the reform introduced by it is to be confined to changes in the machinery of conveyancing only, leaving the substantive general law of real property untouched, and if registration of title is to be compatible with the continued existence of all those rights, privileges, conditions and charges permitted by the general law."[48]

---

[46] See L.R.A. 1925, s.3 (xvi).
[47] Using the same lettering as in the section.
[48] Ruoff and Roper, *Registered Conveyancing* (4th ed.), at p. 95.

In practice, many overriding interests will be shown on the register of the title adversely affected. For example, at the time of first registration the registrar is under an obligation to enter a note on the register of any easement or right which appears adversely to affect the land.[49] And the registrar has a wide discretion to enter a notice of any overriding interest on the register of the land affected.[50] Inspection of the land itself is likely to provide apparent evidence of most of those which are not noted on the register. Nevertheless the basic principle remains that an overriding interest will bind a transferee whether or not it is known to him; and a purchaser must do his best to discover any which affect the land.

Easements, profits, etc. It is convenient to deal here with the protection of easements affecting registered land. There are a number of statutory provisions and some of them are difficult to reconcile.

Although they are registrable interests,[51] legal easements cannot be registered under a separate title; but can only appear on the register of title of the dominant or servient property or both.

Legal easements are overriding interests. In general, this means that they will bind a purchaser of the servient property even though not shown anywhere on the register. However, an express easement created by a registered proprietor (*i.e.* subsequent to first registration) is a disposition and will not exist as a legal easement until completed by registration.[52] And until then, since it is not legal, it will not be an overriding interest.

Legal easements existing at the time of first registration of the servient land, will continue to be enforceable overriding interests, though in practice a note of them will normally be entered on the register.[53]

Equally, legal easements arising by implied grant or prescription, will be overriding even though not shown on any register; though, again, in normal practice there is likely to be mention of them on the register of either the dominant or servient land or both.

There is some argument both as to what interests the term equitable easements embraces and as to whether, in the case of registered land, they are overriding or minor interests. It seems

---

[49] L.R.A. 1925, s.70(2).
[50] *Ibid.* s.70(3).
[51] L.R.A. 1925 ss.2, 3.
[52] L.R.A. 1925, ss.18(1), 19, 20(1).
[53] See L.R.A. 1925, ss.5, 70(2), (3).

likely that they are not overriding interests and must be protected on the register.[54]

Common land. Under section 2(*b*) of the Commons Registration Act 1965 "no rights of common shall be exercisable" unless registered either under the Land Registration Act 1925 or the Commons Registration Act 1965.

Adverse possession. The rules relating to adverse possession help to illustrate the distinction between registered and unregistered land. In the case of unregistered land, 12 years' adverse possession extinguishes the title of the previous owner in law and equity.[55] In the case of registered land the same principles of adverse possession apply. But the basic rule of registered conveyancing is that it is only the removal of his name from the register which puts an end to the registered proprietor's ownership. Therefore, section 75(1) of the Land Registration Act 1925 provides that the proprietor will remain owner but will hold in trust for the person who has acquired by adverse possession. The rest of the section then goes on to provide how the registrar can register the adverse possessor as proprietor in place of the present proprietor.

But the practical effect is the same in registered and unregistered land—ownership is lost by adverse possession. It has been said that " . . . neither a conveyance nor a land certificate retains its value if the landowner is so lax or indifferent as to lose physical control of his land."[56]

Rights of person in actual occupation or in receipt of rents. The rights of any person in actual occupation or in receipt of the rents will in general be overriding interests. A somewhat similar principle applies to equitable non-registrable interests in unregistered land in that a purchaser is generally fixed with constructive notice of any such interests which inspection of the land would have revealed.[57]

In the important case of *Williams and Glyn's Bank Ltd.* v. *Boland*[58] H and W (husband and wife) were equitable tenants in common of the matrimonial home (as joint contributors to the

---

[54] See Ruoff and Roper, *Registered Conveyancing*, (4th ed.), p. 97; and (1969) 33 Conv.(N.S.) 135.

[55] Limitation Act 1980, s.17.

[56] Ruoff and Roper (n. 54, above), p. 102.

[57] See above, p. 516.

[58] [1980] 2 All E.R. 408 (H.L.); and see *Hodgson* v. *Marks* [1971] Ch. 892 (Ungoed-Thomas J.). See also *Blacklocks* v. *J.B. Developments (Godalming) Ltd.*, [1981] 3 All E.R. 392.

purchase price) and both occupied, though only H was registered as proprietor. There was no indication of W's interest on the register. Without W's knowledge, H mortgaged the property to the bank by way of legal charge. The bank made no inquiry at the time as to any possible interest of W. Subsequently, when H defaulted on the mortgage, the bank claimed possession. The House of Lords held[59] that the claim failed. It held that the words "actual occupation" had their ordinary meaning (denoting physical rather than legal occupation); that the occupation by the husband did not exclude the possibility of an independent occupation by the wife; and that consequently, the wife, being in actual occupation as a tenant in common under the trust for sale, was protected.

Local land charges.   These are registered on the appropriate register of local land charges and not usually on the register of title. They are overriding interests and their enforceability is governed by the Local Land Charges Act 1975.

Short term leases.   If a legal lease is granted for a term not exceeding 21 years at a rent, without taking a fine, it is an overriding interest.[60]

Principle 4.   Minor interests

All interests in land which are not registered interests and not overriding interests will be minor interests.[61]

Minor interests may for convenience be classified as follows:

(1) Those interests which should have but have not been registered substantively.

(2) The beneficial interests under a strict settlement or a trust for sale.

(3) All other minor interests.

The general rule is that a transferee of registered land for valuable consideration in good faith[62] will take it free of any minor interests which have not been protected by an appropriate entry on the register whether or not he knows of the interest.[63]

---

[59] Disapproving *Cedar Holdings Ltd.* v. *Green* [1979] 3 All E.R. 117 (C.A.); *Bird* v. *Syme Thomson* [1978] 3 All E.R. 1027 (Templeman J.); and also *Caunce* v. *Caunce* [1969] 1 W.L.R. 286 (C.A.).
[60] See further below, p. 544.
[61] L.R.A. 1925, ss.2(1), 3 (xv).
[62] *Peffer* v. *Rigg* [1978] 3 All E.R. 745 (Graham J.).
[63] L.R.A. 1925, ss.20(1), 23(1). Valuable consideration includes marriage but not a nominal consideration in money; *ibid.* s.3 (xxxi).

When a registrable interest is registered it will cease to be a minor interest. The other two categories of minor interests can be protected by one of the following types of entry on the register:

(a) Notice.

(b) Caution.

(c) Inhibition.

(d) Restriction.

The degree of protection given to a minor interest depends on which of these is used.

Explanation

There are two methods by which interests in registered land can be put on the register:

(i) Substantive registration. This has already been dealt with and is only possible in the case of legal ownership and legal third party rights. Substantive registration carries a guarantee of title as explained earlier.[64]

(ii) Protection by one of the four types of entry listed above. Here in contrast to substantive registration entry does not guarantee the validity of the interest. But if it is valid, the entry protects it to the extent shown below, depending on the type of entry.[65]

Notices. Section 52 of the Land Registration Act 1925 provides that:

> "(i) A disposition by the proprietor shall take effect subject to all estates, rights, and claims which are protected by way of notice on the register at the date of the registration or entry of notice of the disposition, but only if and so far as such estates, rights and claims may be valid and are not (independently of this Act) overriden by the disposition."

Assuming that the interest protected by the notice is valid it will be effective against any transferee of the land.

If an interest is not enforceable against a purchaser for any reason, registration of a notice will not help it. If, for example, a mortgagor grants a lease without the authority of the mortgagee, this will not bind the mortgagee and if the mortgagee exercises his power of sale the purchaser will take free of the lease even though notice of it is entered on the register of the mortgagor's title.

---

[64] p. 533.

[65] See *Kitney* v. *M.F.P.C. Ltd.* [1978] 1 All E.R. 595 (C.A.).

Only certain interests can be protected by notice.[66] Examples include the right of a spouse to occupy the matrimonial home; restrictive covenants[67]; annuities and rentcharges,[68] the severance of mines and minerals from the surface of the land.[69]

A notice can be entered only if the land certificate is produced. If the proprietor is not co-operative a caution or some other form of protection will have to be resorted to.

Cautions. The registration of a caution against the title entitles the cautioner to be warned and to object before any subsequent dealing by the proprietor is registered.[70] The caution, unlike the notice, does not itself protect the interest or make it binding on a purchaser. It merely gives the cautioner warning and the chance to protect his interest, for example, by getting it entered on the register as a notice.

If the cautioner fails to protect his interest when warned of an application to register a subsequent dealing, he loses all the protection to which he might have been entitled against that dealing. If he does object, the registrar (or court, if necessary) can decide the respective rights and priorities of the parties. The caution will thus have preserved any priority to which the cautioner's interest was originally entitled when created.

The case of *Re White Rose Cottage*[71] shows the rules working. V was the registered freehold proprietor. He created an equitable mortgage in favour of B who entered a caution. Next J, a creditor, obtained a charging order on the property to enforce his judgment debt and this too was protected by a caution. The position at this stage was therefore that there were two cautions entered in the order B, J.[72] What happened then was that B applied to enter a *notice* of his mortgage J, as cautioner, was warned of the application and objected. It was therefore for the court to decide their respective rights. B had priority—preserved by his caution—and was therefore entitled to enter notice of his mortgage with priority over J's charging order.

---

[66] See Ruoff and Roper (n. 54, above), at p. 704.

[67] L.R.A. 1925, s.50.

[68] *Ibid.* s.49. If a rentcharge is capable of being overriden under a strict settlement or a trust for sale (*e.g.* a voluntary rentcharge for life), it must be protected by restriction and not notice; *ibid.* s.49(2).

[69] *Ibid.* s.49(1)(*b*).

[70] *Ibid.* s.55.

[71] [1965] Ch. 940 (C.A.). See also *Barclays Bank Ltd.* v. *Taylor* [1973] 2 W.L.R. 293 (C.A.); *Smith* v. *Morrison* [1974] 1 All E.R. 957 (Plowman J.).

[72] Lord Denning M.R. said that prima facie the order of priority was the order in which cautions were registered.

J was also warned as cautioner that V had sold the property and that the purchaser had applied for registration. This sale was subsequent to his charging order and so—as he objected when warned of it—his caution protected him against the sale which could only take place subject to the charging order.[73]

It will be seen from the above that the disadvantage of the caution (compared to the notice) is that its effectiveness depends on the cautioner making the necessary objection when warned. On the other hand, the caution—unlike the notice—can be entered without producing the land certificate and might therefore be the only possibility in some cases.

Inhibitions.[74] The inhibition is an entry which the court or the registrar can order to be made, on the application of any interested person, preventing any further dealing with the land either for a time, or until a specified event, or generally until further order.

The only inhibition commonly found is the bankruptcy inhibition entered after the making of a receiving order, in the following terms: "Bankruptcy inhibition: No disposition or transmission is to be registered until a trustee in bankruptcy is registered."[75]

Restrictions.[76] The purpose of a restriction is to limit the powers of the registered proprietor to deal with the land. Unlike cautions and inhibitions which are hostile, a restriction is said to be friendly in that it is generally made by the registered proprietor himself. It is the device used to ensure observance of any limit on the proprietor's absolute right to deal with the land for his own benefit.

For example, it is the method used to protect the interests of beneficiaries under a strict settlement or a trust for sale and to ensure that the statutory requirements as to number of trustees, necessary consents, etc. are observed. Thus, in the case of a strict settlement, the following sort of entry on the register might be found: "No disposition by the proprietor of the land under which capital money arises is to be registered unless the money is paid to A.B. of, etc., and C.D. of, etc. Except under an order of the

---

[73] On the facts it was not clear whether there was a sale by V with B joining in to release his mortgage (the view taken by the court), or a sale by B in exercise of his statutory power of sale. If the latter had been the case, J's interest would have been overreached.
[74] See L.R.A. 1925, s.57.
[75] See Ruoff and Roper (above, n. 54), at p. 621.
[76] See L.R.A. 1925, s.58.

registrar no disposition is to be registered unless authorised by the Settled Land Act 1925."[77]

Other cases where a restriction would be appropriate include: to protect the beneficiary under a bare trust; to prevent an unauthorised lease by a mortgagor; and to prevent any disposition by a joint proprietor who will not have power to give a valid receipt for capital money arising on a disposition of the land.

It will be appreciated that in accordance with the modern principles of trust ownership of land, the purchaser is not concerned with the beneficial interests in the registered land. These will not be set out on the register at all. The purchaser will merely be concerned to see that he observes the restrictions entered on the register.

Principle 5.   Leases of registered land

(a) **First registration.**   Substantive registration of a legal lease is necessary in the following cases:

(i) Where the reversionary title is registered, the grant of a lease for a term exceeding 21 years is a disposition and must be completed by substantive registration of the lease.[78]

(ii) Where the reversionary title is not registered, the grant of any lease for a term of not less than 40 years or the assignment on sale of a lease with at least 40 years to run, must (in an area of compulsory registration) be substantively registered.[79]

A lease granted for 21 years or less is not capable of substantive registration with a separate title.

(b) **Dealings.**   A transfer of a registered leasehold interest must be completed by registration of the transferee as proprietor as in the case of freehold land.[80]

(c) **Overriding interests.**   The following leases will be protected as overriding interests:

(i) A lease not exceeding 21 years granted at a rent without a fine.

(ii) Any lease where the lessee is in actual occupation.

Any lease not substantively registered and not an overriding

---

[77] See Ruoff and Roper (n. 54, above), at p. 778 *et seq.*
[78] L.R.A. 1925, ss.18(1), 19(2), 21(1), 22(2). And notice must be entered on the register of the reversionary title.
[79] L.R.A. 1925, s.123.
[80] L.R.A. s.22(1).

interest, must be protected as a minor interest by appropriate entry on the register.

Explanation

As with freehold interests, the basic rules of land law in general govern the creation, transfer and determination of leasehold interests in registered land.

Again, in general, the same principles which govern registration of freehold interests, also govern leasehold interests.

The following points should, however, be noted:

1. Not all leasehold estates are subject to the system of compulsory registration. The Principle above sets out those which are.

2. As in the case of freehold, the effect of registration depends on the class of title registered. However, in addition to overriding and minor interests protected on the register, the registered title is subject to the covenants and obligations incident to the lease. This means, in particular, the express and implied terms of the lease.

More important, there is a fourth class of possible title in the case of leasehold, that is good leasehold.[81] A good leasehold title is the same as absolute title except that the title of the lessor to grant the lease is not guaranteed.[82] In the course of time, by virtue of the Limitation Act 1980, any claim to the freehold adverse to the lessee, will be barred and there are provisions for converting good into absolute leasehold title.[83]

3. Finally, it should perhaps be emphasised, that there may be a registered freehold and a separate registered leasehold (and further sub-leasehold) title in respect of the same piece of land. In addition to having its own register, the leasehold will be noted on the freehold title.[84] Thus, any person dealing with the freehold proprietor will have notice of and take subject to the lease. Any person dealing with the leasehold proprietor will in general only be concerned with (and only entitled to inspect) the leasehold title register.[85] Any burden, such as restrictive covenants (other than

---

[81] L.R.A. 1925, ss.10, 23(2).

[82] Compare in unregistered conveyancing, L.P.A. 1925, s.44, under which on a contract to grant or assign a lease the lessee cannot (in the absence of provision to the contrary in the contract) call for the title to the freehold.

[83] L.R.A. 1925, s.77, under which qualified and possessory titles can also be upgraded.

[84] L.R.A. 1925, s.19(2).

[85] But note that on the grant of a lease by a registered proprietor (in the absence of provision to the contrary in the contract), the lessee has no right to inspect the register; L.R.A. 1925, s.110.

overriding interests), will only bind the leasehold if shown on the leasehold title register.[86]

Principle 6.   Mortgages of registered land

In general, a mortgage of registered land can be created in the same ways as a mortgage of unregistered land.

It may be protected either

(a) as a registered charge; or

(b) by entry of a notice or caution against the title of the land charged; or

(c) by notice of deposit of the land certificate.

Explanation

Registered charge.[87]   This is the usual method of mortgaging registered land. The mortgage must be by deed and identify the property by reference to the register; otherwise, no particular form is necessary. In practice, building societies use the same form for registered and unregistered land.

The essential difference (as in the case of other dispositions of registered land) is that the mortgage must be completed by registration. This is done by entering it on the charges register of the property mortgaged naming the mortgagee as proprietor of the charge. A charge certificate is issued to the mortgagee and the land certificate is retained in the land registry until redemption.

Any number of registered charges can be created in this way.

The proprietor of a registered charge has all the powers of a legal mortgagee.[88]

Priority of registered charges is governed (subject to any entry on the register to the contrary) by the order in which they are entered on the register.[89]

Entry of notice or caution.[90]   Any mortgage of registered land which is not registered substantively as a registered charge, will only take effect in equity as a minor interest and must be protected by a notice under the Land Registration Act 1925, section 49, or a caution under section 54, against the title of the mortgaged land.

---

[86] But in the case of good leasehold title, the grantee may be affected by covenants, etc., only shown on the freehold title which he has no right to see; see *White* v. *Bijou Mansions Ltd.* [1938] 1 All E.R. 546 (C.A.).

[87] L.R.A. 1925, ss.25–27.

[88] L.R.A. 1925, s.34.

[89] L.R.A. 1925, s.29. As to tacking, see L.R.A. 1925, s.30.

[90] See Administration of Justice Act 1977, s.26, amending L.R.A. 1925, s.106.

Deposit of the land certificate. A registered proprietor of land can create a lien by deposit of the land certificate with the lender similar to the way in which the owner of unregistered land can create a mortgage by deposit of title deeds. Such a deposit will not itself protect the priority of the lender[91] and will need to be protected by obtaining entry of a notice on the mortgagor's title under Land Registration Rule 239, such a notice operating as a caution under section 54 of the Land Registration Act 1925.[92]

Principle 7. Rectification and indemnity

Under the Land Registration Act 1925, section 82(1), the registrar has a wide power to rectify the register.

Under the Land Registration Act 1925, section 82(3),[93] this will not be done so as to affect the title of a registered proprietor in possession unless (1) it is to give effect to an overriding interest; or (2) the proprietor has caused or substantially contributed to the error or omission by fraud or lack of proper care; or (3) the disposition to him (or an earlier disposition without a subsequent transfer for value) was void.

Under section 83, a person suffering loss as a result of any rectification of the register, or as a result of an error or omission not being rectified, is entitled (subject to exceptions) to compensation from a public fund. A person will not be entitled to compensation where he has caused or substantially contributed to the loss by fraud or lack of proper care.

Explanation

The liability to rectification is a limit on the absolute guarantee given by registration of title; but, in general, there will be compensation for any resulting loss.

An example will illustrate how the provisions may operate.

O is the unregistered, beneficial freehold owner of Blackacre. He sells and conveys part of it to P who intends to build a house for his retirement; but for the time being does nothing to fence off or occupy the land and no memorandum of the conveyance is endorsed on O's title deeds. O, then, in error, sells and conveys the whole of Blackacre (including P's portion) to R who (the area

---

[91] Though in practice, it will be difficult for the mortgagor to deal with the land without the land certificate.

[92] See *Re White Rose Cottage* [1965] Ch. 940.

[93] As amended by Administration of Justice Act 1977, s.24, reversing the effect of the decision in *Re 139 High St. Deptford* [1951] Ch. 884.

having become one of compulsory registration) is registered as proprietor. R takes possession. P may claim rectification[94]; but he is unlikely to be granted it because R is in possession and has not (on the facts given) contributed to the error by his fraud or lack of proper care. Failing rectification, P could claim indemnity; but again his claim is likely to be defeated since, by his failure to fence, etc., he may be said to have shown lack of proper care.

If P had gone into occupation, he would have had an overriding interest. Rectification would have been granted to give effect to it and, since R's title is only guaranteed subject to overriding interests, R would not have suffered loss for which compensation could be claimed.[95]

---

[94] *e.g.* under L.R.A. 1925, s.82(1)(*g*): "Where a legal estate has been registered in the name of a person who if the land had not been registered would not have been the estate owner."

[95] For the measure of compensation, when it is granted, see L.R.A. 1925, s.83(6).

CHAPTER 26

THE SALE OF LAND[1]

This chapter is concerned specifically with the sale of the legal estate; but the same rules apply in general to other dealings with the legal estate such as mortgages and leases, and to dealings with an equitable interest.

Principle 1. Stages in the transaction

A sale of land transaction generally consists of the following stages:

(1) Pre-contract steps.

(2) The formation of a valid and enforceable contract the terms of which will govern the rights and obligations of the parties.

(3) The steps between contract and completion.

(4) Completion by the conveyance of the legal estate to the purchaser in accordance with the terms of the contract.

Each of these stages will be considered separately.

Principle 2. The pre-contract stage

Until there is a valid contract, neither side is bound and either side has absolute liberty to withdraw from the negotiations and the purchaser to recover any "deposit" paid.[1a]

Any agreement which is expressed to be "subject to contract" or contains any other words which show an intention not to create legal relations, will not constitute a binding contract.

In general the principle *caveat emptor* applies to a contract for the sale of land as it does to any contract. However, the vendor may be liable in the following cases:

(1) For misrepresentation.

(2) For non-disclosure of latent defects of title and latent physical defects in the property.

(3) For breach of the contract of sale or some collateral contract.

The purchaser will normally make the following searches and inquiries before binding himself by contract:

---

[1] See, generally, J.T. Farrand, *Contract and Conveyance* (3rd ed.); D.G. Barnsley, *Conveyancing Law and Practice* (1973).

[1a] For the position where a pre-contract "deposit" is paid to an estate agent, see *Sorrell* v. *Finch* [1976] 2 All E.R. 371 (H.L.); and see Estate Agents Act 1979, s.19.

(a) Search in the local land charges register and additional inquiries of the local authorities.[2]
(b) Inquiries of the vendor.
(c) Inspection of the property.

Explanation

Agreements subject to contract. In general a contract for the sale of land is subject to exactly the same rules as any other contract. Subject to section 40 of the Law of Property Act 1925 there is nothing to stop a person making a contract to buy land with as little forethought and formality as he buys a morning newspaper.

For obvious reasons—particularly the amount of money likely to be involved and the legal complexities of land ownership—the prospective purchaser will probably want to have the property surveyed, take legal advice, find out more about the property and the area (amenities, educational facilities, etc.) and possibly to arrange finance, before committing himself.[3] And the vendor will be advised to find out just what he has a legal right to sell before agreeing to sell it.

It is quite usual for the parties—if they are inclined to proceed—to agree a price and make an agreement for sale "subject to contract," and even for the intending purchaser to pay a token deposit, before putting the matter in the hands of their respective solicitors.[4]

An agreement made "subject to contract" is not a contract and has no binding effect in law. The reason is that the words "subject to contract" expressly negative the intention to create legal relations which is one of the essential elements of a valid contract.[5] Any other words which convey the same meaning, *e.g.* "this agreement is intended to be binding in honour only"—will produce the same result; but the following cautionary points need to be noted:

(a) It is essential to use words which the courts will understand to indicate a denial of intention to create legal relations. In one

---

[2] As to need to search in Commons Register, see *G.L.K. Ladenbau (U.K.) Ltd.* v. *Crawley and De Rega* [1978] 1 W.L.R. 266.
[3] But see *Mountford* v. *Scott* [1974] 1 All E.R. 248 (Brightman J.).
[4] In the case of a sale by auction, instead of private treaty, there is no room for any such preliminary agreement; and there is a much greater danger of money spent on surveys, searches, etc. being wasted by the appearance of a higher bidder at the auction.
[5] See *Eccles* v. *Bryant and Pollock* [1948] Ch. 93 (C.A.); compare *Munton* v. *Greater London Council* [1976] 2 All E.R. 815 (C.A.).

case,[6] The agreement described itself as being "provisional . . . " and the court held that this indicated an intention *to be* bound from the outset although possibly only for a temporary period. This sort of case shows the desirability in legal documents of using expressions the meaning of which has become fixed by judicial interpretation. And it is for this reason that the expression "subject to contract" is preferable to any other.[6a]

If an agreement contains terms which the court decides to be meaningless, the agreement will be void for uncertainty,[7] unless the meaningless words can be ignored under the principle in *Nicolene* v. *Simmonds*[8] as a subsidiary and meaningless addendum to an otherwise complete agreement.

(b) The denial of intention must be made express in the agreement. In transactions of a business (as opposed to a family) nature, the intention to create legal relations is presumed in the absence of express provision to the contrary.

(c) Once there is a binding, even though oral, contract, a party cannot unilaterally free himself from liability by introducing the words "subject to contract" into subsequent correspondence.[9]

(d) A contract subject to a condition is not the same as an agreement subject to contract. If an agreement is subject to contract, either party can withdraw for any or no reason. In the case of a conditional contract—for example, a contract to purchase

---

[6] *Branca* v. *Cobarro* [1947] K.B. 854 (C.A.).

[6a] But see J.T. Farrand (n. 1 above), p. 36.

[7] See *Lee Parker* v. *Izzet (No.2)* [1972] 1 W.L.R. 775 (Goulding J.), where the inclusion of the words "subject to satisfactory mortgage" were held to make the agreement void for uncertainty; see also *Bushwell Properties Ltd.* v. *Vortex Properties Ltd.* [1976] 2 All E.R. 283 (C.A.). Contrast *Fe* v. *Kakur* (1978) 40 P. & C.R. 223 (Walton J.) where an agreement "subject to survey" was held *not* void for uncertainty.

[8] [1953] 1 Q.B. 543 (C.A.); and see *Michael Richards Properties Ltd.* v. *St. Saviour's Parish, Southwark* [1975] 3 All E.R. 416 (Goff J.) in which the words "subject to contract" were, surprisingly, held on the facts to be meaningless and ignored; but note the comments on this case in *Munton* v. *Greater London Council* [1976] 2 All E.R. 815 (C.A.).

[9] But a contract in writing can be discharged by subsequent oral agreement. Conversely, a written agreement subject to contract can, by subsequent oral agreement, be converted into a binding contract. Note the doubtful decision in *Michael Richards Properties Ltd.* v. *St. Saviour's Parish, Southwark* [1975] 3 All E.R. 416 (Goff J.) in which the court appears to have confused the question whether a contract has been formed with the question whether that contact has been sufficiently evidenced in writing. A more satisfactory analysis of the facts of this case is perhaps that the parties had by their subsequent conduct converted an agreement subject to contract into an unconditional, binding contract; s.40 was not relevant to the decision. Compare *Cohen* v. *Nessdale* [1981] 3 All E.R. 118 (affirmed on appeal—[1982] 2 All E.R. 160) in which the same confusion appears to have crept in.

subject to planning permission to build a house being obtained—only the failure of the condition will release the parties.[10]

Exchange of contracts. The usual practice, where solicitors act, is for two copies of the contract containing the agreed terms to be prepared and for each party to sign one copy. In such a case the contract will normally become binding when contracts have been exchanged[11]; that is when each party or his solicitor has received the copy signed by the other party. It is sufficient if the copy is held by someone else as agent to the order (and so under the immediate control) of the party or his solicitor. In *Domb* v. *Isoz*[12] the purchaser's solicitors sent the copy signed by the purchaser to the vendor's solicitors, asking them to hold it to their order until they agreed by telephone to exchange. The vendor's solicitors also had in their possession the copy signed by the vendor. At this point, the two solicitors agreed over the telephone that contracts should be treated as exchanged as from that moment. The vendor's solicitors did not forward the part signed by the vendor and the vendor refused to complete. It was held that exchange had taken place and so there was a binding contract. After the telephone conversation, the vendor's solicitors held the copy signed by him as agent for the purchaser's solicitors who had the right to call for its physcial production at any time and so had constructive possession of it.[13]

In some situations, there is no place for exchange. In such cases, as with any contract, the court looks at all the evidence to decide whether a contractual agreement has been reached.[14]

Where the same solicitor acts for both parties[15] there is again no place for exchange; and here the contract will normally be binding as soon as both parties have signed.[16]

---

[10] See, *e.g. N.W. Investments (Erdington) Ltd.* v. *Swani* (1970) 214 E.G. 1115 (Plowman J.). If a condition is wholly for the benefit of one party, that party will be allowed to waive it and enforce the rest of the contract; see *Heron Ltd.* v. *Moss* [1974] 1 All E.R. 421; *Ee* v. *Kakar* (1979) 40 P. & C.R. 223 (Walton J.).

[11] See *Eccles* v. *Bryant & Pollock* [1948] Ch. 93 (C.A.). In this way, each party will hold a copy of the contract signed by the other which will constitute the evidence, necessary under L.P.A. 1925, s.40, to enforce the contract. For the possibility of rectification where, by mistake, the two copies do not correspond, see *Harrison* v. *Battye* [1974] 3 All E.R. 830; *Domb* v. *Isoz* (below).

[12] [1980] 1 All E.R. 942 (C.A.).

[13] The Law Society has issued guidance on the procedure to be adopted by solicitors when exchanging by telephone; see (1980) 77 Law Society Gazette 144.

[14] See *Storer* v. *Manchester City Council* [1974] 3 All E.R. 824 (C.A.); contrast *Gibson* v. *Manchester City Council* [1979] 1 W.L.R. 294 (H.L.).

[15] In general, it is against the Solicitors Rules of Practice for the same solicitor to act for both vendor and purchaser.

[16] *Smith* v. *Mansi* [1963] 1 W.L.R. 26 (C.A.).

Caveat emptor. *Caveat emptor* is the basic rule. The vendor is under no obligation to tell what he knows about the property; and it is for the purchaser to satisfy himself that the property is satisfactory and suitable for the purpose for which he wants it. However, there are important exceptions to this rule.

(1) Misrepresentation. This applies to all contracts. The vendor may remain silent but if he speaks by word or gesture he must tell the truth. Any false statement of fact which influences the purchaser will be misrepresentation and the purchaser will have his remedy.[17] And if he makes a false statement it is no defence that the purchaser could with little effort have discovered the truth.

(2) Non-disclosure. The vendor is under a positive duty to disclose latent defects of title and latent physical defects unless they are already known to the purchaser.[18] Latent, in contrast to patent, defects are those which are not apparent on a reasonable inspection of the property. If a building has no roof on this is likely to be patent. If the windows of a neighbouring building overlook the property, this is likely to make any right of light to the window a patent defect of title. On the other hand, defective foundations are likely to be latent; similarly, a mortgage on the property, or a restrictive covenant against building, are likely to constitute latent defects of title. There is nothing to suggest their existence on inspection of the property.

A defect in title is any adverse interest which burdens the property. Two quite separate questions relating to such possible adverse interests need to be distinguished. First, is the vendor under a duty to disclose it? This is the question now being considered. The answer is that if it is latent and unknown to the purchaser it must be disclosed. In the case of a defect in title, it is no excuse that the vendor himself did not know about it. In general however the vendor will only be liable for non-disclosure of physical defects of which he himself is aware. The second question is whether, if the purchaser does complete and take a conveyance of the land, the adverse interest will be binding on him. The principles which decide this question have been cosidered in the previous two chapters.

Registration of a registrable interest does not relieve the vendor

---

[17] See *Watts* v. *Spence* [1975] 2 W.L.R. 1039 (Graham J.). And see *Walker* v. *Boyle* [1982] 1 All E.R. 634.

[18] Under ss.1, 3 of the Defective Premises Act 1972 the builder/vendor owes a duty of care to the purchaser and his successors in title to see that the building has been erected in a workman-like manner with proper materials.

of his duty of disclosure.[19] On the other hand it does make an adverse interest binding on a purchaser if he completes. Thus, for example, if the vendor fails to disclose a registered restrictive covenant and the purchaser completes—for some reason not having discovered the existence of the covenant for himself—the position is that (i) the purchaser will be bound by the covenant; but (ii) he may have a remedy against the vendor in damages, etc., for non-disclosure.

(3) Remedies for breach of contract.   In addition to misrepresentation and non-disclosure, the purchaser may have a remedy for breach of contract. On the other hand his remedies for misrepresentation or non-disclosure may be limited more or less by the express terms of the contract.

Pre-contract steps.   The purpose of these steps is for the purchaser to find out as much as possible about the property and its suitability for his particular purpose. This is particularly important in respect of those matters which the vendor is not under a duty to disclose and in respect of which the purchaser therefore has no remedy after contract.

(a) (i) *Search in the register of local land charges.*   The usual practice is for the vendor to put an express term in the contract making the sale subject to any local land charges which might affect the property, thus relieving himself of his duty of disclosure and making it essential for the purchaser to search before committing himself.[20]

(a) (ii) *Additional inquiries of the local authorities.*   A local authority is likely to be in possession of much useful information about properties within its area. The usual practice is for the prospective purchaser to use a standard printed set of inquiries agreed between the Law Society and the various local government representative bodies. The local authority answers these on the understanding that it is not liable for any inaccuracy in the replies except for negligence, and it will generally, if it is able, answer any extra inquiries on the same understanding. An example of one of the standard inquiries is: "Is the property within a Conservation Area designated under section 277 of the T. & C.P. Act 1971?"

[19] See L.P.A. 1969, s.24(1), as to unregistered land. The position was previously uncertain because of L.P.A. 1925, s.198.
[20] In any case there are certain matters registrable as local land charges which are not incumbrances and in respect of which the vendor is therefore not under any duty of disclosure; see *Re Forsey and Hollebone's Contract* [1927] 2 Ch. 379. As to what are and what are not local land charges, see Local Land Charges Act 1975, ss.1, 2.

(b) *Inquiries of the vendor.*   Naturally, the prospective purchaser will ask questions of the vendor. It is the usual practice for his solicitor to address a standard form of Inquiries Before Contract to the vendor containing a standard set of printed inquiries to which the purchaser's solicitor will add any others that he considers necessary. An example of one of the standard inquiries is: "Please specify and where possible supply a plan showing to whom all the boundary walls, fences, hedges and ditches belong."

The replies to these inquiries will not usually constitute part of the contract of sale, but if they contain false statements of fact the vendor may be liable for misrepresentation.[20a]

(c) *Inspection of the property.*   This is necessary in particular to discover any patent physical or title defects.

Principle 3.   Formation of enforceable contract: Formalities

In general, the ordinary rules of contract law apply to a contract for the sale of land.

However, under section 40 of the Law of Property Act 1925,[21] any contract for the sale or disposition of land or any interest in land will be unenforceable unless either

(a) all its terms are evidenced in writing signed by the defendant or his authorised agent; or

(b) it is supported by a sufficient act of part performance by the plaintiff.

Explanation

Distinction between contract and conveyance.   When considering formalities in relation to land transactions the following should be distinguished:

(i) the contract;

(ii) the creation or transfer of an equitable interest[22];

(iii) the creation or transfer of a legal estate.[23]

In general, under English law, no formality whatsoever is needed to create a valid fully enforceable contract. By way of exception, section 40 requires any contract to dispose of any interest in land to be evidenced in writing signed by the defendant or his authorised agent. A deed is not essential and is not normally used.

[20a] See *Walker* v. *Boyle* [1982] 1 All E.R. 634.
[21] Re-enacting part of the Statute of Frauds 1677.
[22] See L.P.A. 1925, s.53.
[23] *Ibid.* s.52.

A contract for the sale of land does two things: first, it creates binding personal obligations enforceable by damages and specific performance. In particular, it imposes on the vendor an obligation to transfer the legal ownership to the purchaser at the contractual date for completion; and an obligation on the purchaser to pay the purchase money.

Secondly it automatically vests *equitable* ownership in the purchaser and the vendor becomes a trustee of the legal estate for the purchaser from the moment of contract.[24]

The deed of conveyance is the document which is delivered to the purchaser at completion and transfers legal ownership to him in performance of the contract. The general rule of English law, with a few exceptions, is that a deed is necessary to transfer or create a legal interest in land.[25]

In relation to section 40, two questions must be kept distinct and asked separately. First, is there a valid contract? The answer to this question is governed by the ordinary rules of contract law. Secondly if (and only if) there is a valid contract, is that contract sufficiently evidenced in writing or supported by part performance? Only if the answer to *both* questions is in the affirmative will there be a fully *enforceable* contract.

Section 40 Memorandum.[26] The contract may be in writing and itself constitute the memorandum; or the contract may be oral supported by a separate written memorandum. In any event the following requirements must be satisfied:

(i) The memorandum must contain all the express material terms of the contract.[27]

(ii) It must come into existence at any time before the commencement of the action in which it is to be used in evidence.

(iii) It must be signed by the defendant or his authorised agent.[28] In the case of a sale by auction, the auctioneer has implied, irrevocable authority to sign on behalf of the vendor and the purchaser provided he signs "at the time and as part of the transaction of sale."[29]

---

[24] No writing is necessary to create the equitable interest in this case; L.P.A. 1925, s.53(2). See above, p. 185. As to the trusteeship, see *Lake* v. *Bayliss* [1974] 1 W.L.R. 1073.

[25] *Ibid.* s.52(1)(2).

[26] See generally, *Emmett on Title* (17th ed.), pp. 49, 58 *et seq.*

[27] See *Tweddle* v. *Henderson* [1975] 1 W.L.R. 1496 (Plowman V.—C); note the possibility referred to there that some terms of a single contract may be and some may not be within s.40.

[28] Note *New Hart Builders Ltd.* v. *Brindley* [1975] 1 All E.R. 1007 (Goulding J.).

[29] See *Chaney* v. *Macklow* [1929] 1 Ch. 461 at p. 468 *per* Maugham J; and see *Bell* v. *Balls* [1897] 1 Ch. 663.

(iv) The memorandum may consist of several documents provided the signed one refers expressly or by necessary implication to the others.[30]

(v) The memorandum must not contain anything which constitutes a denial that the agreement was intended to be legally binding or indicates that there was no concluded agreement.[31] Thus, for example, if the document setting out the terms of the contract is itself expressed to be subject to contract, it will not be a sufficient memorandum.[31a] However, if the signed document incorporates an earlier, subject to contract, document merely for the purpose of identifying the agreed terms, the two together will be sufficient.[32] If it is not possible to say, on a balance of probabilities, that the document on its face relates to a concluded agreement between the parties, it will not, it is submitted, be sufficient.[32a]

It may be that the document must, in addition, contain some express recognition that it relates to a legally binding contract. It has been said that the law requires "a signed admission that there was a contract and a signed admission of what that contract was."[33] The authorities are not clear[34], but it is difficult to see the justification for such an additional requirement. The courts do not require implied terms to be set out in the memorandum.[35] At least where the transaction is of a commercial (as opposed to family) nature, the intention to create legal relations is implied.

It has been decided (the "written offer" cases) that, if the defendant makes an offer in writing which is subsequently, unconditionally, accepted orally by the plaintiff, the written offer will provide a sufficient section 40 memorandum.[36] The principle is, perhaps, an exception to the general rule since the written offer, on the face of it, (by virtue of being expressed as an offer) indicates that there is as yet no concluded agreement. However,

[30] See *Timmins* v. *Moreland Street Property Co.* [1957] 3 All E.R. 265 (C.A.).
[31] *e.g.* if P writes to V: "I recall that last week we discussed the possibility of my buying Blackacre on the following terms. . . ."
[31a] See *Cohen* v. *Nessdale* [1981] 3 All E.R. 118 (Kilner-Brown J.). Affirmed on appeal [1982] 2 All E.R. 160.
[32] If, *e.g.* P writes to V: "I agree to purchase on the terms set out in your letter dated 1st June last," that previous letter being headed "subject to contract."
[32a] If, for example, the defendant's writing was on the back of an envelope and might be a note of the terms he was intending to propose or terms he had agreed. See references in n. 34 below.
[33] *Thirkell* v. *Cambi* [1919] 2 K.B. 590, at p. 597, *per* Scrutton L.J.
[34] See *Law* v. *Jones* [1973] 2 W.L.R. 994 (C.A.); *Tiverton Estates Ltd.* v. *Wearwell Ltd.* [1974] 1 All E.R. 209 (C.A.); and *Daulia Ltd.* v. *Four Millbank Nominees Ltd.* [1978] 2 W.L.R. 621 (C.A.), particularly the judgment of Buckley L.J. at p. 635. See (1979) 95 L.Q.R. 7 (H.W. Wilkinson).
[35] See Megarry & Wade *Law of Real Property*, (4th ed.), at p. 558.
[36] *Reuss* v. *Picksley* (1866) L.R. 1 Ex. 342.

the underlying principle of section 40 is that there is a signed statement by the defendant of all the terms to which he is committing or has committed himself; and an unconditional, written offer satisfies this principle.[37]

Doctrine of part performance. The purpose of section 40 (and its predecessor) was to prevent fraud; to prevent the plaintiff persuading the court of the existence of a contract which he had never in fact made. On the other hand, such a provision could itself be used as an engine of fraud, allowing a person who had made a contract to escape his obligations merely because written, as opposed to oral, evidence was not available.

Equity therefore developed the doctrine of part performance, creating an exception to the statutory requirement. Oral evidence of the contract by itself, however convincing, will not suffice; but if the plaintiff has been allowed by the defendant to take some irreversible step in the performance of the contract, the court will then not allow the defendant to hide behind section 40. It will permit the plaintiff to give oral evidence of the contract and will order specific performance of the contract as proved.

For the doctrine of part performance to operate the following requirements must be satisfied:

(i) There must have been acts by the plaintiff which indicate on a balance of probabilities the existence of some contract between the parties and are consistent with the contract alleged. The usual act of part performance relied on is taking possession. But of course, no act, not even taking possession, points unequivocally to any particular contract. If I let P into possession of my property, it is not necessarily because he has agreed to buy it; he may be going to rent it; or he may just be a friend looking after it while I am away. But the point is that the plaintiff has obviously altered his position in reliance on some sort of agreement and coupled with the other requirements this is enough.[38]

---

[37] Indeed, in the ordinary case of exchange of contracts, at the moment when the purchaser signs his half of the contract (which will invariably constitute the section 40 memorandum if the vendor needs to enforce), there will be no contract in existence; though, in such a case, it is true that the whole contract itself (including the vendor's acceptance) is, after exchange, *in* writing. For suggestion that s.40 should be reformed or repealed, see H.W. Wilkinson, (1967) 31 Conv. (N.S.) 182, 254.

[38] On the nature of the act required see *Steadman* v. *Steadman* [1974] 2 All E.R. 977 (H.L.). See also *Maddison* v. *Alderson* (1883) 8 App.Cas. 467; *Kingswood Estate Co. Ltd.* v. *Anderson* [1962] 3 All E.R. 593 (C.A.); *Wakeham* v. *Mackenzie* [1968] 2 All E.R. 783; *Re Gonin* [1979] Ch. 16 (Walton J.); also *Daulia Ltd.* v. *Four Millbank Nominees Ltd.* [1978] 2 W.L.R. 621 (C.A.) where the acts pointed to the contemplation of a contract possibly to be made rather than part performance of one already made.

(ii) There must be sufficient oral evidence of the contract. The act of part performance is not itself expected to prove the contract. The plaintiff must prove the contract and its precise terms like any other disputed fact; but the act of part performance means that oral, instead of just written evidence, is admissible to do this.

(iii) The contract must be specifically enforceable. Part performance cures the absence of a section 40 memorandum. It will not help if there is any other reason which makes the contract not specifically enforceable—if, for example, the plaintiff has been guilty of delay.

(iv) The act must have been done with the consent of the defendant and must be such as to make it a fraud on his part to rely on the absence of writing. If the defendant has not consented to the act—if for example the plaintiff has taken possession without his consent—there is no reason in equity why he should not rely on the statute.

The same reasoning applies if the plaintiff's act can be reversed. For example, the payment of money by itself is not normally likely to constitute a sufficient act of part performance.[39] Apart from the fact that it is equivocal and does not point to the existence of any particular contract at all, the plaintiff can be restored by repayment of the money to him. He has not irreversibly altered his position.

Enforceability of oral contract.   An agreement for the sale of land will fall into one of the following categories:

(i) No binding contract at all, for example, where it is made "subject to contract," or where it is void for uncertainty. In this case neither party will be under any obligation at all.

(ii) A valid oral contract, but one which is not evidenced in writing or supported by part performance. An oral contract is said to be unenforceable, but is a valid contract and it is not without legal effect. First, it will only be unenforceable if the defendant chooses to plead the absence of written evidence as a defence.[40] Secondly, if the purchaser repudiates the contract, the vendor, like any vendor in such circumstances, will be entitled to retain any deposit paid by the purchaser.

(iii) A valid oral contract, not evidenced in writing but supported by a sufficient act of part performance by the plaintiff.

---

[39] See *Steadman* v. *Steadman* [1974] 2 All E.R. 977 (H.L.), where, coupled with other acts it was held to be sufficient. And see comment on *Steadman* in *Elsden* v. *Pick* [1980] 1 W.L.R. 898 (C.A.). See also *Cohen* v. *Nessdale* [1981] 3 All E.R. 118 (Kilner-Brown J.).

[40] But note *Re Gonin, decd* [1979] Ch. 16 (Walton J.), for right of defendant to amend pleadings to raise a s.40 defence.

Here, in addition to the consequences mentioned in (ii) above, the plaintiff will be able to claim specific performance of the contract. But he will not be able to bring an action for damages.[41]

(iv) A valid contract sufficiently evidenced in writing. Here the contract will be fully enforceable by specific performance and at law by a judgment for damages.

Principle 4.   The rights and obligations of the parties

The rights and obligations of the parties are determined by the terms of the contract.

The contract must include express agreement as to the identity of the parties, the identity of the property and the price to be paid. In the absence of agreement on these matters the contract will be void for uncertainty.

The contract will normally (but not necessarily) contain other express terms. A contract which contains agreement only as to property, parties and price, and no other express terms, is often referred to as an "open contract."[42]

Any contract for the sale of land is governed by terms implied by the courts in so far as these implied terms are not modified by any express terms of the contract itself. If the contract is a contract by correspondence, the implied terms are the statutory conditions of sale. The terms implied into any other contract are usually referred to as "the terms implied under an open contract."

Explanation

Express terms.   All that is needed to create a valid contract is a sufficiently certain agreement as to parties, property and price to be paid.[43]

Such a simple agreement, though valid and enforceable, leaves many gaps which must be filled if the contract is to proceed to completion and any disputes arising on the way settled. For example, what if a dispute arises as to whether the vendor has proved his title; or as to the date on which completion should take

---

[41] But, under the Chancery Amendment Act 1858 (and the Statute Law Revision and Civil Procedure Act 1883, s.3 and Sched.) there is jurisdiction to order damages in substitution for specific performance; see below, p. 568.

[42] See A.M. Prichard, An Aspect of Contracts and their Terms, (1974) 90 L.Q.R. 55.

[43] Contrast the sale of goods where, in the absence of agreement as to price, the courts are able to imply a "reasonable" price; Sale of Goods Act 1979, s.8(2). See *Sudbrook Trading Estate Ltd.* v. *Eggleton* [1981] 3 All E.R. 105 (C.A.).

place? The answer is that any gaps left by the express terms will be filled by the implied terms.

In the vast majority of cases, however, the parties, through their respective solicitors, will draw up a detailed contract containing express terms covering more or less every possible eventuality. Again, in the vast majority of cases, they will use one of the standard form contracts, such as the Law Society's form (incorporating the Law Society's General Conditions of Sale); or the National Conditions of Sale published by the Solicitors' Law Stationery Society. These standard form contracts are simply ready drafted contracts containing a standard set of general conditions governing all those matters which need not vary from transaction to transaction. The solicitors in general only have to add those terms which will vary from transaction to transaction, such as the parties, the description of the property, the price to be paid, the date for completion, the root of title (in the case of unregistered land), and so on.

Implied terms. The implied terms are a sort of long stop. They govern where there is no applicable express term. In most cases, where a standard form contract is used with a comprehensive set of express terms, there will be little scope for any implied terms. In the occasional case of the informal contract with few if any express terms, apart from those specifying the parties, property and price, the contract will consist largely of implied terms.[44]

In any contract one of two sets of implied terms will be available.

(a) If the contract is a contract by correspondence, it will be governed by the Statutory Conditions of Sale. This is a set of terms drawn up for this purpose by the Lord Chancellor under the authority of section 46 of the Law of Property Act 1925.

(b) Otherwise, the implied terms which govern any other contract for the sale of the land will apply. These are commonly referred to as the "terms implied under an open contract."

Principle 5. The terms implied under an open contract.

The following are some of the important terms implied under an open contract.

Similar terms are found in the Statutory Conditions of Sale and in standard form contracts.

These terms only apply in so far as not modified by the express terms of the particular contract.

---

[44] For a contract containing express agreement on parties, property and price and one other express term, see *Hawkins* v. *Price* [1947] Ch. 645 (Evershed J.).

(1) The vendor must be in a position, on the date fixed for completion, to convey to the purchaser the fee simple absolute in possession in law and equity free from incumbrances.

(2) He must prove his title in the manner required by law.[45]

(3) From the moment of contract, the vendor becomes trustee of the legal estate for the purchaser who becomes owner in equity. This means that:

   (a) the purchaser will benefit from any increase in value of the property; but

   (b) he will have to pay the agreed purchase price and bear any decrease in value. In particular, this means that the purchaser will need to have the property insured against fire and other damage from the moment of contract.[46]

(4) The vendor's trusteeship is a limited one. In particular, unlike the ordinary trustee.

   (a) he is entitled to retain any income and profits from the property (and must pay any outgoings) up to the date *fixed* for completion; and

   (b) he is entitled to a lien, giving him the right to retain the property until he has been paid the purchase money.

(5) The purchaser is not under any obligation to pay a deposit on exchange of contracts. But in practice, the contract expressly stipulates for a deposit (usually of 10 per cent.) to be paid, and states to whom it is to be paid (generally a solicitor or estate agent), and the capacity in which it is to be held by the payee (whether as stakeholder or agent for the vendor).

(6) The purchaser must complete as soon as the vendor has fulfilled his obligation to show a good title. In return the vendor must deliver the conveyance transferring legal ownership to the purchaser and put him into vacant possession[47] of the property (or into receipt of the rents if the property is sold subject to a lease).

(7) In the case of unregistered land, with certain exceptions, the vendor must hand over the title deeds to the purchaser at completion.[48] In the case of registered land, he must hand over the land certificate.

(8) The vendor must convey as beneficial owner.[49]

---

[45] See next Principle for proof of title.

[46] On the question whether frustration applies to a contract for the sale of land, see *Amalgamated Investment & Property Co. Ltd.* v. *John Walker & Sons* [1976] 3 All E.R. 509 (C.A.).

[47] See *Topfell* v. *Galley Properties* [1979] 1 W.L.R. 446 (Templeman J.).

[48] And supply the statutory acknowledgment and undertaking in respect of any retained documents.

[49] See below, p. 568.

Principle 6. Steps between contract and completion: Proof of title

Before completion takes place the vendor must prove his title to the purchaser in accordance with the contract. The method of proving title depends on whether the land is registered or unregistered.

Explanation. Unregistered land

Method of proof. In the absence of express provision to the contrary in the contract, the vendor must prove that he owns the interest in the land as described in the contract.

To prove title, the vendor must:

(a) produce a good root of title—that is a document at least 15 years old which deals with the whole interest being sold, adequately identifies the property, and does not contain anything to cast doubt on the title;

(b) produce the documents and other proper evidence showing how the title has devolved from the root of title down to his own ownership.

Steps in proving title. After the exchange of contracts, the vendor must deliver to the purchaser an abstract of title, that is a copy in chronological order of the above documents.

The purchaser will examine (peruse) the abstract and if he has any queries about the title arising from the abstract or elsewhere (*e.g.* his search in the Land Charges Registry) he will raise these in the form of Requisitions on Title. In a very simple example, the abstract might show that the property was mortgaged five years ago but no discharge of the mortgage is abstracted.[50] The vendor will deal with any Requisitions by means of Replies to Requisitions.

If any dispute arises which cannot be resolved by agreement, legal action will have to be initiated by one of the parties. For example, if the purchaser has raised a requisition which the vendor claims he is not entitled to raise; or if there is a dispute as to whether the vendor has given a satisfactory answer to a requisition.

Under the Law of Property Act 1925, section 49(1), there is available a summary method of resolving such disputes without the expense and delay of a full scale legal action. This is the Vendor and Purchaser summons.

---

[50] The reply to this inquiry is likely to be very simple—either that there is a mortgage but it is going to be redeemed before completion; or that the mortgage has been redeemed but somebody in the vendor's solicitor's office has forgotten to abstract the discharge endorsed on the mortgage.

The purchaser will also need to examine the actual deeds and documents of title to ensure that they do exist and are as abstracted; and also to make an official search in the Land Charges Registry before completion.[51]

When he is satisfied with the title, the purchaser will accept title and it will then be too late to raise further requisitions. In practice, acceptance is implied from the purchaser proceeding to the next stage without pressing requisitions, if any, which are outstanding. Once the vendor has proved title in the manner required by law, the purchaser is under an obligation to accept and proceed to completion.

Two general points may be made about these steps between contract and completion. First, the contract usually stipulates expressly the number of days within which each of the steps must be taken. Secondly, proof of title does not give an absolute guarantee that the vendor does own what he has agreed to sell. But it is the only proof to which the purchaser is entitled under general conveyancing law. And in practice, because of the operation of the Limitation Act 1980,[52] it is invariably sufficient. In the unlikely event of a defect in title appearing after completion, even after such a proper investigation, the purchaser may have a claim under the covenants for title implied into the conveyance.[53]

Registered land. Two of the chief advantages of registered conveyancing are:

    (a) the proof of title is a simpler matter[54];

    (b) the title offered, assuming that it is absolute, is a title that is in general guaranteed by the state.

The method of proving title in registered land is that the vendor will, after contract, supply the purchaser with an office copy of the entries on the register together with the filed plan and authority to inspect the register. The office copy corresponds with the abstract in the case of unregistered conveyancing.

Matters will then proceed to completion in much the same way as with unregistered conveyancing. Instead of searching in the Land Charges Registry,[55] the purchaser will, before completion, make an official search in the Land Registry to check that no

[51] See above, p. 524.
[52] See above, Chap. 23.
[53] See below, p. 568.
[54] But, with title now reduced to 15 years, even unregistered conveyancing is not generally likely to be complicated.
[55] But he does need to search (generally before contract), for local land charges which are overriding interests.

entries have been made since the date of his office copy and to give himself protection against any entries made after his search and before he has chance to apply for registration.

Principle 7. Remedies and completion

Breach by the purchaser. If the purchaser fails to complete where time is of the essence or otherwise repudiates the contract,[56] the vendor has the following remedies:

(1) To sue for specific performance[57]; or

(2) To accept the repudiation and treat the contract as discharged, and in addition:

(a) to forfeit any deposit paid by the purchaser[58];

(b) re-sell the property and keep any profit made on the re-sale;

(c) claim damages for any loss due to the repudiation including any loss made on a re-sale of the property; but in claiming damages credit must be give for any deposit forfeited.

If the purchaser merely delays where time is not of the essence, or commits a breach which does not amount to repudiation, the vendor is not entitled to treat the contract as discharged and must complete. However,

(i) The purchaser will generally be liable to pay interest on any outstanding purchase money from the date fixed for completion to the date of actual completion.

(ii) The purchaser will be entitled to the profits and income from the property from the date fixed for completion but will have to pay outgoings from that date.

(iii) The purchaser may be liable, in addition to paying interest on the purchase money, to pay damages for any further loss suffered by the vendor.

Breach by the vendor. If the vendor repudiates or is in breach of condition, the purchaser will be entitled either to claim specific performance; or he will be entitled to accept the repudiation and treat the contract as discharged. In the latter case, he will be entitled to recover his deposit with interest and costs.

---

[56] See, *e.g. Myton Ltd.* v. *Schwab-Morris* [1974] 1 All E.R. 326 (Goulding J.).

[57] In which case the position of the parties will be as where there is a breach not amounting to repudiation by the purchaser.

[58] Even where, under common law, the vendor has a right to retain the deposit, the court has a wide discretion under L.P.A. 1925, s.49, to order its return to the purchaser; see *Schindler* v. *Pigault* (1975) 30 P. & C.R. 328; and *Universal Corp.* v. *Fiveways Properties Ltd.* [1979] 1 All E.R. 552 (C.A.).

If the vendor's breach does not amount to repudiation, the purchaser will be obliged to complete.

In any case, the purchaser will be entitled, subject to the ordinary rules as to remoteness, to claim damages in respect of any loss. However, where the vendor's breach arises from a defect in title, the rule in *Bain* v. *Fothergill*[59] will normally apply to restrict the purchaser's claim for damages to the return of his deposit with interest and costs. But the rule in *Bain* v. *Fothergill* was developed at a time when the title to land was a complex matter, and in recent years the courts have perhaps tended to restrict its ambit. In any case, it only applies where the defect is irremovable[59a] and the vendor has acted in good faith.[60] In *Watts* v. *Spence*[61] it was held not to apply to a claim for damages under the Misrepresentation Act 1967. Nor, so it has been held,[62] does it apply to a right of occupation, registered between contract and completion by a wife under the Matrimonial Homes Act 1967.[62a]

Liens. The unpaid vendor has an equitable lien on the land enforceable by a court order for sale in respect of any unpaid purchase money.

Similarly, a purchaser has a lien on the land to secure any money (such as a deposit) which he is entitled to have repaid by the vendor.

Both types of lien are registrable.

Time of the essence. Where the time fixed by the contract for completion is *not* of the essence, failure by either party to complete on time is a breach of contract and the innocent party can claim damages. But it is not a repudiatory breach; the innocent party cannot treat the contract as discharged. Where time *is* of the essence, failure to complete at that time is a repudiatory breach.[63]

---

[59] (1874) L.R. 7 H.L. 158.
[59a] See *Re Daniel* [1917] 2 Ch. 405, where the vendor had the right to pay off an outstanding mortgage (even though he did not have the money). It is doubtful on present day authorities whether the rule in *Bain* v. *Fothergill* would apply in *Bain* v. *Fothergill*.
[60] See *Malhotra* v. *Choudry* [1978] 3 W.L.R. 825 (C.A.), where the vendor failed to show that he had used his best endeavours to obtain the consent of his wife as joint tenant.
[61] [1975] 2 W.L.R. 1039 (Graham J.).
[62] *Wroth* v. *Tyler* [1973] 1 All E.R. 897 (Megarry J.).
[62a] For criticisms of the rule, see A. Sydenham, (1977) 41 Conv. (N.S.) 341; J. Berryman, (1981) 44 M.L.R. 571. Contrast C.T. Emery, (1978) 42 Conv. 338.
[63] For the important distinction (which is often not made clear) between rescission and repudiation, see *Buckland* v. *Farmar & Moody* [1978] 3 All E.R. 929 (C.A.).

Time may be, or become, of the essence in any one of three ways. First, where the contract itself expressly makes it so. Secondly, where, because of the nature of the contract, time is of the essence by implication—for example, on the sale of a wasting asset such a short lease.[64] Thirdly, where one party fails to complete within a reasonable time after the contractual date, the innocent party may make time of the essence by serving notice giving the other a fixed time (which must be reasonable) within which completion must take place.[65] In this case, service of the notice does not deprive the innocent party of his right to sue for damages for the failure to complete on the original date; it gives him the additional remedy of treating the contract as repudiated if the notice is not complied with.[66]

Where a contract is made conditional on some act being done by a certain date, that date will (in the absence of express provision to the contrary) be of the essence.[67]

Specific performance and damages. In general, repudiatory breach does not automatically discharge the contract. It is only discharged if the innocent party elects to treat it as discharged. Where he chooses, instead, to sue for specific performance,[68] the contract remains in existence until it is performed or he applies to the court to treat it as discharged.[69]

There are certain cases in which only specific performance can be claimed; for example, where the contract is supported only by part performance and not a written memorandum.[70]

In any case in which specific performance is being claimed, the court has a discretion to refuse it (on certain, well established grounds).[71] Further, in any case in which the court has jurisdiction to grant specific performance, it has a discretion to award damages

[64] *Hudson* v. *Temple* (1860) 29 Beav. 536. The express terms may of course negative the implication.
[65] Such a notice makes the stipulated time of the essence for *both* parties; *Quadrangle Development and Construction Co. Ltd.* v. *Jenner* [1974] 1 All E.R. 729 (C.A.).
[66] *Raineri* v. *Miles* [1980] 2 All E.R. 145 (H.L.).
[67] *Aberfoyle Plantations Ltd.* v. *Cheng* [1960] A.C. 115.
[68] In an appropriate case, specific performance can be applied for before any breach has actually taken place; see *Woods* v. *Mackenzie* [1975] 2 All E.R. 170 (Megarry J.).
[69] See *Singh* v. *Nazeer* [1978] 3 W.L.R. 785 (Megarry V.—C); *Johnson* v. *Agnew* [1980] A.C. 367 (H.L.).
[70] Also, *e.g.* in a claim for breach of an equitable interest such as a restrictive covenant.
[71] See, *e.g.* *Wroth* v. *Tyler* [1973] 1 All E.R. 897 (Megarry J.) Moreover, in granting or refusing specific performance, the court can override the strict terms of the contract; see *e.g.* *Becker* v. *Partridge* [1966] 2 Q.B. 155; and *Walker* v. *Boyle* [1982] 1 All E.R. 634.

instead[72] (or in addition).

The same rules govern the assessment of damages whether awarded under common law or under the Chancery Amendment Act 1858 in lieu of an equitable remedy.[73] Thus, in both cases, while the normal date at which damages are assessed is the date of breach, a later date may be more appropriate to avoid injustice.[74]

Effect of completion on remedies. Once completion has taken place and the property conveyed to the purchaser, the general rule is that the contract merges with the conveyance. This means that it will generally be too late for the purchaser to claim damages for breach of contract after completion. However, he will be able to claim damages:

(1) For breach of an independent collateral contract.

(2) For breach of any duty owed by the vendor as trustee for the purchaser between contract and completion.

(3) For fraud by the vendor.

(4) For breach of any covenants for title implied into the conveyance.

The covenants for title. The following covenants for title are implied where the vendor conveys as beneficial owner:

(a) that he has full power to convey;

(b) that the purchaser shall have quiet enjoyment;

(c) that the property is free from adverse interests;

(d) that the vendor will take any necessary step to complete the purchaser's title.

These covenants are qualified, protecting only against acts of the vendor and any person claiming under or in trust for him and any predecessor in title, but only back to the last purchaser for value.

If the vendor conveys a leasehold as beneficial owner, two additional covenants are implied:

(e) that the lease is valid and subsisting;

(f) that the rent has been paid and all covenants performed to date.

Where the vendor conveys as trustee, the only covenant implied (and the only one to which the purchaser is entitled in the absence of agreement to the contrary) is that the vendor himself has done nothing to incumber the title.

---

[72] Chancery Amendment Act 1858 and Statute Law Revision and Civil Procedure Act 1883, s.3 and Sched.

[73] See generally, on damages, A.J. Oakley, Pecuniary Compensation for Failure to Complete a Contract for Sale of Land, (1980) 39 C.L.J. 58.

[74] See *Wroth* v. *Tyler* [1973] 1 All E.R. 897; *Johnson* v. *Agnew* [1980] A.C. 367 (H.L.); *Domb* v. *Isoz* [1980] 1 All E.R. 942 (C.A.). And see S.M. Waddams, (1981) 97 L.Q.R. 445, partic. at p. 453. See also *Perry* v. *Sidney Phillips* [1982] 1 All E.R. 1005.

CHAPTER 27

TRANSFER ON DEATH

Principle 1.   Passing of property on death[1]

When a person dies all his property (commonly called his "estate") passes to his personal representatives. Personal representatives may be either executors or administrators.[2]

If the deceased has appointed personal representatives by will, they are known as executors. The property vests in them automatically at the moment of death; but they must generally obtain probate of the will as evidence of their title.

If the deceased has not appointed executors by will, the court will make a grant of administration appointing administrators to act and the grant will vest the property in the administrators.[3] The Supreme Court of Judicature (Consolidation) Act 1925, specifies who may be appointed. The person appointed will receive letters of administration as evidence of his appointment.[4] Usually it will be someone with a claim to the property of the deceased either under the will or intestacy.

Probate or administration of the same property cannot be granted to more than four persons.[5]

Land which continues to be subject to a strict settlement on death will pass to the trustess of the settlement as special personal representatives.[6]

Explanation

Executors and probate. A person is entitled to make a will appointing personal representatives to administer his property after his death and distribute it to the beneficiaries. An executor derives his authority directly from the will and the deceased's property will pass to him automatically on the death. Once an executor has signified his acceptance of the office (for example by performing acts of administration or intermeddling with the estate)[7] it is too late for him to renounce his appointment and he

---

[1] See generally, A.R. Mellows, *The Law of Succession* (3rd ed.).
[2] A.E.A. 1925, s.1.
[3] Until appointment, the property vests in the President of the Family Division of the High Court; see Administration of Justice Act 1970, s.1.
[4] J.A. 1925, s.162.
[5] J.A. 1925, s.160(1).
[6] A.E.A. 1925, s.22(1); J.A. 1925, s.162(1).
[7] See Mellows (n. 1, above), p. 298.

must prove the will (*i.e.* take the necessary steps to obtain probate).

The term "probate" means either the official proving of the will by the Family Division of the High Court or the certified copy of the will which is issued to the executor after proof. With a few minor exceptions[8] the executor will not be able to deal with the testator's property unless he can produce probate as evidence of his title. In the case of unregistered land it is a vital link in the documents of title. In the case of registered land the executor will have to produce probate if he wishes to be registered as proprietor in place of the deceased.[9]

A will may be proved in either common or solemn form. Proof in common form means that probate is granted by the principal or district probate registry of the Family Division of the High Court on the application of the executor without any judicial hearing. This is the usual procedure where there is no dispute and no likelihood of a dispute as to the validity of the will. If the application is supported by the executor's oath that the will is the "true, whole and last will and testament of the deceased" and is accompanied by the will containing a proper attestation clause and perfect on the face of it, then the registry will issue probate as a matter of course.

Where there is any dispute about the will or likelihood of dispute—since probate in common form is open to subsequent challenge—proof will need to be in solemn form. This means that the validity of the will and the right to probate will be decided judicially after a court action in which all those interested in the dispute are given a hearing. In general, probate in solemn form is not open to subsequent challenge.

Administrators and letters of administration. If the deceased has not made a valid will, or if he has made a will without appointing executors, or if the executors appointed are not able and willing to act, it will be necessary for the court to appoint administrators. In this case the title of the administrator of the deceased's property actually derives from the grant of administration by the court. Until a grant has been made, title is vested in the President of the Family Division of the High Court. The grant is evidenced by letters of administration—the official document issued by the court to the administrator as proof of his title in the same way and serving the same purpose as probate.

---

[8] See A.E. (Small Payments) Act 1965.
[9] Or if he wishes to deal with the estate without having himself registered; see L.R.A. 1925, s.37.

Where the deceased has made a will but there is no executor, letters of administration will be granted "with the will annexed."

The Judicature Act 1925 as amended determines who is entitled to apply for a grant of administration. In general the person who has the first claim on the deceased's estate will be appointed.[10] Thus if a husband dies intestate leaving a surviving widow she will normally be appointed administrator.

The procedure is similar to that of proving a will in common form. The person applying will make his application stating his interest and supported by an oath duly to administer the deceased's estate. In some cases he may have to obtain two sureties to guarantee the proper administration of the estate.[11] If all is in order, the application will be granted as a matter of course.

Principle 2. Administration by the personal representatives[12]

It is the duty of personal representatives to:

(1) Take control of the deceased's property as soon as possible.

(2) Manage it properly and realise it if necessary.

(3) Distribute the estate to those entitled either under the will or the rules of intestacy.

Explanation

In general, since 1925, the same rules govern the administration and distribution of both the real and personal property of the deceased.[13] One of the important objects of the 1925 legislation was to assimilate the two types of property. However, this explanation is concerned more particularly with land.

Control. The personal representatives of a deceased are under a duty to "collect and get in the real and personal estate of the deceased and administer it according to law."[14] Thus, for example, they will need to take control of the title deeds relating to land or, if it is registered, the land certificate.

Management. Until the administration is complete and the property can be distributed, the personal representatives are responsible for its management. Quite apart from any powers given by the will, statute gives personal representatives wide

[10] See J.A. 1925, s.160.
[11] See A.E.A. 1971, s.8 (replacing administration bonds).
[12] See generally, Mellows (n. 1, above), Pt. VI.
[13] A.E.A. 1925, s.34.
[14] A.E.A. 1925, s.25, as amended by A.E.A. 1971, s.9.

powers of management including all the powers of management given to trustees by the Trustee Act 1925.[15] Thus, for example, they have the power to invest in trustee securities, to insure the property against loss and pay the premiums out of income, to deposit money at a bank while an investment is being sought, and so on.

Further, "for the purposes of administration, or during a minority of any beneficiary, or the subsistence of a life interest, or until the period of distribution arrives" they have all the powers of trustees for sale.[16] In the case of property passing by intestacy, they *are* trustees for sale to sell and hold the proceeds of sale (subject to paying debts) for the benefit of those entitled on intestacy.[17]

The powers of the personal representatives thus include not only management but the power to sell and mortgage the estate.[18]

Sale and mortgage by the personal representatives. Sale or mortgage of the deceased's property may be justified for a number of possible reasons. For example, it may be necessary to pay his debts or capital transfer tax; to raise the capital sum of money to which a surviving spouse is entitled on intestacy; or to pay pecuniary legacies; and on intestacy there is in any case a trust to sell.

In the case of land, section 36(8) of the Administration of Estates Act 1925 provides:

> "A conveyance of a legal estate by a personal representative to a purchaser[19] shall not be invalidated by reason only that the purchaser may have notice that all the debts, liabilities, funeral, and testamentary or administration expenses, duties and legacies of the deceased have been discharged or provided for."

Thus, the purchaser (including mortgagee) does not have to concern himself with whether the personal representatives had proper reason to sell.[20]

---

[15] See T.A. 1925, s.68(1) (17).

[16] A.E.A. 1925, s.39(1); L.P.A. 1925, s.38(1). This means they have all the powers of the tenant for life and the trustees of the settlement under a strict settlement.

[17] A.E.A. 1925, s.33.

[18] A sale by a personal representative will be an overreaching conveyance. See L.P.A. 1925, s.2(1).

[19] "Purchaser" means a person who acquires the property in good faith for valuable consideration; A.E.A. 1925, s.55(1) (xviii).

[20] But if he knows of a breach of trust he may not be in good faith and so not protected. See Williams and Mortimer, *Executors, Administrators and Probate* (1970), p. 626.

A sole personal representative is able to give a valid receipt for capital money in respect of land.[21] This means that it is never essential to have more than one personal representative though in practice there will commonly be two or a trust corporation[22]— perhaps one of the clearing banks which do trustee and executorship work.

Principle 3. Distribution

The personal representatives must pay the deceased's funeral expenses and debts out of his assets.

Where the estate is insolvent the Administration of Estates Act 1925[23] lays down the order of priority in which creditors are entitled to be satisfied out of what assets are available.

The Administration of Estate Act 1925 also lays down the order in which the various assets must be resorted to for the payment of debts.[24]

Subject to the payment of funeral expenses and debts the personal representatives must distribute the estate as follows:

(1) To meet any claim under the Inheritance (Provision for Family and Dependants) Act 1975.

(2) Subject thereto, in accordance with the provisions of the will.

(3) In the case of property not disposed of under (1) or (2), in accordance with the rules of intestacy.

Explanation

Debts. Section 32(1) of the Administration of Estates Act 1925 provides:

> "The real and personal estate, whether legal or equitable, of the deceased person, to the extent of his beneficial interest therein, and the real and personal estate of which a deceased person in pursuance of a general power . . . disposes by will, are assets for the payment of his debts (whether by specialty or simple contract) and liabilities, and any disposition by will inconsistent with this enactment is void as against the creditors, and the court shall if necessary, administer the property for the payment of the debts and liabilities."

---

[21] L.P.A. 1925, s.27(2), as amended by L.P.(A.)A. 1926, s.7 and Sched.; S.L.A. 1925, s.18(1).
[22] For the meaning of "trust corporation" see Mellows (n. 1, above), p. 689.
[23] s.34(1) and Pt. I of Sched. 1.
[24] *Ibid.* s.34(3) and Pt. II of Sched. 1.

Where the estate is insolvent, that is where the deceased has left more debts than property, it will be necessary to decide the order of payment. This order of priority is contained in Part I of the First Schedule of the Administration of Estates Act 1925. For example, the funeral, testamentary and administration expenses have priority over all other claims. Subject to this the order is the same as for bankruptcy. Under the bankruptcy rules the position is briefly as follows:

(a) Secured debts. The creditor has priority in respect of the property on which the debt is secured.

(b) Certain debts are preferred and, subject to the rights of secured creditors, will have preference over other creditors. For example, the unpaid wages of employees for up to four months before the death are preferred.

(c) Other debts (apart from those in (d)) rank equally in priority.

(d) Certain debts are deferred and must wait until all creditors in previous classes have been paid. For example, money lent by the deceased's husband for the purposes of her trade or business.

All creditors in the same class are paid *pari passu*.

Another important question, important this time to the beneficiaries, is the order in which the personal representatives must resort to the assets to meet the various debts. If a testator leaves his house to A and his money in the bank to B, and he leaves debts of £5,000, then A and B are going to be interested in where the money is going to come from to pay the debts.

The order in which assets are to be resorted to is contained in Part II of the First Schedule to the Administration of Estates Act 1925. For example, the personal representatives must first resort to any property of the deceased not disposed of by will; if that is not sufficient, they must next resort to the residuary property; and so on.

Distribution and family provision. Before the passing of the Inheritance (Family Provision) Act 1938, there was no limit on the absolute freedom of the testator to dispose of his property by will. As a result of that Act as amended,[25] the court has a wide jurisdiction to disregard the terms of the will and the rules of intestacy where it considers that no "reasonable financial provision"[26] has been made for certain specified surviving dependants.

---

[25] The legislation is now contained in the Inheritance (Provision for Family and Dependants) Act 1975.

[26] *Ibid.*, ss.1, 2.

A claim can be made on behalf of any of the following:
- (a) spouse or former spouse who has not remarried;
- (b) a child;
- (c) any person treated as a child of the family by the deceased in his marriage;
- (d) any other person who at the time of death was being wholly or partly maintained by the deceased.

On application the court must decide whether or not by virtue of the will and rules of intestacy, "reasonable financial provision" has been made for the applicant. If it has not the court has a wide discretion to order periodic payments, a lump sum, or a transfer of a property out of the deceased's estate for the benefit of the applicant. In reaching its decision the court must take into account, *inter alia*,[27] the nature of the property, the means and conduct of the applicant, any physical or mental disability of the applicant, and any other relevant circumstances.

Principle 4. Disposition by will and on intestacy[28]

Subject to the above rules about family provision there is absolute freedom of testamentary disposition.

To be valid a will must comply with the Wills Act 1837 as amended. Any alteration or revocation must also comply with the necessary formalities.

In certain exceptional cases a person can make a valid "privileged will" which does not have to comply with any formal requirements.

If a beneficiary dies before the testator the general rule is that the gift lapses.

Any property of the deceased not disposed of by will must be distributed in accordance with the rules of intestacy contained in the Administration of Estates Act 1925 as amended.

Where it is uncertain which of two persons died first the general presumption is that the younger survived the elder; but in applying the intestacy rules an intestate is presumed to have survived his spouse.

Explanation

Formalities of valid will. Briefly, the rules governing the making of a valid will are as follows;

---

[27] Inheritance (Provision for Family and Dependants) Act 1975, s.3.
[28] See generally Mellows (n. 1, above), Pts. I, III.

(a) the testator must be of full age;
(b) it must be in writing;
(c) it must be signed by the testator or by someone else in his presence and by his direction;
(d) the signature must be "at the foot or end" of the will;
(e) the signature must be made or acknowledged in the presence of two witnesses present at the same time;
(f) each witness must himself sign in the presence of the testator.

It is usual, though not essential, to have an attestation clause in words something like the following: "Signed by the above named testator AB as his last will in the presence of us both present at the same time who in his presence and the presence of each other have hereunto subscribed our names as witnesses."

The advantage of having an attestation clause is that it will normally avoid the need for further proof when probate in common form is eventually sought.

If a witness or his spouse receives a gift under the will the gift will be void; but where the signature of the witness is not essential the gift will be valid.[29]

Whilst the requirements of a valid will as set out above are stringent, liberal interpretation by the courts has modifed their effect in many cases. For example, in *In b. Hornby*[30] the will was written on a sheet of paper with an oblong space drawn half way down on the right-hand side, the will filling the rest of the sheet. The testator's signature was in this oblong space in ink different from the rest of the will. It was held to have been signed "at the foot or end thereof" and was therefore admitted to probate. The judge came to the conclusion that the testator must have prepared this space beforehand for his signature and that he "intended the signature sufficiently to authenticate the whole of the document written on that side of the paper."[31]

Alteration and revocation. Any alteration made after the execution of the will must itself be executed in accordance with the above rules. But if any part of the will is not "apparent"[32] as a result of the alteration, probate will be granted without that part. A provision in the will is still considered to be apparent if it can be read without physical interference or making copies—for example by infra red photography.

[29] See Wills Act 1968, s.1.
[30] [1946] P. 171 (Wallington J.), "In b." is short for "*in bonis*" meaning "in the goods of."
[31] *Ibid.* headnote.
[32] Wills Act 1837, s.21.

A will once made can be revoked in any one of three ways:

(a) By a later will or codicil which revokes the earlier either expressly or impliedly to the extent of any inconsistency between the two. The later will or codicil must of course be executed in accordance with the Will Act 1837.

(b) By destruction: Destruction does not itself revoke a will. There must be destruction by the testator coupled with an intention to revoke.

(c) By marriage: With certain exceptions a will is automatically revoked by the marriage of the testator.

Privileged wills. Certain persons can make privileged wills. This privilege extends to a soldier (including a member of the Royal Air Force) in actual military service and a member of the Royal Navy or Royal Marine who would, if a soldier, have been considered in actual military service. It also extends to a mariner or seaman at sea.

A person in one of these categories can validly make or revoke a valid will even though an infant. And the will or revocation does not have to be in any particular form. It may be in writing or oral; and does not have to be signed or witnessed. In *Re Stable*[33] Lieutenant Stable who was a minor and engaged to the plaintiff in 1917, had been told by the family solicitor that he could not make a will until he came of age. However, he told his fiancée that "If anything happens to me, and I stop a bullet, everything of mine will be yours." Shortly afterwards he was killed in action. It was held that his words constituted a valid will.

Lapse. A will is said to be ambulatory. It has no effect until death. A beneficiary gets nothing until the death. It follows that if a named beneficiary dies before the testator, the gift will lapse and, unless otherwise disposed of by the will, it will pass as on intestacy.

Under sections 32 and 33 of the Wills Act 1837 a gift is saved from lapse on the death of the beneficiary in two cases. First, where the beneficiary is given an entail and leaves issue surviving the testator capable of inheriting the entail. Secondly, where the beneficiary is a child or other issue of the testator and issue of the beneficiary survive the testator. In both these cases the property passes as if the beneficiary has died immediately *after* the testator.

Section 33 does not prevent lapse of an appointment by will made under a special power. Neither does it apply to a class gift to issue (*e.g.* "to all my children") since in this case the issue is not a

---

[33] [1919] P. 7. And see *Re Jones* (*decd.*) [1981] 1 All E.R. 1.

beneficiary unless he survives the testator and there is no gift to him to save from lapse.

Commorientes. Where it is uncertain which of two persons died first, the general presumption for the purpose of succession to property is that the elder died first.[34]

However, for the purpose of intestate succession this presumption does not apply between husband and wife and the intestate is deemed to have survived his spouse.[35] For example, if H and W die together in an air crash; H is intestate whilst W has made a will leaving all her property to X. In dealing with H's estate he will be presumed to have survived W. His property will therefore not go to W and so to X.

Intestacy. Since 1925 the same rules govern intestate succession to all property real and personal.[36]

The personal representatives hold all property in respect of which the deceased is intestate upon trust for sale and conversion. This property is known as the "residuary estate of the intestate."[37]

For the purposes of distribution, surviving relatives can be divided into three categories[38]:

(a) The spouse of the intestate.

(b) Issue, *i.e.* children and more remote descendants of the intestate.

(c) "Near relations": *i.e.* parents, brothers and sisters of the whole blood and the issue of such brothers and sisters of the intestate.

The distribution of the residuary estate depends on which of these relatives survive and will be as follows:

1. Surviving spouse but no issue and no near relations: The surviving spouse will be absolutely entitled.

2. Surviving spouse and issue (whether or not there are near relations): The surviving spouse will take the personal chattels; £25,000[39] absolutely with interest at a rate fixed by the Lord Chancellor[40] until payment; a life interest in half the rest. The residue will be held on the statutory trusts for the issue.

3. Surviving spouse and either parent but no issue: The spouse will take the personal chattels; £55,000 absolutely with interest at

---

[34] L.P.A. 1925, s.184.

[35] Intestates' Estates Act 1952, s.1(4).

[36] A.E.A. 1925, s.33.

[37] *Ibid.* s.33(4).

[38] See A.E.A. 1925, as amended by Intestates' Estates Act 1952, Family Provisions Act 1966, and Family Law Reform Act 1969.

[39] See Family Provision Act 1966, s. 1, and S.I. 1977 No. 415.

[40] Administration of Justice Act 1977, s.28; S.I. 1977 No. 1491.

at rate fixed by the Lord Chancellor until payment; half the residue absolutely. The parents will take the rest (equally if two of them).

4. Surviving spouse and any brothers or sisters of the whole blood (but no issue and no parents): The spouse will take as in 3. The rest will be held on the statutory trusts for the surviving brothers or sisters.

5. Surviving issue but no surviving spouse (whether or not there are near relations): The whole will be held on the statutory trusts for the issue.

6. Parents but no issue and no spouse: The parents will take the whole absolutely (in equal shares if two of them).

7. No spouse, no issue and no parents: The residuary estate will be held for other surviving relatives in the following order of priority: (a) on the statutory trusts for brothers and sisters of the whole blood; (b) on the statutory trusts for brothers and sisters of the half blood; (c) for the grandparents (if more than one in equal shares), (d) on the statutory trusts for uncles and aunts (*i.e.* brothers and sisters of the whole blood of parents of the intestate); (e) on the statutory trusts for uncles and aunts being brothers and sisters of the half blood of the intestate's parents. The first of these classes to contain survivors will take to the exclusion of all subsequent classes.

Failing any of the above relations surviving him, the property of the deceased will pass to the Crown as *bona vacantia*.

The personal chattels of the deceased (not to be confused with personal property) refers to those chattels listed in the Administration of Estates Act 1925[41] which are generally thought of as a person's personal belongings and include indoor and outdoor furniture, motor cars, jewellery, books, etc.

The legislation provides for the property to be held on the statutory trusts in those cases where the class of beneficiaries may be uncertain in size or include minors. The term "statutory trusts" is defined in section 47 of the Administration of Estates Act 1925 as amended. It means that the residuary estate will be held in trust for those members of the class in question (in equal shares if more than one) who survive the intestate and either reach the age of 18 or marry under that age. The issue of any member of the class who has predeceased the intestate will take the parent's share. Thus if John dies intestate leaving a son and two grandsons (the sons of a deceased son) and no widow, the residuary estate will be held on the statutory trusts for the benefit of the son as to a half and the

[41] s.55(1) (x).

two grandsons as to a quarter each—assuming they attain the age of 18 or marry.[42]

The surviving spouse may require the personal representatives to appropriate the matrimonial home in partial satisfaction of his or her entitlement.[43]

In the case of a partial intestacy, the sums of £25,000 and £55,000 must be diminished by the value of any beneficial interest under the will.

Entails, of course, still descend to the descendent heir in accordance with the old common law rules.

Transfer of land by the personal representatives. An assent is necessary to transfer the legal estate in land from the personal representatives to the beneficiary entitled under the will or intestacy. The assent does not have to be by deed but it must be in writing signed by the personal representatives and name the person in whose favour it is given.[44] If the personal representative is entitled to the property as trustee or beneficiary he will have to sign an assent in his own favour.[45]

A purchaser from a personal representative will get a good title (in spite of any previous assent) provided the conveyance contains a statement by the personal representative that he has not made any previous assent or conveyance and provided no notice of a previous assent has been endorsed on the probate or letters of administration.[46] Further, in the absence of any such endorsement, a purchaser of a legal estate is entitled to rely on the assent as sufficient proof that it has been made in favour of the person entitled.[47] These provisions are designated to keep the beneficial interests in the deceased's property behind the curtain.

---

[42] As to powers of maintenance and advancement in respect of infants, see T.A. 1925, ss.31, 32.

[43] Intestates' Estates Act 1952, s.5.

[44] A.E.A. 1925, s.36 (4).

[45] *Re King's Will Trusts* [1964] Ch. 542 (Pennycuick J.).

[46] A.E.A. 1925, s.36(6). But this will not upset the title of a previous purchaser for value: *ibid.* s.36(6).

[47] *Ibid.* s.36(7).

CHAPTER 28

LEASEHOLD AND FREEHOLD: COMPARISON

Principle 1.   Real and personal property

Under English law all property is classified as either real or personal.

Real property includes only freehold interests in land. All other property (including leasehold interests in land) is classified as personal property (personalty).

Personal property is further divided into chattels real (leasehold interests in land) and chattels personal or pure personalty (all other personal property).

Today, with certain exceptions, the same rules apply to real and personal property interests in land and the distinction is not generally important.

Under modern law, the distinction between land and goods is more likely to be important than the distinction between real and personal property.

Explanation

This short chapter is an attempt to indicate the significance, past and present, of the distinction between freehold and leasehold ownership.

Real and personal property. From the early days of the common law,[1] the real actions (actions *in rem*) were available to protect freehold interests in land—the fee simple, fee tail and the life interest—enabling the tenant deprived of his seisin (the freeholder's possession) to recover it in the common law courts. He had a right to recover the *res*, the thing itself.

For reasons which are not certain,[2] these actions were not made available to the leaseholder (the "termor"). It was decided that he did not have seisin and that he did not have the protection of the real actions. Instead, if he was wrongfully dispossessed, his remedy was in the personal actions (actions *in personam*) which were available in the case of ordinary moveable chattels. And the personal actions gave the defendant the option to restore the

---

[1] See generally Pollock and Maitland, *History of English Law* (2nd ed., 1968), Vol. II, pp. 106–117; D.R. Denman, *Origins of Ownership* (1958), Chaps. 5 and 6; F.H. Lawson, *Introduction to the Law of Property* (1958), Chap. II; T. Plucknett, *A Concise History of the Common Law* (5th ed.), Chap. 6.

[2] See Pollock and Maitland (n. 1, above), Vol. II, pp. 113 *et seq.*

chattel or pay damages. And so leaseholds together with all other types of property except freehold interests in land came to be classified as personal property.

Before 1926 this distinction between freehold and leasehold, between real and personal property, was important. In a number of vital respects separate rules governed the two categories. For example, the rules of descent on intestacy were quite different; personal property could not be entailed; and in general freehold property was not liable for the debts of the deceased.

The distinction still exists. Correctly speaking, the term "real property," still only refers to freehold land; and leasehold is still personalty. The distinction may still be important. For example:

(1) If a person, such as a testator making his will, uses the term "real property" it will be presumed not to include any of his leaseholds.

(2) The burden of positive covenants can run with leasehold where there is privity of estate but not with freehold.[3]

The policy of the 1925 legislation was, however, to assimilate as far as possible the rules relating to real and personal property. Thus, all property passes in the same way on intestacy[4]; entails can now be carved out of personal property[5]; and all of a deceased's property is equally liable for his debts.[6]

Today, the distinction which is more frequently important is that between land and goods. The importance of this distinction has already been considered.[7]

Principle 2. Commercial and family interests

The 1925 legislation is based on a division of land ownership into two categories:

(1) *Commerical interests.* Those interests which are commonly dealt with for money or money's worth and which derive their value from the access to and use of the land itself which they give. The ownership interests in this category are the fee simple absolute in possession and the term of years absolute.

(2) *Family interests.* Those which generally represent the gratuitous distribution of property amongst the landowner's family, which can satisfactorily be represented by money and

---

[3] See above, p. 419.
[4] See above, p. 578.
[5] L.P.A. 1925, s.130.
[6] A.E.A. 1925, s.32.
[7] Above, at p. 22.

which are therefore amenable to the device of overreaching. The ownership interests in this category are the freehold interests less than the fee simple absolute in possession.

Explanation

Commercial and family interests. As already stated, the leasehold was never given the protection of the real actions or the status of real property. It should not be concluded, however, that those involved in dealings with leaseholds regarded this as a disability or a drawback. The distinction reflects rather perhaps the different purposes which freeholds and leaseholds were required to serve in those early days of the common law.

The freehold interests were designed to give the tenant the security of a place in the feudal agricultural community, and to guarantee the material needs of his life particularly somewhere to live and a source of food—not just to the tenant and his family but to the succeeding generations of his family. Similarly, sub-infeudation was not regarded as the use of a capital asset (the land) to provide an income return. Rather it served to provide the lord with *his* material needs and the support of his tenants. This purpose was reflected in all the feudal burdens and limitations attached to freehold land.

Leasehold land, the term of years, appears to have been designed to serve a different purpose. Leasehold and its classification as a chattel reflected the view of land as a commercial asset; a scheme to use land as a capital investment. Thus, the earliest common use of the term of years was not the husbandry lease; nor was it the periodic occupation tenancy.[8] It was the mortgage. The person with money to invest could lend it in return for a long term of years. His purpose was not occupation of the land but the security of his capital and a satisfactory return on his investment.

It was appropriate for the law to insist that land as the sustainer of the family (freehold) should pass to the heir on death; it was equally appropriate that land as a form of capital investment (leasehold) should be bequeathable like chattels.

Thus, perhaps it is true to say that the emergence of the leasehold and its treatment as personal property represented the gradual development of a money economy and a land market—the antithesis of feudalism—at a time when freehold was still shackled by its feudal origins.

By 1925 a great change had taken place. The fee simple and the leasehold had been largely assimilated in the practices of landown-

[8] These were developed later.

ers; though the old legal distinctions remained and could not, be abolished without the aid of Parliament. Feudalism had long since disappeared for most purposes. The fee simple had acquired the free disposability of an ordinary commercial asset.

The term of years and the periodic tenancy had been recognised as useful means of giving occupation of land—having the advantage of certainty of duration over the lease for life or lives.[9]

On the other hand, the lesser freehold interests, the life interest and the fee tail had remained as the machinery by which landowners settled their land on successive generations of their families.

By 1925 therefore, the natural division was not between freehold and leasehold; it was between commercial ownership interests (the fee simple absolute in possession and present and future leaseholds) on the one hand and family interests (the lesser freehold interests) on the other.

The 1925 legislation had adopted this basic division of ownership as is shown by the following principles:

(1) The fee simple absolute in possession and the term of years absolute (which means most leasehold interests)[10] are the only ownership interests which can still exist as legal estates. And the legal estate is the basis of ordinary commercial dealings in land.

(2) Both these interests, whether legal or equitable, are kept outside the overreaching machinery. This means that they enjoy the guaranteed right to possession of the land (either actual occupation or the receipt of rents).

(3) On the other hand, the successive (family) interests (life interests, fee tails, and future fee simples), can now only exist in equity behind a trust and are subject to overreaching.

This same distinction is applied to third party rights. With some exceptions, those third party rights which are commercial are kept outside the overreaching machinery; those which are family interests are made subject to overreaching. This is illustrated by the case of the rentcharge, an interest which can be employed for a family or a commercial purpose. The legislation therefore provides that if land is charged with the payment of a rentcharge either "voluntarily or in consideration of marriage or by way of family arrangement . . . for the life of any person or any less

---

[9] See Holdsworth, *History of English Law*, Vol. VII, pp. 239 *et seq*. The lease for life or lives was in common use as a husbandry lease down to the end of the 18th century. It had a number of advantages, *e.g.* being classified as freehold, it gave parliamentary franchise.

[10] Except the lease for lives which, if at a rent, is converted into a term of years by the L.P.A. 1925, s.149(6).

period. . . ." then the land will be treated as settled and the overreaching machinery will apply.[11]

On the other hand, any other rentcharge will generally be treated as a commercial third party right not subject to overreaching.[12]

The lease for lives has had to be subdivided in a similar way.

The lease for life or lives. The rule governing these leases has already been set out.[13] They are interesting in the present context because they illustrate the dividing line between commercial and family interests—and also how artificial this dividing line can sometimes be. The lease for life was popular as a means for granting husbandry leases up to the eighteenth century. It was peculiar in that although classified as freehold it did not fall neatly into either the leasehold or the freehold category. Although it was used as a limitation under family settlements it was also commonly granted in consideration of rent. The 1925 legislation had to fit these leases into the twofold division mentioned above. It did this by providing that where the lease was given in consideration of rent or fine, it would be converted into a 90-year term—and thus come within the category of commercial interests.[14] Where there was no rent or consideration the lease would remain a freehold interest and take effect in equity under the settlement and overreaching provisions as a family interest.[15] This test—whether or not there was rent or a fine—is not doubt adequate. But what is in reality a commercial lease for life may be granted without rent or a fine; and conversely what is in essence a family interest may be created for some rent. In *Re Catling*[16] a testator left land instructing his trustees to let it to his widow if she so wished for the rest of her life on a yearly tenancy at £1 per annum. Clearly this was in substance a family interest. But it was held that since she was paying rent she could not be tenant for life under section 20(1)(iv) of the Settled Land Act 1925 and presumably section 149(6) of the Law of Property Act 1925 operated to convert her interest into a 90-year term. On the other hand, in *Bannister* v. *Bannister*,[17] the defendant agreed to sell her cottage to the plaintiff, it being agreed

---

[11] S.L.A. 1925, s.1(1) (v).
[12] But by way of exception some commercial interests may sometimes be overreached. Thus a general equitable charge on land may be overreached on sale, see S.L.A. 1925, s.72 (above, p. 236).
[13] Above, p. 105.
[14] L.P.A. 1925, s.149(6).
[15] S.L.A. 1925, s.1(1) (v).
[16] [1931] 2 Ch. 359 (Bennett J.).
[17] [1948] 2 All E.R. 133 (C.A.).

that she should be allowed to live there as long as she wished rent-free. Clearly this was a commercial arrangement although no rent or fine[18] was paid.

Principle 3. Leasehold as a form of ownership

Leasehold is as much a form of ownership as freehold; though the value of any particular leasehold will depend on its duration and the degree of security of tenure available.

Explanation

There always has been and still is a tendency to regard leasehold as something less than "ownership." Some of the reasons for this have been considered—particularly the early importance of the term of years as a form of investment rather than as a means of obtaining occupation of the land; there has also been the tendency to think of the lease as a tenurial—or even just contractual— relationship between landlord and tenant rather than as a property interest in the land.

This attitude has little if any justification in law today; but it persists both in the legal and the non-legal mind. For example, one survey comparing ownership to renting in the U.S.A. has stated that[19] "home ownership, then, does not appear to be an economic matter as much as it is a psychological or emotional one." A remarkable fact about this survey is that it does not appear to distinguish between short and long tenancies. And, in England, even the Law Commission makes a somewhat grudging distinction,[20] saying that where a lease is for a long term such as 999 years, "the additional benefits arising from owning the freehold are of less significance."

In some cases, such as the block of flats, leasehold ownership— enabling positive covenants to run—may be preferable.

The distinction which is more significant than the distinction between freehold and leasehold ownership is the distinction between the long and the short lease. For most purposes a 999-year lease may be indistinguishable from freehold ownership; a weekly tenancy is much less valuable and its value will depend on

---

[18] Unless the transfer of the cottage could be regarded as a "fine." In fact the court did not need to decide in this case whether s.149 (6) of the L.P.A. 1925 applied.

[19] Glenn-Beyer, *Housing, A Factual Analysis* (Macmillan: New York, 1958), p. 167.

[20] Law Com.W.P. No. 24 (Rentcharges), para. 14.

the degree of security available. In the case of a 999-year lease the whole of the capital value more or less has been transferred to the tenant. In the case of a weekly tenant—apart from his security— the tenant is receiving nothing but the present use of the property and the capital value remains in the landlord.

INDEX